REVELATION

Verse by Verse

A Commentary

by B.L. Turner

Revelation Verse by Verse, A Commentary

© 2016, 2023 by B.L. Turner. All rights reserved.

Fig Press
3631 NE 102nd Avenue
Portland, OR 97220

ISBN: 978-1-961528-01-7

All rights are reserved by the author.

Unless otherwise indicated, all Scripture quotations are from the American Standard Version (ASV).

Dedication

I gratefully dedicate this commentary to Eugene Mitchell. His insistent requests for me to teach the book of Revelation to the Church of Christ at 35th Avenue in Portland, Oregon, in which he serves with distinction as an elder, ultimately led to its being published.

Acknowledgment and Appreciation

I am deeply grateful for the competent assistance that I have had in getting this commentary ready for publication. Jonathan Turner has skillfully produced the twelve maps[1] which will help students visualize the spatial concepts which are integral to the graphic account given through the Apostle John. Eugene Mitchell, to whom this commentary is dedicated, serves as the librarian for Key Communications. He patiently and expertly helped confirm many of the reference materials of which mention is made in the footnotes. Lisa DiVincenzo competently, patiently and graciously converted the dictated text of this commentary into the book form which you are reading. In addition to the textual work which she so accurately rendered, she also designed the cover of the book.

---

1   The maps in this volume were drawn using The Generic Mapping Tools by Paul Wessel and Walter H. F. Smith, School of Ocean & Earth Science & Technology, University of Hawai'i. Topographic data was derived from the Shuttle Radar Topography Mission.

Other books by the author include:

Withering Wind From Arabia: The Story of the Followers of Christ Whose Countries Were Conquered by Islam

The Definitive Battle For Palestine, An Exposition of Ezekiel 38 and 39

God's Game Plan

Table of Contents

Introduction..1

Outline of the Book of Revelation 3

The Location of Exposition and Comments by Chapters in Revelation:

Revelation Chapter 1..5

Revelation Chapter 2..25

Revelation Chapter 3..49

Revelation Chapter 4..71

Revelation Chapter 5..79

Revelation Chapter 6..87

Revelation Chapter 7..103

Revelation Chapter 8..115

Revelation Chapter 9..129

Revelation Chapter 10..151

Revelation Chapter 11..157

Revelation Chapter 12..173

Revelation Chapter 13..193

Revelation Chapter 14..213

Revelation Chapter 15..229

Revelation Chapter 16..237

Revelation Chapter 17..271

Revelation Chapter 18..289

Revelation Chapter 19..309

Revelation Chapter 20..325

Revelation Chapter 21..343

Revelation Chapter 22..359

Appendices:

Appendix A	Correlating and Harmonizing Seventeen Eschatological Passages in the New Testament With the Account Given in Revelation	375
Appendix B	Anchor Points in the Book of Revelation's Panorama of History	409
Appendix C	The Birth of the Muslim Empire	419
Appendix D	The Fall or Collapse of Babylon	423
Appendix E	Expanded Comments on Revelation 16:13, The Dragon, the Beast and the False Prophet Form a Coalition of Evil	427
Appendix F	The Christology of Islam	441
Appendix G	Darwin at the University	455
Appendix H	Scriptures Which Point to The Millennium	465
Appendix I	Which Way Iran?	469

Maps:

Map 1	Contrasting Asias	473
Map 2	Patmos and the Dodecanese Islands	474
Map 3	The Location of the Seven Churches	475
Map 4a	The Vandals	476
Map 4b	The Visigoths	477
Map 4c	Attila and the Huns	478
Map 5	Rome's Three Regions	479
Map 6	The Three Regions of the Mediterranean Sea	480
Map 7	The Arab Empire in Circa A.D. 712	481
Map 8	The Four Countries of the Euphrates	482
Map 9	The Location of Byzantium	483
Map 10	Megiddo	484

Alphabetical Index...485

About the Author..543

Introduction

In reading the book of Revelation, one may feel frustration because he may be unable to identify precise depictions of many familiar historical landmarks, like the Crusades, World War I or II, and personages such as Lenin, Marx, Stalin, Hitler or Mao Tse-tung, along with many other important people in world history. Though many specifics are unmistakably depicted, the Revelation account runs deeper and more extensively than any bare enumeration of people and events. It not only gives us a very broad perspective but also a deep analysis of history. To borrow the words of a great geographer, which he used in another connection, the account in Revelation gives us "the ability to see through the hurly-burly of current events and reveal [the most] basic truths."[2] Accordingly, Revelation, Verse by Verse, as a commentary, also identifies and evaluates many pivotal historic events and developments.

Initially, Revelation was committed in written form to seven local congregations of Christians which had been established in the Roman province of Asia. In addition to the messages in the specific letters to those individual churches, the visions of Revelation cover the most important highlights of the whole panorama of human history, from the apostolic period to the end of the Christian age, to the point at which time blends back into eternity. The bulk of the text of Revelation portrays conditions and events which obviously belong to periods of history which were to occur centuries after the initial recipients of the text would have died. It is therefore logical to conclude that the astounding revelatory message of this book is intended to inform, encourage, warn and buttress, not only churches in the apostolic period but all Christians till the end of time.

The message of Revelation is in harmony with the visions given to Paul and Peter. Paul warned of the defection which he calls "the falling away" (II Thessalonians 2:3), and Peter prophesied of the rise of ruthless skeptics who would hold the faith in utter disdain (II Peter 3:3-4). Those developments are identified and thoroughly analyzed in the message of Revelation.

This commentary, as its title implies, is intended to be comprehensive. As needed, analyses, clarifications and expositions of each verse have been given. Hopefully, every important doctrinal issue, such as the Rapture and the Millennium, has been clarified. Also, many great human migrations with their attendant consequences are identified and evaluated.

Diligent effort has been made to share helpful insights from other commentators, as well as calling them to account where I have deemed them to have been in error. The book of Revelation certainly merits Peter's commendation in which he wrote, "We have the word of prophecy made more sure: whereunto you do well that you take heed, as unto a lamp shining in a dark place, until the day dawn, and the day star arise in your hearts." (II Peter 1:19) May this commentary be a great blessing to you as you study the Revelation.

---

[2] Robert D. Kaplan, The Revenge of Geography, (New York: Random House, 2012), p. 92.

Outline of the Book of Revelation

I. Orientation 1:1-8
    A. The classification of the book
    B. The divisions of the book.
    C. The geography of the book
    D. The transmission of the message
    E. The writer of the book
    F. The date of writing
    G. The recipients of the book
    H. The authorship of the book

II. Messages to the <u>Seven Churches</u> of the Province of Asia 1:9-3:22
    A. The circumstances through which the messages to the churches were revealed. 1:9-20
        1. John's location and spiritual attitude 1:9-10
        2. Instructions given to John 1:11
        3. The one who spoke to John 1:12-18
        4. Final instructions and clarifications about writing to the churches 1:19-20
    B. The identity of the seven churches 2:1-3:22
        1. The church in Ephesus 2:1-7
        2. The church in Smyrna 2:8-11
        3. The church in Pergamum 2:12-17
        4. The church in Thyatira 2:18-28
        5. The church in Sardis 3:1-6
        6. The church in Philadelphia 3:7-13
        7. The church in Laodicea 3:14-22

III. Transition from the historic and the present to the prophetic 4:1

IV. Activity in heaven prior to opening the seven seals 4:2-5:14

V. The opening of the scroll sealed with <u>seven seals</u> 6:1-8:2
    A. The first seal 6:1-2
    The white horse bearing the crowned conqueror
    B. The second seal 6:3-4
    The red horse is bearing the rider with a great sword who takes peace from the earth and instigates slaughter among the inhabitants of the world.
    C. The third seal 6:5-6
    Black horse bearing the rider has the balance in his hand. A voice proclaims the price of wheat and barley.
    D. The fourth seal 6:7-8
    A pallid horse bearing death has authority over one fourth of the earth to kill by sword, famine, death and wild beasts.
    E. The fifth seal 6:9-11
    From beneath the altar, white-robed souls of martyrs cry to God for justice. They are told to rest till their brethren also finish their course.

Revelation Verse by Verse

- F. The sixth seal 6:12-7:17
    1. A great earthquake occurs. The sun becomes black, the moon blood, and the stars fall. The heavens vanish. The islands and mountains moved out of their places. Humanity hides in the earth from the wrath of God and Christ. 6:12-17
    2. Gospel victory among both Jews and Gentiles 7:1-17
        a. Four angels holding four destructive winds stand at four corners of earth and are prohibited by another angel who has the seal of the Living God from hurting the earth till God's servants are sealed. 7:1-3
        b. The number and description of those who are sealed on their foreheads. 7:4-8
        c. The great international throng before God's throne. 7:9-17
- G. The seventh seal 8:1-2
    1. Silence in heaven 8:1
    2. Seven angels are given trumpets 8:2

VI. The blowing of the <u>seven trumpets</u> 8:3-14:20
- A. The power of prayer 8:3-6
- B. Sounding of the trumpets 8:7-14:20
    1. The first trumpet 8:7
    2. The second trumpet 8:8-9
    3. The third trumpet 8:10-11
    4. The fourth trumpet 8:12-13
    5. The fifth trumpet 9:1-12
    6. The sixth trumpet 9:13-11:14
    7. The seventh trumpet 11:15-14:20

VII. The pouring out of the <u>seven bowls</u> of God's wrath (plagues) 15:1-17:18
These bowls of wrath contain "the seven last plagues." 21:9
- A. Preliminary activities in heaven 15:1-16:1
    1. The bowl of God's wrath on the earth 16:2
    2. The bowl of God's wrath on the sea 16:3
    3. The bowl of God's wrath on the rivers 16:4-7
    4. The bowl of God's wrath on the sun 16:8-9
    5. The bowl of God's wrath on the throne of the beast 16:10-11
    6. The bowl of God's wrath on the Euphrates 16:12-16
    7. The bowl of God's wrath on the air 16:17-17:18

VIII. Supplementary visions
- A. The origin and doom of Babylon 18:1-19:5
- B. The marriage of the Lamb 19:6-10
- C. Christ defeats the Beast and the False Prophet 19:11-21
- D. The binding and loosing of Satan 20:1-10
- E. The judgment of the Great White Throne 20:11-15
- F. The New Heaven and New Earth 21:1-8
- G. The wife of the Lamb and New Jerusalem 21:9-27
- H. The River of Life and the Tree of Life 22:1-5
- I. Corroboration and exhortation 22:6-20

Revelation Chapter 1

I. *Orientation: 1:1-8*

    A. *The classification of the book.*

        1.   <u>Revelation</u>. In 1:1 the book is called a revelation. The Greek word from which our word revelation is translated is *apokalupsis*. The Greek word means, to pull off a cover to see what is underneath it or to pull back a curtain to see what is behind it. In either case, the thing which is beneath the cover or behind the curtain is revealed or exposed, therefore that action is called a <u>revelation</u>. Please see also the comments under 5:4.

        "As its contents clearly show, the revealing [in the book of Revelation] is done through words, signs, and symbols, and includes things both present and future at the time John wrote."[3]

        2.   <u>Prophecy</u>. In 1:3 the book is called a prophecy. Our English word comes from the Greek word *prophates* which means a <u>prediction</u>, that is, it foretells events or conditions before they take place or transpire.

    B. *The divisions of the book.*

        1.   The book is divided into three sections: historic, current and prophetic. These sections are seen clearly in 1:19:

            a.   [the historic] "Write therefore the things that you have seen,

            b.   [the current] those that are and

            c.   [the prophetic] those that are to take place after this." (ESV)

        2.   The historic section of the book of Revelation is divided into two descriptive groups of texts. The first group refers to rather recent events concerning which John himself was a witness. Those events are summarized in 1:2, which says, "who [i.e., John] bore witness to the word of God and to the testimony of Jesus Christ, even to <u>all that he saw</u>." (ESV) Those events and conditions which "he saw" probably included those situations and events which were then prevailing in the seven churches. The apostle John seems to have been personally acquainted with each of those churches. The more remote sections of history are alluded to in 2:5 and 3:3 by the word "remember."

        3.   The prophetic sections of the book are divided between the imminent and the remote events which were to take place. The imminent prophetic events are emphasized in 1:1 which tells us about, "<u>things that must soon take place</u>." (ESV)

---

[3]   John T. Hinds, <u>A Commentary on the Book of Revelation</u> (Nashville, Tenn.: Gospel Advocate Company, 1976), p. 15.

or "must shortly come to pass." (ASV) These are the events for which "the time is at hand." (1:3) An example of such an imminent event is found in the message to the church in Smyrna to whom the Lord said, "Fear not the things which thou art <u>about to suffer</u>: behold, the devil is <u>about to cast some of you into prison</u>, that ye may be tried; and ye shall have tribulation ten days." (Revelation 2:10) Another example of an imminent prophetic event is found in Revelation 22:10 which says, "He saith unto me, Seal not up the words of the prophecy of this book; for <u>the time is at hand</u>."

In contrast, the words "the things which <u>shall come to pass hereafter</u>" in 1:19 refer to future events which were to occur more remotely, that is to events which would take place and to people who would appear at more distant times.

The textual discussion of the historic events in the recent past, the current events which were happening as John wrote, and those predicted events which were to take place in the near-term future, take us to 3:22 which makes it clear that, at that point, the messages to the seven churches of Asia are complete. Then at 4:1 the account crosses the threshold into the portrayal of the more remote future. It is expressed by the words, "I will show you <u>what must take place after this</u>.'" (ESV)

C. *The geography of the book. (See also 1:4.)*

Just as the time span is distinctly different in the near-term and long-term prophesies, so also the geographic scope differs. The area related to the prophesies regarding the seven churches encompasses only the Roman province of Asia (See Maps 1 and 3), while the remote-time-frame prophesies cover developments in various far-flung places throughout much of the world.

D. *The transmission of the message.*

1:1 "The Revelation of Jesus Christ, which God gave him to show unto his servants, even the things which must shortly come to pass: and he sent and signified it by his angel unto his servant John;"

The very first verse of Revelation tells us how the message has reached us. The words "God gave him" tell of the transmission of the revelation from God to Christ. Its purpose was that he might, "show his servants." This obviously portrays Christ as the pivotal or central figure in delivering divine revelation. This role of Christ in administering revelation is emphasized at the end of 19:10 which tells us that, "The testimony of Jesus is the spirit of prophecy." Divine, angelic and human are the three categories of participants involved in the transmission of divinely-inspired prophecies to mankind at large. Thus, Christ, the divine participant in transmitting the message, "made it known [signified it - ASV] by sending an angel to his servant John. [the human participant]." (NASV)

E. *The writer of the book.*

1:2 [John] "who bare witness of the word of God, and of the testimony of Jesus Christ, even of all things that he saw."

Revelation Chapter 1

In 1:11, John is said to have been ordered to write in a book that which he was shown. By doing so, he was able to "bare witness." Note that the writer is distinguished from the author of the book. See "H" below.

The identity of the writer of the book has been hotly debated. Those who think the writer of Revelation was not the same person as the one who wrote the Gospel of John base their arguments mainly on writing style. They think "it is well nigh impossible that the same man could have written the *Revelation* and the Fourth Gospel, if for no other reason than that the Greek is so different that the same man could not have written both books. The Greek of the Fourth Gospel is simple but correct enough; the Greek of the Revelation is rugged and virile and vivid, but notoriously incorrect."[4] This evaluation of the style and of the lack of refinement in the Greek language found in Revelation was made by William Barclay who was eminently qualified to render such a judgment for he was Lecturer in New Testament Language and Literature and in Hellenistic Greek in the University of Glasgow.

Though Barclay was eminently qualified to pass judgment on the quality and style of the Greek language found in the oldest manuscripts of Revelation, his sweeping conclusion that the apostle John was not the one through whom the book has been given to us, neglects consideration of several important issues. First, the rough style of writing probably reflects the very rough circumstances under which John was obliged to write. He was in exile on the Isle of Patmos. (1:7) (See Map 2.) Secondly, it was commonly acknowledged that John had never received a sophisticated education. The religious authorities of his time said about both Peter and John that they "were uneducated, common men." (Acts 4:13 ESV) Therefore, it should not surprise us that under circumstances which made it impossible for John to utilize the services of a secretary, as both Peter and Paul sometimes did (See I Peter 5:12 and Romans 16:22.), that his written language in the book of Revelation would be rough. Rather than the unsophisticated Greek language in the manuscripts of the book of Revelation, being an indication that John had not written it, such crude writing supports the conclusion that John, indeed, did write Revelation.

John's lack of sophistication reminds us, "that Christianity entered upon its career almost void of literary and philosophical culture and social standings."[5] It is one of the many indications that the birth and early career of the church, though it involved men, resulted from a divine initiative.

Plummer has pointed out on the words in Revelation 19:13, "his name is called the word of God," that "only in St. John's writings does this title appear – a strong argument in favor of his authorship of the Apocalypse (cf. John 1:1; I John 1:1)."[6]

Additionally, the second verse of Revelation (1:2) seems to settle the question of the identity of the man "John" to whom Christ's angel delivered the divine message. There, we are told that John is the one "who bare witness of the word of God, and of the testimony of Jesus Christ, even of all things that he saw." (Revelation 1:2)

---

4   William Barclay, The Revelation of John, Vol. I, (Edinburgh: St. Andrews Press, 1962), p. 16.
5   Albert Henry Newman, A Manual of Church History, Vol. I, (Philadelphia: The Baptist Publication Society, 1939), p. 148.
6   A. Plummer, The Pulpit Commentary [on] Revelation, (Chicago: Wilcox & Follett Co., no date), p. 449.

The similarity of the descriptive self disclosure in Revelation 1:2 with that which is given in I John 1:1-4 is so close, emphasized here by the underlined expressions, that it must be referring to the same person. In I John 1:1-4 we are told, "That which was from the beginning, <u>that which we have heard</u>, that which we <u>have seen with our eyes</u>, that which we beheld, and our hands handled, concerning the Word of life (and the life was manifested, and <u>we have seen</u>, and <u>bear witness</u>, and declare unto you the life, the eternal life, which was with the Father, and was manifested unto us); that which <u>we have seen</u> and heard declare we unto you also, that ye also may have fellowship with us: yea, and our fellowship is with the Father, and with his Son <u>Jesus Christ</u>: and these things we write, that our joy may be made full."

The identity of the writer of Revelation which is gained by comparing his self disclosure with that given by the writer of I John is buttressed by the fact that, "There was no dispute among the apostolic fathers as to the authorship ["authorship" is used to mean "writer"] of the Revelation. The author identifies himself four times simply as 'John' (1:1; 1: 4; 1:9; 22:8). The earliest fathers – e.g., Justin Martyr (d. 165), Irenaeus (c. 180), Clement of Alexandria (d. 215), Tertullian (d. 220) – unanimously identified this author with John, the son of Zebedee, one of the twelve apostles, and the 'beloved disciple' of Christ, to whom the writing of the fourth Gospel and three epistles is also attributed."[7] Further assurance of the authorship of Revelation comes from scrutiny of the vocabulary which has been used. See the comments under "he that is true" at 3:7.

F.   Date of writing. (See also 1:9.)

External Testimony. Irenaeus[8] "said that John 'beheld the apocalyptic vision ... almost in our day, toward the end of Domitian's reign.' This was in A.D. 96."[9]

"Revelation now forms the last book in the New Testament, an open letter addressed to a number of named church communities in what today is southern Turkey. It is likely to have been written in the time of the Emperor Domitian (81-96 CE) and to be the product of Christian fury at his brutal campaign to strengthen the cult of emperor worship."[10]

Internal Evidence. In addition to those statements from history, there is strong internal evidence that the book of Revelation was written after the destruction of Jerusalem. That powerful assurance comes from the fact that, though Revelation is the revelation of Jesus Christ (Revelation 1:1), nowhere in it does he alert his followers to the imminent destruction of the holy city. From Matthew chapter 24 (See Appendix A.) it becomes clear that Jesus urgently warned his followers of that impending pivotal event. He wanted them to understand the impact it would have on their lives so they could make preparations to avert personal and corporate disaster. Jesus was also careful to inform his apostles about the impact the Roman destruction of Jerusalem would have on the Jewish people. (See comments on Matthew 24:29-30 in Appendix A.) If Revelation had been written before the destruction of Jerusalem we would expect Jesus to have warned his

---

7   <u>Revelation, Four Views: A Parallel Commentary</u>, ed. Steve Gregg, (Nashville: Thomas Nelson Publishers, 1997), p. 12.
8   Irenaeus was born between 120 and 140 A.D. and died between 200 and 203 A.D. He grew up in Smyrna in the province of Asia where as a boy he listened to the sermons of Polycarp who was thought to be a disciple of the apostles. He became a Christian in Smyrna and later was sent to southern Gaul where he became a presbyter at Lyon.
9   Lee G. Tomlinson, <u>The Wonder Book of the Bible: A Commentary On the Book of Revelation</u>, (Joplin, Missouri: College Press, 1963), p.5.
10 Diarmaid MacCulloch, <u>Christianity: The First Three Thousand Years</u>, (New York: Viking, 2010), p. 103.

Revelation Chapter 1

people even more urgently about the coming destruction of Jerusalem and its impact upon his followers. Since the Revelation account is totally silent about any impending attack on Jerusalem and its consequences, it is not only reasonable but essential to conclude that the book of Revelation was written subsequent to the epochal destruction of Jerusalem and its temple, along with the dispersion of the Jewish people.

For additional internal evidence on the date of writing, see the first three paragraphs in the comments on 2:3. Also see the fifth and following paragraphs of the comments on 2:9 and the comments on "rise and measure the temple of God" under 11:1.

G. *The recipients of the book*

1. The literate and illiterate

1:3 **"Blessed is he that readeth, and they that hear the words of the prophecy, and keep the things that are written therein: for the time is at hand."**

The third verse describes the audience to whom the book of Revelation is directed. Part of that group was literate and, therefore, they could read the words of the prophecy. They are told, "blessed is he that readeth." Some among those to whom the book was sent were apparently illiterate or not able to acquire a personal copy of the book. The book was to be read to them, probably in church meetings, so they could "hear the words of the prophecy." We are assured that whether we are literate or illiterate, if we keep the prophecies of this book, we will receive a blessing. This promise of blessing is repeated in 22:7.

2. The seven churches and their angels

1:4 **"John to the seven churches that are in Asia: Grace to you and peace, from him who is and who was and who is to come; and from the seven Spirits that are before his throne;"**

1:4 **"to the seven churches that are in Asia"**

Verse 4 of chapter 1 records John's committal of the message "to the seven churches that are in Asia." Be sure not to confuse the geographical term "Asia" as it is used in the designation "the seven churches that are in Asia" (Revelation 1:4) with the currently used term "Asia." The Asia of the book of Revelation was a Roman province on the eastern shore of the Aegean Sea in what is now western Turkey. Please consult Maps 1 and 3. The Roman province of Asia was just inside the western boundary of the area we now call Asia. It was situated in the far western part of modern Asia in the area which is now called the Near East.

The modern term Asia refers to the great land mass stretching thousands of miles from the eastern shore of the Aegean Sea all the way to the Pacific Ocean. Because it comprises such a huge area, regional terms such as the Near East, the Middle East,[11] the Levant, Central Asia, South Asia, the Far East[12] and Southeast Asia are used to make more precise and specific descriptions possible.

---

11 Alfred Thayer Mahan in 1902 was the first one to use the term "Middle East." See Robert D. Kaplan, The Revenge of Geography, (New York: Random House, 2012), p. 104.
12 The biblical term for the Far East is "the [region of the] sun rising." (Revelation 16:12). Compare Isaiah 41:2 and 46:11.

Asia, in the book of Revelation, was the Roman province of Asia which was comprised, "of Mysia, Lydia and probably Cairia also."[13] It came into being when, "the king of Pergamum, Attalus I, bequeathed his kingdom to the Romans, who in 129 B.C. converted it into the province of Asia."[14] (See also the discussion at 2:12 under "Pergamum.")

Please note specifically who it was to whom the message to the seven churches in Revelation was committed. First of all the message was entrusted to each of **the seven "angels"** of the seven churches. The phrase is, "To the angel of the church in ____ write:" (See 2:1, 2:8, 2:12, 2:18, 3:1, 3:7, 3:14.)

The word "angel" means "messenger." For example, when Mark, at the beginning of his Gospel, quotes Malachi 3:1 saying, "I send my messenger," the word in the Greek text of the Septuagint for "messenger" is *anggelon*, angel. Therefore, the expression "to the angel of the church in ____ " probably refers to the one who regularly preached to the church. It was the duty of that leader who is referred to as "the angel" to convey the message, probably accompanied with comment and exposition, to the whole church.

Paul highlighted the importance of preaching when he asked the rhetorical question, "How shall they hear without a preacher?" (Romans 10:14) The preacher in each of the seven churches might have been an evangelist who had taken up a settled ministry like Timothy who was ordered by Paul to "tarry in Ephesus." (I Timothy 1:3-4) However, it is more likely that the term "angel" refers to one of the elders who had been recognized for his special teaching talent. Paul describes such elders as "those who labor in the Word and in teaching." (I Timothy 5:17)

It was not till "the early second century," that "the Church's leadership was beginning to be concentrated in the hands of single individuals styled bishops."[15] The apostle Paul predicted that the heretical system based on metropolitan and monarchical bishops would, in one instance, rise from among the bishops (elders, Acts 20:17) of the church in Ephesus, one of the seven churches of Asia. (See Acts 20:28-30.)

Next, the message was directed not only to the "angels" of the seven churches, but to the individual churches themselves. It is important to note that Jesus deals with the churches as individual congregations. There were no district, state or national headquarters involved. Not only does Christ address each corporate body, but he sometimes specifically singles out an individual within that body. For example, there is a specific message to the woman who is called Jezebel in 2:20-21. Further, the message was directed to all who were spiritually sensitive and receptive, that is to everyone who "hath an ear." (cf. 2:7, 2:11, 2:17, 2:29, 3:6, 3:13, 3:22.)

The messages to the seven churches were intended to inform not only the seven individual churches, but, ultimately, all of Christ's churches. This becomes clear from the following statement Jesus made to the church in Thyatira: "I will strike her children dead.

---

13 M. C. Hazard, A Complete Concordance to the American Standard Version of the Holy Bible, (New York: Thomas Nelson & Sons, 1922), p. 61.
14 Rand McNalley Atlas of World History, ed. R. R. Palmer, (New York: Rand McNalley & Company, 1965), p. 33.
15 Diarmaid MacCulloch, Christianity: The First Three Thousand Years, (New York: Viking, 2010), pp. 115-116.

Revelation Chapter 1

And <u>all the churches will know</u> that I am he who searches mind and heart, and I will give to each of you according to your works." (Revelation 2:23 ESV)

How inclusive was "all" intended to be in the expression "all the churches?" Does it mean only all seven churches that were in Asia (1:4) or does it mean all churches at all times wherever they might be located? The word "all" not only raises the spatial or geographic question of which churches in which areas are intended, but it also raises the question of time. Does it mean all the churches only during the apostolic period or all churches for all time?

One commentator tells us, "each church represents a church epoch or period. This apocalyptic uncovering is entrusted to the preachers throughout the seven-fold history of the church."[16] A far more reasonable answer to the question of who is included in "all the churches" of 2:23 tells us, "It is unquestionably true that the instruction given the Asiatic churches was for any and all churches in like conditions."[17]

The idea that church history may be accurately made to correspond to seven epochs or periods is evidently erroneous and misleading. For example, if one embraces that concept of church history, how is it to be applied? If one should try to categorize the Reformation as one period of church history in Western Europe, how should he then depict the totally different situation prevailing at the same time in the churches in North Africa and in the Middle East? Those churches were simultaneously undergoing radically different experiences.

1:4 "Grace to you and peace, from him who is and who was and who is to come"

Verse 4 gives us John's prayer for a blessing on the seven churches in which he says, "Grace to you and peace from him who is and who was and who is to come; and from the seven Spirits that are before his throne." The terms "who is and who was and who is to come" express eternity. They can rightfully be applied to God, to Christ and to the Holy Spirit.

John makes it clear that the message of the book of Revelation did not originate with him, but that he is only conveying it to others. It came "from him who is and who was and who is to come; and from the seven Spirits that are before his throne." (1:4) Though the verbs "is," "was," and "is to come" may legitimately be used in reference to Jesus, here, in 1:4, they clearly refer to God since Christ is differentiated in the next verse.

1:4 "the seven Spirits that are before his throne"

John specifically identifies the Holy Spirit as "the seven Spirits that are before his throne." The expression "the seven Spirits" in 1:4 is not in conflict with Paul's exhortation "to keep the unity of the Spirit in the bond of peace." Paul went on to tell us that, "There is one body, and one Spirit." (Ephesians 4:3-4)

The identity of the "seven Spirits" comes from statements in Isaiah 11:2 which express the fullness of the one Spirit. That verse says, "[1] the Spirit of Jehovah shall rest upon

---

[16] Lee G. Tomlinson, <u>The Wonder Book of the Bible: A Commentary On the Book of Revelation</u>, (Joplin, Missouri: College Press, 1963), p. 25.
[17] John T. Hinds, <u>A Commentary on the Book of Revelation</u> (Nashville, Tenn.: Gospel Advocate Company, 1976), p. 19.

him, [2] the spirit of wisdom [3] and understanding, [4] the spirit of counsel [5] and might, [6] the spirit of knowledge [7] and of the fear of Jehovah."

    3.   The international audience

In addition to the literate and illiterate and the seven churches, the messages of the Revelation given to John were intended to impact society internationally. John was told that he "must prophecy again over many peoples and nations and tongues and kings." (Revelation 10:11)

H.   *The authorship of the book.*

1:4   **"from him who is and who was and is to come; and from the seven Spirits that are before his throne"**

The fourth verse of the first chapter makes it clear that the message originated with and from God, that is, with "him who is and who was and is to come; and from the seven Spirits that are before his throne." See also the comments on the words "what the spirit sayeth to the churches" at 2:11.

1:5   **"from Jesus Christ, who is the faithful witness, the first born of the dead, and the ruler of the kings of the earth. Unto him that loveth us, and loosed us from our sins by his blood;"**

1:5   **"the faithful witness, the first born of the dead"**

In the fifth verse, in addition to the statement in verse 4 that the revelation came "from him who is and who was and who is to come; and from the seven Spirits that are before his throne," here it is made unmistakably clear that the message also originated from Christ. In this verse, Jesus is called "the faithful witness." This refers to Jesus' confession before the High Priest as recorded in Mark 14:61-62 which says, "The high priest asked him, and saith unto him, Art thou the Christ, the Son of the Blessed? And Jesus said, I am: and ye shall see the Son of man sitting at the right hand of Power, and coming with the clouds of heaven." Further, Jesus repeated his confession in the presence of Pilate. This is referred to in I Timothy 6:13 which says, "I charge thee in the sight of God, who giveth life to all things, and of Christ Jesus, who before Pontius Pilate witnessed the good confession." (See Matthew 27:11, Mark 15:2, Luke 23:3, John 18:33-37.)

When Jesus told Caiaphas, "Ye shall see the son of man sitting at the right hand of Power, and coming with the clouds of heaven," he made it clear that he was the one predicted in a vision of Daniel which says, "There came with the clouds of heaven one like unto the son of man, and he came even to the ancient of days, and they brought him near before him. And there was given unto him dominion, and glory, and a kingdom that all the peoples, and nations, and languages should serve him: his dominion is an everlasting dominion, which shall not pass away, and his kingdom that which shall not be destroyed." (Daniel 2:13-14)

Denial of who he was could have saved Jesus from gruesome death by crucifixion. By forfeiting his life through the good confession, he then, at his resurrection, became the "first born from the dead." (1:5) This terminology is also quoted in Colossians 1:18.

Revelation Chapter 1

Though Jesus raised the widow's son, Jairus' daughter, and Lazarus, they all ultimately had to die again. In contrast, "Christ being raised from the dead, dieth no more; death no more hath dominion over him." (Romans 6:9) Thus, "he is alive for evermore." (Revelation 1:18) In this sense, Jesus is "the first born of the dead." (Revelation 1:5)

1:5 "the ruler of the kings of the earth"

In addition to Christ being "the faithful witness and the first born of the dead," verse 5 tells us he is also "the ruler of the kings of the earth." "John is lifting the horizon of his readers' perspective above the earthly rulers, who are the visible source of their sufferings, to Him who sits enthroned above the kings of the earth, exercising sovereignty over them (Proverbs 21:1; Daniel 2:21; 4:17). In times of persecution, the kings of the earth who 'set themselves ... against the Lord and against his Anointed' (Psalm 2:2) loom large in the view of the afflicted church. But when the veil is pulled aside, as it is here, to reveal the One who 'sits in the heavens and laughs' (Psalm 2:4), who has not relinquished any part of his sovereignty to tinhorn tyrants, the church takes courage and comfort – and such encouragement may be the principle reason God sent these visions to the exile on Patmos."[18]

1:6 "and he made us to be a kingdom, to be priests unto his God and Father; to him be the glory and the dominion for ever and ever. Amen."

1:6 "he made us to be a kingdom"

John exults with a hymn of praise to Christ, in which he exalts him as the one "who ... made us to be a kingdom." This assertion is very important and is repeated in 5:10. (See also 1:9.) It gives us understanding by which we may determine whether one of the main concepts of pre-millennialism is correct or not. The pre-millennial doctrine states that Christ will return just before (pre) The Millennium which is predicted in Revelation 20:1-3. The pre-millennialists assert that at that alleged point of his second coming Jesus will establish his kingdom on earth. That view is obviously wrong because the Christians to whom John wrote had already been constituted a kingdom.[19] (See also Colossians 1:13 and Acts 2:30-31. See also "The Post-millennial View" in the discussion of 20:3.)

1:6 "to be priests"

Obedient believers in Christ are priests (see I Peter 2:5 and 9).

1:7 "Behold, he cometh with the clouds; and every eye shall see him, and they that pierced him; and all the tribes of the earth shall mourn over him. Even so, Amen."

1:7 "he cometh with the clouds"

As previously noted, this description of his glorious return is a quotation from Jesus' confession before Caiaphas, the High Priest (Matthew 26:57-64) in which he said, "Ye shall see the Son of man sitting at the right hand of Power, and coming with the clouds of heaven." (Mark 14:62). Compare Acts 1:9-11.

---

18 <u>Revelation, Four Views: A Parallel Commentary</u>, ed. Steve Gregg , (Nashville: Thomas Nelson Publishers, 1997), p. 55.
19 The rendering in the King James Version, "he made us kings" is clearly in error. The best Greek texts give *basileian*, a kingdom, not *basileus*, a king. Though the King James wrongly rendered 1:6 and 5:10 as kings, it rendered 1:9 correctly.

Revelation Verse by Verse

1:7 "every eye shall see him"

The statement that "every eye shall see him, and they that pierced him; and all the tribes of the earth shall mourn over him" is a quotation from Zechariah 12:10. In view of Matthew 25:31-46, the coming of Christ to which Revelation 1:7 refers, is his coming for final judgment, not as pre-millennialists would have us believe, to establish his kingdom on earth. (See the comments on "he made us to be a kingdom" at 1:6.)

1:8 "I am the Alpha and the Omega, saith the Lord God, who is and who was and who is to come, the Almighty."

The authorship of the book of Revelation is summarized here in 1:8. The words "Alpha" and "Omega" are the names for the first and last letters of the Greek alphabet. They are used to express the concept of the ultimate, that reality before which and after which nothing else exists or could take precedence. (See 21:6 and especially the comments at 22:13.)

II.   Messages to the <u>Seven Churches</u> of the Province of Asia 1:9-3:22

    A.   The circumstances through which the messages to the churches were revealed. 1:9-20

        1.   John's location and spiritual attitude 1:9-10

1:9 "I John your brother and partaker with you in the tribulation and kingdom and patience which are in Jesus, was in the isle that is called Patmos, for the word of God and the testimony of Jesus."

    1:9   "I John your brother and partaker with you in the tribulation and kingdom"

Though an apostle, John does not mention his status or rank. He simply introduces himself as a brother who is not exempt from the sufferings of ordinary Christians but is, rather, a "partaker" with them in "the tribulation." His statement pointed to the widespread persecution of the Christians which was being carried out at that time. That tribulation in no way contradicted the fact that they were citizens of the "kingdom," a kingdom which ultimately would become triumphant.

    1:9   "the isle that is called Patmos"

Patmos is one of the islands of the Dodecanese group, "in the Aegean Sea about 70 miles southwest of Ephesus – [and] 37 miles from Miletus. It is about 8 miles long by six miles wide and comprises approximately 22 square miles. See Map 2. It was used by the Roman government as a place for the banishment of criminals, who were forced to work the island's mines. The Apostle John was sent here by the Emperor Domitian in 95 A.D. and it was while in exile on Patmos he received the visions recorded in the book of the Revelation (Revelation 1:9-10)."[20]

"Rhodes is the most substantial and fertile of a belt of limestone islands – the Dodecanese, the twelve islands – that stretches for a hundred miles along the coast of Asia Minor. Rhodes lies at the southwest end of the group; the northern marker is the whitewashed monastery island of Patmos, one of Orthodox Christianity's holy sites,

---

[20] Guy P. Duffield, <u>Handbook of Bible Lands</u>, (Glendale, California: Regal Division G/L Publications, 1969), p. 23.

Revelation Chapter 1

where Saint John the Divine received the revelations [of the last book] of the New Testament. These islands are so closely intertwined with the bays and headlands of the Asian shore that the mainland is always a presence on the horizon. From Rhodes the crossing is a bare eleven miles, just a couple of hours' sailing time with a smart wind, so near that on clear winter days the snowy Asia mountains, refracted through the thin air, seem almost within touching distance."[21]

1:9 "for the word of God and the testimony of Jesus"

John was on Patmos for two reasons. First, because of tribulation. He tells us, "I John, your brother and partaker with you in the tribulation …" John was not free to leave Patmos. He was a prisoner. (Revelation 1:9) Secondly, he was on that island because of "the word of God and the testimony of Jesus." John apparently had gone to Patmos to preach "the word of God" and to give "the testimony of Jesus."

The situation: John received the Revelation during the reign of the Roman Emperor Domitian (A.D. 81-96). "With the exception of Caligula, he was the first Emperor to take his [self-proclaimed] divinity seriously and to *demand* Caesar worship. … In particular he launched his hatred against the Jews and the Christians. When he arrived in the theatre with his empress, the crowds were urged to rise and shout: 'All hail to our Lord and his Lady!' He enacted that he himself was a god. He informed all provincial governors that government announcements and proclamations must begin: 'Our Lord and God Domitian commands …' Everyone who addressed him in speech or in writing must begin: 'Lord and God.' Here is the background of the *Revelation*. All over the Empire men and women must call Domitian god – or die. Caesar worship was the deliberate policy; all must say: 'Caesar is Lord.' There was no escape."[22]

"Irenaeus [130 - 202 A.D.] in the late second century was the first, so far as we know, to place the work [that is, the writing of the book of Revelation] at the end of the reign of Domitian, who died in 96."[23]

"Victorinus, who wrote towards the end of the third century A.D., says in his commentary on the *Revelation*: 'John, when he saw these things was in the island of Patmos, condemned to the mines by Domitian the Emperor.'"[24]

Under Domitian, failure to recognize the deity of the Emperor often led to death. For example, "In 95 [A.D.] Clemens was *consul ordinarius* for some four months, but scarcely had he resigned his office when, with his wife and with several others, he was called upon to answer an accusation of neglect of the State religion (*atheotes*). It may be that this accusation was due to their being favourers of Jewish or Christian rights, but whatever the precise implications attaching to the word *atheotes*, it proved fatal to Clemens and to the exiled Aciliul Glabrio, for both were executed."[25]

John held fast to the truth in his teaching and preaching. He had held fast to the "word of God and the testimony of Jesus." Jesus, not the emperor, was Lord. The Almighty, not

---

21 Roger Crowley, Empires of the Sea, (New York: Random House, 2009), pp. 5-6.
22 William Barclay, The Revelation of John, Vol. I, (Philadelphia: The Westminster Press, 1976), p. 19.
23 G. W. Bowersock, *Apocalypse Then*, The New York Review of Books, April 5, 2012, p. 61.
24 William Barclay, The Revelation of John, Vol. I, (Philadelphia: The Westminster Press, 1976), p. 14.
25 M. P. Charlesworth, *The Flavian Dynasty*, The Cambridge Ancient History, Vol. XI, (Cambridge: The University Press, 1954), pp. 31-32.

Domitian, was God. Because he had refused to compromise, he was, along with countless other Christians, suffering tribulation.

1:10 **"I was in the Spirit on the Lord's day and heard behind me a great voice, as of a trumpet"**

1:10 "in the Spirit on the Lord's day"

"John, though denied the privilege of joining in the exercises of a Christian assembly, evidently, devoted the day to meditation and prayer, thereby setting an example for every lonely saint; and his soul was lifted to a spiritual exaltation that peculiarly fitted him for communion with God."[26] (See the note on 4:2).

Undoubtedly, "the Lord's day" refers to the first day of the week. It was on that day, the day of Pentecost which always comes on the first day of the week, (see Exodus 23:15-16) that the church was established. (See Acts chapter 2.) It was also the first day of the week on which Jesus rose from the dead. (Matthew 28:1-10, Mark 16:1-9, Luke 14:1-7) Further, it was the first day of the week when Jesus revealed himself to his disciples. (John 20:19-20) Finally, the first day of the week was the regular meeting day when Christians assembled. (Acts 20:7 and I Corinthians 16:2)

1:10 "a great voice"

The fact that it was "a great voice" indicates that it demanded attention and obedience.

2. Instructions given to John 1:11

1:11 **"saying, What thou seest, write in a book and send it to the seven churches: unto Ephesus, and unto Smyrna, and unto Pergamum, and unto Thyatira, and unto Sardis, and unto Philadelphia, and unto Laodicea."**

1:11 "What thou seest, write in a book"

Here, in chapter 1:11 we are told that John was commanded by a voice as piercing as the sound of a trumpet, (See 1:10.) "what thou seest write in a book and send it to the seven churches." John had seen the vision and had heard the message but they were "not something to receive selfishly [only] for one's own edification; they were something to be transmitted to men, even if the price of the transmission were costly indeed. It may be that a man must withdraw to see his vision, but he must also go forth to tell his vision."[27]

1:11 "send it to the seven churches"

Not only is John told to write the vision in a book, he is told to "send it to the seven churches." So there could be utterly no misunderstanding, those seven churches are enumerated. It will give each student of the book of Revelation a lasting heritage to memorize the names of those churches.

---

26 B. W. Johnson, <u>A Vision of the Ages</u>, (Hollywood, California: Old Paths Book Club, n.d.), p. 26.
27 William Barclay, <u>The Revelation of John</u>, Vol. I, (Philadelphia: The Westminster Press, 1976), p. 55.

Revelation Chapter 1

Using an acronym may help us to remember their names. I suggest the following:

    E - Ephesus   (2:1)

    S - Smyrna   (2:8)

    P - Pergamum   (2:12)

    T - Thyatira   (2:18)

    S - Sardis   (3:1)

    P - Philadelphia   (3:7)

    L - Laodicea   (3:14)

See Map 3, which shows the location of the seven churches. However, the seven churches were not all the churches which were located in the province of Asia at the time John wrote. There were at least four others. Two notable churches which were not included in the seven were the churches at Colossae and at Hierapolis. (See Colossians 4:13.)

Colossae was the third of the Lycus Valley cities. It "lay near the upper end of the valley about eleven miles east and a little south of Laodicea. At Colossae the valley narrowed to approximately two miles, and the city was overshadowed by great mountain heights. Colossae itself stood at an altitude of 1,150 feet: Mount Cadmus towered above it some three miles to the south at an altitude of 8,013 feet."[28]

Hierapolis was visible from Laodicea. From that vantage point one "could see the white cliffs of Hierapolis, six miles away, gleaming in the sunshine. ... 'The holy city' (*hierapolis*) [literally, priestly city] was situated on a shelf about 1100 feet above sea level and about 150 to 300 feet above the plain. ... It stood on the north side of the Lycus [river] while Laodicea was on the south."[29]

A third Asian church not mentioned in the book of Revelation was at Miletus. Intimation of its existence is found in Acts 20:13-38 and in II Timothy 4:20. Also, there was another well-known church at Troas. (See Acts 20:5-12.)

Hinds suggests that, "There was evidently some divine reason why letters were sent [only] to the seven named [churches]. As seven is supposed to be a sacred number indicating perfection, it has been suggested that seven were addressed to signify the perfection of the instruction given or, that the seven would represent the whole church and the combined instruction be complete and applicable to all congregations for all time. It is unquestionably true that the instruction given the Asiatic churches was for any and all churches in like conditions."[30]

---

28 Charles F. Pfeiffer and Howard F. Vos, <u>The Wycliffe Historical Geography of Bible Lands</u>, (Chicago: Moody Press, 1967), p. 381.

29 Charles F. Pfeiffer and Howard F. Vos, <u>The Wycliffe Historical Geography of Bible Lands</u>, (Chicago: Moody Press, 1967), p. 379.

30 John T. Hinds, <u>A Commentary on the Book of Revelation</u> (Nashville, Tenn.: Gospel Advocate Company, 1976), p. 19.

"The number seven was ubiquitous in Temple ritual and in the scriptures: 'composed of the first of the evens and the second of the odds and of the first of the odds and the second of the evens, it is called by the early sages a *mispar kolek* (a 'complete' or 'inclusive' number), and it hints at one of the mysteries of creation.'"[31]

I had two mathematicians review the *mispar kolek*. Both of them are in agreement. Mark Troutt wrote: "It seems to be referring to 7 = 2+5 and 7 = 3+4, which is true. However, the number 1 is usually considered the "first of the odds" when taught in math classes today, which would change the given equations to 2+3 and 1+4 which both equal 5 instead of 7. It's possible that in the Hebrew numbering system 3 was considered the first odd number, and it probably was considered a 'complete' or 'inclusive' number by the Israelites, but it doesn't make total sense based on the current classification of odd numbers."[32]

If we knew more about the interrelationships of the geographic, economic and ethnic features of each of the seven churches, we probably would find that each was uniquely complimentary to each of the others. Therefore, each of the churches in the seven cities enhanced the influence and outreach of her six sister churches. Together, their lamp stands functioned analogously like the golden candelabra with seven lamps which illuminated the Holy Place of both the Tabernacle and the Temple. (See Exodus 25:31-40 and 37:17-24.) Presumably, the other churches in the Roman province of Asia were not situated so they had the mutual and reciprocal relationship with their fellow churches comparable to that which the seven had with each other. When any one of the seven churches allowed conditions to prevail which endangered the continuance of its candlestick in its assigned place, all its fellow congregations in that giant Roman-Asian Christian *menorah*, formed by the seven churches, would be adversely impacted.

It is important to note that, through John, Jesus sends letters directly to each of the seven churches of the Roman province of Asia. He does not send the message to any regional or national church organization to be forwarded to the individual congregations. From this fact it seems logical and scriptural to conclude that, up to this point in church history, there was no formal church organization above individual congregations.

The letters from Jesus to seven churches in the Roman province of Asia give us an invaluable, in-depth opportunity to examine church life in the apostolic period. The accounts of life in several of the churches will shatter any uncritical, idyllic, inclusive concept we may have had for Christian corporate life in the apostolic period of church history. Sexual immorality, indifference and selfishness mar the records of some of the churches. On the other hand, in several of the churches uplifting and inspiring examples of tenacious faithfulness, to the point of martyrdom, along with triumph in the face of poverty and opposition, challenge us to live lives fully committed to Jesus.

3. The one who spoke to John 1:12-18

1:12 "And I turned to see the voice that spake with me. And having turned I saw seven golden candlesticks;"

---

31 Frederic Raphael, *Duran Duran*, Commentary, January 2016, p. 52.
32 Mark Troutt, from an email dated May 18, 2016.

Revelation Chapter 1

When he turned to see who was speaking, it must initially have been disappointing, for he only "saw seven golden candlesticks." Those candlesticks are identified in 1:20 as the seven churches.

John had to identify the commanding voice before he could agree to comply with the strict order which had directed that, "what thou seest, write in a book [compare Jeremiah 30:1-2] and send it to the seven churches." (1:11) His need for complete and certain identity of the one who spoke to him is comparable to that need which motivated Saul, on the road to Damascus to ask, "who art thou, Lord?" (Acts 9:5)

In response to John's inquiring gaze Jesus revealed himself to John in an extended, multifaceted, overwhelming series of self disclosures. Jesus probably did this to fortify John to faithfully and fully convey the phenomenal series of revelations which it would be his duty to make known.

When Daniel was given one of his world-impacting revelations, he "fainted, and was sick certain days." (Daniel 8:27) Jesus undoubtedly knew that John would similarly be traumatized by some of the global disasters the coming prophesies would foretell. Therefore, John's assurance of the reality of the mandate under which he was to work had to be impressed upon him indelibly. Consequently, Jesus reveals himself to John in an extraordinary series of visions.

1:13 **"In the midst of the candlesticks one like unto a son of man, clothed with a garment down to the foot, and girt about at the breasts with a golden girdle."**

That initially disappointing vision (he <u>only</u> "saw seven golden candlesticks" 1:12) was almost immediately compensated for by the vision of "a son of man." The descriptive phrase, "son of man" is a term which Jesus often used, referring to himself. For example, on the occasion of healing a man with palsy, Jesus said, "that ye may know that the Son of man hath authority on earth to forgive sins (then saith he to the sick of the palsy), Arise, and take up thy bed and go unto thy house." (Matthew 9:6) Compare also Mark 2:10 and Luke 3:24.

In using the name "son of man," Jesus was clearly appropriating terminology from Old Testament prophecies which looked forward to the coming of Christ. For example, Daniel wrote, "I saw in the night visions, and, behold, there came with the clouds of heaven one like unto a son of man, and he came even to the ancient of days, and they brought him near before him. And there was given him dominion, and glory, and a kingdom, that all the peoples, nations, and languages should serve him: his dominion is an everlasting dominion, which shall not pass away, and his kingdom that which shall not be destroyed." (Daniel 7:13-14) As we have seen previously, in his confession before Caiaphas, Jesus unmistakably applied that Messianic description to himself. (See Matthew 26:63-64 and Mark 14:61-62.)

As man was made in the image of God (see Genesis 1:26), so God, in reciprocal response, affirms his affinity with man by the term, "son of man." Of course, while it carries the idea of intimate relationship with man, it implies none of the limitations and restraints within the confines of which man must live and act.

Revelation Verse by Verse

The being who spoke to John was clothed with a garment, a robe, which reached to his feet while his chest was covered by a golden girdle, like a vest, worn over the robe. John probably recognized the close resemblance of this apparel to that which was worn by the Jewish High Priest who, when on duty, was to wear: a linen coat and a linen girdle. (See Leviticus 16:4.)

The robe that the risen Christ was wearing not only denoted priestly rank but also the rank of royalty. (See I Samuel 18:4.) "No longer was he a criminal on a cross; he was dressed gloriously and majestically like a king. So here we are shown the royalty of Christ. Christ is Priest and Christ is King."[33]

1:14-15 "And his head and his hair were white as white wool, white as snow; and his eyes were as a flame of fire; and his feet like unto burnished brass, as if it had been refined in a furnace; and his voice as the voice of many waters."

1:14-15 "His head ... his hair ... his eyes ... his feet ... his voice."

In 1:14-15 our attention is drawn away from his apparel to the visage or appearance of the one who spoke to John.

The commanding voice, which earlier had been likened to the piercing sound of a trumpet (1:10), is here likened to the roar of a great waterfall, "the voice of many waters." This deafening, demanding voice probably reminded John of the vision given to Ezekiel in which he beheld "the glory of the God of Israel [who] came from the way of the east: and his voice was like the sound of many waters." (Ezekiel 43:2)

The whiteness of the head of that being who spoke to John and his white hair align this vision with one described by Daniel who recorded, "I beheld till thrones were placed, and one that was the ancient of days did sit: his raiment was white as snow, and the hair of his head like pure wool." (Daniel 7:9)

The whiteness which John saw is also a symbol, used by Isaiah, of sinlessness. Isaiah said, "Though your sins be as scarlet, they shall be as white as snow; though they be red like crimson, they shall be as wool." (Isaiah 1:18)

1:14-15 "His eyes were as a flame of fire and his feet like unto burnished brass"

These descriptions take us to Daniel's vision of God in which it is recorded that, "His eyes [were] as flaming torches, and his arms and his feet like unto burnished brass, and the voice of his words like the voice of a multitude." (Daniel 10:6)

1:16 "And he had in his right hand seven stars: and out of his mouth proceeded a sharp two-edged sword: and his countenance was as the sun shineth in his strength."

1:16 "had in his right hand seven stars."

The divine personage whom John beheld, "had in his right hand seven stars." Those stars are clearly identified in verse 20, which informs us that "the seven stars are the angels of the seven churches."

---

[33] William Barclay, <u>The Revelation of John</u>, Vol. I, (Philadelphia: The Westminster Press, 1976), pp. 57-58.

Revelation Chapter 1

1:16 "Out of his mouth proceeded a sharp two-edged sword:"

This description is borrowed from Isaiah 11:4 in which the characteristics are given for the "shoot out of the stock of Jesse, and the branch out of his roots." In that passage, we are told that "with righteousness shall he judge the poor, and decide with equity for the meek of the earth; and **he shall smite the earth with the rod of his mouth**, and with the breath of his lips shall he slay the wicked." (See also Revelation 19:15.)

"The symbolism tells us of the penetrating quality of the Word of God. The Word of God, if we listen to it, is such that no shield of self-deception can withstand it; it strips away our disguises and our self-deludings, and lays bare our sin and then leads to pardon."[34]

This description of the Word proceeding out of the mouth of God as "a sharp two-edged sword" is in harmony with Hebrews 4:12 where we are told, "the word of God is living, and active, and sharper than any two-edged sword, and piercing even to the dividing of soul and spirit, of both joints and marrow, and quick to discern the thoughts and intents of the heart."

1:16 "his countenance was as the sun shineth in his strength"

At this point, the vision must have had its full impact on John. Now, beyond all doubt, the identity and the reality of the one who spoke to him must have been fully certified, for John saw that the one who spoke to him had a "countenance [which] was <u>as the sun shineth in his strength</u>." This segment of the vision was a duplication of the phenomenon which he had seen on the Mount of Transfiguration, concerning which Matthew wrote that Jesus took "with him Peter, and James and John his brother and bringeth them up into a high mountain: and he was transfigured before them; and his face did shine <u>as the sun</u>, and his garments became white as the light." (Matthew 17:1-2)

1:17 "And when I saw him, I fell at his feet as one dead. And he laid his right hand upon me, saying, Fear not; I am the first and the last,"

1:17 "when I saw him, I fell at his feet as one dead"

John tells us of the impact which the vision of the transfigured Christ had on him. He said, "when I saw him, **I fell at his feet as one dead**." His description is completely analogous to the experience which Paul had when Jesus appeared to him. He had gone to the High Priest in Jerusalem and had "asked of him letters to Damascus unto the synagogues, that if he found any that were of the Way, whether men or women, he might bring them bound to Jerusalem. And as he journeyed, it came to pass that he drew nigh unto Damascus: and suddenly there shown round about him a light out of heaven: and **he fell upon the earth**, and heard a voice saying unto him, Saul, Saul, why persecutest thou me?" (Acts 9:1-4) Daniel experienced a similar impact when he beheld a man whose "face was as the appearance of lightning, and his eyes as flaming torches." (Daniel 10:6) When Daniel "saw this great vision, [he said] there remained no strength in me. [When] I heard the voice of his words, then I was fallen into a deep sleep on my face, with my face toward the ground." (Daniel 10:8-9)

---

34 William Barclay, <u>The Revelation of John</u>, Vol. I, (Philadelphia: The Westminster Press, 1976), p. 63.

1:17   "laid his right hand upon me, saying, Fear not"

John was comforted and reassured because the one speaking to him not only laid his right hand upon him, but said, "Fear not." "The command, 'fear not' was intended to give John assurance so he would carefully hear that which would be revealed to him. Once before, Jesus gave a similar command to his apostles, saying, 'It is I; be not afraid.' (Matthew 14:27) In the midst of manifestations of divine power, man needs assurance from God to calm his fears."[35]

1:17   "I am the first and the last."

"As we have seen, in the Old Testament this is nothing other than the self description of God Himself (Isaiah 44:6; 48:12). It is the promise of Jesus that He is there [is present] at the beginning and the end."[36] (See especially the comments on 22:13.)

1:18   "and the Living one; and I was dead, and behold, I am alive for evermore, and I have the keys of death and of Hades."

1:18   "[I am] the Living one; and I was dead, and behold, I am alive for evermore"

This is not only a post-resurrection appearance of Jesus, but a post-ascension appearance. The apostles and many others had received assurance from Jesus' victory over death by his post-resurrection appearances. Here, their confidence is augmented by the assurance that the victory they had beheld had not been reversed or terminated. Through this appearance Jesus makes it clear that he is not only alive, but alive forevermore.

1:18   "I have the keys of death and Hades"

Science and Medicine have valiantly tried to fend off death. Though by that effort the human life span, on average, has been extended, the key to the phenomenon of death still eludes man's best efforts. Death still prevails. Jesus proved that he has the key of death by his resurrection.

But more than that, Jesus also has the key of Hades. When Jesus died, he went into Hades, the unseen abode of the spirits of the dead. This is made clear by Peter, who by inspiration wrote, "He went and preached unto the spirits in prison." (I Peter 3:19) Hades is a spirit prison, the two parts of which were separated and isolated by a moat, a chasm or a great gulf. Jesus made that clear when he told of the situation of the rich man who had selfishly disregarded the grievous needs of a beggar named Lazarus who was laid at his doorstep every day. In Hades that rich man besought Abraham to send Lazarus, who was in the other part of Hades known as Abraham's bosom, to alleviate his thirst. But Abraham told him it was impossible to respond to his request because "there is a great gulf fixed, that they that would pass from hence to you might not be able, and that none may cross over from thence to us." (Luke 16:26)

Jesus used the key of Hades when he ascended. Paul reminds us of this triumphant fact when he quotes Psalm 68:18 saying, "When he ascended on high he led captivity captive." (Ephesians 4:8) What was that captivity? It was the upper part of Hades called

---

35   John T. Hinds, A Commentary on the Book of Revelation (Nashville, Tenn.: Gospel Advocate Company, 1976), p. 30.
36   William Barclay, The Revelation of John, Vol. I, (Philadelphia: The Westminster Press, 1976), p. 64.

Revelation Chapter 1

Abraham's bosom where Lazarus was detained. Jesus took with him all of the captive spirits from that temporary abode when he ascended on high. They could not have been liberated earlier because a death had to take place for their redemption before they could receive, "the promise of the eternal inheritance." (Hebrews 9:15, See also Romans 3:25.) Now, for Christians there is no Hades, that is, no spirit prison. When we Christians die, we "depart to be with Christ which is very far better." (Philippians 1:23) (See also II Corinthians 5:1-4). Now, since Jesus has used the keys of death and Hades, we shall not enter into captivity at death but into the presence of Christ. This is just one way in which Hades shall not prevail against the church. (See Matthew 16:18).

        4.   Final instructions and clarifications about writing to the churches 1:19-20

1:19   "Write therefore the things which thou sawest, and the things which are, and the things which shall come to pass hereafter;"

See the discussion of this verse under "The divisions of the book" at "B. 3" beginning on page 5.

1:20   "the mystery of the seven stars which thou sawest in my right hand, and the seven golden candlesticks. The seven stars are the angels of the seven churches: and the seven candlesticks are seven churches."

For a discussion of the "seven stars" which are "the angels of the seven churches" see the discussion at 1:4 under "the seven angels" on pages 9-11. For a discussion of the meaning of "candlesticks" see the discussion under 2:5 on page 30.

Revelation Chapter 2

> B.   The identity of the seven churches 2:1-3:22
>
> 1. The Church in Ephesus 2:1-7

2:1   "To the angel of the church in Ephesus write: These things saith he that holdeth the seven stars in his right hand, he that walketh in the midst of the seven golden candlesticks:"

Reasoning from clues in scripture and from statements in post-biblical church history, it is quite certain that the church in Ephesus was the home church of the apostle John during the latter part of his life. (See paragraphs six and seven below.) Though John lived in Ephesus and worked in the church there, he was not the person to whom the word "angel" refers, for obviously he was not writing to himself.

There is a strong possibility that the angel of the church in Ephesus was Timothy, for Paul had written to Timothy saying, "I urge you, as I did when I was on my way to Macedonia, to remain in Ephesus so that you may instruct certain people not to teach any different doctrine, and not to occupy themselves with myths and endless genealogies that promote speculations rather than the divine training that is known by faith." (I Timothy 1:3-4 NRSV)

While it is probable that Timothy was the angel of the church in Ephesus, it is also possible that the term may refer to Onesiphorus about whom Paul wrote that in many things "he ministered at Ephesus." (II Timothy 1:16-18)

It is clear that the apostles used an organized approach to world evangelism. Jesus had told them, "You will be my witnesses in Jerusalem, in all Judea and Samaria, and to the ends of the earth." (Acts 1:8 NRSV) However, the apostles did not haphazardly approach the global work which Jesus had mandated, but organized their evangelistic outreach. From Galatians 2:9 it is obvious that, on one level, the apostles divided their work between Gentiles and Jews (also called "the circumcision"). The passage says, "when they perceived the grace that was given unto me, James and Cephas and John, they who were reputed to be pillars, gave to me and Barnabas the right hands of fellowship, that we should go unto the Gentiles and they unto the circumcision."

Note that the apostle John's area in worldwide evangelism was to be among those known as "the circumcision," that is, among the Jewish people. The apostle Peter made it clear that part of the Jewish Dispersion lived in the Roman province of Asia. (See I Peter 1:1.) Thus, if John worked with the church in Ephesus it would have given him opportunity to reach out to those Jewish people in harmony with his assignment which is recorded in Galatians 2:9.

From Jesus' letter to the church in Smyrna (2:8-11), it seems probable that the apostle John had worked among the Jews in that Asian city. Jesus characterized those Jews as "a synagogue of Satan," reflecting what seems to have been an understanding which someone, probably John, had reached by working among them. (Revelation 2:9) Jesus also found the Jews in Philadelphia to be of that same degraded sort. (See 3:9.)

The inferential clue that John worked among the churches of Asia, which is drawn from the statement about the Jews in Smyrna and Philadelphia, is powerfully augmented by a statement in Eusebius' Church History.[37] While enumerating the parts of the world where Christ was preached by the apostles, Eusebius recorded, "The holy apostles and disciples of our Saviour, being scattered over the whole world, Thomas, according to tradition, received Parthia as his allotted region; Andrew received Scythia, and John [received] Asia, where, after continuing for some time, he died at Ephesus." Eusebius even gives us his source for this information about John. He tells us, "This account is given by Origen, in the third book of his exposition of Genesis."[38] Origen was born about 185 and died in approximately 254 A.D.

"While living in Ephesus it is believed that he [John] had with him Mary, the mother of Jesus, for a few years."[39] If Mary was alive at the time John moved to Ephesus, he certainly would have taken her with him because at the crucifixion Mary, Jesus' mother, had been entrusted to his care. The record says, "When Jesus saw his mother there, and the disciple whom he loved standing nearby, he said to his mother, 'Dear woman, here is your son,' and to the disciple, 'Here is your mother.' From that time on, this disciple took her into his home." (John 19:26-27 NIV)

There is strong tradition that the apostle John took Mary with him when he moved to Ephesus. However, there is also countervailing tradition which says Mary died in Palestine before John made Ephesus the center of his ministry. We simply do not have historical records which make it possible to decide between these two traditions.

2:2 **"I know thy works, and thy toil and patience, and that thou canst not bear evil men, and didst try them that call themselves apostles, and they are not, and didst find them false;"**

2:2 "I know thy works, and thy toil and patience"

This description seems to indicate that the church in Ephesus had been diligent in its effort to weed out heresy and restore proper order.

2:2 "thou canst not bear evil men, and didst try them that call themselves apostles"

The letter which Jesus wrote to the church in Ephesus confirms Paul's prophecy about the Ephesian church in which he said, "I know that after I leave, savage wolves will come in among you and will not spare the flock. Even from your own number men will arise and distort the truth in order to draw away disciples after them. So be on your guard! Remember that for three years I never stopped warning each of you night and day with tears. 'Now I commit you to God and to the word of his grace, which can build you up and give you an inheritance among all those who are sanctified.'" (Acts 20:29-32 NIV)

---

37 Eusebius, who died in 341, is known as the father of Church History because there is no coherent church history which antedates his.
38 Eusebius Pamphilius, The Ecclesiastical History, trans. Christian Frederick Cruse (Grand Rapids: Baker Book House, 1979), p. 82
39 William Steuart, McBirnie, The Search For the Twelve Apostles, (Wheaton, Illinois: Tyndale House, 1988), p. 110.

Revelation Chapter 2

Paul's prophecy which is recorded in Acts 20:29 is shown to have been fully accurate by the description which Jesus gave of events which had subsequently taken place in the church. He said, "Thou canst not bear evil men, and didst try them that call themselves apostles, and they are not, and didst find them false." (Revelation 2:2) Paul had not only warned the leaders of the church of the coming danger but had exhorted them to be on guard. It is obvious that ultimately the church had successfully responded to Paul's warning. They had rejected the men who were making false claims about their true standing. Those false apostles had even turned against Paul. See the discussion of the church trial under 2:3.

How vicious did the opposition to Paul at Ephesus become? The answer to that question will help us understand the perilous and miserable conditions into which the church in Ephesus had fallen before Jesus wrote this letter to them. To clarify the issue we must understand Paul's imprisonment record. Paul was imprisoned twice in Rome. That implies, of course, that he had been released from the first imprisonment and was later imprisoned again. This becomes clear if we read the Biblical record carefully: Paul was released from the imprisonment described in the final chapter of Acts during which, "he abode two whole years in his own hired dwelling, and received all that went in unto him, preaching the kingdom of God, and teaching the things concerning the Lord Jesus Christ with all boldness, none forbidding him." (Acts 28:30-31).

Two considerations indicate that the imprisonment mentioned in II Timothy 2:9 is later and distinct from that with which the narrative in Acts closes. The passage says, "I suffer hardship unto bonds, as a malefactor; but the word of God is not bound."

First of all, the imprisonment mentioned in II Timothy is much harsher than the one described in Acts. According to the account in his letter to Timothy, he had been indicted under a criminal charge: "I suffer hardship unto bonds as a malefactor ("criminal" - NIV, "chained like a criminal" - NRSV). Paul expects the death penalty to be imposed. He says, "I am already being offered, and the time of my departure is come." (II Timothy 4:6). He must have written from Rome, just before his execution. This is in vivid contrast to his earlier imprisonment from which he expected to be released. At that time he said, "I am confident in the Lord that I myself will come soon." (Philippians 2:24 NIV). On another occasion he said, "Prepare a guest room for me, because I hope to be restored to you in answer to your prayers." (Philemon v. 22 NIV). Furthermore, according to the account in Acts, no indictment had been made (Acts 25:25-27) and he certainly was not in jeopardy of the death penalty. (Acts 26:30-32).

Part of Paul's ministry, which he rendered between his two imprisonments, clearly took place in the Roman Province of Asia (Cf. II Timothy 1:15) and probably in Ephesus itself (Cf. I Timothy 1:3; II Timothy 1:18). The trouble which resulted in Paul's second imprisonment unquestionably began in Asia, while that resulting in his imprisonment described in Acts chapter 28 obviously began in Jerusalem. (By comparing II Timothy 1:15 and 4:16 it seems that Paul's preliminary judicial hearing, leading to his second imprisonment, took place in Asia and that all the brethren who were in a position to have testified in Paul's favor declined to do so.) Without doubt, some men from Ephesus, the chief city of Asia, had a key role in causing Paul's trouble. This is clear from what he says of a trouble maker by the name of Alexander: "Alexander the coppersmith did me much evil:" (II Timothy 4:14) Then Paul warns Timothy of the danger which this same man may cause him. He said, "... of whom do thou also beware; ..." (II Timothy 4:15) Since Timothy seems to have been ministering in Ephesus (Cf. I Timothy 1:3; II Timothy 1:16-18; 4:19) it seems logical to conclude that Alexander also resided there. In I Corinthians 15:32 Paul says, "I fought with beasts at Ephesus." The NIV renders it, "wild beasts." while the NRSV translated it, "wild animals."

2:3 **"and thou hast patience and didst bear for my name's sake, and hast not grown weary."**

With the degree and extent of vicious opposition to Paul, which centered on the church in Ephesus, in the face of which the church had shown despicable cowardice (see II Timothy 4:16), it is truly remarkable that Jesus could now say, "thou hast patience and didst bear for my name's sake and hast not grown weary." Obviously, there must have been a fundamental recovery in the spiritual life of the church in Ephesus. It must have taken place between the time when Paul, just prior to his execution which probably took place in 68 A.D., wrote to Timothy and this point at which Jesus commends the Ephesian church. Previously, the Ephesian church had been in the clutches of men who had falsely brought criminal charges against Paul and who subsequently threatened Timothy. The time needed for recovery must have been lengthy.

By the time Jesus had written to them, a church trial must have taken place in the Ephesian church. That trial is clearly indicated in Revelation 2:2 in the words, "thou ... didst try [test - ESV, NIV] them that called themselves apostles."[40] Such a trial would have been in complete harmony with Paul's instructions to the church in Corinth which are given in I Corinthians 6:1-5. That trial process would have required considerable time. First of all, someone had to get the parties involved in the serious contention in the church to agree to participate in a church trial. They had to reach agreement on who would pronounce judgment and the criteria upon which that judgment would be reached.

Following all that, charges and counter-charges had to be allowed and testimony had to be heard and evaluated. Subsequent to the decision which grew out of that trial, time would have been necessary to see church harmony and equilibrium restored. Probably, that cumulative time would have been extensive enough that it would indicate that the book of Revelation was written after the destruction of Jerusalem in 70 A.D. This internal clue about the date when the book of Revelation was written supplements the incontrovertible historical evidence that Revelation was written after Titus destroyed the Jewish temple in 70 A.D. (See "F., Date of Writing" on page 8.) For additional internal evidence that the writing of the book took place after the destruction of the city of Jerusalem, see the exposition of 2:9.

As we study Christ's epistle to the church in Ephesus, we should also try to understand how the church came into being, not only in Ephesus but throughout the province of Asia. According to Acts 2:9, there were men from the province of Asia who listened to Peter's sermon on the Day of Pentecost. We can only guess whether any of those Asians

---

40 The King James, The American Standard, the Revised Standard Version and the Interlinear Greek-English New Testament translate the Greek word *epeirasas* by the English word "try" which implies a judicial procedure. The NIV, the ESV and the NRSV rendered the Greek word by the English word "test." While the latter translations are not as emphatic as those which rendered the meaning of the Greek word by the word "try," it seems clear that a judicial procedure had taken place in the church at Ephesus before Jesus' letter reached them.

Revelation Chapter 2

were converted to Christ. If so, they probably became charter members of churches when they returned to their hometowns. Though that might be how Christ's church began in one or more of the towns in Asia, we have no explicit confirmation of it in the New Testament.

The apostle Paul had wanted to preach in the province of Asia during his second missionary tour. However, God had other priorities. Luke tells us, "they went through the region of Phrygia and Galatia having been forbidden of the Holy Spirit to speak the word in Asia." (Acts 16:6) Shortly after that, Paul received the vision of the "man of Macedonia standing, beseeching him, and saying, Come over into Macedonia, and help us." (Acts 16:9) Macedonia was on the western shore of the Aegean Sea while Asia was on the eastern shore.

The earliest clue from scripture about how the church began in Ephesus is found in Acts 18:19 which tells us that Paul interrupted his trip to Syria by a layover at Ephesus during which he "entered into the synagogue and reasoned with the Jews." While converts to Christ resulting from that period of preaching are not mentioned, presumably there were some, and they may have become charter members of the church in Ephesus.

Not only could this have been the beginning of the church in Ephesus, but it could also have been the beginning of the church in the whole province of Asia as well. It would have been appropriate that the Asian church should have started in Ephesus because it was not only the largest city in that Roman province, but was the economic and cultural capital as well, though Pergamum was Asia's political capital.

The origin of the churches in Asia, in part, grew out of the dynamic cultural and economic activity centering on Ephesus. More specifically, they came into being through the converts resulting from Paul's ministry, which "continued for the space of two years, … [so that] all they that dwelt in Asia heard the word of the Lord both Jews and Greeks." (Acts 19:10) Was this province-wide triumph the result of evangelistic preaching trips which Paul made? Though there is no mention in scripture of Paul having made such trips, it is difficult to think that he would have confined his evangelistic outreach solely to the city of Ephesus. Also, undoubtedly, citizens from other cities in Asia would have visited Ephesus, because of business or other issues, during the time Paul was preaching there. Some of them, doubtless, heard the Gospel, were converted, and took the message back to their home cities.

2:4 **"But I have this against thee, that thou didst leave thy first love."**

Though the church in Ephesus had recovered from its terrible failure to stand with Paul when Alexander had falsely accused him and had brought criminal charges against him, they were still not fully exonerated before Christ. Consequently, he said, "I have this against thee that thou didst leave thy first love." This indictment not only conveys the idea that the church had lost its initial exuberance but some of its fidelity to the word of Christ. Jesus had clearly taught "If ye keep my commandments, ye shall abide in my love; even as I have kept my Father's commandments, and abide in his love." (John 15:10) He summed it up by saying, "Ye are my friends, if ye do the things which I command you." (John 15:14)

2:5 "Remember therefore whence thou art fallen, and repent and do the first works; or else I come to thee, and will move thy candlestick out of its place, except thou repent."

At that point, the church could only distance itself from the precarious standing it had with Christ if it followed his command to "remember therefore whence thou art fallen, and repent and do the first works." Loss of fervor for and conformity to the will of Christ will not be tolerated, not only in the church at Ephesus but in any church.

2:5 "I come"

Please see the discussion of this warning under 2:16 on page 39.

2:5 "will move thy candlestick out of its place"

Why are churches figuratively called "candlesticks" or "lamp stands?" They have been given this descriptive designation because they are to be "seen as lights in the world, holding forth the word of life." (Philippians 2:14-15) Churches are to illuminate the way to God in the midst of a dark and misleading world. This is one apostolic application of Jesus' exhortation that we should let our light shine before men that they may see our good works and glorify our Father who is in heaven. (See Matthew 5:16.)

What does removing the church's candlestick out of its place mean? It could mean the utter and total extinction of the church. Commentators and expositors who take this position usually point to the conquest of the churches in the Roman province of Asia by the military triumph of Islam, brought to this area by the conquering Turks, an event which ultimately led to the destruction of these churches.

Any church which should refuse to repent will lose Jesus' presence. That would make such a church vulnerable to destructive and fatal attacks. Also, moving the church's candlestick out of its place may mean that some significant role which a church might have filled, due to its circumstances, would be withheld from it, just as the talent was taken from the unworthy servant and given to a worthy one. (Matthew 25:28)

There are crucial opportunities which if not utilized at the right moment will be lost forever. As Mordecai said to Esther, "Who knoweth whether thou art not come to the kingdom for such a time as this?" (Esther 4:14) Similarly, churches must keep themselves alert and faithful so Christ may work through them to forward his cause at critical junctures in history. Should a church, like the five foolish virgins (Matthew 25:1-13), be unprepared, Jesus will take that church's candlestick out of its place. He will not allow such a church to occupy a critical and advantageous position in the future, otherwise it would be "wasting the soil." (Luke 13:7 NRSV)

2:6 "But you have this in your favor: You hate the practices of the Nicolaitans, which I also hate."

While extensive details of the doctrinal system which was embraced and advocated by the Nicolaitans are not known, it is widely thought that they were named after Nickolaus, the seventh one in the group of deacons ordained by the church in Jerusalem to care for the widows. (See Acts 6:5-6.)

Revelation Chapter 2

The Nicolaitans not only had been able to influence the church in Ephesus, but also the church in Pergamum. While the wording in Revelation 2:14-15 leaves some room to question whether the teaching of Balaam is stated to have been the same as that of the Nicolaitans, probably that is the intent. If so, the teaching of the Nicolaitans was based on raw sensualism. (See II Peter 2:13-16 and Numbers 31:15-16.)

It is very sobering to realize that men, like Nickolaus, who have been entrusted with places of responsibility in the church may use the advantages which come from their position as a base from which to promote a corrupt personal agenda. The apostle Paul warned the elders of the church in Ephesus of this danger, when he foresaw by divine insight that one or more of those elders would seek self aggrandizement. (See Acts 20:28-30.)

2:7 **"He that hath an ear, let him hear what the Spirit saith to the churches. To him that overcometh, to him will I give to eat of the tree of life, which is in the Paradise of God."**

2:7 **"He that hath an ear let him hear what the Spirit saith to the churches."**

From this often repeated exhortation, it becomes obvious that God will hold us responsible for the use of our opportunities and our natural abilities. Hearing is one of the gates through which we may acquire knowledge, in this case, knowledge of the will of God. To either negligently or deliberately keep one's self in ignorance of God's purpose and will, is a sin for which God will hold us accountable.

The members of the church in Ephesus were not only to give heed to what God's Spirit said to the Ephesian church but what he "said to [all] the churches." (Revelation 2:23) While existing conditions in one's home church may not duplicate conditions in some of the other churches, certainly the potential for duplication exists. Therefore, knowledge of problems existing in other congregations could fortify one's own church from an attack by those advocating godless destructive perversions.

2:7 **"To him that overcometh,"**

Capitulation in the face of wrong or evil is not an option for those who would be faithful to Jesus. Triumph, success or overcoming are the only choices. Similarly, in the fight against evil, yielding to weariness or exhaustion, which are forms of capitulation, cannot be allowed. We must remember that "a man's goings are established of Jehovah and he delighteth in his way. Though he fall, he shall not be utterly cast down; for Jehovah upholdeth him with his hand." (Psalm 37:23-24) With that reassurance we can accept Paul's exhortation to the Thessalonian church that we should "be not weary in well doing." (II Thessalonians 3:13)

2:7 **"to him will I give to eat of the tree of life, which is in the paradise of God."**

For those who overcome, access to the tree of life will reverse the curse brought upon the human race by the sin of Adam due to which God "placed at the east of the garden of Eden the Cherubim, and the flame of a sword which turned every way, to keep the way of the tree of life." (Genesis 3:24) Those who gain access must "wash their robes, that they may have the right to come to the tree of life, and may enter in by the gates into the city." (Revelation 22:14)

2. The Church in Smyrna 2:8-11

2:8 **"And to the angel of the church in Smyrna write: These things saith the first and the last, who was dead and lived again."**

2:8 **"the angel of the church in Smyrna"**

Though we cannot be dogmatically certain, probably Smyrna's angel was Polycarp, a disciple of the apostle John, though not mentioned in scripture. Polycarp was born about 69 A.D. and died by martyrdom on Saturday, February 23, 155. John's imprisonment on the Isle of Patmos took place about 96 A.D. at which time Polycarp would have been 27 years old, certainly old enough to have been the angel or the messenger to the church in Smyrna. Both Irenaeus[41] and Tertullian[42] in their writings, tell us that Polycarp was a disciple of the apostle John. Though we do not know where their lives first intersected, John probably made itinerant preaching trips to all of the seven churches of Asia. That would have given him opportunity to meet Polycarp at Smyrna. Though the date is not known, according to Jerome, the apostle John appointed Polycarp to be a bishop at Smyrna. Of Polycarp's writings, only his epistle to the church in Philippi has survived. A letter from Bishop Ignatius of Antioch in Syria, addressed to Polycarp, has also survived. Ignatius traveled through Smyrna, on his way to Rome to be executed because of his steadfast loyalty to Christ.

2:8 **"These things saith the first and the last, who was dead and lived again."**

For a discussion of "the first and the last," see the comment on 1:17 on page 22. The speaker's identity which is further stated as the one, "who was dead and lived again" is a renunciation of the swoon theory which states that Jesus never really died but was merely in a comatose state in the tomb from which he recovered by natural bodily vitality. The expression "lived again" tells us that the finality and immutability of death have been broken.

2:9 **"I know thy tribulation and thy poverty (but thou art rich), and the blasphemy of them that say they are Jews and they are not, but are a synagogue of Satan."**

Smyrna was a very prosperous Roman city whose prosperity was undergirded by being the terminus of land routes coming through Asia Minor and by robust sea trade sustained by shipping on the Aegean Sea which utilized Smyrna's excellent port. Living where there was a flourishing economy, why were the Christians in poverty? The Christians in Smyrna lived under a double jeopardy resulting in penury:

First. At the time Jesus dictated these letters to John, Roman persecution was severe. Undoubtedly, that Roman governmental opposition to Christians was a serious impediment to their economic activity. Though on the eastern shore of the Aegean Sea all seven churches of Asia faced the same Roman persecution, yet only Smyrna is noted to have been in poverty. This is in contrast to the poverty, in an earlier time frame, of all the churches in Macedonia which were located on the western shore of the Aegean Sea. (See II Corinthians 8:1-2.)

---

41 At 202 A.D., Irenaeus was bishop of the church in Lugdunum which is now Lyon in southern Gaul, which is now France.
42 Tertullian lived c. 160-c225 A.D. He was a Christian author living in Carthage.

Revelation Chapter 2

Second. In Smyrna there was an additional important factor. The large Jewish population was fanatically trying to thwart Christian activity. For example, when Polycarp was burned at the stake, many from the Jewish community in Smyrna broke their own Sabbath to assist the Roman soldiers by carrying wood for the fire which killed Polycarp.

"In going to his martyrdom at Smyrna in the second century Polycarp is said to have observed the Jews of the city zealously helping its Roman citizens by adding wood to the pyre on which he would be burned alive, and they did this 'as they habitually did.'"[43]

The apostle John died about 55 years before Smyrna's Jews helped the Romans burn the aged Polycarp. But, even at that time, by the power of the Holy Spirit, he could see the dissolute and degraded state of those Jews and called them "a synagogue of Satan." That intense Jewish hatred for Christians is a strong clue that Revelation was written after the destruction of the Jewish temple in 70 A.D., for it was that event which more than anything else elicited vicious widespread persistent Jewish hatred against Christians. (See the comments on 2:3 for additional internal evidence on the date of writing).

Earlier, before widespread virulent hatred against Christians engulfed Jewish communities everywhere, synagogues had not only been very important in Jesus' ministry (See John 18:20), they had also been extremely important for the successful spread of the Gospel in the early years of the apostolic age. (See Acts 13:14, 14:1, 17:1-2, 17:10, 17:17, 18:4, 18:19 and 19:8.) However, Jesus certainly foresaw the time when synagogues would be centers of the persecution of his followers. (See Mark 13:9 and Luke 12:11.)

Subsequent to the Roman destruction of the Jewish temple in Jerusalem, in 70 A.D., vitriolic hatred against Christians engulfed Jews, not only in Palestine, but throughout Jewish communities worldwide. This occurred because Jewish Christians living in Judea had followed Jesus' instructions to flee when the Roman armies gathered in preparation for attack against the Jewish Rebellion. (See Luke 21:20-24.)

Non-Christian Jews saw that flight not only as an act of cowardice but a gross betrayal of the Jewish cause. In A.D. 80, and possibly earlier, the Jewish Jamnia Academy issued a curse on Christians. That curse, "had every day consequences, not least the expulsion from the synagogues of those Christians of Jewish origin who still went to these common places of worship. [See James 2:2.] The last remaining places of contact after the destruction of the Temple had become inaccessible. And with them, the most natural sites of dialogue or indeed missionary activity, had vanished for good. Jamnia only sealed a development marked by four momentous episodes which had begun in A.D. 62 with the killing of James. The cumulative effect resulted in a complete break, which the (Jewish) Christians were unable and probably also unwilling to mend."[44]

From the characterization of the synagogues in Smyrna and in Philadelphia as synagogues of Satan (See Revelation 2:9 and 3:9.) it is unmistakably clear that Jewish post-temple-destruction hatred against Christians had flooded into the cities in the Roman province of Asia where the famous seven churches were located. Undoubtedly, in the case of the church in Smyrna, that Jewish hatred had an economic impact from which

---

43 G. W. Bowersock, *Apocalypse Then*, The New York Review of Books, April 5, 2012, p. 63.
44 Carsten, Peter Thiede and Matthew D'ancona, Eyewitness to Jesus, (New York: Doubleday, 1996), pp. 50-51.

those Christians were thrown into poverty. Here is yet another internal clue that the book of Revelation was written after the destruction of Jerusalem in 70 A.D.

2:10 **"Fear not the things which thou art about to suffer: behold the devil is about to cast some of you into prison, that ye may be tried; and ye shall have tribulation ten days. Be thou faithful unto death and I will give thee the crown of life."**

The Christians in Smyrna were already being severely tried by tribulation, poverty and blasphemous accusations. However, Jesus made it completely clear that additional suffering would be part of their future near-term experience. <u>Imprisonment</u> awaited some of the Christians in Smyrna which would be a part of additional <u>tribulation</u>, that was to last ten days. Some of the Christians, like Polycarp, would be put to <u>death</u>. Jesus encouraged them to face their destiny without fear because he would reward them with the crown of life.

Even while facing such daunting prospects in their near future, Jesus exhorts the Christians in Smyrna to "fear not." "Fearlessness, however, may not necessarily mean the total absence of dread, but rather the refusal to succumb to intimidation, so that threats of harm do not turn them back from their duty to Christ."[45]

Identification of the ten day period during which the Christians were to suffer additional tribulation and trial is disputed. "Ten natural days would be too insignificant for such a grave thing. It might have been ten years. [Calculated as prophetic days, meaning a day for a year. See Ezekiel 4:6] ... It seems probable that the statement was made to encourage the brethren not to falter in their fidelity to God. If so, then by 'ten days' Jesus meant to say that the tribulation would be comparatively short. This would stimulate them to faithfulness."[46]

2:11 **"He that hath an ear, let him hear what the Spirit saith to the churches. He that overcometh shall not be hurt of the second death."**

2:11 "what the Spirit saith to the churches"

Though Jesus is dictating these letters to the apostle John, he says that listeners are to "hear what the Spirit saith to the churches." He does not say that listeners are to hear what I say to the churches. From this it is obvious that the Holy Spirit had an active major role in composing these communications to the churches in Asia.

How to distinguish the role of the Spirit from the role of Christ in generating these messages is an issue so profound that we will have to wait to ask Christ for the full explanation. The union between Christ and the Spirit is so intimate and profound that it reminds us of that union expressed by Isaiah when he wrote, "Come ye near unto <u>me</u>, hear ye this; from the beginning <u>I</u> have not spoken in secret; from the time that it was, there am <u>I</u>: and now <u>the Lord Jehovah</u> hath sent <u>me</u>, and <u>his Spirit</u>." (Isaiah 48:16)

The Christians to whom the Revelation was addressed were exhorted to "hear what the Spirit saith to <u>the churches</u>." It does not say, only hear what the Spirit saith to your own individual church. From this it seems quite clear that each of the seven churches was

---
45 <u>Revelation, Four Views: A Parallel Commentary</u>, ed. Steve Gregg, (Nashville: Thomas Nelson Publishers, 1997), p. 67.
46 John T. Hinds, <u>A Commentary on the Book of Revelation</u>, (Nashville, Tenn.: Gospel Advocate Company, 1976), p. 42.

Revelation Chapter 2

intended to have access to all seven of the letters. Not only were they to give heed to all seven of Christ's messages to the churches but we, too, are to follow that counsel. Presumably, a church in any one of the Asian towns would not only be benefitted by the letter addressed specifically to its own body of Christians, but by the messages to all of the others as well.

2:11   "he that overcometh"

Nothing short of overcoming is acceptable to the Saviour. That, obviously, does not mean to avoid tribulation, suffering and other forms of satanic pressure by compromise. Contrariwise, if steadfast loyal adherence to Jesus should result in prison, in torture or even in death, we are assured that the second death can never hurt us.

2:11   "the second death"

Please see the comment on this expression which is tersely given in 21:8 on page 347.

3. The Church in Pergamum 2:12-17

2:12   "And to the angel of the church in Pergamum write: These things sayeth he that hath the sharp two-edged sword:"

2:12   "Pergamum"

While the ASV spells the name of the city "Pergamum," the King James translation says, "And to the angel of the church in Pergamos write." In addition to these two spellings of the city's name, secular renditions of the name usually give it as "Pergamon." This is the spelling used in the great Pergamon Museum in the city of Berlin. "*Pergamos* is the feminine form of the name, and *Pergamum* is the neuter form. In the ancient world it was known by both forms of the name; but *Pergamum* was much the commoner, and the newer translations are right to prefer it."[47] Pergamon is a variant spelling of the feminine form, Pergamenos. There is a small Turkish town on the location of the biblical Pergamum by the name of Bergama.

Discussion of the church in Pergamum should start with a basic understanding of the historical background of that ancient city in the Roman province of Asia. Between 277 and 241 B.C. the Gauls, ancestors of the New Testament Galatians as well as of present-day France, invaded the area around Pergamum. "Pergamum for a time paid the Gauls tribute, but she retained her general independence, and at last, under Attalus I, refused her tribute and defeated them in two decisive battles. For more than a century thereafter (until 133 B.C.), Pergamum remained free and was perhaps during that period the most highly civilized state in the world."[48]

Subsequently, "The influence of a new power began to be felt in the Eastern Mediterranean, the power of the Roman Republic, [initially] friendly to Greece and to Greek civilization; and in this power the Hellenic communities of Pergamum and Rhodes [See Maps 2 and 3.] found a natural and useful ally and supporter against the Galatians

---
47 William Barclay, The Revelation of John, Vol. I, (Philadelphia: The Westminster Press, 1976), p. 106.
48 H. G. Wells, The Outline of History, Vol. I, (New York: Doubleday & Co., Inc, 1971), p. 312.

and against the Orientalized Seleucid Empire [which had made Pergamum its westernmost capital city]. ...

"[When] at last the Roman power came into Asia, ... it defeated the Seleucid Empire at the Battle of Magnesia (190 B.C.), and drove it out of Asia Minor and beyond the Taurus Mountains, and ... finally in 133 B.C. Attalus III, the last king of Pergamum, bowing to his sense of inevitable destiny, made the Roman Republic the heir to his kingdom, which, when he [Attalus III] died, became then the Roman province of 'Asia.'"[49]

"From 133 B.C. when king Attalus III bequeathed his kingdom into the hands of Rome, ... for two and a half centuries, Pergamum became the official center [the capital] in Rome's province of Asia. It was a seat of sovereign government, therefore, for around four centuries (from 282 B.C. to 120 A.D.)."[50]

As surprising as it may seem, our word "parchment" is derived from the name Pergamum. There is an interesting historical account of how this association of names took place. "Pergamum was famous for its library, which contained no fewer than 200,000 parchment rolls. In the ancient world, it was second only to the unique library of Alexandria. ...

"For many centuries ancient rolls were written on papyrus. ... In the third century B.C., a Pergamene king called Eumenes was very anxious to make the library of the city supreme. In order to do so, he persuaded — or even bribed — Aristophanes of Byzantium, who was the librarian at Alexandria, to agree to leave Alexandria and come to Pergamum. Ptolemy of Egypt was enraged at this seduction of his outstanding scholar. He promptly imprisoned Aristophanes, and by way of retaliation, he put an embargo on the export of papyrus to Pergamum. Faced with this situation, the scholars of Pergamum invented parchment or vellum, which is made of the skins of beasts, smoothed and polished and prepared for writing upon."[51] In the ancient world, parchment was known as the Pergamene sheet.

Subsequent to the apostolic era, it is also of note that Pergamon was the home of the Greco-Roman physician, Galen. His medical text is one of the most influential ancient treatises on medical practice. During the Abbasid Caliphate, Galen's works were translated into Arabic. "The most famous of these translators was a Nestorian (Christian) Arab by the name of Hunayn ibn Ishaq al-Ibadi (808-873 A.D.). Together with a handful of students, he is responsible for the translation of most of the Galenic medical corpus, as well as many other Greek philosophical and scientific treatises."[52]

2:12   "he that hath the sharp two-edged sword"

For discussion of the words, "he that hath the sharp two-edged sword" please consult the discussion of a similar statement under 1:16 on page 21.

---

49 H. G. Wells, The Outline of History, Vol. I, (New York: Doubleday & Co., Inc, 1971), p. 314.
50 http://www.arlev.co.uk/pergamum.htm, p. 2
51 William Barclay, The Revelation of John, Vol. I, (Philadelphia: The Westminster Press, 1976), p. 107.
52 Ahmad Dallal, *Science, Medicine, and Technology, The Making of a Scientific Culture*, The Oxford History of Islam, (Oxford: Oxford University Press, 1999), p. 160.

Revelation Chapter 2

2:13 "I know where thou dwellest, even where Satan's throne is; and thou holdest fast my name, and didst not deny my faith, even in the days of Antipas my witness, my faithful one, who was killed among you, where Satan dwelleth."

2:13 "I know where thou dwellest, even where Satan's throne is."

The identification of "Satan's throne" has brought a great variety of suggestions from commentators. One quite common explanation says, "The throne of Satan was undoubtedly the great altar built in the second century B.C. that is now installed in the Pergamon Museum in Berlin. Anyone who has seen it will know that it bears an uncanny resemblance to a gigantic throne."[53]

A far more probable explanation is, "that Pergamum was the capital of the province and, as such, [was] also the center of emperor-worship. Here the government was carried on and here were the temples dedicated to the worship of Caesar. Here believers were asked to offer incense to the image of the Emperors and to say 'Caesar is Lord.' Hence, here Satan has his throne; here he has free rein."[54]

Hendriksen's conclusion about the identity of the expression "Satan's throne" is also given more expansively by Barclay who said, "Rome's problem was to find a unifying bond in her vast and heterogeneous Empire. ... Rome saw in the spread of Caesar worship that very unifying principle which she needed; and so it became the law that once a year every Roman citizen should go to the temple of the Emperor, burn a pinch of incense to the godhead of Caesar, and say: 'Caesar is Lord.' Having done that, the citizen was given a written certificate to prove that he had made this act of worship. ... But the one thing no Christian would say was: 'Caesar is Lord.' For him Jesus Christ, and none other was Lord. ... Undoubtedly that is why Pergamum was Satan's seat; it was the place where men must take the name of the Lord and give it to Caesar instead of to Christ; and to a Christian there could be nothing more Devilish and Satanic than that."[55]

In addition to the great altar from Pergamum which is now housed in the Pergamon Museum in Berlin, there are many other art treasures which have been recovered from the ruins of the city of Pergamum. The ruins of Pergamum were discovered "in the 1860s by the Germans, who began excavations in 1878. Today the site is widely considered the finest surviving example of its kind. ... Sculpture takes pride of place here, with Hellenism's striving for realism embodied in vigorous portrait busts, vivacious terra cotta character pieces and bronze statuettes of heroes as well as the aged or diseased. Their boldness and detail were influenced by Alexander's innovative court sculptor, Lysippos of Sikyon, whose works survive only in later copies. Even fragments are powerfully arresting."[56]

---

53 G. W. Bowersock, *Apocalypse Then*, The New York Review of Books, April 5, 2012, p. 61.
54 W. Hendriksen, More Than Conquerors: An Interpretation of the Book of Revelation, (Grand Rapids: Baker Book House, 1952), p. 82.
55 William Barclay, The Revelation of John, Vol. I, (Philadelphia: The Westminster Press, 1976), pp. 110-111.
56 Barrymore Laurence Scherer, *An Empire of Treasures,* The Wall Street Journal, May 10, 2016, p. D5.

2:13 **"thou holdest fast my name, and didst not deny my faith, even in the days of Antipas my witness, my faithful one, who was killed among you, where Satan dwelleth"**

It is relatively easy to embrace and practice a faith against which no law has been enacted. As we have just seen, it had become illegal to hold Jesus of Nazareth to be one's exclusive supreme Lord. Undoubtedly, it had been the tenacious unwavering commitment of Antipas to the Lordship of Jesus which had resulted in his execution at Pergamum. In that dangerous context, it is extremely exemplary that the other Christians had refused to compromise their commitment to Jesus. Jesus acknowledges that they had held his name fast and had not denied the faith, even in the presence of the very real danger of paying the ultimate price which Antipas had given. (See addendum on page 47.)

Jesus calls Antipas "my witness." The Greek word for witness is *martus*. It means to faithfully give witness when by doing so one must forfeit his life. That was precisely how Polycarp at Smyrna had persistently given witness, that Jesus was his only Lord, to the exclusion of Caesar, as they led him to be burned to death. It is from the Greek word *martus* that the English word "martyr" is derived. In this sense, Jesus is called the faithful *martus*, "the faithful witness," in 1:5 on page 12 and also at 3:14.

2:14 **"But I have a few things against thee, because thou hast there some that hold the teaching of Balaam, who taught Balak to cast a stumbling block before the children of Israel, to eat things sacrificed to idols, and to commit fornication."**

2:14 **"I have a few things against thee"**

As courageous and steadfast as the Christians in Pergamum had been, there still were some grievous deficiencies in their church life. This account, in addition to offering other priceless lessons, makes it clear that virtue in one quadrant of a person's life cannot compensate for sin in another quadrant. When Jesus said to the church in Pergamum, "I have a few things against thee," he made it clear that their virtues had not mitigated their sins nor absolved them from those sins' consequences. He still held them accountable as he does everyone who still harbors sin in his life, either personally or corporately.

2:14 **"because thou hast there some that hold the teaching of Balaam"**

A glaring deficiency in the members of the church in Pergamum was their failure to have excluded from their fellowship those who held "the teaching of Balaam." Not only is that teaching condemned here in the letter to the church in Pergamum, it was so pernicious and destructive that it had previously been condemned both by Moses and by the apostle Peter.

God had prevented the false prophet Balaam from uttering a curse against Israel, which Balaam wanted to give in order to collect the rich reward offered to him by Balak, king of Moab. As an alternative, he then counseled the king to send sensuous, lascivious Moabite women into the camp of Israel to seduce the men to commit fornication as part of sensual Moabitish idol worship. Subsequently, an Israelite army annihilated all the Moabite/Midianite tribal population except the women. Consequently, "Moses said unto them, Have ye saved all the women alive? Behold, these [Midianite/Moabite women, see

Revelation Chapter 2

Numbers 25:1-9] caused the children of Israel, **through the counsel of Balaam**, to commit trespass against Jehovah in the matter of Peor, and so the plague was among the congregation of Jehovah." (Numbers 31:15-16)

Peter's second epistle was addressed to those who had "obtained a like precious faith, in the righteousness of our God and the Saviour Jesus Christ" (II Peter 1:1). It is probable that those people to whom he addressed his second epistle lived in the same areas as those to whom his first epistle had been sent. Among those to whom he wrote the first time were the members of the Dispersion in Asia. (I Peter 1:1) Since the sin of adhering to the doctrine of Balaam was known to have been a blemish in the church at Pergamum, it is probable that Peter was trying to eradicate that very sin.

Peter acknowledged the great damage the adherents to the sin of Balaam had caused by saying, "They will be paid back with harm for the harm they have done. Their idea of pleasure is to carouse in broad daylight. They are blots and blemishes, reveling in their pleasures while they feast with you. With eyes full of adultery, they never stop sinning; they seduce the unstable; they are experts in greed — an accursed brood! They have left the straight way and wandered off to follow the way of Balaam son of Beor, who loved the wages of wickedness. But he was rebuked for his wrongdoing by a donkey — a beast without speech — who spoke with a man's voice and restrained the prophet's madness." (II Peter 2:13-16 NIV)

Between Peter's execution in Rome, about 69 A.D., and Jesus' letter to Pergamum which was written between 96 and 100 A.D., approximately thirty-years had elapsed. In all those years, the sin of Balaam in the church at Pergamum had not been overcome. It is no wonder that Jesus told them, "I have a few things against you."

2:15 **"So hast thou also some that hold the teaching of the Nicolaitans in like manner."**

For a discussion of the "teaching of the Nicolaitans" see comments at 2:6 on pages 30-31.

2:16 **"Repent therefore; or else I come to thee quickly, and I will make war against them with the sword of my mouth."**

2:16 **"I come to thee quickly"**

Commentators are generally agreed that the urgent coming of Jesus which is mentioned in this verse, is not pointing to his final, visible, triumphant return which is predicted in Acts 1:10-11. The word "quickly" indicates that Jesus' coming was both urgent and imminent.

Jesus threatened a similar personal appearance in his letter to the Ephesians in which he said, "Remember therefore whence thou art fallen, and repent and do the first works; or else I come to thee, and will move thy candlestick out of its place, except thou repent." (Revelation 2:5)

Plummer commented that "The coming, of course, refers to a special visitation, not to the second advent."[57] Hinds asserted that "This does not mean a personal coming, but in some kind of judgment that would fall upon the church. Just how or what that would be is

---
57 A. Plummer, The Pulpit Commentary [on] Revelation, (Chicago: Wilcox & Follett Co., no date) p. 58.

not stated."[58] Tomlinson wrote that, "He would not come in person, but in providence and judgment."[59] Gregg says, "It probably does not refer to the Second Coming, since this church no longer exists."[60]

2:16 "I will make war against them with the sword of my mouth."

The identification of the sword is generally thought by commentators to point to the sword mentioned in Hebrews 4:12 which says, "The word of God is living, and active, and sharper than any two-edged sword, and piercing even to the dividing of soul and spirit, of both joints and marrow and quick to discern the thoughts and intents of the heart." Concurring with this understanding, Barclay wrote, "Paul speaks of 'the sword of the Spirit which is the word of God' (Ephesians 6:17). The sword of Christ is the word of Christ. In the word of Christ there is *conviction of sin*; in it a man is confronted with the truth, and is thereby confronted with his own failure to know and obey the truth. In the word of Christ there is [also] *invitation to God*; it convicts a man of sin and then invites him back, not to the judgment, but to the love of God."[61]

While the identification of the sword mentioned in 2:16 as the "word of Christ" is undoubtedly correct, one is still left to ponder who it would have been who would have wielded that sword. The angels to whom the letters to each of the seven churches were addressed, as earlier indicated, "probably referred to the one in each congregation who regularly preached to the church." That being the case, was not the angel of the church in Pergamum already wielding that sword each time he preached to the church?

Does Jesus' coming imply that the ability of the local preacher was to be enhanced or augmented in some powerful way by Jesus indwelling him more personally, powerfully and effectively? Does Jesus mean he will animate and invigorate the preacher in some special way to wield the sword of the Spirit with greater impact? Perhaps, Jesus would endow the preacher with qualities like those possessed by Apollos about whom it is written that he was "an eloquent man ... and mighty in the scriptures." (Acts 18:24) There is still at least one other possibility. Perhaps, Jesus would make himself present by sending an evangelist to the church in Pergamum who would be able to preach the message of Christ more powerfully than the local preacher had been able to do.

2:17 "He that hath an ear, let him hear what the Spirit saith to the churches. To him that overcometh, to him will I give the hidden manna, and I will give him a white stone, and upon the stone a new name written, which no one knoweth but he that receiveth it."

2:17 "to him that overcometh"

The key to understanding the meaning of the "hidden manna," the "white stone" and the "new name" is the identification of the overcoming mentioned in this verse. While there are many subsidiary triumphs in a Christian's life-long experience, this overcoming probably points to a Christian's final victory, our joining that great throng, "out of every

---

58 John T. Hinds, <u>A Commentary on the Book of Revelation</u> (Nashville, Tenn.: Gospel Advocate Company, 1976)., p. 38.
59 Lee G. Tomlinson, <u>The Wonder Book of the Bible: A Commentary On the Book of Revelation</u> , (Joplin, Missouri: College Press, 1963), p. 27.
60 <u>Revelation, Four Views: A Parallel Commentary</u>, ed. Steve Gregg , (Nashville: Thomas Nelson Publishers, 1997), p. 69.
61 William Barclay, <u>The Revelation of John</u>, Vol. I, (Philadelphia: The Westminster Press, 1976), p. 116.

Revelation Chapter 2

nation and of all tribes and peoples and tongues, standing before the throne and before the Lamb arrayed in white robes." (Revelation 7:9)

Following that ultimate triumphant victory, the redeemed Christian will have an exhilarating role to fill in God's eternal purpose in which the manna, the white stone and the new name will have practical value.

2:17   "will I give … hidden manna … a white stone … a new name"

We are indebted to the message God gave through Paul to help us understand the eternal role for which God is now preparing us. In Ephesians 2:6-7 we are told that not only will we be raised up with Christ, but we will be made "to sit with him, in the heavenly *places*, in Christ Jesus: that in the ages to come he might show the exceeding riches of his grace in kindness toward us in Christ Jesus." Compare the statement, "in the ages to come" with Paul's earlier statement in which he said, "not only in this world, but also in that which is to come." (Ephesians 1:21)

What is to be included in "the exceeding riches of his grace" which he will show in kindness to redeemed men and women, in the ages to come or in the world to come? Probably, it is partially summarized in Revelation 2:17 as the manna, the white stone and the new name. First, the manna points to divine sustenance. While we have been sustained throughout our mortal journey, we will also be sustained for the eternal work God wants to achieve through us.

The white stone gets its identity from "the ancient law courts [in which] white and black stones were used for registering the verdict of juries."[62] A white stone was given to the one whom the jury found innocent. Up till the time when Satan is ultimately consigned to the pits of eternal fire (Revelation 20:10), should he still be able, as the accuser of the brethren (Revelation 12:10), to make the charge that any redeemed person has no right to his position in heaven, all that person will need to do is to show his white stone. That would prove his triumphant eternal exoneration through the redemption that is in Christ. Anyone who should be falsely accused would be reminded that, "it is God that justifieth; who is he that condemneth?" (Romans 8:33-34)

The new name reminds us how Jesus gave unique new names to the disciples whom he called. He gave names which were indicative of the roles each one would fill in his place in the kingdom. Similarly, it seems, redeemed humans upon entering their ultimate triumph, will be given names which will be appropriate for the eternal ministries in which we will serve.

The passage says that no one would know that name but the one who will have received it. Obviously, such a private endowment is for eternal, personal encouragement and reassurance. If one should ever be questioned about the legitimacy of his inclusion in the vast throng of the redeemed, all he would need to do would be to glance at the name God has given him, a name reassuring him of his ownership and inclusion, which would also give God's evaluation of him.

C. Austin Miles, author of the hymn "A New Name in Glory" must have had some premonition or anticipation of the glorious status that the personal, unique individual

---

62   William Barclay, The Revelation of John, Vol. I, (Philadelphia: The Westminster Press, 1976), p. 118.

name mentioned in Revelation 2:17 confers on each redeemed soul. He wrote, "There's a new name written down in glory, and it's mine, O yes, it's mine. And a white robed angel sings the story, 'a sinner has come home.'"

4. The Church in Thyatira 2:18-29

2:18 **"And to the angel of the church in Thyatira write: these things saith the Son of God, who hath his eyes like a flame of fire, and his feet are like unto burnished brass:"**

Surprisingly, this is the only occurrence of the expression "Son of God" in the book of Revelation. The statement that his eyes are "like a flame of fire, and his feet like unto burnished brass" powerfully declare his deity. In addition to the notes given previously in the comments on 1:15 (page 20), Barclay makes this insightful comment, "the flaming eyes must stand ... for the blazing anger against sin in the eyes of the Risen Christ; and they must stand for the awful penetration of that gaze which strips the disguises away and sees into a man's innermost heart. The brazen feet must stand for the inflexible, immovable strength and power of the Risen Christ."[63]

The history and geography of Thyatira are more prosaic and commonplace than those for Pergamum and Sardis. The Roman government kept a company of soldiers quartered in Thyatira because it was situated on a road which led to nearby Pergamum, capital city of the Roman province of Asia. Their function was to engage, and hopefully destroy, any hostile force marching to attack the capital. Since there were no natural barriers such as narrow defiles or passes nor any commanding height in the topography, which could impede an enemy's advance, the soldiers billeted at Thyatira would be in a very disadvantageous position. They certainly would be able to harry an invading force but probably could not destroy one.

Thyatira, despite its rather monotonous and commonplace geographic site, was nevertheless a thriving economic center. Its economy was based on crafts, prominent among which was the manufacture of an elegant purple fabric. (See the comments on 18:12 on pp. 295-297.) It was marketing that cloth, highly desired by royalty and the aristocracy, which took Lydia from Thyatira to Philippi where the apostle Paul met her and led her to Christ as he preached to a small band of devout Jewish women who maintained a place of prayer on the river bank. (See Acts 16:14-15.)

2:19 **"I know thy works, and thy love and faith and ministry and patience, and that thy last works are more than the first."**

This beautiful commendation is exceptionally remarkable when one realizes that at the same time the church was manifesting such Godly virtues there was also the presence of a powerful, widespread scandalous immorality in the life of some members of the congregation. Does the pronoun "thy" refer only to the "angel" of the church (2:18) or does it include the corporate body? (See the discussion of the next verse, 2:20.)

2:20 **"But I have this against thee that thou sufferest the woman Jezebel, who calleth herself a prophetess; and she teacheth and seduceth my servants to commit fornication, and to eat things sacrificed to idols."**

---

63 William Barclay, The Revelation of John, Vol. I, (Philadelphia: The Westminster Press, 1976), p. 128.

Revelation Chapter 2

2:20   "thou sufferest the woman Jezebel"

We cannot be certain whether the name Jezebel was the woman's real name or whether Jesus was using it metaphorically with reference to the wife of Ahab. If the second possibility should have been the case, then Jesus used the name appropriately because both women were committed to the basest levels of sensuality. (See I Kings 16:29-33 and II Kings 9:22.)

The Koine Greek language did not have two separate and distinct words for "woman" and "wife." The Greek word *gunaika*, which is translated here as "woman," could be translated as "wife" if its grammatical setting were right. Should the context in this verse allow the word *gunaika* to be translated as "wife," then the shocking question would arise whether Jezebel could have been the wife of the one preaching at Thyatira, whom Jesus called "the angel" or messenger of the church. Every devout Christian sincerely hopes that such would not have been the case. Barclay concluded that, "this interpretation must be rejected, because the evidence for inserting the word *sou* [in the Greek text] is not good enough."[64] The word *sou* is the possessive pronoun "your." An example of its occurrence is found in Luke 1:13 in the words "your wife."

2:20   "who calleth herself a prophetess; and she teacheth and seduceth my servants to commit fornication, and to eat things sacrificed to idols"

Whoever the woman was whom Jesus called Jezebel, she was undoubtedly a person with a very magnetic, attractive, persuasive and, obviously, seductive personality. Might she have been a former pagan-temple prostitute who had obeyed the Gospel but had subsequently slipped back into the grasp of her former sensualism? A patron of a temple prostitute was supposed to achieve union with the supposed deity by coming to the ecstasy of orgasm in union with the temple prostitute. Perhaps this Jezebel persuaded her patrons that a union with her would similarly bring them into closer union with Christ.

2:21   "And I gave her time that she should repent; and she willeth not to repent of her fornication."

God has no obligation to give any of us time to correct evil behavior. Should he strike us down at our first sin, he would not have violated justice. To give any of us time to re-evaluate and correct a sinful life style is purely a manifestation of God's goodness. In a rhetorical question, the apostle Paul points out the purpose for which God shows reticence in bringing judgment. He said, "Or despisest thou the riches of his goodness and forbearance and long suffering, not knowing that the goodness of God leadeth thee to repentance?" (Romans 2:4) The Thyatiran Jezebel, by willing "not to repent of her fornication," had slapped God's hand of mercy. Only judgment was left.

2:22   "Behold, I cast her into a bed, and them that commit adultery with her into great tribulation, except they repent of her works."

---

64 William Barclay, <u>The Revelation of John</u>, Vol. I, (Philadelphia: The Westminster Press, 1976), p. 130.

2:22 "cast her into a bed"

The word "bed" in the statement saying, "I cast her into a bed" is rendered in the New English Version, the New King James translation and in the Revised Standard Version as "sickbed." William Barclay was certainly qualified as a translator for he was Lecturer in New Testament Language and Literature and in Hellenistic Greek in the University of Glasgow. Though in the text of his personal translation, which accompanies his commentary on Revelation, he rendered the Greek word simply as "bed," still, in his comment on this sentence he wrote, "She will be cast into a bed of sickness."[65] Plummer says, "The bed of sin becomes a bed of suffering."[66]

In verse 25, Jesus exhorts the Christians in Thyatira to hold fast that which they had till he should come. Probably one way in which his coming was to be manifest was in turning the bed, in which the adulterous members of the church were enjoying the pleasures of sin, into a bed of sickness which would culminate in death. This is the same sequence of events that the homosexuals whom Paul rebuked were doomed to follow. They were to receive "in themselves that recompense of their error which was due." (Romans 1:27)

More contemporary translations help us understand the consequences of the sin in which those men persisted who are mentioned in Romans 1:27. For example, the ESV says, "men committing shameless acts with men and receiving in themselves the due penalty for their error." And the NIV rendered it with these words, "Men committed indecent acts with other men, and received in themselves the due penalty for their perversion."

2:22 "great tribulation"

"This 'great tribulation' was to punish a false prophetess in the Lord's church in Thyatira along with those who followed her. Christ warned that if she and her followers did not repent, He would cast them into 'great tribulation.' It would be the Lord's punishment on specific sinning Christians. There is no way to fit this situation [i.e., tribulation] into the context of either Matthew 24 [v. 21] or Revelation 7 [v.14]."[67] (See Appendix A.)

2:23 "And I will kill her children with death; and all the churches shall know that I am he that searcheth the reins and hearts: and I will give unto each one of you according to your works."

2:23 "I will kill her children with death"

Not only is Jezebel herself to be judged, but those whom she leads into sin will suffer capital punishment. They are to be killed. Their death will probably grow out of the consequences of their perversion, such as some variety of venereal disease which results in death.

2:23 "I am he that searcheth the reins and hearts"

Both the King James and the ASV have translated the Greek as "reins and hearts." The use made here of the word "reins" is very archaic and will not be understood by many.

---

65 William Barclay, The Revelation of John, Vol. I, (Philadelphia: The Westminster Press, 1976), p. 138.
66 A. Plummer, The Pulpit Commentary [on] Revelation, (Chicago: Wilcox & Follett Co., no date), p. 65.
67 David Vaughn Elliott, Nobody Left Behind, Insight into "End-Time" Prophecies, (Methun, Massachusetts, 2004), p. 125.

Revelation Chapter 2

The English Standard Version renders it "mind and heart" while the New International Version renders it "searches hearts and minds."

2:23 **"I will give unto each one of you according to your works"**

Though there was corporate sin in the church at Thyatira, Christ judges individually.

2:24 **"But to you I say, to the rest that are in Thyatira, as many as have not this teaching, who know not the deep things of Satan, as they are wont to say: I cast upon you none other burden."**

The clumsy wording, "as they are wont to say" is made much clearer in the ESV which says, "But to the rest of you in Thyatira, who do not hold this teaching, who have not learned what some call the deep things of Satan, to you I say, I do not lay on you any other burden."

2:25 **"Nevertheless that which ye have, hold fast till I come."**

This exhortation is repeated in 3:11 in the letter to the church in Philadelphia. Many times we fail to appreciate what we have. It may possess more significance and potential than we have recognized. In a similar sense, Paul exhorts us that "whereunto we have attained, by the same rule let us walk." (Philippians 3:16)

2:26 **"And he that overcometh, and he that keepeth my works unto the end, to him will I give authority over the nations:"**

2:26 **"he that overcometh, and he that keepeth my works unto the end"**

The second clause, "he that keepeth my works unto the end," gives the definition of the one who triumphantly overcomes.

2:26 **"to him will I give authority over the nations"**

Please see the significance of this promise in the discussion of the next verse.

2:27 **"and he shall rule them with a rod of iron, as the vessels of the potter are broken to shivers; as I also have received of my Father:"**

2:27 **"he shall rule them with a rod of iron"**

The one who is going to have "authority over the nations" (2:26) and who will "rule them with a rod of iron," leading to those nations at times being shattered "as the vessels of the potter are broken to shivers," is the Christian who has held fast (2:25), who has overcome (2:26) and who has kept Christ's works (2:26). To such a one, Jesus says, "to him will I give authority over the nations" (2:26). Such a Christian shares in Christ's rule. (See 12:5 and the comments on page 181.)

2:27 **"as the vessels of the potter are broken to shivers"**

Undoubtedly, this expresses the same reality which was predicted in Daniel's interpretation of Nebuchadnazzar's dream. In it Nebuchadnazzar was told that "in the time of those kings, the God of heaven will set up a kingdom that will never be destroyed, nor will it be left to another people. <u>It will crush all those kingdoms</u> and bring them to an end, but it will itself endure forever." (Daniel 2:44 NIV)

The shattering mentioned in Revelation 2:27 and the crushing predicted in Daniel 2:44 are two descriptions of the same reality. Such an impact on the world's anti-God philosophical, political and social systems will be the ultimate influence of Christ's church. Such a revolutionary role for the church will probably occur repeatedly in the future. By seducing the church into the rankest and basest sensualism of common society, the woman called Jezebel in the church at Thyatira would ultimately have robbed the church of its destined role in world history, if her demonic ministry were not stopped.

Has the church ever shattered pagan society? Since its birth, has the presence of the church ever led to the fundamental societal and political changes foreseen in these prophecies? Church historians, as seen in the following quotations, affirm that this mission of the church was first accomplished shortly after the apostolic period.

Yale University historian, the late Kenneth Scott Latourette, tells us "Beginning as a seemingly obscure sect of Judaism, one of scores, even hundreds of religions and religious groups which were competing within that realm, revering as its central figure one who had been put to death by the machinery of Rome, and in spite of having been long proscribed by that government and eventually having the full weight of the state thrown against it, Christianity proved so far the victor that the Empire sought alliance with it and to be a Roman citizen became almost identical with being a Christian."[68]

Latourette went on to say, "Certainly in the first half of the second century thousands were flocking into the churches. The Christian communities had long been growing, the uncertainties of the times were moving many to seek security in religion, especially in one which was giving rise to so inclusive and strong a fellowship as the Christian Church, and the weakening of existing patterns of society and the popularity of cults from the Orient which were esteemed as having the authority of hoary antiquity were easing the path to the Church."[69]

A younger church historian fully corroborates the analysis given by Latourette about the impact of the church on Roman government and society in the early post-apostolic period. He wrote, "During the period of peace after Valerian's death in Persia [260 A.D.], the church grew rapidly. Cities and city cults grew less popular, and Christianity was displaying impressive intellectual leadership, organizational strength, and, in persecution, courage. Christians were increasingly integrated into all aspects of imperial society, and despite disputes over lapsed bishops and monarchianism,[70] the church was resilient. Though only ten percent of the empire was Christian, by the end of the third century the church was too big and well organized to be safely ignored. ... Christianity could not be assimilated into the Roman system without cracking the system wide open. It could not be ignored."[71]

---

68 Kenneth Scott Latourette, <u>A History of Christianity</u>, (New York: Harper & Row, Publishers, 1975), p. 65.
69 Kenneth Scott Latourette, <u>A History of Christianity</u>, (New York: Harper & Row, Publishers, 1975), p. 87.
70 "A Christian heresy that developed during the second and third centuries. It opposed the doctrine of an independent, personal subsistence of the Logos affirmed the sole deity of God the Father, and thus represented the extreme Monotheistic view. Though it regarded Christ as Redeemer, it clung to the numerical unity of the Deity. Two types of Monarchianism developed: The Dynamic (or adoptionist) and the Modalistic (or Sebellium)." [Britannica Online Encyclopedia]

Revelation Chapter 2

One final quote from Leithart will be helpful to understand that Christianity did exercise authority over the nations, and did shatter them, "as the vessels of the potter are broken to shivers." He recorded that, "When things went badly, Diocletian adopted the time-tested policy of finding someone to blame. He blamed the Christians for failing to honor the gods, just as later pagans would blame Christians for the evils suffered at the hands of barbarians. Once Diocletian got started persecuting, however, he had no chance of success. Too many Christians stood their ground, and the church was clearly not going anywhere. ... Something would have to budge, either the demands of Roman citizenship or the church, and the church showed no signs of budging."[72]

2:28 **"And I will give him the morning star."**

Jesus says, "I am the root and the offspring of David, the bright, the morning star." (Revelation 22:16) From this it seems that to the ones who hold fast, the ones who overcome and the ones who keep his works unto the end, Christ will give an immeasurably greater endowment of himself. This will be an infinite enhancement of one of the great realities we now enjoy, "which is Christ in you, the hope of glory." (Colossians 1:27)

2:29 **"He that hath an ear, let him hear what the Spirit saith to the churches."**

For the frequency with which this exhortation is used in the letters to the seven churches, please see the summary under 3:6 on page 55. For additional implications which this exhortation carries, please see the comments on 2:7 at page 31.

Addendum to Revelation 2:13

It is surprising that though Jesus called Antipas "my witness, my faithful one" and acknowledged that he had been martyred at Pergamum, there is, in addition to the account in Revelation 2:13, almost no historical record of his life and death. In addressing the church at Pergamum, Jesus said that Antipas "was killed among you." This tells us he was a member of the church in that Roman city. It is believed that he was martyred in the year 92 A.D.. It seems obvious that through faithfully giving witness to Jesus, Antipas triggered belligerent antagonism in the hearts of those who listened to him. They silenced an unwelcome message by killing the messenger. The sparse and succinct account of the life and martyrdom of Antipas is ominously reminiscent of the way Stephen became a martyr. (See Acts chapter 7.)

---

71 Peter J. Leithart, <u>Defending Constantine: The Twilight of an Empire and the Dawn of Christendom</u>, (Downers Grove, IL: IVP, 2010)., pp. 39-40.

72 Peter J. Leithart, <u>Defending Constantine: The Twilight of an Empire and the Dawn of Christendom</u>, (Downers Grove, IL: IVP, 2010)., p. 51.

Revelation Chapter 3

5. The Church in Sardis 3:1-6

3:1 **"And to the angel of the church in Sardis write: These things saith he that hath the seven Spirits of God, and the seven stars: I know thy works, that thou hast a name that thou livest, and thou art dead."**

> **3:1** **"And to the angel of the church in Sardis write"**

For a more complete discussion of the identity of the angel who is mentioned in the address to each of the seven churches of Asia, please see the discussion of "the seven spirits that are before his throne" beginning on page 11.

"The church in Sardis had no Nicolaitans, no Balaam, no Jezebel. But, there was worse evil than the presence of what is morally and doctrinally corrupt. The numbness of spiritual torpor and death is more hopeless than unwise toleration [of evil]. The church in Sardis, scarcely out of its infancy, had already the signs of an effete [i.e., exhausted] and moribund [i.e., stagnant] faith; and it is possible that their deadness was a result of the absence of internal enemies."[73]

Sardis had been the capital of the ancient kingdom of Lydia. In 133 B.C., the Lydian king, Attalus III, whose capital had been moved to Pergamum, bequeathed his kingdom to Rome. Subsequently, Rome joined Lydia politically with other areas to form the Roman province of Asia. Though Pergamum was the capital city of the new province of Asia, Sardis continued to have political significance because it was "the seat of a proconsul under the Roman Empire, and the metropolis of the province of Lydia in later Roman and Byzantine times."[74] Its most famous king in ancient times was Croesus who ruled Lydia from 560 B.C. to 547 B.C. During his reign Persia was becoming a world power under the inspiration and competent rule of Cyrus. Only "one monarch in the world was alive to the threat of the new power that lay in the hands of Cyrus. That was Croesus the Lydian king.

"[Because] his son had been killed in a very tragic manner, which Herodotus relates: 'For two years, then, Croesus remained quiet in great mourning, because he was deprived of his son; but after this period of time, ... the growing greatness of the Persians, caused Croesus to cease from his mourning, and led him to a care of cutting short the power of the Persians if by any means he might, while yet it was in growth and before they should have become [even more] great.'

"He then made trial of the various Oracles [by searching and evaluating their utterances which they had made for the alleged deity they represented]: [Since Oracles demanded

---

[73] Slightly edited from A. Plummer, The Pulpit Commentary [on] Revelation, (Chicago: Wilcox & Follett Co., no date), p. 107.
[74] http://en.wikipedia.org/wiki/sardis, p. 1.

remuneration for their ministry], "to the Lydians who were to carry these gifts to the temples, Croesus gave charge that they should ask the Oracles this question: whether Croesus should march against the Persians, and if so, whether he should join with himself any army of men as his friends.

"And when the Lydians had arrived at the places to which they had been sent and had dedicated the votive offerings, they inquired of the Oracles and said: 'Croesus king of the Lydians and other nations, considering that these are the only true Oracles among men, presents to you gifts such as your revelations deserve, and asks you again, now, whether he shall march against the Persians, and, if so, whether he shall join with himself any army of men as allies.' They inquired thus and the answers of both the Oracles agreed in one, declaring to Croesus that if he should march against the Persians he should destroy a great empire. ... So when the answers were brought back and Croesus heard them, he was delighted with the Oracles, and expecting that he would certainly destroy the kingdom of Cyrus, he sent again to Pytho, and presented to the men of Delphi, having ascertained the number of them, two staters of gold for each man: ...

"While Croesus was preparing to march against the Persians, one of the Lydians, who even before this time was thought to be a wise man, but in consequence of this opinion got a very great name for wisdom among the Lydians, advised Croesus as follows: 'O king, thou art preparing to march against men who wear breeches of leather, and the rest of their clothing is of leather also; and they eat food not such as they desire, but such as they can attain, dwelling in a land which is rugged and, moreover, they make no use of wine but drink water; and no figs have they for dessert, nor any other good thing. On the one hand, if thou shalt overcome them, what wilt thou take away from them, seeing they have nothing? And on the other hand, if thou shalt be overcome, consider how many good things thou shalt lose; for once having tasted our good things, they will cling to them fast, and it will not be possible to drive them away. I, for my own part, feel gratitude to the gods that they do not put it into the minds of the Persians to march against the Lydians.' Thus he spoke, not persuading Croesus; for it is true indeed that the Persians before they subdued the Lydians had no luxury nor any good thing.'

"Croesus and Cyrus fought an indecisive battle at Pteria, from which Croesus retreated. Cyrus followed him up, and he gave battle outside his capital town of Sardis. The chief strength of the Lydians lay in their cavalry; they were excellent, if undisciplined horsemen, and fought with long spears.

"Cyrus, when he saw the Lydians being arrayed for battle, fearing their horsemen, did on the suggestion of Harpagos, a Mede, as follows: all the camels which were in the train of his army carrying provisions and baggage he gathered together, and he took off their burdens and set men upon them provided with the equipment of cavalry; and, having thus furnished them forth, he appointed them to go in front of the rest of the army toward the horsemen of Croesus; and after the camel-troop he ordered the infantry to follow; and behind the infantry he placed his whole force of cavalry. Then, when all his men had been placed in their several positions, he charged them to spare none of the other Lydians, slaying all who might come in their way, but Croesus himself they were not to slay, not even if he should make resistance when he was being captured. Such was his charge: and he set the camels opposite the horsemen for this reason — because the horse has a fear of

Revelation Chapter 3

the camel and cannot endure either to see his form or to scent his smell: for this reason then the trick had been devised, in order that the cavalry of Croesus might be useless, that very force wherewith the Lydian king was expecting most to shine. And as they were coming together to the battle, so soon as the horses scented the camels and saw them, they turned away back, and the hopes of Croesus was at once brought to naught. In [the next] fourteen days Sardis was stormed and Croesus taken prisoner."[75]

The ultimate successful storming of the city was made possible by the carelessness of the leaders and citizens of Sardis. "For fourteen days as Herodotus the Greek historian tells the story, Cyrus besieged the city. He then offered a reward to any of his soldiers who could find a way into the impregnable Sardis. A certain Mardian soldier called Hyeroeades had been watching the battlements of Sardis, and at a certain point he had seen a Sardian soldier accidentally drop his helmet over the battlements, and then make his way down the precipice to retrieve it. Hyeroeades knew that there must be a crack in the rock there, by means of which an agile man could climb up. That night he led a party of Persian troops up by the fault in the rock. When they reached the top they found the battlements completely unguarded. The Sardians had thought themselves too safe to need a guard; and so Sardis fell. A city with a history like that knew what the Risen Christ was talking about, when he said: 'Watch!'"[76] (See 3:2-3.)

3:1 "he that hath the seven Spirits of God, and the seven stars"

On the expression "seven Spirits of God" please see the discussion under 1:4 on pages 11-12. Succinctly, John gave us the identification of "the seven stars" when he wrote, "The seven stars are the angels of the seven churches." (Revelation 1:20)

3:1 "I know thy works"

While Jesus mentions the works of the church in Sardis, he gives us no description or definition of them. However, in the very next verse, he tells the church in Sardis, "I found no works of thine perfected before my God." Thus their works, being incomplete and unfinished, were neither useful nor productive. Those incomplete works had absorbed funds and effort but were giving no return on the investment.

3:1 "a name that thou livest, and thou art dead."

The reputation of the church in Sardis far exceeded its accomplishments. Their advertising was deceptive. Their product was deficient, not meeting the standards claimed for it. It should have been exactly the reverse, so people would have been impressed like the Queen of Sheba was when she saw the wealth, applied wisdom and administrative excellence of Solomon's kingdom. She said, "I believed not the words, until I came, and mine eyes had seen it: and, behold, the half was not told me; thy wisdom and prosperity exceed the fame which I heard." (I Kings 10:7)

3:2 "Be thou watchful, and establish the things that remain, which were ready to die: for I have found no works of thine perfected before my God."

---

75 Edited from H. G. Wells, <u>The Outline of History</u>, Vol. I, (New York: Doubleday & Co., Inc, 1971), p. 256-258.
76 William Barclay, <u>The Revelation of John</u>, Vol. I, (Philadelphia: The Westminster Press, 1976), p. 144.

3:2 "Be thou watchful, and establish the things that remain"

Vestigial remnants of better days still existed. There were things that remained, as certified by 3:1. The remedial exhortation is "be thou watchful." It is very likely that this exhortation called to mind the much earlier pre-Christian experience of the residents of Sardis during the Persian period of the city's history. The city had been conquered and ruined because neither the leaders nor the citizens had been watchful. Their negligence allowed the enemy to conquer and control them. Similarly, we are exhorted to "be sober, be watchful: your adversary the Devil, as a roaring lion, walketh about, seeking whom he may devour: whom withstand steadfast in your faith." (I Peter 5:8-9a)

3:2 "I have found no works of thine perfected before my God."

It is relatively easy to begin kingdom-related undertakings. While we may be commended for beginning a needed or a noble project, the real accolades can only come if we carry the endeavor all the way to completion. We must follow the example set for us by the apostle Paul who said, "Forgetting the things which are behind, and stretching forward to the things which are before, I press on toward the goal unto the prize of the high calling of God in Christ Jesus. Let us therefore, as many as are perfect, be thus minded." (Philippians 3:13b-15a)

"Once a church has a good reputation [see 3:1] in the public eye, it is possible to mechanically continue in the same activities but lose the original motivation that made it great. The incentive to good works can shift from a desire to serve and please God to simply a desire to maintain the good public face that the church has come to enjoy."[77]

3:3 "Remember therefore how thou hast received and didst hear; and keep it, and repent. If therefore thou shalt not watch, I will come as a thief, and thou shalt not know what hour I will come upon thee."

3:3 "Remember therefore how thou hast received and didst hear; and keep it, and repent"

The church in Sardis had had some admirable periods of achievement in the past toward which Christ exhorts them to look. His exhortation "may have reference to the sincerity and enthusiasm with which they [had initially] accepted the Gospel. If so, then, like the church at Ephesus, they had fallen from their first love. Hence after urging them to keep what they had received at the first, he tells them to repent – that is, they should decide to turn back to their former zeal for the church. This church is not charged with tolerating any wicked doctrine, as in the cases of Ephesus and Thyatira, but rather with slowly dying from loss of interest in what they had accepted."[78]

3:3 "If therefore thou shalt not watch, I will come as a thief, and thou shalt not know what hour I will come upon thee."

Jesus repeatedly warns the churches of his imminent and sudden coming. For discussion of his warning, please see the final paragraph in the discussion of 2:16.

---

77 Revelation, Four Views: A Parallel Commentary, ed. Steve Gregg, (Nashville: Thomas Nelson Publishers, 1997), p. 73.
78 Slightly edited from John T. Hinds, A Commentary on the Book of Revelation (Nashville, Tenn.: Gospel Advocate Company, 1976), pp. 53-54.

Revelation Chapter 3

3:4 **"But thou hast a few names in Sardis that did not defile their garments: and they shall walk with me in white; for they are worthy."**

Corporate congregational life had broken down in the church at Sardis. Jesus could not speak of them as a unified body. For them it was no longer true that, "we, who are many, are one bread, one body." (I Corinthians 10:17) Only a few of the members, referred to as, "a few names," were still committed to Christ's intent that, "now unto the principalities and the powers in the heavenly places might be made known through the church the manifold wisdom of God, according to the eternal purpose which he purposed in Christ Jesus our Lord." (Ephesians 3:10-11)

Those referred to by the expression "a few names" were "individuals who were known by name to the Father in heaven. They were known individually, each separately. God knew exactly who and what they were, for, He knows his own. They were as shining lights in the midst of the darkness of their world. Those few who had kept unspotted the garment of grace here, would by and by wear the white garment of glory. White indicates holiness, purity, perfection, festivity, Isaiah 61:10; Revelation 19:8."[79]

Since there were only a few Christians in Sardis who had not defiled their garments, apparently the majority had, thus dividing the church. It was an extremely damaging division because it gave those who were in the wrong the advantage of being in the majority. Consequently, the power which should have been generated by the entire congregation working in concert had been thwarted. The impact of the church in fulfilling Christ's great eternal purpose had been negated.

Christians are to be harmoniously associated with one another in congregations for at least three very important reasons: First, <u>evangelism</u> (Ephesians 3:10-11, Philippians 4:10-20 and I Thessalonians 1:8), second, <u>benevolence</u> (Galatians 2:10, Romans 15:25-27, II Corinthians 9:1-15), and third, <u>mutual edification</u> (Romans 1:12 and Ephesians 4:15-16).

There are indications in the writings of the Apostolic Fathers as well as in the writings of the Church Fathers[80] that the New Testament Scriptures were widely available and accessible even to the very earliest churches. In the Roman province of Asia, and probably over a much wider area, churches cooperated among themselves to make sure each church had access to all the Scripture. Such cooperation is clearly indicated in Colossians 4:16. That being the case, the Christians at Sardis had probably read the exhortation which inspires us to, "follow after righteousness, Godliness, faith, love, patience, meekness." (I Timothy 6:11) They had probably also read about, "the enemies of the cross of Christ whose end is perdition, whose God is their belly, and whose glory is

---

79 Edited from W. Hendriksen, <u>More Than Conquerors: An Interpretation of the Book of Revelation</u>, (Grand Rapids: Baker Book House, 1952)., p. 91.

80 Those early Christian leaders who personally had had fellowship with one or more of the twelve apostles are called Apostolic Fathers, while those early Christian leaders, though not having personally met an apostle, but knew the Apostolic Fathers are called Church Fathers. The Church Fathers are divided into two groups. "Christian writers who were born after the death of the apostles but before 325 A.D., are called Ante-Nicene Fathers. They wrote before the Council of Nicea which marked the triumph of the Christian religion in the empire. Ancient writers who lived after the Council of Nicea are called Post-Nicean Fathers. There are many writings which have survived and been preserved from those times." [Fred P. Miller, <u>Revelation: A Panorama of the Gospel Age</u>, (Claremont, Florida, Moellerhaus Publisher, 1991), p. 55].

their shame, who mind earthly things. For our citizenship is in heaven; whence also we wait for a Saviour, the Lord Jesus Christ." (Philippians 3:18b-20)

In addition to the churches having access to Scripture, which should have kept them from folly, both the apostle Paul and the apostle John had ministered extensively among the churches in Asia. Therefore, it is inconceivable that the Christians in Sardis could have been in ignorance about right and wrong, purity and filthiness. The soiling or "defiling" of their garments, undoubtedly and sadly, had occurred in the face of ample restraining knowledge and repeated exhortations.

3:5 **"He that overcometh shall thus be arrayed in white garments; and I will in no wise blot his name out of the book of life, and I will confess his name before my Father, and before his angels."**

The expression "overcometh" is equivalent to being "faithful unto death." It was with that second expression of Christian determination that Christ set the level of the bar for the Christians in Smyrna. He said, "Be thou faithful unto death, and I will give thee the crown of life." (Revelation 2:10) No matter what the circumstances, there can be no opting out. We must complete the course. We must be able to say with the apostle Paul, "I have fought the good fight, I have finished the course, I have kept the faith." (II Timothy 4:7)

We must not follow the example of Elijah who, when opposition became extremely harsh and dangerous, "requested for himself that he might die." (I Kings 19:4) When God did not immediately grant his request, he fled. Then God spoke to Elijah at the mouth of the cave in which he had sought protection, and said, "What doest thou here Elijah?" Elijah's answer was, "I, even I only, am left; and they seek my life to take it away." (I Kings 19:13-14) God made it clear that in spite of the daunting circumstances which Elijah faced, there was still work to be done and he was the one to fill that role. He was commanded to go to the wilderness of Damascus to anoint Hazael to be king over Syria and also to anoint Elisha to fill the role from which Elijah was seeking dismissal. At that point, God also made it clear that Elijah's analysis of the horrible situation, which he described by saying, "I only am left," was badly in error. God said that Elijah was not the only one left, rather, in Israel there were seven thousand who had not bowed the knee to Baal. (See I Kings 19:18.) Therefore, whatever our circumstances, we must triumph, we must be faithful, we must overcome.

To those who do overcome, there are three marvelous promises. <u>First</u>, such a person shall "be arrayed in white garments." Those garments will be a sign of eternal triumph, for God covers himself "with light as with a garment." (Psalm 104:2) White garments, indicative of triumph, are mentioned in Revelation 6:11, 7:9, 7:13-14 and in 19:14.

<u>The second promise</u> which God makes to those who overcome is that "in no wise [will God] blot his name out of the book of life." "The book of life is a conception which occurs often in the Bible. Moses is willing to be wiped out of the book which God has written, if by his sacrifice he can save his people from the consequences of their sin (Exodus 32:32-33). It is the hope of the Psalmist that the wicked will be blotted out of the book of the living (Psalm 69:28). In the time of judgment, those who are written in the

Revelation Chapter 3

book will be delivered (Daniel 12:1). The names of Paul's fellow-laborers for God are written in the book of life (Philippians 4:3). He who is not written in the book of life is cast into the lake of fire (Revelation 20:15); only they who are written in the Lamb's book of life shall enter into blessedness (Revelation 21:27)."[81] (For additional discussion of the book of life, see 20:15 on page 339.)

Jesus makes the third promise when he says, "I will confess his name before my Father, and before his angels." Jesus had previously promised that for "everyone who shall confess me before men, him will I also confess before my Father who is in heaven." (Matthew 10:32) This will be the ultimate recognition ceremony. Let each of us determine in his heart that we will be one of those for whom this ultimate acknowledgment of triumph is given.

3:6 **"He that hath an ear, let him hear what the Spirit saith to the churches."**

This is the fifth time Jesus has given this same exhortation. He will give it two more times. It calls our attention to a matter of extreme importance toward which he wants us to be fully alert.

There is a scale of priority in the various sections of divine revelation. Some revealed truths are more important than others. Some aspects of the divinely inspired message should be given greater attention and urgency than others. For example, at least on two occasions, Jesus said some enactments in the Mosaic Law were weightier than others. He made this clear when he rebuked the Scribes and Pharisees saying, "Woe unto you, Scribes and Pharisees, hypocrites! for ye tithe mint and anise and cummin, and have left undone the weightier matters of the law, justice, and mercy, and faith: but these ye ought to have done, and not to have left the other undone." (Matthew 23:23) Again, Jesus made priorities clear when a scholar of the Law questioned him about emphases in the Mosaic Law. That scholar asked, "Teacher, which is the great commandment in the law? And he said unto him, Thou shalt love the Lord thy God with all thy heart, and with all thy soul, and with all thy mind. This is the great and first commandment." (Matthew 22:36-38)

Jesus puts great emphasis on the messages which he gave to the seven churches of Asia by saying seven times, "He that hath an ear to hear let him hear what the Spirit saith to the churches." (See 2:7, 2:11, 2:17, 2:29, 3:6, 3:13 and 3:22.) Christians who do not follow his entreaty are impoverishing and endangering themselves through their gross negligence, indifference and unresponsiveness. Jesus' exhortation becomes even more conspicuous when we realize that he gave no comparable exhortation in the later prophetic sections of Revelation. That being the case, we should understand the urgency with which he expects us to heed the messages which God's Spirit has given to the seven churches.

6. The Church in Philadelphia 3:7-13

3:7 **"And to the angel of the church in Philadelphia write: These things saith he that is holy, he that is true, he that hath the key of David, he that openeth and none shall shut, and that shutteth and none openeth:"**

---

[81] William Barclay, The Revelation of John, Vol. I, (Philadelphia: The Westminster Press, 1976), pp. 155-156.

3:7 "the church in Philadelphia"

"As in the letter to the church in Smyrna, this church receives no rebuke nor call to repentance."[82]

The name "Philadelphia" comes from the Greek word *philadelphos*. It "is the Greek word for '*one who loves his brother*.' Such was the love of Attalus [king of Lydia] for his brother Eumenes that he was called Philadelphos, and it was after him that [the city of] Philadelphia was named."[83]

3:7 "he that is holy"

"Christ, the Speaker, here claims to be 'the Holy One.' ... In the Old Testament 'the Holy One' is a frequent name of God, especially in Isaiah 1:4, 24; 10:17, 20; 12:6, etc. ... Its radical meaning is separation."[84]

"All through the Old Testament God is the Holy One; and now that title is given to the risen Christ. We must remember the meaning of the word *holy* (hagios). It means *different, separate from*. God is holy, because he is different from men; he has that quality of life and being which men can never have by themselves and which belongs to Him alone."[85]

As the name is applied to Christ, it also points to his sinlessness. In Christian theology, it is clear that Christ's sinlessness was utterly essential to his being man's Saviour. There are repeated affirmations in the New Testament about Jesus' righteousness. There he is called, "Him who knew no sin." (II Corinthians 5:21) It is also affirmed that in all points, he was, "tempted like as we are, yet without sin." (Hebrews 4:15) Further it is stated that he was, "holy, guileless, undefiled, separated from sinners." (Hebrews 7:26) He, "did not sin, neither was guile found in his mouth." (I Peter 2:22) He was, "manifested to take away sins; and in him is no sin." (I John 3:5)

3:7 "he that is true"

Here, the English word "true" is the translation of the Greek word *alethinos*. It "means *real* or *genuine* as opposed to that which is shadowy or unreal. ... When we are confronted with Jesus Christ, we are confronted with no shadowy outline and image of the truth, but with the truth itself. ... In Him we are confronted, not with a substitute for divinity and godhead, but with the genuine reality of God Himself."[86]

The use of *alethinos* is characteristic of the apostle John. The use of the word is one of the ways we know that the apostle John is the author of the Gospel of John, the epistles of John as well as the book of Revelation. It "serves to bind together Gospel, Epistle and Apocalypse. It occurs nine times in the Gospel, four times in the First Epistle, and ten times in the Apocalypse; twenty-three times in all; in the rest of the New Testament only five times."[87]

---

82 Revelation, Four Views: A Parallel Commentary, ed. Steve Gregg, (Nashville: Thomas Nelson Publishers, 1997)., p. 75.
83 William Barclay, The Revelation of John, Vol. I, (Philadelphia: The Westminster Press, 1976), p. 158.
84 A. Plummer, The Pulpit Commentary [on] Revelation, (Chicago: Wilcox & Follett Co., no date), pp. 110-111.
85 William Barclay, The Revelation of John, Vol. I, (Philadelphia: The Westminster Press, 1976), pp. 160-161.
86 William Barclay, The Revelation of John, Vol. I, (Philadelphia: The Westminster Press, 1976), p. 161.
87 A. Plummer, The Pulpit Commentary [on] Revelation, (Chicago: Wilcox & Follett Co., no date), p. 111.

Revelation Chapter 3

3:7 "the key of David"

Here, Jesus makes "an allusion to Isaiah 22:22, in which the same privilege and prerogative [to open and shut] is assigned to a man named Eliakim, who was steward over the house of King Hezekiah. This man had the power either to admit persons or deny entry into the king's house. Jesus is claiming to have a corresponding right [among others] to admitting people into heaven."[88]

The full relevant passage from Isaiah 22:20-22 says, "In that day I will summon my servant, Eliakim son of Hilkiah. I will clothe him with your robe and fasten your sash around him and hand your authority over to him. He will be a father to those who live in Jerusalem and to the house of Judah. I will place on his shoulder the key to the house of David; what he opens no one can shut, and what he shuts no one can open." (NIV)

"In possessing 'the key of the house of David,' Eliakim had control over the house of David. Therefore in this passage, Christ claims control of that of which the house of David was a type. He is the Regent [one who rules, reigns or governs] in the kingdom of God."[89]

3:8 "I know thy works (behold, I have set before thee a door opened, which none can shut), that thou hast a little power, and didst keep my word, and didst not deny my name."

3:8 "I have set before thee a door opened"

No doubt, the door which Jesus opened for the church in Philadelphia had been opened by his use of the key of David. Thus, it is clear that the key of David is not only used to grant or deny someone entrance into heaven, but is also used to open doors of opportunity for the church.

At Ephesus Paul had been the beneficiary of Jesus' use of the key of David to open a door of opportunity. He said, "a great door and effectual is opened unto me, and there are many adversaries." (I Corinthians 16:9)

It is encouraging to know, that by the use of the key of David, Jesus can open doors for his people in the midst of and in the face of adversaries. It is probable that the door which was opened at Ephesus was the same one which Paul mentions in II Corinthians 2:12 in reference to Troas. Those open doors seem to have provided all of the opportunities which Paul had found during his first missionary tour. When he and Barnabas reported to the church in Antioch which had sent them out, "they rehearsed all things that God had done with them, and that he had opened a door of faith unto the Gentiles." (Acts 14:27) It is obvious from another statement made by the apostle Paul, that we can pray for Christ to use the key of David. He besought the Christians at Colossae to continue praying, "that God may open unto us a door for the word, to speak the mystery of Christ." (Colossians 4:3)

---

[88] Revelation, Four Views: A Parallel Commentary, ed. Steve Gregg , (Nashville: Thomas Nelson Publishers, 1997)., p. 75.
[89] A. Plummer, The Pulpit Commentary [on] Revelation, (Chicago: Wilcox & Follett Co., no date), p. 111.

3:8 "thou hast a little power, and didst keep my word, and didst not deny my name"

For small congregations, for congregations with stringent financial resources, for congregations with inadequate buildings and for congregations limited by social status and legal strictures, this letter to the church at Philadelphia should be a great encouragement. It was written to a church which had little power or strength. Though the details of the weakness of the Philadelphia church are not given, they may have included weaknesses in many categories. Despite the disadvantageous circumstances of the church in Philadelphia, Jesus said they had kept his word and had not denied his name. Their persistent on-going loyalty to Christ was rewarded by an imminent breakthrough with the local antagonistic Jewish community.

3:9 "Behold, I give of the synagogue of Satan, of them that say they are Jews, and they are not, but do lie; behold, I will make them to come and worship before thy feet, and to know that I have loved thee."

3:9 "the synagogue of Satan"

The corporate body of Jews in Philadelphia had departed so far from God's plan for their lives and destinies that their collective life had come under Satan's control. Yet, it is out of this shockingly degenerate synagogue of Jews that Jesus was going to give a stunning breakthrough to the little church in Philadelphia.

3:9 "of them that say they are Jews, and they are not, but do lie"

The church in Philadelphia faced a similar situation, originating from the Jewish synagogue in their city as the Christians did in Smyrna in which the synagogue was noted for blasphemy uttered by, "them that say they are Jews, and they are not, but are a synagogue of Satan." (Revelation 2:9) In Philadelphia, there was a group, perhaps even the entire congregation in the synagogue, "that say they are Jews and they are not, but do lie." It was their lie which disqualified them from being Jews. Ultimately, "the only true Jews are those who accept the Christ."[90] (See Galatians 3:29.)

3:9 "I will make them to come and worship before thy feet, and to know that I have loved thee"

"Against the Jewish accusers and scoffers it [the church in Philadelphia] will not only prevail – like Smyrna – but will gain the victory, in which the vanquished, through their conversion, will share!"[91]

When it is said that the Jews from the satanically-controlled synagogue in Philadelphia will be made to come to the Christians and will worship at their feet, it points, for example, to the learning experience of Saul of Tarsus before becoming a Christian. He says about that period of his life, that he had been brought up "at the feet of Gamaliel, instructed according to the strict manner of the law of our fathers." (Acts 22:3)

---

90 A. Plummer, The Pulpit Commentary [on] Revelation, (Chicago: Wilcox & Follett Co., no date), p. 112.
91 W. Hendriksen, More Than Conquerors: An Interpretation of the Book of Revelation, (Grand Rapids: Baker Book House, 1952), p. 93.

Revelation Chapter 3

Another example of what it meant for those Jews to worship before the feet of the Christians is found in the life of Mary, sister of Martha and Lazarus. Of her, it is written that she "sat at the Lord's feet, and heard his word." (Luke 10:39)

Jesus is predicting that through the church in Philadelphia, which had "little power" but had kept Christ's word and had not denied his name, there would come a startling, victorious breakthrough among some in the Jewish community which was under satanic dominance.

William Barclay wrote a commentary on the book of Revelation which, on the whole, is helpful and rewarding. However, his explanation of what is meant by the Jews of Philadelphia coming to worship before the feet of the Christians is certainly mistaken. He sees those Jews coming in groveling submission as though they had been taken captive on the battlefield. He points to Isaiah 45:14 and 60:14 as examples which he thinks portray what was predicted to happen to the Jews in Philadelphia. Those verses in Isaiah point to militarily subdued Gentiles bowing before the feet of Jews who had been victorious on the battlefield. That is not an example of how Christians are to triumph with the Gospel.

When Jesus told the church at Philadelphia that he would make the Jews from the local "synagogue of Satan" come and worship before their feet, he was predicting that, surprisingly, the Jews from that radical synagogue would come with the desire to learn from the Philadelphia Christians. Presumably, that would result in many of those Jews becoming Christians. Jesus, therefore, predicts a great, triumphant Gospel break-through among those who had previously shown only enmity and rejection. This probably is one consequence of Jesus' promise, recorded in verse 8, that he had set before them, "a door opened, which none can shut."

3:10 **"Because thou didst keep the word of my patience, I also will keep thee from the hour of trial, that hour which is to come upon the whole world, to try them that dwell upon the earth."**

3:10 "Because thou didst keep the word of my patience, I also will keep thee"

"It is the promise of the risen Christ that he who keeps will be kept. 'You have kept my commandment,' He says, 'Therefore, I will keep you.' … Loyalty has its sure reward."[92]

3:10 "the hour of trial, that hour which is to come upon the whole world, to try them that dwell upon the earth"

To understand the trial from which Jesus said he would keep the Christians of Philadelphia, one must understand the expression "the whole world." The Greek word here for "world" "is not *kosmos* [cosmos], 'the ordered universe' (as in 11:15; 13:8; 17:8), [that is, the entire globe] but the *oikoumene*, 'the inhabited earth' (as in 12:9; 16:14)."[93] The inhabited earth is equivalent to the civilized world. This, undoubtedly, refers to the Roman Empire. Most probably, the cataclysm from which Jesus promised to save the

---

92 William Barclay, The Revelation of John, Vol. I, (Philadelphia: The Westminster Press, 1976), p. 166.
93 A. Plummer, The Pulpit Commentary [on] Revelation, (Chicago: Wilcox & Follett Co., no date), p. 112.

Christians of Philadelphia was empire-wide persecution by Rome. The extent of that persecution is said to impact "the whole world."

"Christians [in the Roman Empire] were always in danger, for their legal status was at best precarious, a local or provincial official might at almost any time proceed against them, and some action of an Emperor might stiffen the backbone of otherwise lenient authorities. They were chronically regarded with suspicion by large elements in the population and among the respectable citizens. Their peril was further accentuated by a procedure which gave their possessions to those who brought a successful accusation against them. Confiscation of goods, imprisonment, and torture might overtake them at any time, followed by hard labor in the mines or by execution."[94]

In any case, the Christians at Philadelphia undoubtedly knew of the apostle John's exile to the Island of Patmos (See 1:9.) and of the martyrdom of Antipas (See 2:13.), a member of their sister church in Pergamum. Jesus promised that he would keep them from a similar hour of trial.

3:11 **"I come quickly: hold fast that which thou hast, that no one take thy crown."**

3:11 "I come quickly"

See the discussion of this promise under 2:16 on page 39.

3:11 "hold fast that which thou hast"

See the comments on 2:25, page 45.

3:11 "no one take thy crown"

The crown to which reference is made is the crown of life. (See Revelation 2:10, p. 34.)

3:12 **"He that overcometh, I will make him a pillar in the temple of my God, and he shall go out thence no more: and I will write upon him the name of my God, and the name of the city of my God, the new Jerusalem, which cometh down out of heaven from my God, and mine own new name."**

3:12 "He that overcometh"

For a discussion of the word "overcometh" see comments on 2:17 at page 40.

3:12 "I will make him a pillar in the temple of my God" (the first reward)

While the symbolism of "a pillar in the temple of my God" is undoubtedly taken from the two pillars of Solomon's temple (See I Kings 7:15, 21 and II Chronicles 3:17.) the reality points to the redeemed Christian's unending participation in the working out of God's eternal purpose. See discussion of God's eternal purpose under 2:17, on pages 40-41.

3:12 "he shall go out thence no more" (the second reward)

"In A.D. 17 there came a great earthquake, the earthquake which destroyed Sardis and ten other cities. In the other cities the earthquake was over and done with; but in Philadelphia the tremors went on for years. ... It is frequently the case that ever-recurring minor

---

94 Kenneth Scott Latourette, A History of Christianity, (New York: Harper & Row, Publishers, 1975), p. 86.

Revelation Chapter 3

shocks over a long period drive people to sheer panic. That is what happened in Philadelphia. ... Those who still dared to live in the city were reckoned mad; they spent their time shoring up the shaking buildings, and every now and then fleeing to the open spaces for safety. ... People in Philadelphia well knew what gratefulness and security lay in the promise that 'they would go out no more.'"[95]

3:12 "I will write upon him the name of my God" (the third reward)

This is the third of five rewards or blessings which are to be bestowed upon those who "overcome." When Jesus says, "I will write upon him the name of my God," is he referring to some process like a tattoo or a stencil emblazoned on one's clothing? Or, does he indicate that the name of God will be impressed in some utterly unforgettable and indelible manner upon the memory and consciousness of victorious Christians?

We have an Old Testament example of this second concept. It is found in the formula by which Moses and Aaron were to perpetually pronounce blessing upon the children of Israel. The biblical account tells us, "Jehovah spake unto Moses, saying, Speak unto Aaron and unto his sons, saying, On this wise ye shall bless the children of Israel: ye shall say unto them, Jehovah bless thee, and keep thee: Jehovah make his face to shine upon thee, and be gracious unto thee: Jehovah lift up his countenance upon thee, and give thee peace. **So shall they put my name upon the children of Israel**; and I will bless them." (Numbers 6:22-27)

Note the word "So" at the beginning of verse 27. It conveys the idea of "in this way," or "in this manner." This is clearly confirmed in David Stern's translation entitled, "*Complete Jewish Bible*." There, verse 27 is rendered as "In this way they are to put my name on the people of Israel, so that I will bless them."

Not only do we have the issue of how Jesus will write the name of his God on those who overcome, but we may also ponder what name he will choose for this purpose. Will it be "Jehovah," (He who exists) or "Adonai," (my Lord) or "Elohim" (the true God) or "El-Shadai" (the powerful One, the Almighty) or "I Am that I Am" (the Eternal One)? No one single name seems to capture the total reality of the Eternal, Infinite One whom we call God. Each of the names just given stresses a particular or specific attribute of the Infinite One. While we may not be able to say what name Jesus will use to write the name of his God on those who overcome, we can be sure it will be definitive and unmistakable.

3:12 "the name of the city of my God, the new Jerusalem" (the fourth reward)

As a fourth reward, Jesus says he will write "the name of the city of my God" upon those who overcome. Just as no one will ever be able to question which deity it is to whom we give our total loyalty after Jesus has written God's name upon us, similarly, when the name of the city of God is written on the overcomers, their citizenship can never be in doubt. Jesus seems to specify that the name of the city of God will be "the new Jerusalem, which cometh down out of heaven from my God." (See notes on Revelation 21:2 on page 342 and following.) When Ezekiel described the new Jerusalem, he said, "The name of the city from that day shall be, Jehovah is there." (Ezekiel 48:35)

---
95 William Barclay, The Revelation of John, Vol. I, (Philadelphia: The Westminster Press, 1976), p. 159.

3:12 "mine own new name" (the fifth reward)

The fifth blessing which Jesus promises to bestow upon those who overcome is that he will write on them "my own new name." At this point in the unfolding of God's eternal purpose, it would be pointless to speculate what Jesus' "new name" might be, for he tells us that, "he hath a name written which no one knoweth but he himself." (Revelation 19:12) Just as we will be vividly aware of the name of God, so also will the name of our Redeemer ever be before us.

3:13 "He that hath an ear, let him hear what the Spirit saith to the churches."

See the exposition under 3:6.

7. The Church in Laodicea 3:14-22

3:14 "And to the angel of the church in Laodicea write: These things saith the Amen, the faithful and true witness, the beginning of the creation of God:"

3:14 "the angel"

There is an ancient document dated in the third century bearing the name "The Apostolic Constitutions." That document in Section 8:46 says "that Archippus was the first bishop of the church in Laodicea. Now when Paul was writing to the neighboring church in Colossae, he says sternly: 'Say to Archippus, Take heed to the ministry which thou hast received in the Lord, that thou fulfill it. (Colossians 4:17). It would seem that Archippus was somehow failing in his duty, and needed a sharp reminder. That was thirty years before the *Revelation* was written; but it may be that as long ago as that the rot had set in in the church in Laodicea, and that an unworthy pastor and an unsatisfactory and unfaithful ministry had sown the seeds of degeneration there."[96]

From the letter to the Colossian church we know of another preacher who had labored with the Laodicean church. The account says, "Epaphras, who is one of you, a servant of Christ Jesus, saluteth you, always striving for you in his prayers, that ye may stand perfect and fully assured in all the will of God. For I bear him witness, that he hath much labor for you, and for **them in Laodicea**, and for them in Hierapolis." (Colossians 4:12 - 13)

3:14 "the church in Laodicea"

Barclay correctly, but almost dismissively, wrote, "Laodicea has the grim distinction of being the only Church of which the Risen Christ has nothing good to say."[97] Though Barclay's observation is correct, still we must not overlook the fact that Jesus assures the church in Laodicea of his love, when he tells them, "As many as I love, I reprove and chasten: be zealous therefore, and repent." (Revelation 3:19) Is it possible that sometimes we may give up on churches before Jesus does?

"The Laodicea of the *Revelation* was called Laodicea on the Lycus [river] to distinguish it from others [which also bore the name of Laodicea]. It was founded about 250 B.C. by Antiochus of Syria, and it was named after his wife Laodice.

---
96 William Barclay, The Revelation of John, Vol. I, (Philadelphia: The Westminster Press, 1976), p. 176.
97 William Barclay, The Revelation of John, Vol. I, (Philadelphia: The Westminster Press, 1976), p. 173.

Revelation Chapter 3

"Laodicea's importance was due entirely to its position. The road from Ephesus to the east and to Syria was the most important road in [the province of] Asia. That road began on the coast at Ephesus and had to find a way to climb up to the central plateau which was 8,500 feet up. It set out along the valley of the river Meander until it reached what were known as the Gates of Phrygia. Beyond these gates lay a broad valley where Lydia, Phrygia and Caria met. That sector of the valley taken by the Meander was a narrow, rocky, precipitous gorge, through which no road could pass. The road, therefore, detoured through the Lycus [river] Valley and climbed up to the plateau by that way. In that valley Laodicea stood. It was literally astride the great road to the east. That road went straight through Laodicea, entering by the Ephesian Gate and leaving by the Syrian Gate.

"That in itself would have been enough to make Laodicea one of the great commercial and strategic centers of the ancient world …[Additionally] two other roads passed through the gates of Laodicea. There was the road from Pergamum and the Hermus Valley to Pisidia and Pamphilia and to the coast at Perga. And the road from eastern Caria to central and west Phrygia also passed through Laodicea.

"As Sir W.M. Ramsay says: 'It only needed peace to make Laodicea a great commercial and financial center.' That peace came with the dominion of Rome. In the previous days of unsettlement Laodicea had been a comparatively small town, but when the Roman peace gave it its opportunity it became, as Pliny called it, 'a most distinguished city.'"[98]

The importance of the route through Laodicea continued for centuries. In the Crusader era, for example, Conrad "advised Louis and his barons that they could expect provisioning difficulties on the Philadelphia road. The best option was to make for the south-west, fully at right angles to their intended course, and follow the coast road to Smyrna and Ephesus. From there, revictualed and rested, they could then take the ancient road up the Meander Valley to Byzantine-held Laodicea before heading south for the Mediterranean and so complete their journey by sea."[99]

3:14   "These things saith the Amen"

To remind the Christians at Laodicea of the divine origin of his message to them, Jesus calls himself "the Amen." This undoubtedly is taken from Isaiah 65:16 in which God calls himself "the God of Amen," which is translated accurately in the marginal reading in the ASV. Unfortunately, when the translators of the Septuagint rendered this divine name from Hebrew into Greek, they chose the word *alethinos*, which means "true," which does not convey the correct meaning. Most English translations of Isaiah 65:16 seem to have followed the Septuagint rendering rather than the Hebrew. This makes it difficult to identify this title with the Amen in Revelation 3:14. Because of this anomaly, superficially, it appears that the name in Isaiah 65:16 is parallel to the name in Revelation 3:7 where Jesus calls himself "he that is true," which is expressed by the Greek word *alethinos*. However, the reality is that "the Amen" is a unique name which Jesus uses for himself and it has its roots in Isaiah 65:16. As Plummer correctly says, "The word

---

98   Slightly edited from William Barclay, The Revelation of John, Vol. I, (Philadelphia: The Westminster Press, 1976), p. 173-174.
99   Jeremy Seal, Meander: East to West, Indirectly, Along A Turkish River, (New York: Bloomsbury, 2011), p. 234.

'Amen' is here [in Revelation 3:14] used as a proper name of our Lord; and this is the only instance of such an application."[100]

The cry or exclamation, "Amen!" means "So be it!" Thus, Christ says by this unique name, that he is the One who can bring desire or aspiration into reality. He can cause it to be, or make it happen. Thus, as Paul, speaking of Christ, wrote, "In him is the yea: wherefore also through him is the Amen, unto the glory of God through us." (II Corinthians 1:20)

3:14 "the faithful and true witness"

"R.C. Trench well points out that a witness must satisfy three essential conditions. (a) He must have seen with his own eyes that of which he tells. (b) He must be absolutely honest, so that he repeats with accuracy that which he has heard and seen. (c) He must have the ability to tell what he has to say, so that his witness may make its true impression on those who hear."[101]

One can only be a witness of that which he has seen or heard or felt. It is on this triple basis that John wrote his first epistle. He said "that which was from the beginning, that which we have heard, that which we have seen with our eyes, that which we beheld, and our hands handled, concerning the word of life ..." (I John 1:1) When Jesus calls himself the "faithful and true witness," it makes it clear that Jesus has total input about what is going on in the churches as well as in our individual lives.

3:14 "the beginning of the creation of God"

"It should not be assumed that this makes Christ out to be a created thing [or being]. The Greek work translated **Beginning** is *arche*, which carries the concept of the 'beginning, origin, active cause.' Rather than the 'first thing created,' the expression could be understood to mean 'he who is the Origin (Source, Creator) of the creation of God.'

"Paul instructed the Colossian church to pass along his letter [which he had written to them] to the church of Laodicea (Colossians 4:16). If these instructions were followed, then this church would have been familiar with the Colossian epistle, where the role of Christ as Creator is strongly affirmed: 'He is the image of the invisible God, the firstborn over all creation. For by him were all things created ... All things were created through Him and for Him.' (Colossians 1:15-16). Thus there is little likelihood that the Laodiceans would interpret Jesus' words here to mean that He was a created being."[102]

However, "The Arians, attempting to disprove the Divinity of our Lord, quoted this passage attributing to it the former sense (that is, a passive sense, which would make Christ the first created thing of all the things which God had created)."[103]

3:15 "I know thy works, that thou art neither cold nor hot: I would thou wert cold or hot."

---

100 A. Plummer, The Pulpit Commentary [on] Revelation, (Chicago: Wilcox & Follett Co., no date)., p. 114.
101 William Barclay, The Revelation of John, Vol. I, (Philadelphia: The Westminster Press, 1976), p. 177.
102 Revelation, Four Views: A Parallel Commentary, ed. Steve Gregg, (Nashville: Thomas Nelson Publishers, 1997), pp. 78-79.
103 A. Plummer, The Pulpit Commentary [on] Revelation, (Chicago: Wilcox & Follett Co., no date), p. 115.

Revelation Chapter 3

The church in Laodicea was not completely dead. That is clear from the fact that they had "works," though they are not described. However, those works must have been trivial and probably were undertaken timorously in spite of the fact that the church had great resources. The church boasted, "I am rich" (3:17), but their works were not carried out in proportion to their means.

For example, though they certainly knew of Paul's evangelistic work, they did not support him financially. When Paul wrote to the Philippian church, he said, "Ye did well that ye had fellowship with my affliction. And ye yourselves also know, ye Philippians, that in the beginning of the gospel, when I departed from Macedonia, no church had fellowship with me in the matter of giving and receiving but ye only: for even in Thessalonica ye sent once and again unto my need." (Philippians 4:14-17)

Jesus shows his revulsion toward an indifferent, tepid lifestyle among his followers. He expects a decisive commitment. Somewhere between cold and hot is not acceptable. Even a frigid or cold life is less repugnant to Jesus than a fence-straddling, uncommitted neutrality, which he expresses as being "lukewarm." (3:16)

3:16 "So because thou art lukewarm, and neither hot nor cold, I will spew thee out of my mouth."

Jesus says, "I will spew thee out of my mouth." He seems to be addressing his message to the whole church rather than to specific individuals in the body. The Greek text is very emphatic. It seems translators have struggled to convey the sense of reflexive repugnance which Jesus feels in the presence of a church with a tepid commitment. The words "spew" (ASV), "spit" (NRSV), and "vomit" (NKJV) have been used to help English speakers feel the sense of loathing, nausea and gagging which Jesus has for those among his followers who are lukewarm. "The one who neither opposes nor serves offers Christ the ultimate insult – affirming His existence, but not taking Him seriously. ... The image of Jesus vomiting is an undignified and shocking one, and its use here warns us that He is not to be taken lightly."[104]

Jesus' warning that he would "spew thee [the church in Laodicea] out of my mouth" seems equivalent in severity to his warning to the church in Ephesus when he said, "Repent and do the first works; or else I come to thee, and will remove thy candlestick out of its place, except thou repent." (Revelation 2:5) It is obvious from the warnings to the churches in Ephesus and Laodicea that Jesus will not perpetually tolerate sin and indifference.

3:17 "Because thou sayest, I am rich, and have gotten riches, and have need of nothing; and knowest not that thou art the wretched one and miserable and poor and blind and naked:"

3:17 "thou sayest, I am rich, and have gotten riches, and have need of nothing"

The church in Laodicea not only had wealth, it boasted of it. The church said "I am rich." The ostentatious wealth of the church in Laodicea put it in glaring contrast to the

---
104 <u>Revelation, Four Views: A Parallel Commentary</u>, ed. Steve Gregg , (Nashville: Thomas Nelson Publishers, 1997), p. 79.

churches in Smyrna and in Philadelphia. About Smyrna, Jesus said, "I know thy tribulation and thy poverty." (2:9) About the church in Philadelphia he said, "Thou hast a little power." (3:8)

The church boasted saying, "I am rich, and have gotten riches, and have need of nothing." There is a distinction between these two flaunting statements. By pridefully saying "I am rich" they were boasting about the residual congregational wealth which they had previously hoarded. Secondly, in the words "I ... have gotten riches" the congregation seems to brag about having successfully augmented their older unspent hoard of wealth. They covetously had kept both hoards of wealth in their treasury, refusing to use either of them to expand or strengthen the work of Christ.

3:17 "thou ... knowest not that thou art the wretched one and miserable and poor and blind and naked"

When Jesus indicted the Laodicean church by saying, "thou knowest not," it emphasizes the fact that wealth and ease can, and often do, blind and limit or distort perception and insight. This probably grew out of indifference to the word of God. As James has pointed out, "If anyone is a hearer of the word and not a doer, he is like unto a man beholding his natural face in a mirror: for he beholdeth himself and goeth away, and straightway forgetteth what manner of man he was." (James 1:23-24)

The church in Laodicea was "wretched" and "miserable." Probably, these words reflect jealousy, bickering, envy and selfishness between the individual members as well as in the church's congregational life. Any church in which such conditions prevail, has been impoverished. Though they may claim to be rich, they are poor. The members will have been robbed of the inspiration and consolation which come from harmoniously and joyously sharing goals and experiences in a local congregation of the Lord's church.

The church in Laodicea, despite having a bulging treasury, was really poor. "If all that one has to meet life with is wealth, then he is poor indeed."[105] But, they did not have feedback on their own condition because, as Jesus said, they were blind. Even though the city of Laodicea was noted for "its medical skill in the care of the eyes, [the church] never realized that, in the sight of God, it was spiritually blind."[106]

The Laodicean church was also vulnerable. That seems to be the significance of Jesus' statement that they were not only "blind," but also "naked." Such conditions of vulnerability will certainly grow out of belligerent divisions within a congregation. As John wrote, "He that hateth his brother is in the darkness, and walketh in the darkness, and knoweth not wither he goeth, because the darkness hath blinded his eyes." (I John 2:11)

3:18 "I counsel thee to buy of me gold refined by fire, that thou mayest become rich; and white garments, that thou mayest clothe thyself, and that the shame of thy nakedness be not made manifest; and eyesalve to anoint thine eyes, that thou mayest see.

---

[105] William Barclay, The Revelation of John, Vol. I, (Philadelphia: The Westminster Press, 1976), p. 181.
[106] William Barclay, The Revelation of John, Vol. I, (Philadelphia: The Westminster Press, 1976), p. 175.

Revelation Chapter 3

3:18   "I counsel thee to buy of me gold refined by fire"

When Jesus says, "I counsel thee," he shows his tenderness and friendship. He did not say, "I command thee," but "I counsel thee." His first bit of counsel was "to buy of me gold refined by fire." It was spiritual rather than metallic gold to which Jesus pointed the Laodicean Christians. It represented the kind of purchasing power which Isaiah lauded centuries earlier, when he said, "Ho, every one that thirsteth, come ye to the waters, and he that hath no money; come ye, buy, and eat; yea, come, buy wine and milk without money and without price." (Isaiah 55:1) Furthermore, such an exchange could not be based on a barter system for we possess nothing of equal worth!

3:18   "that thou mayest become rich"

Jesus impoverished himself in order to enrich his true followers. The apostle Paul pointed that out when he wrote, "Ye know the grace of our Lord Jesus Christ, that though he was rich, yet for your sakes he became poor, that ye through his poverty might become rich." (II Corinthians 8:9)

Paul had not personally visited the church in Laodicea for he said, "I strive [in prayer?] for you, [the Christians at Colossae] and for them at Laodicea, and for as many as have not seen my face in the flesh." (Colossians 2:1) Still, he prayed for them that they would become truly rich by being, "knit together in love, and unto <u>all riches</u> of the full assurance of understanding, that they may know the mystery of God, even Christ, in whom are <u>all the treasures</u> of wisdom and knowledge hidden." (Colossians 2:2-3)

3:18   "white garments, that thou mayest clothe thyself"

"Later in Revelation, we read of a bride dressed in 'fine linen, clean and bright,' which is said to represent 'the righteous acts of the saints' (19:8). [We may conclude, then, that] Righteous acts were lacking from this church."[107]

3:18   "that the shame of thy nakedness be not made manifest"

Paul wrote, "Christ loved the church, and gave himself up for it; that he might sanctify it, having cleansed it by the washing of water with the word, that he might present the church to himself a glorious church not having spot or wrinkle or any such thing; but that it should be holy and without blemish." (Ephesians 5:25-27)

When a church is without "spot or wrinkle or any such thing" but is holy and without blemish, the closest scrutiny by others will not bring shame. However, when a church is as seriously blemished as was the Laodicean church, for anyone to see their faults, shortcomings and blemishes brings an intense feeling of shame.

3:18   "eyesalve to anoint thine eyes, that thou mayest see"

Ironically, "despite the fact that a world-renowned eyesalve was produced in that very city, the church had lost its spiritual perception. It was just as Peter indicated, people who

---

107 Edited from <u>Revelation, Four Views: A Parallel Commentary</u>, ed. Steve Gregg , (Nashville: Thomas Nelson Publishers, 1997), p. 80.

have failed to persevere in Christian growth are 'shortsighted, even to blindness' (II Peter 1:9)."[108]

The church in Laodicea boasted about its wealth but had been unable to see where and how that wealth should have been spent to further and enhance the work of Christ. The church could see its hoard of money but could not see its own shameful nakedness.

A cure for their blindness was available, but certainly not from the local medical market. Their blindness was reversible, but only with the medication which Jesus exclusively dispenses. The salve which Jesus could have given them would have been something analogous to the remedial mixture which he compounded from saliva and clay and applied like a salve to restore the sight of a man who had been blind from birth. (See John 9:5-7.)

In actuality the salve which Jesus would give probably suggests, "that they carefully consider God's Word, applying its teaching to themselves [as if it were a salve], till they could fully see their pitiable and sinful condition. This would bring them back to a full realization of their true state and bring about a happy reformation."[109]

3:19 **"As many as I love, I reprove and chasten: be zealous therefore, and repent."**

Despite the fact that the church in Laodicea had not demonstrated a single virtue for which Jesus could commend them, still, remarkably, Jesus expresses his reproof and chastening as evidence of his love. Two things were necessary for the church's restoration, one was zeal and the other was repentance.

The word "reprove," used in the ASV, is rendered in the King James and New International Version by the word "rebuke." "The Greek word is *elegchein*, and it describes, not simply rebuke, but the kind of rebuke which compels a man to see the error of his ways and to admit that he was wrong."[110]

Along with reproof or rebuke, Jesus administers chastening. None of us who are his followers can escape it for he says, "As many as I love, I ... chasten." His chastening is a confirmation of our relationship with him. Therefore, "It is for chastening that you endure; God dealeth with you as with sons; for what son is there whom his father chasteneth not?" (Hebrews 12:7)

3:20 **"Behold, I stand at the door and knock: if any man hear my voice and open the door, I will come in to him, and will sup with him, and he with me."**

3:20 **"Behold, I stand at the door and knock"**

The most basic or fundamental problem in the Laodicean church was its exclusion of Christ from its corporate life as well as from the lives of the individuals who made up the church. He had not been allowed in their affairs, in their decisions or in their activities. Jesus was on the outside. He was knocking, trying to gain access to the church! He had

---
108 Edited from Revelation, Four Views: A Parallel Commentary, ed. Steve Gregg , (Nashville: Thomas Nelson Publishers, 1997), p. 80.
109 John T. Hinds, A Commentary on the Book of Revelation (Nashville, Tenn.: Gospel Advocate Company, 1976), p. 62.
110 William Barclay, The Revelation of John, Vol. I, (Philadelphia: The Westminster Press, 1976), p. 183.

Revelation Chapter 3

died for the church but even so, had been excluded from its life! Can any church flourish which ignores or excludes Christ?

"Christ stands at the door of the human heart [and of the church] and knocks. One unique new fact that Christianity brought into this world is that God is the seeker of men. No other religion has the vision of a seeking God. ... It would be great enough to think of a God who accepted men when they came back; [but] it was beyond belief to think of a God who actually went out and searched."[111] The seeking Saviour is also powerfully portrayed in the Parable of the Good Shepherd (Luke 15:3-7).

Christ is not only standing at the door, he is knocking on it. If he were merely standing there, we might be able to plead ignorance of his presence, but he makes it impossible for us not to have noticed him. How does that knock come? Is it a pang of conscience? Is it a casual true comment from someone whom, perhaps, we may not even know? Is it some passage in Scripture or in something else we are reading which reminds us that we have left Jesus completely outside of our thinking and decision-making process?

3:20 "if any man hear my voice and open the door, I will come in to him"

Jesus not only knocks on the church's door but that of each individual as well. Thus, he says, "If any man hear my voice and open the door, I will come in to him."

It is not only indifference which keeps many from hearing the Lord's voice, but there are also competing voices to which Satan wants us to give priority. Whenever the voice of the Lord breaks through the jumble of competing voices, we must give it the utmost priority.

"This voice of the Lord as applied to the heart by the Spirit is the *power of God unto salvation!* Hence, we find that this passage does full justice both to divine sovereign grace and to human responsibility."[112] The knocking on the door of man's heart, the calling to man's intellect and conscience, is the divine part in salvation, but man's part is opening the door. To everyone who opens the door of his heart Jesus promises, "I will come in to him." It is a visit which will transform and ennoble the host. Paul expresses this divine visit as, "Christ in you, the hope of glory." (Colossians 1:27)

3:20 "will sup with him, and he with me."

"He, as it were, descends from the throne of his glory in order to dine with this individual who in himself is so poor and pitiable. Christ and the believer dine together, which in the Orient was an indication of special friendship and of covenant relationship. In other words, the believer has blessed fellowship with his Savior and Lord, ... That fellowship begins even in this present life."[113]

"The [Greek] word translated 'sup' is *deipnein,* and its corresponding noun is *deipnon.* The word is very significant. The Greeks had three meals in the day. There was *akratisma,* breakfast, which [often] was no more than a piece of dried bread dipped in

---

111 William Barclay, The Revelation of John, Vol. I, (Philadelphia: The Westminster Press, 1976), pp. 185-186.
112 W. Hendriksen, More Than Conquerors: An Interpretation of the Book of Revelation, (Grand Rapids: Baker Book House, 1952), p. 97.
113 W. Hendriksen, More Than Conquerors: An Interpretation of the Book of Revelation, (Grand Rapids: Baker Book House, 1952), p. 97.

wine. [Next], there was *ariston*, the midday meal. A man did not go home for it; it was simply a picnic snack eaten by the side of the pavement, or in some colonnade, or in the city square, a meal eaten in the passing. [Finally], there was *deipnon*; this was the evening meal; it was the main meal of the day; people lingered and sat long and talked over it, for the day's work was done; there was time now for unlimited and unhurried fellowship together. It was the *deipnon* that Christ would share with the man who answered His knock. This was no hurried meal, no visit in the passing, no hasty, conventional call; it was the meal where people lingered in fellowship together."[114]

3:21 **"He that overcometh, I will give to him to sit down with me in my throne, as I also overcame, and sat down with my Father in his throne."**

"There are two points to be noticed in this promise: (1) The position promised to the conqueror ['he that overcometh'], 'I will give to him to sit down with me in my throne.' (2) The two thrones mentioned. (a) Note the expression 'in my throne' (not *epi* [on], but *en* [in] *to throno*), which occurs nowhere else. The mother of St. James and St. John had requested for them a place on the right hand and the left of our Lord — the highest dignity which she could conceive. The twelve apostles are promised to sit on twelve thrones [Luke 22:29-30], to judge the tribes of Israel. But Christ offers a yet higher honor, that is to say, to sit in his throne; placing us in the closest relationship with himself, and exalting us to his own glory. (b) The throne promised is not that which Christ now occupies with his Father, but his own. Christ is now sitting on his Father's throne, mediating for his church on earth, and waiting till his enemies be made his footstool (Psalm 110:1). To that throne there is no admission for humanity although Christ shares it in virtue of his Godhead. But when his enemies have been made his footstool and death, the last enemy, is destroyed (I Corinthians 15:26), and the necessity for his mediation exists no longer, since the Church militant will have become the Church triumphant, then will be erected Christ's own throne, which glorified man may share in common with him who was man, and who has so exalted humanity as to render such a condition and such a position possible."[115]

"Reigning with Christ was also promised to the overcomers in Thyatira (2:26ff), and additional references to the co-regency of the saints are found in 5:10 and 20:4."[116]

3:22 **"He that hath an ear, let him hear what the Spirit saith to the churches."**

On this seven-times-repeated exhortation, see the comments on 2:7, 2:11, 2:17, 2:29, 3:6 and 3:13. In addition to those insightful comments, we should realize that, "the seven messages were not merely separate admonitions addressed only to each particular Church, but all the epistles were meant for all the seven Churches, and, after them, for the universal Church."[117]

---

[114] William Barclay, The Revelation of John, Vol. I, (Philadelphia: The Westminster Press, 1976), pp. 186-187.
[115] A. Plummer, The Pulpit Commentary [on] Revelation, (Chicago: Wilcox & Follett Co., no date), p. 118.
[116] Edited from Revelation, Four Views: A Parallel Commentary, ed. Steve Gregg, (Nashville: Thomas Nelson Publishers, 1997), p. 80.
[117] A. Plummer, The Pulpit Commentary [on] Revelation, (Chicago: Wilcox & Follett Co., no date), p. 118.

Revelation Chapter 4

Introduction: Hendriksen astutely observed that "Chapters 4 and 5 teach one main lesson. Unless we clearly grasp this point, we shall never see the glorious unity of the Apocalypse. We shall lose ourselves in allegorization. That *one main* lesson may be expressed in the words of the Psalmist: '*Jehovah* reigns; let the peoples tremble! He sits above the cherubim; let the earth be moved.' [Psalm 99:1] The assurance of this truth should impart comfort to believers in the midst of fiery trials. Hence, this vision of the universe governed by The Throne precedes the symbolic description of the trials through which the church must pass. ...The universe of the Bible is ... theocentric. ... The real mind, the real will which – while fully maintaining the responsibility and freedom of individual instruments – controls this universe is the mind, the will of *the Almighty God*! Nothing is excluded from his dominion. Hence, the term Throne occurs seventeen times in these two chapters."[118]

III. *Transition from the historic and the present to the prophetic 4:1*

4:1 **"After these things I saw, and behold, a door opened in heaven, and the first voice that I heard, a voice as of a trumpet speaking with me, one saying, "Come up hither, and I will show thee the things which must come to pass hereafter."**

4:1 "a door opened in heaven"

"The scene is transferred to heaven and John is permitted to view it through the door open for that purpose. This is similar to the words of Ezekiel, 'The heavens were opened, and I saw visions of God.' (Ezekiel 1:1)"[119] "The 'open door' significantly declares that the secrets of heaven are to be revealed."[120]

"A door standing open in heaven!" This is "the door of revelation."[121] "He appeared to enter the door, and a new world in heavenly glory burst upon his view."[122] John was given the rare privilege of observing the throne room from which the ultimate destiny of the universe is determined.

4:1 "a voice as of a trumpet speaking with me"

We are not told whose voice it was but it was a commanding one, "as of a trumpet," not to be ignored.

4:1 "Come up hither"

John explains in the next verse how he was enabled to make the journey from earth to heaven.

---

118 W. Hendriksen, More Than Conquerors: An Interpretation of the Book of Revelation, (Grand Rapids: Baker Book House, 1952), p. 103.
119 John T. Hinds, A Commentary on the Book of Revelation (Nashville, Tenn.: Gospel Advocate Company, 1976), p. 66.
120 B. W. Johnson, A Vision of the Ages, (Hollywood, California: Old Paths Book Club, n.d.), p. 33.
121 William Barclay, The Revelation of John, Vol. I, (Philadelphia: The Westminster Press, 1976), p. 150.
122 B. Steward, *Revelation Fulfilled in History*, (London: John Bale, Sons & Danielsson, Ltd., 1934), p. 15

Revelation Verse by Verse

4:1 **"the things which must come to pass hereafter"**

This vision of the hereafter assures us that there is a future. The fragility of any uncertain situation is not to be seen as the flickering out of a transient existence which would be followed by endless, vacuous nothingness and non-being. This vision is a total repudiation of any concept of Nihilism. The Revelation does not lead us to anticipate a nihilistic boundless void, but to an awareness of a much higher level of existence, a celestial panorama. Life, reality and existence, as we have experienced them, are not illusions but are reaffirmed along with the assurance of a limitless future, anchored in the One who inhabits the epicenter as well as the periphery of all existence and reality.

John has been invited to behold "things which must come to pass hereafter." How far in the future does the word "hereafter" indicate? Most human perspective is limited spatially to our universe and chronologically to time which is measured by the rotation of the earth, its journey around the sun and the changing inclination of its axis. With the fourth chapter of Revelation, we begin to step across those limiting boundaries by visualizing time merging back into eternity and by spatial concepts which infinitely exceed those bounded by galactic space. This verse should greatly expand our concepts of reality. (See the discussion of the concept of time under "How long?" at 6:10 on page 97.)

It will be helpful in answering the question, "how far in the future does the word 'hereafter' indicate," if we understand Paul's phrase, "the ages to come" (Ephesians 2:7) First of all, according to biblical reckoning, the Christian era is considered to be the final major age or epoch in world history. This evaluation was made clear at the very outset of the Gospel age, the Christian era, which Peter initiated with a quotation from the prophet Joel which begins by saying, "it shall be <u>in the last days</u> ..." (Acts 2:17) Peter further emphasized that evaluation of history when he tells us Christ "...was foreknown indeed before the foundation of the world, but was manifested at <u>the end of times</u> for your sake." ("in these last times" - NIV, "at the end of the ages" - NRSV) (I Peter 1:20)

Visualizing the final period of human history in its proper place in the eternal scheme of things, in no way blinded biblical prophets, apostles and teachers to significant developments within the Christian age, which is the final epoch of temporal history. They did not see the Christian age as a monotonous series of events, all of equal importance. For example, Isaiah clearly foresaw a climactic period of Gospel triumph when he wrote, "And he will judge between the nations, and will decide concerning many peoples; and they shall beat their swords into plowshares, and their spears into pruning-hooks; nation shall not lift up sword against nation, neither shall they learn war any more." (Isaiah 2:4) Similarly, God allowed John to behold the same triumph, The Millennium, which Isaiah had been permitted to see. He was also given a pre-event vision recorded in Revelation 7:2-10 of a massive worldwide turning to Christ. He was also allowed to see a time when Satan would no longer be able to "deceive the nations." (Revelation 20:3)

Not only did they see great periods of Gospel triumph, but the apostles also clearly saw periods of Gospel crisis. For example, an entity called the "man of sin," and "the son of perdition" would wreak havoc on the church. (II Thessalonians 2:1-12) That predator, whom Paul called "the man of sin," was called "the anti-Christ" by John. (See I John 2:18-28.)

Revelation Chapter 4

Paul, in his inspired expression, "the ages to come" is pointing to aeons beyond the Christian age rather than to any succeeding future periods within the great climactic Christian era. Accordingly, he very clearly understood the Christian age to be the concluding period of all temporal human history. For example, his message to the church in Corinth makes it clear that the Christian age is the ultimate and climactic age of all time-bound human history. He said, "Now these things happened unto them by way of example; and they were written for our admonition, upon whom <u>the ends of the ages</u> are come." (I Corinthians 10:11) He also expressed the same concept when he wrote to the Hebrew Christians, telling them that "…now once at <u>the end of the ages</u> hath he been manifested to put away sin by the sacrifice of himself." (Hebrews 9:26)

The "hereafter" into which John was invited to look certainly takes us to the end of the Christian age and, very probably, at places, even beyond that threshold into the distant period called, "the ages to come." (See addendum at page 78.)

IV. *Activity in heaven prior to opening the seven seals 4:2-5:14*

4:2 "Straightway I was in the Spirit: and behold, there was a throne set in heaven, and one sitting upon the throne;"

4:2 "I was in the Spirit"

While Johnson's fine comment was cited on the identical statement in Revelation 1:10, his portrayal is almost certainly inadequate to fully describe what John meant as he used the words "in the Spirit" here at 4:2. Johnson thought it implied that "his soul was lifted to a spiritual exaltation which peculiarly fitted him for communion with God." While that no doubt was true, here the statement seems to take us further, pointing to John coming under the spiritual guidance of the Holy Spirit. It probably was like that guidance Jesus has promised to any of his disciples should they be persecuted. He said, "Beware of men: for they will deliver you up to councils and in their synagogues they will scourge you; yea and before governors and kings shall ye be brought for my sake, for a testimony to them and to the Gentiles. But when they deliver you up, be not anxious how or what ye shall speak: for it shall be given you in that hour what ye shall speak. For it is not ye that speak, but the Spirit of your Father that speaketh in you." (Matthew 10:17-20)

4:2 "a throne set in heaven, and one sitting upon the throne"

In the heavenly realm or venue, there are orders and categories of reality which go beyond those we encounter in our present mortal experience. In the book of Revelation, those higher levels of existence, or being, are made known through similes or comparisons based on things we encounter in our present temporal human experience. Also, the new dimensions which we encounter through the book of Revelation add significance to the choices we make from the alternatives presented to us in the present order of things. There is a throne and it is occupied. The Most High ruleth and will ultimately triumph. Life, history and existence are, therefore, not haphazard. This vision is a dramatic reaffirmation that "the Most High ruleth in the kingdom of men." (Daniel 4:25)

4:3 **"and he that sat was to look upon like a jasper stone and a sardius: and there was a rainbow round about the throne, like an emerald to look upon."**

John "never mentions any kind of shapes or forms. It is the Bible's way to see God in terms of light. … John sees his vision in terms of the lights which flash from precious stones. … It may well be that the *jasper* stands for the unbearable brightness of the *purity* of God; that the blood-red *sardian* stands for the avenging *wrath* of God; and that the gentle green of the *emerald* stands for the *mercy* of God, by which alone we can meet the purity and the justice of God."[123]

The names used in the book of Revelation to identify gemstones do not in every case fully correspond to their current use. For example, the stone which we now call jasper is dull and opaque, while at the time John was transcribing the book of Revelation, jasper was "a stone most precious, … clear as crystal." (21:11) (See the chart at Revelation 21:20.)

4:4 **"And round about the throne were four and twenty thrones: and upon the thrones I saw four and twenty elders sitting, arrayed in white garments; and on their heads crowns of gold."**

4:4 "four and twenty elders"

Based on a statement in Revelation 5:8-9 as rendered in the King James Version, the identification of these elders seemed very simple. It reads "And when he had taken the book, the four beasts and four *and t*wenty elders fell down before the Lamb, having every one of them harps, and golden vials full of odours, which are the prayers of saints. And they sung a new song, saying, Thou art worthy to take the book, and to open the seals thereof: for thou wast slain, and hast redeemed us to God by thy blood out of every kindred, and tongue, and people, and nation." Basing his comments on that translation, Barnes wrote, "they [the twenty-four elders] are human beings … manifestly of our race – persons from this world before the throne. They are designed in some way to be symbolic of the church as redeemed. Thus they say (ch. v. 9), 'Thou hast redeemed us to God by thy blood.'"[124]

However, later it was noted that there was an error in the Greek text of Revelation 5:9-10 from which the King James Version had been translated. For example, Johnson called attention to the problem when he wrote, "the Greek text has been corrupted. It is found that the oldest Greek manuscripts give a different sense, and it is the testimony of the great critics and scholars that this passage has been corrupted. Tischendorf, Alford and Lange agree in saying that the correct Greek text is translated as follows:

"Thou wast slain, and hast redeemed to God by thy blood, out of every kindred, and tongue, and people, and nation, and hast made *them* [not 'us'] unto our God kings and priests; and *they* shall reign on the earth. — *Lange on Revelation*, p. 152.

---

[123] William Barclay, The Revelation of John, Vol. I, (Philadelphia: The Westminster Press, 1976), pp. 191-192.
[124] Albert Barnes, Notes, Explanatory and Practical on the Book of Revelation, (New York: Harper & Brothers Publishers, 1864), pp. 134-135.

Revelation Chapter 4

"This gives an entirely different idea. They do not praise the Lamb for their own redemption, but for the redemption of the world."[125]

However, even without the pronoun "us" in Revelation 5:9, it still seems that the twenty-four elders are redeemed human beings who are rendering service in God's presence. The evidence for this conclusion was given succinctly by Barclay when he wrote, "We think that the likeliest explanation is that the twenty-four elders are the symbolic representatives of the faithful people of God. Their white robes are the robes promised to the faithful (Revelation 3:4), and their crowns (*stephanoi*) are those promised to those who are faithful unto death (Revelation 2:10). The thrones are those which Jesus promised to those who forsook all and followed him (Matthew 19:27-29). The description of the twenty-four elders fits well with the promises made to the faithful."[126]

Since believers are priests (See I Peter 2:5, 9.), the twenty-four elders, as glorified Christians, serve in presenting the prayers of their fellow saints before the throne. (See Revelation 5:8.) Presenting the incense before God was the work of priests. (See Exodus 30:1-8, II Chronicles 13:10-11 and Luke 1:5-9.) Thus, the twenty-four elders continue to do the work of Christians who are priests in the new-covenant period. As there were twenty-four courses of the Levitical priesthood (I Chronicles 24:1-19), the number of these elders and their activities correspond with the pattern. (See Hebrews 8:5.)

4:4 "thrones ... and on their heads crowns"

It is obvious that the twenty-four elders not only give eternal worshipful adoration to the One on "the throne," but, in subordination to that One, are themselves reigning and ruling. Their thrones and their crowns can point to nothing less. In this vision, we have a clear confirmation of Paul's prediction in which he said, "Know ye not that the saints shall judge the world? And if the world is judged by you are ye unworthy to judge the smallest matters? Know ye not that we shall judge angels?" (I Corinthians 6:2-3)

4:5 "And out of the throne proceed lightnings and voices and thunders. And there were seven lamps of fire burning before the throne, which are the seven Spirits of God;"

4:5 "out of the throne proceed lightnings and voices and thunders"

Barclay reasonably stated that what was "primarily in the mind of John is the description of Mt. Sinai as the people waited for the giving of the Law: 'There were thunders and lightnings and a thick cloud upon the mountain, and the voice of the trumpet exceeding loud.' (Exodus 19:16) Here, John is using the imagery which is regularly connected with the presence of God."[127]

Probably, the lightning represents divine energy while voices and thunders represent divine authority. Similarly, in Revelation 19:6, "the voice of many thunders" tell us that "God, the Almighty, reigneth."

---

125 B. W. Johnson, A Vision of the Ages, (Hollywood, California: Old Paths Book Club, n.d.), pp. 35-36.
126 William Barclay, The Revelation of John, Vol. I, (Philadelphia: The Westminster Press, 1976), p. 194.
127 William Barclay, The Revelation of John, Vol. I, (Philadelphia: The Westminster Press, 1976), p. 195.

4:5 "there were seven lamps of fire burning before the throne, which are the seven Spirits of God"

The location of the seven Spirits before the throne is exactly the same position which they are described as occupying in 1:4. For a discussion of the seven Spirits of God versus the "One Spirit" mentioned in Ephesians 4:4, please see the comments on Revelation 1:4 on page 11.

Here, the Spirit of God is represented by "seven lamps of fire." Probably, this explains the most fundamental reason why the seven churches are represented by candlesticks or lamp stands in Revelation 1:20. Those churches possessed the Spirit of God who is the ultimate source of light, portrayed here as "seven lamps of fire." It is the presence of God's Spirit within individual Christians and corporately in Christ's churches which makes it possible for them to be "seen as lights in the world." (Philippians 2:15)

4:6 "and before the throne, as it were a sea of glass like a crystal; and in the midst of the throne, and round about the throne, four living creatures full of eyes before and behind."

4:6 "a sea of glass like a crystal"

It is not a raging sea but a sea at rest. It is placid with no turbulence, probably depicting everything as harmonious and under control in God's presence.

This sea like shining glass symbolizes "(i)... preciousness. In the ancient world glass was usually dull and semi-opaque, and glass as clear as crystal was as precious as gold. In Job 28:17 gold and glass are mentioned together as examples of precious things. (ii) It symbolizes dazzling purity. The blinding light reflected from the glassy sea would be too much for the eyes to look upon, like the purity of God. (iii) It symbolizes immense distance. The throne of God was in the immense distance, as if at the other side of a great sea. Swete writes of 'the vast distance which, even in the case of one who stood in the doors of heaven, intervened between himself and the throne of God.'"[128]

4:6 "four living creatures"

Hendriksen asserts that the living creatures represent "a very high order of angels."[129] But he surely is mistaken because in 5:11 those angels around the throne are clearly distinguished from the living creatures. Thus, the "living creatures" are to be understood in a more literal sense. Not only is the redemption of man portrayed by the twenty-four elders but the redemption of the animal kingdom is shown by the presence of the four living creatures in this panorama of heaven. This concept is in harmony with the teaching of the book of Romans in which we are told that, "the earnest expectation of the creation waiteth for the revealing of the sons of God. For the creation was subjected to vanity, not of its own will, but by reason of him who subjected it, in hope that **the creation itself also shall be delivered from the bondage of corruption into the liberty of the glory of the children of God.**" (Romans 8:19-22)

---

[128] William Barclay, The Revelation of John, Vol. I, (Philadelphia: The Westminster Press, 1976), pp. 197-198.
[129] W. Hendriksen, More Than Conquerors: An Interpretation of the Book of Revelation, (Grand Rapids: Baker Book House, 1952), p. 106.

Revelation Chapter 4

The redemption of the animal kingdom is also in harmony with Psalm 150:6 which says, "Let everything that hath breath praise Jehovah." (See especially the comments at 6:1-2 under "one of the four living creatures" on page 87.)

4:7 "And the first creature was like a lion, and the second creature like a calf, and the third creature had a face as of a man, and the fourth creature was like a flying eagle."

"The four living creatures stand for everything that is noblest, strongest, wisest and swiftest in nature. Each has the preeminence in his own particular sphere. The lion is supreme among beasts; the ox is supreme among cattle; the eagle is supreme among birds; and man is supreme among all creatures. The beasts represent all the greatness and the strength and the beauty of nature; here we see nature praising God. In the verses which are to follow we see the twenty-four elders praising God; and when we put the two pictures together we get the complete picture of both nature and man engaged in constant praise and adoration of God."[130]

4:8 "And the four living creatures, having each one of them six wings, are full of eyes round about and within: and they have no rest day and night, saying, Holy, holy, holy, is the Lord God, the Almighty, who was and who is and who is to come."

4:8 "having each one of them six wings, are full of eyes about and within"

Not only have the living creatures been redeemed, but their faculties will have been marvelously augmented and multiplied.

4:8 "Holy, holy, holy"

Many explanations have been offered to explain why this triple expression of adoration is used by repeating the adjective "Holy" three times. This triple repetition of "Holy" is called the Doxology which means, the attribution of glory to God. The purpose for its use is clear from the verse itself. First, they adore the One "who was" with the cry of "Holy." Secondly, they praise the One "who is" by exuberantly shouting, "Holy." And thirdly, they worship the One "who is to come" by victoriously proclaiming, "Holy."

4:9-10 "And when the living creatures shall give glory and honor and thanks to him that sitteth on the throne, to him that liveth for ever and ever, the four and twenty elders shall fall down before him that sitteth on the throne, and shall worship him that liveth for ever and ever, and shall cast their crowns before the throne, saying,"

4:10 "living creatures ... the four and twenty elders"

"The living creatures stand for nature in all its greatness and the twenty-four elders for the great united Church in Jesus Christ. So when the living creatures and the elders unite in praise, it symbolizes nature and the Church both praising God."[131]

4:10 "cast their crowns before the throne"

"When one king surrendered to another, he cast his crown at the victor's feet. ... The picture looks on God as the conqueror of the souls of men; and on the Church as the body

---

[130] William Barclay, The Revelation of John, Vol. I, (Philadelphia: The Westminster Press, 1976), p. 200.
[131] William Barclay, The Revelation of John, Vol. I, (Philadelphia: The Westminster Press, 1976), p. 163.

of people who have surrendered to him. There can be no Christianity without submission."[132]

4:11 **"Worthy art thou, our Lord and our God, to receive the glory and the honor and the power: for thou didst create all things, and because of thy will they were, and were created."**

God's right to receive adulation, worship and dominion is based on his role as the sole creator. In that capacity he stands absolutely alone. It is our duty and privilege to acknowledge him for who he is!

Addendum to Revelation 4:1

The utterly unique character of true prophecy is highlighted by a well-known and highly respected writer and foreign correspondent who wrote, "a journalist simply cannot be expected to predict the distant future, or even the exact details of the near future. That is impossible, for so much depends not only on impersonal forces like geography and technology, but on the actions of individuals – themselves motivated often by the disfiguring whirlwinds of passion. However, a journalist, through his or her own observations, might be expected to make the reader measurably less surprised by the advance to come in a given place within the space of a few years: the middle-term future."[133]

---

132 William Barclay, The Revelation of John, Vol. I, (Philadelphia: The Westminster Press, 1976), p. 163-164.
133 Robert D. Kaplan, In Europe's Shadow, (New York: Random House, 2016), pp. 10-11.

Revelation Chapter 5

5:1 "And I saw in the right hand of him that sat on the throne a book written within and on the back, close sealed with seven seals."

5:1 "written within and on the back"

"John was in Patmos in the year ninety-six, and ninety-six years of the Christian dispensation had passed by [that is, if we consider the Christian dispensation to have started at the birth of Christ rather than, more accurately, on the day of Pentecost as described in Acts 2] when John saw this vision in Patmos; and that much of the history of the Christian dispensation was [written] on the back part of the book, [it] was not sealed up; it was a matter of history already, and [therefore] on the outside. All men could read it without a seal being broken. About that part of the history there is not one word said in the opening of the seals, because it was already plain."[134]

5:1 "close sealed with seven seals"

"This sealed book is the book of the future."[135] Though "God has a book in which the history of [the] time to come is already written, [it] does not mean that everything is settled long ago and that we are in the grip of an inescapable fate. What it does mean is that God has a plan for the universe and that the purpose of God will be in the end worked out."[136] Even more, it has been suggested that, "The closed scroll indicates the Plan of God unrevealed and unexecuted. If that scroll remains sealed God's purposes are not realized; his plan is not carried out. To open that scroll by breaking the seals means not merely to reveal but to carry out God's plan."[137]

5:2 "And I saw a strong angel proclaiming with a great voice, Who is worthy to open the book, and to loose the seals thereof?"

Here, we encounter heaven's search for someone who would be able to sort out and reveal the significant developments and complexities of the future. While we often are puzzled by the history of the past, we contemplate the future with much greater incomprehension. Jesus' redemptive death and resurrection qualified him (See verse 5.) to tell us of the great panoramas and vistas which will appear in the future. To everyone except Jesus, the future is opaque. Jesus experienced both sides of death. Before death he experienced the realities, boundaries and limitations of time, along with all the complexities and frustrations of human experience, but his resurrection put him back into the boundless expanse of eternity. Because of his totally unique experience, he alone is "worthy" and can, therefore, tell us what lies ahead. As one perceptive scholar has said, Jesus' "resurrection triumph over death supremely confirms his right to speak

---

134 J. L. Martin, The Voice of Seven Thunders or Lectures On the Apocalypse, (St. Louis: Christian Board of Publication, 1870), p. 101.
135 B. W. Johnson, A Vision of the Ages, (Hollywood, California: Old Paths Book Club, n.d.), p. 39.
136 Slightly edited from William Barclay, The Revelation of John, Vol. I, (Philadelphia: The Westminster Press, 1976), p. 211.
137 W. Hendriksen, More Than Conquerors: An Interpretation of the Book of Revelation, (Grand Rapids: Baker Book House, 1952), p. 109.

authoritatively about the future and about the world beyond the grave."[138] Though heaven was ransacked, no one else was found with the qualifications which would enable him to perform this great ministry.

5:3 **"And no one in the heaven, or on the earth, or under the earth, was able to open the book, or to look thereon."**

This statement refers to the time of Jesus' earthly ministry, before he had overcome (see 5:5), and thus had not yet become qualified to open the book of the future.

5:4 **"And I wept much, because no one was found worthy to open the book, or to look thereon:"**

John keenly wanted someone to open the seals so he could gain greater insight into the spiritual significance of future historical developments. We too must have a great desire, even to the shedding of tears because of our longing for spiritual perception, before understanding will be granted. Do we care enough to weep? Note the many exhortations in the book of Revelation to seek understanding: 2:7, 2:11, 2:17, 2:29, 3:6, 3:13, 3:22 and 13:9. Many things in the book of Revelation will not be understood without heavenly wisdom, "the wisdom that is from above." (James 3:17) As Revelation itself in 17:9 tells us, "This calls for a mind with wisdom." (NIV) Please notice also the following translations of 17:9: "But here is the clue for those who can interpret it" (NEB), "Here is a problem for a profound mind!" (Goodspeed), "Here is something for the intelligent to ponder" (Berkeley) "This calls for a mind that has wisdom" (NRSV), "Here is the mind that has wisdom" (NKJV).

Revelation 17:9 puts us on notice that there are some facts, some realities and some truths expounded in the book of Revelation which are hard to understand. Because of this, someone may ask, if this is really a revelation, why is it so hard to understand? It is hard because the realities, facts and truths which are uncovered, in and of themselves, are often complicated, obtuse, convoluted and intricate. We must pray as David did, "Open thou mine eyes, that I may behold wondrous things out of thy law." (Psalm 119:18)

Though some realities are now difficult to comprehend, "there will be developments hereafter which will make that clear which is now obscure; developments which will make this book [of Revelation], in all past ages apparently so enigmatical, as clear as any other portion of the inspired volume, as it is now, even with the imperfect view which we may have of its meaning, beyond all question one of the most sublime books that has ever been written."[139]

5:5 **"and one of the elders saith unto me, Weep not; behold, the Lion that is of the tribe of Judah, the Root of David, hath overcome to open the book and the seven seals thereof."**

5:5 **"the Lion that is of the tribe of Judah"**

The book of Hebrews tells us, "it is evident that our Lord hath sprung out of Judah." (Hebrews 7:14) The words "sprung out of Judah" mean he "descended from Judah."

---

138 Carl F. H. Henry, God, Revelation and Authority, Vol. III, (Waco, TX: Word Books, 1979), p. 23.
139 Albert Barnes, Notes, Explanatory and Practical on the Book of Revelation, (New York: Harper & Brothers Publishers, 1864), p 162.

Revelation Chapter 5

(NRSV) Undoubtedly, by calling Jesus "the Lion that is of the tribe of Judah," we are taken back to Jacob's pre-death blessing on his son Judah which is recorded in Genesis 49:8-12. In verse 9 of that passage, Judah is said to have "crouched as a lion." The identity of that lion is given to us here in Revelation 5:5. As the lion crouches preparing to overcome its prey, so Jesus has overcome the horrible phenomenon of death, which he made his prey.

5:5   "the Root of David"

"The Lion that is of the tribe of Judah" is said to be "of the Root of David." David was from "the root of Jesse." (Isaiah 11:10) Jesse, David's father, was of the tribe of Judah. (See Genesis 38:24-30, Ruth 4:18-21 and Matthew 1:1-6.)

5:5   "hath overcome to open the book and the seven seals thereof"

As noted in the comments on verse 2, it was the death, burial and resurrection of Jesus, his overcoming, which qualified him to open the book describing the future. The death, burial and resurrection of Christ are, indeed, central events which must be acknowledged and understood to gain a perspective and grasp of human history – past or future. Until and unless all is studied in reference to the great primal truths in Christ's experience, all will remain sealed, a mystery.

5:6   "And I saw in the midst of the throne and of the four living creatures, and in the midst of the elders, a Lamb standing, as though it had been slain, having seven horns, and seven eyes, which are the seven Spirits of God, sent forth into all the earth."

5:6   "in the midst of the throne"

Jesus' position following his death, burial and resurrection is not peripheral, but central, "in the midst of the throne," ("in the center of the throne" - NIV). This is in harmony with Paul's statement to the church in Philippi that "God highly exalted him." (Philippians 2:9) It also is completely in harmony with Peter's declaration on Pentecost that, following his resurrection, Christ had been "exalted at the right hand of God." (Acts 2:33)

5:6   "the four living creatures"

See the comments on 4:4 and 4:6-8.

5:6   "standing as though it had been slain"

The fact that the Lamb was standing points to his having been raised from death, yet, visible evidence remains that the Lamb had been slain. This description reminds us of Jesus, following his resurrection, inviting Thomas to "reach hither thy finger, and see my hands; and reach hither thy hand, and put it into my side: and be not faithless, but believing." (John 20:27) Here, we see confirmation of the axiom that "historical evidence is not confined to the written word."[140]

---

140 J. H. Elliott, History In the Making, (New Haven: Yale University Press, 2012), p. 145.

5:6 **"having seven horns, and seven eyes, which are the seven Spirits of God"**

Seven, the number of perfection and entirety (See page 17, last paragraph.), reflects the fact that Jesus not only received the Holy Spirit without measure, but also gives the Spirit without measure. (See John 3:34.) On the issue of the "Seven Spirits of God" versus "one Spirit" (Ephesians 4:9), see comments on 1:4 at page 11. His seven horns represent his unlimited power, his omnipotence, while his seven eyes represent his limitless powers of perception. For the reason why the number seven has been considered the number of perfection, see the discussion at 1:11 on page 16 under "send it to the seven churches."

5:7 **"And he came, and he taketh it out of the right hand of him that sat on the throne."**

The pronoun "it" refers to the book which God was holding in his hand, mentioned in 5:1.

5:8 **"And when he had taken the book, the four living creatures and the four and twenty elders fell down before the Lamb, having each one a harp, and golden bowls full of incense, which are the prayers of the saints."**

5:8 **"the four living creatures and the four and twenty elders"**

See 4:4 and 4:6-8.

5:8 **"fell down before the Lamb"**

The living creatures and the elders are worshiping Christ, the Lamb of God, in recognition of his deity. For the scriptural affirmations of the deity of Christ, see the comments at 15:3 under "great and marvelous are thy works, O Lord God" on page 233.

5:8 **"the prayers of the saints"**

These prayers, probably, were somewhat like the one recorded in Revelation 6:10 in which martyred saints cry out, "How long, O Master, the holy and true, dost thou not judge and avenge our blood on them that dwell on the earth?" However, here the bowls of incense seem to represent the prayers of the living saints, that is, Christians. (See I Corinthians 1:1-2.) These saints, who have not yet suffered martyrdom are still living on the earth, and are probably imploring the God of heaven and earth to speedily bring about the full realization of his great eternal purpose.

5:9 **"And they sing a new song, saying, Worthy art thou to take the book, and to open the seals thereof: for thou wast slain, and didst purchase unto God with thy blood men of every tribe, and tongue, and people, and nation,"**

5:9 **"they sing a new song"**

Heaven seems to have a hymn book and a massive choir accompanied by a string section dominated by harps (5:8). No doubt, those heavenly harmonies and chords reverberating through the concert hall of heaven excel anything which Bach, Beethoven or Handel could have written, even Handel's immortal "Hallelujah Chorus."

William Cushing, who lived from 1823 to 1902, probably had this passage in mind when he wrote the words for his triumphant "Ring the Bells the Heaven," which he composed

Revelation Chapter 5

to be sung to the tune of G. F. Root's Civil War song, "Tramp, Tramp, Tramp the Boys Are Marching." In the chorus, Cushing wrote:

> Glory!, glory! How the angels sing!
> Glory!, glory! How the loud harps ring!
> 'Tis the ransomed army, like a mighty sea,
> Pealing forth the anthem of the free.

5:9   "saying worthy art thou to take the book and open the seals thereof"

Following the word "saying" we are given a brief but highly significant verbal quotation from heaven's hymn book. Declaring the worthiness of the Lamb is a persistent theme in heaven. (See 5:12.) The "book" is the book of the future, including the future God has prepared for those who love him and whose future could not have been realized without the sacrifice which Jesus made on their behalf. (See Romans 3:25-26 and Hebrews 9:15.)

5:9   "didst purchase unto God with thy blood"

How extensive and how inclusive was that purchase? The theme of being purchased by the blood of Jesus which he shed at Calvary receives major emphasis in scripture. For examples, see Acts 20:28, I Corinthians 6:20 and 7:23. The problem introduced through sin is so deep that we need far greater help understanding our dilemma than most of us have imagined. Historically, acquiring such understanding took generations.

Slowly, one of the complications into which sin has entrapped us became evident through the practice of animal sacrifice in religious rituals. That religious rite was inaugurated very soon after the entrance of sin into human experience. An obvious message from the practice of sacrifice was that there are some obligations in which sin has trapped us which are transferable. This seems to be the significance of worshipers putting their hands on the head of the sacrificial animal. (See Exodus 29:10, 15, 19 and Leviticus 1:4.)

It took many centuries longer to get the message across, that there is also something in which sin ensnares us which is so heinous that it cannot be transferred. Awareness of this truth came very slowly, even though this sobering point was first made clear long ago, immediately following Noah's flood. At that point, God said, "Whoever sheds the blood of man, by man shall his blood be shed; for in the image of God has God made man." (Genesis 9:6 NIV) Those words make the truth clear that by sinning we become involved in a result for which no substitution can be made. This truth was made obvious by presenting the example of murder. In it, the stated consequence of the sin of murder is the death of the murderer, not some sacrifice given on his behalf. From this we should be able to realize that sin does, indeed, snare us in guilt for which no substitution is allowed.

The concept that some consequences of sin are not transferable, is clearly carried over into the teaching of the apostles of Christ. For example, the apostle Paul gave us this essential information when he said, "Faithful is the saying: For if we died with him, we shall also live with him." (II Timothy 2:11)[141] Thus, though Christ died for us, we still must also die, in this case, "with him," that is, with Christ.

The apostle Peter, in harmony with Paul's teaching, wrote, "we, having died unto sins, might live." (I Peter 2:24) Both apostles base their statements on the ancient recognition that there is an element in sin which cannot be transferred. There is something so horrendous in sin that substitution for it cannot be allowed. Therefore, the sinner himself must die.

Sin involves us in both debt and in crime. Debt is transferable, crime is not. When Jesus died, he paid our fathomless debt (See I Peter 1:18-19.) – but not for our crime – we still must die for it. But Jesus, through his death, made a new way for us to die. Now, because of what Jesus did, we may die with him (See Colossians 2:20.) and, subsequently, live with him. If we choose not to die with him, we shall still have to die for our sin, because as Ezekiel so definitively expressed it, "the soul that sinneth, it shall die." (Ezekiel 18:20) Obviously, if we choose not to die with Christ, we will not be allowed to live with him.

5:9   "every tribe, and tongue, and people, and nation"

On the meaning of the descriptive words "tribe … tongue … people … and nation," please see the exposition at 7:9, under "out of every nation …" on page 108.

Every tribe, tongue and people collectively constitute a resounding confirmation that there will have been a positive worldwide response to the egalitarian "whosoever" invitations extended by the Lord to sinners who seek cleansing and redemption. It is just such an invitation given to us in Revelation 22:17 which says, "The Spirit and the bride say, Come. And he that heareth, let him say, Come. And he that is athirst, let him come: he that will, let him take the water of life freely." (See also Isaiah 55:1, Matthew 11:28 and 12:50, Mark 3:35, John 6:40 and Acts 10:35.)

While the verses just cited express the inclusiveness of the Gospel, there is also an exclusionary aspect in the Gospel message. That reality is clearly enunciated in Jesus' statement that, "many are called, but few are chosen." (Matthew 22:14) That exclusionary aspect of the Gospel system is given in more detail in I Corinthians 3:10-15.

5:10 "and madest them to be unto our God a kingdom and priests; and they reign upon the earth."

Not only heavenly beings, but redeemed people, whose redemption is based on the purchase price paid by Christ (5:9), are given the honor of participating in the full maturing of God's eternal purpose. Ultimately, therefore, we shall reign. Here, such sovereignty is said to be exercised "upon the earth." Beyond that, redeemed man's sovereignty may well extend to much more extensive and remote venues because, as Paul said, "Know ye not that we shall judge angels?" (I Corinthians 6:3) Paul's statement is in fulfillment of Isaiah 32:1.

The promise that redeemed people shall "reign upon the earth" must have seemed ironic to John, who was suffering in a prison-laborers' gang, working in a mining operation on

---

141 If one searches for "the saying" to which Paul refers, he only finds it where Peter said of Christ, "who his own self bare our sins in his body upon the tree, that we, having died unto sins might live unto righteousness; by whose stripes ye are healed" (I Peter 2:24).

Revelation Chapter 5

the isle of Patmos. (For a discussion of the reason why John was on Patmos, please see the comments under 1:9.)

For the dispensational and millennial significance of the words "madest them to be unto our God a kingdom" please see the discussion under 1:6 on page 13.

5:11 **"And I saw, and I heard a voice of many angels round about the throne and the living creatures and the elders; and the number of them was ten thousand times ten thousand, and thousands of thousands;"**

The "**angels ... living creatures ... elders**" are the cadres of God's administrative staff as he governs the universe to bring it to the ultimate triumph of his eternal purpose. Each category is discussed at other references. For "angels," see 7:3 and 8:2; for "living creatures," see 4:6; for "elders," see 4:4.

5:12 **"saying with a great voice, Worthy is the Lamb that hath been slain to receive the power, and riches, and wisdom, and might and honor, and glory, and blessing."**

5:12   "worthy is the Lamb"

This is a glimpse of the heavenly ceremony by which the crucified Christ was exalted. Peter referred to this ceremony of triumph in his sermon on Pentecost in which he said, "This Jesus did God raise up, whereof we all are witnesses. <u>Being therefore by the right hand of God exalted</u>, and having received of the Father the promise of the Holy Spirit, he hath poured forth this, which ye see and hear. For David ascended not into the heavens: but he saith himself, The Lord said unto my Lord, <u>Sit thou on my right hand</u>, Till I make thine enemies the footstool of thy feet. Let all the house of Israel therefore know assuredly, that God hath made him both Lord and Christ, this Jesus whom ye crucified." (Acts 2:32-36)

Paul also briefly referred to this heavenly exaltation of the Christ in his letter to the church in Ephesus in which he told of God's power, "which he wrought in Christ, when he raised him from the dead, and <u>made him to sit at his right hand in the heavenly places</u>, far above all rule, and authority, and power, and dominion, and every name that is named, not only in this world, but also in that which is to come: and he put all things in subjection under his feet, and gave him to be head over all things to the church." (Ephesians 1:20-22)

5:12   "power ... riches ... wisdom ... might ... honor ... glory ... blessing"

These seven rewards have been granted to the Lamb of God in recognition and appreciation for his making it possible for God to be both "just and the justifier of him that hath faith in Jesus." (Romans 3:26) The differences in translations of these seven rewards are minimal. Some render "might" as "strength," and "riches" as "wealth," and the NIV renders "blessing" as "praise."

5:13 "And every created thing which is in the heaven, and on the earth, and under the earth, and on the sea, and all things that are in them, heard I saying, Unto him that sitteth on the throne, and unto the Lamb, be the blessing, and the honor, and the glory, and the dominion, for ever and ever."

> This homage, this worshipful adoration, is rendered by every created thing which is in heaven and on earth as well as under the earth and on the sea. Many will willingly, gratefully and joyfully render this worship to God and to the Lamb. Others will bow unwillingly, even belligerently. But all will bow, for "in the name of Jesus every knee should bow, of things in heaven and things on earth and things under the earth, and that every tongue should confess that Jesus Christ is Lord, to the glory of God the Father." (Philippians 2:10-11)

5:14 "And the four living creatures said, Amen. And the elders fell down and worshiped."

> For a discussion of the "four living creatures … and the elders," please see the comments on 4:4 and 4:6-8.

Revelation Chapter 6

Introduction: The opening of the first four of the seven seals introduces us to a series of horses and their riders who are famously known as The Four Horsemen of the Apocalypse. Those horsemen do not depict single one-time events, but rather, recurring developments which repeatedly take place throughout the entire Christian era. The horses are color-coded in harmony with the character of the development which each one represents.

V. *The opening of the scroll sealed with* <u>*seven seals*</u> *6:1-8:2*

    A. *The first seal 6:1-2*

    The white horse bearing the crowned conqueror

6:1-2 "And I saw when the Lamb opened one of the seven seals, and I heard one of the four living creatures saying as with a voice of thunder, Come. And I saw, and behold, a white horse, and he that sat thereon had a bow; and there was given unto him a crown: and he came forth conquering, and to conquer."

    6:1-2 "one of the four living creatures saying as with a voice of thunder"

The members of the redeemed animal kingdom (See comments at 4:6-8.), are here represented by one of the four living creatures, having highly enhanced abilities, in this case, the power of speech. The creatures who have been mute for millennia, with the exception of Balaam's donkey (See Numbers 22:26-30 and II Peter 2:16.), are now endowed with attention-demanding power of speech, "a voice of thunder."

The redemption of the animal realm will be transformative, allowing the members of their dominion to be highly useful, filling roles far beyond those in which they are currently able to function. Their personalities will undoubtedly be restored as well as marvelously enhanced. In the Garden of Eden, Satan was able to seduce, persuade, impress or force the serpent, a living creature, to become his agent. There, the serpent had the ability to communicate with humans by speech. Prior to the fall, the living creatures in Eden must have been docile and friendly, for Eve was neither startled nor frightened by the serpent's visit. In harmony with the vision of the redemption of living creatures given to us in Revelation, Isaiah saw, as part of the work of the Messiah, the restoration of docility and companionability to even the most vicious and venomous living creatures. (See Isaiah 11:1-9.) Those characteristics of personality, now so prized in cats and dogs, will, according to Isaiah's prophecy, be extended to their genetic relatives, tigers and wolves. (See also the comments at 4:6-8 under "four living creatures." Also, see the comments under 21:1 on pages 341-342.)

Revelation Verse by Verse

6:1-2 "come"

This was an authoritative command given to John to behold a preview of coming events rather than being an order to the rider on the white horse to begin his role in history.

6:1-2 "a white horse, and he that sat thereon"

If one compares this vision of the rider on the white horse with the similar description given in Revelation 19:11-16, it is obvious that the rider on the white horse in Revelation 6:1-2 portrays Christ. However, Johnson disagreed. He wrote, "There is one circumstance, however, that has as yet found no fitting explanation. The rider of the white horse was armed with a *bow*. This significant fact indicated that Christ was not signified."[142]

Johnson was surely mistaken, because Christ is shown prophetically to be armed with a bow. For example, Hebrews 1:8-9 quotes Psalms 45:6-7 and applies the passage to Christ. In reference to the same person, Psalms 45:5 says, "Thine arrows are sharp." Note also that the same person is described in Psalms 45:4. There he is not only armed with a bow but is portrayed as a mounted bowman who in his majesty rides on prosperously.

Barclay also thought that the rider on the white horse, portrayed in 6:1-2, was not Jesus. He wrote, "It is to be noted that the crown in this passage is different from that in *Revelation* 19. Here the crown is *stephanos*, which is the *victor's* crown; in *Revelation* 19 it is *diadema* which is the royal crown. The passage we are here studying is telling of woe upon woe and disaster upon disaster; any picture of the victorious Christ is quite out of place in it. This picture tells of the coming not of the victor Christ but of the terrors of the wrath of God."[143]

Barclay also was undoubtedly mistaken. The Greek word in Revelation 14:14 for Christ's crown is *stephanos*, the crown of victory. Thus, he wears either crown, the royal crown or the crown of victory, depending on his given role. Also, verses 1-2 do not tell, as Barclay alleged, "of woe upon woe and disaster upon disaster [so that] any picture of the victorious Christ is quite out of place in it." There is a startling contrast between the work of the first and the next horseman. While the rider on the white horse comes "forth conquering, and to conquer," it is the rider on the red horse who takes "peace from the earth." Thus, the conquering of the first rider did not take peace from the earth. That was the distinction of the second rider. Obviously, then, the conquering to which reference is made in 6:1-2 is spiritual rather than military or physical.

The words "Conquering and to conquer" in 6:2 point to many triumphs; however, two of those triumphs are of special significance. **First**, will be the victory among the Jews (See 7:1-8.). Though delayed for centuries by Jewish hardness of heart (See Romans 11:25.), it will probably occur in the relatively near future.[144] **Second**, as a consequence (See Romans 11:15.), the conversion of the Jews to Christ will be followed by an unparalleled triumph among the Gentiles. (See 7:9-17.) Here, the account in 6:3-17 helps us understand the recurring events which take place in reaction to Gospel triumphs which lead up to those two unparalleled victories.

---

142 B. W. Johnson, A Vision of the Ages, (Hollywood, California: Old Paths Book Club, n.d.), p. 48.
143 William Barclay, The Revelation of John, Vol. II, (London: Westminster John Knox Press, 2004), p.4.
144 See God's Game Plan by B.L Turner, available through Amazon and www.CreateSpace.com.

Revelation Chapter 6

Since the rider on the white horse surely represents Christ, the question arises whether shortly after John wrote Revelation there was a triumphant period of successful Gospel progress, here called "conquering." The following brief historical accounts will help answer that question.

"During the period of peace after Valerian's death in Persia [in 260 A.D.], the church grew rapidly ... City cults grew less popular, and Christianity was displaying impressive intellectual leadership, organizational strength, and, in persecution, courage. Christians were increasingly integrated into all aspects of imperial society, and despite disputes over lapsed bishops and monarchianism[145] the church was resilient. Though only 10 percent of the empire was Christian, by the end of the third century the church was too big and organized to be safely ignored."[146]

"Crude and misinformed though many of the criticisms of Christianity were, there was an awareness that a force was entering the world which if given free scope would overrun the existing culture. Dimly, to be sure, and imperfectly, but with an appreciation of the actualities, non-Christians sensed that because of its revolutionary nature, its uncompromising character, and its claim on the allegiance of all mankind, Christianity was more to be feared by the established order than any of its many competitors, not even excepting Judaism."[147]

Principles introduced by Christ and his apostles are still challenging those governments which are based on anti-God concepts. Though obviously the filling of the whole earth with the knowledge of Jehovah (See Isaiah 11:9.) is not yet complete, Isaiah helps us understand the magnitude of the transcendent victory which will have ultimately resulted from the coming of the Messiah. He said, "the wolf shall dwell with the lamb, and the leopard shall lie down with the kid; and the calf and the young lion and the fatling together; and a little child shall lead them. And the cow and the bear shall feed; their young ones shall lie down together; and the lion shall eat straw like the ox. And the sucking child shall play on the hole of the asp, and the weaned child shall put his hand on the adder's den. They shall not hurt nor destroy in all my holy mountain; for the earth shall be full of the knowledge of Jehovah, as the waters cover the sea. And it shall come to pass in that day, that the root of Jesse, that standeth for an ensign of the peoples, unto him shall the nations seek; and his resting-place shall be glorious." (Isaiah 11:6-10)

B.   *The second seal 6:3-4*

The red horse is bearing the rider with a great sword who takes peace from the earth and instigates slaughter among the inhabitants of the world.

6:3   **"And when he opened the second seal, I heard the second living creature saying, Come."**

The word "come" as noted in 6:1-2, was an invitation to John to behold a vision which would further fulfill his deep longing for understanding.

---

[145] Monarchianism is defined as, "An attempt to stress Monotheism against those who would make Jesus Christ ... a second God." - Kenneth Scott Latourette, A History of Christianity, (New York: Harper & Row, Publishers, 1975), p. 143.

[146] Peter J. Leithart, Defending Constantine: The Twilight of an Empire and the Dawn of Christendom, (Downers Grove, IL: IVP, 2010), p. 39.

[147] Kenneth Scott Latourette, A History of Christianity, (New York: Harper & Row, Publishers, 1975), p. 82.

6:4 "And another horse came forth, a red horse: and to him that sat thereon it was given to take peace from the earth, and that they should slay one another: and there was given unto him a great sword."

6:4 "a red horse"

The red horse and its rider, wielding "a great sword," represent slaughter as an extreme form of persecution. But it is slaughter, sometimes expanding to full-scale war. Such war is instigated in reaction to, and in opposition to, triumphant Christian evangelism, represented by the rider on the white horse who goes forth conquering and to conquer. Is it possible that the proclamation of the Gospel can stir the winds of such lethal opposition? As a partial answer to that question, we should note that this certainly was not only one of the consequences of the Lutheran Reformation, but also of the preaching of Peter Waldo as well as the evangelism of the Huguenots. Here we have only space to give a few details from the power of Lutheran preaching.

As a result, many Catholics in Scandinavia, particularly in Sweden, embraced concepts which, though not in full conformity, were much nearer to New Testament teaching than their previous Catholic theology had been. Subsequently, they had to defend themselves against Catholic reprisals during the Thirty-Year War, fought mainly in Germany. "The German issue was complicated by the fact that various non-German peoples, the Bohemians and the Swedes (who had a new Protestant monarchy which had arisen under Gustavus Vasa as a direct result of the Reformation), were entangled in the struggle."[148]

"Luther's doctrines also spread into Scandinavian lands. The rulers of Denmark, Norway, and Sweden closed the monasteries and compelled the Roman Catholic bishops to surrender ecclesiastical property to the Crown. Lutheranism became henceforth the official religion of these three countries."[149]

Persecution, as portrayed in this section of Revelation, is reactionary, rising in protest and in opposition to Gospel advance and success, represented by the conquest of the rider on the white horse. Wherever and whenever the Gospel message has notable success throughout the Christian age, persecution will probably follow. Persecution may raise its ugly and gory head at many levels. Often, it begins on the **personal**, the domestic or family level. As Jesus said, "a man's foes shall be they of his own household ... brother shall deliver up brother to death, and the father his child: and children shall rise up against parents, and cause them to be put to death." (Matthew 10:21 and 10:36)

The next level of persecution is **institutional**. The most ironic form of institutional persecution of Christians is that which took place in and through Jewish synagogues. The synagogue was an institution ostensibly devoted to recognizing, embracing and promoting the truth revealed in the Jewish Scriptures – our Old Testament. However, Jesus said to his followers who had accepted that very truth, "Beware of men: for they will deliver you up to councils, and in their synagogues they will scourge you." (Matthew 10:17)[150]

---

148 H. G. Wells, The Outline of History, Vol. II, (New York: Doubleday & Co., Inc, 1971), p. 686.
149 Hutton Webster, World History, (Boston, D.C. Heath & Co. Publishers, 1921), p. 261.
150 While I cite here Matthew's account of Jesus' warnings, see also Luke 21:12-19.

Revelation Chapter 6

The most widespread form of persecution of all has been, and will continue to be, **governmental**. Jesus warned all of us who are his disciples about this ominous danger when he said, "Before governors and kings shall ye be brought for my sake, for a testimony to them and to the Gentiles." (Matthew 10:18) In summary, Jesus said, "Ye shall be hated of all men for my name's sake: but he that endureth to the end, the same shall be saved." (Matthew 10:22)

6:4 "take peace from the earth"

Plummer correctly tells us that though "'the earth' has been, [by numerous commentators], erroneously restricted to the Roman Empire or to Judea, the whole world is meant."[151] However, from the Euphrates boundary which divided the Roman Empire from the Persian Parthian Empire, all the way to the Atlantic seaboard, initially it was the Roman government which wielded the "great sword." "Clement of Alexandria, who was the head of the catechetical school [in Alexandria], wrote sometime before the close of the second century: 'Many martyrs are daily burned, crucified, and beheaded before our eyes.'"[152]

The Roman emperors who became notorious for persecuting the followers of Christ were: (1) Nero (reigned 54-68), to whom Paul appealed his case. (See Acts 25:10-11.) Ironically, after freeing Paul from that imprisonment later, in approximately 68 A.D., he had him decapitated at Rome. (2) Domitian, (c. 90-96) was the one who, in imposing widespread persecution, had John imprisoned on Patmos. (3) Trajan (98-117 A.D.) From a surviving letter to Trajan from Pliny the Younger, governor of the Roman province of Bythinia, asking how to interrogate Christian prisoners, we learn a great deal about Roman persecution. (4) Hadrian (117-138) During his reign, "Christianity was still a *religio illicita*. The pastor of the Roman church, Telesphorus, and many others, suffered martyrdom at this time."[153] (5) Marcus Aurelius (161-181) "The enthusiasm of Christians seemed to him mere fanaticism, and their steadfastness under persecution he looked upon not as fidelity to a higher principle, but rather as obstinancy in disobedience to constituted authority."[154] (6) Septimus Severus (202-211) "It does not appear to have been his purpose to attempt the extermination of Christianity, but simply to put a check upon proselytizing. But the enforcement of the Trajanic law against Christianity as an unauthorized religion involved many Christians in severe suffering."[155] (7) Maximus the Thracian (235-251) who "was responsible for a brief persecution in the 230's, was from Thrace … Galerius, a notorious persecutor of the next century, was from the same general region."[156] (8) In 250, during the reign of Decius (249-251), "was issued the first imperial edict aiming at the universal suppression of Christianity. Christians everywhere were required to conform to the state religion by participating in its ceremonies, and officials were commanded, under heavy penalties, rigorously to enforce the requirement."[157] (9) Valerian (257-260) in 257 "issued an edict commanding all Christians to conform to the state religion on pain of banishment. He directed that pastors be separated from their

---
151 A. Plummer, The Pulpit Commentary [on] Revelation, (Chicago: Wilcox & Follett Co., no date), p. 184.
152 Albert Henry Newman, A Manual of Church History, Vol. I, (Philadelphia: The Baptist Publication Society, 1939), p. 160.
153 Albert Henry Newman, A Manual of Church History, Vol. I, (Philadelphia: The Baptist Publication Society, 1939), p. 154.
154 Albert Henry Newman, A Manual of Church History, Vol. I, (Philadelphia: The Baptist Publication Society, 1939), p. 156.
155 Albert Henry Newman, A Manual of Church History, Vol. I, (Philadelphia: The Baptist Publication Society, 1939), p. 160.
156 Kenneth Scott Latourette, A History of Christianity, Vol. I, (New York: Harper & Row, Publishers, 1975), p. 87.
157 Albert Henry Newman, A Manual of Church History, Vol. I, (Philadelphia: The Baptist Publication Society, 1939), p. 165.

churches, and prohibited Christian assemblies of every kind."[158] (10) Diocletian (303-311), in 303 "declared in a series of cruel edicts, his intention of abolishing the Christian name."[159]

Roman imperial persecution ended in 313 through a joint declaration by Constantine and Licinius which was made at Milan. That declaration is often erroneously called The Edict of Milan. They declared that "no man should be denied leave of attaching himself to the rights of the Christians, or to whatever other religion his might [that is, his strength] directed him."[160]

East of the Roman/Persian Euphrates boundary, during the time of both the Parthian Empire and its successor the Sassanian Empire, which came to power in 226 A.D., governmental persecution of Christians was sometimes much worse than it was in the Roman Empire. The following is just one account from the fifth century:

"In 438 A.D. [Sassanian Emperor] Yazdgerd II succeeded his father Bahram. At first he tolerated the Christians, but after eight years (for reasons which are not altogether clear to us) he turned against them. On 24 and 25 August 446 Christians from a number of provinces, including the bishops, senior clergy and many members of distinguished families, were collected at Karka (modern Kirkuk) and put to death. They met their martyrdom with great courage. The way in which one of the Christian women, Shirin, and her two sons met their death so touched the King's officer in charge of the proceedings that he too confessed faith in Christ and on 25 September was himself crucified. The next year saw the death of the famous martyr, Pethion, who had been a notable evangelist in Western Persia. He had many followers among the important families in the area, including a high-ranking military officer and the chief of Police of Shahin. Eventually he was imprisoned and after being tortured for several days was beheaded and his head was exposed on the Royal Road near Kholwan. The persecution extended to Jews and Armenians and was so fierce that it has remained in the minds of Christians up to the present day. The little Christian community in Kirkuk still gathers together year by year to celebrate the faith and courage of their martyred forebears."[161]

There are many examples of later governmental persecution in Europe such as that which was waged against the Waldensens by the Papacy when it exercised governmental power in Western Europe. Pope Innocent III preached "a crusade against these unfortunate sectaries, and permitting the enlistment of every wandering scoundrel at loose ends to carry fire and sword and rape and every conceivable outrage among the most peaceful subjects of the King of France. The accounts of the cruelties and abominations of this crusade are far more terrible to read than any account of Christian martyrdoms by the pagans, and they have the added horror of being indisputably true."[162]

War which is waged to stamp out a significant advance of Christian evangelism is a form of persecution which historically has been known to wipe out whole segments of society.

---

158 Albert Henry Newman, A Manual of Church History, Vol. I, (Philadelphia: The Baptist Publication Society, 1939), p. 166.
159 B. W. Johnson, A Vision of the Ages, (Hollywood, California: Old Paths Book Club, n.d.), p. 62.
160 Peter J. Leithart, Defending Constantine: The Twilight of an Empire and the Dawn of Christendom, (Downers Grove, IL, IVP, 2010), p. 99.
161 Robin E. Waterfield, Christians in Persia, Assyrians, Armenians, Roman Catholics and Protestants, (London, George Allen & Unwin Limited, 1973), pp. 25-26.
162 H. G. Wells, The Outline of History, Vol. II, (New York: Doubleday & Co., Inc, 1971), p. 574.

Revelation Chapter 6

Obviously, such vicious and widespread carnage will usually also destroy segments of the economy such as food production and distribution. <u>Such devastation leads to inflation and economic upheaval, represented by the black horse and, ultimately, to widespread death, represented by the pale horse.</u>

Almost unbelievably, the government of the U.S.A. has become a persecuting power, punishing many who hold to and act on Christian teaching. For example, the pharmacist who refuses to fill anti-pregnancy prescriptions faces fines and jail. Also, the administrative personnel of hospitals and medical clinics who refuse to perform abortions on demand face fines and the closure of their medical facilities. Other examples on the state and local governmental level may also be cited. For example, the proprietors of the American Pulverizer Company in St. Louis, Missouri are faced with a government mandate which violates their Christian beliefs. The new health care law which is enforced by the Department of Health and Human Services (HHS) "requires employers with more than fifty full-time workers to provide insurance to their employees or face fines. The HHS mandate requires employers to provide a range of 'preventative services' in those insurance plans, including birth control pills, sterilization, and 'emergency contraception' that may act as abortifacients."[163]

Another example of persecution by the government of the U.S.A. has just become notorious. "A county clerk who, through her defiance of a Federal Court Order to issue marriage licenses to gay couples, became a national symbol of religious opposition to same-sex marriage was jailed Thursday after a Federal judge here (Ashland, Kentucky) declared her in contempt of court. The clerk, Kim Davis of Rowan County, KY, was ordered detained and later rejected a proposal to allow her deputies to process same-sex marriage licenses that could have prompted her release. Instead, on a day when Ms. Davis' lawyer said she would not retreat from or modify her stand despite a Supreme Court ruling legalizing same-sex marriage, Judge David L. Bunning of United States District Court secured commitments from five of Ms. Davis' deputies to begin providing the licenses ... 'The court cannot condone the willful disobedience of its lawfully issued order,' Judge Bunning said. 'If you give people the opportunity to choose which orders they will follow, that's what potentially causes problems.' The judge's decision to jail Ms. Davis, a 49-year-old Democrat who was elected last year, immediately intensified the attention focused on her, a long-time government worker who is one of three of Kentucky's 120 county clerks who contend that their religious beliefs prevent them from recognizing same-sex nuptials."[164]

C.   The third seal 6:5-6

Black horse bearing the rider has the balance in his hand. A voice proclaims the price of wheat and barley.

6:5   **"And when he opened the third seal, I heard the third living creature saying, Come. And I saw, and behold, a black horse; and he that sat thereon had a balance in his hand."**

---

163 James Dean, *Where They Stand*, <u>WORLD</u>, February 9, 2013, p. 35.
164 Alan Blinder & Tamar Lewin, *Clerk Chooses Jail Over Deal on Gay Unions*, <u>The New York Times</u>, September 4, 2015, p. A1.

6:5 "a black horse"

Black is a somber, foreboding, ominous color which according to the book of Lamentations is associated with famine. There we read, "Our skin is black like an oven, Because of the burning heat of famine." (Lamentations 5:10)

6:5 "a balance in his hand"

A balance is indicative of extreme stringency, scarcity and famine. "Food is weighed carefully as something very rare and precious."[165]

6:6 "And I heard as it were a voice in the midst of the four living creatures saying, A measure of wheat for a shilling, and three measures of barley for a shilling; and the oil and the wine hurt thou not."

6:6 "the four living creatures"

See the comments on 4:6-8.

6:6 "a measure of wheat"

The NRSV renders it "a quart of wheat for a day's pay." The NKJV words it as "a quart of wheat for a denarius."

6:6 "three measures of barley"

"In return for his work he [a laborer] is to get a mere quart of wheat, or about one person's daily ration. ... To feed a family he must turn to [barley,] a cheaper grain."[166]

6:6 "a shilling"

The Greek word is *denarius*, a laborer's daily wage. Compare Matthew 20:1-2.

6:6 "the oil and the wine hurt thou not"

The grapevine and the olive tree are perennial rather than seasonal as wheat and barley are. The chaos resulting from widespread persecution often would not allow seasonal sowing and harvesting to be properly carried out. In contrast, the produce of the olive tree and the vine likely would not be so badly impacted. It is very probable that the growing cycle for wheat and barley would often be aborted, resulting in exorbitant prices. If one had wine and olive oil with which to bargain, there might be hope of survival.

As an example, the economic and social consequences of war, growing out of persecution, were clearly visible at the end of The Thirty Years' War. During that war which was fought from 1618 to 1648, "Germany had seen most of the fighting. She suffered from it to the point of exhaustion. The population dwindled from about sixteen million to one-half, or as some believe, to one-third that number. The loss of life was partly due to fearful epidemics such as typhus fever and the bubonic plague, which spread over the land in the wake of the invading armies. A great many villages were destroyed or abandoned by their inhabitants. Much of the soil went out of cultivation, while trade and manufacturing nearly disappeared. Added to all this was the decline of

---

165 A. Plummer, The Pulpit Commentary [on] Revelation, (Chicago: Wilcox & Follett Co., no date), p. 185.
166 Revelation, Four Views: A Parallel Commentary, ed. Steve Gregg , (Nashville: Thomas Nelson Publishers, 1997), p. 110.

Revelation Chapter 6

education, literature, and art, and the brutalizing of the people in mind and morals. It took Germany at least one hundred years to recover from the injury inflicted by The Thirty Years' War; complete recovery, indeed, came only in the nineteenth century."[167]

D. The fourth seal 6:7-8

A pallid horse bearing death has authority over one fourth of the earth to kill by sword, famine, death and wild beasts.

6:7-8 "And when he opened the fourth seal, I heard the voice of the fourth living creature saying, Come. And I saw, and behold, a pale horse: and he that sat upon him, his name was Death; and Hades followed with him. And there was given unto them authority over the fourth part of the earth, to kill with sword, and with famine, and with death, and by the wild beasts of the earth."

6:7-8 "a pale horse: and he that sat upon him, his name was Death;"

The consequences of persecution which had been focused upon those who followed Christ have a much wider impact, engulfing society at large. Extremely harsh and stringent economic conditions brought about by the events represented by the second and third horses, lead to further strife and killing. People will kill for food and other basic essentials. Due to the disruption in food production and distribution, famine also will ensue, leading to the death of many more.

6:7-8 "the fourth part of the earth"

While the macabre forces enumerated here operate globally, God mercifully sets a limit — "the fourth part of the earth." While tragedies from other causes may exceed this limit, death resulting from persecution of Christians seems to be limited, at any one time, to one-fourth of the earth.

6:7-8 "to kill with sword, and with famine, and with death, and by the wild beasts of the earth."

Based on comparison with Ezekiel 14:21, some translators think the word "death" refers to death by pestilence. Hence, the NRSV and the ESV translate it "pestilence," while the NIV renders it "plague."

Some commentators think that "the wild beasts" point to the sadistic spectacles in Roman stadiums in which starving wild animals were released upon helpless Christian victims. Though such barbarous and torturous ordeals were inflicted on many defenseless Christians, here "wild beasts" more probably refers to the wider phenomenon in which the economy will have been so disrupted by widespread vicious opposition initiated in response to Gospel triumph that wild beasts will have been deprived of normal food sources. Consequently, they turn on human beings to satisfy their hunger.

---
167 Hutton Webster, <u>World History</u>, (Boston: D.C. Heath & Co. Publishers, 1921), p. 277.

E. *The fifth seal 6:9-11*

From beneath the altar, white-robed souls of martyrs cry to God for justice. They are told to rest till their brethren also finish their course.

6:9 **"And when he opened the fifth seal, I saw underneath the altar the souls of them that had been slain for the word of God, and for the testimony which they held:"**

6:9 "the altar"

This altar cannot be an altar upon which sacrifice is offered for expiation or atonement for sin, as numerous commentators would have us believe. Those commentators seem to have forgotten that Jesus "offered one sacrifice for sins forever." (Hebrews 10:12) This altar, therefore, must be equated with that which is described in 8:3, see page 115, as "the golden altar which was before the throne." That is the altar upon which the prayers of the saints are placed and from which they rise into the presence of God. This is the fulfillment of the pattern in which incense rose from a similar prototype altar located just before the curtain dividing the holy place from the most holy place in both the Tabernacle and the Temple. This identification is substantiated in the very next verse (6:10) in which is recorded a fervent prayer of the martyred saints in their appeal to God.

6:9 "underneath the altar"

In what sense are the souls of them who had been slain for the word of God underneath the altar? Though being souls, that is spirit beings, they obviously still had a visual appearance despite not having flesh and bones (See Luke 24:39.), otherwise John could not have seen them. Probably, those souls were congregated around the base of the altar of incense. That position would certainly put them in the presence of Christ, a concept which would be in harmony with Paul's statement that he had "the desire to depart and be with Christ." (Philippians 1:23)

6:9 "slain for the word of God, and for the testimony which they held"

These glorified Christians had been faithful to the divine message which is here called "the word of God." They had done so even though the environment in which they conveyed God's message was so hostile it was mortally dangerous. They had been "slain." In spite of the peril which they had faced, they had given "testimony" which substantiated not only the message itself, but their sincere commitment to it. The word "testimony" is from the Greek word *marturian* which means to give one's life as the ultimate expression of sincerity and reality in conveying and corroborating a message.

Some commentators see the persecution which is depicted here as historically limited. For example, one commentator wrote, "The historical interpretation of the book of Revelation sees the fulfillment of the fifth seal in the persecution of the early church by the Roman Empire. This persecution culminated in Emperor Diocletian's attempt to blot out Christianity, A.D. 303-311."[168] However, the series of consequences rising out of the persecution of the church is certainly not limited to the persecution by Diocletian. The dire consequences of the persecution of the people of Christ, which are enumerated here, will be repeated whenever and wherever such widespread opposition arises.

---

168 David Vaughn Elliott, Nobody Left Behind, Insight into "End-Time" Prophecies, (Methun, Massachusetts, 2004), p. 124.

Revelation Chapter 6

6:10 **"and they cried with a great voice, saying, How long, O Master, the holy and true, dost thou not judge and avenge our blood on them that dwell on the earth?"**

6:10 "how long"

Though these martyred Christians had crossed the threshold from time to timeless eternity, they were still aware of the earthly phenomenon of time with its finite ongoing progress. Though in eternity there may be no calibrations like winter and summer or sunset and sunrise (See Revelation 21:23-25.) by which to mark linear movement or progress, distinguishing one event from another, yet even in that environment, discreet events and developments are somehow kept distinct from each other.

The essence of the phenomenon of time, from a purely human perspective, is still under debate. "In the late seventeenth century, [Gottfried Wilhelm] Leibniz and [Isaac] Newton staked out competing positions on time's true nature. Newton took the 'absolutist' position, holding that time transcended the physical world and all that went on within it. 'Absolute, true and mathematical time, of itself and from its own nature, flows equably without relation to anything external,' Newton declared. Leibniz took the opposite, 'relationist' position. He argued, against Newton, that time was merely a relation among events. In a static world – a world without change, without 'happenings' – time would simply not exist. Grunbaum, in contending that there was no time before the Big Bang, seemed to be echoing Leibniz. He was assuming that it would be meaningless to talk of time in a clock-less and event-less state of Nothing."[169] (See addendum, page 101.)

(See also the discussion of time in the exposition of "the things which must come to pass hereafter" under 4:1 on page 72.)

6:10 "O Master"

The word "Master" is the translation of the Greek word *despotais*. "This is the only instance of its occurrence in the Apocalypse."[170] Though our word "despot" derives from this Greek word, here it means the one who is the Lord of the house, a house in which there are servants or slaves. The house in this case is defined as the earth by the phrase, "them that dwell on the earth."

6:10 "avenge our blood"

To avenge means to impose the penalty on a criminal which corresponds to the crime he has committed. In this case, those who martyred Christians had committed murder. According to the divine edict which says, "whoso sheddeth man's blood, by man shall his blood be shed: for in the image of God made he man" (Genesis 9:6), capital punishment should have been imposed. The cry of the martyrs is an appeal for justice, not an expression of hatred. The martyrs had been summarily executed as though they had been convicted criminals. Their execution, in many if not most cases, was carried out with no trial and no due process of law. The record on earth had not been corrected. Their names had not been cleared. They had not been exonerated. The opening of the sixth seal (6:12-

---

169 Jim Holt, Why Does The World Exist?, (New York: Liveright Publishing Corporation, 2012), p. 71.
170 A. Plummer, The Pulpit Commentary [on] Revelation, (Chicago: Wilcox & Follett Co., no date), p. 189.

17) reveals an answer to their prayers. It tells them that the corrupt political system, under which the crime against them had occurred, would fall.

6:11 "And there was given them to each one a white robe; and it was said unto them, that they should rest yet for a little time, until their fellow-servants also and their brethren, who should be killed even as they were, should have fulfilled their course."

6:11 "a white robe"

Probably, these robes were bestowed as a reminder of the cleansing from sin which each one of them had experienced when they yielded their lives to Christ. As Isaiah made clear, white is the color representing cleansing and pardon. He wrote, "Though your sins be as scarlet, they shall be as white as snow; though they be red like crimson, they shall be as wool." (Isaiah 1:18)

6:11 "they should rest"

Rest had been granted to them, a benefaction in harmony with the blessing recorded later in Revelation which tells us, "Blessed are the dead who die in the Lord from henceforth: yea, saith the Spirit, that they may rest from their labors; for their works follow with them." (Revelation 14:13) They should not allow their reward of rest to be destroyed by anxiety about the timing of God's ongoing administration of justice.

6:11 "a little time"

See the discussion of the concept of time under 6:10 in "how long."

6:11 "brethren who should be killed"

The testimony with the greatest impact is that which is given by signing it with one's blood. By allowing martyrdom to proceed, God gives the perpetrators of, and the witnesses to, the brethren's martyrdom the most powerful message it is possible to convey. In sharp contrast, the current death cult in Islam is a crude, grotesque counterfeit and caricature of Christian martyrdom. The Muslim concept of martyrdom is suicide committed by becoming a human bomb, so that one kills as many of his opponents as possible. It is recorded that Christian martyrs prayed for those who put them to death. (Acts 7:60) There is no record that any of them tried to inflict punishment on those who were inflicting death on them.

F.   The sixth seal 6:12-7:17

1.   A great earthquake occurs. The sun becomes black, the moon blood, and the stars fall. The heavens vanish. The islands and mountains were moved out of their places. Humanity hides in the earth from the wrath of God and Christ. 6:12-17

6:12 "And I saw when he opened the sixth seal, and there was a great earthquake; and the sun became black as sackcloth of hair, and the whole moon became as blood;"

Revelation Chapter 6

6:12   "a great earthquake"

For identification, it is important to compare and very probably equate this earthquake, which is further described in verse 14, with the one predicted in Ezekiel 38:19-20. By comparing the two prophesies, it becomes obvious that in both accounts the "earthquake" is described as taking place just prior to and as contributing to the turning of the Jewish people to Jesus Christ. Compare Ezekiel 39:7 and 39:22-28 with Revelation 7:3-8.

From the description in Revelation 6:12-17, the question arises whether this portrays a geological-seismic earthquake or a political-social earthquake, or both.

In either case, it is an earthquake which takes place during a war. Ezekiel chapters 38 and 39 describe this same war-related upheaval in great detail. The equivalent of "the chief captains" who are mentioned in Revelation 6:15 is found in Ezekiel 39:20 as the "mighty men" and "men of war." Such a war is just beginning to get underway in our time with Russia and Iran militarily and politically upholding the Shi'ite-Alawite Assad regime in Syria.

The dramatic failure of the massive, widespread, multinational military coalition, described in Ezekiel chapters 38 and 39, in its attempt to destroy the nation of Israel, will inevitably be followed by extensive political upheavals and many regime changes, as severe as "a great earthquake." Accordingly, political confusion and chaos will ensue.

The kings and princes who are predicted in Revelation 6:15 to flee to the rocks, caves and mountains are clearly paralleled by the princes mentioned in Ezekiel 39:18 who similarly will not be successful in their attempt to avoid death.

6:12   "the sun became black as sackcloth of hair"

Violent seismic earthquakes may throw so much dust into the air that the visual appearance of the sun and moon are either distorted or completely blocked out. In social and political earthquakes, even the highest ranks of leaders, here represented by the word "sun," may fall or lose political and social power.

6:12   "the whole moon became as blood"

This probably points to second tier officials in comparison to those represented by the sun.

6:13   "and the stars of the heaven fell unto the earth, as a fig tree casteth her unripe figs when she is shaken of a great wind."

These stars probably represent people who hold positions of prominence and authority. Such use of the word "star" is found in Genesis 37:9-10, Numbers 24:17, Daniel 8:9-10, Luke 21:25-26, Revelation 1:16, 1:20 and 9:1.

6:14   "And the heaven was removed as a scroll when it is rolled up; and every mountain and island were ["was"- ESV, NIV] moved out of their places ["its place" - ESV, NIV]."

This certainly does not point to an atmospheric or astronomical collapse, but indicates that the whole political structure, in this verse represented by "every mountain and island," will be discredited, repudiated and overthrown.

Revelation Verse by Verse

6:15 "And the kings of the earth, and the princes, and the chief captains, and the rich, and the strong, and every bondman and freeman, hid themselves in the caves and in the rocks of the mountains;"

As emphasized in the comments on the words "a great earthquake" in 6:12, the description of the events included under the sixth seal is to be aligned with that of those events which will transpire during the invasion of Israel by a vast coalition of nations, led by Gog, the great power from the uttermost parts of the north. That invasion is described prophetically in great detail in chapters 38 and 39 of Ezekiel. In Revelation 6:15-16, "the princes and chief captains" will hide from the "wrath" or "from the face of him that sitteth on the throne." Similarly, according to Ezekiel's prophecy, carrion birds "shall eat the flesh of the mighty, and drink the blood of the princes of the earth." (Ezekiel 39:18)

6:16 "and they say to the mountains and to the rocks, Fall on us, and hide us from the face of him that sitteth on the throne, and from the wrath of the Lamb:"

The pronoun "they" points to the roster of leading political dignitaries and supporting personnel cited in 6:15. Stricken by fear, kings, princes, chief captains, the rich, the strong, as well as bondmen and freemen will desperately flee, vainly seeking refuge and protection from a catastrophe resulting from a huge military adventure which will have gone terribly wrong.

Where in biblical prophecy can we find such a constellation of people from every level of society who will be impacted so adversely by war that they are driven to embrace such panic measures? Certainly, the war described prophetically in the 38th and 39th chapters of Ezekiel presents us with just such a roster of participants who shall take part in the currently looming futile war to destroy the nation of Israel. From nine distinct countries, many of them Islamic, they will bring their troops, accompanied by all the necessary supporting personnel and equipment, in a collaborative joint effort to wipe Israel off the map. Without giving the lengthy documentation from which these identities are made,[171] the following succinct enumeration is given of the participants in the ultimate war against Israel:

1. Tubal, Ezekiel 38:2, refers to the area covered by the drainage basin of the Tobolsk River in north-central Russia. **2. Meshech**, Ezekiel 38:3, is the ancient name for Moscow. **3. Rosh**, Ezekiel 38:2, is the biblical name for Russia. These first three participants all fall within the boundaries of present-day Russia and are part of that group which come from "the uttermost parts of the north." (Ezekiel 38:15). **4. Togarmah**, Ezekiel 38:6, is the biblical terminology for the Turkish people. **5. Gomer**, Ezekiel 38:6, is to be identified with France and Germany. **6. Persia**, Ezekiel 38:5, is the alternate name for Iran. **7. Sheba**, Ezekiel 38:13, is the ancient name for Yemen. **8. Dedan**, Ezekiel 38:18, is the ancient country now governed by Jordan. **9. Cush** (Kush), Ezekiel 38:5, is the ancient name for the area now occupied by Ethiopia and Sudan. **10. Put**, Ezekiel 38:5, is an alternate biblical name for Libya. **11. Tarshish**, Ezekiel 38:13, is the biblical name for ancient Spain. By New Testament times, the geographical name of Spain is used. (See Romans 15:28.)

---

[171] For more detailed documentation, see The Definitive Battle for Palestine by B. L. Turner. (Available through Amazon and www.CreateSpace.com.)

Revelation Chapter 6

6:17   **"for the great day of their wrath is come; and who is able to stand?"**

    This refers to the simultaneous coordinated wrath of "him that sitteth on the throne and … the wrath of the Lamb." (See 6:16.) Normally, we think of lambs as docile like the description of the Lamb of God in the 53rd chapter of Isaiah. But, at this point in the development of God's eternal purpose, the Lamb of God becomes wrathful.

Addendum to Revelation 6:10

Albert Einstein had a "vision of a universe in which space and time are interwoven and dynamic, able to stretch, shrink and jiggle. … A century of innovation, testing, questioning and plain hard work after Einstein imagined it on paper, scientists have tapped into the deepest register of physical reality, where the weirdest and wildest implications of Einstein's universe became manifest." On February 11, 2016 astronomers announced that these new areas of understanding have been authenticated by using the "Laser Interferometer Gravitational-Wave Observatory." "When Einstein announced his theory in 1915, he rewrote the rules for space and time that had prevailed for more than 200 years, since the time of Newton, stipulating a static and fixed framework for the universe. Instead, Einstein said, matter and energy distort the geometry of the universe. … A disturbance in the cosmos could cause space-time to stretch, collapse and even jiggle."[172]

---

[172] Dennis Overbye, *With Faint Chirp Scientists Prove Einstein Correct*, The New York Times, February 12, 2016, pp. A1 & A12.

Revelation Chapter 7

Note: As an aid in understanding chapter 7, one should study Appendix B, page 407.

> 2. *Gospel victory among both Jews and Gentiles 7:1-17*
>
>   a. *Four angels holding four destructive winds stand at four corners of earth and are prohibited by another angel who has the seal of the Living God from hurting the earth till God's servants are sealed. 7:1-3*

7:1 **"After this I saw four angels standing at the four corners of the earth, holding the four winds of the earth, that no wind should blow on the earth, or on the sea, or upon any tree."**

7:1 "the four corners of the earth"

This precise phrase is used only once in the Old Testament, in Isaiah 11:12. A similar phrase was used by Ezekiel in 7:2, but it only refers to the land of Israel. John uses the phrase only one more time, in Revelation 20:8. It is an idiomatic expression meaning the whole earth. It does not, as Barclay surprisingly suggests, imply a flat earth. He commented, "This vision is expressed in ideas about the world which were current at the time in which John wrote. The earth is a square, flat earth, and at its four corners are four angels waiting to loose the winds of destruction."[173]

Twice, the concept of a global earth has been enshrined in Old Testament scripture. Those biblical statements clearly indicate that we live on a spherical world, not on a flat earth. God told the Jewish people that "it is he [God] that sitteth above the circle of the earth." (Isaiah 40:22) He also revealed that "he set a circle upon the face of the deep." (Proverbs 8:27) The apostle John was obviously thoroughly acquainted with the Old Testament scripture. Therefore, he surely knew and believed that the earth is a globe. When he uses the expression "the four corners of the earth," he undoubtedly was simply employing a well-known idiom, meaning the entire earth.

7:1 "that no wind should blow on the earth, or on the sea, or upon any tree"

The words "that no wind should blow on the earth" do not point to a climatological wind which would indicate that there would be no movement of air. Rather, this absence of wind points to a period of political and military quiescence. Historical examples would lead us to expect that such a period of quiescence would develop due to widespread systemic exhaustion resulting from a major war. For example, in Europe there was a century of peace between the Battle of Waterloo in 1815 and the beginning of World War I in 1914. The occurrence of global war, focused on the land of Israel, which is predicted in Ezekiel chapters 38 and 39 and in Revelation 6:12-17, will undoubtedly be followed

---

173 William Barclay, <u>The Revelation of John</u>, Vol. II, (London Westminster: John Knox Press, 2004), p. 21.

by an extensive period without conflict due to worldwide economic and military exhaustion.

Here, by the activity of four angels, major political, social, and military upheavals will be held in abeyance for a prolonged period. That period will begin following a devastating world war. It will allow important major developments to take place in the outworking of God's eternal purpose. Among those developments will be the epochal conversion of the Jews to Christ. Most probably this period of quiescence will coincide with The Millennium. (See 20:2-7.) This angelic intervention, carried out by "four angels" in the course of human events, is one of the ways we see that "the Most High is sovereign over the kingdoms of men." (Daniel 4:17 NIV)

7:2 **"And I saw another angel ascend from the sunrising, having the seal of the living God: and he cried with a great voice to the four angels to whom it was given to hurt the earth and the sea,"**

7:2   "the seal of the living God"

From the definition given in the following verse, it is clear that this "seal of the living God" should in no way be equated with the "mark on the forehead" mentioned in Ezekiel 9:4-6. This distinction needs to be emphasized because some commentators have made such a misleading association. For example, one of them asserted that this seal "is the symbolic instrument used in Ezekiel 9 to mark the righteous Jews in Jerusalem for preservation against the coming Babylonian destruction."[174] The identification of this seal is given below in the discussion of verse 3.

7:2   "the four angels to whom it was given to hurt the earth and the sea"

The "earth and the sea" speak of the area or arena in which the four angels will be authorized to bring about damaging and detrimental developments. In other words, they will have a global mandate. Historic developments, even those which are destructive, here implied by the word "hurt," are under divine control.

7:3 **"saying, Hurt not the earth, neither the sea, nor the trees, till we shall have sealed the servants of our God on their foreheads."**

7:3   "Hurt not the earth, neither the sea, nor the trees"

Though the restriction on the scope of the angels' activity is here emphasized again, a terminal point on that restriction is given in the next phrase.

7:3   "till we shall have sealed the servants of our God on their foreheads"

The restriction on the activities of the four angels indicates that political and economic conditions would remain benign till the major movement of Jews toward Christ (7:3-8) should have been accomplished. We are not told how long that period will last.

In harmony with II Corinthians 1:21-22, Ephesians 1:13 and 4:30, this sealing of the servants of God on their foreheads points to the 144,000 Jewish converts' receiving the

---
[174] Loren Brink, <u>Rethinking Revelation In Light of the Old Testament Prophets</u>, (Portland, Oregon: Northwest Publications, 1986), p. 87.

Revelation Chapter 7

gift of the Holy Spirit. This will take place when Jewish converts to Christ, like all Gentile converts, being baptized into Christ, receive the Holy Spirit. (See Acts 2:36-38.)

Receiving the Holy Spirit will allow those Jews, as natural branches, to be grafted back into the olive tree, the epochal event which is predicted in Romans 11:23-24. This will also be the time when ungodliness, which is totally incompatible with the Holy Spirit, will be turned away from Jacob, an event foretold in Romans 11:26-27.

That this sealing is something far more extensive and significant than anything related to those Jews who were saved either from the Babylonian captivity or the Roman destruction of Jerusalem becomes even more clear from the prophecy in Revelation 9:4. There, many centuries later than either the Jewish captivity in Babylon or the Roman destruction of Jerusalem, but well before this sealing of the Jews, a group of victims who suffered under the yoke of Islam will have been granted their lives because they had this very same seal. The Islamic predators were free only to hurt, that is to kill, anyone who did not have "the seal of God on their foreheads." (See the comments on Revelation 9:4.)

We may reasonably ask, why "on their foreheads?" Probably, it points to the Holy Spirit helping the recipient of this seal to control his or her mental powers, thus bringing "every thought into captivity to the obedience of Christ." (II Corinthians 10:5)

Control of thought processes and bringing them into harmony with God's will is an invaluable blessing. It helps thwart Satan's efforts to capture and control our minds. That he works at that level is made clear from II Corinthians 4:4 and 11:3.

We Christians are exhorted to be "transformed by the renewing of [our] minds, that [we] may prove what is the good and acceptable and perfect will of God." (Romans 12:2) The renewing of our minds is one of the great ministries of the Holy Spirit which he carries out, but only with our total cooperation and acquiescence. In Titus 3:5-6, we are told that "he saved us through the washing of regeneration and the renewing of the Holy Spirit, which he poured out upon us richly, through Jesus Christ our Saviour." This is how we "put off [our] old self, which belongs to [our] former manner of life and [which was] corrupt through deceitful desires, and [therefore requires that we must] be renewed in the spirit of [our] minds, [as we] put on the new self, created after the likeness of God in true righteousness and holiness." (Ephesians 4:22-24 ESV) (See also Philippians 2:5, 2:13, and Galatians 5:22-25.)

Angels are the ones referred to by the pronoun "we" in the statement "till we shall have sealed the servants of our God on their foreheads." This indicates that angels share in the impartation of the Holy Spirit to those who yield their lives to Christ. This is a significant dimension of the angelic ministry mentioned in Hebrews 1:14.

Jews receiving the Holy Spirit upon their acceptance of Christ is a development which has been stressed many times in prophecy. (See, for example, Isaiah 44:1-5, Ezekiel 11:17-21, 36:22-28, and 39:29. Finally, see Zechariah 12:10.)

> b. *The number and description of those who are sealed on their foreheads. 7:4-8*

7:4 **"And I heard the number of them that were sealed, a hundred and forty and four thousand, sealed out of every tribe of the children of Israel:"**

7:4 "a hundred and forty and four thousand"

These Jews who come to Christ do so in calculable numbers in contrast to the Gentiles who will have come to Christ in such enormous multitudes that, according to 7:9, no one will be able to calculate their total number. Though the number of Jews, at the beginning of their breakthrough conversion, is easily comprehended, still, it certainly is no paltry or insignificant number. That number constitutes one percent of the current number of Jewish people. Based on current population figures, a comparable portion of Gentiles would number eighty million. However, if one should add all the Gentiles who will have obeyed the Gospel before the Jewish people yield to Christ, the number of Gentile converts becomes really phenomenal.

Also, clearly the number 144,000 does not convey the total number of Jewish people who will ultimately yield their allegiance to Christ. We know this because in Revelation 14:3-4, this same number is said to be only "the first fruits unto God and unto the Lamb." So, after this initial period of Gospel triumph among the Jewish people, we should anticipate an ongoing Gospel victory in that special segment of humanity.

It seems evident that, "the 144,000 is a definite for an indefinite number, for it is not a reasonable supposition that there would be exactly 12,000 from each tribe, or that amount would be all that would be saved. It means that a large number of Abraham's descendants [from each of the twelve tribes] would be saved in the period of prosperity for the church that followed the [opening of the] sixth seal."[175]

7:4 "every tribe of the children of Israel"

This verse states that those who will be sealed will have come from every tribe of the children of Israel, notwithstanding the fact that Dan, from whose offspring was formed one of the original twelve tribes of the children of Israel, is not included in the enumeration given just below in 7:6-8. Just as there was one who became a renegade traitor from among the twelve disciples whom Jesus chose to be his apostles, so earlier there was a tragic and persistent betrayal of Israel's high calling by one of the twelve tribes. Had a corrective move not have been made, that betrayal would have marred, if not thwarted, the ultimate fulfillment of the profound purpose which God wanted to bring to pass through Jacob's progeny.

Dan's betrayal prefigured the even greater betrayal of Judas. Just as Judas lost his place in the enumeration of Christ's apostles (Compare Matthew 10:2-4 with Acts 1:13.), so here in Revelation 7:6-8, Dan's infamous name is not included. The apostasy of the tribe of Dan is recorded in the 18th chapter of the book of Judges. The tribe of Dan disqualified itself from remaining a member in the nation of Israel by gross inclusive tribal idolatry and by practicing unprovoked and unjustified violence. As Peter, quoting from Psalm

---

175 John T. Hinds, A Commentary on the Book of Revelation (Nashville, Tenn.: Gospel Advocate Company, 1976), p. 110.

Revelation Chapter 7

109:8, says about Judas, "His office let another take" (Acts 1:20), so here Dan's name is replaced by that of Levi, who, though a son of Jacob, had previously not been listed as one of the twelve tribes, probably because he had been given no tribal territory.

7:5 **"Of the tribe of Judah were sealed twelve thousand: Of the tribe of Reuben twelve thousand; Of the tribe of Gad twelve thousand;"**

In verses 5-8, the name of each Jewish tribe is given from which thousands of converts will have ultimately been won to Christ. In the following exposition, comments are only given regarding those tribes for which there has been some significant or unique development.

7:5 **"the tribe of Judah"**

It is surprising that Barnes wrote that "There seems to be no particular reason why the tribe of Judah was mentioned first. Judah was not the oldest of the sons of Jacob, and there was no settled order in which the tribes were usually mentioned."[176]

Though biologically Judah was not the firstborn son of Jacob, he gained precedence over his brethren, a precedence clearly indicated first in Jacob's pre-death prophecy of the future careers of his sons. In that prophecy, Jacob predicted that the scepter would not depart from Judah, nor the ruler's staff from between his feet until Shiloh should come unto whom the obedience of the people would be. (See Genesis 49:10.) Jacob's prophecy about the unique preeminence of Judah was confirmed in the Chronicles of Israel where we are told that "Judah prevailed above his brethren, and of him came the Prince." (I Chronicles 5:2) Further, we are told that God "hath chosen Judah to be Prince." (I Chronicles 28:4) Through the prophet Hosea, God said, "Ephraim compasseth me about with falsehood, and the house of Israel with deceit; but Judah yet ruleth with God, and is faithful with the Holy One." (Hosea 11:12) In the 60th Psalm God says, "Judah is my scepter." (Psalm 60:7) Psalm 76:1 declares "In Judah is God known." "Moreover he refused the tent of Joseph, And chose not the tribe of Ephraim, But chose the tribe of Judah, The mount Zion which he loved. (Psalm 78:67-68) Further, God has said, "Gilead is mine; Manasseh is mine; Ephraim also is the defence of my head; Judah is my sceptre." (Psalm 108:8) (See also Psalm 114:1-2.) Later, Zechariah prophesied that from Judah "shall come the cornerstone, from him the nail, from him the battle bow, from him every ruler together." (Zechariah 10:4) "The glory of the house of David and the glory of the inhabitants of Jerusalem [are not to be] magnified above Judah." (Zechariah 12:7) The ultimate accolade for Judah comes when we are told that "The Lion that is **of the tribe of Judah**, the Root of David, hath overcome to open the book and the seven seals thereof." (Revelation 5:5)

7:6 **"Of the tribe of Asher twelve thousand; Of the tribe of Naphtali twelve thousand; Of the tribe of Manasseh twelve thousand;"**

The touching moment when Jacob told Joseph that his first two sons "are mine; Ephraim and Manasseh, even as Reuben and Simeon shall be mine" is recorded in Genesis 48:5-6. In the tense interchange which arose between Joseph and his father Jacob at the moment of formal adoption (See Genesis 48:17-20.), though Manasseh was not given precedence

---
[176] Albert Barnes, Notes, Explanatory and Practical on the Book of Revelation, (New York: Harper & Brothers Publishers, 1864), p. 203.

for being Joseph's first born son, still Jacob said, "He also shall become a people and he also shall be great: howbeit, his younger brother shall be greater than he, and his seed shall become a multitude of nations." (Genesis 48:29)

7:7 **"Of the tribe of Simeon twelve thousand; Of the tribe of Levi twelve thousand; Of the tribe of Issachar twelve thousand;"**

7:8 **"Of the tribe of Zebulun twelve thousand; Of the tribe of Joseph twelve thousand; Of the tribe of Benjamin were sealed twelve thousand."**

7:8 **"the tribe of Joseph"**

Though Joseph initially had protested that Jacob had given Ephraim, the youngest son, greater honor than Manasseh, here the name of Joseph is listed in place of Ephraim. This, perhaps, suggests that Joseph ultimately acquiesced in the unusual precedence and sequence demanded by his father, Jacob.

c. The great international throng before God's throne. 7:9-17

7:9 **"After these things I saw, and behold, a great multitude, which no man could number, out of every nation and of all tribes and peoples and tongues, standing before the throne and before the Lamb, arrayed in white robes, and palms in their hands;"**

7:9 **"a great multitude which no man could number"**

In contrast to the Gospel victory among the Jewish people, this multitude indicates the presence of an innumerable collective aggregation of redeemed Gentile men and women, the fruit garnered by Gospel preaching and teaching during a period, undoubtedly covering many years, starting with Pentecost. The startling numerical disparity between the number of Jews converted to Christ, compared to the number of Gentiles, reflects the minority position which Jews hold in world population. In mid-2015, world population is predicted to be 7,324,782,000[177], out of which only approximately 14,000,000 would be Jews.

Through Paul, God made it clear that a universal Gospel triumph among Gentiles would result from this initial major Jewish conversion to Christ. He wrote, "If the casting away of them [that is, the Jews] is the reconciling of the world, (See Acts 13:46.) what shall the receiving of them be [for the world], but life from the dead?" (Romans 11:15) The Jewish people are remarkably gifted. They have received more Nobel prizes per capita than any other people. The outstanding linguistic, perceptual and persuasive talents found uniquely in the Jewish people, will, following their conversion to Christ, be dedicated to promoting among the Gentiles the message of redemption through Christ with thrilling and astonishing results.

7:9 **"out of every nation and of all tribes and peoples and tongues"**

The message of Christ will have been projected in such inclusive, pervasive and persuasive ways that multitudes from all ethnic backgrounds ("every nation" *ethnous*), every genetic group ("all tribes" *phulon*), every people ("peoples" *laon*) and from every

---
[177] Todd M. Johnson, Gina A. Zurlo, Albert W. Hickman and Peter F. Crossing, *Christianity 2015: Religious Diversity and Personal Contact*, International Bulletin of Missionary Research, Vol. 39, No. 1, January 2015, p. 29.

Revelation Chapter 7

linguistic background ("tongues" *glosson*),[178] will have yielded their allegiance to Jesus Christ. This prophetic summary of Gospel triumph probably covers many years, the whole Christian era including The Millennium. It probably represents the collective fruit resulting from the efforts of many dedicated linguists, publishers, broadcasters, experts in social media, preachers and teachers.

To everyone in the varied ranks of dedicated laborers in the harvest field, this triumphant vision sends the clear and encouraging message that our labors in the Lord are not in vain. (Philippians 2:16)

7:9 "standing before the throne and before the Lamb, arrayed in white robes, and palms in their hands"

They are standing on the podium of ultimate eternal triumph. They hold in their hands the symbol of their sublime victory – the palm branch – while being clothed in white robes, the symbol of purity, the significance of which is clearly indicated in Revelation 19:8. On the expression, "arrayed in white robes," please also see the comments on 7:14.

7:10 "and they cry with a great voice, saying, Salvation unto our God who sitteth on the throne, and unto the Lamb."

7:10 "they cry"

The pronoun "they" refers to the great multitude mentioned in verse 9. Their cry is not one of anguish, pain, regret, defeat or sorrow but is the triumphant, exultant, exuberant exclamation of irrepressible joy. Stern translated it, "they shouted."[179]

7:10 "Salvation unto our God … and unto the Lamb"

By this exclamation the redeemed attribute their salvation exclusively to the combined work of God and Christ. The meaning of "unto our God" is made more clear in some of the newer translations. For example, the NRSV and the NIV have rendered it, "salvation belongs to our God," that is, it is attributable solely to God's initiative.

These recipients of eternal salvation are expressing exuberant awe of God and Christ because they have, at this point in their new experience, probably realized much more fully than ever before the exquisite genius with which God negotiated the delicate legal conundrums involved in fashioning and devising the process of salvation. One of the most intractable problems which God solved was how he could be both "just and the justifier of him that hath faith in Jesus." (Romans 3:26)

7:11 "And all the angels were standing round about the throne, and about the elders and the four living creatures; and they fell before the throne on their faces, and worshiped God,"

7:11 "the elders and the four living creatures"

Please see the comments on 4:4 and 4:6-8.

---

[178] According to the latest edition of *Ethnologue: Languages of the World*, the comprehensive online reference catalog of every known language (ethnologue.com), flagship publication of SIL (former Summer Institute of Linguistics), there are currently 7,105 languages. RESPONSE, Spring 2014, pp. 38-39.

[179] David H. Stern, Complete Jewish Bible, (Jerusalem, Israel: Jewish New Testament Publications, Inc., 1998).

7:11 "the angels ... fell before the throne on their faces, and worshiped God"

Not only do eternally redeemed human beings stand in awe of God, having realized the tangled legal, ethical and moral thickets through which God surveyed a route making salvation possible, but in addition, all God's angels express their reverent veneration. This scene is certainly one fulfillment of Jesus' assertion in which he said, "There is joy in the presence of the angels of God over one sinner that repenteth." (Luke 15:10)

7:12 "saying, Amen: Blessing, and glory, and wisdom, and thanksgiving, and honor, and power, and might, be unto our God for ever and ever. Amen."

The words "amen ... blessing ... glory ... wisdom ... thanksgiving ... honor ... power ... might," are the words of praise to God from heaven's angels who are exulting because they see the eternal triumph of redeemed sinners who are praising God for facilitating their singular and unique victory. The angels have been allowed to witness the moment in which God brought "many sons unto glory." (Hebrews 2:10) This moment has fulfilled the angel's long-term desire to look into this salvation process. (See I Peter 1:12.)

7:13 "And one of the elders answered, saying unto me, These that are arrayed in white robes, who are they, and whence came they?"

7:13 "who are they"

They are members of the "great multitude." (See 7:9.)

7:13 "whence came they?"

The rendering given by the NIV asks, "where did they come from?" If we want that question answered geographically, linguistically, ethnically or genetically, see verse 9 and its comments. If we want the question to be answered chronologically, it is clear that they will have come from that period in history when it was possible to have sin washed away, as indicated by their white robes, the Christian era.

7:14 "And I say unto him, My lord, thou knowest. And he said to me, These are they that come out of the great tribulation, and they washed their robes, and made them white in the blood of the Lamb."

7:14 "they that come out of the great tribulation"

The words "come out of" do not indicate that those who are "arrayed in white robes" somehow evaded, eluded, escaped from or were raptured out of "the great tribulation" and thus had been spared its rigors and sufferings. On the contrary, having endured all the arduous trials of "the great tribulation," they have emerged from it victoriously. The term "great tribulation" is rendered by Stern as "the great persecution" and by the NRSV as the "great ordeal." (See comments on 2:10.)

Participants in a magnificent series of individual conversions of Gentiles to Christ here collectively constitute the innumerable throng gathered around God's throne (7:9). It was a victory achieved by many Christians, who will have endured great persecution and pain. These converts, along with their mentors, will have gone through "great tribulation." Some aspects and details of their tribulation are given below in 7:16 where

Revelation Chapter 7

the phrases "no more" and "anymore" clearly indicate they had indeed suffered. They had not been delivered from sufferings by some sort of a pre-tribulation rapture. This tribulation refers to opposition, persecution and hardship endured everywhere, from time-to-time, by followers of Christ throughout the whole Christian era. It certainly is not, as Tim LaHaye visualized it, a period of "unparalleled visitation of plagues"[180] from which Christians will have been spared by the Rapture. (See additional notes on the Rapture in Appendix A, especially in the comments on Matthew 24:9 and 24:40, and also in the comments on Acts 1:9.)

Also, this "great tribulation" is not to be equated with the "great tribulation" mentioned in Matthew 24:21. Though verbally identical, the tribulation predicted in Matthew describes only the terrible fate which befell those unfortunate Jews who were trapped in Jerusalem because they did not believe in Christ and consequently did not follow his instruction to flee as the armies of Titus gathered to besiege Jerusalem in 70 A.D. Jesus prophesied about that siege that no fully comparable suffering had ever occurred in the past nor would ever occur in the future. (Matthew 24:21) That means, for example, that the horrible sufferings, unspeakable as they were, of thousands of Russians trapped in Stalingrad when the Germans besieged that city in World War II, did not equal the suffering which the citizens of Jerusalem endured under the Roman siege. It should clearly be noted that those who suffered in the agony of the Roman siege of Jerusalem were not Christians, but unbelieving Jews. Jesus had instructed his disciples to flee from Jerusalem when they saw the Roman troops massing outside the city walls. (Matthew 24:15-16) Consequently, the Christians, followers of Jesus, did flee from the besieged city. (See Appendix A on Matthew 24:21.)

7:14 "washed their robes and made them white"

This cleansing will have occurred in fulfillment of Zechariah 13:1 and 14:8. It is the cleansing John mentioned earlier when he wrote in his first epistle, "If we walk in the light, as he is in the light, we have fellowship one with another, and the blood of Jesus his Son cleanseth us from all sin." (I John 1:7; See also the comments on 22:14.)

7:15 "Therefore are they before the throne of God; and they serve him day and night in his temple: and he that sitteth on the throne shall spread his tabernacle over them."

7:15 "therefore"

The word "therefore" explains the reason why they have been allowed to be present before God's throne. They will have been victorious because they will have persevered in their faith through that segment of "the great tribulation" which they will have had to face. Their victory qualifies them to stand in the most coveted of all venues, that which is "before the throne of God."

---

180 Tim LaHaye, The Beginning of the End, (Wheaton, Illinois: Tyndale House Publishers, 1972), p. 28.

7:15 "they serve him day and night"

Though, on occasion, that service may take them far afield to some distant place in the universe, their position before God's throne will neither be compromised nor forfeited. "Day and night" is an idiomatic way to express "continuously." Those words do not affirm that there will be sunrise and sunset in heaven. (See Revelation 22:5.)

7:15 "spread his tabernacle over them"

Barclay points out that, "The Authorized Version has it that the one who sits upon the throne shall *dwell* among them. That is a perfectly correct translation; but there is more in it than meets the eye. The Greek for *to dwell* is *skenoun*, from *skene*, which means a *tent*. It is the same word as is used when John says that "the word became flesh and *dwelt* among us. (John 1:14)."[181] Literally, God will erect his "tent" among them. (See 21:3.)

7:16 "They shall hunger no more, neither thirst any more; neither shall the sun strike upon them, nor any heat:"

7:16 "no more ... any more"

In harmony with the comments on 7:14, these two phrases clearly indicate that the servants of Christ had grievously suffered. They had not been delivered from suffering, pain, anguish and humiliation by any kind of a rapture.

7:16 "hunger ... thirst ... sun ... heat"

Many varieties of persecution are summarized by these four nouns. They epitomize the despicable kinds of torture utilized during "the great tribulation" mentioned in 7:14. Those who are here depicted as rejoicing before God's throne had endured great agony in order to remain faithful to Christ. They had not been rescued by a rapture. On the contrary, they had persevered through times when these four categories of affliction, which characterize the agonies of "the great tribulation," had been implemented or utilized.

Captives, whether confined in jails or restricted by house arrest from leaving their houses or communities, are often brought to their knees through depriving them of food and water, an excruciating form of torture which is here vividly brought before us by the words, "hunger" and "thirst."

A more fiendish form of persecution consists of tying a victim so he or she, with no recourse, is exposed hour after hour to the full force of the terrible dehydrating and blinding rays of the sun. All of us remember what happened to Jonah when he was exposed to the sun even minimally. The scripture records that "The sun beat upon the head of Jonah [so] that he fainted." (Jonah 4:8) The brief time Jonah was exposed to the sun was trivial compared to the vulnerability of those chained or tied to be exposed hour after hour to the full brilliance and heat of the sun. While the word "heat" may well refer to the heat of the sun, it may also point to the heat of branding irons or heated ovens into which helpless Christians were forced to hold their hands to induce those men and women to deny their faith in Christ.

---

181 William Barclay, The Revelation of John, Vol. II, (London Westminster: John Knox Press, 2004), pp. 39-40.

Revelation Chapter 7

These gruesome realities remind us of "the medieval dungeon: the scrape of shackles, the screams of agony, the groans of despair. ... An ancient form of adjudication known as trial by ordeal became commonplace after 500 A.D. In trial by ordeal, a defendant submits to a grueling physical test, the outcome of which is taken as a sign from God, an indication of guilt or innocence. ... Trial by ordeal was also practiced throughout Latin Christendom. It was a favorite device for trying traitors, slaves, and foreigners. ... Trial by fire involved grasping an iron bar [heated till it was red]. A plea was offered to God: 'If this man is innocent of the charge from which he seeks to clear himself, he will take this fiery iron in his hand and appear unharmed; if he is guilty, let your most just power declare that truth in him, so that wickedness may not conquer justice but falsehood always be overcome by the truth.' The [Catholic] Church's sanction for trial by ordeal was withdrawn in 1215, by order of the Fourth Lateran Council. ... The first criminal jury trial took place in Westminster, in 1220. It included elements of ordeal. Swearing an oath was a means of bringing God's judgment into the proceedings. And there remained the threat of pain. The accused had to consent to trial by jury.

"The other choice according to a thirteenth century treatise, was *prisone forte et dure* [French for "hard and forceful imprisonment"]: 'Let their penance be this, that they be barefooted, ungirt and bareheaded, in the worst place in the prison, upon the bare ground continually night and day, that they eat only bread made of barley or bran, and that they drink not the day they eat; nor eat the day they drink, nor drink anything but water, and that they be put in irons.' Most people chose trial by jury. ... In time, the rule of law, revulsion at torture, the abolition of blood sanctions,[182] and the law of evidence became the means by which the nations of the West came to distinguish themselves from the rest of the world (including, not least, non-states like the Taliban insurgency and terrorist organizations like Al Qaeda)."[183]

7:17 "for the Lamb that is in the midst of the throne shall be their shepherd, and shall guide them unto fountains of waters of life: and God shall wipe away every tear from their eyes."

7:17 "the Lamb ... shall be their shepherd"

What an ironic, dramatic and unprecedented reversal of roles this is! But who would know better what ministry a shepherd should render than a lamb, especially the Lamb of God?

7:17 "guide them unto fountains of waters of life"

Please see the comments at 21:6 and 22:1.

7:17 "God shall wipe away every tear from their eyes"

Here again, it becomes clear that these Christians will not have been saved from torture and persecution by a rapture; they will have grievously suffered and therefore, will be comforted by God. This assurance of divine solace is given to everyone who will have been called upon to suffer for Christ in "the great tribulation." (7:14) A very similar

---
182 Blood sanction involved an executioner dismembering a condemned person's limbs from his torso.
183 Jill Lepore, *The Dark Ages, Terrorism, Counterterrorism, and the Law of Torment*, The New Yorker, March 18, 2013, p. 30.

promise is recorded in 21:3-4. There, however, it seems to refer to a more inclusive consolation to be given also to those who will have suffered more general miseries like sickness, accidents, droughts, famines, wars, and other calamities.

———

Revelation Chapter 8

Note: The realities prophesied in this chapter will become more vivid if the student relates the descriptions in the commentary to the depictions given in Maps 4a, 4b and 4c.

    G.   The seventh seal 8:1-2

        1.   Silence in heaven 8:1

8:1 "And when he opened the seventh seal, there followed a silence in heaven about the space of half an hour."

It appears that there is no description of what happens when the seventh seal is opened. Instead of beholding an event-filled scene, all we receive from heaven is silence. Why do we have this blank, this discontinuity? It probably occurs to accentuate the opening of the seventh seal which is extremely momentous. To emphasize the consequential character of the impending events, to borrow Barnes' phrase, heaven stands in suspense. With the opening of the seventh seal, we are introduced to the period of the seven trumpets.

        2.   Seven angels are given trumpets 8:2

8:2 "And I saw the seven angels that stand before God; and there were given unto them seven trumpets.

There is a hierarchy among the angels. The seven angels mentioned here, who "stand before God," along with others who stand in that sacred place (See 5:11.), belong to the highest order of angels. However, we only know the name of one of them. When Zacharias thought that because of his advanced age the announcement about fathering a child must be a mistake, the rebuffed angel said to him, "I am Gabriel, that stand in the presence of God." (Luke 1:19) Undoubtedly, these seven angels who stand in God's presence constitute or belong to that elite group known as archangels, that is ruling angels, who are mentioned in I Thessalonians 4:16 and in Jude verse 9.

VI.   The blowing of the <u>seven trumpets</u> 8:3-14:20

    A.   The power of prayer 8:3-6

8:3 "And another angel came and stood over the altar, having a golden censer; and there was given unto him much incense, that he should add it unto the prayers of all the saints upon the golden altar which was before the throne.

This altar is near the throne of grace, highlighted in Hebrews 4:16. There, we are encouraged to "draw near with boldness unto the throne of grace, that we may receive mercy, and may find grace to help us in time of need." Here, in Revelation 8:3, we have assurance that the prayers of God's saints have, indeed, reached the throne of grace. Just as Cornelius was assured that his prayers had been heard (See Acts 10:4.), so here, we Christians are assured that our prayers are not in vain. Encouragingly, we will see in verse 5 that Christians' prayers may well have a significant impact on earth.

8:4 **"And the smoke of the incense, with the prayers of the saints, went up before God out of the angel's hand."**

This verse describes the corresponding spiritual reality toward which the altar of incense in the Mosaic tabernacle pointed. The pattern or "blueprint" is described in Exodus 30:1-10 and Psalm 141:1-2.

8:5 **"And the angel taketh the censer; and he filled it with the fire of the altar, and cast it upon the earth: and there followed thunders, and voices, and lightnings, and an earthquake."**

8:5 **"cast it upon the earth"**

Barnes took the position that these words show that Christians' "prayers were not heard any longer" and that "the prayers of the saints did not prevail to turn them [fearful calamities] away."[184] Unfortunately, he came to a very wrong conclusion. The words "cast it upon the earth" do not indicate the rejection or the futility of the prayers of the saints but rather the impact on earth which ensues because of those prayers.

8:5 **"there followed thunders, and voices, and lightnings, and an earthquake"**

These phenomena were a direct consequence of the prayers of the saints. Those prayers had reached God's throne of grace. Consequently, the conditions and circumstances were overturned which collectively had brought about the period called "the great tribulation," (7:14) a period in which the Christians had grievously suffered. That revolution is implied by the word "earthquake." That "earthquake" was brought about by the seven trumpet-blowing angels who are called forth in response to the prayers of the saints. A series of disturbances culminate in an "earthquake." Though it brought Roman persecution to an end, did not immediately usher in a period of bliss but a long period of largely chaotic conditions, brought on by invasion and barbarism.

8:6 **"And the seven angels that had the seven trumpets prepared themselves to sound."**

This does not imply that the angels had been preoccupied. Rather, it probably points to their carrying out the necessary preparatory work of putting the essential social, economic, political and climatological circumstances in order.

B. Sounding of the trumpets 8:7-14:20

   1. The first trumpet 8:7

8:7 **"And the first sounded, and there followed hail and fire, mingled with blood, and they were cast upon the earth: and the third part of the earth was burnt up, and the third part of the trees was burnt up, and all green grass was burnt up."**

---

184 Albert Barnes, Notes, Explanatory and Practical on the Book of Revelation, (New York: Harper & Brothers Publishers, 1864), p. 222.

Revelation Chapter 8

8:7 "hail and fire, mingled with blood"

If climatological phenomena are referred to, then "hail and fire" would be hail accompanied by lightning. However, because the hail and fire are "mingled with blood," it is quite certain that the phrase refers to the violence of war.

8:7 "the third part of the earth"

The Roman Empire, denoted by the word "earth," consisted of three distinct regions: (See Map 5)

(1) North Africa was a region consisting of the coastal strip along the southern shore of the Mediterranean, roughly one-hundred miles deep, stretching west to east from the Atlantic to the border of the Nile Valley. The Roman Empire began to include this area in its expanding domain by the defeat of Carthage in the Third Punic War in 146 B.C.

(2) Eastern Rome consisted of the area beginning at approximately the middle of the Balkan Peninsula and extending to the Euphrates River. It included all of the Levant,[185] that is, the eastern seaboard of the Mediterranean, and Egypt. (Eastern Rome eventually became the Byzantine Empire, the rise of which is prophesied in Revelation 13:1.) The inclusion of this region into the Roman Empire began by the defeat of the army of the Ptolemaic/Selucid Empire at the Battle of Magnesia in 190 B.C. The full inclusion of Ptolemaic territory was completed by the Roman victory in the Battle of Actium in 31 B.C.

(3) Western Rome, from east to west, covered the area stretching from approximately the middle of the Balkan Peninsula to the Atlantic. In addition to half of the Balkan Peninsula, it also included two other great peninsulas: the Italian Peninsula, the original home of the Empire, and the Spanish Peninsula. On the south, Western Rome was bordered by the Mediterranean. On the north, it was bordered by the Danube and Rhine rivers but for a time also crossed the English Channel. During the days of its greatest extent it included England all the way north to the city of York. There, Hadrian (who ruled 117-138) built a wall to protect Roman territory from attacks by the Picts from the north. At approximately 450 A.D., Rome had to relinquish its hold on England and pull back to the European side of the English Channel. The Western Empire survived till "in the year 476 Romulus Augustulus ... was deposed."[186]

It seems beyond question that this three-fold division of the Roman Empire is reflected in the remarkable twelve-times-repeated phrase "the third part" in only six verses, that is, in 8:7-12. At the end of the apostolic age, when John was writing the Revelation, an alert informed reader would probably have known of the long-standing three-fold division of the Roman Empire. Therefore, he/she would have recognized that this repetitiously highlighted phrase pointed to judgment on that empire. Any Christian who was suffering from Roman state-sponsored persecution would have been assured by this prophecy that God was bringing judgment on that government which was so unjustly misusing its power.

---

185 Levant from Italian *levante*, the east [where the sun rises]. The Levant, derivative of the Latin levare, to raise. The EAST: orient. Specifically, the countries washed by the eastern part of the Mediterranean and its contiguous waters.
186 Kenneth Scott Latourette, A History of Christianity, Vol. II, (New York: Harper & Row, Publishers, 1975), p. 272.

Revelation Verse by Verse

8:7 "the third part of the earth was burnt up and the third part of the trees was burnt up and all green grass was burnt up"

This is a prophetic description of the consequences of the Vandal invasion of western North Africa which took place in 428/429 A.D. (See Map 4a.) It initially engulfed the three westernmost provinces of Roman North Africa: Mauretania, Numidia and Proconsular Africa. The well-known cities of Carthage and Hippo were located in the province of Proconsular Africa.

Obviously, to attack North Africa, the Vandal army, coming from southern Spain, could not cross the 8.9-mile-wide Strait of Gibraltar, narrow though it is, without an adequate flotilla. Ironically, the required fleet was provided through treachery. The Vandals were given the use of Roman ships because Boniface, an offended imperial general, wanted to take vengeance on the empire. Succinctly the story is this:

"Count Boniface, embittered by the attitude of the Augusta which was fostered, as we know, by the intriguer Aetius, had decided to call in the help of the Vandals. Partly from anger and partly from fear, Boniface sent to Gonderic, the king of the Vandals, who was encamped in Spain, a trusted messenger charged with an offer to hand over to him, in return for his aid, a third of the Roman possessions in Africa. Gonderic's death placed Genseric, his son, at the head of the Vandal army (mixed with Goths and Alans), estimated as numbering eighty thousand fighters. Through the Strait of Gibraltar they passed from Spain into Africa in May 428, Boniface having placed at their disposition a large part of his navy."[187] Previously, "The vandals had been able to come in [to Western Europe] by way of Gaul, then had occupied Spain, and finally had settled permanently in North Africa. [Ultimately] Carthage was the vandal capital."[188]

Augustine, the great Roman Catholic bishop, whose headquarters were at Hippo, boldly and sternly exhorted Boniface to reverse course and save North Africa from the depredations of the Vandals. At great personal risk, a priest named Paul delivered Augustine's letter to Boniface in which the great but traitorous general was confronted starkly with his responsibility for the disaster and his duty to rise against the Vandals. Augustine first asked, "You say you have just reasons for your action?" Without waiting for an answer Augustine turned to accusation <u>in words which fully correspond to the triple description of earth, trees and grass being burnt up</u>. He said, "What shall I say of Africa's devastation by the barbarians which is met by no resistance? You do nothing to prevent this calamity! Who could have believed such a thing! **They ravage, pillage, change into a desert this prosperous and populous land. Not even a single fruit tree remains standing.** But, you reply, these things should be blamed on those who have offended you, those who have repaid your loyalty with bitter enmity. ... But Boniface was committed to the rebellion he had begun – too proud to denounce it, too involved to withdraw."[189]

---

187 Jacques Chabannes, <u>St. Augustine</u>, trans. Julie Kernan (Garden City, New York: Doubleday & Company, Inc., 1962), p. 197
188 Downey Glanville, <u>Constantinople In the Age of Justinian</u>, (Norman, Oklahoma: University of Oklahoma Press, 1960), p. 80.
189 Jacques Chabannes, <u>St. Augustine</u>, trans. Julie Kernan (Garden City, New York: Doubleday & Company, Inc., 1962), pp. 198-199.

Revelation Chapter 8

Even yet, a visitor to North Africa is reminded of its dreadful history when he drives past Roman "aqueducts dismembered during the Vandals' century of anarchic misrule and [are] now bleaching like stone bones in the sun."[190]

North Africa's ability to resist the Vandal invasion was not only neutralized by the betrayal of Boniface, the governor/general, but was also undermined by the weakness, disorganization and distraction growing out of the long-running Donatist-Catholic feud, usually called "The Donatist Controversy." That feud was so extensive and hard-fought that it nearly became a civil war. Augustine led the Catholic side of that horrible confrontation. That feud became so damaging that Emperor Constantine called a church council at Rome in 313 in a vain attempt to solve the problem.

2. The second trumpet 8:8-9

8:8 "And the second angel sounded, and as it were a great mountain burning with fire was cast into the sea: and the third part of the sea became blood;"

8:8 "the third part of the sea"

This sea is the Mediterranean. Just as the Roman Empire was divided into three regions, so, as a consequence of geography, the Mediterranean was and still is similarly divided into thirds. (See Map 6.) Going from west to east, the first one-third is that part of the Mediterranean which lies between the Strait of Gibraltar, western gateway to the Mediterranean, and the Strait of Sicily where the seaway is narrowly confined between the Island of Sicily on the north and on the south by the northern tip of Cape Bon which protrudes toward Sicily from the North African shore. This is the western Mediterranean, constituting one-third of the entire sea. It is unmistakably defined by two narrow waterways, the Strait of Gibraltar, being only 8.9 miles wide, and the Strait of Sicily, being about 90 miles wide. It is this western "third part of the sea" in which we should look for the fulfillment of the second-trumpet prophecy.

The eastern two-thirds of the Mediterranean are divided by the Island of Crete. Islands west of Crete "provided a stopping route from Venice to Crete; from Crete a busy trade route linked Cyprus and Syria."[191] Thus, the strategic Island of Crete was, and still is, the fulcrum between the central Mediterranean and the eastern Mediterranean, both of which featured prominently in Paul's voyage to Rome. (See Acts 27:7-21.)

8:8 "a great mountain burning with fire was cast into the sea"

This "great mountain" points either to the incendiary Vandals or to their talented but ruthless fiery leader, Genseric (also spelled Gaiseric), or to both, becoming the totally dominating sea power in the western Mediterranean.

When <u>the Germanic Gothic people (See Map 4b.), of whom the Vandals were a part</u>, migrated from Scandinavia, their earliest known home, "they came in contact with the old Greek population of southwestern Russia (the great land bridge for migration between Asia and Europe), [and there] the Goths learned how to build a fleet of ships and soon

---

190 Rick Atkinson, <u>An Army at Dawn The War in North Africa</u>, 1942-1943, (New York: Henry Holt and Company, 2002), p. 168.
191 Fernand Braudel, <u>The Mediterranean and the Mediterranean World in the Age of Philip II</u>, Vol. 1, (New York: Harper & Row Publishers, 1972), p. 149.

were raiding and pillaging the famous old cities of mainland Greece and along the coasts of the Aegean Sea."[192]

"As we have seen [in the comments on the first-trumpet prophecy at 8:7], approximately 80,000 Vandals crossed over into North Africa at the invitation of [Boniface] the Roman governor. Gaiseric [Genseric], the Vandal king and one of the ablest of the German rulers, then proceeded to take over all of [western Roman] Africa; it was during his siege of Hippo that the great St. Augustine ... died. From their kingdom in North Africa the Vandals now dominated the [western] Mediterranean with their ships. In 455 they even sacked Rome. The destruction they are believed to have wrought everywhere has given rise to the term *vandalism*, 'senseless destruction.'"[193]

The ability to acquire the ships which the Vandals used to dominate the western Mediterranean grew out of their capture of Carthage. From that point, being "in possession of the best harbor west of Alexandria with its shipyards and experienced ship builders, Gaiseric [Genseric] could be expected in a short time to have a fleet able to carry the Vandalic pirates anywhere in the Mediterranean."[194]

In accordance with that expectation, "After the conquest of Carthage, 'they created a fleet of light cruisers and attacked the empire by sea, as no other Teutonic people had done or was to do in the Mediterranean'"[195]

The Vandals not only raided and conquered, but also established a kingdom in the areas over which they triumphed. As previously noted, "the Vandals of the south of Spain, under their king Genseric [Gaiseric], embarked *en masse* for North Africa (in 429), became masters of Carthage (in 439), secured the mastery of the sea, raided, captured, and pillaged Rome (in 455), crossed into Sicily, and set up a kingdom in West Sicily, which endured there for a hundred years (up to 534). At the time of its greatest extent (477) this Vandal kingdom included also Corsica, Sardinia, and the Balearic Isles, as well as much of North Africa."[196]

"The sack of Rome by [Genseric] Gaiseric's Vandals in 455, left the city gutted and prostrate. Only the most strenuous and heroic efforts could now raise Rome and Italy from the slough, whereas in fact the remains of Roman political power fell into the hands of German mercenary leaders."[197]

Only forty-five years before the Vandals sacked the city of Rome, "it had been pillaged thoroughly by Alaric and his Visigoths in 410."[198] "The sack of their city was a tremendous shock to the Romans, evoking the famous response of St. Augustine's *City of God*, yet as a military event it was far less momentous. Although for three days the

---

192 Deno J. Geanakoplos, Medieval Western Civilization and the Byzantine and Islamic Worlds, (Lexington, Massachusetts: D. C. Heath & Company, 1979), p. 48.
193 Deno J. Geanakoplos, Medieval Western Civilization and the Byzantine and Islamic Worlds, (Lexington, Massachusetts: D. C. Heath & Company, 1979), pp. 51-52.
194 J. Otto Maenchen-Helfen, The World of the Huns, Studies in Their History and Culture, (Berkeley: University of California Press, 1973), p. 108.
195 J. Otto Maenchen-Helfen, The World of the Huns, Studies in Their History and Culture, (Berkeley: University of California Press, 1973), p. 100.
196 H. G. Wells, The Outline of History, Vol. I, (New York: Doubleday & Co., Inc, 1971), p. 432.
197 James Westfall Thompson and Edgar Nathaniel Johnson, An Introduction to Medieval Europe, 300-1500, (New York: W. W. Norton & Co., Inc., 1937), p. 101.
198 Downey Glanville, Constantinople In the Age of Justinian, (Norman, Oklahoma: University of Oklahoma Press, 1960), p. 81.

Revelation Chapter 8

Visigoths pillaged Rome, they left untouched most of the main buildings, especially the churches. Alaric then moved southward in the direction of Africa, probably in search of food for his people, but in southern Italy he died. [In a procedure like that which, some say, was later employed in the burial of Attila], a river was diverted from its course, Alaric and his treasures were buried in its bed, and the river allowed to flow again over the grave."[199]

8:8 "the third part of the sea became blood"

These prophetic words anticipated the violent and bloody conquest and utter domination of the western third part of the Mediterranean Sea by the Vandals. The Romans were not able to resist the Vandal triumph by challenging it with organized naval warfare. This permitted the Vandals to challenge and violently destroy all Roman seagoing vessels between the Strait of Gibraltar and the Strait of Sicily. It was a naval and maritime disaster from which Rome was never able to recover.

8:9 "and there died the third part of the creatures which were in the sea, even they that had life; and the third part of the ships was destroyed."

8:9 "third part of the creatures which were in the sea, even they that had life;"

The death of these "creatures" probably does not imply an extinction of the third part of aquatic life, but points to the death of Rome's active-duty naval personnel – her sailors and seaman in the western third part of the Mediterranean. Should anyone think that the word "creature" may not point to humans, then note that the same basic Greek word *ktismaton* is used in James 1:18, II Corinthians 5:17 and Galatians 6:15 in which it clearly points to humans. "They that had life" probably points to the seamen on active duty and those still capable of active sea duty.

8:9 "the third part of the ships was destroyed"

This means that most, if not all, Roman ships in the western third of the Mediterranean Sea would be destroyed. This actually happened because Rome had gone on "its way quite stupidly, oblivious to the growth of a newer and more powerful piracy in the north. The same unimaginative quality made the Romans leave the seaways of the Mediterranean undeveloped. When presently the barbarians pressed down to the warm water, we read of no swift transport of [Roman] armies from Spain or Africa or Asia to the rescue of Italy and the Adriatic coasts. Instead, we see the Vandals becoming masters of the western Mediterranean without so much as a naval battle."[200]

Rome's western naval power, at this point, had suffered a disastrous, unrecoverable reversal. Much earlier, "it was the Roman control of the water that forced Hannibal 'to that long perilous march through Gaul in which more than half his veteran troops wasted away. Throughout the war, the [Roman] legions passed by water, unmolested and unwearied, between Spain, which was Hannibal's base, and Italy.' Mahan points out that there were no great sea battles in the Second Punic War [218-201 B.C.], because Rome's

---

[199] Deno J. Geanakoplos, Medieval Western Civilization and the Byzantine and Islamic Worlds, (Lexington, Massachusetts: D. C. Heath & Company, 1979), p. 50.
[200] H. G. Wells, The Outline of History, Vol. I, (New York: Doubleday & Co., Inc, 1971), pp. 419-420.

mastery of the Mediterranean was a deciding factor in Carthage's defeat."[201] However, during the 655 years between the end of the Second Punic War and the Vandals' sacking of the city of Rome, the Roman Empire had lost naval control of the Mediterranean.

The Romans, then ruling from their eastern capital of Constantinople, did have a naval fleet stationed on the island of Sicily. However, "as soon as they learnt that a major Hun attack had developed, Theodosius and his ministers recalled the fleet from Sicily, where, owing to the subtle diplomacy of Gaiseric it had achieved nothing against the Vandals and had served only to oppress the Sicilians."[202]

Historical background for the third trumpet. In the brief prophecy of Revelation 8:10-11 we are given a very succinct anticipatory account of the second great migration of an ethnic people group which was destined to significantly impact both Christianity and Western Civilization. The account points to the people known as the Huns. A prior comparable major ethnic population shift, highlighted at 8:8 in the prophetic account of Revelation, was that of the Germanic people to whom, it should be noted, both the Goths and the Vandals belonged. As the existence of the country of Germany reminds us of the coming of the Germanic people to the West, so the presence of the country of Hungary gives testimony to the arrival and settlement of the Huns. The impact of the Germanic people on both Christianity and European civilization has proven to have been much greater than that of the Hungarian people.

Before the Huns invaded Europe, Christian missionaries had been sent among them by John Chrysostom (lived 345-407), bishop at Constantinople. He dispatched those missionaries "to some of the nomadic Scyths who were encamped along the Danube. The term 'nomadic Scyths' is one which our authority uses elsewhere of the Huns and of no one else, and we have no doubt that the great patriarch of Constantinople had endeavored to have the new barbarians converted. But again no claim is made that the missionaries met with the slightest success. One of their greatest difficulties must have been that of language. John Chrysostom himself could find an interpreter easily enough when he wished to preach to the Goths in the capital; but as we shall see later, the number of Romans who knew the Hun language was exceedingly small, so that churchmen qualified to preach among them could only have been acquired with the utmost difficulty, if, indeed, at all."[203]

3. The third trumpet 8:10-11

8:10 "And the third angel sounded, and there fell from heaven a great star, burning as a torch, and it fell upon the third part of the rivers, and upon the fountains of the waters;"

8:10 "fell from heaven"

What "heaven" was this? It seems correct to identify the "great star" as Attila the Hun. The heaven from which he fell was the marvelous, abundant and collective endowment of perception, charisma, magnetism, dynamism and analytical ability residing in his personality, a heavenly constellation of exceptional gifts. Because of that generous

---
201 Robert D. Kaplan, The Revenge of Geography, (New York: Random House, Inc., 2012), p. 107.
202 E. A. Thompson, The Huns, (Oxford: Blackwell Publishers Ltd., 1999), p. 90.
203 E. A. Thompson, The Huns, (Oxford: Blackwell Publishers Ltd., 1999), p. 44.

Revelation Chapter 8

genetic benefaction, he could lead and inspire his fellow Huns. Had he devoted those great heavenly gifts to lead his fellow Huns in developing fruitful productive lives rather than to careers in systematic organized plunder and massacre, the Huns could have led the world in benevolence and creativity. The fall was the astoundingly horrible misuse of his magnificent gifts.

"Did the Huns make no *direct* contribution to the progress of Europe? Had they nothing to offer besides the terror which uprooted the Germanic nations and sent them fleeing into the Roman Empire? The answer is, 'No,' they offered nothing. Their society was such that they could make no contribution like those of the Germans, the Persians, and the Arabs. They were mere plunderers and marauders."[204]

8:10   "a great star, burning as a torch"

The great star was Attila, but his career was brief. He began joint rule with his brother in 434. His term as sole ruler of the Huns began with his murder of Bleda, his elder brother, in 445. Thus, we might say that the "torch" soon burned out since his death occurred in 453. "The end [of Attila's entire dynasty] came only [16 years later] in 469. Marcellinus Comes[205] has the short entry, 'the head of Dinzic, son of Attila, king of the Huns, was brought to Constantinople.' The *Chronicon Paschale* gives more details: 'Dinzirichus [the longer form of his name], Attila's son, was killed by Anagastes, general in Thrace. His head was brought to Constantinople, carried in procession through the Middle Street and fixed on a pole at the Wooden Circus. The whole city turned out to look at it.' The few Huns south of the Danube who did follow the Ostrogoths, like the Bittugur, gradually lost their ethnic identity or joined the Bulgarian raiders."[206]

"Despite his victory on the river Utus in 447, Attila suffered bloody losses in the battle there. He was heavily defeated in Gaul in 451, and in 452 he was repulsed from Italy by plague and famine. The following year he died and his empire was divided among his sons. They at once quarreled among themselves. After internal struggles they engaged in a series of costly battles with their subjects, and were routed in the struggle on the river Nadao."[207]

But as the prophecy says, it was "a great star." For one thing, "Attila's greatness lay in his remarkable insight into the potentialities of Hun society. He saw the direction in which the changes taking place in that society in his day were tending. He realized more clearly than any of his predecessors that, if all the tribes could be united under an unquestioned and absolute leader, the Huns would form an unparalleled instrument for the exploitation of the peoples of central Europe."[208]

Probably, it was Attila's vision of a totally unified leadership for the Huns which motivated him to murder his brother. In any case, "there can be little doubt that Attila murdered his elder brother in the year 445. Of the origin of the dispute we know nothing.

---

204 E. A. Thompson, The Huns, (Oxford: Blackwell Publishers Ltd., 1999), p. 237.
205 Comes died about 534 A.D. He was a Latin historian of the Eastern Roman Empire. He spent most of his life at the court in Constantinople.
206 J. Otto Maenchen-Helfen, The World of the Huns, Studies in Their History and Culture, (Berkeley: Univ. of California Press, 1973), p. 168.
207 E. A. Thompson, The Huns, (Oxford: Blackwell Publishers Ltd., 1999), p. 198.
208 E. A. Thompson, The Huns, (Oxford: Blackwell Publishers Ltd., 1999), p. 230.

Its result was that the peoples formerly governed and exploited by Bleda now came under the direct control of Attila."[209]

8:10 "the third part of the rivers"

The impact of the Huns under Attila was not maritime as was that of the Vandals, but was uniquely and overwhelmingly riverine. Professor J. Otto Maenchen-Helfen reflects this emphasis as he relates the history of the Huns by citing their activities in relation to many of those rivers. (Any interested student may compile the list of those rivers from the index of Professor Maenchen-Helfen's The World of the Huns, Studies in Their History and Culture.)

First, they impacted the watershed of the eastern "third part of the rivers" by many attacks on that segment of the empire, and subsequently, the western rivers by attacking the western "third part" of the empire. Cumulatively, the size of the empire of the Huns, which resulted from their aggression, was breathtaking. "We may conclude that all the Germanic and other nations between the Alps and the Baltic, and between the Caspian (or somewhat west of it) and a line drawn an unknown distance east of the Rhine, recognized Attila and Bleda [Attila's older brother] as their masters. Although the two brothers always acted in concert, so far as we know, and regarded their empire as a single property, they divided it between them and ruled separately; but we do not know which portion was allotted to each."[210] (See Map 4c.) "Attila's empire stretched from the Caucasus to the confines of France and Denmark."[211]

8:11 "and the name of the star is called Wormwood: and the third part of the waters became wormwood; and many men died of the waters, because they were made bitter."

8:11 "the name of the star is called Wormwood"

Botanically, the name wormwood refers to "any of a genus (*Artemisia*) of composite woody herbs; *esp*: a European plant (*A. absinthium*) yielding a bitter slightly aromatic green oil used in absinthe [a distilled, highly alcoholic drink]. Thus, [it means] something bitter or grievous."[212]

The concept which is carried by the name "Wormwood" as it is applied to "the star" may be understood by its previous eight-times use in scripture. In Deuteronomy 29:18 it is paralleled with gall. In Proverbs 5:4 it expresses the epitome of bitterness. In both Jeremiah 9:15 and 23:15 it is associated with the water of gall. In Lamentations 3:15 the word expresses the ultimate degree of bitterness, while in Lamentations 3:19 it is associated with misery and gall. In Amos 5:7 wormwood expresses the antithesis to justice, and similarly, in Amos 6:12 it is expresses the epitome of unrighteousness.

8:11 "the third part of the waters became Wormwood"

The location of those riverine waters has been identified in the comments on 8:10. (See Map 4c.)

---

209 E. A. Thompson, The Huns, (Oxford: Blackwell Publishers Ltd., 1999), p. 97.
210 E. A. Thompson, The Huns, (Oxford: Blackwell Publishers Ltd., 1999), p. 85.
211 E. A. Thompson, The Huns, (Oxford: Blackwell Publishers Ltd., 1999), p. 196.
212 Webster's Seventh New Collegiate Dictionary, (Springfield, MA: G. & C. Miriam Company, Publishers, 1971), p. 1030.

Revelation Chapter 8

8:11 "many men died of the waters because they were made bitter"

There were many categories and intensities of that bitterness. There was the bitterness of being maimed, of being crippled, of being paralyzed, of being impoverished, of being looted, of being raped, of being orphaned, of being widowed, of being made a refugee, of being starved, of being humiliated, of being enslaved, and by countless other varieties of degradation and deprivation, most of which, sooner or later, led to death.

4. The fourth trumpet 8:12-13

8:12 "And the fourth angel sounded, and the third part of the sun was smitten, and the third part of the moon, and the third part of the stars; that the third part of them should be darkened, and the day should not shine for the third part of it, and the night in like manner."

8:12 "third part"

In just this one verse, the phrase "the third part" is stressed five times. This five-times-emphasized "third part" refers to the western one-third of the Roman Empire which was brought to an end in 476 by the crowning of Odovacar. "The German mercenaries in the army, quartered on the Italian landholders, demanded what their fellow Germans had received in other parts of the empire, one-third of the land of Italy. When this was refused they crowned Odovacar, a Scirian chieftain and one of themselves killed Orestes, and deposed the twelve-year-old Emperor Romulus in 476. So the line of Roman emperors in the west ended."[213]

8:12 "sun ... moon ... stars"

The loss of luminescence from the sun, moon and stars not only points to the total overthrow of the Roman political system in the western third part of the empire, but also to the beginning of a prolonged period of darkness. That period is usually called the Dark Ages due to the loss of enlightenment growing out of the death of the educational process, a process dependent upon political order, vigor and stability.

What the educational system had been, before its vast area-wide collapse, may be conceptualized by estimating the number of specialists who would have been required to establish and maintain the great Roman civilization. It was essential to have highly trained engineers, surveyors, quarrymen, cartographers, coordinators, masons, landscapers, architects, designers, administrators, transportation experts, accountants, carpenters, shipwrights and other categories of highly-skilled workers. These were necessary to plan and develop new townships, and to bring into being the great coliseums, triumphal arches, forums, public buildings, aqueducts and far-flung road systems. Even today the surviving segments of those great engineering triumphs, some still functioning, amaze any thoughtful beholder. Such an unparalleled infrastructure could not have been created without a skilled, talented and experienced workforce. Such an elect body of capable people points to a long-standing educational system of an unusually high standard. "Even when it [Europe] suffered severe changes and considerable disintegration, as during the barbarian invasions of the fifth century, enough

---

213 James Westfall Thompson and Edgar Nathaniel Johnson, <u>An Introduction to Medieval Europe, 300-1500</u>, (New York: W. W. Norton & Co., Inc., 1937), p. 101.

of its past always survived to provide real continuity. The greatest turbulence never destroyed all elements of the old order."[214]

The collapse of the process and the means of learning in the area of the Western Roman Empire, an area equivalent to that of modern Western Europe, was so devastating, pervasive and long-lasting that the scholars and politicians who later substantially contributed to its eventual recovery should be gratefully acknowledged.

Chronologically, the first recognition should go to Cassiodorus and Boethius, two ministers who served in the court of the Ostrogothic king, Theodoric. "When he died, on August 30, 526, Italy lost the greatest of her early medieval rulers, unequaled until the days of Charlemagne."[215] In 488, after freeing northern Italy from the barbaric rule of the Huns by murdering Odovacar, their ruthless leader, and having all the Hunnish troops and their families slaughtered, Theodoric established an Ostrogothic kingdom. During his long period of rule, "few of the existing institutions in Italy were changed."[216] That gave stability to society. Also, he gave enough freedom to Cassiodorus and Boethius that they were able to undertake some fundamental work in what later proved to have been an initial phase of the renewal of learning. For example, while Boethius was in prison on false charges, he wrote *The Consolation of Philosophy* which became "fundamental to all subsequent medieval speculative thought."[217] Also, his translations of Aristotle "were virtually all of Aristotle that was known in the West for half a millennium."[218] In spite of the great work he did while in prison, Theodoric "ordered [him] to be garrotted [that was death by strangulation which was carried out by using an iron collar]."[219] At the same time, "the inspiration of Cassiodorus helped to make monasteries oases of learning in the West until the early eleventh century."[220] "During this time he collected from Italy and North Africa Greek and Latin manuscripts of such wide variety and scope that his monks had a considerable library to work with."[221]

Space does not permit description of the works of Gregory, Bishop of Tours, who wrote the *History of the Franks*, Jerome, translator of the *Latin Vulgate* edition of the Bible, and Augustine, who wrote *Confessions* and *The City of God*. Writings of all of those scholars ultimately made noteworthy contributions to the revival of learning in the West. However, attention must be given, at least briefly, to two other notable scholars.

First, is Bede (c. 673-735), a monk whose work centered in a monastery at Jarrow in the far northeast corner of England. "His *Ecclesiastical History of the English People* ranks as the best history written in the West between the sixth and twelfth centuries. Composed in a good Latin style, the work also exhibits a genuine historical sense. Bede almost

---

214 David Thomson, Europe Since Napoleon, (New York: Penguin Books Ltd., 1978), p. 82.
215 John Julius Norwich, Absolute Monarchs, A History of the Papacy, (New York: Random House, 2011), p. 29.
216 James Westfall Thompson and Edgar Nathaniel Johnson, An Introduction to Medieval Europe, 300-1500, (New York: W. W. Norton & Co., Inc., 1937), p. 184.
217 Deno J. Geanakoplos, Medieval Western Civilization and the Byzantine and Islamic Worlds, (Lexington, Massachusetts: D. C. Heath & Company, 1979), p. 74.
218 Deno J. Geanakoplos, Medieval Western Civilization and the Byzantine and Islamic Worlds, (Lexington, Massachusetts: D. C. Heath & Company, 1979), p. 73.
219 John Julius Norwich, Absolute Monarchs, A History of the Papacy, (New York: Random House, 2011), p. 28.
220 Deno J. Geanakoplos, Medieval Western Civilization and the Byzantine and Islamic Worlds, (Lexington, Massachusetts: D. C. Heath & Company, 1979), p. 74.
221 James Westfall Thompson and Edgar Nathaniel Johnson, An Introduction to Medieval Europe, 300-1500, (New York: W. W. Norton & Co., Inc., 1937), p. 206.

Revelation Chapter 8

invariably cites his sources of information."[222] He also "popularized the common B.C./A.D. dating system. ... [He] showed how to calculate the date of Easter and explicitly taught that the earth was round 'like a ball.' From this, he showed why the length of days and nights changed with the seasons, and how tides were dragged by the moon."[223]

Second, in any account of the ultimate revival of learning in the West one must not forget the remarkable work done by Alcuin (735-804). His work actually antedated that done by Hunayn ibn Ishaq (808-873), known in the West as Joannitius, the great Christian translator who worked in Baghdad under Caliph Harun al-Rashid (reigned 786-809) and his son, Caliph al-Ma'mun, in a translation center known as The House of Wisdom.

"Charlemagne ordered that reading and writing would be taught in all monasteries. [To implement that great vision], in 782 he brought the Northumbrian scholar Alcuin to his capital at Aachen as, in effect, minister of education. Alcuin founded flourishing schools, and established standards in teaching. At his scriptoria, thousands of books from the ancient world were scrupulously copied. Almost all those Latin classics which have survived in Europe have come down to us through these copyists. The Carolingian Renaissance thus begun was to blossom in the reign of Charlemagne's grandson Charles the Bald."[224]

"Alcuin wrote a number of educational manuals. He encouraged questions of his pupils, of whom several were later famous, rather than being content with memorization. In material content, he made Augustine basic. For method, he featured the Latin grammarians. Most of his public work was, of course, a fight for simple literacy in an ocean of barbarism."[225] The work of Alcuin had such an uplifting impact upon society that it has been called the Carolingian Renaissance.

The main reason these great educational and intellectual initiatives did not contemporaneously spark a widespread revival of learning in Europe was because of the economic stranglehold which the Muslim world had on Europe, forcing its people into dire penury. That Islamic stranglehold was only broken by the voyages of Vasco da Gama which began in 1498.

8:13 **"And I saw, and I heard an eagle, flying in mid heaven, saying with a great voice, Woe, woe, woe, for them that dwell on the earth, by reason of the other voices of the trumpet of the three angels, who are yet to sound."**

8:13 "mid heaven"

See the comments on 14:6 at page 218.

8:13 "Woe, woe, woe"

Events thus far portrayed had been devastating to the cause of Christ. Worse developments, measured in intensity, duration and scope lay ahead. Three additional

---

222 Deno J. Geanakoplos, Medieval Western Civilization and the Byzantine and Islamic Worlds, (Lexington, Massachusetts: D. C. Heath & Company, 1979), p. 78.
223 Carl Wieland, quoting Gary Baxter in *Getting The Word Out*, CREATION, Vol. 35, No. 3, 2013, p. 21.
224 Michael Worth Davison (ed.), When, Where, Why & How It Happened (London: The Reader's Digest Association Ltd., 1995), p. 81.
225 Franklin H. Littell, The Macmillan Atlas History of Christianity, (New York: Macmillan Publishing Co. Inc., 1976), p. 29.

historic movements would prove to be so destructive that each one is announced with the word, "woe."

———

Revelation Chapter 9

5. The fifth trumpet 9:1-12

9:1 **"And the fifth angel sounded and I saw a star from heaven fallen unto the earth: and there was given to him the key of the pit of the abyss."**

9:1 "the fifth angel sounded"

While in the overall sequence of the seven trumpet angels (8:2) this angel is number five, he is the first of the three angels who are called "the woe angels." (See 8:13.) The culmination of the career of this first Woe angel will be announced at 9:12.

The events indicated by the blasts on the trumpets of the first four angels, as we have seen, have taken us to 476 A.D. Thus, the sounding of the trumpet by the fifth angel must be subsequent to those events.

9:1 "I saw a star"

Clearly, the "star" represents a person, since it is referred to by the pronoun "him" in verse 1. (The NIV says the key was given to the star. However, in verse 2 the personal pronoun is used in reference to the star, "when *he* opened the abyss.") So, it is clear that the "star" refers to a person.

It is well known that in the Bible a star is often used as a symbol for people in positions of leadership. Note three familiar passages: First, is Genesis 37:9-10 which tells us, "He dreamed yet another dream, and told it to his brethren, and said, 'Behold, I have dreamed yet a dream; and, behold, the sun and the moon and eleven **stars** made obeisance to me.' And he told it to his father, and to his brethren; and his father rebuked him, and said unto him, 'What is this dream that thou hast dreamed? Shall I and thy mother and thy brethren indeed come to bow down ourselves to thee to the earth?'"

A second passage is Revelation 22:16, "I Jesus have sent mine angel to testify unto you these things for the churches. I am the root and the offspring of David, the bright, the morning **star**."(See also Numbers 24:17.)

A third passage is Revelation 1:20. It describes how Jesus holds seven **stars** in his right hand. Those stars are identified as "the angels [messengers, that is, preachers] of the seven churches."

9:1 "a star from heaven fallen unto the earth"

Be sure to read the comments at Revelation 8:10 about a previous star which had fallen from heaven. Some think that the star mentioned here represents Satan. However, if we assume that it does, then John's chronology is badly distorted. Satan seems to have fallen initially sometime before the creation of Adam. Of course, theoretically, the expression may refer to some later fall of Satan. An example of such a fall is found in Jesus' statement at the return of the seventy: "And the seventy returned with joy, saying, Lord even the demons are subject unto us in thy name. And he said unto them, I beheld Satan fallen as lightning from heaven." (Luke 10:17-18)

But this fallen star in Revelation 9:1 does not seem to refer to the fall of Satan because this fallen star seeks the help of Satan, who is clearly referred to in this vision as "the angel of the abyss" whose "name in Hebrew is Abaddon, and in the Greek tongue he hath the name Apollyon." (Revelation 9:11) The word Apollyon means destroyer. We know Satan comes to destroy. (cf. John 10:10) Satan himself is the true Apollyon.

When it is said that, "They have over them as king the angel of the abyss:" (Revelation 9:11a), it seems the "star" is included in the pronoun "they." When anyone uses the key to Satan's abode to get help for his cause, he first must surrender his own autonomy to Satan. This requisite surrender to Satan is clearly seen in the demand which he made of Jesus when he unsuccessfully ordered, "Fall down and worship me." (Matthew 4:9)

Many evil systems, movements or entities start with a fall. See, for example, Revelation 18:2 which says, "Fallen, fallen is Babylon the great, and is become a habitation of demons, and a hold of every unclean spirit, and a hold of every unclean and hateful bird." The fall mentioned in Revelation 18:2 describes the origin of spiritual Babylon, not its doom. It was once something noble, grand and exalted. It was once Christ's church in Rome. But it fell. Once, as a church following the apostles' teaching, it was part of the new Jerusalem (See Galatians 4:26 and Hebrews 12:22.) but, abandoning that standard, it became Babylon.

The fall from "heaven" represents a series of great misfortunes which befell the "star's" family which brought about the fall of the star. The star mentioned in Revelation 9:1 fell both economically, and socially. Often, many of the elements of social acceptability rest on one's economic standing. If one loses his economic advantage it is almost predictable that his social standing will also suffer.

An ethical and moral fall is clearly indicated in this passage. When the key of the abyss was given to the star, he was willing to use it to enlist the powers of darkness in his cause. He used the key to open the abyss, the abode of Satan and evil. (9:2) In short, he embraced the concept that "the end justifies the means." From this we may judge what the future of the movement would prove to be which was ultimately founded by this fallen luminary.

In a series of questions the Koran reveals the initial stages of the fall of the star: "Did He not find thee an orphan and protect thee? Did He not find thee wandering and direct thee? Did He not find thee destitute and enrich thee?" This poignant passage comes from verses 6-8 of the Koran's Surah 93. With near universal agreement, the words are thought to refer to the very precarious early life of Muhammad.

The earliest surviving biography of Muhammad is that written by Ibn Ishaq (b. 85 - d. 150/151 A.H.[226]) The great Arabist, A. Guillaume, who translated Ibn Ishaq's Life of

---

[226] AH stands for the Latin, Anno Hegirae, i.e., in the year of the Hegira (Hijra), Muhammad's flight from Mecca to Medina, which occurred in 622 A.D.

Revelation Chapter 9

Muhammad into English, says of Ishaq's work, "no book known to the Arabs or to us can compare in comprehensiveness, arrangement, or systematic treatment, with Ibn Ishaq's work."

The "fall" represents a series of tragedies which befell his family and changed Muhammad's status in life. In deft strokes, Ibn Ishaq recorded the crucial events which substantiate the arresting and touching account given to us in the quotation from Surah 93.

First, was the death of Muhammad's father. Ibn Ishaq's account tells us that, "'Abdullah the apostle's father died while his mother was still pregnant."[227]

Second, was the death of Muhammad's mother. "When he was six years old his mother Amina died. … Thus the apostle was left to his grandfather ['Abdul-Muttalib] for whom they made a bed in the shade of the Ka'ba."[228]

Third, was the death of Muhammad's grandfather. "When the apostle was eight years of age, eight years after the 'year of the elephant,'[229] his grandfather died. … After the death of 'Abdul-Muttalib the apostle lived with his uncle Abu Talib, for (so they allege) the former had confided him to his care because he and 'Abdullah, the apostle's father, were brothers by the same mother, … It was Abu Talib who used to look after the apostle after the death of his grandfather and he [Muhammad] became one of his family."[230]

Johnson succinctly summarized the star's fall by reminding us that Muhammad "belonged by birth to the princely house of Koreish, the ruling family of Mecca. At his birth his grandfather was the ruling prince. His grandfather and his father, in the view of the surrounding nations, were prominent stars. But, just [before] his birth his father died, and very soon after his grandfather also. The boy, apparently destined to rule his country, was set aside, and a different family received the headship of the tribe, the governorship of Mecca, and the keys of the Caaba. Though by birth a star he becomes now a *fallen star*, his prospects for life apparently blasted, and at manhood he entered into the service of a rich widow as a servant, in which capacity he visited Damascus, to traffic in the markets of that great city."[231]

Clan and Family Affiliation: Muhammad was born into the Beni Hashim clan of the Arab Quraish tribe, in which the members of the Beni Umaiya clan were long-time rivals. Ultimately, the great Sunni-Shia rift in Islam grew out of the rivalry and animosity between those two clans in the Quraish tribe.

The Illiterate Prophet: Though Muhammad's uncle, Abu Talib, never became a Muslim, until death he remained completely and unfailingly loyal to his nephew. But, being a poor man he could not afford to give him an education. Appropriately therefore, Surah 7:157, according to Pickthall's translation, calls Muhammad, "the Prophet who can neither read nor write." However, Yusuf Ali translated it: "The unlettered Prophet."

---

227 Ibn Ishaq, The Life of Muhammad, Trans. A. Guillaume, (Karachi: Oxford University Press, 1982), p. 69.
228 Ibn Ishaq, The Life of Muhammad, Trans. A. Guillaume, (Karachi: Oxford University Press, 1982), p. 73.
229 In 570, when Abraha was Ethiopian viceroy in Yemen, a pagan from Mecca desecrated the resplendent church building which Abraha had constructed in San'a, capital of Yemen. In vengeance, Abraha unsuccessfully led an army against Mecca., in which was one war elephant.
230 Ibn Ishaq, The Life of Muhammad, Trans. A. Guillaume, (Karachi: Oxford University Press, 1982), pp. 73-79.
231 B. W. Johnson, A Vision of the Ages, (Hollywood, California: Old Paths Book Club, n.d.), p. 96.

Revelation Verse by Verse

"About A.D. 609 [specifically 610 A.D.], in the deserts of Arabia, one of the most remarkable, most talented, most brilliant leaders of men that the world has ever known, began his work. He claimed to be the prophet of God. He was a star, but a fallen star; a prophet, but a false prophet. To extend his religion and reign he resorted to the sword and his converts became a race of warriors."[232]

The "heaven" from which the "star" fell most probably refers to the high standing of his forebears who were held in honor. Having traced the genealogy of Muhammad, his most renowned biographer says, "So the apostle of God was the noblest of his people in birth and the greatest in honor both on his father's and his mother's side."[233]

First, his ancestors were highly capable people. The diplomatic and economic expertise of Muhammad's ancestors clearly illustrate the superior gifts of the line. "There is ample evidence of the increasing commercial prowess of Mecca in the period immediately before Muhammad's mission. Their defeat of Abraha, attacking from the south in A.D. 570, [See footnote 229.] enhanced the position of the Quraish. Hashim, the Prophet's great-grandfather, had been the moving spirit in a wide extension of Mecca's access to Syrian and other markets, by safe conducts he was able to negotiate from Byzantium, Ethiopia and Persia. Within the Hijaz and among the tribes he seems to have been successful also in developing a popular stake in the trade encouraged by security pacts (the *ilaf* of Surah 106) which 'bought off' marauders but also 'interested' them in the profits that might accrue from non-molestation. There is a revealing hint in Surah 9:28 that loss of trade might be involved in the denial of access, by Islam, to the sacred house. Though the passage belongs to a late date in the evolution of events after the Hijrah,[234] it seems fair indication of how mercantile factors married with cultic ones in the Meccan situation prior to Islam. In its success, of course, Islamic power came to provide the same trading 'umbrella' with vastly more reach and authority. Surah 2:198 makes it clear that Muslim pilgrimage would not preclude trade at the accompanying fairs. Allahu akbar[235] spells a far more resounding guarantee of pilgrim/merchant immunity for worship/trade than any antecedent system of pagan haram prestige."[236]

The triumphant shout "Allahu akbar," that is, "God is great," became the password giving entrance into what was, in effect, a vast Muslim common market! That market was extremely advantageous to those on the inside and devastating to those on the outside!

Secondly, in addition to being exceptionally capable people, Muhammad's ancestors were also influential people. "He belonged to one of the most distinguished tribes in Arabia, and was a member of a highly aristocratic family. His relations were men of great political and social influence and that was used [especially by his uncle, Abu Talib] for his personal protection."[237]

---

232 B. W. Johnson, A Vision of the Ages, (Hollywood, California: Old Paths Book Club, n.d.), p. 95.
233 Ibn Ishaq, Sirat Rasul Allah, trans. A. Guillaume (Karachi: Oxford University Press, 1982), p.69. Muslims as well as western scholarship consider this to be the best authenticated biography of Muhammad, the founder of Islam. Therefore, it is the most widely accepted of all existing biographies.
234 The Hijrah is the Arabic name for Muhammad's migration from Mecca to Medina, the event which marks the beginning of the Muslim era.
235 Allahu Akbar is a universal declaration made many times a day by Muslims throughout the world. It occurs several times in each of the five daily calls to prayer. It means, God is Great or the Greatest.
236 Kenneth Cragg, Muhammad and the Christian, (Maryknoll, New York: Orbis Books, 1984, p. 37.
237 Rev. Canon Sell, The Historical Development of the Qur'an (People International Reprint), p. 7.

Revelation Chapter 9

"Indeed if it had not been for the powerful protection of Abu Talib, Muhammad would have been in great danger now; but that generous-hearted uncle, though not always pleased with the actions of his nephew, stood manfully by him...."[238]

9:1 "there was given to him the key of the pit of the abyss."

At this desperate moment in the career of Muhammad a diabolical opportunity was presented to him. "There was given to him the key of the pit of the abyss." Had he lived in harmony with his noble background he would have refused this gift. What a contrast between the career of this individual and the career of Jesus the Christ! Jesus was offered many diabolical gifts, but he refused them all! Though it is not stated who gave "the key of the pit of the abyss" to the fallen star, probably it was "the angel of the abyss." (9:11) Ultimately heaven will take custody of that key. (See Revelation 20:1.)

"The abyss is the intermediate place of punishment of the fallen angels, the demons, the beast, the false prophet and of Satan (9:1-2, 9:11, 11:7, 20:1 [-3], 20:3). Their final place of punishment is the lake of burning fire and brimstone (20:10, 20:14-15)."[239]

9:2 "And he opened the pit of the abyss; and there went up a smoke out of the pit, as the smoke of a great furnace; and the sun and the air were darkened by reason of the smoke of the pit."

9:2 "And he opened the pit of the abyss"

Since the pit is the abode of demons (See Luke 8:30-31.) this event marks the beginning of greater satanic activity in human affairs. This is a very important element in the development of the suffering during the period of "Woe" announced in 8:13.

9:2 "there went up a smoke out of the pit, ... and the sun and the air were darkened by reason of the smoke of the pit."

This smoke originated from the abode of Satan, "the deceiver of the whole world." (Revelation 12:9) The smoke undoubtedly represents confusion and obscurity, constituting a satanic smokescreen hiding and camouflaging truth and reality.

Since "the sun and the air were darkened by reason of the smoke of the pit," it was now no longer easy to see things clearly. Accordingly, the emergence of Islam was accompanied by great misunderstanding and confusion. Many people, even leaders in a wide array of categories, were deceived. Those leaders, represented by the sun, now darkened by the smoke from the pit, did not recognize the true nature of that which was emerging from the pit.

By conquest, many areas which had formerly been governed by the Byzantines from Constantinople, came under Muslim rule. At that point, many times Christians living in the newly conquered areas only slowly came to realize the true nature of their new masters. This reality is emphasized by a perceptive passage from Cragg: "But if the burden of the Byzantine nexus [connection] was lifted, the new and untried burden of the

---

238 Rev. Canon Sell, <u>The Historical Development of the Qur'an</u> (People International Reprint), p. 38.
239 William Barclay, <u>The Revelation of John</u>, Vol. II, (London: Westminster/John Knox Press, 2004), p. 53.

Islamic presence had to be shouldered with its implications, [which were] only slowly disclosed as the decades passed and then the centuries."[240]

Even today many people are deceived about the nature of Islam. This is amazing in view of its commitment to expediency, violence, denial of freedom and its constant use of deceit.[241]

Glacially slow though it has been, an awakening is taking place even in the Muslim World: Kanan Makiya is professor of Islamic and Middle Eastern Studies at Brandeis University. Though himself an Arab, he has come to a deep understanding of the malaise afflicting not only the Arab world, but more widely, the entire Islamic world. He recently wrote, "No Arab Spring protester…would think today to attribute all the errors of Arab polities to empty abstractions like 'imperialism' and 'Zionism.' [even though "today's Arab media culture is drenched in Nazi-style anti-Semitism."[242]]… Generations of Arabs have paid with their lives and their futures because of a set of illusions that had nothing to do with Israel; these illusions come from deep within the world that we Arabs have constructed for ourselves, a world built upon denial, bombast, and imagined past glories, ideas that have since been exposed as bankrupt and dangerous to the future of the young Arab men and women who set out in 2011, against all odds, to build a new order."[243]

Those bankrupt and dangerous ideas which Professor Makiya repudiates are all expressions of the Arab commitment to Islam. When recognition of that fact finally dawns among Muslims, by eventually being able to see through the smokescreen which emerges from the pit, there will be a vast renunciation of Islam. At that point we will see at least one magnificent fulfillment of Jeremiah's prophecy which tells us, "The nations will come from the ends of the earth and say, 'Our fathers possessed nothing but false gods, worthless idols that did them no good.'" (Jeremiah 16:19b NIV)

9:3 **"And out of the smoke came forth locusts upon the earth; and power was given them, as the scorpions of the earth have power."**

The true nature of the movement eventually became clear. It shortly became apparent that it was a religious-political movement enforced by military power. Part of that reality is made obvious by comparing it to a plague of locusts.

In scripture, locusts often represent armed multitudes, armies: "For they [the Midianites, the Amalekites, and the children of the east - Judges 6:3] came in as locusts for multitude; both they and their camels were without number: and they came in to the land to destroy it." (See Judges 6:5.) (cf. also Nahum 3:15 and Isaiah 33:4)

Biblically, locusts also often represent horses: "Hast thou given the horse his might? Hast thou clothed his neck with the quivering mane? Hast thou made him to leap as a locust?" (Job 39:19-20) (cf. also Jeremiah 51:27 NIV)

---

240 Kenneth Cragg, The Arab Christian A History in the Middle East, (Louisville: Westminster/John Knox Press, 1991), p. 178.

241 Knowledge of the deceptive nature of the system comes from the Quran itself. "The third verse of Sura 9 of the Quran, which has already been cited in connection with the *Hajj* of the year 9 (630 A.D.) contains what it itself announces is a formal proclamation (*adhan*): "And a proclamation from God and His Apostle on the Day of the Great Pilgrimage - that God and His Apostle dissolve treaty obligations with the pagans. If you repent, it is better for you. But if you turn your backs, then know that you cannot frustrate God. Inform those who disbelieve of a painful punishment." [F.E. Peters, Muhammad and the Origins of Islam, (Albany: State University of New York Press, 1994), p. 251.]

242 Charles Hill, Trial of a Thousand Years, (Stanford: Hoover Institution Press, 2011), p. 75.

243 Kanan Makiya, *The Arab Spring Started in Iraq*, The New York Times, April 7, 2013, p. 7.

Revelation Chapter 9

The locusts in this passage certainly represent war horses. The scripture clearly says, "And the shapes of the locusts were like unto horses prepared for war; ..." (Revelation 9:7) These conquering hordes emanate from the same source, that is the pit, the abyss (See 9:2.), as does the entity which is called "the beast" mentioned in Revelation 11:7.

By use of the simile of locusts, "the scene is transferred from the West to East. ... The locust, the groundwork of the symbolism, is peculiarly Arabic. It was the 'east wind' [Exodus 10:12-15], the wind that swept from Arabia that brought the locusts into Egypt, ... The sandy wastes of Arabia have always been a breeding ground for locusts."[244]

9:4 "And it was said unto them that they should not hurt the grass of the earth, neither any green thing, neither any tree, but only such men as have not the seal of God on their foreheads."

9:4 "not hurt the grass of the earth, neither any green thing, neither any tree"

This restraint in attacking vegetation of any kind is clearly unique, and points to early Islam. (For contrast, see Revelation 8:7 and the comment on "the third part of the trees," page 118.) "It is significant that from the days of their first attack, the followers of Islam showed great concern for the trade and material prosperity of the lands they swept over. The care they took, for example, in Syria and Egypt to prevent the ruin of the crops, to guard the non-combatants, and to organize their new dominion with an eye to the well-being of agriculture and manufacture proves this. In their Indian conquests the Turks are not known to have destroyed aimlessly the objects of material prosperity."[245]

"It was the duty of the Commander-in-Chief to persist in war against the infidels, and not to abandon it until the enemy either accepted Islam and received equal rights and duties with the rest of the Muslims, or was completely reduced to subjection, or capitulated on payment of tribute to the Muslim ruler and entered into his protection. ... [In the course of military attacks] it was also permitted to fell trees and palms belonging to the enemy, but only for good reasons. Wanton waste, however, was never sanctioned. Moreover, it was permitted to destroy the sources of water, even if women and children were to suffer thereby; since this was considered eminently suited to bring the enemy to bay."[246] (cf. Revelation 7:3)

From the information in footnote 245, it is obvious that the prohibition against destruction of vegetation came after Muhammad's ruthless suppression of the Jewish tribes at Medina. In those vicious campaigns Muhammad personally ordered the destruction of vineyards and palm orchards.

---

244 B. W. Johnson, A Vision of the Ages, (Hollywood, California: Old Paths Book Club, n.d.), p. 93.
245 H.C. Verma, Medieval Routes to India, (Lahore: Book Traders, 1977), p. 22. Perhaps Muhammad ordered the protection of crops and orchards because he saw what damage earlier destruction of them had brought upon the Muslims who occupied the devastated areas. "Just as in the sequel of [the battle of] Badr Muhammad turned to the Jewish tribe of the Qaynuqa`, so the direct or indirect consequence of [the battle of] Uhud was the expulsion of a second Jewish tribe from the Medina association, the Banu al-Nadir., In this case the provocation was the report of a threat by members of the Banu al-Nadir against the Prophet's life. The response was prompt and direct, an assault on their redoubts in the Medina oasis. The Jews took refuge in their forts and the Messenger ordered the palm-trees should be cut down and burnt." [F.E. Peters, Muhammad and the Origins of Islam, (Albany: State University of New York Press, 1994), p. 219.]
246 Von Kremer, The Orient Under the Caliphs, trans. S. Khuda Bukhsh (Beirut: United Publishers, 1973), pp. 278-282.

Revelation Verse by Verse

9:4 "they should not hurt the grass ... but only such men ..."

Obviously, this limitation does not refer to ordinary locusts. If they were ordinary locusts, they would hurt only the grass but not the men. These, in contrast, hurt only men. The words "hurt" and "torment" (See 9:5.) are not to be equated. The two words are not used synonymously; consequently, the result of being hurt or being tormented is not the same. To be hurt is to receive a fatal attack like the attack of a swarm of locusts on grass, green plants or trees. Locusts kill vegetation, denuding the ground. Those who have "the seal of God on their foreheads" will be tormented but not "hurt," thus not killed.

This distinction is made very clear in verse 5. One group is hurt, i.e., killed, but regarding the others, those who have the seal of God, it is written, " they should not kill them ..." Obviously, the other categories were killed.

9:4 "only such men as have not the seal of God on their foreheads"

It is the servants of Christ who have the "seal of God on their foreheads," cf. Revelation 7:3. This seal refers to the gift of the Holy Spirit which God gives to those who obey the Gospel. This phenomenon is equivalent to that experienced by the Christians in Ephesus who were told, "Ye were sealed with the Holy Spirit of promise." (Ephesians 1:13)

Initially, Islam offered a three-fold choice to the people in the vast areas which it militarily subjected. Those choices were stark. "Muhammad had specified Jews and Christians as being people with religious books, who were to be left to practice their religion if they paid tribute. Apart from them, 'heathen' were to be offered the alternatives of conversion or death. The Persians were Zoroastrians and therefore not entitled to the toleration accorded to Jews and Christians. Yet it was obviously impossible to put them all to death. Circumstances made it inevitable for them also to be accepted as 'people of the book,' and admitted to the status of tolerated tributaries."[247] Thus was born the saying, "Islam, tribute or the sword." Initially, everyone had the first choice, that is, Islam. Only the people of the book, that is Jews, Christians, and eventually Zoroastrians, had the second choice, that is, tribute. They could pay tribute and retain their own religion under harsh Muslim regulation. However, the tribute consisted of a ruinous poll tax, called *jizya* in Arabic. Often, the heathen who did not quickly convert to Islam were executed.

9:5 "And it was given them that they should not kill them, but that they should be tormented five months: and their torment was as the torment of a scorpion, when it striketh a man."

9:5 "should not kill them, but that they should be tormented"

The meaning is that they "should not kill them"as they did those who were deemed to be heathens. The Christians, along with others in the category known as "people of the book," were not killed but tormented. The ruinous tax which was imposed upon those "people of the book" who elected to retain their own religion was so harsh that it was a torment. After their tax was paid they had only enough left for the barest subsistence living. Furthermore, the tax was imposed in the most demeaning manner possible.

---

247 Sir John Bagot Glubb, The Great Arab Conquests, (Englewood Cliffs: New Jersey, Prentice-Hall, Inc., 1963), p. 200.

Revelation Chapter 9

Many Zoroastrians from Iran, to avoid the torment of rigorous and demeaning suppression under Islam, successfully fled to India. Today, their descendants constitute the famous Parsee community which is centered on Mumbai (Bombay).

9:5   "five months"

This five-month-long period is emphasized again in 9:10. "We are told in Ezekiel, [Ezekiel 4:6] that a day shall stand for a year. We will find that such is its usual meaning in the book of Revelation. Thus, this torment would then be continued for a period of one hundred and fifty years."[248]

Five months, according to Ezekiel's formula, translates into a century and a half. What are the landmarks which delineate this crucial period? It is obvious that the period begins at some point at the very dawn of Islamic history. That initial period was purely an Arabic one. Following Muhammad's personal oversight, Islam was governed by the first four caliphs ruling from Medina. Ali, fourth caliph, moved his capital to Kufa where he was assassinated. Then the following caliphs of the Umayyad Caliphate ruled from Damascus. The rule of the Umayyad Caliphate was terminated by the total defeat of that caliphate's army at the epochal battle on the Great Zab River in 750 A.D. That river flows into the Tigris River from the northeast.

The Battle of the Zab not only brought the Arab Umayyad Caliphate to an abrupt end, it also gave birth to the Persian-dominated Abbasid Caliphate which made its capital in Baghdad, a resplendent new city which the Abbasids founded on the Tigris. Further, that battle defined the termination of the specifically designated five-month-long period of torment (Revelation 9:5).

It only remains to calculate the event with which that 150-year-long period began. That event was Muhammad's marriage in 600 A.D. to Khadija, a remarkably wealthy Meccan merchant widow. His marriage to Khadija was a great enabling event, immediately allowing Muhammad to regularly indulge in deep and prolonged meditation in a cave near Mecca. During one of those early seances, Muhammad was visited by a spirit-being who ordered him to recite words which became one of the center points of Islamic doctrine. They are preserved in the first five verses of Surah 96, which was revealed at the very beginning of Islam. The words were, "Read: In the name of thy Lord who createth, createth man from a clot. Read: And thy Lord is the Most Bounteous, Who teacheth by the pen, Teacheth man that which he knew not."[249]

9:5   "as the torment of a scorpion when it striketh a man"

Ordinary locusts (9:3) do not strike men. They are herbivorous, feeding only on grass, plants and trees. This points to the torment of living under Muslim rule which was as excruciating as the sting of a scorpion.

9:6   "And in those days men shall seek death, and shall in no wise find it; and they shall desire to die, and death fleeth from them."

---
248 B. W. Johnson, A Vision of the Ages, (Hollywood, California: Old Paths Book Club, n.d.), p. 93.
249 Marmaduke Pickthall, The Meaning of the Glorious Koran, An Explanatory Translation, (New York: Alfred A. Knopf, 1930), p. 659.

"The suffering caused by the locusts will be so great that people will long for death but will not be able to die. Job speaks of the supreme misery of those who long for death and for whom it does not come (Job 3:21); and Jeremiah speaks of the day when people will choose death rather than life (Jeremiah 8:3). A Latin writer, Cornelius Gallus, says: 'Worse than any wound is to wish to die and yet not be able to do so.'"[250]

The Islamic torment was so grievous that men sought to die. Before coming to that death decision many Christians tried unsuccessfully to flee from those areas which had come under Islamic dominance. Two historic examples help us understand the utter desperation of those Christians.

First, "On the conquest of the upper Mesopotamia a small tribe, consisting of some 4,000 souls, professing Christianity, fled to the [Byzantine] Roman territory. [The caliph] Omar, thereupon, wrote to the Greek Emperor: 'An Arab tribe has forsaken my territory and fled to thine. I swear by God that if thou dost not deliver them to me, I shall expel every Christian from my territory to thine.' The Greeks did not hesitate to send back the fugitives, and Omar distributed them in the adjoining provinces of Mesopotamia and Syria."[251]

Secondly, "Among the regions to the West of the Nile, Islam spread most rapidly in Libya which the Muslim armies entered in 640. The country lost the core of its Christian population when a Berber tribe, the Louata, departed with its bishop to Morocco. All traces of them had been removed by the time the [vicious Arab tribe known as] Banu Hilal passed through in their march towards the west."[252] It is likely that the Christian Louata Berber tribe could not have imagined that after a few years following their flight Islam would also inundate their Moroccan refuge! Did they flee again? If so, the only direction by land, which offered refuge from the Islamic juggernaut, would have been very far to the south.

For a Christian to renounce his faith in and his loyalty to Christ is to embrace spiritual death. (See Hebrews 10:26-31.) Yet, because of the rigors and oppression of paying *jizya* (the poll tax) which was levied on Christians, many of them tried to renounce their loyalty to Christ and embrace Islam. However, they were not permitted to do so! Thus, they sought death but could not find it!

"Rulers sought *dhimmi*[253] subjects because the Shari'a sanctioned more taxes from them than from Muslims. As presently will be seen, Islamic taxes hardly ever covered government needs, so additional sources of legal revenues were prized. This had the curious consequence that the more pious a ruler was and the more concerned to follow

---

250 William Barclay, The Revelation of John, Vol. II, (London: Westminster/John Knox Press, 2004), p. 58.
251 Von Kremer, The Orient Under the Caliphs, trans. S. Khuda Bukhsh (Beirut: United Publishers, 1973), pp. 121-122.
252 Youssef Courbage and Philippe Fargues, Christians and Jews Under Islam, trans. Judy Mabro (New York: I.B. Tauris Publishers, 1998), pp. 39-40.
253 *Dhimmatude* was a status which was only granted to Jews and Christians who wished to retain their religion. Muslims are exhorted to, "Fight against such of those who have been given the Scripture as believe not in Allah nor the Last Day, and forbid not that which Allah hath forbidden by His messenger, and follow not the religion of truth, until they pay the tribute readily, being brought low." (Surah 9:29) Marmaduke Pickthall, The Meaning Of The Glorious Koran, An Explanatory Translation, (New York: Alfred A. Knopf, 1930), p. 195. It is obvious that not only did the Christians and Jews have to pay a repressive tax, they had also to be humiliated, brought low.
"It is the duty of a Muslim, wherever he may be, to bring the faith to the unbelievers. ... It is, however, strictly forbidden to a *dhimmi* to try to convert a Muslim to his religion, and if by any mischance he succeeds, the penalty for apostasy is death. From a Muslim religious point of view, this discrepancy is both logical and proper. To promote the true faith is a divine commandment. To abandon it, or to persuade another to do so, is both a mortal sin and a capital crime." Bernard Lewis, Islam And The West, (New York: Oxford University Press, 1993), p. 53.

Revelation Chapter 9

Shari'i regulations, the greater his incentive was to encourage *dhimmi* subjects not to convert. Quite contrary to the Muslims' reputation for imposing their religion on others, rulers in Dar al-Islam [the world of Islam] sometimes prevented *dhimmi* subjects from becoming Muslim; as early as the seventh century, the governor of Iraq, Hajjaj ibn Yusuf, refused to recognize the conversion of some of his subjects and called out the troops to return them to their villages."[254]

Not only was *jizya* odious and oppressive because of the financial burden it imposed upon the non-Muslims, but for its social implications as well. The Koran states in Surah 9:29 (Yusuf Ali's translation): "Fight those who believe not In Allah nor the Last Day, Nor hold that forbidden Which hath been forbidden By Allah and His Apostle, Nor acknowledge the Religion Of Truth, (even if they are) Of the People of the Book, Until they pay the *Jizya* With willing submission, And feel themselves subdued."

Thus, not only did the Christians and Jews have to pay a repressive tax, they also had to be humiliated. History tells us what that meant in practical terms: "Thus, for Mahmud ibn 'Umar al-Zamakhshari (1075-1144), author of a standard commentary on the Qur'an, the meaning of these words is that 'the *jizya* shall be taken from them with belittlement and humiliation. He [the *dhimmi*, i.e., the non-Muslim subject of the Muslim state] shall come in person, walking not riding. When he pays, he shall stand, while the tax collector sits. The collector shall seize him by the scruff of the neck, shake him, and say: Pay the jizya, and when he pays it he shall be slapped on the nape of his neck.' Other authorities add similar details – such as, for example, that the *dhimmi* must appear with bent back and bowed head, that the tax collector must treat him with disdain and even with violence, seizing his beard and slapping his cheeks, and the like.

"A piece of symbolism prescribed in many law books is the *dhimmi's* hand must be below, the tax collector's hand above, when the money changes hands. The purpose of all this is made clear by a fifteenth-century jurist of the rigorous Hanbali school who, after prescribing these and similar acts of ritual humiliation to be performed in public 'so that all may enjoy the spectacle,' concludes: 'Perhaps in the end they will come to believe in God and His Prophet, and thus be delivered from this shameful yoke.'"[255] No wonder that in those conditions "men shall seek death," that is, through apostasy from their faith in Christ but "shall in no wise find it." (9:6)

9:7 **"And the shapes of the locusts were like unto horses prepared for war; and upon their heads as it were crowns like unto gold, and their faces were as men's faces."**

9:7 "horses"

"Naturalists consider Arabia the native country of the horse, and from time immemorial it has produced the most famous horses of the world. ... The zoology of the symbolism points beyond a doubt to the portion of the world in which Arabia is located."[256] cf. Joel 2:4-25

---

254 Daniel Pipes, In the Path of God, Islam and Political Power, (New York: Basic Books, Inc., Publishers, 1983), p.52. See also Laura Veccia Vaglieri, "The Patriarchal and Umayyad Caliphates," The Cambridge History of Islam, ed. P.M. Holt, Ann K.S. Lambton, Bernard Lewis (Cambridge: The University Press, 1970), Vol. I, pp. 90-91.
255 Bernard Lewis, The Jews of Islam, (Princeton: Princeton University Press, 1984), pp. 14-15.
256 B. W. Johnson, A Vision of the Ages, (Hollywood, California: Old Paths Book Club, n.d.), p. 93.

9:7 "prepared for war"

Since the horses are prepared for war, they will have riders. Thus, the description which follows includes the description of the riders as well as that of the horses.

9:7 "crowns like unto gold"

Probably, "crowns" refer to the turbans of the riders which were dyed a golden color.

9:7 "their faces were as men's faces"

This detail confirms that the vision is that of a mounted or cavalry army. There were not simply horses but horses mounted by cavalrymen.

9:8 "And they had hair as the hair of women, and their teeth were as the teeth of lions."

9:8 "hair of women"

This points to the long hair which was customary among Arab men in the time of Muhammad. "Pliny, who was the contemporary of John, speaks (Nat. History 7:28) of 'the turbaned Arabs with their uncut hair.' Ammianus Marcellinus in the fourth, and Jerome in the fifth century, each speak of the long-haired Arabs. An Arabian poem, *Antar* written in Mahomet's time, often speaks of the hair of its heroes flowing down upon their shoulders. We quote: 'He adjusted himself, twisted his beard, and folded his hair under his turban, drawing it up from his shoulders'"[257]

9:8 "teeth as the teeth of lions."

Doubtless, these words reflect the vicious aggressive appearance of attacking desert warriors. cf. Proverbs 30:14.

9:9 "And they had breastplates, as it were breastplates of iron; and the sound of their wings was as the sound of chariots, of many horses rushing to war."

9:9 "breastplates of iron"

According to Koranic testimony the earliest Muslim soldiers used iron-chain mail for body protection. In the Yusuf Ali translation of the Koran we read:

> "It is God who made.
> Out of the things He created,
> Some things to give you shade;
> Of the hills He made some
> For your shelter; He made you
> Garments to protect you
> From heat, and *coats of mail*
> To protect you from
> Your (mutual) violence." (Surah 16:81)

---

[257] B. W. Johnson, A Vision of the Ages, (Hollywood, California: Old Paths Book Club, n.d.), p. 94.

Revelation Chapter 9

In a footnote on "coats of mail" Yusuf Ali, the translator, wrote, "Our clothes protect us from heat and cold, just as our armor protects us from the hurt which we might otherwise receive in battle."

Describing a display of military power, Ibn Ishaq, who wrote the earliest surviving biography of Muhammad, recorded, "Finally, the apostle passed with his greenish-black squadron in which were Muhājirs and Ansār whose eyes alone were visible because of their armour."[258]

9:9   "the sound of their wings"

These armies of cavalrymen are presented under the simile of locusts. The wings refer to the wings of the locusts. However, the reality was the sound of the many horses rushing to battle.

9:9   "the sound of chariots" (See Joel 2:5.)

Though not generally known, the Arabs did utilize chariots in some of their military operations. This fact comes out in "The *Doctrina Jacobi*[259], this is a Greek anti-Jewish tract [which was] spawned by the Heraclean persecution.[260] It is cast in the form of a dialogue between Jews set in Carthage in the year 634; it was in all probability written in Palestine within a few years of that date. At one point in the argument reference is made to current events in Palestine in the form of a letter from a certain Abraham, a Palestinian Jew:

"A false prophet has appeared among the Saracens ... They say that the prophet has appeared coming with the Saracens, and is proclaiming the advent of the anointed one who is to come. ... I, Abraham, went off to Sykamina and referred the matter to an old man very well versed in the Scriptures. I asked him: 'What is your view, master and teacher, of the prophet who has appeared among the Saracens?' He replied, groaning mightily: 'He is an impostor. Do the prophets come with sword and chariot?'"[261]

9:10   "And they have tails like unto scorpions, and stings; and in their tails is their power to hurt men five months."

9:10   "in their tails is their power to hurt men"

Though the head (9:7), that is, the initial phase, of the Muslim invasion was painful, it did not result in the greatest pain and damage. The whole time of the first period, the Arabian period, of Muslim history was extremely hurtful to the Christian subjects of the Arabian

---

258 Ibn Ishaq, The Life of Muhammad, Trans A. Guillaume, (Karachi: Oxford University Press, 1967), p. 548.
259 This refers to the document known as Doctrina Jacobi ("Teachings of Jacob"). It purportedly was composed in Africa in July 634. For details see Robert G. Hoyland, Seeing Islam As Others Saw It, A Survey and Evaluation of Christian, Jewish and Zoroastrian Writings on Early Islam, (Princeton: The Darwin Press, Inc., 1997), p. 55ff.
260 This refers to persecution which took place during the reign of Heraclius, the Byzantine emperor who was reigning when the Muslim attacks took place on the eastern territories (the Levant) of the Byzantine Empire.
261 Patricia Crone and Michael Cook, Hagarism, The Making of the Islamic World, (Cambridge: Cambridge University Press, 1977), p. 3. Daniel Pipes gives the same reference to the use of chariots by Muhammad. He writes, "Challenged by Muslims for power and for souls, Europeans responded by viewing Islam as the epitome of evil, a fiendishly clever amalgam of doctrines designed to exploit human weakness. Initial Christian reactions to Muslims set the tone. In a conversation that apparently took place in July 634, two years after Muhammad's death, an old Byzantine scribe was asked what he made of 'the prophet who has appeared among the Saracens?' He replied that Muhammad 'is deceiving. For do prophets come with swords and chariots?'" Daniel Pipes, In The Path of God, Islam And Political Power, (New York: Basic Books, Inc., 1983), p. 85.

Muslim Empire. However, it was after the initial invasion and occupation of "Christian" lands, at the tail end of the Arabian period, when the Muslims were able to impose their system. At that time, the Arab-Muslim occupation began to hurt even more. For example, as already noted, punishing and demeaning taxes were imposed which excruciatingly hurt those who had to bear them.

9:10 "five months"

See the comment on 9:5.

9:11 "They have over them as king the angel of the abyss: his name in Hebrew is Abaddon, and in the Greek tongue he hath the name Apollyon."

9:11 "They have over them"

Ostensibly, it was Muhammad, followed by a retinue of astonishingly capable caliphs and generals, who led the military forces of Islam during the period of Arabian domination of its history. But over them, guiding and inspiring, was "the angel of the abyss." (Please see also the discussion at 9:1.) It is the guidance of this angel which explains the tenacity and stunning victories of the Arab armies which they achieved time-after-time against forces which were generally considered to have been far superior!

9:11 "the angel of the abyss"

Satan originally seems to have been an angel who, at some point, rebelled against God, thus entering that category of angels which Jude identified when he wrote that, "Angels that kept not their own principality, but left their proper habitation, he hath kept in everlasting bonds under darkness unto the judgment of the great day. (Jude 1:6)

The biblical record of Satan's rebellion is probably the event given to us by Ezekiel, using the symbolism of the King of Tyre. (See Ezekiel 28:11-19.) Isaiah seems to record the same event under the symbolism of the king of Babylon. (See Isaiah 14:12-20.)

9:11 "his name in Hebrew is Abaddon, and in the Greek tongue he hath the name Apollyon."

This reveals the true character of Islam. The movement is under the direction of the "angel of the abyss" whose name is Abaddon and Apollyon. Abaddon means "destruction" or "ruin." It is used three times in the Old Testament: Job 26:6, Proverbs 15:21 and 27:20. Apollyon means "the destroyer," clearly referring to Satan. (See John 10:10.) For example, he tries to destroy men's faith by sifting them (Luke 22:31-32). He also destroys people's ability to think clearly (II Corinthians 4:3-4 and 11:3).

9:12 "The first Woe is past: behold, there come yet two Woes hereafter."

Though the first Woe itself has passed, its woeful impact will go on for many centuries. For its impact during the first century of Islam's existence and beyond, see Appendix C.

Note: To visualize the initial geographic expanse of Islam, please consult Map 7.

Revelation Chapter 9

6. The sixth trumpet 9:13-11:14

9:13 "And the sixth angel sounded, and I heard a voice from the horns of the golden altar which is before God"

This was probably the voice of one of the archangels who stand in the presence of God. (See the comments on 8:2.)

9:14 "one saying to the sixth angel that had one trumpet, Loose the four angels that are bound at the great river Euphrates."

9:14 "angels that are bound"

These words indicate a time lapse, a delay in the occurrence of some major historical event or series of events. The delay indicated by the words "angels that are bound" probably is not the same period of delay clearly denoted in 10:6 with the words, "there shall be delay no longer." Here, the angels whose duty it was to inaugurate or allow the next historical development were bound, making it impossible for them to carry out their role at that point in history. Because of the delay, the activity of "the four angels" does not immediately follow the event depicted by the fifth trumpet. The "four angels" will not be allowed to act till the right circumstances are in place.

The activity which begins when "the four angels" are eventually unleashed probably will be related to activity initiated by and focused on the Muslim world. However, that activity is not to be equated with the epochal rise of the Turks to dominance in the Islamic world nor their spectacular military exploits which they carried out both in Europe and Asia. Rather, it will be fulfilled by something far more significant. By overlooking the obvious time lapse implied by the words "angels that are bound," many commentators feel this description, especially in verse 15, refers to the rise of the Turks to predominance in Islam. For example, Hinds mistakenly wrote "If applying the fifth trumpet vision to Mahometanism [his unique spelling] was correct, then this doubtless refers to the Turkish power."[262]

The numerical strength of the military forces which is cited in 9:16 and its implications about the size of world population decisively confirm the fact that the events related to "the four angels" could not have been fulfilled exclusively by the Turks. Also, if we treat the visions as though they are sequential, with no gaps, the next period of Islamic history, immediately following the Arab period, was the Iranian-dominated period of the Abbasid Caliphate, not the Turkish.

In any case, we should not lose sight of the fact that the description of satanic and angelic activities which occurs in this section of Revelation relates to the ultimate destiny of human society. That destiny is determined by the outcome of the contest between the forces emanating from the throne of God on the one hand and those emanating from the pit on the other hand.

---

[262] John T. Hinds, A Commentary on the Book of Revelation (Nashville, Tenn.: Gospel Advocate Company, 1976), p. 136.

9:14 "bound at the great river Euphrates"

Today there are four countries which are touched by the Euphrates River, each of them is Muslim and each one is in significant upheaval. (See Map 8.) It is highly probable that the areas of ministry for the four angels who are bound correspond to these four countries, each angel monitoring, influencing, and perhaps even guiding affairs in his respective country. The countries are, in order from north to south: Turkey, Syria, Iraq, and Iran. Iran's border touches the Euphrates along the lower half of the 120-mile-long Shatt al-Arab (The River of the Arabs), the combined river formed by the confluence of the Tigris with the Euphrates.

The work of the four angels who were bound at the Euphrates needs to be seen in conjunction with the ministry of the sixth wrath angel, who is the second woe angel, whose work is prophetically portrayed in 16:12-16.

9:15 "And the four angels were loosed, that had been prepared for the hour and day and month and year, that they should kill the third part of men."

9:15 "hour and day and month and year"

Sometimes it may seem that those superhuman evil forces which were unleashed by opening the pit are the only ones at work in the arena of human society. That illusion will have come about because divine intervention usually comes only at the precise time, at "the hour and day and month and year," when maximum potential beneficial impact will ensue. These time designations emphasize the precision of divine intervention in human affairs.

9:15 "they should kill"

Instead of only one death angel, like the one who brought death to the Egyptians during the events related to the Exodus of the Jews from Egypt, at this point in the development of human history there will be four death angels! Clearly, the four angels are to serve as God's agents of judgment. They have remained under restraint, "bound," probably because analogously, "the sin of the Amorites has not yet reached its full measure." (Genesis 15:16 NIV)

It does not seem that the four death angels will personally and directly kill "the third part of men," but will allow those conditions to develop which will permit a hideous war to take place during which the third part of men shall be killed. That such a war is involved in the "Woe" which is initiated when the four angels are loosed, becomes clear from verse 16 in which the cumulative size of the armies is given.

9:15 "the third part of men"

According to many commentators, "third part" refers to "the eastern third, or Grecian portion of what had been the Roman Empire. This was the Byzantine Empire. ... In 1453, the Turks – by this time known as the Ottoman Empire, conquered Constantinople, bringing to an end the last vestige of the Roman Empire in the east."[263]

---

263 Revelation, Four Views: A Parallel Commentary, ed. Steve Gregg, (Nashville: Thomas Nelson Publishers, 1997), p. 186.

Revelation Chapter 9

<u>In the first place</u>, their position is in error because the time lapse noted in the comments on 9:14 seems to take us chronologically far beyond the rise of Turkish power in the Islamic world and the Turkish conquest of the Byzantine Empire. Thus, the killing of "the third part of men" points not to the conquest of the eastern third of the old Roman Empire, but to a more gruesome cataclysmic conflict in which fatalities will reach shocking and astronomically high numbers, "the third part of men."

<u>Secondly</u>, those commentators, who assert that "the third part of men" mentioned in chapter 9 refers to the Byzantine Empire, the eastern third of the Roman Empire, overlook the fact that the passage stresses that "they should kill the third part of men" (9:15) and "by these three plagues was the third part of men killed" (9:18). They think that when in 1453 Constantinople was finally conquered by the Ottoman Turks, this prophecy of "the third part of men" was fulfilled, since Byzantium had been constituted out of the eastern one-third of the old Roman Empire. Surprisingly, those historicist commentators completely overlooked the fact that <u>the population of the Byzantine Empire was subjugated, not killed, by the Ottoman Muslims</u>. Obviously, therefore, we must look to later times for the fulfillment of this startling prophecy.

<u>Thirdly</u>, there is also an additional factor which helps us understand that, here, the phrase "the third part of men" does not refer to the Byzantine Empire. The prophecy of the rise and career of Byzantium is clearly the emphasis of Revelation 13:1-10.

9:16 **"And the number of the armies of the horsemen was twice ten thousand times ten thousand: I heard the number of them."**

The number "twice ten thousand times ten thousand" calculates to be a total of 200 million men who are simultaneously under arms. Certainly the Turks did not and could not have marshaled such an enormous army. The largest army whose tally is recorded in the Bible came from Ethiopia. Scripture says, "There came out against them Zerah the Ethiopian with an army of a thousand thousand, [that totals 1 million men] and three-hundred chariots; and he came unto Mareshah." (II Chronicles 14:9) The appearance of Ethiopia's vast army caused King Asa to turn to God in fervent prayer. His appeal was, "There is none besides thee to help, between the mighty and him that hath no strength: help us, O Jehovah our God; for we rely on thee, and in thy name are we come against this multitude. O Jehovah, thou art our God; let not man prevail against thee." (II Chronicles 14:11)

As vast as that Ethiopian army was, it was utterly puny compared with this gargantuan apocalyptic army of 200 million fighting men. A brief survey of world population growth shows that such gargantuan military forces could be mustered and sustained only in modern times.

"World population [in the year 1000] is estimated to have been 275 million, with 25 percent evangelized and about 19 percent professing to be 'Christians.' Widespread fear of the Second Coming and Judgment Day attended the turn of millennium."[264]

---

264 Erich Bridges, *The March of Time*, <u>The Commission</u>, December 1999, p. 6.

In 1350, world population stood at approximately 370 million. It had been slowed to this number by the Black Death and a great famine.[265] From this census number it is obvious that Turkish military forces in 1453 were not those which were prophesied to number 200 million. That would have been clearly impossible when total world population would probably have been not more than 500 million.

In 1798 "Thomas Malthus published *An Essay on the Principle of Population*, arguing that the world population would increase faster than the food supply."[266]

In 1800 world population reached 1 billion. Protestant missionaries numbered only about 100, but the 'Great Century' of evangelical missions was about to begin, sweeping the world with the gospel by 1914.[267]

"By 1863, London – the first city since the fall of Rome to reach a population of more than one million – could boast several mail deliveries a day. A letter posted early in the morning to another London address could not only bring a reply, but do so in time for a further letter from the first writer to be delivered before the day was out."[268]

In 1927, a full century and a quarter after world population had reached 1 billion, "World population reached 2 billion."[269] From that point, world population began to increase exponentially. In 1960, only thirty-three years after reaching the 2 billion level, "World population reached 3 billion."[270] Then the pace accelerated almost frighteningly. In the next fourteen years, by 1974, "World population reached 4 billion."[271] In the next thirteen years, by 1987, "World population topped 5 billion."[272] It only took another twelve years, till 1999, when "World population topped 6 billion."[273] "Somebody who is 85 years old was born into a world that had a third as many people as the world does today."[274]

During World War II, the combined cumulative total of men under arms, both in the allied and axis forces, came to 82,350,000. Since both the allies and the axis were making their maximum effort it is obvious that, as recently as 1945, armed forces totaling 200 million could not have been mustered and supported. However, by March 12, 2012 world population had exceeded 7 billion. "By 2050, the earth's current 7.3 billion people will swell by one-third to 9.7 billion."[275] At current world population levels, an army of 200 million would represent only 2.86 percent of total world population. Thus, such enormous military forces are well within the realm of possibility at the current point in world history.

---

265 https://en.wikipedia.org/wiki/World_population.
266 WIRED [Magazine] January 2002, p. 77.
267 Erich Bridges, *The March of Time*, The Commission, December 1999, p. 8.
268 Jeremy Rifkin, The European Dream, How Europe's Vision of the Future Is Quietly Eclipsing the American Dream, (New York: Tarcher/Penguin Books, 2004), p. 95.
269 Erich Bridges, *The March of Time*, The Commission, December 1999, p. 10.
270 Erich Bridges, *The March of Time*, The Commission, December 1999, p. 12.
271 Erich Bridges, *The March of Time*, The Commission, December 1999, p. 12.
272 Erich Bridges, *The March of Time*, The Commission, December 1999, p. 13.
273 Erich Bridges, *The March of Time*, The Commission, December 1999, p. 12.
274 Dan Brown, TIME, May 27, 2013, p. 64.
275 The Week, August 21, 2015, p. 19.

Revelation Chapter 9

9:17 "And thus I saw the horses in the vision, and them that sat on them, having breastplates as of fire and of hyacinth and of brimstone: and the heads of lions; and out of their mouths proceedeth fire and smoke and brimstone."

This statement obviously points to an era when warfare will have become far more sophisticated and lethal than that referred to in 9:9 when the breastplates were only body armor, fashioned from iron mesh. Those earlier breastplates were purely defensive while these seem to have great offensive potential. Here the breastplates probably refer to defensive armor equipped with portholes from which protrude high-powered guns. The fire probably represents gunfire or rocket fire. Hyacinth refers to the sapphire stone, of deep purplish blue color, probably describing one hue of the flame generated by gunfire or rocket fire. The word brimstone comes from a root word meaning "to burn," but has become a synonym for sulfur. This probably refers to the chemical composition of the explosives used to propel lethal military projectiles.

9:18 "By these three plagues was the third part of men killed, by the fire and the smoke and the brimstone, which proceeded out of their mouths."

9:18 "these three plagues"

These are the fire, hyacinth and brimstone mentioned in 9:17.

9:18 "the third part of men killed"

As emphasized in the comments on 9:14-15, this one-third does not refer to the eastern one-third of the Roman Empire. This should be taken more literally to predict a war so devastating that one-third of the world's population perishes. Based on the current world population figure, that total reaches the repulsive number of 2 and 1/3 billion people who will perish due to this coming global conflict. It seems probable, with such vast butchery, that this global conflict finally will be brought to an end by the sheer exhaustion of the combatants. Agriculture will have suffered disastrously and, consequently, widespread hunger will prevail. The death toll will be twenty-seven times higher than the highest estimate (85 million) of the fatalities in World War II.

When one contemplates this diabolical total number of fatalities, one wonders what may motivate nations to commit their forces to such a destructive conflict. Undoubtedly, economic factors will have their part. For example, at the present moment in Portugal "the country's youth-unemployment rate is over 40 percent. In Spain it's 57 percent, and in Greece just shy of 63 percent."[276] Such unthinkable unemployment generates desperation which may reach such a level that war seems to be the only alternative. But motivating the nations more than economic hardship and frustration will be demonic forces which were unleashed when the pit was opened. (See 9:1-2 with comments.)

9:18 "the smoke"

In addition to the fire, the hyacinth and brimstone discussed in the comments on verse 17, here an additional lethal element in the weaponry employed in this coming conflict is mentioned. It is called "the smoke." While the acrid smoke of battle may become so

---

276 Mark Steyn, *Happy Warrior, The Graffiti on the Wall*, National Review, July 15, 2013, p. 48.

dense that people are asphyxiated, this mention of smoke probably refers to clouds of poison gases to be used by the antagonists. The effectiveness of this combination of weaponry and other killing agents is seen in the fact that one-third of humanity will be killed. It is no wonder, therefore, that this vision is the second one of those which are categorized by the word "Woe." (See 8:13.)

9:19 **"For the power of the horses is in their mouth, and in their tails: for their tails are like unto serpents, and have heads; and with them they hurt."**

These are not ordinary horses. The description probably envisions battle tanks which are able to spew out lethal projectiles, both fore and aft, from "their mouth and in their tails."

Whether this hideous gargantuan war is the same war as that which is usually referred to as the Battle of Armageddon is discussed at Revelation 16:14-16, page 261ff.

9:20 **"And the rest of mankind, who were not killed with these plagues, repented not of the works of their hands, that they should not worship demons, and the idols of gold, and of silver, and of brass, and of stone, and of wood; which can neither see, nor hear, nor walk:"**

9:20 "the rest of mankind who were not killed … repented not"

The curse of the worldwide war had been permitted to occur so that both individuals and society might realize the consequences of their grossly misguided and misplaced priorities. Surprisingly, the moral and spiritual lessons of the just-completed frightening and devastating war are totally ignored. The impenitence of world society stubbornly and flagrantly continues to persist.

The unbelievers' lack of repentance at this time is breathtakingly astonishing. Fully one-third of the world's population will have died due to the war. How many of these fatalities have resulted directly from conflict and how many as a result of the disruption of the ecosystem, the economy, transportation, food production and lack of medical services is not known. The survivors, rather than acknowledging the massive failure of human society and their own alienation from God, will have hardened their hearts. They are walking "in the vanity of their mind, being darkened in their understanding, alienated from the life of God, because of the ignorance that is in them, because of the hardening of their heart; who being past feeling gave themselves up to lasciviousness, to work all uncleanness with greediness." (Ephesians 4:17-19)

9:20 "should not worship demons"

It is amazing that society refuses to see where its devotion to demons and to unbridled and unlimited materialism, indicated by "the idols of gold, and of silver, and of brass, and of stone, and of wood" has taken it. The demons are, in addition to those to which Paul made reference in I Corinthians 10:20, new myriads of demonic beings which emerged when Muhammad opened the pit (9:2), the home of the demons. (See Luke 8:30-31.)

9:21 **"and they repented not of their murders, nor of their sorceries, nor of their fornication, nor of their thefts."**

Revelation Chapter 9

In addition to societal worship of materialism, society will be characterized by four disastrous habitual commitments to evil. They are: (1) vengeance, greed or jealousy, resulting in "murder," (2) corrupted religious activities in which "sorceries" play a significant role, (3) ongoing sensualism summarized by the word "fornication," and (4) by unbridled greed indicated by the word "thefts."

The word "sorceries" comes from the Greek word *pharmakeion*. You undoubtedly will recognize this Greek word as the source from which we get the word "pharmacy." This word clearly implies that at this point in human history drug addiction will be widespread. Though the majority of translations have rendered it "sorceries," William Beck rendered it as "magic arts" and Moffatt as "magic spells." The NIV translated it as "magic arts." All of these translations fall short of the real impact the Greek seems to have. David Stern, in his translation entitled *Complete Jewish Bible*, helps us grasp the true impact of this word. His translation of verse 21 is "Nor did they turn from their murdering, their involvement with the occult and with drugs, their sexual immorality or their stealing."

Revelation Chapter 10

Introduction: Barclay says "The verses from 10:1-11:14 are a kind of interlude between the sounding of the sixth and the seventh trumpets. The sixth trumpet has already sounded; but the seventh does not sound until 11:15, and in between there are terrible things."[277] Barclay does not clearly indicate the event or events to which he thinks the passage which he calls an interlude refers. Though Barclay did not see it, the passage from 10:1 to11:14 is to be understood as part of the portrayal of events related to the sixth-trumpet angel.

The "little book" (10:10) contained both good and bad news. Unfortunately, the bad news predominated. The good news was that the war, (9:15 ff) that is, the actual fighting, was finally over. But then reality dawned and it was sickening, nauseous, "bitter" in the belly. (10:9) The war had not sparked or spawned any moral or spiritual recovery. Though hostilities had ceased, the conflict had been so prolonged, so widespread, and so fierce that it undoubtedly left a shattered infrastructure causing starvation, fatal exposures and untreated and rampant disease. These abominable conditions will have kept adding to the direct fatalities from the war, till the total will have reached the abominable and repulsive sum of one-third of world population. Even then there will have been no moral and spiritual recovery! Societal commitment to evil would undoubtedly result in persecution of the church, causing her to flee and take refuge in the wilderness.

Gregg, in summarizing the historicist position, says, "The prophesies of Chapter 10 and 11:1-15 are about the Reformation period in the early 16th century. This follows naturally the identification of the second Woe with the fall of the Byzantine (Greek) Empire in 1453."[278] As comments on Revelation 9:15 and 9:18 have tried to make unmistakably clear, the Woe introduced when the sixth angel sounds his trumpet (8:6) portrays neither the fall of the Byzantine Empire, nor the Reformation period, but the occurrence of an imminent ghastly worldwide war in which a third of world population will become fatalities.

10:1 **"And I saw another strong angel coming down out of heaven, arrayed with a cloud; and the rainbow was upon his head, and his face was as the sun, and his feet as pillars of fire;"**

> The words "another strong angel" indicate a comparison. One asks, who is this "strong angel" and who is the other strong angel or angels with whom comparison is being made? Probably this "strong angel" is being compared to the four angels mentioned in 9:14.
>
> The persistent mercy of God is remarkably demonstrated by his unwillingness to abandon the human race even at this abominably low point in its societal behavior. (See 9:20-21.) Rather than abandoning society as he did in the days of Noah, he will make another

---

277 William Barclay, The Revelation of John, Vol. II, (London: Westminster/John Knox Press, 2004), p. 61.
278 Revelation, Four Views: A Parallel Commentary, ed. Steve Gregg, (Nashville: Thomas Nelson Publishers, 1997), p. 202.

magnificent effort to bring about human redemption. He will send yet "another strong angel." That angel will come with a message of regeneration and reclamation.

Without citing corroborating evidence, many commentators assert that this strong angel is Christ himself. They base their conclusion on his appearance. He is said to be "arrayed with a cloud; and the rainbow was upon his head, and his face was as the sun, and his feet as pillars of fire." Their conclusion about the identity of this "strong angel" is very likely incorrect since it is based on skimpy evidence. Out of the striking characteristics of his visage, <u>only</u> the statement that "his face was as the sun" is confirmed as a facet of Christ's appearance. That single confirmation is found in Revelation 1:16 where it tells us "his countenance was as the sun shineth in his strength." It is probable that the description points not to Christ but to a very strong angel.

10:2 "and he had in his hand a little book open: and he set his right foot upon the sea, and his left upon the earth"

10:2 "a little book"

At this point God's message is going to be extremely concise, thus "a little book" will be adequate. It is being revealed through the agency of an angel, a process which is in harmony with the method by which other segments of scripture have been revealed. (See "the word spoken through angels" at Hebrews 2:2.) It will be so concise that it will be entirely contained in "a little book." It will probably contain a summary of or selections from the "book of the future" mentioned in the comments on 5:1 and 5:9. Thus we can say that this "little book" is also a "book of the future," but it is small, containing only the residual prophesies of those unfulfilled events portrayed in the "book of the future" which was mentioned earlier. Because so much history will have already taken place, the book can be small. These remaining coming events are so important and significant that God gives them special emphasis in the "little book."[279]

Barclay's comment, though not as specific as the position I have expressed about the "little book" being a summary of the remaining events from the "book of the future," is still compatible with that understanding. He wrote, "The angel has a little scroll, unrolled and opened. That is to say, he is giving John a limited revelation about a quite small period of time."[280]

However, students should be aware that many, probably the majority of conservative Protestant Bible commentators, think this "little book" represents the opportunity developed through the Protestant Reformation for people to have access to the Bible. Albert Barnes, writing in 1851, took the position that the "little book" pointed to the great work of Bible translation, publication and distribution, which was one of the great achievements of the Reformation. Barnes wrote, "The Bible became at the Reformation, in fact an 'open' book."[281] B. W. Johnson, writing in 1880-81, took the position that the open book mentioned here "appears as the divine measure by which the church and its

---

[279] After coming to this understanding of the meaning of the "little book" I was surprised and pleased to find that another commentator had also come to this same conclusion. His name is David S. Clark, whose comment is found on page 204 in Gregg's summary of expositions of the book of Revelation.
[280] William Barclay, <u>The Revelation of John</u>, Vol. II, (London: Westminster/John Knox Press, 2004), p. 62.
[281] Albert Barnes, <u>Notes, Explanatory and Practical on the Book of Revelation</u>, (New York: Harper & Brothers Publishers, 1864), p. 285.

Revelation Chapter 10

worship are measured."[282] He goes on to identify that divine standard as the New Testament. Hendriksen, writing in 1940, said that, "The scroll is the word of God, his Gospel in which the mystery of salvation is set forth."[283] Finally, Hinds, writing in 1937, commented that, "If applying this vision to the Reformation movement is correct, then it is easy to understand that a book would be involved, for the Reformation largely pertained to the work of giving back to the people the word of God."[284]

10:2 "he set his right foot upon the sea and, his left upon the earth"

The message, though concise, will be global. It will be relevant and applicable, whether one is at home, "upon the earth" or traveling, "upon the sea."

10:3 "and he cried with a great voice, as a lion roareth: and when he cried, the seven thunders uttered their voices."

10:3 "a great voice, as a lion roareth"

Not only will the message be global, applicable on both sea and land, and concise, being contained in "a little book," it will also demand attention. It will be impossible for anyone to plead ignorance because the message will come, not with a whisper, but with a startling, attention-getting roar, like that of a lion. From this point on, man's ability to plead ignorance of God's plan and purpose will diminish to zero.

10:3 "the seven thunders uttered their voices"

Quite forthrightly, Hendriksen says "What they [the seven thunders] are we do not know."[285] Hinds took a surprising view when he wrote that John "was in the act of writing what the thunders said when a voice from heaven forbade it. [See 10:4.] This shows that God would not allow them to be recorded as part of the revelation. To do so might have left the impression that they came from God; refusing them a place in the record shows that they came from some power which was in fact against God's will."[286] Hinds' position is untenable. John was not repulsed by a message he deemed to have been wicked or inappropriate. He did not cry out in revulsion as Peter did when he protested "Not so, Lord." (See Acts 10:14.) Thus, John certainly felt the message was compatible with the previous revelation which he had been commanded to write or to transcribe (1:19).

A number of commentators in the group known as the Historicists think the "seven thunders" refer to the papal anathemas hurled against Luther and other reformers. That view is not credible because those anathemas were not sealed as the voices of the seven thunders were (10:4). Rather, church historians know what was written in them.

Barclay has probably pointed in the right direction when he said in explanation of "the seven thunders," "they are most likely a reference to the seven voices of God in Psalm 29."[287] Those voices are here epitomized as being "seven thunders." Those thunderous voices probably constituted a personal or private message to guide, strengthen and

---

282 B. W. Johnson, A Vision of the Ages, (Hollywood: California, Old Paths Book Club, n.d.), p. 119.
283 W. Hendriksen, More Than Conquerors: An Interpretation of the Book of Revelation, (Grand Rapids: Baker Book House, 1952), p. 151.
284 John T. Hinds, A Commentary on the Book of Revelation (Nashville, Tenn.: Gospel Advocate Company, 1976), p. 143.
285 W. Hendriksen, More Than Conquerors: An Interpretation of the Book of Revelation, (Grand Rapids: Baker Book House, 1952), p. 150.
286 John T. Hinds, A Commentary on the Book of Revelation, (Nashville, Tenn.: Gospel Advocate Company, 1976), p. 145.
287 William Barclay, The Revelation of John, Vol. II, (London: Westminster/John Knox Press, 2004), p. 62.

encourage John and enable him to finish the great work which had been entrusted to his care. Because those voices were a personal message to John, they were not to be written for general perusal. (See also the comments on 4:5, page 75.)

10:4 **"And when the seven thunders uttered their voices, I was about to write: and I heard a voice from heaven saying, Seal up the things which the seven thunders uttered, and write them not."**

It is as though God were saying, "for now, the message of the seven thunders is just for you, John." Presumably, this part of the divine message will ultimately be declared to the right people at the right time and for the right purpose. We may wonder why John was given insight by means of seven thunderous voices but was not allowed to share that insight with others. It may help us understand if we remember that Jesus, on one occasion, withheld information from his closest disciples. He told them, "I have yet many things to say unto you, but ye cannot bear them now." (John 16:12) Sometimes, for reasons which we may not know, God chooses to withhold information or refuses to answer our questions. For example, just before Jesus ascended back to the Father, the apostles "asked him, saying, 'Lord, dost thou at this time restore the kingdom to Israel?' And he said unto them, 'It is not for you to know times or seasons, which the Father hath set within His own authority.'" (Acts 1:6-7)[288]

Knowledge and insight are powerful and must be handled with mature discretion. As a non-negotiable minimum, one must have secure control of his pride before God will grant understanding of some realities, because "knowledge puffeth up, but love edifieth." (I Corinthians 8:1)

Paul experienced a breakthrough in understanding, similar to that which John was granted, and was also put under constraint regarding those to whom he might share the insight. He tells us, "I know a man in Christ, fourteen years ago (whether in the body, I know not; or whether out of the body, I know not; God knoweth), such a one caught up even to the third heaven. And I know such a man (whether in the body, or apart from the body, I know not; God knoweth), how that he was caught up into Paradise, and heard <u>unspeakable words, which it is not lawful for a man to utter.</u>" (II Corinthians 12:2-4)

10:5 **"And the angel that I saw standing upon the sea and upon the earth lifted up his right hand to heaven,"**

10:5 "standing upon the sea and upon the earth"

See the comments on 10:2.

10:5 "lifted up his right hand to heaven"

"The action was customary among the Jews in swearing [legal oaths, 10:6 makes it clear that the angel was swearing a legal oath] (See Genesis 14:22; Deuteronomy 32:40)."[289]

---

[288] Jesus' statement is not a ban on historical inquiry as Daniel J. Boorstin thought Eusebius' position was. To take that position would negate the whole historical and prophetic emphasis of the book of Revelation. Boorstin's analysis is in <u>The Discoverers</u> (New York: Random House, 1983), p. 573.

[289] A. Plummer, <u>The Pulpit Commentary [on] Revelation</u>, (Chicago: Wilcox & Follett Co., no date) p. 274.

Revelation Chapter 10

10:6 **"and sware by him that liveth for ever and ever, who created the heaven and the things that are therein, and the earth and the things that are therein, and the sea and the things that are therein, that there shall be delay no longer:"**

Divine patience has its limits. God had been holding back a time of judgment and of punishment. Up to this point, not only will have God's patience intervened to delay judgment, but one wonders if someone will also have been pleading with God on behalf of human society as Abraham did on behalf of Sodom. (See Genesis 18:17-33.) It seems God is saying that the period of probation is now over, "there shall be delay no longer." As has been clearly indicated in 9:20-21, certainly society will have become impenitent.

10:7 **"but in the days of the voice of the seventh angel, when he is about to sound, then is finished the mystery of God, according to the good tidings which he declared to his servants the prophets."**

The event/events in the period of the seventh-trumpet angel will be so important that they are here being announced during the historic period of events which are to take place under the oversight of the sixth-trumpet angel. Apparently, the voice from heaven (See 10:4 and 10:8.) is still addressed to John. It informs him that "the mystery of God" is not yet "finished" but will reach that climactic point when the seventh-trumpet angel sounds. ("Then is finished the mystery of God, according to the good tidings …" 10:7)

The account of the actual coming of the seventh-trumpet angel, who is the third Woe angel, begins at 11:15. The significance of the ministry of the third Woe angel will be so great that a pre-announcement is given here at 10:7 during the period under the supervision of the second Woe angel. This verse gives us a locator message. It helps us understand what point has been reached historically in God's overall scheme, as narrated in the Revelation.

10:8 **"And the voice which I heard from heaven, I heard it again speaking with me, and saying, Go, take the book which is open in the hand of the angel that standeth upon the sea and upon the earth."**

10:8 **"Go, take the book"**

See a very similar experience in Ezekiel's ministry as narrated in Ezekiel 2:8-3:3.

10:8 **"the angel that standeth upon the sea and upon the earth"**

See the comment on 10:2 under "he set his right foot upon the sea, and his left upon the earth."

10:9 **"And I went unto the angel, saying unto him that he should give me the little book. And he saith unto me, Take it, and eat it up; and it shall make thy belly bitter, but in thy mouth it shall be sweet as honey."**

It will be sweet in his mouth. These words represent John's initial jubilant reaction to receiving this summary of the remaining events which were predicted in this "little book" of the future. However, this concise revelation will make John's belly bitter. This indicates that when he will have begun to digest or understand the realities which lie ahead, they will not seem sweet but repulsively bitter. This repugnant aspect notwithstanding, the revelation of these coming events is so important that a special "little book," a compendium, is given to John in which they are emphasized, perhaps with explanations.

10:10 "And I took the little book out of the angel's hand, and ate it up; and it was in my mouth sweet as honey: and when I had eaten it, my belly was made bitter."

There is no specific time line given which tells us how long it was between the time John ate the book and his belly was made bitter. The bitterness, as indicated before, probably came from understanding the repugnant and distasteful nature of the events enumerated in the little book. It seems that John quickly grasped the abhorrent nature of coming developments within human society.

10:11 "And they say unto me, Thou must prophesy again over many peoples and nations and tongues and kings."

10:11 "they say"

The pronoun "they" most probably points to "the voices of the seven thunders" mentioned in 10:4.

10:11 "Thou must prophesy again over many peoples and nations and tongues and kings"

This "again" statement is very important. It clearly indicates that the narrative in subsequent chapters in Revelation may once more focus on some of the same centuries which have already been highlighted. Of course, the focus and emphasis which will be featured will be distinct from those to which attention was given previously.

For the distinction between peoples, nations and tongues, please see the comments at Revelation 7:9 under "every nation and of all tribes and peoples and tongues."

Revelation Chapter 11

11:1 "And there was given me a reed like unto a rod: and one said, Rise, and measure the temple of God, and the altar, and them that worship therein."

11:1 "a reed like unto a rod"

The reed which was like a rod was a measuring rod, comparable to the common yardstick. It refers to the scripture by which we may determine whether concepts, conditions or practices in the church and in our private lives are legitimate, fully developed and measure up or not. This function of scripture is clearly set forth in the following passages: Isaiah 8:20, I Corinthians 4:6, II Timothy 3:16-17 and Hebrews 8:5.

That part of the divine message which was given orally by the apostles was later incorporated into the written message of the New Testament. This basic truth is emphasized in II Thessalonians 2:5 in which Paul tells us, "Remember ye not, that, when I was yet with you, **I told you these things**?" Those were the very things he was then putting into written form. The same truth is made clear in II Peter 3:1-2 in which Peter says, "I write unto you … that ye should remember the words which were spoken before by the holy prophets, and the commandment of the Lord and Saviour through your apostles."

That being the case, the message which is like a measuring rod cannot be elastic, but preserves a standard which is not to be compromised, just as Paul made clear in Galatians 1:8. The measuring rod has a permanently established set of objective values not subject to revision, for as Jude said, the faith "was once for all delivered to the saints." (Jude 3) The reed which was like a rod was "given." We have no liberty to invent our own. We must take it as it is because eternal truth is inflexible. This quality of the measuring rod, the divinely revealed word, is emphasized by calling it "a rod of iron." (19:15) Accordingly, God's word is "settled ("firmly fixed" - ESV, "stands firm" - NIV) in heaven." (Psalms 119:89)

11:1 "rise and measure the temple of God, and the altar"

Though this command was given specifically to John, every Christian has the duty of utilizing this very same measuring rod. We must begin by evaluating ourselves. Every time we come to the Lord's table we are to measure ourselves by this method, for Paul wrote, "Let a man prove ["examine" - KJV, ESV, NIV] himself, and so let him eat of the bread, and drink of the cup." (I Corinthians 11:28) When we examine, evaluate or measure ourselves, we are measuring the temple of God, for each individual Christian's body is the temple of the Holy Spirit. (See I Corinthians 6:19.)

Personal measuring or evaluation is not only to be done at the Lord's table, but should be a regular personal discipline. "For if a man thinketh himself to be something when he is nothing, he deceiveth himself. But let each man prove his own work, and then shall he have his glorying in regard of himself alone, and not of his neighbor. For each man shall bear his own burden." (Galatians 6:3-5) Accordingly, all of us are exhorted to "try your own selves, whether ye are in the faith; prove your own selves." (II Corinthians 13:5) (See also Romans 12:2, Galatians 6:4, and I Thessalonians 5:21.)

Faithfully measuring ourselves in this way will develop within us the skill we need to avoid the pitfalls which an eminent historian mentioned in discussing the ability of nations to evaluate their own status and progress. He said, "The difficulty of measurement is enhanced by the influence of perceptions."[290] This same difficulty is also encountered at the personal level. Therefore, we are exhorted not to think of ourselves more highly than we ought ["the influence of perceptions"], but, "to think soberly, according as God hath dealt to each man a measure of faith." (Romans 12:3)

Here, the order to "measure the temple of God" cannot refer to the Jewish temple in Jerusalem which had been built by Herod the Great. That temple had been destroyed by Roman armies under the command of General Titus in 70 A.D., a full quarter century before the book of Revelation was written. Please read Section F in the Introduction to Chapter 1, page 8.

Realization of the historical impossibility that the command to "measure the temple of God" might refer to the temple built by Herod is buttressed by geography and theology. Could John or the people to whom the book of Revelation was addressed have traveled to Jerusalem? Should they have been able to make that journey, would Gentile Christians have been allowed into that temple to take the measurements? If by some expedient they could have taken the measurements, would they have been allowed to make repairs, additions, or adjustments to that structure?

Though, as we have seen, "the temple of God" refers to our own body, collectively it also refers to the "church." Please see I Corinthians 3:16-17, II Corinthians 6:16 and Ephesians 2:19-22 where the church is referred to as God's temple.

This verse refers to a time when the church, the temple of God, is subjected to careful scrutiny based on scripture, that is, to a time when it will be measured. The seven churches of the Roman province of Asia had been scrutinized, a form of careful measuring, by Christ the Incarnate Word (John 1:14). Here the global church, the temple of God, is to be measured by the written word which is given to us in scripture.

11:1 "the altar"

The altar which is to be measured is that one which is identified in Hebrews 13:10.

11:2 "And the court which is without the temple leave without, and measure it not; for it hath been given unto the nations: and the holy city shall they tread under foot forty and two months."

---

290 J. H. Elliott, <u>History In the Making</u>, (New Haven, Yale University Press, 2012), p. 133.

Revelation Chapter 11

11:2   "the court which is without"

The unbelieving Gentile world, depicted as "the court which is without," at this time is not subjected to the same standards of scrutiny as those to which the church must be held. This is in harmony with Paul's question, "What have I to do with judging them that are without?" (I Corinthians 5:12) However, the participation of Christians in evaluating the world will come later when "the saints shall judge the world." (I Corinthians 6:2)

11:2   "the holy city"

The holy city is another simile picturing the church. That is the clear implication of Hebrews 12:22, which says, "Ye are come unto mount Zion, and unto the city of the living God, the heavenly Jerusalem and to innumerable hosts of angels." This concept is buttressed in Revelation 22:14 which says, "Blessed are they that wash their robes, that they may have the right to come to the tree of life, and may enter in by the gates into the city." For further identification of "the holy city," see also Galatians 4:26.

The holy city of Revelation 11:2 is to be equated with the city of God which is mentioned prophetically in Psalm 46:4 and 48:1. Historically, geographic Jerusalem was called "the holy city," prefiguring the true holy city. (See Nehemiah 11:1, Isaiah 52:1, Matthew 4:5 and Matthew 27:53.) However, Jerusalem ruined its already deeply compromised reputation (See Luke 13:34.) by allowing itself to become the site where Christ was crucified.

In 413 A.D., Augustine, the great North African Metropolitan Bishop and theologian, began writing his seminal classical work, *The City of God*. He bestowed labor on it for the next fifteen years. Beginning in chapter 14 he wrestled with the concept and career of the city of God. By failing to properly draw the boundaries between the city of God and "the great city" of Revelation 11:8, Augustine, by his persuasive theological dissertation, laid the foundation for theological Babylon, the misbegotten concept in which the church wields secular power to coerce people into submission to its dictates. That Augustine fell into this grievous error is confirmed by his role in the Donatist controversy of justifying brutality in his effort to stamp out the very vigorous Donatist Movement.[291] The true city of God stands in stark contrast both to "the great city" (11:8) and to "Babylon." On the characteristics of the "great city," see the comment on 11:8.

11:2   "the holy city shall be tread under foot forty and two months"

During those forty-two months it will seem that the world is totally triumphant, for the church will be, as it were, dirt under the world's feet. See the explanation of this period of time in the comment on "a thousand two hundred and threescore days" at 11:3.

11:3   "And I will give unto my two witnesses, and they shall prophesy a thousand two hundred and threescore days, clothed in sackcloth."

---

[291] "By 412 Augustine had lost patience and he backed harsh new government measures against the Donatists. He even provided theological reasons for the repression: he pointed out to one of his Donatist friends that Jesus had told a parable in which a host had filled up places at his banquet with an order, 'compel them to come in.' That meant that a Christian government had the duty to support the Church by punishing heresy and schism, and the unwilling adherents which this produced might be the start of a living faith. This was a side of Augustine's teaching which had much appeal to Christian regimes for centuries to come." [Diarmaid MacCulloch, Christianity: The First Three Thousand Years, (New York: Viking, 2010), p.304.]

11:3   "I will give unto my two witnesses"

The two witnesses are clearly identified in 11:4-5. Please see the comments on those verses. The ASV, though faithfully and literally translating the elliptical Greek text, is clumsy because it, like the Greek text, does not tell us what was given to the two witnesses. The ESV says, "I will grant authority to my two witnesses." The NIV says, "I will give power to my two witnesses." And the NRSV says, "I will grant my two witnesses authority to prophesy one thousand two hundred sixty days, wearing sackcloth." The words "authority," "power" and "authority to prophesy" have been supplied by the translators.

11:3   "a thousand two hundred and threescore days"

This countdown and the one in 11:2 has not yet started because only one of the two witnesses who are described as "my two witnesses" are currently on the scene. The Gentile Christian church, one member of God's two-member witness team, is now on duty but the Jewish contingent, the second witness, is not yet giving testimony. That member of the two-party witness team will present itself for duty when 144,000 Jewish people eventually accept Christ (See Revelation 7:1-8.) and consequently will be grafted back into the olive tree. (See Romans 11:23.)

The calculation of the length of time during which the two witnesses will prophesy is given by months in 11:2 and by days, here, in 11:3. According to the statement in Ezekiel 4:6, one day equals a year. Forty-two months multiplied by 30, the days per month, gives the 1260 days of 11:3. From this calculation we have the assurance that from the time the Jewish people accept Christ as their Messiah (see 7:2-8), world history will continue for at least another 1260 prophetic days, that is, 1.26 millennia.

The time designations of "forty and two months" in 11:2 and the "thousand two hundred and threescore days" in 11:3 are of the same length. If they both describe the same period of time, as they seem to, then the two witnesses will be working in a hostile environment.

11:3   "clothed in sackcloth"

The wardrobe of the two witnesses depicts their humility, a character trait which will marvelously magnify the power of their testimony. The high-mindedness of Gentile Christians, rebuked by Paul in Romans 11:20, will have been totally repudiated at this point. Also, the Jewish arrogance manifested in their persistent centuries-long rejection of the Messiah, for which they are indicted in Romans 11:23, will have been totally forfeited and renounced by the Jewish Christians, who collectively will constitute one of the two witnesses.

11:4   "These are the two olive trees and the two candlesticks, standing before the Lord of the earth."

11:4   "these are the two olive trees"

The pronoun "these" refers to the two witnesses (11:3) which are here, first of all, epitomized by a simile of two olive trees. One of these two olive trees, the one which the apostle Paul described as "a wild olive [tree]" (Romans 11:17, 24), portrays Gentile

Revelation Chapter 11

Christians or Christ's Gentile church. The second olive tree is the "natural" olive tree (clearly implied as that tree which has "natural branches." (Romans 11:21, 24) It is the "good olive tree" (Romans 11:24) ["a cultivated olive tree" - NRSV and Stern], representing Jewish Christians or Christ's Jewish church.

It is highly probable that Christ's Jewish church will be composed of converts to Jesus who will have come from stunningly remote and diverse locations. This will make it possible for them to take the Gospel of Christ to some of the most remote and difficult areas of the world. One Jewish scholar recently said "There are multitudes of people whose forefathers were once part of us and who now seek a way back into the fold." For example, he tells us, "From the Jews of Kaifeng, China, whose Sephardic ancestors traveled along the Silk Road, to the Bnei Menashe of northeastern India, who claim descent from a lost tribe of Israel, and to the Hidden Jews of Poland from the Holocaust, there are multitudes with a historical connection to the Jewish people."[292]

11:4 "the two candlesticks"

In a second simile, the two witnesses are further identified as being "the two candlesticks, standing before the Lord of the earth." As we have seen in Revelation 1:20, candlesticks, because they give light, represent the church. (See Matthew 5:16 and Philippians 2:15.) The two candlesticks, therefore, also represent the Jewish and Gentile churches.

Though the witnesses present themselves humbly, as indicated by wearing "sackcloth" garments (11:3), they are flourishing for they are "standing before the Lord of the earth." This is the triumph which was prophesied in Revelation 7:2-10.

11:5 "And if any man desireth to hurt them, fire proceedeth out of their mouth and devoureth their enemies; and if any man shall desire to hurt them, in this manner must he be killed."

11:5 "fire proceedeth out of their mouth"

The fire which proceeds out of their mouth is the word of God, for fire is one of the graphic similes portraying God's word. Here are three examples:

(1) "Is not my word like fire? saith Jehovah; and like a hammer that breaketh the rock in pieces?" (Jeremiah 23:29) (2) "Wherefore thus saith Jehovah, the God of hosts, Because ye speak this word, behold, I will make my words in thy mouth fire, and this people wood, and it shall devour them." (Jeremiah 5:14) (3) "Behold, the name of Jehovah cometh from far, burning with his anger, and in thick rising smoke: his lips are full of indignation, and his tongue is as a devouring fire." (Isaiah 30:27)

11:5 "out of their mouth"

One of the reasons the testimony of the two witnesses will be powerful and effective is because they will speak with only one mouth. They will give witness through "their mouth," not their mouths. Though genetically, historically, ethnically and culturally different, their witness will be completely harmonious. This certainly will be one fulfillment of Jesus' prayer in which he implored God to "keep them in thy name which

---

292 Michael Freund, *Symposium: The Jewish Future*, <u>Commentary</u>, November 2015, pp. 26-27

thou hast given me, that they may be one, even as we are." (John 17:11) This will also demonstrate the power of verbal unity to which Paul pointed as he wrote to the church in Rome. He said, "Now the God of patience and of comfort grant you to be of the same mind, one with another, according to Christ Jesus: that with one accord ye may <u>with one mouth glorify the God and Father of our Lord Jesus Christ</u>." (Romans 15:5-6)

It is extremely important to recognize the obvious conclusion that the two witnesses cannot be the Old and New Testaments, since the message, the fire, coming out of their mouth is itself the message of those Testaments. If the fire proceeding out of their mouth, as many commentators indicate, is God's word (the Old and New Testaments) then the witnesses, out of whose mouth that word proceeds, must be something or someone other than the Old and New Testaments.

11:5 "devoureth their enemies"

One example of the word of God "devouring" the enemies of the church is found in the ministry of Stephen. Simply put, "they were not able to withstand the wisdom and Spirit by which he spake." (Acts 6:10) Comparably, during their ministry, the two witnesses, by God's Spirit, will demonstrate such wisdom that consequently the enemies of the Gospel will be totally discomfitted, thus eaten up or devoured.

11:5 "in this manner must he be killed"

The pronoun "he" refers to "any man [who] desireth to hurt them." The words "in this manner" refer to the fire which proceeds out of the mouth of the witnesses, that is, by the transforming power of the divine message. Preaching of the message spiritually impacts the lives of everyone who accepts it so they spiritually put the sinful personality, the "old man," to death (Romans 6:6), and thus are killed.

Obviously, in view of these scriptures, the two witnesses give their testimony by teaching or preaching the word of God. In that way, "in this manner," that is, with the fire which proceeds out of their mouth, not with clubs, swords, spears, arrows or other martial weapons, they will "kill" the opposition. (See also Isaiah 11:4 and Revelation 19:15.)

11:6 "These have the power to shut the heaven, that it rain not during the days of their prophecy: and they have power over the waters to turn them into blood, and to smite the earth with every plague, as often as they shall desire."

11:6 "power to shut the heaven ... power over the waters ... and to smite the earth"

In addition to being able to wield the power of prayer, which Elijah used to control rainfall in his time (See James 5:17-18.), the total numerical strength of the combined Jewish/Gentile body of believers/witnesses, though probably still a minority in the total world population, will be very large. (See Revelation 7:9.) Their numerical strength will be so great that they could, if they should so choose, exert great and awesome power, enough not only to skew normal weather patterns, but to impact society in many other ways and even wage war.

Revelation Chapter 11

Whenever the preaching of the Gospel becomes overwhelmingly triumphant, as that of the two witnesses is here prophesied to become, great social, economic and even political power will be within the grasp of the church. The success of the two witnesses will be so extensive and numerically significant that ecclesiastical power could be exerted over a wide spectrum of human life and activity, even malevolently. <u>It is important to note that the prophecy only says they "have" these powers, it does not say that they ever use them</u>. It is startling to realize that some commentators overlook this important observation. For example, Hendriksen wrote, "Be very, very careful, O wicked world. If anyone is *fully determined* to harm the church, fire proceeds out of the mouth of God's witnesses. But even if anyone would like to harm the true ministers and missionaries, he will be destroyed similarly, verse 5."[293] It seems Hendriksen was advocating something like the policy carried out by Augustine whose "arguments were used for centuries to justify Christian persecution of dissent, the presence of unworthy men in sacramental offices, and the neglect of church discipline — none of which was allowed in the Early Church."[294]

The fact that the two witnesses will not yield to the temptation to grasp and use economic, political or military power, will be a great spiritual triumph over the enticements which accompany victorious and numerically significant success. They will not use any of their powers for their own advantage or to coerce people to align themselves with the church, or to punish dissenters or backsliders. They will not be among those who will be punished when the time comes "to destroy them that destroy the earth." (Revelation 11:18)

If the two witnesses should choose to use the social and political power malevolently, which their success will have made available to them, they could disastrously impact the ecology to the extent that weather patterns would be skewed or altered. Think of desiccated areas which only for economic gain have been denuded of trees and other plant life, like some of those great rain forests in the Amazon River basin in Brazil. Such activity would "shut the heaven, that it rain not."

"It is impossible to overstate the importance of humankind's clearing of the forests. The transformation of forested land by human actions represents one of the great forces in global environmental change, and one of the great drivers of biodiversity loss. … Forests influence local climate and weather. Rain forests transport great quantities of water to the atmosphere via [a biological process called] plant transpiration. … Much of that transpired water replenishes the clouds and rain that maintain the rain forest. If the forest is cut, much more of that rain will become river water [due to unimpeded runoff where the forest used to stand], flow to distant seas, and the region will become permanently drier. No rain forest can regenerate if this occurs. Rain forests maintain local climate and strongly influence global fluxes of oxygen and carbon dioxide."[295]

The two witnesses will also have enough power to incite terrible wars, should they wish to utilize their power in such a diabolical way. The resultant killing would be so widespread and devastating that the waters would be turned into blood. The potential for

---

293 W. Hendriksen, <u>More Than Conquerors: An Interpretation of the Book of Revelation</u>, (Grand Rapids: Baker Book House, 1952), p. 157.
294 Franklin H. Littell, <u>The Macmillan Atlas History of Christianity</u>, (New York: Macmillan Publishing Co. Inc., 1976), p. 16.
295 http://www.globalchange.umich.edu/globalchange2/current/lectures/deforest/deforest.htm. Accessed 7/20/13.

such a disaster occurring is clear if one remembers the Vandal naval war which turned the sea into blood. (See 8:8 and comments.)

Further, their success will be so great that should they use the power which such success makes available in a malicious way, they would be able to "smite the earth with every plague as often as they shall desire."

11:7 **"And when they shall have finished their testimony, the beast that cometh up out of the abyss shall make war with them, and overcome them, and kill them."**

11:7 "finished their testimony"

Their testimony will be given for a long time. It will continue for 1,260 years. (See 11:3.) It will only be "finished" when that global saturation by God's Word has been achieved which Isaiah foresaw when he prophesied, "the earth shall be full of the knowledge of Jehovah, as the waters cover the sea." (Isaiah 11:9)

11:7 "the beast that cometh up out of the abyss"

This beast which comes up out of the abyss should not be identified with the one portrayed in Revelation 17:8, unless he emerges multiple times on various occasions. The beast mentioned in 17:8 depicts the revival of persecuting Roman power in the form of the Holy Roman Empire, whose first and greatest emperor was Charlemagne, grandson of Charles Martel. "The empire of Rome, which had died at the hands of Odoacer in 476, rose again in 800 as the 'Holy Roman Empire.' While its physical strength lay north of the Alps, the center of its idea was Rome."[296]

The prolonged period of Gospel triumph predicted in 11:3-6 will elicit intensified satanic opposition. It will come directly from the abyss, Satan's abode. (Luke 8:30-31) Ultimately he will be doomed to forever inhabit the lake of fire.

This beast which comes up out of the abyss will make his appearance centuries later than the tenure of the Holy Roman Empire or even that of its extension and continuation in the Hapsburg Empire. In contrast to the Holy Roman Empire, which was a political entity, this beast which comes up out of the abyss clearly seems to be a powerful satanically-inspired, anti-Christian philosophical entity.

11:7 "shall make war with them"

This will be a war of clashing and conflicting concepts. The war will be initiated and facilitated by the powerful advocacy of a satanically inspired anti-gospel philosophical doctrine. (See Colossians 2:8.) It will be a specious, subtle, and secular idea. That idea will appear to be a total rebuttal, a nullification, of the triumphant Christian Gospel message preached by the two witnesses.

11:7 "overcome them and kill them"

This triumph of evil will be achieved by the propagation of a cunning, trendy, revised and rejuvenated, godless doctrine. It will be globally embraced with such widespread acclaim and enthusiasm that it will temporarily seem to genuinely negate the message of the two

---

296 H. G. Wells, The Outline of History, Vol. I, (New York: Doubleday & Co., Inc, 1971), p. 547.

witnesses. The two witnesses and their message will have been "overcome." From dazzling success (vv. 5-6) both they and their message will seem to have lost all relevance. Their message suddenly will become ineffective, eliciting sneers, jeers and disdain. They, so to speak, will have been "killed."

The unbelievers' new lethal philosophical argumentation will consist of something like the current scourge of popular, aggressive, evangelical atheism. Though polemical books attacking the message of Christ are nothing new, going back at least to the attack made by Celsus in 180 A.D., still, "in 2004, the unexpected happened. First came Sam Harris' *The End of Faith*, which was a *New York Times* bestseller and [contra factually] winner of the 2005 PEN Award for Nonfiction. Soon after followed Daniel C. Dennett's *Breaking the Spell: Religion as a Natural Phenomenon*; [Richard] Dawkins' *The God Delusion*; Harris' second book, *Letter to a Christian Nation*; Victor J. Stenger's *God: The Failed Hypothesis – How Science Shows That God Does Not Exist*; and Christopher Hitchens' *God is Not Great: How Religion Poisons Everything*.

"These books weren't just publishers' rash responses to a surprise bestseller. Rather, they've been hot commodities in the book marketplace. Take Dawkins' *The God Delusion*, for example. According to Amy Heidel, Houghton Mifflin's assistant director of publicity, it's been on *The New York Times* nonfiction bestseller list for more than a year and has 1.5 million copies in print worldwide."[297] These authors incessantly attack the Christian concept of God, which they contemptuously call "the God hypothesis." It is these anti-God philosophers who conceive of and promote the virulent godless concepts which undergird the open moral and spiritual rebellion described in 11:10.

In addition to the revival and rejuvenation of the doctrine of aggressive atheism, Christianity will doubtless also be simultaneously confronted by a revival of ancient diatribes, challenging the validity of the foundational history of Christian doctrine. These will probably take a form similar to Dan Brown's *The DaVinci Code*, or to that of the Muslim writer Reza Aslan, the Iranian-born academic and author of *Zealot: The Life and Times of Jesus of Nazareth*. "His Jesus is an essentially political figure, a revolutionary killed because he challenged Roman rule, who was then mysticized by his disciples and divinized by Paul of Tarsus."[298]

These attacks against the testimony of Jesus are based on fabrications and distortions of both biology and history. Please see the analysis of these fraudulent polemical positions at the exposition of Revelation 19:10 under the heading "thy brethren that hold the testimony of Jesus" on page 312.

11:8 "And their dead bodies lie in the street of the great city, which spiritually is called Sodom and Egypt, where also their Lord was crucified."

---

[297] Kara Gebhart Uhl, *Religious Wars*, Writer's Digest, April 2008, p. 27. Some books which refute the atheists' books should be noted: Richard Dawkins, "*The God Delusion* has spurred several direct responses, including Alister McGrath and Joanna Colicutt McGrath's *The Dawkins Delusion?* And Walter Thirring's Cosmic Impressions: *Traces of God in the Laws of Nature*." [Uhl, op.cit., p. 27] Especially, Dinesh D'Souza, What's So Great About Christianity. "D'Souza offers a persuasive, scholarly, and intelligent rebuttal to the main charges made by those who proudly carry the banner of atheism." [Peter Wehner, *God's Advocate*, The Weekly Standard, February 18, 2008, p. 46.]

[298] Ross Douthat, *Return of the Jesus Wars*, The New York Times, Sunday Review, August 4, 2013, p. 11.

11:8 "their dead bodies lie in the street"

Both the Jewish and the Gentile churches will lose their vitality and dynamism. As James tells us, "The body apart from the spirit is dead." (See James 2:26.) The witnesses will still have public contact with society, a vestigial superficial contact, "in the street," a presence through that which Revelation calls "their dead bodies." Sadly, their presence will have become like a corpse, no longer having vital or dynamic power to leaven society.

11:8 "the great city"

We can leave Babylon, the corrupt church. In fact, God's people are ordered to leave Babylon. (See Revelation 18:4.) In contrast, short of the occurrence of death, we cannot leave <u>this</u> great city, worldwide unholy secular society. This is in harmony with Paul's statement, in which he said, "I wrote unto you in my epistle to have no company with fornicators; not at all meaning with the fornicators of this world, or with the covetous and extortioners, or with idolaters; for then must you needs go out of the world." (I Corinthians 5:9-10)

11:8 "Sodom and Egypt, where also their Lord was crucified"

This is not the crucifixion of Jesus which took place on Golgotha in Roman-controlled Jerusalem, but another crucifixion taking place in "the great city." (11:8) This refers to the treading underfoot of the Son of God (Hebrews 10:29), which is a form of crucifying afresh the Son of God (Hebrews 6:6). The unholy deed of initially crucifying the Lord Jesus Christ was carried out in the "holy city" (Revelation 11:2), ironically, the city which by intent was to have been attuned to the will of God. Therefore, it should not surprise us that repeat occurrences of crucifying the Lord Jesus Christ would take place in the "great city" which depicts unholy secular society. That city's true spiritual character is portrayed by the terms "Sodom" and "Egypt," which respectively epitomize sensualism and idolatry.

11:9 "And from among the peoples and tribes and tongues and nations do men look upon their dead bodies three days and a half, and suffer not their dead bodies to be laid in a tomb."

The church, both Jewish and Gentile, will not be forgotten; the "great city" will keep their corpses on display for international ridicule by taunters "from among the peoples and tribes and tongues and nations." This mockery will go on for "three days and a half" which, translated according to the formula given in Ezekiel 4:6, will last three and a half years.

11:10 "And they that dwell on the earth rejoice over them, and make merry; and they shall send gifts one to another; because these two prophets tormented them that dwell on the earth."

Revelation Chapter 11

11:10 "they that dwell on the earth rejoice over them, and make merry"

Worldly people (those "that dwell on the earth") will hold "them" (the seemingly discredited Jewish/Gentile churches) up to scorn. They will "rejoice over them and make merry." (Compare Psalms 79:1-4.)

11:10 "because these two prophets tormented them that dwell on the earth"

Note that God's two witnesses (11:3) are here called "prophets." Since "the church of the living God, [is] the pillar and ground of the truth," (I Timothy 3:15) it is to present the facts as witnesses. The church is to call people to acceptance of the truth and repentance, one of the great works of prophets. The torment was caused by the powerful, spiritual, moral, doctrinal, conceptual, and philosophical content of the Gospel of Christ. Until the beginning of the "three days and a half," (11:9) unbelievers, though unable to counter the message, squirmed and writhed, as it were, in the torment of their total frustration.

11:11 "And after the three days and a half the breath of life from God entered into them, and they stood upon their feet; and great fear fell upon them that beheld them."

11:11 "after the three days and a half"

Satan made his move through the beast that came up out of the abyss (See 11:7.); now God, "after the three days and a half" which translates into three and a half years, (See comment on 11:9.) makes a victorious counter move.

11:11 "the breath of life from God entered into them, and they stood upon their feet"

The two witnesses, that is the Gentile and Jewish churches, will gain the ability to successfully counteract the secular philosophical anti-God concepts which seemingly will have negated the power of the Gospel message. This spiritual victory will clearly be the result of a divine initiative, for the passage says, "the breath [or "Spirit" - KJV] of life from God entered into them."

This vision is one confirmation of Jesus' prediction that the gates of Hades shall not prevail against the church. (Matthew 16:18) Satan may reduce it to "dead bodies in the street," (Revelation 11:8) but eventually God will give it new life. This is a corporate fulfillment of Jesus' prediction that "he that believeth on me though he die, yet shall he live." (John 11:25)

11:12 "And they heard a great voice from heaven saying unto them, Come up hither. And they went up into heaven in the cloud; and their enemies beheld them."

11:12 "they went up into heaven in the cloud; and their enemies beheld them"

Some might consider this to be the concept of the Rapture, the widely acclaimed concept popularized in the *Left Behind* series of books. (See additional comments on the Rapture at 7:14-17 and in Appendix A on Matthew 24:40 and Acts 1:9-11.) The church had been triumphantly successful in its evangelistic efforts, devouring, as it were, the enemies, those who oppose the message (11:5). This propelled the church to a position of great power. (See 11:6 and the comments.) That extended period of phenomenal success, lasting much of the twelve- hundred-sixty-years, will have been brought to an abrupt and humiliating end by a unique unprecedented satanic attack (11:7). That attack will have been so successful that the church will be overcome and killed (11:7).

After three and a half years, during which the church was considered to be only a despised rotting corpse, compared to its previous exalted status (11:9), the church again becomes vital and triumphant. This resuscitation of the church caused "great fear" (11:11) in the hearts of those who had previously rejoiced over its demise. At that triumphant point, in some sense, the Jewish/Gentile church "went up into heaven."

This "heaven" does not seem to be the place where "the Lamb that is in the midst of the throne shall be their shepherd, and shall guide them unto fountains of waters of life: and God shall wipe away every tear from their eyes." (Revelation 7:17)

Probably this "heaven" refers to a place of high earthly honor, power and exaltation. It will be a status held, at this point, in which the church is once again truly dominant. Consideration of this second possibility is rendered logical because the church's new status seemingly is what causes the revolution described in the next verse.

Some commentators consider that this "heaven" refers to the eternal triumphant abode of the redeemed of all ages in the presence of almighty God. Though superficially seeming to be the intent of the words, the conclusion to which those commentators have come has caused them consternation. For example, Barclay says, "What makes this passage difficult is that it seems to indicate that things have come to an end and final victory, while there is still half the book to go."[299]

11:13 "And in that hour there was a great earthquake, and the tenth part of the city fell; and there were killed in the earthquake seven thousand persons: and the rest were affrighted, and gave glory to the God of heaven."

11:13 "in that hour"

"That hour" probably is not to be considered a sequential time marker. Rather, it marks a definite point in historical development. Thus, it is equivalent to saying, "at that point." However, it is an important point.

11:13 "there was a great earthquake"

The earthquake took place in "the city," "the great city." (See 11:8.) It was this "city" which, under the influence of its leaders, had rejoiced (11:10) over the nearly fatal blow the church had received. The church's two constituent elements, the two witnesses, were comatose, lying in the street (11:8) of this city like decaying unburied corpses. But after three-and-a-half years "the breath of life from God entered into them; and great fear fell upon them that beheld them." (11:11) This created a backlash leading to a conceptual rebellion, the "great earthquake."

11:13 "a tenth part of the city fell"

While this development took place throughout the world, it was not world-enveloping because only "a tenth part of the city fell." This "tenth part of the city" probably refers to

---

[299] William Barclay, <u>The Revelation of John</u>, Vol. II, (London: Westminster/John Knox Press, 2004), p. 82.

Revelation Chapter 11

centers of academia. The fall of the "tenth part" probably refers to the complete discrediting of those pseudo academic centers where the chairs of false philosophy and theology were located. Those were the centers in which the devastating false doctrines had been contrived, which had killed the two witnesses (11:7) and from which people had been led to mock those two witnesses.

11:13 "there were killed in the earthquake seven thousand persons"

Apparently, an enraged citizenship rebelled and then murdered – either physically or conceptually or both – that part of perverted academia which had led them so far astray.

11:13 "the rest were affrighted and gave glory to the God of heaven"

This statement seems to indicate that the rebellion against those forces in academia which had misled people first sparked a rebellion, killing seven thousand people, and ultimately led many people to glorify God.

11:14 "The second Woe is past: behold, the third Woe cometh quickly."

11:14 "the second Woe is past"

We should review some of the developments which took place during the time of the sixth trumpet. They are depicted in 9:13-11:14 and warranted the use of the proper noun "Woe" to describe that historic period. Though the events foretold in the foreboding prophecy of the second Woe are yet to take place, it seems they will occur in the very near rather than the remote future. From the turmoil currently seething in the four nations contiguous to the Euphrates River (See Map 8.), it is possible that the four angels (See 9:14 and comments.) have already been unshackled. Current ongoing developments could well expand so dramatically that the major nations of the world would feel compelled to ally themselves with one faction or the other, resulting in that gargantuan world war due to which one-third (9:18) of the world's inhabitants will die.

One would think that the extent of the war-generated carnage, plus the destruction and suffering out of which a third of the world's population will perish, would be so shocking that people would turn to God. Yet, "the rest of mankind who were not killed with these plagues, repented not of the works of their hands, that they should not worship demons, and the idols of gold, and of silver, and of brass, and of stone, and of wood ... and they repented not of their murders, nor of their sorceries, nor of their fornications, nor of their thefts." (9:20-21) Not only are the astronomical numbers of deaths generated by the war shocking, but so is the widespread resolute, rebellious hardness of heart which will continue to prevail in the surviving multitudes of mankind.

Undoubtedly, the war will have destroyed extensive portions of the world's infrastructure, inevitably making economic recovery very difficult, resulting in ongoing and widespread human suffering. During that inauspicious time, God's two witnesses, the Jewish/Gentile church, will preach and teach the Gospel of Christ with phenomenal success. However, satanic forces will generate a backlash based on specious philosophical arguments which will temporarily seem to negate the Gospel message of the church.

Surprisingly, out of that environment of extensive ongoing woe, the church recovers and is once again able to project the Gospel of Christ so powerfully that it will cause "a great earthquake," (11:13) leading to the death of seven thousand people, an elite, those who had conceived and promoted the doctrines which decisively impeded the church's testimony for three-and-a-half years. Finally, "the rest [of mankind] were affrighted, and gave glory to the God of heaven." (11:13)

11:14 "the third Woe"

The woe of the third Woe angel is to take us through a review of history, showing us some difficult periods, including the prolonged persecution of the church. This review will occur under the mandate of the very important "again" clause in 10:11.

11:14 "the third Woe cometh quickly"

This indicates that there will be no intervening undescribed period of history between the events under the supervision of the second Woe angel and those which are to follow during the period of the third Woe angel.

7. The seventh trumpet 11:15-14:20

11:15 "And the seventh angel sounded; and there followed great voices in heaven, and they said, The kingdom of the world is become the kingdom of our Lord, and of his Christ: and he shall reign for ever and ever."

11:15 "the seventh angel sounded; and there followed great voices in heaven"

The impact of the seventh angel's ministry will be so dramatic that it causes excited discussion even in heaven, implied by "great voices in heaven." From 11:16 we should conclude that this "heaven" refers to the place where God's universal throne is. This statement implies that, to all those gathered around his throne, God had not previously divulged the full scope of impending events. Thus, the "great voices in heaven" are voices of surprise and excitement.

11:15 "the kingdom of the world is become the kingdom of our Lord, and of his Christ"

This epochal transition is not the end of the Christian dispensation or epoch which would terminate terrestrial human history but expresses another period of unprecedented phenomenal Gospel triumph. That triumph will be the pinnacle of the twelve-hundred-sixty-year period of Gospel success. It will be achieved despite intense satanic opposition. The calculation for the twelve-hundred-sixty-year period has been explained in the comments on 11:2-3. (See also the comments on 13:5 on page 201.)

11:16 "And the four and twenty elders, who sit before God on their thrones, fell upon their faces and worshiped God,"

While the historically climactic Gospel triumph will elicit a profound worshipful response in heaven, it also will have simultaneously sparked urgent satanic efforts to counter and thwart the success of the Gospel growing out of the revival of the church.

Revelation Chapter 11

(See 11:11.) Some of Satan's renewed efforts will be described in the twelfth chapter of Revelation. (See especially 12:12.) For the "four and twenty elders," see 4:4 and 4:6-8.

11:17 "saying, We give thee thanks, O Lord God, the Almighty, who art and who wast; because thou hast taken thy great power, and didst reign."

This reign does not refer to God's rule over the universe which has been continuously going on without any cessation or interruption, but to his rule over those people who will have become followers of Christ as indicated in 11:15 by the words "become the kingdom of our Lord and of his Christ." They have sanctified Christ as Lord in their hearts (See I Peter 3:15.), thus allowing God to reign.

11:18 "And the nations were wroth, and thy wrath came, and the time of the dead to be judged, and the time to give their reward to thy servants the prophets, and to the saints, and to them that fear thy name, the small and the great; and to destroy them that destroy the earth."

11:18 "And the nations were wroth"

This wrath expresses the nations' response growing out of the ultimate futility of their venomous anti-God activities. This prophetic description replicates the one in the second Psalm. There the question is asked, "Why do the nations rage and the peoples meditate on a vain thing? The kings of the earth set themselves, and the rulers take counsel together, against Jehovah and against his anointed, *saying*, Let us break their bonds asunder, and cast away their cords from us. He that sitteth in the heavens will laugh; the Lord will have them in derision. Then will he speak unto them in his wrath, and vex them in his sore displeasure; yet I have set my king upon my holy hill of Zion." (Psalm 2:1-6)

11:18 "thy wrath came, and the time of the dead to be judged and the time to give their reward to thy servants the prophets, and to the saints, and to them that fear thy name, the small and the great"

In mercy, God's wrath may be delayed but because of justice its coming will not be canceled. The coming of God's wrath, which is noted here, is not that judgment which is foretold in Revelation 20:11-15. While the nations on this occasion "were wroth," God expresses his wrath by nullifying or negating the anti-gospel vengeful efforts of the unbelieving nations. God expresses his wrath by a vindicating judgment concerning "the dead," those who have died in the cause of the Gospel. The purpose for which they spent their lives will have been achieved. That will constitute a judgment in their favor. It will be part of "their reward." Christians of every category who labored, expending their lives for the Gospel, here categorized as "the dead," will be rewarded by seeing or knowing that their efforts and deaths were not in vain. The dead are specifically identified as "thy ["Lord God, the Almighty" 11:17] servants the prophets, ... the saints and ... them that fear thy name, the small and the great."

11:19 "And there was opened the temple of God that is in heaven; and there was seen in his temple the ark of his covenant; and there followed lightnings, and voices, and thunders, and an earthquake, and great hail."

11:19 "the ark of his covenant"

God will keep his covenant. He has not forgotten his documented promises and commitments. He keeps the "ark of his covenant" on display, not to remind himself of his covenanted commitments but to reassure us that he will keep them meticulously. This assures us that he will be with the church during those times when the nations manifest their wrath against it in many devious and destructive ways.

11:19 "there followed lightnings, and voices, and thunders, and an earthquake, and great hail"

In "his covenant" are stipulations which if ignored or violated bring about consequences on earth. We know the five consequences, which are itemized here, take place on earth because one of them is an earthquake not a "heavenquake." Satanically inspired opposition to those committed to God's program has been fatal to many of God's servants. In 11:18 they are called "the dead." Those who brought about their deaths will now suffer God's "wrath." (11:18) The carrying out of his wrath is here expressed by five nouns: lightnings, voices, thunders, earthquake and hail.

Revelation Chapter 12

Introduction: For an accurate understanding of the Book of Revelation it is essential to correctly identify the glorious woman whose career is foretold in chapter 12. This commentary takes the position that she represents the church and that her life portrays some of the critical periods of political, ecclesiastical and philosophical history through which the church will have to pass.

12:1 "**And a great sign was seen in heaven: a woman arrayed with the sun, and the moon under her feet, and upon her head a crown of twelve stars;**"

12:1   "a great sign was seen in heaven"

This heaven is the atmospheric heaven which was being used as a backdrop for a revelation like that mentioned in Acts 9:3, 22:6 and 26:13-14. On the meaning of the various uses of the word "heaven" in the book of Revelation, please see the introduction to chapter 15. The "heaven" mentioned here is number six in that summary.

12:1   "a woman arrayed with the sun, and the moon under her feet, and upon her head a crown of twelve stars"

The following seven clear indicators (pp. 173, 174, 176, 180, 181, 182 & 184) help us understand that this glorious woman represents the church.

First, the fact that the symbol being used is that of a woman itself points to the church. The depiction of the church as a woman in this chapter of Revelation is in full harmony with other related passages of scripture. For example, in the exposition of matrimonial harmony which Paul gave to the church in Ephesus, he said that a man should "cleave to his wife; and the two should become one flesh. This mystery is great but I speak in regard of Christ and of the church." (Ephesians 5:31-32) Earlier in that same passage we are told that Jesus sanctified the church "having cleansed it by the washing of water with the Word, that he might present the church to himself [as a bride], a glorious church, not having spot or wrinkle or any such thing; but that it should be holy and without blemish." (Ephesians 5:25-27) There is no doubt that the "glorious church" mentioned in Ephesians 5:27 is here in Revelation represented by the glorious woman who is arrayed ("clothed" - NIV) with the sun.

The church being portrayed as a woman betrothed to Christ is also clear in Paul's second letter to the church in Corinth. In it he reminded those Christians of their bond with Christ when he said "I espoused you ["promised you in marriage" - NRSV] to one husband, that I might present you as a pure virgin to Christ." (II Corinthians 11:2) Paul's statement is in full harmony with Jesus' teaching in which he referred to himself as the bridegroom. (See Matthew 9:15.) But, there are also many additional facts which assure us of this identity.

Second, the woman may also be identified by her glorious wardrobe which consists of two elegant outfits. <u>Her first outfit is truly stellar</u>. When she puts it on, she is "arrayed with the sun" and has "the moon under her feet" and also "upon her head [she has] a crown of twelve stars." (12:1)

Being "arrayed" or clothed with the sun describes the high level of the glorious woman's spiritual enlightenment – it is dazzling apparel. As God's eternal purpose has been disclosed during the course of history, the biblical account shows there has been progress, increasing advancement and growth in spiritual revelation, comprehension, understanding and enlightenment. One indication of that progress is seen, for example, in the account of Jesus' visit to Capernaum. Matthew, quoting Isaiah 9:1-2, tells us that "the people that sat in darkness saw a great light and to them that sat in the region and shadow of death, to them did light spring up." (Matthew 4:16) This implies that additional and enhanced spiritual light or perception had been made available to those who listened to Christ.

However, the increase in spiritual enlightenment was not limited to that one incident from the ministry of Jesus. Therefore, subsequent to that time, the Christian era or dispensation has often been appropriately called the sunlight age. That designation is given in contrast to the Mosaic period, which scholars have frequently epitomized as the moonlight dispensation, while the more remote patriarchal period of biblical history is correspondingly and appropriately characterized as the starlight age.

The concept that both the clarity and scope of revealed spiritual knowledge had increased through the centuries, from the time of Adam till the conclusion of the ministry of Christ's apostles, may be called progressive revelation. This concept, in embryonic form, is clearly expressed in Isaiah 28:9-10. There, the idea of being weaned from milk while learning "line upon line, line upon line; here a little, there a little" makes the progressive concept clear. Even earlier, this idea was expressed to Moses when God said "I am Jehovah and I appeared unto Abraham, unto Isaac, and unto Jacob as God Almighty; but by my name Jehovah I was not known to them." (Exodus 6:3)

This idea of a gradually increasing, more expansive and in-depth revelation of the eternal purpose of God is very clearly expounded in the book of Hebrews. There we are told that during the era in which the Mosaic revelation predominated, the people served only "a copy and shadow of the heavenly things." (Hebrews 8:5) However, it was a great blessing that in the time of Christ people could come out of those shadows because Christ was "a high priest of the good things to come through the greater and more perfect tabernacle, not made with hands, that is to say not of this creation." (Hebrews 9:11) As a reiteration for added emphasis, the epistle to the Hebrews again stresses the point that the law had only "a shadow of the good things to come, not the very image of the things." (Hebrews 10:1)

The concept of increasing fullness and inclusiveness of divine revelation, reaching a climax at the end of the apostolic era, was unmistakably made clear when Paul spoke about his "understanding in the mystery of Christ; which in other generations was not made known unto the sons of men, as it hath now been revealed unto his holy apostles and prophets in the Spirit." (Ephesians 3:4-5) The same concept is conveyed in I Corinthians 13:9-12 in which the growth in the scope and clarity of revelation is

Revelation Chapter 12

compared to the more precise and extensive concepts a person has in his maturity, compared with that which he has in his infancy.

Further conclusive evidence that divine revelation was given progressively comes to us in another passage in Paul's writings. He said "the mystery hidden for long ages past [is] now revealed and made known through the prophetic writings by the command of the eternal God, so that all nations might believe and obey Him." (Romans 16:25-26 NIV)

The vision of the glorious woman who is clothed with the sun indicates that a spectacular culmination of a more complete revelation has occurred, allowing those people whom the woman represents to come out of the shadows of ignorance and incomprehension into the brilliance of much greater understanding, epitomized by the dazzling brightness of the sun with which the woman is clothed.

In addition to being clothed with the sun, the glorious woman has the "moon under her feet." This indicates that she is standing upon, and thus having the advantage of, the prior spiritual enlightenment which had been received up to and including that of the Mosaic period, the moonlight era of divine revelation. Paul gave us an explicit example of this when he wrote, "whatsoever things were written aforetime [the written revelations given during the Patriarchal and Mosaic periods] were written for our learning, that through patience and comfort of the scriptures we might have hope." (Romans 15:4)

This progress from starlight to moonlight and on into the era in which the glorious woman is clothed with the sun makes it possible for her, as the church, to be the agency through which "the wisdom of God in its rich variety might now be made known to the rulers and authorities in the heavenly places." (Ephesians 3:10 NRSV)

Though this woman wears dazzling apparel, being clothed with the sun, and uses, as it were, the moon as her footstool, still she is neither proud, contemptuous nor self-willed. She lives under authority, having "upon her head a crown of twelve stars." This refers to her recognizing, acknowledging and abiding in the authority and guidance of the twelve apostles. That commitment was made by the church from its very beginning. From its birth, it "continued steadfastly in the apostles' teaching." (Acts 2:42) [300]

The second outfit in the woman's wardrobe is also glorious. It is purity. It is showcased clearly and explicitly in Revelation 19:7-8. There John recorded that "the marriage of the Lamb is come, and his wife hath made herself ready. And it was given unto her that she should array herself in fine linen, bright and pure: for the fine linen is the righteous acts of the saints."

In apostolic writings the church is referred to as "the saints." For example, in his letter to the church in Rome, Paul addressed his epistle "to all that are in Rome, beloved of God, called to be saints." (Romans 1:7) In his first epistle to the Corinthian Church, Paul addressed his letter to "the church of God which is at Corinth, even them that are sanctified in Christ Jesus, called to be saints." (I Corinthians 1:2) In his second epistle to

---

[300] The power of the symbolism of the twelve stars is seen in the fact that, "Even the European Union's flag - a circle of 12 yellow stars on a blue background - has a coded Christian message. Arsene Heitz, a French Catholic who designed the flag in 1955, originally for the Council of Europe, drew inspiration from Christian iconography of the Virgin Mary wearing a crown with 12 stars. But official accounts of the flag today make no reference to this." - [Andrew Higgins, *At European Parliament, Pope Bluntly Critiques a Continent's Malaise*, The New York Times, November 26, 2014, p. A10.]

that church he wrote to "the church of God which is at Corinth, <u>with all the saints</u> that are in the whole of Achaia." (II Corinthians 1:1)

The identity of the glorious woman as the church is reinforced in Revelation 21:2 in which John tells us that he "saw the holy city, new Jerusalem [another simile for the church] coming down out of heaven from God, made ready as a bride **adorned** for her husband."

"The Jerusalem that is above" (Galatians 4:26) is the same one which John saw "coming down out of heaven from God, made ready as a bride adorned for her husband." (Revelation 21:2) To refresh one's memory of the truth that the bride of Christ is the church, please see Ephesians 5:25-32. Also, Paul wrote to the church in Corinth saying, "I espoused you to one husband ["I promised you to one husband" - NIV], that I might present you as a pure virgin to Christ." (II Corinthians 11:2)

Finally, John was given an invitation which said, "come hither, I will show thee the bride, the wife of the lamb ... the holy city Jerusalem, coming down out of heaven from God, having the glory of God: her light was like unto a stone most precious, as it were a jasper stone, clear as crystal." (Revelation 21:9-11 - See the comment on 4:3.) On the identification of the church being "the holy city Jerusalem" see also Galatians 4:26.

12:2 "and she was with child; and she crieth out, travailing in birth, and in pain to be delivered."

12:2 "she was with child"

<u>In the third place</u>, the glorious lady's maternal condition gives us another strong clue to the identity of this stunningly glorious woman. "She was with child." In 12:5 we are told "she was delivered of a son." Additionally, she also has offspring who are called "her seed, that keep the commandments of God and hold the testimony of Jesus." (Revelation 12:17) The significance of the glorious woman's pregnancy is unmistakable if we compare her condition with that of Paul's when he said, "My little children, of whom I am again in travail until Christ be formed in you." (Galatians 4:19) Paul's period of pregnancy was not complete till the embryo was fully developed, that is, until Christ was formed in that embryo. Based on this poignant glimpse into Paul's experience in winning people to Christ, we can say with assurance that the church is pregnant when it is leading people to Christ, through the process of the new birth. (See John 3:3-11 and Titus 3:3-5.) The recognition of this reality solves the problem which perturbed Barclay when he wrote, "The persecution of the woman by the dragon suggests she might be identified with the Christian Church. The objection is that the Christian Church could hardly be called the mother of the Messiah."[301] When the church, on the pattern of Paul's experience, is "in travail until Christ be formed" in the convert, then the church is the mother of the Messiah!

12:2 "she crieth out, travailing in birth, and in pain to be delivered"

Her pregnancy was not an easy one. The pain was so intense that she cried out, "travailing in birth." The word "travail" may be either a noun or a verb. As a verb it

---

301 William Barclay, <u>The Revelation of John</u>, Vol. II, (Philadelphia: The Westminster Press, 1976), p. 76.

Revelation Chapter 12

means to labor hard; as a noun it means performing work that is painful or laborious. The NRSV says that she "was crying out in birth pangs, in the agony of giving birth." This vividly depicts the painful struggle of many of the church's pregnancies in her effort to bring potential converts to a full-term new birth. The church must agonize to help people to be born again.

12:3 **"And there was seen another sign in heaven: and behold, a great red dragon, having seven heads and ten horns, and upon his heads seven diadems."**

12:3 **"a great red dragon, having seven heads and ten horns"**

At this point it is beneficial to recall the comment made on 10:11. There it was emphasized that the "again" statement in that verse clearly indicates that the narrative in subsequent chapters in Revelation may review some of the same centuries and areas which have already been highlighted. Of course, the focus and emphasis which would be featured would be distinct from those to which attention had been given previously. By looking at a previous example of satanic persecution through the Roman Empire, Christians living in a later time will be more adequately equipped and thus able to understand and triumph over satanic attacks coming through governmental persecution.

While there have already been many references in this commentary to persecutions initiated by the Roman Empire, here we get an even more dramatic vision of that persecuting political entity as "a great red dragon." At this point, a graphic review of Roman persecution is given to prepare Christians living in later eras to understand the torturous tyranny they may have to face. As Rome did Satan's work, Rome got Satan's name, that of the dragon (the dragon is identified as Satan in Revelation 12:9). We should never forget that Satan often does his work through political structures. (See Ephesians 6:12.) The "great red dragon" is mentioned less ornately as "the dragon" in verses 4, 7, 13, 16, and 17. He is also called "the old serpent" in verse 9, and simply "the serpent" in verses 14 and 15.

As the serpent caused the downfall of the glorious woman in Eden, so here, the serpent, the "great red dragon," is depicted as trying to cause the downfall of her counterpart, the even more glorious woman portraying the church. However, thankfully, the Devil will not be able to duplicate his initial victory.

The seven heads and ten horns refer to subordinate administrative and defensive centers utilized by the Roman Empire to administer its far flung dominions. Those seven heads and ten horns were subordinate to the capital city, the ultimate seat of power.

Those heads and horns were "guardians of the frontiers of the Republic." Those "petty chiefs ruled over districts that served as buffer-states between the province and the desert, and they protected the land belonging to the towns from the incursions of nomads. In this way from the very beginning that policy took root by which Rome was always to abide, the policy of maintaining Hellenism [not only in the eastern areas of the Empire but wherever the Greek language was commonly spoken[302]] and of strengthening the city-states, which were its home, against the threat of the 'barbarians.'"[303]

While the passage just quoted describes the administrative arrangement which prevailed, especially on the eastern frontier of the empire, history makes it clear that the same system prevailed everywhere. For example, though "Egypt was most directly controlled by Augustus through a prefect ... the rest of North Africa was provincial territory: Cyrenaica (eastern Libya) had been organized since 74 B.C., and the province of Africa (western Libya and Tunisia) was still older, dating from the destruction of Carthage in 146 B.C. [See Map 5.] But the circle was not complete, and Augustus did not seek to close it: beyond the province of Africa, in the lands of modern Algeria and Morocco, Roman control was indirect, being exercised through the client kingdom of Mauretania."[304]

12:3 "upon his heads seven diadems"

The seven diadems refer to splendid gifts given to the rulers of newly subdued regions when they acknowledged their submission. For example, in the month of January in the year 95 A.D., "Domitian [under whom John was suffering on Patmos] might well have been satisfied as he surveyed the world beneath his feet: there was peace in the Empire, the Dacian king had acknowledged his overlordship and sent his brother Diegis to accept the diadem from his hands ..."[305]

Another form of diadem consisted of special rewards. "Loyal and efficient client rulers were rewarded by personal honors, ordinarily receiving Roman citizenship (which Augustus's highly restrictive citizenship policy made an important privilege); but no honor or title could confer genuine equality in a world where none could equal Roman power. More tangible rewards were also given, primarily territorial."[306]

Obviously, as circumstances required, the number of heads, horns and diadems would change from time to time. At the time John wrote the book of Revelation, the numbers which he recorded, like a photo, captured the actual situation at that moment in Rome's history.

12:4 "And his tail draweth the third part of the stars of heaven, and did cast them to the earth: and the dragon standeth before the woman that is about to be delivered, that when she is delivered he may devour her child."

---

302 "Greek became so much the general language of educated people in Egypt that the Jewish community there found it necessary to translate their Bible into the Greek language, many men of their own people being no longer able to understand Hebrew. Attic Greek for some centuries before and after Christ was the language of all educated men from the Adriatic to the Persian Gulf." H.G. Wells, The Outline of History, Vol. I (New York: Doubleday and Co. Inc., 1940), p. 316.
303 Franz Cumont, *The Frontier Provinces of the East*, The Cambridge Ancient History, Vol. XI, (Cambridge: The University Press, 1954), p. 615.
304 Edward N. Luttwak, The Grand Strategy of the Roman Empire From the First Century A.D. to the Third, (Baltimore: The Johns Hopkins University Press, 1981), pp. 9-12.
305 M. P. Charlesworth, *The Flavian Dynasty*, The Cambridge Ancient History, Vol. XI, (Cambridge: The University Press, 1954), p. 31.
306 Edward N. Luttwak, The Grand Strategy of the Roman Empire From the First Century A.D. to the Third, (Baltimore: The Johns Hopkins University Press, 1981), p. 32.

Revelation Chapter 12

12:4 **"his tail draweth the third part of the stars of heaven, and did cast them to the earth"**

The emperor, the head, set the policies and gave the orders to persecute,[307] but it was the lower members of the governmental structure, the centurions and foot soldiers, constituting the "tail," who had to carry out the orders. This organizational scheme prevailed not only in the Roman Empire, governing the area from the Euphrates River to the Atlantic, but also, similarly, in the Persian Empire to the east of the Euphrates. In Persia, during the rule of both the Parthian and Sassanian empires, persecution of Christians was common. For a glimpse of the persecution of Christians in Persia see the comments under 6:4 on page 90ff.

"The stars of heaven" refer to the leaders of the churches who occupy a very precarious exposed position. Satan has targeted them and will kill a "third part" of them, that is "cast them to the earth." This identity of the "stars" is made clear in the comments on Revelation 1:16 and 1:20. For historic examples of the persecution and killing of church leaders see the accounts of Ignatius, bishop of Antioch, in the comments under 2:8 and of Polycarp in the comments under 2:13.

The "heaven" refers to the churches, "the heavenly places in Christ." (Ephesians 2:6) which is to be equated with "the kingdom of heaven." (See Matthew 16:18-19.) From this passage it is obvious that Satan does have some success in his campaign of eternal destruction. He did draw "the third part of the stars of heaven, and did cast them to the earth:" But, thank God, when he pushed for total victory he was thwarted!

12:4 **"the dragon standeth before the woman that is about to be delivered"**

As at times in the past, Roman political power, here portrayed by the simile of the dragon, will again become extremely confrontational ("standeth before the woman"). One reason is that, "no authoritarian state can tolerate those with absolute moral standards by which they can judge the state."[308]

When the church, depicted by this glorious woman, is pregnant, when it is leading people to Christ, she is extremely vulnerable. At that time the attention of the church and her leadership is focused on growth, not on self defense. In that circumstance she cannot effectively defend herself. Her condition makes her an easy target for the wrath of her worst enemy. Satan wants to disrupt her pregnancy. He wants to cause a miscarriage, to stop conversion to Christ. Should he fail in that demonic effort, then he wants to devour her child. When the church is growing significantly by redeeming people through the new birth, opposition leading to persecution proliferates.

12:4 **"that when she is delivered he may devour her child"**

A newborn Christian, one who has just come through the process of the new birth, is in his or her most vulnerable condition. He or she is not even yet a toddler. At that vulnerable moment, Satan does his utmost to devour the church's child. He works through casting doubt, through intimidating threats or through creating confusion in a baby Christian's mind. This insight should give leaders in every congregation guidance

---

[307] See the list of persecuting Roman emperors in the comments under 6:4.
[308] Yvonne S. Smith, WORLD, January 26, 2013, p. 67.

about protecting and strengthening those who have just been born anew. Every newborn baby Christian is in danger and is extremely vulnerable. That is a moment when Satan's special attacks come. The church must give special care to new converts!

A fourth way we may understand the reality which is typified by this glorious woman is to see her in contrast with the notorious woman who is depicted in Revelation 17:1-6. This glorious woman is in the final phase of pregnancy. We are told that "she crieth out, travailing in birth and in pain to be delivered." (Revelation 12:2) It is clear that her child is not the offspring of fornication or adultery. Her purity is made clear by the fact that to protect herself and her child she "fled into the wilderness, where she hath a place prepared of God." (Revelation 12:6) The fact that God prepared the refuge in the wilderness shows his approval of the woman. It testifies of her purity even though she is pregnant. The apostle Paul clearly identifies this woman by saying, "The Jerusalem that is above is free, which is our mother." (Galatians 4:26.) Though her marriage has not yet taken place, (Revelation 21:2) her pregnancy does not imply any form of sin or illegitimacy. That purity identifies her as the church. (See Ephesians 5:27.)

The woman described here in the twelfth chapter of Revelation is depicted as pure and glorious, while the contrasting woman is notoriously corrupt. She is called the harlot (Revelation 17:1-6) because of her illicit union with political and economic powers. She is the false church, a counterfeit, an imposter who is clothed, not with the sun but with "purple and scarlet, and decked with gold and precious stones and pearls." (Revelation 17:4) Those are some of the rewards given to her for endorsing and facilitating injustice and unscrupulous practices.

"Think of Medieval popes waging the Crusades – raising armies, sacking cities and conquering territory – in the name of Jesus Christ. Or torturing apostates and heretics during the Inquisition. Or Pope Pius V expelling Jews from the Papal States in 1569. Or Pope Pius XI signing the Reichskonkordat with Hitler, which, in return for winning a measure of freedom for German Catholics under the Nazis, assured silence from the Holy See over the forced sterilization of 400,000 people and then only the faintest of objections to the Holocaust. Or more recently, bishops and other church officials concealing widespread and repeated child sexual abuse by priests.

"All of these and many other well-known acts of complicity with the ways of the world are touched on in Gerald Posner's new book, [God's Bankers: A History of Money and Power at the Vatican] but its main subject is a somewhat more arcane form of corruption. 'God's Bankers' provides an exhaustive history of financial machinations at the center of the church in Rome, from the final decades of the nineteenth century down to Pope Francis' sincere but as yet inconclusive efforts to reform the church's labyrinthine bureaucracy (the Curia) and the Vatican Bank (named Istituto per le Opere di Religione, or Institute for the Works of Religion, also known as the I.O.R.)."[309] An even more recent exposé of financial and other forms of corruption in the Vatican is given with extensive documentation by Gianluigi Nuzzi, an Italian journalist, non-fiction writer and TV anchorman, in his book entitled <u>Merchants in the Temple</u>.

---

309 Damon Linker, *Pass the Collection Plate,* <u>The New York Times</u>, Book Review, March 22, 2015, p. 14.

Revelation Chapter 12

Notwithstanding the overwhelming testimony of history to the contrary, the harlot tries through imitation (by wearing gaudy apparel and jewelry) to present herself as glorious, while at the same time, diverting attention from the splendor of the truly glorious woman.

12:5 "And she was delivered of a son, a man child, who is to rule all the nations with a rod of iron: and her child was caught up unto God, and unto his throne."

<u>The fifth way</u> the glorious woman may be identified is by her unique son. Without question, the son is Christ, "who is to rule all the nations with a rod of iron." This is made clear from Revelation 19:11-16. But this being "delivered of a son" does not point to the manger in Bethlehem. Rather, it points to the ongoing birth of Jesus in the hearts of those who yield themselves to him. This spiritual birth of Christ starts with a begetting which Paul identified when he said, "I begat you through the Gospel." (I Corinthians 4:15) We are told that "the Jerusalem that is above … is our mother." (Galatians 4:26) Like every Christian, Paul was part of that "Jerusalem that is above." That Jerusalem is further identified as "the heavenly Jerusalem," the "church of the first born." (Hebrews 12:22-23) That church is additionally identified as "the bride, the wife of the Lamb." (Revelation 21:9) It is "the wife of the Lamb," not the virgin Mary, who is "delivered of a son, a man child, who is to rule all the nations with a rod of iron."

It is the Christian, her son who is faithful unto death, who will be given "authority over the nations and he shall rule them with a rod of iron." (Revelation 2:26-27) For the identification of "the rod of iron," see Revelation 19:15 and its comment.

This passage says "her child was caught up unto God and unto His throne." "Her child," that is, Christ, has been enthroned in the hearts of people who submit to him: "For this is what the high and lofty One says – he who lives forever, whose name is holy: I live in a high and holy place, but also <u>with him who is contrite and lowly in spirit</u>, to revive the spirit of the lowly and to revive the heart of the contrite." (Isaiah 57:15 NIV)

Every conversion to Christ involves a struggle between God and the devil. Consequently, every conversion is not only a defeat for Satan but a victory for Christ who is exalted and enthroned in peoples' hearts in the process of the new birth. Every person who yields his allegiance to Christ obeys the divine command to "sanctify in your hearts Christ as Lord." (See I Peter 3:15.) If Christ has become Lord in our hearts, he has been enthroned. <u>The heart yielded to Jesus is the throne of God</u>. God's throne is located, as it should be, in his temple. Christ is said to be "in" the Christian. (See the words "Christ in you" in Colossians 1:27.) That temple is identified as the Christian's body, which "is a temple of the Holy Spirit which is in you, which ye have from God." Consequently, "ye are not your own; for ye were bought with a price: glorify God therefore in your body." (I Corinthians 6:19-20)

12:6 "And the woman fled into the wilderness, where she hath a place prepared of God, that there they may nourish her a thousand two hundred and threescore days."

12:6 "the woman fled into the wilderness"

The wife of the first Adam, unfortunately, did not flee from Satan. The wife of the second Adam, the church, perhaps learning from the experience of Eve, is wiser and flees from

181

the presence of Satan. (Remember that we have been told that "the dragon standeth before the woman that is about to be delivered, that when she is delivered he may devour her child." 12:4)

She flees because she knows the enemy. She is, "not ignorant of his devices." (II Corinthians 2:11) While the harlot, the counterfeit church, basks in the splendor of fawning political and financial powers whom she has scandalously endorsed, embraced and facilitated, the true church is in the wilderness of disdain, scorn and obscurity.

By fleeing, the glorious woman becomes the underground church. We American Christians can visualize the church in China or in Iran becoming an underground church as their tiny, yet vibrant, house churches try to survive under the vicious attacks of Satan's proteges, the Communist or Islamic governments. However, it is very hard for us to imagine that the church in America may one day have to become an underground church, though it is almost certain to happen.[310]

The sixth way we can identify the glorious woman is by the length of her career. It will be so long that it is obvious that she is no mortal woman. She takes refuge in "the wilderness, where she hath a place prepared of God, that there they may nourish her a thousand two hundred and threescore days." (Revelation 12:6 RV)

As noted earlier, based on a statement in Ezekiel 4:6, we concluded that each of the days represents a year. Ezekiel wrote, "And again, when thou hast accomplished these, thou shalt lie on thy right side, and shalt bear the iniquity of the house of Judah: forty days, each day for a year, have I appointed it unto thee."

Though the twelve-hundred-sixty-days do refer to a specific historic period of persecution, there are principles in this account which are timeless and apply to periods of persecution at all times during the entire Christian dispensation. It is also important to notice that the period of the church's obscurity is limited to "a thousand two hundred and threescore days." Following her period in the wilderness, she will experience another period of triumph!

Alert readers will recognize from the comments on 11:3 that the period of time when the glorious woman will take refuge in the wilderness for protection against Satan's onslaughts is identical in duration to that of the period when the two witnesses will triumphantly be giving their united testimony. From this identity it is clear that the triumph of the Jewish/Gentile church will be achieved in the face of great satanic opposition. It will be a flamboyant rebuke to Satan that during a period when his persecution of the church is so extreme that the church must, in some sense, flee into the wilderness, it also experiences phenomenal growth! To encourage Christians living in a later period, as an example, the history of the Roman Empire (prior to its demise in 476

---

310 For example, "Project 10 is a Los Angeles based pro-homosexual counseling program for public schools. ... On April 23 & 24 [1992], a coalition of homosexual groups and government agencies will hold a two-day state-wide conference at the Greenwood Inn in Beaverton. Teachers, social workers, counselors and others who work with children will be addressed by Project 10 founder, Virginia Uribe, and leader of similar organizations from around the country. Materials to be introduced in the conference include a government report which blames homosexual youth suicide on conservative Christianity and urges legal sanctions against Christians who refuse to alter their theology." [underlining mine, BLT] A much more current indication of which way the wind is blowing comes from a notice that on September 20, 2014 "Supreme Court Justice Elena Kagan officiated a same-sex wedding in Maryland ... [and] retired Justice Sandra Day O'Connor and Justice Ruth Bader Ginsburg have both officiated at similar occasions. [Also] U.S. Attorney General Eric Holder's legacy includes vigorous activism for homosexual marriage: The attorney general declared the Defense of Marriage Act unconstitutional and refused to defend it in court. Holder also declared gay marriage 'the defining civil rights issue of our time.'" WORLD, October 18, 2014, pp. 7, 10.

Revelation Chapter 12

when it was persecuting the church) is reviewed in the following section, 12:7-10. Thus, when some political or ecclesiastical entity, like the Roman Empire, shall also persecute the church, Christians will have been forewarned and prepared.

12:7 **"And there was war in heaven: Michael and his angels going forth to war with the dragon; and the dragon warred and his angels;"**

12:7 **"there was war in heaven"**

For a definition of this "heaven," please see the eighth use of the word "heaven" in the introduction to chapter 15. This war takes place on several battle fronts. **First** is the war which Satan wages in the heart of every Christian. On that battle front he tries to defeat the power of God's Spirit in the struggle for loyalty and commitment. This heaven is the place where the special presence of God, the Son of God, and the Spirit of God is found. (See note on 12:8.) It is the place where God's throne is located. While this in no way denies the omnipresence of God, it does acknowledge the place of the special presence of God.

The heart of the Christian is the temple of God. This is clear from Peter's exhortation in which he tells us, "Sanctify in your hearts Christ as Lord ..." (I Peter 3:15 ARV) This is also in harmony with Paul's teaching in which he asks, "Know ye not that your body is a temple of the Holy Spirit which is in you, which ye have from God? and ye are not your own; for ye were bought with a price: glorify God therefore in your body." (I Corinthians 6:19-20)

Secondly, this "war in heaven" is fought in places of authority in which Christians are involved as a consequence of being a citizen in a governmental structure. (Please see the second use of the word "heaven" in the introduction to chapter 15 where it discusses the word "heaven" used to describe a political structure.) This is not that primeval war in which Satan first rebelled which is mentioned in Jude, verse 6, and in II Peter 2:4 and which is expounded by Ezekiel under the metaphor of the king of Tyre (Ezekiel 28:14-15) and by Isaiah under the metaphor of the king of Babylon (Isaiah 14:4-15). Rather, it is that conflict or war which Paul describes when he says, "our wrestling ["struggle" - NIV] is not against flesh and blood, but against the principalities, against the powers, against the world rulers of this darkness, against the spiritual hosts of wickedness in <u>the heavenly places</u>." (Ephesians 6:12 RV) The words "principalities," "powers," and "world rulers" point to governments which permit, sponsor or facilitate persecution.

12:7 **"the dragon warred and his angels"**

Surely the war mentioned in Ephesians 6:12 is the same one mentioned here in Revelation 12:7. Certainly, "the spiritual hosts of wickedness" are to be equated with the angels of the dragon. The war in "the heavenly places" which Paul mentions is the same as the "war in heaven" which John mentions in this verse.

12:7 **"Michael and his angels"**

Michael and his angels belong to that heavenly group who are called "ministering spirits sent forth to do service for the sake of them that shall inherit salvation." (Hebrews 1:14) The angels under Michael perform an invaluable ministry by helping us in our war against Satan. When Satan attacks, the angels are there to help us! The epistle to the Hebrews tells us in 12:22 that these angelic beings are "innumerable." In addition to the angelic ministry of protection, which is emphasized in this text in Revelation, some other invaluable aspects of their ministry are: (1) They motivate and direct preachers of the Gospel (Acts 8:26). (2) They motivate and direct potential converts (Acts 10:3, 10:7 and 10:22), thus helping the woman remain pregnant, thereby helping the church grow, as seen here. (3) Overall, they help us fight the war against Satan.

12:8 "And they prevailed not, neither was their place found any more in heaven."

As noted earlier, this "heaven" also refers to the churches, "the heavenly places in Christ." (Ephesians 2:6). That is just one venue where this war takes place. Even more fundamentally, it takes place in the hearts of individual Christians. And as we have just seen, the war also involves Christians' relationships to the state. See the introduction to chapter 15 for a discussion of the various uses of the word heaven.

12:9 "And the great dragon was cast down, the old serpent, he that is called the Devil and Satan, the deceiver of the whole world; he was cast down to the earth, and his angels were cast down with him."

When Satan is cast out of the heart of the convert to Christ, one of the venues of the temple of God (one heaven where this spiritual war takes place, see 12:8), he has only one realm left in which he may operate. He is "cast down to the earth," being the hearts of worldly people who constitute "the earth" of Revelation 12:9.

Satan therefore now operates with special vigor in the hearts of those "whose end is perdition, whose god is the belly, and whose glory is their shame, **who mind earthly things.**" (Philippians 3:19) He now works with great urgency and zeal in the hearts of those who have a wisdom that is "**earthly, sensual, devilish.**" (James 3:15)

Satan, the Dragon, in conjunction with his angels, after being cast out of heaven, is "the spirit that now worketh in the sons of disobedience." (Ephesians 2:2).

12:10 "And I heard a great voice in heaven, saying, Now is come the salvation, and the power, and the kingdom of our God, and the authority of his Christ: for the accuser of our brethren is cast down, who accuseth them before our God day and night."

12:10 "salvation ... power ... kingdom ... authority"

Whenever "the accuser" is "cast down," whenever his enticements and blandishments are refused, it is a victory in the continuous "day and night" struggle that goes on "before our God." God never lets Satan have an uncontested victory. The Christian is assured of God's presence in all of the venues of his battle against Satan. It is during such contests that we see divine salvation, power, kingdom and authority assert and manifest themselves.

12:10 "our brethren"

A seventh way the glorious woman may be identified is by her relationship with the "brethren," her extended family. From Revelation 12:17, it is clear that these "brethren"

Revelation Chapter 12

are all sons of the glorious woman. That verse tells us that "the dragon waxed wroth with the woman, and went away to make war with the rest of **her seed**, that keep the commandments of God, and hold the testimony of Jesus." (Revelation 12:17 RV) Her seed, or children, not only keep the commandments of God, they also "hold the testimony of Jesus." Obviously, then, they are Christians, "our brethren" in Christ.

12:11 "And they overcame him because of the blood of the Lamb, and because of the word of their testimony; and they loved not their life even unto death."

12:11 "And they overcame him because of the blood of the Lamb, and because of the word of their testimony"

The verbal content of and the motivation behind "the word" which constitutes "their testimony" is given to us in I John 5:10-11. It tells us, "he that believeth on the Son of God hath the witness in him!" This points to the mutual inherent relationship between faith and life. Paul called our attention to this same relationship when he explained the dynamics of his ministry. Quoting Psalm 116:10 which says, "I believed, and therefore did I speak," he makes it clear that the same dynamic is at work in us. Consequently, since "we also believe, … therefore also we speak." (II Corinthians 4:13 RV) Thus, if one really believes the Gospel he cannot keep that fact hidden or secret. He will witness of its great truths. This is "the word of their testimony."

According to I Timothy 1:15, if a person believes the saying "that Christ Jesus came into the world to save sinners" is a "faithful" saying, meaning it is true, he will inevitably say also that this saying is "worthy of all acceptation." Once a person acknowledges that "faithful saying," then he will do all he can to help others accept it. It is only natural, therefore, that such a one will witness to others, for he "hath the witness in him." (I John 5:10 RV) This organic and spontaneous witness which inevitably springs from faith, also expresses the broader meaning of Paul's affirmation that "with the heart man believeth unto righteousness; and with the mouth confession is made unto salvation." (Romans 10:10 RV)

But what does one say when he gives witness? "The witness is this, that God gave unto us eternal life, and this life is in His Son. He that hath the Son hath the life; he that hath not the Son of God hath not the life." (I John 5:11-12 RV)

If we do not speak, if we do not convey that truth, it is because we do not believe it. Should we speak from unbelief, our words would be hollow and powerless. Only the existence of faith, that faith which God is pleased to accept, will bring about fruitful evangelism. When faith flourishes in his heart, the Christian will show love for the lost of the world by witnessing to them of the life which God has given him in Christ.

12:11 "they loved not their life even unto death."

There are times when our testimony must be buttressed by great bravery. We must be prepared to face mortal jeopardy, even death.

12:12 "Therefore rejoice, O heavens, and ye that dwell in them. Woe for the earth and for the sea: because the devil is gone down unto you, having great wrath, knowing that he hath but a short time."

12:12 "Therefore rejoice, O heavens"

This rejoicing is to take place because of the victory which was declared in 12:11 by the words "they overcame him." The "heavens" are the various regions in the kingdom of heaven, "the heavenly places in Christ." (Ephesians 2:6)

12:12 "Woe for the earth and for the sea: because the devil is gone down unto you"

Since Satan's direct attack on the church was largely repulsed, "they overcame him" (12:11), now Satan will make the environment more hostile in which the church must live. Thus, individually and corporately, the triumph of the church (the kingdom of heaven which rejoices) makes society at large, here represented by the earth and the sea, even more vulnerable to Satan's attacks. He seeks a more promising environment in which to focus his destructive work. This helps us understand the current rapidly accelerating and expanding moral and spiritual disintegration of society at large. The decline of moral and ethical standards is seen in the widespread increase in the use of narcotics, the general acceptance of gross sexual perversion (such as same-sex marriage) and governmental efforts to enforce these perversions as societal norms.[311]

12:12 "the devil is gone down unto you, having great wrath, knowing that he hath but a short time"

The hurricane or tsunami of moral and spiritual decline which we are both experiencing and witnessing throughout global society is the result of expanded and intensified satanic activity. Somehow Satan is aware of God's timetable and knows that "he hath but a short time." He, therefore, being aware that opportunities to snare and destroy men and women are to rapidly end, is frantically making a final all-out effort to bring individuals and society to utter eternal calamity.

12:13 "And when the dragon saw that he was cast down to the earth, he persecuted the woman that brought forth the man child."

12:13 "the earth"

"The earth" refers to society at large, that is, secular society. (See the comments on "earth and sea," 12:12.)

12:13 "persecuted the woman"

Just one day before Christmas 1996, *The Wall Street Journal* raised its editorial voice on behalf of Christians around the world who were suffering persecution. We should be deeply grateful that this major secular business newspaper cried out against the persecution of the followers of Jesus Christ. The editorial writer informed the paper's readers that, "religious persecution is still common; the truth is that when the victims are Christians, too little attention is often paid to their plight." Then, quoting an analysis by

---

[311] For example, "Washington State can force pharmacies to dispense Plan B or other emergency contraceptives a federal appeals court said Thursday in a lawsuit brought by pharmacists who said they have religious objections to providing the drugs. The unanimous decision by a three-judge panel of the United States Court of Appeals for the Ninth Circuit overturned a 2012 ruling by a Federal District Court judge, who had found that the rules violated the religious freedom of pharmacy owners. ... A pharmacy in Olympia and two pharmacists sued on religious rights grounds, and argued that they should be allowed to refer patients to a nearby drugstore, but the appeals judges said that was not good enough. Judge Susan P. Graber wrote that speed was a consideration. 'The time taken to travel to another pharmacy, especially in rural areas where pharmacies are sparse, may reduce the efficacy of those drugs,' she wrote." The New York Times, July 24, 2015, National Briefing, p. A17.

Revelation Chapter 12

another writer, the editorialist informs us that "Christians today are the most persecuted religious group in the world and that persecution is intensifying."

The greatest perpetrators of this crime are "communism" and "militant, politicized Islam." For instance, regarding Communist China, "Both Catholic and Protestant leaders say this year has seen the harshest persecution of their faiths since the Cultural Revolution of the 1960s." In the Muslim world, "Freedom House reports that Sudan has abducted or killed more than one million of its people in a *jihad*, or holy war, against non-Muslims. Young Christian boys are held captive, forced to convert to Islam and then sold as slaves." In Saudi Arabia, the State Department confirms, "freedom of religion does not exist. … The Mutawa religious police raid houses, confiscate Bibles and arrest people for practicing their faith."

That enlightened and enlightening editorial concludes with a suggested course of action. It says, "An appropriate New Year's resolution for leaders in the U.S. government and in the Christian denominations themselves would be to make a greater effort than they did the past year at ensuring that religious persecution is challenged and condemned."

There is probably no more effective way to accept that editorial exhortation than to understand and propagate the teaching of the twelfth chapter of Revelation.

To become aware of the situation subsequent to that 1996 *Wall Street Journal* article, consult the informative book by John L. Allen Jr., The Global War on Christians, Dispatches From the Front Line of Anti-Christian Persecution, (New York: Image, 2013). Also, to monitor the ongoing day-to-day situation see the website of World Watch Monitor at www.worldwatchmonitor.org.

Most recently, on July 26, 2015, *The New York Times Magazine* devoted a nine-and-a-half page section to the current persecution of Christians. They highlighted the article on the cover by writing that "Christians in the Middle East are being forced out of their homes, enslaved and killed. Why is no one coming to their aid?" When secular scholars and journalists are deeply concerned about satanic attacks on Christians, should not we Christians in churches in the West, who are currently free from brutal deadly attacks on our persons and assemblies, be in fervent, constant prayer for our suffering fellow Christians in many places throughout the world?

12:14 "And there were given to the woman the two wings of the great eagle, that she might fly into the wilderness unto her place, where she is nourished for a time, and times, and half a time, from the face of the serpent."

12:14 "there were given to the woman the two wings of the great eagle, that she might fly"

God's provision of the symbolic "wings of the great eagle" is reminiscent of how he delivered Israel from Egypt. Regarding that deliverance God said, "I carried you on eagles' wings and brought you unto myself." (Exodus 19:4 NIV) This statement of God's provision for the church when it is under persecution also reflects and enhances David's prayer in which he pled, "Oh that I had wings like a dove! Then would I fly away, and be at rest. Lo, then would I wander far off, I would lodge in the wilderness." (Psalm 55:6-7)

12:14 "And the woman fled into the wilderness, where she hath a place prepared of God,"

God always prepares a place which becomes "the way of escape." "There hath no temptation taken you but such as man can bear; but God is faithful, who will not suffer you to be tempted above that ye are able; but will with the temptation make also <u>the way of escape</u>, that ye may be able to endure it." (I Corinthians 10:13) The servant of God can call that place "my place of shelter." (Psalm 55:8 NIV; See also Isaiah 43:1-2.) Though they are not identical, compare this wilderness with that which is described in Revelation 17:3. The woman is the church. Though the church will survive, sometimes perilously, many of her members will become martyrs.

12:14 "a time, and times, and half a time"

This is another way of expressing twelve-hundred-sixty-days or three-and-a-half-years, the word "time" is used as an equivalent for the word "year." This system of noting, recording or predicting time is a duplication of that which was used in Daniel 4:16, 4:23, and 4:25 to calculate the period of time during which Nebuchadnezzar would roam as a grass-eating animal. And finally, the same computation also occurs in Daniel 7:25.

12:15 "And the serpent cast out of his mouth after the woman water as a river, that he might cause her to be carried away by the stream."

What do we expect to come out of the mouth of the serpent? Only one thing – a river of lies; lies which he spreads against the Gospel message, against individual Christians and against the church. Satan's lies are not only against the church itself but against the truth to which she is committed and for which she stands. We must always remember that "the church of the living God, [is] the pillar and foundation of the truth." (I Timothy 3:15 NIV) Satan's purpose in spewing forth his river of lies is that the glorious woman might lose her footing on the great rock on which she stands (Matthew 16:18), "that he might cause her to be carried away by the stream."

Jesus told us of the true nature of Satan when he said, "He was a murderer from the beginning, and standeth not in the truth, because there is no truth in him. When he speaketh a lie, he speaketh of his own: for he is a liar, and the father thereof." (John 8:44)

12:16 "And the earth helped the woman, and the earth opened her mouth and swallowed up the river which the dragon cast out of his mouth."

12:16 "the earth helped the woman"

For the identity of "the earth," see the comments on 12:12. The thrilling account of how the earth helps the woman is succinctly told in the very next sentence.

12:16 "the earth opened her mouth and swallowed up the river which the dragon cast out of his mouth"

It is non-Christian worldly people who initially swallow the devil's lies. By doing so, they actually help the church by eventually exposing satanic propaganda as totally ridiculous, preposterous and untenable. Then the truth becomes more obvious! When members of worldly society finally realize they have been deceived and can no longer

Revelation Chapter 12

swallow the devil's lies, the truth is reinforced. Thus, the earth helps the glorious lady! One example of such help is the exposure of the Piltdown-Man hoax.[312] Other deceptions in this biological category are "Lucy,"[313] the "Neanderthal Man,"[314] and the "Nebraska Man."[315]

Other secular revulsions against historical fraud which have been motivated by Satan also help the church. An example in this category is "the so-called Donation of Constantine [which] is now known to have been a forgery – fabricated, probably during the eighth century, within the Roman Curia; it was, however, to prove of inestimable value to the territorial claims of the Papacy until the fraud was finally exposed (by the Italian humanist Lorenzo Valla) in 1440."[316] (See Appendix D for more details.) Thus they, non-Christian worldly people, help the church as Herod Antipas helped Jesus when he hired Chuzas to be his steward. Chuzas sent his wife and his money to help Jesus! Thus Antipas supported Jesus! (See Luke 8:2-3.) Analogously, from time to time, "the earth," consisting of non-Christians, helps the church.

12:17 "And the dragon waxed wroth with the woman, and went away to make war with the rest of her seed, that keep the commandments of God, and hold the testimony of Jesus:"

12:17 "waxed wroth"

Satan's wrath comes, in part, from a sense of urgency because he knows the time in which he can act is short. (See 12:12.)

12:17 "the rest of her seed"

See the comment on the words "she was with child" at 12:2. The emphasis here in the twelfth chapter, by historical allusion, is to persecution in the Roman Empire which will be replicated through the course of history by other political entities where "the rest of her seed" will be living.

12:17 "her seed, that ... hold the testimony of Jesus"

While this passage emphasizes the bravery and tenacity of Christians, those who hold the testimony of Jesus in the face of severe threats and persecution, there is another aspect of holding the testimony of Jesus in the face of subtle and ingenious philosophical attacks. That second challenge is discussed in the comments on 19:10 on pages 312-313.

Two Alternate Views

The Catholic concept: Catholic expositors have generally concluded that this symbol of the woman clothed with the sun refers to the Virgin Mary. Superficially, this view seems compelling. They present four main points: (1) They remind us that Mary did give birth to the one who is to rule with the rod of iron. (See 12:5) (2) They point out that Satan did try to destroy Mary's child, the Christ child. (3) And further, Mary did flee into the wilderness. She certainly had to go through much desolate wilderness as she fled from

---

312 See http://en.wikipedia.org/wiki/Piltdown_Man.
313 See http://theevolutionhoax.blogspot.com/2012/01/lucy-missing-link-australopithecines.html.
314 See http://www.apologeticspress.org/apcontent.aspx?category=9&article=1500.
315 See http://www.uark.edu/~cdm/creation/shame3.htm.
316 John Julius Norwich, Absolute Monarchs, A History of the Papacy, (New York: Random House, 2011), p. 17.

Bethlehem to Egypt. (4) Roman Catholic commentators interpret the "thousand two hundred and threescore days" (Revelation 12:6, cf. Revelation 12:14) as three-and-a-half years, pointing to the duration of Mary and Joseph's stay in Egypt.[317]

As a result of that type of exposition Catholics give Mary extreme exaltation and veneration. Thus, from their point of view the Hail Mary seems very reasonable. It says:

> Hail Mary full of grace
> The Lord is with thee.
> Blessed art thou among women and
> Blessed is the fruit of thy womb – Jesus.
> Holy Mary, Mother of God
> Pray for us sinners now
> And at the hour of our death. Amen.

There are, however, at least three solid reasons for rejecting the simplistic view of the Catholic interpreters: (1) First, the Roman Catholic position requires that we break the continuity of the prophetic section of the book of Revelation. Their view throws chapter 12 back into the historical section. Revelation 1:19 says, "write therefore the things which thou sawest, and the things which are, and the things which shall come to pass hereafter." When we reach Revelation 4:1, we are clearly in the section of the Revelation designated, "the things which shall come to pass hereafter."

(2) Secondly, it exalts Mary to a position which neither Christ nor his apostles ever gave her! "The Bible-oriented Christian must marvel at the way in which the mother of our Lord has, in Roman Catholic piety and dogma, gradually been lifted out of her humanity and elevated to the position of a quasi deity. In spite of repeated denials, Mary has, to a considerable extent, replaced Christ Himself in the affection and devotion of millions of people. ... The growing cult of Mary has caused a deep and ever widening rift in Christendom. There is a considerable element of truth in the remark attributed to the famous British statesman, Benjamin Disraeli: 'Half of Christendom worships a Jewish man, and the other half a Jewish woman.'" [318]

(3) In the third place, the Revelation account in 12:14-15 makes it clear that the glorious woman was persecuted even in her refuge in the wilderness. That wilderness is the place where Satan inundated the glorious woman with "a river, that he might cause her to be carried away by the stream." However there is not even a hint in either scripture or in history that Mary was persecuted while she was in Egypt. Thus, the glorious woman cannot be factually and truthfully identified as Mary, wife of Joseph of Nazareth.

"An important stage in the [development of the] Marian cult was reached with the official adoption by the Council of Nicea of the Greek term *theotokos* – Mother of God, as a description of Mary. This term gained wide currency during the heated disputes of the third and fourth centuries concerning the two natures of Christ – the human and the divine. The Council of Nicea in 325, after condemning the anti-trinitarian position of

---

[317] It is very unlikely that Joseph, Mary and Jesus stayed so long in Egypt. For startling historic insights about the length of their stay see Ernest L. Martin, The Birth of Christ Recalculated (2nd Ed.), (Pasadena: Foundation for Biblical Research, 1980).
[318] Victor Buksbazen, Miriam the Virgin of Nazareth, (Philadelphia: The Spearhead Press, 1963), p. 178.

Revelation Chapter 12

Arius, affirmed the perfect divinity of Christ. God the Son, the Council declared, was 'con-substantial' with the Father. Henceforth Mary was to be considered as *theotokos* – the Mother of God. The purpose of this title was not to glorify Mary, but rather to express the belief that the eternal God humbled Himself and came down into the world 'in the form of a servant' (Philippians 2:7), and was born of the virgin Mary. However, the term *theotokos* was pregnant with possibilities of misinterpretation and mischief, which later history proved only too abundantly.

"The exact meaning and significance of *theotokos* was disputed with vehemence and venom at the Councils of Ephesus in 431 and Chalcedon in 451. ...

"Nestorius, bishop of Constantinople, found the term *theotokos* misleading because God cannot be born, nor can He die, but Christ the Son of God was born and did die on the cross. He therefore proposed that Mary should be called *Christotokos* – the Mother of Christ. His opponent, Cyril, bishop of Alexandria, who championed the complete and perfect union of the human and divine nature of Christ insisted on the term *theotokos*, that Mary was the Mother of God."[319]

Roman Catholic commentators take the position that the glorious woman depicts the Virgin Mary. The scriptural and historical analysis given above in this commentary shows the error of the Catholic position.

A second position should also be evaluated. Commentators who are designated *futurists* "take the **woman** (v. 1) to be Israel, and her child (v. 5) to be Christ. ... The faithful remnant in Israel throughout the ages is pictured as God's instrument for bringing the Messiah into the world."[320] Similarly, those commentators who are known as *preterists* agree when "The Woman is usually identified with the faithful remnant of Old Testament Israel."[321]

Pertinent scripture passages help us evaluate the position of those who affirm that the woman represents the nation of Israel. First, the woman was pregnant, she was "with child." (v. 2). Secondly, she gave birth, "she was delivered of a son" (v. 5). Thirdly, she had additional children who not only "keep the commandments of God" but also "hold the testimony of Jesus" (v.17). That description lets us know that her children are Christians. The apostle Paul explicitly says that we Christians cannot look to Sinai, that is, to "the legitimate Jewish religion which began with Moses," to discover our spiritual maternal parentage. That relationship bears "children unto bondage." (Galatians 4:24) In

---

[319] "To speak of Mary as 'The Mother of God' Nestorius maintained, makes the Christian doctrine ridiculous in the eyes of pagans, because God cannot be born. "In spite of the objections of Nestorius, the Council of Ephesus, confirmed the title *theotokos* as orthodox and proper.

"What to the theologians assembled at Ephesus was a theological formula designed to express the perfect union of the human and divine natures of Christ, to the common people, especially to the inhabitants of Ephesus, became a question of local pride, honor and piety. It must be remembered that according to local tradition, Mary died in Ephesus and her tomb was shown as being located not far from the tomb of the Apostle John. It is hard to say how much this strong local sentiment for Mary influenced the outcome of the Council of Ephesus in 431. It should also be remembered that Ephesus was the city where the Apostle Paul was nearly lynched by an incensed mob of worshipers of The Great Goddess Diana (Acts 9:23-24).

"After confirming the position of the Council of Nicea, the Council of Ephesus declared: 'We confess that the Holy Virgin is Mother of God (*theotokos*), by the fact that God the Word is incarnated and made man, and from her conception has united to his very self the temple taken from her.

"It was this formula *theotokos* which became the doctrinal foundation for the cult of Mary. Thus it can be said that in the year 431 official sanction was given to the Marian cult, which at first was only a popular expression of a Mary-centered piety, but later became the basis of church dogma." Victor Buksbazen, Miriam The Virgin of Nazareth, (Philadelphia: The Spearhead Press, 1963), pp. 185-187.

[320] Revelation, Four Views: A Parallel Commentary, ed. Steve Gregg, (Nashville: Thomas Nelson Publishers, 1997), pp. 255 & 257.

[321] Revelation, Four Views: A Parallel Commentary, ed. Steve Gregg, (Nashville: Thomas Nelson Publishers, 1997), p. 256.

sharp contrast, he tells us, "**the Jerusalem that is above is free, which is our mother**.' (Galatians 4:26)

We Christians are citizens of the city which Paul called, "the Jerusalem that is above." Collectively, we constitute the church which makes up the bride of Christ. As Paul wrote to the Christians in Corinth, "I espoused you to one husband, that I might present you as a pure virgin to Christ." (II Corinthians 11:2; Compare Ephesians 5:25-32.) It is Christ's bride, not the virgin Mary or the nation of Israel, who gives birth to those who "hold the testimony of Jesus."

———

Revelation Chapter 13

Introduction: Tracking the Narrative of Revelation. The narrative of the book of Revelation follows the major developments in Christianity resulting from being impacted from various non-Christian power centers within the Christian world. The narrative of Revelation also tracks internal developments in the church like the one from which we see Babylon, the corrupt theological city, emerge. Ironically, it arises out of the City of God, the true church!

By the term "Christian world," as used here, is meant the area, culture or society in which the Christian message has become the dominating or pervading spiritual, intellectual, moral and ethical concept. In such an area one sees the Gospel concept reflected in social mores, art, literature, architecture, music and law. The term "Christian world" is, therefore, here being used in a much broader and more inclusive sense than if one should conceptually limit the boundaries of Christianity to only those people who have conformed to the Gospel message on the composite pattern drawn from the examples of those whose positive response to the Gospel message is recorded in the book of Acts.

The message of Christ, in fulfillment of the remarkable prophecies in Zechariah 13:1 and 14:8, not only spread to the west but also made notable inroads in many areas east of the Euphrates River. It achieved especially strong standing in Iran, including, by the preaching of the apostle Thomas, the conversion of the Iranian Parthian King Gondophares, who ruled from Taxila in far eastern Parthian Iran (now part of northern Pakistan). From Taxila Thomas journeyed on to South India where he continued to win many to Christ till he died as a martyr at Mylapore, near Madras/Chennai.

From their base in Iran, Christian evangelists took the message to Turfan (in Xinjiang Province), in far western China as well as all the way to Changan, the Chinese Tang Dynasty capital. That evangelistic thrust all the way to the capital of China was a feat to which the magnificent Nestorian Monument gives indisputable witness. However, despite those marvelous triumphs of Christian evangelism, the Gospel of Christ never became the dominating concept in any broad area of that vast region.

The remnant church is now dying out in most places in the Euphrates River basin due to the dominance of Islam and the vicious, bestial and destructive attacks of ISIS/ISIL, one of Islam's many factions. For many centuries, serving as spiritual beacons (Please see Philippians 2:15.), minority communities of Christians courageously survived east of the Euphrates River. They served in an environment that theologically, culturally, socially and legally was, and continues to be, very intimidating and harsh for those who follow Christ.

At the dawn of the Christian era, starting from the Euphrates River and going from west to east, Zoroastrianism, Buddhism and Hinduism were the dominant ideologies in the extensive area extending all the way to Indonesia. Both Zoroastrianism and Buddhism were eliminated as dominating ideologies by intentional and deliberate destruction brought by Islam during its rise and early expansion. That has left Islam and Hinduism, the two dominant contestants, confronting each other in India. Islam now also dominates Indonesia, Malaysia and Borneo.

The narrative in Revelation first tells us of those enactments, events and developments emanating from Rome which impacted the cause of Christ. Rome was the initial great power center in the Mediterranean world which had come to be ideologically dominated by the Gospel message. Chronologically, that status continued till 330 A.D., the point at which Constantine dedicated the new and soon-to-be dominating power center of Constantinople. The Revelation narrative prophetically foretells that shift in the first half of chapter 13. After many centuries, the center of power in the eastern part of the Christian world again shifted, this time from Constantinople to Kiev and, later, from Kiev to Moscow. Those two later shifts are together prophetically predicted in the second half of chapter 13.

While the emphasis in the narrative of the book of Revelation is on the Christian world, the overall account also takes note of the more remote locations when they have an impact on those areas in which Christianity had become the dominant ideological concept. An example is found in 16:12 which tells us of kings who shall come from "the sunrising," a term which certainly includes the area we normally denote as the Far East. However, the concept may take us much further east than China. It may go all the way across the Pacific Ocean to North and South America. Certainly, the nation-states of North and South America will be drawn into the war described in 16:12.

13:1 **"And he stood upon the sand of the sea. And I saw a beast coming up out of the sea, having ten horns, and seven heads, and on his horns ten diadems, and upon his heads names of blasphemy."**

13:1 "he stood upon the sand of the sea"

It is unfortunate that this phrase was not included in verse 17 of chapter 12, of which it is the logical ending. Doubtless it was carried over to the beginning of chapter 13 by an editorial error or oversight. The antecedent in 12:17 to the pronoun "he" is "the dragon," referring to Satan. (See 12:9.) The seashore upon which he was standing was that of the Sea of Marmara out of which an economically vibrant and culturally resplendent yet bestial political power was about to emerge. (See Map 9, The Location of Byzantium.) The fact that the emerging political power was bestial rather than benign doubtless reflects the influence of Satan who, standing on that seashore, was overseeing and influencing the rise of that power.

13:1 "a beast coming up out of the sea"

The beast rising out of the sea, having seven heads and ten horns, was the Eastern Roman-Byzantine Empire. It arose on a promontory or peninsula which protrudes into the Sea of Marmara. That sea borders the peninsula on the south and east, while an inlet from that sea, known as the Golden Horn, borders it on the north. Its larger maritime environment consists of the Aegean and Mediterranean Seas on the south and the Bosporus and the Black Sea on the north. Constantinople, magnificent capital of the Eastern Roman Empire, which eventually morphed into the Byzantine Empire, is situated

Revelation Chapter 13

at the south end of the Bosporus, the strait linking the Black Sea and the Sea of Marmara, which, along with the Dardanelles and the Aegean Sea forms the connecting link between the Mediterranean and the Black Seas. One scholar graphically stated the case by saying that Constantinople, capital of the Byzantine Empire, was, "garlanded by water."[322]

Emperor Constantine laid the foundation for the fabulous city of Constantinople in 324 A.D. and dedicated it in 330 A.D. Saint Sophia, the world's greatest domed cathedral, became the city's most renowned adornment and the epicenter of the Orthodox Church. It was built by order of Justinian who dedicated it in 538 A.D. "From the fifth century to the fifteenth, Constantinople remained the greatest market and shipping center in the world. Alexandria, which had held this supremacy from the third century B.C., now ranked in trade below Antioch. All Syria throve with commerce and industry; it lay between Persia and Constantinople; between Constantinople and Egypt its merchants were shrewd and venturesome, and only the effervescent Greeks could rival them in the extent of their traffic and the subtlety of their ways."[323]

Since this rising political entity, as seen from its name, "Beast," (13:1) was clearly evil from its very inception, one must review the biblical statements about the rise and nature of civil political entities. One well-known passage evaluating political powers is Romans 13:1-7. In verse 1 the apostle Paul says, "Let every soul be in subjection to the higher powers: for there is no power but of God; and the powers that be are ordained of God." Consequently he concludes in verse 2 that, "he that resisteth the power withstandeth the ordinance of God: and they that withstand shall receive to themselves judgment." These statements endorsing and commending civil government must be seen as limited, referring to a specific moment in the life of the Roman Empire, rather than as an inclusive endorsement covering all governments in all places, at all times and in all circumstances.

Such a limitation in one's viewpoint is necessary because of the evaluation of governments which Paul gave to the church in Ephesus. In his letter to that church he wrote, "Our wrestling is not against flesh and blood, but against the <u>principalities, against the powers, against the world rulers of this darkness, against the spiritual hosts of wickedness in the heavenly places</u>." (Ephesians 6:12) Also, should we not see the limitations on Paul's endorsement of civil government which he gave to the Roman church, it would create a clash with John's vision of "a beast" which comes up out of the sea. (Revelation 13:1) There is no doubt that the designation "beast" is given to this emerging political entity because of its rapacious, repressive and unjust nature.

The concept of and the mandate for the existence of civil government had their origin in and through Christ at some point before his incarnation. Paul made that clear in his letter to the Colossians. Referring to Christ he said, "He is the image of the invisible God, the firstborn over all creation. For by him all things were created: things in heaven and on earth, visible and invisible, whether <u>thrones or powers or rulers or authorities</u>; all things were created by him and for him." (Colossians 1:15-16 NIV) That being the case, it is not surprising that Jesus recognized both the legitimacy of and the limitations of civil

---

[322] Roger Crowley, <u>Empires of the Sea</u>, (New York: Random House, 2008), p. xiii.
[323] Peter Charanis, "Byzantium and the West," <u>Great Problems in European Civilization</u>, (Englewood Cliffs, N.J.: Prentice-Hall, Inc., 1954), Ed's: Kenneth M. Setton & Henry R. Winkler, p. 90.

government when he said, "Give to Caesar what is Caesar's and to God what is God's." (Matthew 22:21 NIV) Jesus' statement gives Christians "a place to stand outside politics, and without it [that is, without Jesus' statement] we're vulnerable to a system in which the state defines everything, which is the essence of tyranny."[324]

Thus, God is the author of political nationalism or civil government, though certainly not of all its forms.[325] For example, God certainly endorses political structures which take "vengeance on evil-doers" and which "praise them that do well." (I Peter 2:14) God continues to give a mandate for political nationalism to exist and function, even in the face of many horrible abuses of political power. (See 13:2, "the dragon gave him his power." See also 13:4 and comments.) Proper political power is that which is "conceived not as intrinsically corrupting, but as an instrument in the service of higher, divinely ordained, ends."[326]

What should a follower of Christ do if the political entity of which he is a citizen restricts or prohibits his activities as a Christian? Such prohibitions may be enforced by fines, by imprisonment and even by death. One option is bold confrontation. That choice can only be embraced by one who is willing to pay not only the personal price but also be willing to endanger his family. Another choice is to flee to a location into which the agents of enforcement from a repressive government are not able to extend their reach. This was the choice which God directed Joseph and Mary to take in the attempt to protect the Christ child. For those who do not live near an international border or cannot get legal permission to cross that border or do not have funds allowing them to abandon their residence and seek refuge, they probably will have to face the alternatives of fines, prison, torture, or martyrdom. Even flight is not a totally sure protection.

13:1   "having ten horns, and seven heads"

The empire arose out of the sea and is symbolized by a beast having seven heads and ten horns. However, it is not to be thought of as some sort of a grotesque misshapen multi-headed animal crawling out of the slurry of some evolutionary slime pit. As noted under 12:3, the heads and horns represent outlying administrative nodes or centers of Byzantine political power. When Constantine moved his capital to the site which became Constantinople, he continued utilizing the Roman administrative structure which was already in place. Therefore, the same description is used here as that in 12:3, where the

---

324 Quoted from a speech which R. R. Reno, Professor of Theology and Ethics at Creighton University in Omaha, Nebraska, made on February 20, 2013 at Hillsdale College National Leadership Seminar.

325 There are several bases upon which civil government currently exists. Some forms and bases of government are clearly against God's concept of a benign political state. The prophet Habakkuk warned of such a venomous political entity when he described the Chaldeans as those whose "judgment and their dignity proceed from themselves" and who "come all of them for violence" and as those who "sweep by as a wind, and shall pass over, and be guilty, even he whose might is his god." (Habakkuk 1:7-11) One political scientist affirms that "Nationalism is the most potent principle of legitimacy in the modern world. The principle of national self-determination holds that nations should be freely and severally institutionally expressed, and ruled by their co-nationals in sovereign nation-states or in power sharing arrangements with their peers in multinational states." - Brendan O'Leary, *Europe's Embers of Nationalism*, Current History, March 2015, p. 101.

   Where there is not a legal basis for the existence of a nation-state, still a political entity may exist like those to which the apostle Paul made reference in his sermon to the Athenians in which he said, God "made of one, every nation of men to dwell on the face of the earth, having determined their appointed seasons, and the bounds of their habitation." (Acts 17:26) Political entities where ethnicity is the basis of legitimacy are called ethnic-based nation-states. However, "the world, after all, is full of multiethnic and multiconfessional states that are successful and prosperous, from Switzerland to Singapore to the U.S. ... In all these places, a social compact – usually based on good governance and economic opportunity – often makes ethnic and religious diversity a source of strength, not an engine of instability." - Yaroslav Trofimov, *The Fractured Legacy of the Map Makers*, The Wall Street Journal Review, April 11-12, 2015, p. C2.

326 Farzana Shaikh, Making Sense of Pakistan, (New York, NY: Columbia University Press, 2009), p. 40.

Revelation Chapter 13

Roman Empire is called "a great red dragon, having seven heads and ten horns." Here, it is "a beast coming up out of the sea, having ten horns and seven heads." Byzantium simply continued to utilize the administrative structure which was previously in place before Constantine established his new capital at the south entrance to the Bosporus. The red dragon mentioned in 12:3 having seven heads and ten horns, represents the bloody persecuting Roman Empire. The heads and horns were the Roman outlying administrative centers which Constantine and the succeeding Byzantine Emperors continued to use. Some centers, the heads, were more important, while the relatively minor centers are represented as horns.

The transition from the Eastern Roman Empire to the Byzantine Empire, though gradual, seems to have reached its consummation during the reign of Heraclius (Herakleios), who ruled from 610 till his death in 641. His regency "marked in many ways the end of the East Roman Empire and the true beginnings of that distinctive, Greek-speaking, Christian, culturally heterogeneous form of civilization known as Byzantine. Its first years saw the final titanic struggle with Persia, so long Rome's most formidable rival, culminating in Heraclius's crushing victory at Nineveh in 628."[327] Concerning the date of the beginning of the Byzantine Empire, see also the discussion of the words "authority to continue forty and two months" under 13:5, on page 201.

13:1   "on his horns ten diadems"

This statement is very similar to the one in 12:3 except for the number of diadems. In the earlier description, it was the "heads" which were adorned with diadems. (Please see 12:3, "upon his heads seven diadems.") Here, the "horns," representing a lower level of administrative control, have been rewarded with diadems.

13:1   "upon his heads names of blasphemy"

The heads which were governmental centers had names of blasphemy by reputation and imputation. Such a category of names was used to describe the spiritual condition of the church in Sardis, concerning whom Jesus said, "Thou hast a name that thou livest, and thou art dead." (Revelation 3:1) In this way, the Byzantine governmental centers were notorious for forcing Christians to make utterances and perform rituals which were blasphemous. Be sure to read the exposition at 13:5 under "a mouth speaking great things and blasphemies."

13:2   "And the beast which I saw was like unto a leopard, and his feet were as the feet of a bear, and his mouth as the mouth of a lion: and the dragon gave him his power, and his throne, and great authority."

13:2   "leopard ... bear ... lion ... dragon"

These similes are given to help us understand the rapacious persecuting nature of the sea-born beast. History fully confirms the prophetic picture given here. For example, "In the court of Constantinople the attraction of power was much greater because it was a power unlimited by laws, regulations, audits, parliamentary interventions, or judicial reviews: the emperor could castrate, blind, behead, and provide succor; promote to any position

---
327 Geoffrey Barraclough (ed.), <u>Harper Collins Atlas Of World History</u>, (Ann Arbor, Michigan: Borders Press, 2001), p. 112.

and demote and exile; give the most valuable gifts and confiscate, endow a man with a rich estate or take away all his possessions."[328]

With seventeen governmental power centers, its ten horns and seven heads, in addition to the central capital, no one could elude or escape the clutches of the sea-born beast unless he could flee, like the Nestorians did, to some place beyond its borders. It was truly bestial as seen in its ruthless persecution of theological dissenters like the Egyptian monophosites, now known as the Copts. It was this background of Byzantine oppression which initially deceived many Christians to think that the conquering Muslims were bringing freedom and emancipation. However, reality soon proved that the coming of the Muslims was a transition from one tyranny to an even more repressive and rapacious one. Additionally, the enormous size of the Islamic world made fleeing almost impossible.

13:2 "the dragon gave him his power and his throne and great authority"

This dragon refers to Satan whose identification is clearly given in 12:9. It is a stunning and frightening confirmation of the fact that Satan can and does intrude into and utilize political structures and activities for his own purposes. The pronoun "him" refers to the "beast coming up out of the sea." (13:1)

13:3 "And I saw one of his heads as though it had been smitten unto death; and his death-stroke was healed: and the whole earth wondered after the beast;"

13:3 "smitten unto death and his death-stroke was healed"

That death-stroke came from Sassanian Iran. Iran was almost perpetually at war with Rome during the time of both the Parthian (50 B.C. - 226 A.D.; See "Parthians" at Acts 2:9.) and Sassanian Dynasties (226 A.D. - 642 A.D.) First, war was with Rome which was governed from the city of Rome, and subsequently with the Eastern Roman/Byzantine Empire, governed from Constantinople. "Most Sassanian rulers were actually moderate in their war aims. In spite of intense suspicion, they too recognized the Roman and Byzantine Empires as their civilized neighbors that were not to be destroyed – so they were mostly content with limited gains in Mesopotamia when they went to war.

"But Khusrau II was entirely more ambitious. … In 610-611, Sassanian armies entered Syria and conquered Antioch, one of the largest cities of the empire. By then they had taken the rich trading center of Edessa – its churches reportedly yielded a booty of 112,000 pounds of silver. In 613 the Sassanians seized Emesa (Homs, Hims) and Damascus, then descending to capture Jerusalem in May 614, where they seized a celebrated fragment of the 'true cross.' Egypt, the largest single source of Byzantine tax revenues and grain supplies was next: by 619 Alexandria had fallen, completing the conquest.

"Sassanian armies threatened the survival of the empire even more directly by penetrating into its core territory of Anatolia. By 611 they won a major victory at Caesarea of Cappadocia (Kayseri), and in 626 a Sassanian army would reach all the way west to the Asiatic shore directly opposite Constantinople across the Bosporus, at that point less than a mile wide. ... Ever since the Sassanian invasion started nineteen years before in 603,

---

328 Edward N. Luttwak, The Grand Strategy of the Byzantine Empire, (Cambridge Massachusetts: Harvard University Press, 2009), p. 129.

Revelation Chapter 13

Byzantine forces had been battered again and again, in defeats, retreats, and the outright collapse of frontier and city defenses. But evidently surviving units, fragments of units, individual veterans, and new recruits rallied around Herakleios (Heraclius), whose ability to lead them to victory was entirely unproven. ... Herakleios set out on March 25, 624, with his newly trained army to launch a counteroffensive. ... On February 23, 628, according to Theophanes, when Herakleios seemed to be on the verge of entering Ctesiphon and finishing off the empire, Khusrau was overthrown and killed in a coup d'etat by his own son Kawadh-Siroy, who opened peace negotiations and offered a prisoner exchange."[329] And so, the Byzantine Empire had been "smitten unto death and his death-stroke was healed: and the whole earth wondered after the beast."

13:4 "and they worshipped the dragon, because he gave his authority unto the beast; and they worshipped the beast, saying, Who is like unto the beast? And who is able to war with him?"

13:4 "they worshipped the dragon, because he gave his authority unto the beast"

The pronoun "they" seems to refer back to the expression "the whole earth" in 13:3 which would point to the individuals comprising the entire population of the Byzantine Empire. Perhaps this worship was not deliberate and overt but was worship in essence through submission to the beast, since the dragon, Satan, (See 12:9.) worked through the Byzantine Empire. (See the comments on 13:1.) Satan provided the inspirational concept and energizing power behind the beast, thus giving "his [the dragon's] authority unto the beast." Here is one of the points of union between the serpent and the beast.

13:4 "who is able to war with him?"

"Obdurate resistance, no matter how sturdy, cannot explain the Byzantine's survival either – they often faced enemies much too strong to be long resisted by defensive combat alone. It was by creative responses to new threats – by strategy, that is – that the empire survived century after century. More than once, successive defeats reduced it to little more than a beleaguered city-state. More than once the great walls of Constantinople came under attack from the sea or by land, or both at once. But time after time, allies were successfully recruited to attack the attackers, allowing the imperial forces to regain their balance, gather strength, and go over to the offensive. And when the invaders were driven back, as often as not imperial control was restored over larger territories than before. The enemies of the empire could defeat its armies and fleets in battle, but they could not defeat its grand strategy. That is what made the empire so resilient for so long – its greatest strength was intangible and immune to direct attack."[330]

Perhaps many Christians who might have desired to defy the beast would have been overwhelmed by a sense of futility leading to submission and conformity. Anyone courageous enough (many would say foolhardy enough) to have defied the beast would have had to be prepared for agonizing suffering and/or death.

---

329 Edward N. Luttwak, The Grand Strategy of the Byzantine Empire, (Cambridge, Massachusetts: Harvard University Press, 2009), pp. 393-407.
330 Edward N. Luttwak, The Grand Strategy of the Byzantine Empire, (Cambridge Massachusetts: Harvard University Press, 2009), p. 12.

13:5 "and there was given to him a mouth speaking great things and blasphemies; and there was given to him authority to continue forty and two months."

13:5 "given to him"

Please see the notes on 13:7. The pronoun "him" refers to the "beast coming up out of the sea," that is, to the Byzantine Empire.

13:5 "a mouth speaking great things and blasphemies"

The mouth was that of the emperor and the blasphemies were his dictatorial orders and proclamations intended to control the personal and corporate life of the Christians. The emperor's despicable role in these matters is clearly documented in history. For example, "Justinian was resolved to see the empire reunited under a revised and authoritative law, but he was no less inclined to regard the Church of his empire as completely subject to his will, with its clergy subject to his appointment, its ecclesiastical affairs subject to his judication, and its dogma subject to his dictation. This is the policy referred to as Caesaropapism: the emperor was not only Caesar, the absolute head of the state, but also pope (*papa*), the absolute head of the church. The policy had its source in the idea of the emperor as the divine representative of God on earth, the head of the divine administration of the Church as well as of the secular administration of the state, the possessor of full temporal and spiritual power. In the east it was transplanted from the pagan world to regulate affairs between the Christian state and the Christian Church. In the west there was the opposite tendency of the Bishop of Rome to regard himself as entitled to assume temporal power because possessed of spiritual authority. To the Byzantine emperor it was necessary to exercise spiritual power in order to maintain the unity of the Church and thus to maintain the Church as a powerful support for the throne."[331]

That analysis, given by secular historians, is completely corroborated by church historians. For example, Latourette tells us that, "Eventually, the Emperor himself, as we have reported, and as we are to see especially in the case of Justinian, declared what was sound doctrine. The Emperors enforced the decrees of councils against those condemned as heretics. They had a voice in appointments to high ecclesiastical office, especially in the east, near the main seat of their authority. As time passed, the assent of the Emperor was required even for the assumption of his powers by each successive Bishop of Rome. [Here is another point at which we see the union of the serpent (satanic power) and the beast (subservient political power).] It was under the Emperors that what came to be called 'ecumenical councils' became the voice of the entire Catholic Church."[332]

Latourette also says, "Beginning with Constantine, the first [emperor] formally to accept the Christian faith, the Emperors sought to control the church and to make it serve the state and society as they had the non-Christian official cults. That tradition was strengthened in the sixth and seventh centuries by Justinian and other strong Emperors, and was what has been termed Caesaropapism."[333]

---

[331] James Westfall Thompson and Edgar Nathaniel Johnson, An Introduction to Medieval Europe, 300-1500, (New York, W. W. Norton & Co., Inc., 1937), pp. 129-130.
[332] Kenneth Scott Latourette, A History of Christianity, Vol. I, (New York: Harper & Row, Publishers, 1975), pp. 184-185.
[333] Kenneth Scott Latourette, A History of Christianity, Vol. I, (New York: Harper & Row, Publishers, 1975), p. 312.

Revelation Chapter 13

Finally, he tells us, "Continuing the pre-Christian tradition that religion and religious cults must be subservient to the state, they had sought, usually successfully, to dominate the Church. They called general councils, expressed themselves on theological issues, and controlled the election of the Patriarchs of Constantinople. Here was preeminently what was known as Caesaropapism, the kind of control of the Church and its hierarchy by the prince to which the lay rulers of Western Europe aspired but which they were not uniformly able to achieve."[334] In Caesaropapism religion "is hijacked by politics. ... It [then]may be used by manipulative leaders to motivate people to wage wars precisely because it inspires people to heroic acts of self-sacrifice."[335]

A similar misuse of civil governing authority is now taking place in the United States of America. One example of this is seen in a "crass ruling handed down on July 14 [2015] by the 10th Circuit Court of Appeals in Denver against the Little Sisters of the Poor, a historic Roman Catholic relief organization, in a case involving Obama Care's contraceptive mandate. Now we're talking about calculated efforts to compel folks to adopt a particular system of belief, or to pay massive fines for their non-compliance. Now we're talking not about incidental slip-ups on the way to justice. We're talking here about applications of the law deliberately designed to override the consciences of our citizens."[336]

13:5 "authority to continue forty and two months"

We previously encountered this identical time-designating expression in 11:2, in which exactly the same verbal description is given, and again in 11:3 where it is transformed into "a thousand two hundred and threescore days." In both those cases the designations were given to delineate the period of time during which God's two unique witnesses would be giving their testimony. The same expression, here in 13:5, gives us the length of the life of the Byzantine Empire. It is exceptional that it denotes a period of time exactly equal to that during which the two witnesses will give their testimony. It is remarkable, though not impossible, that the length of those two very separate, distinct and different historical periods would both be identical!

If we consider this to be a twelve-hundred-sixty-year period (translated from "forty and two months" according to the principal given in Ezekiel 4:6), then when should we understand the period to have begun and to have ended? One might start his calculation from the point when the Byzantine Empire started provisionally when "in 293 Emperor Diocletian split his empire into four, [making] his capital at Nicomedia – now Izmit, in the northeastern corner of the Sea of Marmara – and none of his other three tetrarchs dreamt of living in what was still technically the imperial capital [that is, in Rome]. The whole focus of the empire had shifted to the east."[337]

If we thus broadly date the beginning of the Byzantine Empire at 293 A.D., then the twelve-hundred-sixty years would take us exactly one-hundred years beyond 1453, the date when the Ottoman Turks finally captured Constantinople, the event usually cited as the terminal point of the Byzantine Empire. However, that additional one-hundred year

---

334 Kenneth Scott Latourette, A History of Christianity, Vol. I, (New York: Harper & Row, Publishers, 1975), p. 568.
335 Jonathan Sacks, *Swords Into Plowshares*, The Wall Street Journal, Review, October 3-4, 2015, p. C1.
336 Joel Belz, *With Justice for All?* WORLD, August 8, 2015, p. 6.
337 John Julius Norwich, Absolute Monarchs, A History of the Papacy, (New York: Random House, 2011), p. 14.

period can well be accommodated in the time when the beast which came up out of the earth exercised "all the authority of the first beast." (13:12)

13:6 "And he opened his mouth for blasphemies against God, to blaspheme his name, and his tabernacle, even them that dwell in the heaven."

13:6 "mouth for blasphemies against God, to blaspheme his name"

See the comments on "a mouth speaking great things and blasphemies" at 13:5.

13:6 "his tabernacle, even them that dwell in the heaven"

The expression "his tabernacle" is rendered in the ESV and NRSV as "his dwelling." The NIV translated it as his "dwelling place." This place undoubtedly refers to the composite Jewish/Gentile church, which is "a habitation of God in the Spirit." (Ephesians 2:22) It is the temple of God which the apostle Paul identified when he wrote to the church in Corinth saying, "If any man destroyeth the temple of God, him shall God destroy; for the temple of God is holy, and such are ye." (I Corinthians 3:17) He further told the church in Corinth, "your body is a temple of the Holy Spirit." (I Corinthians 6:19) Also compare the affirmation that "Christ [is] in you, the hope of glory." (Colossians 1:27) The obvious truth that "his tabernacle" refers to Christians is buttressed by the statement which says he "shall give life also to your mortal bodies through his Spirit that dwelleth in you." (Romans 8:11) Finally, the book of Hebrews flatly states that "we [Christians] are his house." (Hebrews 3:6 NIV)

John equates "his tabernacle" with "them that dwell in the heaven." This is a further confirmation that "his tabernacle" refers to Christians, for it is the Christians who have been blessed "with every spiritual blessing in the heavenly *places* in Christ." (Ephesians 1:3, see also Ephesians 2:6.)

13:7 "And it was given unto him to make war with the saints, and to overcome them: and there was given to him authority over every tribe and people and tongue and nation."

13:7 "and it was given unto him"

The words "it was given unto him" may point to the working of Satan or, on the other hand, to the momentum of events. In such a case, circumstances would have coalesced, which made the exercise of a totalitarian government possible. With such a power in place, internal dissent and criticism, which might come from an independent church, could not be tolerated. This resulted in empire-wide enforced conformity. The enforcement of that conformity could be sustained by economic strength coming from a successful system of internal taxation and custom fees imposed on flourishing international trade. That commerce was sustained by Byzantine dominance of seaborne trade in the eastern two-thirds of the Mediterranean, the Aegean Sea, the Sea of Marmara and the entire Black Sea.

Additional significant state revenue was garnered by control of the entry points for the cargoes carried from the east on the fabled vigorous land-based Silk Route. The stimulus for the silk trade came from the wealth and opulence of Rome, where ostentation and extravagance increased with prosperity. Pliny, in his Natural History describes the vast

Revelation Chapter 13

amount of labor involved in acquiring silk fabrics and then says, "So has toil to be multiplied; so have the ends of the earth to be traversed: and all that a Roman dame may exhibit her charms in transparent gauze."[338] That silk "sold for $800,000 a pound in the Sybaritic markets of Rome."[339] Because of such a vigorous economy, military forces could be raised and sustained, not only to guard the borders of the empire but also to suppress any significant internal dissent.

13:7   "make war with the saints"

Because the church formed a very significant percentage of the population of the empire, from the emperor's viewpoint it must not be allowed to exercise independent autonomy. Thus, this war was a war forcing Christians into submission, uniformity and conformity.

13:7   "overcome them"

Many would be overcome by poverty and obscurity, which had resulted from their resistance to the beast. Others would be overcome by imposed death. Still others would be overcome by capitulation to the demands of the beast. Last of all, some would obviously be overcome by flight across the border, beyond the reach of the beast.

13:7   "every tribe and people and tongue and nation"

These nouns (tribe, people, tongue and nation) express the extensive and inclusive ethnic composition of the population of the Byzantine Empire. Among the various people comprising the citizenry of the Empire were to be found Bulgars, Avars, Egyptians, Arabs, Jews, Huns, Slavs and Berbers, as well as others. The adjective "every" is pointing to every tribe, people, tongue and nation resident in the empire; it does not point to those living outside the empire, thus it does not point to global persecution.

13:8   "And all that dwell on the earth shall worship him, every one whose name hath not been written from the foundation of the world in the book of life of the Lamb that hath been slain."

The expression "all that dwell on the earth" is to be understood as a contrast to "them that dwell in heaven" (13:6), referring to Christian citizens of the kingdom of heaven, as clearly indicated in the comments on that expression. "The earth" is that society made up of those "whose name hath not been written from the foundation of the world in the book of life of the Lamb." Thus, in contrast, "all that dwell on the earth" refers to the members of secular society, including the fallen church, distinguished from the true church. The fallen church is later indelibly depicted in the sentence, "Fallen, fallen is Babylon the great, and is become a habitation of demons and a hold of every unclean spirit and a hold of every unclean and hateful bird." (Revelation 18:2)

13:9   "If any man hath an ear, let him hear."

For the significance of this exhortation, please see the comments on 3:22 along with the cross references given there.

---

338 Owen & Eleanor Lattimore, Silks, Spices, and Empire (New York: Dell Publishing Co., Inc., 1968), p. 12.
339 Nancy Hatch Dupree, An Historical Guide to Afghanistan, (Kabul: Afghan Tourist Organization 1971) p. 26.

13:10 "If any man is for captivity, into captivity he goeth: if any man shall kill with the sword, with the sword must he be killed. Here is the patience and the faith of the saints."

13:10 "If any man is for captivity, into captivity he goeth"

Often circumstances may dictate an inevitability of the most repugnant kind. William Wilberforce (1759-1833), who brought slavery to an end in the British Empire, and Abraham Lincoln (1809-1865), who brought emancipation for slaves in America, are notable exceptions in the broad flow of human history. The message of Revelation is letting us know that the circumstances prevailing in the lives of many of God's people, perhaps even our own, may sweep us away to a detestable fate which proves to be unavoidable. Think, for example, of the repulsive fate of millions of Jewish people who were trapped in Hitler's rabid anti-Semitism. We must determine in our hearts that we will be faithful to Christ, even unto death.

13:10 "if any man shall kill with the sword, with the sword must he be killed"

It is entirely conceivable that some of the followers of Christ, when confronted with the despicable alternatives described just above, might resort to mortal combat. Here, the message given to John underlines and emphasizes the prediction made by Jesus when he said, "All they that take the sword shall perish with the sword." (Matthew 26:52)

13:11 "And I saw another beast coming up out of the earth; and he had two horns like unto a lamb, and he spake as a dragon."

13:11 "I saw another beast coming up out of the earth"

This vision depicts the birth of the Russian Empire. No civilization or political power is more fitly described as "coming up out of the earth" than Russia. "Russia is the world's preeminent land power, extending 170 degrees of longitude, almost halfway around the globe."[340]

This geographic evaluation remained relevant even after "1991, when the Soviet Union [was] officially disbanded. Russia was reduced to its smallest size since before the reign of Catherine the Great [reigned July 9, 1762-Nov. 17, 1796]. It had lost even Ukraine, the original heartland of Kievan Rus. But despite the loss of Ukraine and the Baltic states [Latvia, Lithuania and Estonia], the Caucasus, and Central Asia, despite the military uncertainties of Chechnya, Dagestan, and Tatarstan, and despite the emergence of outer Mongolia as an independent state free of Moscow's tutelage, Russia's territory still surpassed that of any other nation on earth, covering over a third of mainland Asia, with land borders still stretching over almost half of the world's time zones from the Gulf of Finland to the Bering Sea."[341] In dramatic language, one scholar helps us grasp the immensity of Russia by telling us, "a third of a world and ten time zones to the east, mid-morning in Vladivostok was still evening of the previous day in St. Petersburg."[342]

---

340 Robert D. Kaplan, The Revenge of Geography, (New York: Random House, 2012), p. 155.
341 Robert D. Kaplan, The Revenge of Geography, (New York: Random House, 2012), p. 175.
342 W. Bruce Lincoln, The Conquest of a Continent, Siberia and the Russians, (Ithica, NY: Cornell University Press, 1994), p. 287.

Revelation Chapter 13

13:11 "he had two horns"

One of the two horns of the beast which came up out of the earth symbolizes the empire's political power. The second horn symbolizes the ecclesiastical or spiritual powers of the Russian Empire. This identification is substantiated by the fact that the Russian Empire became known as the "Third Rome." "The Vatican Secretary of State, Cardinal Casaroli ... spoke of Moscow as the 'Third Rome,' referring to the Russian idea that the mantle of religious leadership moved from Rome to Constantinople, and from Constantinople, after the Moslem conquest [in 1453], to Moscow.[343] While one assumes Casaroli sees no need for a second or third Rome, it was striking that he admitted religious leadership has more than one address."[344] Political Rome, the Roman Empire, exercised spiritual power in addition to its political power through its union with Spiritual Rome, the Roman Catholic Church. Similarly, Russia, the Third Rome, in conjunction with the Greek Orthodox Church, also has two horns, exercising both spiritual and political power.

Though "medieval Muscovy had fashioned itself as the 'Third Rome,' the rightful successor of both Rome itself and Constantinople,"[345] the empire collapsed in the sixteenth century. That led to a period known as the Time of Troubles. "And yet Russia was not finished, in spite of how it seemed at the time. Within a few short years, in 1613, Michael Romanov was installed as the Czar, and a new dynasty as well as a new chapter in Russian history commenced."[346]

The Russian Empire had its birth in the area which is now known as the Ukraine. It was first known as Kievan Rus because the city of Kiev, located on the Dnieper River, was its first capital. The "two horns" were the two concentrations of governing power. The first horn was that of secular political power headed by the Grand Prince while the second horn represented the religious power headed by the Russian Orthodox Metropolitan.

"The Christian Church, administered by the Patriarch of Constantinople, ... worked 'in symphony' with the emperor and helped the secular authorities in many ways – a spiritual arm, moral authority, provider of social services, and mobilizer of the Christian populations. She also observed the effectiveness of Christianity in holding the people in thrall."[347]

The power of the two horns was not equal, for "The Grand Prince's wishes on ecclesiastical appointments were heeded. [Even so], the Church also provided a major source of political advice and administrative skill for him to draw on."[348]

Kiev remained the capital till 1240 when it was destroyed by the Mongol Tatars. The Tatar capital was at Sarai, located on the eastern bank of the Volga River, not far upstream from the Volga estuary at the northwest corner of the Caspian Sea.

---

[343] In 476 A.D. the first Rome ceased. It had been supplanted by Constantinople, the second Rome. In 1456 A.D. the second Rome came to an end when the Turks captured Constantinople and gave the coup de grace to the Byzantine Empire. Constantinople, the second Rome, was supplanted by Kiev and ultimately by Moscow, the third Rome. Let us not forget that the Russian Emperor called himself the Czar, the word comes from the Latin word Caesar, meaning the emperor.

[344] Jim Forest, Religion in the New Russia, (New York: The Crossroad Publishing Company, 1990), p. 23.

[345] Robert D. Kaplan, The Revenge of Geography, (New York: Random House, 2012), p. 165.

[346] Robert D. Kaplan, The Revenge of Geography, (New York: Random House, 2012), p. 165.

[347] Philip Longworth, Russia, the Once and Future Empire From Pre-History to Putin, (New York: Saint Martin's Press, 2005), p. 35.

[348] Philip Longworth, Russia, the Once and Future Empire From Pre-History to Putin, (New York: Saint Martin's Press, 2005), p. 43.

"The [Tatar] Empire of Batu comprised central and south Russia and the region east of the Urals; [the great north-south mountain range which separates European Russia from Asian Russia, see Map 1] it is known also as the empire of Kipchak or the Golden Horde."[349]

After the destruction of the city of Kiev, the center of Russian power shifted to the north, to Moscow, which meanwhile had gained pre-eminence over Novograd. Moscow, "had come to command a strategic central sector of Russia's great network of rivers and portages, and developed an adequate agriculture and food supply. It was part of the Grand Principality of Vladimir, 'a complex of ... valuable territories, which were the source of great military and financial resources.'"[350] Later the Russian capital shifted to the newly built grandiose city of Saint Petersburg, built by order of Peter the Great, who ruled from 1672 to 1725. It was later renamed Petrograd and finally, Leningrad. The capital was moved from that location during World War I and was brought back to Moscow. That the capital should shift back to Moscow is not surprising if one understands its highly advantageous location. "Moscow stood at the center of the upland in which the great rivers of European Russia had their beginnings and that it was a hub from which Russia's river highways zigged and zagged outward like the irregularly shaped spokes of a lopsided wheel. From Moscow, an army could move along Russia's frozen river highways in any direction or, if it was large enough, could advance in several directions at once."[351]

13:11 "he had two horns like unto a lamb, and he spake as a dragon"

The entire Russian system was deceptive. The two horns presented a docile appearance "like unto a lamb." However, its state activities were very often extremely vicious, "as a dragon." When "he spake as a dragon" it reflected the satanic powers which brought the beast into being.

13:12 "And he exerciseth all the authority of the first beast in his sight. And he maketh the earth and them that dwell therein to worship the first beast, whose death-stroke was healed."

13:12 "he exerciseth"

The pronoun "he" clearly refers back to the emerging land-based beast of 13:11. It carries that meaning as it is used in many subsequent places in this chapter of Revelation.

13:12 "the first beast"

This points to the beast which came up out of the sea (13:1-10), that is, the Byzantine Empire.

13:12 "in his sight"

The rulers of the Byzantine Empire saw the rise of the Russian State and beheld how it exercised those very same powers which had previously been exercised from Constantinople. This continued as long as the first beast was still living, that is, till the

---

349 Rand McNally Atlas of World History, R. R. Palmer, editor, (New York: Rand McNally & Company, 1968), p.125.
350 Philip Longworth, Russia, the Once and Future Empire From Pre-History to Putin, (New York: Saint Martin's Press, 2005), p. 53.
351 W. Bruce Lincoln, The Conquest of a Continent, Siberia and the Russians, (Ithaca: Cornell University Press, 1994), p. 19.

Revelation Chapter 13

Ottoman Turkish Sultan Mehmed the Conqueror captured Constantinople in 1453, bringing the Byzantine Empire to its end. (On the question of the length of time the Byzantine Empire was in existence, see the comments on 13:5 under "authority to continue forty and two months.") For an extended period of time the second beast, the one out of the earth, was simultaneously exercising full authority along with that which emanated from Constantinople. Thus, there was historic overlap. That overlap seems to have gone on even beyond 1453. (See the comments on 13:5.)

13:12 "he maketh the earth and them that dwell therein"

Here the words "the earth" do not convey the global concept, but refer to the very extensive steppe regions of Russia on both sides of the Ural Mountains. The distinction in the phrases (1) "maketh the earth" and (2) "them that dwell therein" seem to indicate (1) enactment of state policy and (2) its enforcement.

13:12 "to worship the first beast"

For centuries Russia has felt great attraction to, attachment to and adoration of Byzantium's Orthodox form of Christianity. That sense of sacred affinity reached a climactic point in 988 A.D. when Prince Vladimir of Kiev ordered the mass baptism of his subjects in the Dnieper River.

The mass baptism ordered by Prince Vladimir was the decisive turning point of the southern Slavic people to the Orthodox form of Christianity. It was a doctrinal commitment which has remained intact right into the twenty-first century, despite the current threatening challenge by Islam coming largely from the Caucasus area, especially from Chechnya.

"The coming of the Magyars or Hungarians into the heart of the Danube valley at the end of the ninth century destroyed all chances of a homogeneous Slavic development. The Magyars formed an alien wedge between the northern and the southern Slavs, and from this time onward the two great branches of the Slavic peoples were driven into widely divergent lines of development. The southern Slavs were drawn into the circle of Byzantine influence; they acquired a version of the Greek alphabet and adopted the Greek form of Christianity. Meanwhile the northern Slavs, i.e., the Poles, the Czechs, and the Slovaks, adopted the Latin letters in use among their German neighbors and the Roman form of Christianity."[352]

The translation of the Bible was begun in 863, a century and a quarter before Vladimir "baptized" his subjects by marching them en masse into the Dnieper River. Prior to the work of Bible translation, the Slavic people had no alphabet and, consequently, of course, were illiterate, having no written language. The monumental work of creating an alphabet which could symbolize the various phonetic values of the Slavic language and then using that alphabet to translate the Bible, was done by two brothers, whose names were Cyril (827–869 A.D.) and Methodius (815-885 A.D.). The alphabet which those two highly gifted brothers devised went through two stages of development. The first stage is known as the Old Glagolitic. That was refined to the present Cyrillic Alphabet, which is still used for the Russian language. Cyril and Methodius did their great creative biblical work

---

[352] William Montgomery McGovern, The Early Empires of Central Asia, (Chapel Hill: The University of North Carolina Press, 1939), p. 13.

among the western Slavic people. They carried out their epochal work in Moravia, located in the present-day Czech Republic where a beautiful church building, the Basilica of St. Cyril and Methodius stands as a tribute to their magnificent work. It is not known how long it was before copies of the Cyrillic Bible were available in Kiev, the first capital of the Russian Empire.

13:12 "to worship the first beast, whose death-stroke was healed"

For comment on this phrase, see 13:3.

13:13 "And he doeth great signs, that he should even make fire to come down out of heaven upon the earth in the sight of men."

13:13 "and he doeth great signs" (See addendum on page 211.)

Regarding "the signs which it was given him to do in the sight of the beast," (13:14) history clarifies the meaning: "The emperor himself was the focus of elaborate court rituals performed by officials in resplendent robes, to better overawe foreign envoys at court. If that was not enough, there was a period when hydraulic machinery elevated the imperial throne just as visitors approached, and activated lions that stamped their tails and roared convincingly enough to shock and awe the unprepared. … Much of what they did was calculated to preserve and enhance the prestige of the imperial court even as it was being exploited to impress, overawe, recruit, even seduce."[353] These signs and the fire are examples of satanically-empowered "lying wonders." (II Thessalonians 2:9)

13:13 "that he should even make fire to come down out of heaven upon the earth in the sight of men"

The fire which they were able to make come down out of heaven in the sight of men, undoubtedly, refers to "Kiev's carefully chosen patron saint, Elias. Vladimir's sponsor, the Emperor Basil, was, after all, a devotee of St. Elias. Moreover, the saint was associated with thunder and lightning, which made the cult particularly attractive to worshipers of Perun.[354] The choice was calculated both to integrate Russia's ruler with the great Emperor and to help wean pagan subjects from their addiction to Perun."[355]

13:14 "And he deceiveth them that dwell on the earth by reason of the signs which it was given him to do in the sight of the beast; saying to them that dwell on the earth, that they should make an image to the beast who hath the stroke of the sword and lived."

13:14 "the signs"

See the comments on 13:13.

---

353 Edward N. Luttwak, The Grand Strategy of the Byzantine Empire, (Cambridge Massachusetts: Harvard University Press, 2009), p. 125.
354 "In Slavic mythology [remember that the Russians are Slavs] Perun is the highest god of the pantheon and the god of thunder and lightning. His other attributes were fire, mountains, the oak, iris, eagle, firmament (in Indo-Eruopean languages, this was joined with the notion of the *sky of stone*), horses and carts, weapons (the hammer, Axe of Perun, and arrow), and war. He was first associated with weapons made of stone and later with those of metal." http://en.wikipedia.org/wiki/Perun, Accessed October 1, 2013.
355 Philip Longworth, Russia, the Once and Future Empire From Pre-History to Putin, (New York: Saint Martin's Press, 2005), pp. 38-39.

Revelation Chapter 13

13:14 "saying to them that dwell on the earth, that they should make an image to the beast who hath the stroke of the sword and lived"

The beast to which they should make an image refers to the beast that came up out of the sea (13:1-10), that is the Byzantine Empire. It was that beast which received "the stroke of the sword and lived." As told before, that sword stroke came from Sassanian Iran. (See 13:3.)

The beast which came up out of the earth (13:11), that is the Russian Empire, itself became that image. The Russians for several centuries and in many aspects, fashioned their state and church affairs according to the pattern of Byzantium. "Kievan Rus ... though imperial in territorial extent, it lacked appropriate imperial institutions. But it soon began to import models and ideals to remedy these deficiencies. The source was the city of Constantinople."[356] In the attempt to pattern their life on the model of the Byzantines, among many other ways, the Russian secular leaders adopted the title of Czar which is derived from the word Caesar.

13:15 "And it was given *unto him* to give breath to it, even to the image of the beast, that the image of the beast should both speak, and cause that as many as should not worship the image of the beast should be killed."

13:15 "it was given *unto him* to give breath to it, even to the image"

The phrase "it was given *unto him*" in the rendering of the ASV is expressed by "it was allowed to give" by the NRSV and the ESV. The NIV says "he was given power to give breath." Obviously, translators labored to express the precise meaning. Was the permission or ability to give life to the image given by an outside entity or by the Russian Empire itself? In any case, the Russian state, "the image," became a living, self-perpetuating political entity which initially mimicked the Byzantine Empire in important aspects.

13:15 "as many as should not worship the image of the beast should be killed"

Dissenters and rebels were "killed" – thus unifying the state. True Christians who were resolute in their faith faced death! The brutality of the image, the Russian State through its various forms, was a reflection of the model, the Byzantine Empire.

13:16 "And he causeth all, the small and the great, and the rich and the poor, and the free and the bond, that there be given them a mark on their right hand, or upon their forehead;"

13:16 "he causeth all, the small and the great, and the rich and the poor, and the free and the bond"

The inclusiveness of this language clearly indicates the birth of a totalitarian political entity. No category of citizens was to be exempted.

---

356 Philip Longworth, Russia, the Once and Future Empire From Pre-History to Putin, (New York: Saint Martin's Press, 2005), p. 34.

Revelation Verse by Verse

13:16 "a mark on their right hand, or upon their forehead"

How far into the future does this vision project Russian history? Minute personal control, like that which is prophesied here to eventually come into being, did not occur during the rule of the Czars or the brutal dictatorships of Lenin, Stalin and their successors. Stalin imposed massive banishment and smothering state control through the vicious imposition of the collectivization of agriculture and by other means, during which thousands perished. Even that brutality did not involve the minute individual control which is here prophesied to eventually be put in place.

The state control which is prophesied here to come into being will certainly go far beyond requiring every citizen to have a national identity card. It probably points to the injecting of an invisible programmed scannable computer chip or an implanted radio-frequency identification tag under the skin of the hand or forehead of every citizen of Russia. At that point, death will become the only certain way of escape.

Deceit will be used to convince or entice people to be branded. Scripture tells us "the beast was taken, and with him the false prophet that wrought the signs in his sight, wherewith he deceived them that had received the mark of the beast." (Revelation 19:20)

Those who submit to this demonic, inclusive, totalitarian branding ultimately will have to face eternal consequences. Those consequences are itemized first in 14:9-12. Those who yield to the beast are contrasted with those who refuse the mark of the beast. The book of Revelation tells us, "I saw thrones, and they that sat upon them, and judgment was given unto them: and I *saw* the souls of them that had been beheaded for the testimony of Jesus and for the word of God, and such as worshiped not the beast, neither his image, and received not the mark upon their forehead and upon their hand; and they lived and reigned with Christ a thousand years." (Revelation 20:4)

13:17 "and that no man should be able to buy or to sell, save he that hath the mark, even the name of the beast or the number of his name."

To borrow the words of Stein Ringen in describing totalitarian China, the Russian government at this point will have become "a totalitarian state of the most sinister kind, the kind in which persons are only 'the masses' and do not matter individually."[357] Those who will have successfully and boldly eluded the injection teams will be able to survive only by furtively participating in a crude, secretly operated underground economy, a barter system through which only the most basic items will occasionally and erratically be available. When that barter system fails, then the only recourse will be garbage cans and garbage dumpsters!

13:18 "Here is wisdom. He that hath understanding, let him count the number of the beast; for it is the number of a man: and his number is Six hundred and sixty and six."

This beast is the one which comes "up out of the earth." (13:11) This is the "third Rome," the Russian Empire. The number of this beast "is the number of a man." It will undoubtedly be the number of the man who will lead the Russian government to impose the state control system based on "a mark" on citizens' "right hand, or upon their

---

[357] Stein Ringen, *The Perfect Dictatorship*, The Wall Street Journal, October 12, 2016, p. A 11.

Revelation Chapter 13

foreheads." (13:16) The man who will impose this shockingly evil system has not yet appeared, unless Vladimir Putin evolves into that diabolical person.

Is it possible that living conditions in Russia could become so utterly stringent that draconian methods like those described here by the mark on the hand or on the forehead could reasonably be imposed on its citizens? "The Soviet economy, at its peak in the 1980s, reached about a third of the size of the U.S. economy. Russia's economy today, Mr. Kotkin [in his upcoming book, Stalin: Waiting for Hitler, 1929-1941] points out, 'is one-15th the size of America's. Russia is very weak, and getting weaker.' Not long ago, Russia was the eighth-largest economy in the world. Today, Mr. Kotkin says, 'you're lucky to get it at 12th or 13th, depending on how you measure things. Another two terms of Putin, and Russia will be out of the top 20.'"[358]

Government control of the citizenry of America, though it has not reached the levels of totalitarianism that are here prophesied to eventually be imposed in Russia, still presents numerous developments that are ominous. Employers who offer medical coverage for their employees must offer policies which include contraceptives and abortion prescriptions (abortifacients), even though the employer has Christian convictions against the use of those drugs or procedures.[359]

Similarly, the pharmacist who refuses to fill a request for abortion pills faces the threat of trial, the loss of his pharmaceutical license, and other penalties. The potential for this type of dictatorial government control which forces people to violate their Christian convictions or suffer severe penalties will probably increase in the near future. "As more states permit gay couples to marry or form civil unions, wedding professionals in at least 6 states have run headlong into state anti-discrimination laws after refusing for religious reasons to bake cakes, arrange flowers or perform other services for same-sex couples. The issue gained attention in August, when the New Mexico State Supreme Court ruled that an Albuquerque photography business violated state anti-discrimination laws after its owners declined to snap photos of a lesbian couple's commitment ceremony."[360]

Addendum to 13:13 "he doeth great signs"

In Byzantium there was a very active "Christian" cult of miracle-working relics. "The idea [of relics] warmed the hearts of Byzantines and of medieval Western Catholics for over a thousand years. Then, in the sixteenth century, this notion was fiercely challenged by the Protestant Reformers and was later treated with contempt in Enlightenment Europe. ... The very texture of the materials used [in making relics] and their ingenious fashioning helped to bridge the chasm between the seen and the unseen. ... We are looking at objects from where one world meets and elevates the other. ... What was revealed at the heart of the *enkolpion* [the ornate enclosure holding the relic] was the tomb of the saint in miniature together with a tiny pile of dust taken from that tomb. It showed that a precious fragment of the holy rested on the breast of its wearers,

---

358 Tunku Varadarajan, *Will Putin Ever Leave? Could He if He Wanted?*, The Wall Street Journal, March 10-11, 2018, p. A11.

359 A tiny ray of light filtered through when the U.S. Supreme Court in the Burwell v. Hobby Lobby lawsuit declared in favor of the Hobby Lobby contention. It was "a landmark decision by the United States Supreme Court allowing closely held for-profit corporations to be exempt from a law its owners religiously object to if there is a less restrictive means of furthering the law's interest." http://en.wikipedia.org/w/index.php?title=Burwell_v._Hobby_Lobby_Stores,_Inc.&printable=yes. Accessed 4/2/15.

360 Nathan Koppell and Ashby Jones, *Firms Balk at Gay Weddings, Photographers, Bakers Face Legal Challenges After Rejecting Jobs on Religious Grounds*, The Wall Street Journal, October 2, 2013, p. A3.

Revelation Verse by Verse

in such a way as to reassure them that a protecting saint was as close to them as their own flesh."[361] For further reading, see <u>Saints and Sacred Matter: The Cult of Relics in Byzantium and Beyond</u> by Holger A. Klein.

---

361 Peter Brown, *The Glow of Byzantium*, <u>The New York Review of Books</u>, July 14, 2016, p. 37.

Revelation Chapter 14

Introduction: In chapter 14 we encounter another review which is presented under the important mandate given in 10:11. As in chapter 12, where we were given a review of Roman persecution under the symbolism of the "great red dragon," so here (14:1-5) we are given an evaluation of the yet-to-come post-apostolic epochal major conversion of Jews to Christ, which was very succinctly predicted in 7:1-8. While this vision starts by predicting the special role of the 144,000 Jews who initially will have acknowledged Christ and yielded themselves to Him, it also makes clear that the first significant group of conversions from among the Jews will only have been the beginning. They will be "the first fruits unto God and unto the Lamb." (14:4b) Obviously, there can only be "first fruits" if there is a subsequent or later harvest of fruit. It is clear then, that the conversion of the Jewish people to Christ will continue after that initial breakthrough of 144,000 takes place. From Romans 11:16 it is obvious that those subsequent conversions of Jews to Christ will be copious or numerically significant because they are designated as "the lump," "the whole loaf" (Stern), "the whole lump" (ESV), "the whole batch" (NIV and NRSV), probably denoting the major portion of the Jewish people.

The vistas to follow in chapter 14 are sweeping. One panorama, a harvest scene, starts at verse 6 on the occasion of the first festival of Pentecost following the resurrection of Christ and at verse 16 takes us all the way to the end of the Gospel age. We know the passage depicts a harvest because of the use of the reaping sickle mentioned in verses 15-16. Though the joyous scene of harvesting ripened grain is marred by grievous developments, still it is reminiscent of Jesus' teaching about the Gospel harvest, recorded in Matthew 9:35-38 and in John 4:35-38.

The second panorama is extremely grim. It is tersely portrayed in verses 17-20. It also is a harvest scene – but the sickle is that of war, a form of judgment. It shows the judgmental aspect of God's hand in the historic wars which have taken place and which are yet to take place during the whole Christian period of history. Collectively, by the end of that era so much blood will have been shed that in an area extending for 200 miles that blood will have risen high enough to reach a horse's bridle! (14:19-20)

From this gruesome depiction of massive bloodshed, it becomes obvious that the book of Revelation does not cast a blind eye on the wars of the Christian era. The depiction of those wars stretches from those fought by Rome at the beginning of the Christian age, through ever-more grim conflicts, to those in our time and on into the future.

Here are to be placed such cataclysmic conflicts as the Muslim wars of conquest beginning in 632 at the death of Mohammad, taking us through those of the Arabic, the Persian and Turkish periods of Islamic expansion and on into the wars of Wahabi expansion and those of the many other varieties of Jihadism. To all of that gore must be added the blood which was shed during the period of the Crusades against Islam, from 1095 through 1291. When the Crusaders conquered Jerusalem "they put to death by sword over 17,000 Muslims on the site of Solomon's temple and burned all the Jews inside their synagogues."[362] Following those crusades were those in Europe which were initiated by the papacy to reconvert or, if reconversion failed, to destroy those who had been declared to be heretics.

Next, one must not overlook the wars of Portugese and Spanish colonialism which followed Vasco da Gama's 1498 discovery of the sea route to India by circumnavigating Africa. In addition to the Spaniards and the Portugese, also the French, the Dutch, the Belgians, the British, the Italians and the Germans, all shed rivers of blood in pursuit of their colonial ambitions.

To this repulsive river of blood one must add the blood flowing from the Thirty Years' War, which ended finally in 1648 with the Peace of Westphalia and the birth of the current nation-state system. Also to be included are the Napoleonic wars, fought in Spain, in Egypt, in Palestine, in Russia, and finally ending in Belgium with Napoleon's defeat at Waterloo in 1815.

Only if we ignore the horrible American Civil War could we think of the century between 1815 and 1914 as one of relative peace which was finally shattered by World War I, beginning at Sarajevo with the assassination of the Archduke of the fading Hapsburg Empire. The American Civil war began on April 12, 1861 with the Confederate shelling of Fort Sumter. More than 600,000 soldiers had been killed by the time it ended in 1865 by General Lee's surrender at Appomattox. Beyond those extensive and lurid conflicts still much greater tributaries were to flow into that sea of blood. They were to come from World War II, the Korean War, the war in Vietnam, the eight-year war between Iraq and Iran from 1980-1988[363], America's wars both in Afghanistan and Iraq, and now the Muslim civil war in Syria.

The repulsive global conflict beginning in 1914 deserves further consideration. The great winepress (14:19) not only points to "the monstrous bloodshed of 1914-1918" but to much greater bloodshed, especially if we consider World War II to be a continuation of the 1914-1918 conflict. Since there were only twenty-three years between the Treaty of Versailles, ending the hostilities of World War I, and the beginning of World War II, one may reasonably consider both conflagrations as a single gargantuan war. If one considers the horrifying 1936-1939 Spanish Civil War as the beginning of World War II, then only eighteen years of breathing space, a brief recess, divided the two parts of one great world war. Added together, the combined total of fatalities is breathtakingly frightening. "In thinking about Europe and its union, [the current European Union, the E.U.] the number that one needs to keep in mind is not the rate of the Euro Exchange or the measure of the Greek deficit, but a simpler one, of sixty-million. That is the approximate (and probably understated) number of Europeans killed in the thirty years between 1914 and 1945, victims of wars of competing nationalisms on a tragically divided continent."[364]

"Few observers in the summer of 1914 anticipated that Austria-Hungary's declaration of war against Serbia would spark an ineluctable [inevitable] chain reaction in which Russia dashed to

---

362 Malachi Martin, The Decline and Fall of the Roman Church, (New York: G.P. Putnam's Sons, 1981), p. 111.

363 "When it mercifully ended in August 1988, neither side had achieved very much: the border was unchanged, no territory had been gained, and both Saddam Hussein and Ayatollah Khomeini remained in power, safely seated in their respective capitals. But well over a million men had given the full measure of devotion, with perhaps four times that number permanently maimed. It was a war of incompetence... Iran's once mighty military had been gutted by the revolution. Instead of using tanks, infantry and aircraft in a combined arms doctrine of a modern military, Khomeini and the revolutionary commanders believed élan and revolutionary zeal in the form of human wave assaults could overcome rows of Iraqi tanks and artillery laid hub to hub." David Crist, The Twilight War, The Secret History of America's 30-Year Conflict with Iran, (New York: Penguin Press, 2012), pp. 84-85.

364 Tim Arango, *Fears of Deeper Sectarian Strife in Syria,* The New York Times, December 7, 2012, p. A6 and A17.

Revelation Chapter 14

Serbia's defense and Germany ran to Austria's, or that France would rally to its Russian allies while Britain sided with the French. Fewer still predicted that Turkey would fail in its efforts to stay clear of the fracas and be driven into an alliance with Germany and Austro-Hungary – the Central Powers – against the Triple Entente of Russia, Britain, and France. The shockingly unexpected, however, happened. World War I, the cataclysm that would last four unspeakable years, [and would] bring about the fall of empires and irrevocably transform the Middle East, had started."[365]

This bare and very incomplete list has not even alluded to many additional wars like those which have brutally and repulsively taken place on the continent of Africa. Those should include the blood shed by the wars involved by participating in the gruesome slaving industry. Also, no mention has been made of the interminable wars in the Far East between the Han Chinese and the Mongolian people, or the Japanese-Russian War of 1904-05, and the Japanese invasion of Manchuria beginning in 1937 during which, in the siege of the city of Changchun alone, 160,000 civilians were killed. Also, one must not forget the Mao Tse-tung/Chiang Kai-shek War which ended in 1949 with the defeat of the Chinese Nationalists and their withdrawal to the island of Taiwan. That was followed by Mao's war of suppression to unify Communist China in which "an estimated five million were killed in the first decade of Maoism."[366]

To this repulsive account of blood-letting, one must add that caused by the Korean War (1950-1953) and the Vietnam War (1959-1975). One must also consider the rivers of blood that are yet to flow from future wars, of which the one predicted in 9:16 will dwarf that of any war yet seen.

14:1 **"And I saw, and behold, the Lamb standing on the mount Zion, and with him a hundred and forty and four thousand, having his name, and the name of his Father, written on their foreheads."**

14:1 "the Lamb standing on the mount Zion"

Jesus of Nazareth is that "Lamb." This is confirmed by the testimony of John the Baptist, which is recorded in John 1:29. In this vision he is standing on mount Zion with his initial major group of post-apostolic converts from Judaism. According to Psalm 48:1-2, mount Zion is "the city of our God." It is then to be equated with "the holy city, new Jerusalem [which ultimately will be] coming down out of heaven from God, made ready as a bride adorned for her husband." (Revelation 21:2) Indisputably therefore, Jesus is standing with those Jewish converts in the church, which is the bride of Christ. It is not only those Jewish converts who have attained that high standing, but also everyone, Jew and Gentile alike, who having yielded his/her heart and life to Christ, will have "come unto mount Zion, and unto the city of the living God, the heavenly Jerusalem." (Hebrews 12:22)

14:1 "a hundred and forty and four thousand, having his name, and the name of his Father written on their foreheads"

The 144,000 will consist of the initial major post-apostolic conversion of Jewish people to Christ. They were first mentioned in chapter 7:3-4. (Please see the comments on that

---

[365] Michael B. Oren, <u>Power, Faith, and Fantasy, Americans in the Middle East, 1776 to the Present</u>, (New York: W.W. Norton & Co., 2007), p. 325.
[366] George Walden, *A Red Book Written in Blood*, <u>The Wall Street Journal</u>, October 5-6, 2013, p. C7.

passage.) The words "having his name" refer to the name of the Lamb, thus it is clear that they will have become Christians. This description enlarges our understanding of the blessing given through the Holy Spirit which will have been bestowed on those first Jewish converts to Christ, who will be sealed on their foreheads. (See 7:3 and the comments.) In that first description of those converts, we saw that the seal of the Holy Spirit transforms, but here we see that it also identifies. (See I Corinthians 6:19-20.)

14:2 **"And I heard a voice from heaven, as the voice of many waters, and as the voice of a great thunder: and the voice which I heard** was as the voice **of harpers harping with their harps:"**

14:2 "a voice from heaven"

This heaven is that which is defined in definition number one in the introduction to chapter 15.

14:2 "the voice which I heard was as the voice of harpers harping with their harps"

Heaven is visualized as a great concert hall and John is privileged to attend one of the concerts. There is a great choir in which each vocalist accompanies himself on a harp. Since there is a clear distinction between "mount Zion," where the 144,000 are standing, and "heaven," where the concert takes place, we know that the heavenly chorus does not consist of the 144,000.

14:3 **"and they sing as it were a new song before the throne, and before the four living creatures and the elders: and no man could learn the song save the hundred and forty and four thousand,** even **they that had been purchased out of the earth."**

14:3 "throne … living creatures … elders"

Please see the comments on 4:4-11.

14:3 "a new song … [which] no man could learn save the hundred and forty and four thousand"

Something in the experience, in the gifts and in the personality of the 144,000 Jewish Christians will have made it possible for them to have deeper comprehension about this heavenly song than other Christians. They will be able to learn the song while others will not. This is a stunning example of the discreet function of each member of the body of Christ, outlined by Paul in I Corinthians 12:12-27.

The "new song" probably is "the song of the lamb" (15:3). If so, it is distinguished from "the song of Moses" (15:3). If this identity is accurate, then the deeper understanding which the Jewish converts will have had of the new song may come from Israel's centuries-long experience with sacrificial lambs.

14:4 **"These are they that were not defiled with women; for they are virgins. These** are **they that follow the Lamb whithersoever he goeth. These were purchased from among men,** to be **the first fruits unto God and unto the Lamb."**

Revelation Chapter 14

Women are not evil and sexual union between a man and a woman is not defiling if it occurs within marriage. Marriage between one man and one woman is not a defilement. However, same-sex marriage certainly is a defilement. (See Romans 1:26-27 and I Corinthians 6:9-11.) Scripture tells us that "marriage [should] be had in honor among all." (Hebrews 13:4) Additionally, I Corinthians 7:28 and I Timothy 4:1-3 also make it crystal clear that marriage is not a sin.

The statement here about being "defiled with women" is not a pro-celibacy teaching, as Barclay surprisingly and with total inaccuracy asserted when he wrote, "We cannot avoid the conclusion that it [the statement that "they that were not defiled with women"] praises celibacy and virginity and belittles marriage."[367] Sadly and dismayingly, Barclay compounds his error by concluding, against all textual evidence, that "the first half of verse 4 does not contain the words of John at all, but is the comment of a scribe."[368]

This passage gives us augmented understanding of what the loyalty of the initial group of 144,000 Jewish converts to Christ will be who were first mentioned in 7:2-8. To consider that all of them could potentially be vulnerable to defilement in a carnal sense by women would imply that each and every one of those converts would be men. But, it is inconceivable that none of those converts would have been women.

Here, the scripture with the words "defiled with women" points to spiritual fornication which may be committed by either males or females. It is that theological fornication which is condemned just four verses later in 14:8. Therefore, verse 14:4 speaks of the theological purity of the 144,000 Jewish converts, not their sexual purity. The plural, "women" is used because the corrupt church, the one which entices "all nations" to commit the spiritual and political fornication of 14:8, is a plural reality having several autonomous manifestations. As mentioned before, political Rome, that is the Roman Empire, exercised spiritual power in addition to its political power. Spiritual Rome, both as the Roman Catholic Church and the Greek Orthodox Church, along with smaller manifestations of the same ecclesiastical deformity, exercise political power in addition to spiritual power.

14:5 **"And in their mouth was found no lie: they are without blemish."**

This group of 144,000 Jewish converts to Christ will have broken with the persistent, lying, theological dishonesty which, regretfully, is even yet embraced by the majority of Jewish people. It is that dishonesty, that lie, which through many centuries has kept the Jewish people from acknowledging and accepting Jesus of Nazareth as their Messiah. Typical of that dishonesty is the definition given by a well-known Jewish lexicographer of the word "Messiah." He wrote, "The concept of a divine or semi-divine 'savior,' whose self-sacrifice will save mortals from the punishment merited by their sins, is a purely Christian idea that has no foundation in Jewish thought."[369] Anyone with even a rudimentary knowledge of the Old Testament scriptures would wonder if that scholar had deleted the 53rd chapter from the book of Isaiah, along with many other passages, for example, Isaiah 9:6-7.

---

367 William Barclay, The Revelation of John, Vol. II, (Philadelphia: The Westminster Press, 1976), p. 121.
368 William Barclay, The Revelation of John, Vol. II, (Philadelphia: The Westminster Press, 1976), pp. 121-122.
369 Ronald L. Eisenberg, Dictionary of Jewish Terms: A Guide to the Language of Judaism, (Rockville, Maryland: Schreiber Publishing, 2008), p. 283.

Two other Jewish lexicographers, giving their joint definition of the term "Messianic Jew" wrote, "Although Messianic Jews share some of the texts and ideas of Judaism, the central tenant of Messianic Jews – that Jesus is the **Messiah** – is diametrically opposed to the very foundations of Judaism."[370] Obviously, the Judaism cited in that definition is not biblical Judaism. The 144,000 Jewish followers of Jesus will decisively have broken the bonds of that kind of collective falsehood which has kept the majority of Jewish people from recognizing, acknowledging and obeying Jesus, who is the Lamb of God.

No lie was found in their mouth because they accepted the message of the Old Testament in which "are hundreds of references to a coming Jewish messiah that are uniquely fulfilled in Jesus. These include his genealogy, his birthplace, the date of his arrival in Jerusalem, details of his death, his burial in a rich man's tomb, and that his body would not see decay. Even just a handful of these prophecies make it a near mathematical certainty that only Jesus fits the person described."[371]

14:6 **"And I saw another angel flying in mid heaven, having eternal good tidings to proclaim unto them that dwell on the earth, and unto every nation and tribe and tongue and people;"**

14:6 "another angel"

The book of Hebrews tells us that the Mosaic Covenant was "the word spoken through angels." (Hebrews 2:2) Similarly, just as there was angelic mediation in transmitting the book of Revelation (See 1:1.), so here an angel has a central role in the inauguration of the Gospel message of Christ. Since they are "ministering spirits, sent forth to do service for the sake of them that shall inherit salvation," (Hebrews 1:14) they probably also have a strengthening role in the ongoing preaching of the Gospel.

14:6 "in mid heaven"

The occurrence of the expression "mid heaven" is used only two other times, in Revelation, in 8:13 and in 19:17, where it is an eagle and "all the birds" which fly in mid heaven. In this passage (14:6) it is an angel which flies in mid heaven. Hendriksen says, in commenting on the occurrence of the expression "mid heaven" in 8:13, that "It [the eagle] is soaring aloft to the zenith so that it may be seen everywhere."[372] Similarly, Plummer wrote, concerning 8:13, "The eagle is thus [because it is flying in mid heaven] plainly visible to all."[373] Barclay, in commenting on 8:13, wrote, "The expression 'mid heaven' means the highest point in the sky, that part where the sun is at mid day. Here we have a dramatic and eerie picture of an empty sky and a solitary eagle winging its way across its highest point, forewarning of the doom to come."[374]

Thus, the expression "mid heaven" is a figure of speech or a metaphor used to illustrate something as being obvious, in the open, equivalent to the common American expression "in the light of day." It means not hidden, in clear sight, so clearly manifest that no one could plead ignorance. Its use here in 14:6 has the implication that people should have

---

370 Joyce Eisenberg and Ellen Scolnic, The JPS Dictionary of Jewish Words, (Philadelphia: The Jewish Publication Society, 2001), pp. 100-101.
371 Paul Ernst, *Betting Your Life*, Challenger, October/December 2013, p. 9.
372 W. Hendriksen, More Than Conquerors: An Interpretation of the Book of Revelation, (Grand Rapids: Baker Book House, 1952), p. 144.
373 A. Plummer, The Pulpit Commentary [on] Revelation, (Chicago: Wilcox & Follett Co.., no date), p. 235.
374 William Barclay, The Revelation of John, Vol. II, (Philadelphia: The Westminster Press, 1976), p. 52.

Revelation Chapter 14

been able to anticipate the dawning of the Gospel era, which was copiously and unmistakably foretold in the writings of the Jewish prophets. (See Isaiah 2:1-3.)

14:6 "eternal good tidings"

These are the tidings which announce the availability of eternal salvation through the life, death, burial and resurrection of Jesus. These marvelous "eternal good tidings" were initially proclaimed on that indelibly memorable first celebration of Pentecost following the resurrection of Jesus. Here, that event is recounted in a very brief retrospective. The destiny of the proclamation of the "eternal good tidings" will ultimately reach a victorious crescendo which is described in 14:16.

14:7 "and he saith with a great voice, Fear God, and give him glory; for the hour of his judgment is come: and worship him that made the heaven and the earth and sea and fountains of waters."

The entire period during which the declaration of the Gospel, "the eternal good tidings" (14:6), takes place is itself "the hour of his judgment." The preaching of the Gospel constitutes a period of judgment because it separates those who love God and his truth from those who do not. (See Acts 13:46.)

14:8 "And another, a second angel, followed, saying, Fallen, fallen is Babylon the great, that hath made all the nations to drink of the wine of the wrath of her fornication."

14:8 "fallen, fallen is Babylon"

These words compose one of the significant judicial pronouncements of doom handed down in the course of "his judgment." (14:7) The words "fallen, fallen" point to the collapse of the false church. This fall or collapse is currently ongoing and will lead to the ultimate judgment of and doom of Babylon, the counterfeit or false church. It is a fall achieved only through costly heroic sacrifice by people who dare to proclaim the truth. In contrast to this fall, a verbally similar announcement in 18:2 refers back to the origin of spiritual Babylon. (See also the comments on 11:8.) This pronouncement in 14:8 is not describing the origin of Babylon, but its character and its collapse, its judgment and its doom. At this point, the declaration, which describes Babylon – the deceitful misleading false church – as fallen, is obviously entirely consistent with the message of the "eternal good tidings." Some of the epochal stages in the ongoing fall or collapse of Babylon are worthy of note to which several pages are devoted in Appendix D. (See also 17:4-5.)

14:8 "Babylon the great, that hath made all the nations to drink of the wine of the wrath of her fornication"

Here, Babylon is called "Babylon the great." This expression may point to the conglomerate made up of all churches which have united with some political power or have assumed political power themselves. More probably it refers to that one church which has excelled in the breach of the church/state separation which Jesus clearly endorsed. (See Matthew 22:21.) We may understand the enormous extent to which such a grotesque union of ecclesiastical and political power may grow if we look at the extent to which the church in Rome grew and how it subsequently shrank. This not only distinguishes the Western Catholic Church from other churches following the same pattern, but should alert us to the extent to which this horrible ecclesiastical perversion may develop. "The popes for many centuries, with brief interruptions, held temporal sovereignty over mid-Italy (the so-called Papal States), comprising an area of some 16,000 square miles, with a population in the nineteenth century of more than 3 million. [Subsequently] this territory was incorporated in the new Kingdom of Italy (1861), the sovereignty of the pope being confined to the palaces of the Vatican and the Lateran in Rome and the villa of Castel Gandolfo, by an Italian law, May 13, 1871.

"A treaty of conciliation, a concordat, and a financial convention were signed February 11, 1929, by Cardinal Gasparri and Premier Mussolini. The documents established the independent state of Vatican City and gave the Roman Catholic Church special status in Italy. The treaty (Lateran Agreement) was made part of the Constitution of Italy (Article 7) in 1947. Italy and the Vatican signed an agreement in 1984 on revisions of the concordat; the accord eliminated Roman Catholicism as the state religion and ended required religious education in Italian schools.

"Vatican City includes the Basilica of St. Peter, the Vatican Palace and Museum [collectively] covering over thirteen acres, the Vatican Gardens, and neighboring buildings between Viale Vaticano and the church. Thirteen buildings in Rome, outside the boundaries, enjoy extraterritorial rights; these buildings house congregations or officers necessary for the administration of the Holy See."[375]

If one compares the extent of the Papal States when they embraced 16,000 square miles with the current statistics, one may understand the extent to which the fall of Babylon has already occurred. Today, in glaring contrast, Vatican City (The Holy See) has only a total area of 0.17 square miles, all located inside the city of Rome. However, we must not imagine that this dramatic decline in the extent of the area over which the papacy has direct political control indicates that Babylon's flame is on the verge of extinction. On the contrary, for example, Pope Francis visited South America in July 2013 and on July 27th held Mass on the beach at Rio de Janeiro which was attended by throngs estimated to number as high as 3.5 million. Obviously, Babylon still has great appeal and power.

It is imperative that Christians understand the true fundamental character of spiritual Babylon. Babylon is not only to be equated with "the harlot" because of her fornication with political powers, but she is also called "the mother of the harlots and of the abominations of the earth." (17:5) Because Babylon is called "the mother of the harlots" we know that her offspring, churches corrupted in a similar way, will arise in various and multiple national settings. Indeed, such prostituting churches have arisen, but the senior most, the mother of them all, is the one in Rome which delights to call herself "The Mother Church."

Babylon is called a harlot (Revelation 17:1-5) because it is a church which either has allowed itself to be corrupted or by its own initiative has embraced corruption. In either case, it has not kept itself pure in its relationship with secular government. Jesus clearly indicated that there is a boundary between church and state when he said "Render unto Caesar the things that are Caesar's, and unto God the things that are God's." (Matthew

---

375 Sarah Janssen, ed., The World Almanac, (New York City: Infobase Learning, 2013), p. 851. For further information, see The Pope and Mussolini: The Secret History of Pius XI and the Rise of Fascism in Europe by David I. Kertzer, Random House, 2014.

Revelation Chapter 14

22:21) When the dichotomy between government and God is honored, "politics will remain politics and not become religion."[376]

Sometimes the violation of that boundary, which by divine precept is intended to separate church and state, is initiated by the state, wishing to use the church for its own purposes, and at other times by the church, seeking favors from the state. When the state wants to adopt or take over the church for its own purposes, it is dangerous to resist the state's overtures. Poignantly, this is seen in the history of the church in Persia.

The Persian Sassanian imperial government, which came to power in 226 A.D. by deposing the Parthian regime (mentioned in Acts 2:9), insisted on the centralization of authority in the church. In general, that organizational change made the process more efficient and easier by which the state could control the extensive membership of the church. "The Church was recognized as a permitted religious community, or *millat* [nation], in a State whose official religion was Zoroastrianism."[377] Later, this same arrangement was basically adopted by Islam after the Battle of Nehawand in 642 when it replaced the Zoroastrian-Persian-Sassanian government. Even today, the Christian church in a Muslim country is only marginally tolerated and must bear many adverse impositions on its freedom and liberty.[378]

Despite great danger, there were Iranian bishops who dared to defy the authority of the state when it was exercised against the followers of Christ. For example, in the reign of Emperor Shapur II who ruled from 309 to 379, the Christians were falsely accused of collusion with Byzantium during an attack by Constantine against Iran. Informers accused Bishop Simon, who was then Bishop in Seleucia-Ctesiphon, the Sassanian dual capital, of conveying state secrets to the Romans. "Shapur II's response was to order a double tax on Christians and to hold the bishop responsible for collecting it. ... [The Emperor gave the following order to his officer], 'When you receive this order ... you will arrest Simon, the chief of the Nazarenes. You will not release him until he has signed this document and agreed to collect the payment to us of a double-tax and a double tribute for all the people of the Nazarenes who are found in the country of our godhead and who inhabit our territory. For our godhead has only the weariness of war while they have nothing but repose and pleasure. They live in our territory [but] share the sentiments of Caesar our enemy.' Bishop Simon refused to be intimidated. He branded the tax as unjust and declared, 'I am no tax collector but a shepherd of the Lord's flock.'"[379]

Bishop Simon's defiance not only led to his execution on Good Friday, April 17, 341, but also to the persecution of the church. In fact, on the same day Simon was put to death "about 100 other Christians, including many clergy and some monks and nuns, were put to death."[380]

---

376 Jonathan Sacks, *Swords Into Plowshares*, The Wall Street Journal, Review, October 3-4, 2015, p. C2.
377 William G. Young, Patriarch, Shah and Caliph, (Rawalpindi, Pakistan: Christian Study Centre, 1974), p. 1.
378 "The Catholicos [the title given to the national reigning bishop in Iran] was made responsible for the behavior of his people and the Christian community became a kind of state within a state, not unlike the position of the religious minorities in the Turkish Empire which persisted into the twentieth century." Kenneth Scott Latourette, A History of The Expansion of Christianity, Vol. I: The First Five Centuries (Grand Rapids, Michigan: Zondervan Publishing House, 1970), p. 229.
379 Samuel Hugh Moffett, A History of Christianity in Asia, Vol. I: Beginnings to 1500 (2nd ed. rev.; Maryknoll, New York: Orbis Books, 1998), p. 140.
380 Robin E. Waterfield, Christians in Persia, Assyrians, Armenians, Roman Catholics and Protestants (London: George Allen & Unwin Ltd., 1973), p. 19.

Revelation Verse by Verse

The name Babylon (14:8), meaning confusion, is also applicable for any church which initiates spiritual fornication or harlotry, that is, ecclesiastical fornication originated not by the state but most repugnantly by the church itself. This is the wantonness about which Paul prophesied in his letter to the Thessalonian church in which he predicted "the falling away" and the appearance of "the man of sin, the son of perdition." (II Thessalonians 2:3) The one who would commit this breach would ultimately arrogate to himself a status in which he would exalt "himself against all that is called God or that is worshipped so that he sitteth in the temple of God, setting himself forth as God." (II Thessalonians 2:4) Paul called the motivation propelling such apostasy "the mystery of lawlessness." However, that apostasy could not immediately take place in Paul's time because there was a blocking presence described as "one that restraineth." (II Thessalonians 2:7) The Roman civil government, centered on the city of Rome, did its utmost to limit the expansion of the church. That blocking influence or force was not removed until the conversion of Emperor Constantine to a pro-Christian stance. At that point, the church began adopting the trappings of the Roman state and subsequently replaced that state.

Whenever a church becomes a partner in an intimate organic relationship with civil government, a relationship which scripture calls fornication, subsequently that church will itself become a persecuting entity, either on its own behalf or as a branch of the state. That was seen when the church which is centered on Rome grasped the powers of civil government. It then became a repugnant, persecuting power. One example is found in its violent suppression of the ministry of Jan Hus, an early leader in the movement which came to be known as The Protestant Reformation. It was a courageous movement, central to the initial and partial fall of Babylon in the West. The final and total fall of Babylon will be achieved by Christ himself who will bring it to naught by his coming. (See II Thessalonians 2:8.)

"In 1402 Hus became the rector and preacher in the Chapel of the Holy Innocents of Bethlehem in Prague. In that post, by his eloquence and earnestness he attracted all classes, from the highest to the lowest, and speedily became one of the most influential men in the country.[381] ... Hus preached in both Latin and Czech and by his use of the latter stimulated a patriotism which was already growing. ... He denounced the evils in the church, from parish priests to Pope, and held that Christ and not Peter was the foundation on which God had founded the Church, and that, far from being inerrant, many Popes had been heretics. He was marked by high ethical purpose rather than radical theological speculation and wished moral reform rather than ecclesiastical revolution. ...

"The [Roman Catholic] archbishop of Prague was antagonistic and obtained a decree from the first Pisan Pope[382] ordering the surrender to the archbishop of all Wyclif's writings [which Hus was promoting in Prague] for burning and what amounted to silencing of Hus. Hus refused to comply, and that in spite of the burning (1410) of several scores of Wyclif's books, and on excommunication by the archbishop he appealed to the new Pisan Pope, John XXIII. Yet he soon placed himself against that pope by openly denouncing the crusade which the latter was invoking against the King of Naples and the indulgences which were being sold in Prague to raise funds for that venture. ... John

---
[381] The country was then known as Bohemia, but is now known as the Czech Republic.
[382] This was Pope Alexander V who was elected to fill the papacy on June 26, 1409, by the Council of Pisa.

Revelation Chapter 14

XXIII retaliated by putting Hus under strict excommunication and issued an interdict[383] against Prague.

"To relieve the situation, Hus left the city (1412). Yet he continued to preach from place to place and generally in the open air. Czech sentiment was with him. ... [Even so,] The Council of Constance formally condemned Wyclif and his writings, an action which made clear its attitude towards Hus. ... Hus declared that he was being accused of maintaining positions which he did not hold, that he was willing to be informed by the council of his errors, and that he was prepared to submit to its judgment but only if by doing so he did not offend God and his conscience. [Hus had been arrested and imprisoned by the Council.] Here it may be added, that he took a position which was closely akin to that maintained by Luther a little over a century later and which was the essence of Protestantism. ... In a formal meeting of the Council the charges against Hus were repeated, and the prisoner, wasted by prolonged imprisonment, illness, and sleeplessness, still protesting his innocence and refusing to abjure his alleged errors, was silenced, degraded from the priesthood, and turned over to the secular arm. He was thereupon (July 6, 1415) burned at the stake. His last audible words were said to have been: 'Lord, into thy hands I commend my spirit.'"[384]

Fornication between church and state is odious to God because it completely diverts the church from the critical role to which God has assigned it. It also stifles the voice of the church in speaking out against corrupt practices of the state.

14:9   "And another angel, a third, followed them, saying with a great voice, If any man worshippeth the beast and his image, and receiveth a mark on his forehead, or upon his hand,"

14:9   "if any man worshippeth the beast and his image"

This "beast" is the one which comes up out of the sea. (See the comments on 13:1 and following.) "His image" is the beast which comes up out of the earth. (See 13:11 and the accompanying comments.) This worship is pandering to the state by "any man," that is, any one whether from the leadership or from the rank and file, the common members of the church, when the two, that is church and state, commit theological/political fornication. This religious/political fornication points to religious perversion which, though initially appearing in the West, here points to the same severe aberration taking place also in the East.

14:9   "receiveth a mark on his forehead, or upon his hand,"

Please see 13:16-18 and the comments.

14:10   "he also shall drink of the wine of the wrath of God, which is prepared unmixed in the cup of his anger; and he shall be tormented with fire and brimstone in the presence of the holy angels, and in the presence of the Lamb:"

---

[383] A Roman Catholic ecclesiastical censure (judgment, condemnation) withdrawing most sacraments and Christian burial from a person or a district.
[384] Kenneth Scott Latourette, A History of Christianity, Vol. I To A.D. 1500, (New York: Harper & Row, Publishers, 1975), pp. 667-669.

14:10 "the wrath of God, which is prepared unmixed in the cup of his anger"

"Here on earth this wrath is still mixed with grace. The Lord makes his sun to rise on the evil and the good, and sends rain on the just and the unjust, Matthew 5:45. By and by, in hell, the wrath will be unmixed!"[385] As Plummer has stated, "God's wrath will not be tempered, but the wicked will feel the full force of his anger."[386]

14:10 "tormented with fire and brimstone"

This description of the torment of the rebels against God is in perfect agreement with Jesus' statement that God will say to those assembled at his left hand, "Depart from me, ye cursed, into the eternal fire which is prepared for the devil and his angels." (Matthew 25:41) It becomes clear that anyone who chooses to endorse and cooperate with Satan's program will share in Satan's doom.

14:10 "in the presence of the holy angels, and in the presence of the Lamb"

This statement does not depict Jesus and the angels as sadists, eagerly beholding an eternal lurid spectator sport, on the pattern of the ancient Romans cheering as they beheld Christians torn by lions or made into human torches in the coliseum. Rather than what Jesus and the angels are seeing, this tells us what the visions of the lost will be during their eternal torments. They will visualize the very ones whose teaching and pleas they had contemptuously ignored. As a consequence, they will be consigned to suffer along with Satan with whom they had allied themselves. Thus, the suffering of the doomed is "in the presence of the holy angels, and in the presence of the Lamb" whom they will vividly visualize in their memory.

14:11 "and the smoke of their torment goeth up for ever and ever; and they have no rest day and night, they that worship the beast and his image, and whoso receiveth the mark of his name."

14:11 "the smoke of their torment goeth up for ever and ever"

Their punishment will be in proportion to their crime. Their torment will last as long as the consequences of their rebellion. Their capitulation to state and/or ecclesiastical tyranny, rather than opposing it, will have brought tragic, perpetual, ongoing ruin to millions of people. It is a ruin, the consequences of which will have eternal impact. It is the "eternal punishment" of which Jesus has warned us. (See Matthew 25:46.)

14:11 "the mark of his name"

This is the mark mentioned in 13:16 and 14:9. (See the comments on those verses.) It is a designation yet to be devised and applied. (See also 13:18 and 15:2, along with the accompanying comments.)

14:12 "Here is the patience of the saints, they that keep the commandments of God, and the faith of Jesus."

---

385 W. Hendriksen, More Than Conquerors: An Interpretation of the Book of Revelation, (Grand Rapids: Baker Book House, 1952), p. 186.
386 A. Plummer, The Pulpit Commentary [on] Revelation, (Chicago: Wilcox & Follett Co., no date) p. 349.

Revelation Chapter 14

This gives us a broader definition of the term "saints" than that which is usually thought of by Christians. The usual concept envisions someone practicing exemplary abstinence, compassion or generosity. Here, the emphasis is on obedience, that is, keeping "the commandments of God, and the faith of Jesus." One who meets this definition will inevitably practice abstinence, compassion and generosity, but will have a lifestyle which goes beyond the embodiment of those three virtues. He will not only endorse the renunciation of evil but will practice active opposition to evil. Keeping God's commandments and the faith of Jesus in defiance of political power, which demands a conformity involving the transgression of God's commandments and the violation of the faith of Jesus, requires a commitment which is here epitomized as the essence of being a saint.

The centrality and importance of Christians living out their faith in opposition to demands that oppose the faith was well expressed by Barclay, who wrote, "The Church was battling for its very existence. If it was to continue, individual Christians must be prepared to face suffering and trial, imprisonment and death. If the individual Christian yielded, the Church died. In our day, individual Christians are still of prime importance; but their function now is not usually to protect the faith by being ready to die for it, but to commend it by being diligent to live for it."[387]

14:13 "And I heard the voice from heaven saying, Write, Blessed are the dead who die in the Lord from henceforth: yea, saith the Spirit, that they may rest from their labors; for their works follow with them."

14:13 "Blessed are the dead who die in the Lord"

Doubtless, many of these "dead" will have died because of standing firm against the perversions brought about by the corrupt church. Only in Christ is death transformed into a blessing. Only in Christ is dying gain! (See Philippians 1:21.) The condition of these blessed dead is in vivid contrast with that of those whose death ushers them into a condition in which they "shall be tormented with fire and brimstone." (14:10) For those who die "in the Lord," the struggle is over, "they may rest from their labors."

14:13 "they may rest from their labors"

Death had brought their labors to an end. However, they seem anxious and concerned lest their labors should prove to have been fruitless and without significant impact.

14:13 "their works follow with them."

No effort will have been lost! Every sincere effort made in the cause of Christ will have made a mark and will have had an enduring impact!

14:14 "And I saw, and behold, a white cloud; and on the cloud I saw one sitting like unto a son of man, having on his head a golden crown, and in his hand a sharp sickle."

---

387 William Barclay, <u>The Revelation of John</u>, Vol. II, (Philadelphia: The Westminster Press, 1976), p. 127.

14:14 "one sitting like unto a son of man"

The term "son of man" seems to have been Jesus' favorite name or designation for himself. For example, in the Gospel of Matthew Jesus is recorded as using this name twenty-eight times in reference to himself. In sharp contrast, in Matthew's account, Jesus is not said even once to have used the term "Son of God" for himself. However, when Peter acknowledged him as "the Son of the living God," (Matthew 16:16) Jesus certainly endorsed the use of that name for himself. Also, Jesus claimed to be "the Son of God" before Caiaphas, the high priest. (Matthew 26:63-64) The term "son of man" expresses the idea of a bridge across the gulf between deity and humanity, God and man. Jesus seems to be saying by the use of that name, *while I am the Son of God, I am also part of the human race. I am not simply a son of man, but the Son of man.* This is what made it possible for him to be tempted in all points like as we are. (See Hebrews 4:15.) Jesus clearly emphasized his being the Son of God. (See John 9:35-37.)

14:14 "in his hand a sharp sickle"

This sickle is the preaching of the Gospel by which the harvest of joy is reaped.

14:15 "And another angel came out from the temple, crying with a great voice to him that sat on the cloud, Send forth thy sickle, and reap: for the hour to reap is come; for the harvest of the earth is ripe."

14:15 "Send forth thy sickle, and reap"

This one who reaps is the one who is "like unto a son of man," (14:14) referring to Jesus Christ. His sickle is the Gospel message and reaping takes place by preaching that message. Here is prophetic assurance that Jesus will keep his promise all the way to the end of the world. It is not only Christians who wield the sickle, but Christ himself. This fulfills his promise that he would be with those who made disciples and baptized them in the name of the Father and of the Son and of the Holy Spirit and went on to teach them to observe all things that he had commanded. (Matthew 28:18-20)

14:16 "And he that sat on the cloud cast his sickle upon the earth; and the earth was reaped."

The word "earth" is to be taken in its global sense as used in 14:7. It is to be equated with the globally inclusive "all the nations" of Matthew 28:19. This prophecy assures us that the Gospel sickle will reach every stalk of grain which is ripe for harvest.

14:17 "Another angel came out from the temple which is in heaven, he also having a sharp sickle."

In bold, glaring contrast to the Gospel sickle mentioned in 14:14-16, this is the sickle of war, one of the means through which the wrath of God is made manifest.

14:18 "And another angel came out from the altar, he that hath power over fire; and he called with a great voice to him that had the sharp sickle, saying, Send forth thy sharp sickle, and gather the clusters of the vine of the earth; for her grapes are fully ripe."

Revelation Chapter 14

The harvest envisioned in 14:14-16 is that of ripened grain, which stands in startling contrast to this harvest of grapes. These are grapes of wrath. That is clear because in the next verse we are told they are to be cast into "the great winepress of the wrath of God."

14:19 "And the angel cast his sickle into the earth, and gathered the vintage of the earth, and cast it into the winepress, the great winepress, of the wrath of God."

14:19 "the angel"

There is a divine factor in the prolonged military conflicts which have ironically characterized nearly the whole time that the "Prince of Peace" (See Isaiah 9:6.) will have been on his throne!

14:19 "the great winepress of the wrath of God"

The great winepress points not only to "the monstrous bloodshed of 1914-1918," but to the much greater bloodshed of all the wars of the Christian era which have partially and briefly been summarized in the introduction to this chapter. However, there are special aspects of the 1914-1918 conflict which deserve special attention. (See also the comments on 17:14.)

Among those special aspects of the 1914-1918 all-out war were the seemingly limitless losses of men, "which destroyed much of a generation of men in Europe and drastically reconfigured its culture and moral outlook."[388] The shocking total of fatalities was given in the introduction to this chapter. However, that summation should not hide the poignancy one inevitably feels when looking at specific encounters, "like Verdun, where French losses in 1916 exceeded 200,000 men. … [and] The battle of Belleau Wood was legendary among United States Marines. … On June 6, 1918 the Marines launched an attack, capturing the entire area by June 26. They lost more men on June 6 than in the entire previous history of the corps."[389]

"Before its self-destructive civil war of 1914-1918 [*the author refers to WWI as a civil war because it was fought between nations, all of whom professed to be Christian*], the Christian world was as sharply defined as the Muslim world. Both were perfectly capable of defining themselves against each other in a cultural sense, and keeping their tolerations and rejections in useful order. What secularism has done, since replacing Christianity as the guiding light of 'the West,' is to cast aside any idea of a distinctly 'Western' social, geographic, and cultural space that should be protected. This was obvious in Europe by the early 1960s, and for the past quarter-century, at least, it has become obvious in the United States. Patriotism rekindled after September 11 [2001] is a reminder that at the grass-roots level the capacity for instinctive self-definition is still alive, but it cannot be sustained if the dominant outlook is that of cultural relativism and anti-historicism."[390] It is this spiritual-cultural vacuum which makes Islam's current massive incursion into the West possible. Previously, that vacuum had made the hippie movement and the drug culture possible.

---

[388] Nancy R. Newhouse, *Honoring the Fallen in the War to End All Wars*, The New York Times, Travel, November 10, 2013, p. 12.
[389] Nancy R. Newhouse, *Honoring the Fallen in the War to End All Wars*, The New York Times, Travel, November 10, 2013, p. 12.
[390] Serge Trifkovic, The Sword of the Prophet, (Boston: Regina Orthodox Press, Inc., 2002), pp. 7-8.

"World War I marked ... the rise of Bolshevism and the advent of America's [period of] pre-eminence. But it was the literary men – poets chiefly, some of them soldiers – who conveyed the magnitude of the carnage, who first grasped that, after this war, things would not be the same. The old world had destroyed itself in the frontal assaults across no man's land."[391]

"As the twentieth century gave way to the twenty-first, the disaster Solzhenitsyn foresaw had been avoided, at least in the form of nuclear holocaust. But that does not diminish the salience of Solzhenitsyn's chief point – that 1914-1918 marked the beginning of a civilizational crisis in Europe, and perhaps especially in Western Europe, whose effects are much with us today."[392]

Subsequently, "Europe, which until 1914 had been a fountain of cultural vitality, was what it remains, a spent force."[393] However, in that exhausted body politic will come new and fearsome vitality. (See 17:8ff and the accompanying comments.)

14:20 "**And the winepress was trodden without the city, and there came out blood from the winepress, even unto the bridles of the horses, as far as a thousand and six hundred furlongs.**"

14:20 "without the city"

The NRSV, the NKJV, the ESV, the NIV and Stern in his *Complete Jewish Bible* have all rendered it "outside the city." This seems to refer to "the holy city" which has been described in the comments on Revelation 11:2. Therefore, "the city" is another simile picturing the church. Thus, the wars which constitute "the winepress" will be fought among entities in general society, rather than in "the city," meaning the true church. However, the church cannot avoid those sufferings which will result from the winepress being trodden.

14:20 "blood from the winepress, even unto the bridles of the horses, as far as a thousand and six hundred furlongs"

As already emphasized, this winepress is the winepress of war. It is not pointing to a single war, but to the summation of all the wars of the Christian era. (See the succinct summary of those wars in the introduction to this chapter.) Collectively, enough blood will have been shed that it would rise high enough to reach the bridles of horses. This depth of blood is made clear in the NIV which says "rising as high as the horses' bridles." That ocean of blood will cover an area extending 1,600 furlongs, the equivalent of 200 miles. (See the NRSV.) The word "furlong" is an approximation for the Greek word "stadia." (See the ESV and the NIV.) From the Greek measurement called a stadia comes the word "stadium." A stadia was "about 606 English feet; it was the length of the race-course at Olympia, and the eighth part of the Roman mile."[394]

---

391 Geoffrey Norman, *A Veteran Who Struggled to Find Peace*, The Wall Street Journal, December 1, 2005, p. D9.
392 George Weigel, The Cube and the Cathedral, Europe, America, and Politics Without God, (New York: Basic Books, 2005), p. 34.
393 George F. Will, *Progress in a Cauldron?*, Newsweek, August 14, 2006, p. 64.
394 A. Plummer, The Pulpit Commentary [on] Revelation, (Chicago: Wilcox & Follett Co., no date), p. 351.

Revelation Chapter 15

Introduction: The fifteenth chapter begins with a statement from the Apostle John, saying "I saw another sign in heaven." The word "heaven" occurs fifty-five times in the book of Revelation. With so many occurrences it is appropriate to give a summary and evaluation of the use of the word.

Each one of its occurrences comes from the same Greek word, *ouranos*. The case endings in each of the variations show the grammatical use of the word in the sentence. So far, from 1:1 through 14:20, the word "heaven" has occurred thirty-six times. In those fourteen chapters the word "heaven" has been used with a wide variety of distinct meanings. This puts a heavy responsibility on the commentator to specify the discreet meaning of the word "heaven" as it appears in its various occurrences.

The **first** meaning of the word "heaven" seems unmistakably clear, though surprisingly difficult to define or explain. For example, in 3:12 the words "the city of my God, the new Jerusalem, which cometh down out of heaven from my God" clearly point to the ultimate or supreme use of the word "heaven," meaning that place of God's special presence, that special aura or environment in which God is the epicenter. This concept of heaven is expressed again in 4:2, which says "there was a throne set in heaven, and one sitting upon the throne." It may be defined as "the place where the Most High ruleth," (See Daniel 4:17, et al.) though this definition in no way is intended to diminish or deny the truth that God rules everywhere.

Also, the concept of heaven being a place which is dominated by God's special presence in no way contradicts, nullifies, or detracts from the omnipresence of God. That reality is powerfully and beautifully presented in the 139th Psalm, which asks, "Whither shall I go from thy spirit? Or whither shall I flee from thy presence? If I ascend up into heaven, thou art there: if I make my bed in Sheol, behold, thou art there. If I take the wings of the morning, and dwell in the uttermost parts of the sea; even there shall thy hand lead me and thy right hand shall hold me. If I say, Surely the darkness shall overwhelm me, and the light about me shall be night; even the darkness hideth not from thee, but the night shineth as the day: the darkness and the light are both alike to thee." (Psalm 139:7-12)

Still, the book of Revelation speaks in 4:1-3 of a throne in "heaven" and "one sitting upon the throne," obviously referring to God Almighty. That place of God's special presence is clearly distinguished in 5:3 from the "earth, or under the earth," a distinction more clearly emphasized in 5:13, which says "every created thing which is in the heaven, and under the earth, and on the sea." Another occurrence of the word "heaven," meaning the place of the special presence of God, is in 8:1-2 which tells about "a silence in heaven" and "the seven angels that stand before God." Again this use is found in 11:13 which talks about giving glory "to the God of heaven." This use of the word "heaven" is found also in 11:15 concerning which I have commented that "this heaven refers to the place where God's universal throne is."

A **second** distinct use of the word "heaven" is found in 6:13, which says "the stars of the heaven fell unto the earth as a fig tree casteth her unripe figs when she is shaken of a great wind." These stars probably represent people who hold exalted positions of precedence or authority. In 6:14 we are told that "heaven was removed." This certainly does not point to an atmospheric or astronomical collapse, but indicates that the whole political structure will be discredited, repudiated and overthrown. Another instance when the word "heaven" is used in reference to the political firmament is found in 11:12, where it is said, "They heard a great voice from heaven saying unto them, 'Come up hither.' And they went up into heaven in the cloud; and their enemies beheld them." This heaven seems to mean a place of high earthly honor, power and exaltation.

A **third** use of the word "heaven" occurs in 8:10, which says "there fell from heaven a great star, burning as a torch, and it fell upon the third part of the rivers, and upon the fountains of the waters." That "great star" was Attila the Hun. The heaven from which he fell was the marvelous and generous endowment of perception, charisma, magnetism, dynamism, and analytical ability inherent in his personality, a heavenly constellation of exceptional gifts. An even more significant use of the word "heaven" in this sense is found in 9:1, which, referring to Muhammad, says "I saw a star from heaven fallen unto the earth: and there was given to him the key of the pit of the abyss." The fall from 'heaven' represents a series of great misfortunes which befell the star's family. That definition was further clarified in the commentary by the statement that "the 'heaven' from which the 'star' fell most probably refers to the high standing of his forbears who were held in high honor."

A **fourth** use of the word "heaven" is found in the expression "mid heaven" which occurs three times in Revelation, that is, in 8:13, 14:6, and 19:17. As noted in the comments on 14:6, it is a figure of speech or a metaphor used to illustrate something as being obvious, in the open, equivalent to the common American expression "in the light of day." It means not hidden, out in the open, in clear sight, so clearly manifest that no one could plead ignorance.

A **fifth** use of the word "heaven" in the book of Revelation refers to the astronomical heaven. We find this use, for example, in 10:6, which says, referring to the one who "liveth forever and ever, who created the heaven and the things that are therein, and the earth and the things that are therein, and the sea and the things that are therein."

A **sixth** meaning of the word "heaven" as it is used in Revelation refers to the atmosphere, specifically to the troposphere, the area in which water-vapors form clouds. This use is clear in 11:6, which says, "These have the power to shut the heaven, that it rain not during the days of their prophecy." This is the heaven from which lightning was seemingly made to come down by the incantations of a false prophet. (See 13:13 and the comments. See also the comments on the word "heaven" at 12:1.)

A **seventh** use of the word "heaven" is found in 12:4, which says, "And his tail draweth the third part of the stars of heaven and did cast them to the earth." The "stars of heaven" refer to the leaders of the churches who occupy a very precarious exposed position. Satan has targeted them and will kill a "third part" of them. This heaven is the "kingdom of heaven," the church, or "the heavenly places in Christ. This identity of the "stars" is made clear in the comments on Revelation 1:16 and 1:20. For historic examples of the persecution and killing of church leaders,

Revelation Chapter 15

see the accounts of Ignatius, bishop of Antioch, in the comments under 2:8, and of Polycarp in the comments under 2:13. This "heaven" refers to the churches, "the heavenly places in Christ" (Ephesians 2:6), also called "the kingdom of heaven." (See Matthew 13:24-52.)

An **eighth** use of the word "heaven" is found in 12:7 where it says "there was war in heaven." This heaven refers to the two distinct places where God and Christ have been invited to rule. The first place is the heart of the Christian who has heeded Peter's exhortation to "sanctify in your hearts Christ as Lord." (I Peter 3:15) The second place is the church, which is called "the heavenly places in Christ." (Ephesians 1:3) These two locales make up the "heavens" where the command is received, "Rejoice, O heavens, and ye that dwell in them." (12:12) This use of the word "heaven" occurs in 13:6, where Satan blasphemes God's "tabernacle, even them that dwell in the heaven." This tabernacle/heaven refers to the church which is "a habitation of God in the Spirit." (Ephesians 2:22) This "war in heaven" is the war against wrong which goes on individually in the Christian's heart and corporately in the churches.

VII. *The pouring out of the <u>seven bowls</u> of God's wrath 15:1-17:18*

These bowls of wrath contain "the seven last plagues." 21:9

    A.   *Preliminary activities in heaven 15:1-16:1*

15:1 "And I saw another sign in heaven, great and marvelous, seven angels having seven plagues, which are the last, for in them is finished the wrath of God."

15:1 "I saw another sign in heaven"

Finally, a **ninth** use of the word "heaven," the one utilized here in 15:1, points to the use of the atmospheric heaven as a backdrop for divine revelation. Though the wording varies somewhat, each of these references seem to point to the same reality. For example, the word "heaven" in the expression "a voice from heaven" (10:4) seems equivalent to divine intervention or, as in 10:8, of divine revelation. In 12:1 we are told "a great sign was seen in heaven." In this chapter, in 15:1, John says, "I saw another sign in heaven," and in 19:11, John tells us, "I saw the heaven opened and behold …" These references remind one of Paul's experience of receiving a divine revelation on the road to Damascus. About that event, the account records that as Paul journeyed to Damascus "suddenly there shone round about him a light out of heaven and … a voice saying unto him, 'Saul, Saul, why persecutest thou me?'" (Acts 9:3-4) Later, Paul called that experience a "heavenly vision." (Acts 26:19) To this group of references we should add Revelation 12:10, which says "I heard a great voice in heaven saying …" This obviously refers to an occurrence of receiving revelation.

15:1 "seven plagues, which are the last, for in them is finished the wrath of God"

Hendriksen emphasizes a very reasonable and helpful consideration. He wrote, "These plagues are the *last*. They leave no more opportunity for repentance. When the wicked, often warned by the trumpets of judgment, continue to harden their hearts, death finally plunges them into the hands of an angry God."[395] At this point, God will no longer try through judgmental plagues to turn human society from the ultimate disaster which lies

---
395 W. Hendriksen, <u>More Than Conquerors: An Interpretation of the Book of Revelation</u>, (Grand Rapids: Baker Book House, 1952), p. 190.

ahead. These seven plagues are the last warning signs on society's downward road to eternal catastrophe! Society's condition will be a duplication of the situation in Roman society described by Paul when he wrote, "Even as they refused to have God in their knowledge, God gave them up." (Romans 1:28; See comments on "it is done" at 16:17.)

15:2 **"And I saw as it were a sea of glass mingled with fire; and them that come off victorious from the beast, and from his image, and from the number of his name, standing by the sea of glass, having harps of God."**

15:2 "sea of glass"

The existence of this sea of glass, sometimes called the crystal sea from its description in 4:6, has captivated and inspired hymn writers. For example, in 1864, referring to this sea, Robert Lowry in his great hymn, *Shall We Gather at the River* wrote, "Shall we gather at the river, Where bright angels feet have trod, With its crystal tide forever, Flowing by the throne of God?" Even more explicitly, in 1914 F.H. Rowley in his great hymn, *I will Sing of My Redeemer*, wrote, "Yes, I'll sing the wondrous story of the Christ who died for me, Sing it with the saints in glory, Gathered by the crystal sea."

15:2 "mingled with fire"

The first mention of the crystal sea (4:6) portrayed tranquility. The appearance of its water being mixed with fire at this time will assure these martyrs that there will be divine judgment and justice which will be rendered through fire. Barclay perceptively commented that, "This is a passage of judgment – and fire in Scripture is often the symbol of judgment. [For example,] there comes upon Egypt hail mingled with fire (Exodus 9:24); the chaff is to be consumed in the fire (Matthew 3:12); our God is a consuming fire (Hebrews 12:29)."[396]

15:2 "them that come off victorious"

The words "come off victorious from the beast" seem clumsy. The King James translation for which the ASV was intended to be a clarification, is more understandable. Its wording is "them that had gotten the victory over the beast." The NIV is, perhaps, the most clear, rendering it "those who had been victorious over the beast."

It is obvious that the ones who had been "victorious over the beast" had encountered death in the course of their victorious struggle. That assertion is based on the fact that they are gathered around the sea of glass. That is one of the venues where the spirits of Christ's faithful servants congregate after death.

15:2 "from the beast, and from his image and the number of his name"

There are three distinct groups of spiritual victors in the throng assembled for the victory rally "by the sea of glass:"

First are those whose faith and courage sustained them all the way to victory over "the beast." That beast refers to the far-flung persecuting Byzantine Empire, the beast which came up out of the sea.. (See 13:1.)

---

396 William Barclay, The Revelation of John, Vol. II, (Philadelphia: The Westminster Press, 1976), p. 133.

Revelation Chapter 15

The second group of victors are those who triumphed over "his image," ("its image" ESV) meaning those who triumphed over the beast which arose out of the earth, (See 13:11.) the structure of which was so closely modeled on that of the Byzantine Empire that it was like a mirror image. The contest depicted here is still underway. The true followers of Christ are facing the daunting power of that political/religious entity, Russia, in its various manifestations, which is here simply called "his image," that is, Byzantium's image. The power and scope of Russia as the "image" of Byzantium is stunning. For example, it was Russia's decision in support of their Slavic brothers, the Serbs, which set World War I ablaze. Again, after the breakup of Yugoslavia, Russia upheld their Serbian/Slavic ethnic comrades in the ethnic cleansing of the Muslim population, a tragic war brought to an end by the Dayton Accords on November 21, 1995.

The third group of victors who will participate in the victory rally on the shores of the crystal sea are those who will have been victorious over "the number of his name." (Please see the comments on 13:18.) This means that the victory rally has not yet begun which is to be held on the shores of the crystal sea because this third group of participants are yet to join those earlier victors. For clarification, be sure to see the comments on these future victors at 13:17-18.

We Christians of the twenty-first century should look forward with great anticipation and expectation to that coming victory rally which is to be held for those who will have triumphed over such appalling odds! This three-fold throng will ultimately become part of that innumerable throng mentioned in 7:9.

15:2   "harps of God"

On the harps in heaven, see 4:8 and 14:2.

15:3   "And they sing the song of Moses the servant of God, and the song of the Lamb, saying, Great and marvelous are thy works, O Lord God, the Almighty; righteous and true are thy ways, thou King of the ages."

15:3   "they sing the song of Moses the servant of God, and the song of the Lamb"

So far, the Revelation of John has introduced us to only one song from the heavenly hymn book. That one is mentioned in 14:3, an exclusive song, the full meaning of which will only be mastered by the initial 144,000 converts to Jesus from the Jewish people. Here in 15:3, we are introduced to additional segments of heaven's hymn book. Initially, one may wonder if "The Song of Moses" and "The Song of the Lamb" are the same song having two names, or are two separate songs. That question is answered in the following phrase of this verse.

15:3   "Great and marvelous are thy works, O Lord God, the Almighty"

Fortunately, the question about whether the titles, "The Song of Moses" and "The Song of the Lamb," refer to one song or two, proves to be simple. From the quotation in verses 3 and 4 from the Song of the Lamb there are words which are applicable only to Jesus, the Lamb, but can in no way be used in reference to Moses. This allows us to say with certainty that "The Song of Moses" is separate and distinct from "The Song of the Lamb." Jesus rightfully and biblically should be called "Lord God, the Almighty." In contrast, while Moses holds a preeminent position among the prophets, he is not divine in any sense. The following scriptural references show us conclusively that Jesus is divine: Isaiah 7:14, Isaiah 9:6-7, Isaiah 11:1-5, Isaiah 15:5, Isaiah 42:1-4, Isaiah 48:16, Isaiah 52:13-15, Isaiah 53:1-12, Isaiah 61:1-3, Matthew 1:23, Matthew 28:19, Luke 1:35, Luke 5:20-21, John 1:1-18, John 5:18, John 20:28, Romans 1:4, Romans 9:5, Romans 10:9, II Corinthians 13:14, Philippians 2:6, Colossians 1:15-20, Colossians 2:9, Titus 2:13, Hebrews 1:1-8, II Peter 1:1, Revelation 1:13-18, and Revelation 22:13.

The stanzas of the epic song of Moses are found in Exodus 15:1-18. It is a preeminent song of victory achieved through the power and blessing of God Almighty in the face of overwhelming forces of opposition and destruction. Similarly, those who are standing by the sea of glass are the ones who will have come "off victorious from the beast, and from his image and from the number of his name." (15:2) Just as the Israelites under Moses' leadership had triumphed over hopeless odds by divine power, so these Christians will have been led through even greater peril to victory by divine strength and power. While, understandably, there are statements and phrases in the song of Moses that can only refer to Israel's victory at the Red Sea, there are also expressions which may be used appropriately to verbalize this upcoming triumph. In the first victory, the exodus from Egypt, it is the story of God working through the man, Moses, to save the tribes of Israel. The second victory shows us God, as the son of man, working to save the human race.

15:4 **"Who shall not fear, O Lord, and glorify thy name? for thou only art holy; for all the nations shall come and worship before thee; for thy righteous acts have been made manifest."**

15:4 "Who shall not fear, O Lord, and glorify thy name? for thou only art holy"

The negation "not" used before the verb "fear" is implied also before the verb "glorify." So, the full meaning is "who shall not fear [thee] O Lord, and [not] glorify thy name?" The impetus to both fear the Lord, and to glorify him, is generated by the overwhelming awareness of his holiness. His holiness not only refers to his sinlessness, but to the impeccable justice of his judgments, such as sending the seven impending plagues. Here is the attempt to fend off accusations against God which may be hurled at him by many who will suffer during the periods dominated by these imminent plagues.

15:4 "for all the nations shall come and worship before thee; for thy righteous acts have been made manifest"

The answer to the question "who shall not fear, O Lord, and glorify thy name?" in the first half of the verse is resoundingly answered in the second half. The answer is <u>utterly no one</u> because "<u>all</u> the nations shall come and worship before thee." The noun "nations" is the translation of the Greek word *ethnai*, that is, ethnic groups or people groups, not political entities. They will consist of discreet ethnic groups like Celts, Arabs, Turks, Kurds, Chinese, Mongols, Bulgars, Spaniards, Gauls, and so forth.

The motivating impulse causing the ethnic people groups throughout the world to glorify God is an awareness to which they will have come: that God's acts are righteous. This scene is a beautiful prologue to the imminent initiation of the seven disastrous plagues

Revelation Chapter 15

during which we are thus assured of God's righteousness. Those plagues will be initiated by angels who emerge from the very center of God's temple.

15:5 **"And after these things I saw, and the temple of the tabernacle of the testimony in heaven was opened:"**

This seems to be a reference to a very similar statement in 11:19 which says, "There was opened the temple of God that is in heaven; and there was seen in his temple the ark of his covenant." Upon the opening of that temple, which is mentioned in 11:19, "there followed lightnings and voices and thunders and an earthquake and great hail." This time, as we see in the following verse (15:6), the reality which emerges is even more ominous, consisting of seven angels who will initiate seven plagues.

"The temple of the tabernacle" in 15:5 is to be equated with "the temple of God that is in heaven" mentioned in 11:19. The statement here in 15:5 that the tabernacle is "the tabernacle of the testimony" is probably pointing to the presence of "the ark of the covenant" which resides there according to 11:19. It is God's covenant which continually gives testimony to his faithful dealings with mankind. God does not act whimsically but by eternal principles, codified in "the testimony."

15:6 **"and there came out from the temple the seven angels that had the seven plagues, arrayed with precious stone, pure and bright, and girt about their breasts with golden girdles."**

15:6 "there came out from the temple the seven angels that had the seven plagues"

The English word "plague" is the transliteration of a Greek word whose root is *plag*. It is often used in a personal, individual sense to describe the lacerations inflicted by a whip or a club. Examples of this use are found in Luke 12:48, Acts 16:23 and 33, II Corinthians 6:5 and II Corinthians 11:23. When that type of laceration brings one to the point of death, the Greek word is translated "death-stroke" or "fatal wound." The word is also used to describe the nature of a physical malady, like the bubonic plague, which involves the extreme and often fatal swelling of the *bubous*, the lymph glands, especially in the groin. This type of plague was seen in the boils which came upon the Egyptians during the period of the ten plagues. (See Exodus 9:8-9.) Such a widespread physical malady may also be called a pestilence. As the word is used here in the seven plagues of the fifteenth chapter of Revelation, it seems to refer to widespread affliction, catastrophe, tragedy or some momentous, very extensive, tragic event.

15:6 "arrayed with precious stone, pure and bright, and girt about their breasts with golden girdles"

The rendering given here from the ASV portrays each of the seven angels as wearing regalia reminiscent of that worn by the high priest during the Mosaic period. On the high priest's vesture was worn or attached "a breastplate of judgment" in which were "settings of stones." They were to "be enclosed in gold in their settings." (See Exodus 28:20, however, also read verses 15-30.)

The words "precious stone" do not occur in the earliest and most reliable manuscript copy of the book of Revelation. The earliest of all surviving transcripts of Revelation is the fourth century Sinaitic manuscript, discovered in 1844 by the great Russian scholar Tischendorf in the library of St. Catherine's Convent, located at the foot of traditional Mt. Sinai. The word "stone" does occur in the Alexandrinus manuscript and the Ephraemi manuscript, both written in the fifth century. While the Vaticanus manuscript is also dated at a time almost equivalent to that of the Sinaitic manuscript and though it does include the word "stone" in its rendering of 15:6, it is thought not to carry the same weight as the text in the Sinaitic manuscript. Perhaps the copyists who transcribed some of the manuscripts mistook the Greek word *linon* (translated in Matthew 12:20 as flax, from which linen is made, its only other occurrence in the New Testament) for the Greek word *lithon*, meaning "stone." In any case, the scholars who produced the majority of recent English translations of the book of Revelation have felt that the evidence points to "linen" and not to "stone." The NRSV renders the passage as "robed in pure bright linen, with golden sashes across their chests." This wording also is reminiscent of the official garments of the Jewish high priest. (See Exodus 39:27.)

15:7 **"And one of the four living creatures gave unto the seven angels seven golden bowls full of the wrath of God, who liveth for ever and ever."**

Please read the comments on 4:6 and 6:1-2 in which I have identified the four living creatures as representatives of the redeemed and transformed animal kingdom. I indicated that their metamorphosis would equip them to fill roles infinitely beyond anything of which the animal kingdom is presently capable. If we compare the injustices which have been endured by the animal kingdom, it far exceeds the cruelty, barbarity and injustices borne by mankind. Therefore, it is fitting that God uses one of the four living creatures, who are indicative of the entire redeemed animal kingdom, to give the "golden bowls full of the wrath of God" to the seven angels who are to initiate and administer God's wrath.

15:8 **"And the temple was filled with smoke from the glory of God, and from his power; and none was able to enter into the temple, till the seven plagues of the seven angels should be finished."**

Once the "bowls full of the wrath of God" are given to the angels, no one can enter with a petition or a prayer to delay or rescind that which has been determined. No appeal, no prayer and no entreaty to modify, to ameliorate or to cancel the missions of the seven angels of wrath can reach God's throne. At this point, the angels' missions have been immutably decreed by God. Any appeal seeking modification or abrogation will be blocked by a reality, resembling smoke, which represents the inscrutable and impenetrable glory of God.

Revelation Chapter 16

Introduction: The sixteenth chapter of Revelation predicts a series of societal and "natural" catastrophes, resulting from divine judgmental decisions, which will cover extremely broad spectrums of human life. Are we to think of these calamities as a sequence of totally separate, one-time, prolonged occurrences, or as cumulative, overlapping events? Certainly, some are overlapping. For instance, the disruption of the normal cycle of atmospheric phenomena (No. 7) would impact the flow of fresh water from its sources. (No. 3) The following succinct preview of the seven wrath-filled periods may help us grasp other unique relationships which exist in the sequence of the seven angelically triggered events which are prophesied to occur during the entire tenure of the wrath angel epoch.

The activity of the first wrath angel brings about endemic problems, called "sores," a calamity which centers in the enormous Russian expanse. (16:2) Those "sores" remained persistently unhealed for they are still a major cause of suffering when the fifth angel pours out his bowl of wrath. (16:10-11)

The actions of the second angel of wrath result in chaotic, worldwide maritime problems. The oceans are not only plagued by naval warfare but probably by other sea-related disasters as well. (16:3)

The ministry of the third angel of wrath impacts freshwater sources. They become inadequate, bringing on excruciating conditions, sparking international wars fought over the ownership of riparian water rights. (16:4-7)

When the bowl of the fourth angel of wrath is poured out, it brings about the disruption of normal solar activity, instigating conditions which "scorch men." (16:8-9)

When the fifth angel of wrath pours out his bowl, it brings political malfunction and misrule in the world's most widespread political entity. This results in conditions augmenting those which had been brought about by the activities of the first wrath angel. This double judgment against Russia is probably meted out because it is the center from which emanates the most explicit and virulent anti-God movement of all, the philosophy of atheistic materialism. (16:10-11)

When the sixth angel pours out his bowl of wrath, it removes the barrier which for centuries has prevented war between a number of irreconcilable world ideologies. The removal of that barrier is represented by the drying up of the Euphrates River. The ultimate consequence is a disastrous world conflict which finally reaches its climax on the Plain of Megiddo. (16:12-16) (See Map 10.)

Last of all, the wrath from the seventh angel's bowl judgmentally impacts the atmosphere with manifold disastrous consequences. (16:17-21)

Though recognizing the coordination between the symbol and the corresponding event may sometimes be difficult, it is even more difficult to recognize the point in history at which each of these seven supernatural events will have begun or ended. As Hinds wrote, "There is perhaps no part of Revelation for which expositors have offered more different explanations than the seven bowls of God's wrath."[397]

Some commentators take the position that the vision of the seven bowls of God's wrath really only rehearses the same periods of history pointed to by the visions of the seven seals and the seven trumpets. An example of that expository position is given by Plummer who wrote, "The events portrayed occupy the same period in time as the seals and the trumpets; that is to say, the period of the world's history terminating with the last judgment day."[398] While the overall span of history may be nearly identical, certainly the discreet events are unique and distinct.

16:1 "And I heard a great voice out of the temple, saying to the seven angels, Go ye, and pour out the seven bowls of the wrath of God into the earth."

16:1 "a great voice out of the temple"

This voice initiates one of the major series of developments in harmony with that declaration revealed to Nebuchadnezzar that "the Most High is sovereign over the kingdoms of men." (Daniel 4:25 NIV) This "great voice" is probably the voice of Christ, the same one which is quoted as speaking in 16:15.

Heaven is not going to secretly bring disaster upon mankind. The coming of these calamities is clearly made known by "a great voice." The voice speaks through multiple phenomena: social turmoil (like the current flood of desperate refugees fleeing terrorism in the Muslim world) or economic disruption (such as unemployment among young workers which has reached 60% – see the comments at 9:18 under "the third part part of men killed"). These painful developments are like a "great voice" indicating that worse calamities are on their way.

16:1 "pour out the seven bowls of the wrath of God into the earth"

The word "earth" in this verse is used in the global sense. However, in the very next verse it is used in a clearly defined, restricted sense. The coming of God's wrath should not be surprising. It follows upon man's persistent refusal to be wooed by God's goodness. That goodness was succinctly summarized by the apostle Paul in his sermon to the city of Lystra, in which he said, God "left not himself without witness, in that he did good and gave you from heaven rains and fruitful seasons, filling your hearts with food and gladness." (Acts 14:17) If we spurn God's goodness, we must expect the eventual appearance of his severity.

---

397 John T. Hinds, A Commentary on the Book of Revelation, (Nashville, Tenn.: Gospel Advocate Company, 1976), p. 223.
398 A. Plummer, The Pulpit Commentary [on] Revelation, (Chicago: Wilcox & Follett Co., no date), p. 392.

Revelation Chapter 16

1. The bowl of God's wrath on the earth 16:2

16:2 "**And the first went, and poured out his bowl into the earth; and it became a noisome and grievous sore upon the men that had the mark of the beast, and that worshipped his image.**"

16:2 "poured out his bowl into the earth"

This is not "the earth" in its total global sense. The word "earth" as it is used here in 16:2 is clearly and specifically limited to that part of the globe in which live "the men that had the mark of the beast and that worshipped his image." This is the same "earth" which is specified in 13:8. (Please see the comments there.) Though the expanse which is here called "the earth" does not encompass the entire globe, still it involves residents occupying wide vistas of the global earth's surface. (See the comment at 13:11 under "another beast coming up out of the earth.") Principally, it impacts those people who inhabit the area under the control of the beast which came up out of the earth (13:8), that is, the extensive Russian state.

16:2 "a noisome and grievous sore"

The word "noisome" is antiquated and probably does not convey a precise concept to most of us. More recent translations help us understand its meaning. The NRSV calls the malady "a foul and painful sore." David H. Stern, in his translation entitled *The Complete Jewish Bible*, rendered it as "disgusting and painful sores." The ESV translated it as "harmful and painful sores," while the NIV expresses it as "ugly and painful sores."

Thus, the language does not indicate a fatal disease, but a repugnant and painful "sore." (See also 16:11 under "their pains and their sores.") Under the symbol of the onset of a widespread disastrous and perhaps infectious epidemic, the reality of manifold failure is vividly depicted. The failure is that of the centuries-long ongoing struggle of the "image" (See the comments on 13:14.); that is, of Russia, to dominate and thrive in proportion to its size and potential.[399] The failure of Russia to excel in relation to its potential is very persistent. For example, when the Mongols attacked the city of Riazan in 1237 A.D., "the prince of Riazan called upon his neighbors for reinforcements. Yet Russia's princes paid no more heed to calls for unity than did the sovereigns of Western Europe. Civil wars had become yearly events in the Russian land, and the dominions of every prince were fair game for any other. Accustomed to internecine warfare and having no regrets about killing their countrymen, Russia's princes sent no reinforcements to help Riazan. As the Mongols closed their siege in December, the people of Riazan faced them alone."[400]

Russia's problems have continued to persist. For example, in 1991, Boris Yeltsin, Chairman of the Russian Supreme Soviet, made an anguished statement which conveys this very idea being applicable to Russia for the previous century of its history. He said, "Our country has not been lucky. It was decided to carry out this Marxist experiment on us. In the end we proved that there is no place for this idea – it has simply pushed us off the path taken by the world's civilized countries."[401]

---

[399] A student wishing to gain extensive knowledge of Russia and its "sores" should read W. Bruce Lincoln's book, The Conquest of a Continent, Siberia and the Russians and Philip Longworth's Russia, the Once and Future Empire From Pre-History to Putin.
[400] W. Bruce Lincoln, The Conquest of a Continent, Siberia and the Russians, (Ithaca: Cornell University Press, 1994), p. 18.
[401] Tony Judt, Postwar, A History of Europe Since 1945, (New York: Penguin Books, 2005), p. 637.

Unfortunately, "Boris Yeltsin who succeeded Mikhail Gorbachev and intended to preside over a democratic renaissance, failed to hold the Communist party accountable for its crimes, to create institutions guaranteeing the rule of law and to ensure that the country's vast mineral and energy resources would be administered for the benefit of the entire Russian people. His failures gave democracy a bad name and sapped whatever confidence a majority of Russian citizens might once have entertained about the virtues of a more Western-oriented political system. It seemed like a miracle when the Soviet Union fell apart with hardly a whiff of violence, but the first Chechen war, which Yeltsin initiated in December 1994, was only a harbinger of the continuing ethnic violence and acts of terrorism that have marred the Russian political landscape ever since – all of which made it easier for a former K.G.B. officer like Vladimir Putin to assume power and pick up the pieces."[402]

Russia's perpetual falling short is like a painful sore that does not heal. Right now, conspicuous success is also being impeded by an extremely low birth rate and by a vigorously encroaching virulent form of Islam. That dynamic ingress of Islam is coming from the Caucasus and from the five "Stans" (Kyrgyzstan, Kazakhstan, Turkmenistan, Tajikistan, Uzbekistan) where there has been a dramatic resurgence of Islam since those areas gained their independence upon the break-up of the Soviet Union.

16:2   "the mark of the beast"

This mark is to be distinguished from the one described as "the mark on their right hand or upon their forehead" (13:16, 14:9), though it is to be associated with the beast which "comes up out of the earth." (13:16-18) This mark is borrowed from the beast which came up out of the sea as highlighted in 13:1-10, thus here the term "beast" points to the Byzantine Empire. Though that first beast will have eventually died, after continuing "forty and two months" (13:5), its mark has remained during all the subsequent centuries up to the present day. That mark, or defining characteristic, is the Greek/Russian Orthodox church. Since 988, when Prince Vladimir "baptized" the citizenry of Kiev in the river, that mark has also consistently and continuously existed as an identification of the beast which came up out of the earth. (See the comments on 13:12.) As just stated, this mark is to be clearly distinguished from the mark mentioned in 13:16, 14:9 and 14:11. It is highly important to notice that <u>the mark of 16:2 identifies a beast, or empire, while at some future date the mark mentioned in 13:16, 14:9 and 14:11 will identify the individual subjects of an empire</u>.

16:2   "worshipped his image"

Closely associated with those who continue to keep or wear "the mark of the beast" are those who worship "his," that is, the first beast's image. Undoubtedly, many people do both. "His image" is another beast, the one which came "up out of the earth," whose description is given in 13:11-18. That entity is clearly called "the image of the [first] beast." (13:15) "His image" through the centuries has taken many forms. First, it was Kievan Russia under its Grand Prince. Next was Czarist Russia, which was followed by Communist or Soviet Russia which was given birth by the Revolution of 1917.

---

402 Joshua Rubenstein, *Tragedy and Farce, From the Collapse of the Soviet Union to Pussy Riot, Two Journalists Examine the Paradoxes of Modern Russia*, <u>The New York Times Book Review</u>, February 23, 2014, p. 13.

Revelation Chapter 16

More recently "his image" has taken the form of the Russian Federation, which came into being at the collapse of the Soviet Union on December 26, 1991, while it was under the oversight of Mikhail Gorbachev.[403] The "image" currently continues to live under the domineering administration of Prime Minister Vladimir Putin, who is striving mightily to re-establish Russia's political boundaries to their pre-Gorbachev status. The most recent phase of Mr. Putin's struggle is dramatically seen in Moscow's all-out effort to keep the Ukraine from joining the European Union which would perpetuate its separation from Russia.[404] As an intermediate step, ultimately leading to full reunion with Russia, Mr. Putin wants the Ukraine to become a member of the Eurasian Union. The Eurasian Union, brought into being by Mr. Putin, consists of an association of former members of the defunct Soviet Union. By this strategy Mr. Putin hopes to counter the gravitational pull of the European Union.

2. The bowl of God's wrath on the sea 16:3

16:3 "And the second poured out his bowl into the sea; and it became blood as of a dead man; and every living soul died, even the things that were in the sea."

16:3 "poured out his bowl into the sea"

Not only will the gargantuan land area where the "mark of the beast" predominates be plagued with troubles, which like foul persistent sores will not heal, but also, worldwide maritime activity will no longer be peaceful. Foreign relations experts call this kind of dispute a transnational problem. It is the kind of dispute which may easily arise from new geopolitical realities, like China's rise to dominance, or from a great shift in global power between countries with widely divergent and narrow national interests. Internationally agreed upon maritime law like the U.N. Convention on the Law of the Sea will no longer be observed by all nations. That law "beyond defining states' rights and responsibilities in territorial seas and exclusive economic zones and clarifying the rules of transit through international straits, provides a forum for dispute resolution on ocean-related issues, including claims to extended continental shelves."[405]

After the second wrath angel pours out the contents of his bowl, shipping lanes will be disputed and obstructed. Hints of such conditions are already clearly seen in disputes over the control of the arctic passage between the Pacific and Atlantic Oceans, and by threats to the freedom to use the shipping lanes in both the East China Sea and the South China Sea. In the near future, probably, critical choke points like the Strait of Malacca will no longer be free for unobstructed shipping for all nations. Piracy on the high seas similar to that recently based in Somalia is likely to increase. Such issues explain why nations have felt and continue to feel it necessary to build, maintain and deploy war fleets. Inevitably, maritime trade will be grievously impacted bringing economic misery to many people.

---

403 "In December 1991, Gorbachev and Yeltsin agreed that the U.S.S.R. would cease to exist as of January 1, 1992." The New York Times 2011 Almanac, Editor: John W. Wright, (New York: Penguin Books, 2012), p. 669.

404 There are very clear reasons why the Ukraine is important to Russia. "Sitting squarely athwart Russia's access routes to the Black Sea (and the Mediterranean) as well as to central Europe, Ukraine was a mainstay of the Soviet economy. With just 2.7% of the land area of the U.S.S.R. it was home to 18% of its population and generated nearly 17% of the country's Gross National Product, second only to Russia itself. In the last years of the Soviet Union Ukraine contained 60% of the country's coal reserves and a majority share of the country's titanium (vital for modern steel production); its unusually rich soil was responsible for over 40% of Soviet agricultural output by value." - Tony Judt, Postwar, A History of Europe Since 1945, (New York: Penguin Books, 2005), p. 648.

405 Stewart Patrick, *The Unruled World*, FOREIGN AFFAIRS, January/February 2014, p. 69.

Such dangerous confrontation and conflict over access to the oceanic shipping lanes grows in part out of the fact that multilateral bodies, like the U.N., lack power to enforce compliance with collective decisions. However, more than any political cause behind the disruption of the sea lanes, and the conflicts which will grow out of it, is the fact that the second angel of wrath has poured his bowl of wrath into the sea.

16:3 "it became blood as of a dead man"

These words point to coming, widespread, persistent maritime war. An example of the gruesome consequence of the second wrath angel's activity, described as the sea becoming "blood as of a dead man," may be taken from an account of the Battle of Lepanto which occurred off the west coast of Greece on October 7, 1571. "The greater fury of the battle lasted for four hours and was so bloody and horrendous that the sea and the fire seemed as one, many Turkish galleys burning down to the water, and the surface of the sea, red with blood, was covered with Moorish coats, turbans, quivers, arrows, bows, shields, oars, boxes, cases, and other spoils of war, and above all many human bodies, Christian as well as Turkish, some dead, some wounded, some torn apart, some not yet resigned to their fate struggling in their death agony, their strength ebbing away with the blood flowing from their wounds in such quantity that the sea was entirely coloured by it, but despite all this misery our men were not moved to pity for the enemy. … Although they begged for mercy they received instead arquebus shots and pike thrusts. There was looting on a grand scale. Men put out rowing boats to fish the dead out of the water and rob them; the soldiers, sailors, and convicts pillaged joyously until nightfall. There was great booty because of the abundance of gold and silver and rich ornaments that were in the Turkish galleys, especially those of the pashas. …

"It was a scene of staggering devastation, like a biblical painting of the world's end. The scale of the carnage left even the exhausted victors shaken and appalled by the work of their hands. They had witnessed killing on an industrial scale. In four hours 40,000 men were dead, nearly 100 ships destroyed, 137 Muslim ships captured by the Holy League. Of the dead, 25,000 were Ottomans; only 3,500 were taken alive. Another 12,000 Christian slaves were liberated. The defining collision in the White Sea gave the people of the early modern world a glimpse of Armageddon to come. Not until the World War I Battle of Loos in 1915 would this rate of slaughter be surpassed. …

"The day drew to its mournful close; the bloody water, heaving thickly with the matted debris of the battle, reddened in the sunset. Burning hulks flared in the dark, smoking and ruined. The wind got up. The Christian ships could barely sail away, according to Aurelio Scetti, 'Because of the countless corpses floating on the sea.' The survivors left with pitiful shouts from the water still ringing in their ears. 'Even though many Christians were not dead, nobody would help them.' As the winners sought secure anchorages on the Greek shore, a storm churned the surface of the sea scattering the debris, as if the ocean were wiping the battlefield away with a great hand."[406]

In addition to causing naval warfare, the pouring out of the second angel's bowl of wrath into the sea probably also points to disastrous sea storms, like tsunamis and rising sea levels.

---

406 Roger Crowley, Empires of the Sea, (New York: Random House Trade Paperbacks, 2008), pp. 275-277.

Revelation Chapter 16

16:3 "every living soul died, even the things that were in the sea"

The effects of this series of maritime disasters will cut across all distinctions. The adjective "every" does not describe entirety, but the scope or degree of inclusiveness. No category of human existence will be exempt from the consequences of this judgment-angel's activity. It cuts across distinctions of age, of sex, of ethnicity, of nationality, of religious affiliation, and of linguistic identity. In that sense, "every living soul died."

3. The bowl of God's wrath on the rivers 16:4-7

16:4 "And the third poured out his bowl into the rivers and the fountains of the waters; and it became blood."

16:4 "the rivers and the fountains of the waters"

With the dramatic increase in world population (See the discussion under 9:16.), fresh water sources for human consumption and irrigation have already become hotly contested. However, the inadequacy of available water is not simply a matter of population increase, or of scanty rainfall, but more importantly there is also divine judgmental involvement, initiated by the activity of the third wrath angel. Consequently, old weather patterns upon which freshwater resources have been predictable will give no clue about what to expect. Ultimately this problem will become much worse when the seventh wrath angel pours out his bowl on the atmosphere. (See 16:17-21.)

16:4 "it became blood"

The pronoun "it," as shown in many other translations, should be "they." Thus, the rivers and the fountains of water "became blood." This points to war breaking out between countries, states and communities over the control and use of freshwater resources. We Americans should appreciate how delicate this issue has become by observing the interstate rivalry and contention over the division and use of the waters of the Columbia and Colorado Rivers.

An example of the danger of international conflict taking place over freshwater rights is seen in Egypt's recent threat of war against Ethiopia because of that country's construction of a great dam on the Blue Nile which will diminish the flow of water to Egypt, water upon which Egyptian agriculture is utterly dependent.

Another flashpoint has arisen from the tension growing between the countries through which the Mekong River flows. There, "water conflict could become a real threat in the next decade: Laos' dam building has already raised concerns among its downstream neighbors over water access and environmental degradation. Laos hosts the headquarters for the Mekong River Commission, an intergovernmental agency that works with Cambodia, Laos, Thailand, and Vietnam on hydroelectric development and water management. But the Laotian government too often flouts its rules. China must also be persuaded by its neighbors to join the Commission, and abide by its strictures."[407]

Why can't nations come to amicable and mutually beneficial decisions about the distribution and use of freshwater resources? The answer is, they cannot agree because

---

[407] Thitinan Pongsudhirak, *The Mekong Region*, FOREIGN AFFAIRS, January/February 2014, pp. 49-50.

the nations which must divide the waters are under divine judgment brought on by the activity of the third angel of wrath.

16:5 **"And I heard the angel of the waters saying, Righteous art thou, who art and who wast, thou Holy One, because thou didst thus judge:"**

Please see the comment on "thy righteous acts" under 15:4 and, especially, the following comments under 16:7.

16:6 **"for they poured out the blood of the saints and the prophets, and blood hast thou given them to drink: they are worthy."**

The first pronoun "they" seems to have a cumulative import, perhaps going back many generations, but finally the time of reckoning has arrived. A later generation, also referred to as "they," had not repudiated and reversed the brutal and atrocious persecuting activities of previous generations. Rather, they had continued such barbarism. God's judgment is seen, in that he has given them blood to drink, an expression pointing to war. God's judgment is completely just, for "they are worthy." The NIV renders it "as they deserve." This accumulation and perpetuation of guilt is very similar to that depicted by Jesus in his denunciation of hypocritical Scribes and Pharisees in the account which is found in Matthew 23:29-32.

16:7 **"And I heard the altar saying, Yea, O Lord God, the Almighty, true and righteous are thy judgments."**

In 6:10 is recorded the anguished cry of some of those who had suffered and died in the cause of Christ. At that point, their cry was one of perplexity, asking "How long?" It seemed to them as though divine justice would never be rendered. Finally, at the opening of the sixth seal (6:12), after long periods of divine patience and forbearance, retributive justice had been righteously rendered. Similarly, here, at the occurrence noted in 16:5-7, again divine judgment is carried out.

When judgment, not in the sense of forming an opinion but of rendering punishment on an entire society, is meted out, the question of its being righteous is paramount. It presents complicated, arresting ethical problems with which God's people have wrestled for many centuries. For example, when the destruction of Sodom was decreed, Abraham raised this central wrenching issue. First he did so by remonstrating with God, "Far be it from you to do such a thing - to kill the righteous with the wicked, treating the righteous and the wicked alike. Far be it from you!" Then he turned to admonition, "Far be it from you! Will not the Judge of all the earth do right?" (Genesis 18:25 NIV)

Here, in the execution of retributive justice, in a case far more extensive than that punishment which was rendered to Sodom, we are assured that God's judgment is "true and righteous." All of us will stand in awe when we see how God will have accomplished that!

Revelation Chapter 16

4. The bowl of God's wrath on the sun 16:8-9

16:8 "**And the fourth poured out his bowl upon the sun; and it was given unto it to scorch men with fire.**"

This bowl of wrath, the work of the fourth wrath angel, probably points to God's manipulation of sunspot and solar flare activity. Both of these phenomena have very significant influence on the environment in which we live. Astronomers know, for example, that there was a period of low sunspot activity from 1645 to 1717, after which there was a renewal of normal sunspot cycles. But then on September 1, 1859, an extremely powerful solar flare, known as the Carrington Event, took place. "It was so powerful that it interrupted electrical telegraph service. From 1900 to the 1960s, the solar maxima trend of sunspot count has been upward. ... Over the last decades the Sun has had a markedly high average level of sunspot activity. ... Solar activity (and the sunspot cycle) are frequently discussed in the context of global warming."[408]

Sunspot activity and solar flares can result in disturbances which are known as geomagnetic storms. Such storms can disrupt navigation because of erroneous readings on magnetic compasses and other direction-giving devices.

The disruptive potential for human life and activities may be gauged by "the March 1989 geomagnetic storm [which] caused the collapse of the Hydro-Québec power grid in a matter of seconds as equipment protection relays tripped in a cascading sequence of events. Six million people were left without power for nine hours, with significant economic loss."[409]

Even wider disruption from geomagnetic storms may be imagined if we realize that they have resulted in "the degradation of homing pigeons' navigational abilities" and also the abilities of "other migratory animals, such as dolphins and whales, [who] demonstrate magnetosensitive behavioral responses."[410]

16:9 "**And men were scorched with great heat: and they blasphemed the name of God who hath the power over these plagues; and they repented not to give him glory.**"

Rather than a penitent reaction by those who suffer because of disruptions growing out of extreme geomagnetic storms, men foolishly and contemptuously continue their blasphemy. "These plagues" seem to be overlapping and cumulative.

5. The bowl of God's wrath on the throne of the beast 16:10-11

16:10 "**And the fifth poured out his bowl upon the throne of the beast; and his kingdom was darkened; and they gnawed their tongues for pain,**"

16:10 "poured out his bowl upon the throne of the beast"

This beast has been identified in 16:2 under "poured out his bowl into the earth." The "throne of the beast" had earlier shifted from its sea girt site in Constantinople (See the

---

408 http://en.wikipedia.org/wiki/Sunspot, accessed January 20, 2014
409 http://en.wikipedia.org/wiki/Geomagnetic_storm, accessed January 20, 2014
410 Adapted from http://en.wikipedia.org/wiki/Geomagnetic_storm, January 20, 2014

comments on 13:1-10.) to its riverine site at Kiev, the first capital of "the image of the [first] beast." Finally it shifted to its present site in Moscow.

16:10 "his kingdom was darkened"

Among other forms of darkness, the beast's kingdom being darkened points to "spiritual darkness which prevails among the subjects of the beast."[411] Further, the impact of this angel's work would also result in extreme political miscalculation and misrule, a form of darkness. That malady first manifested itself in the tyranny of the czars, followed by the dictatorship of the proletariat, a distinct and unique feature of Russian Communism, and now continues to be manifested in the iron-fisted rule of Vladimir Putin.

16:11 "and they blasphemed the God of heaven because of their pains and their sores; and they repented not of their works."

16:11 "they blasphemed the God of heaven"

Such blasphemy is the well-known contemptuous trademark of that branch of communism which is centered in Moscow, the throne of this beast. It has imposed the blasphemy of the denial of God on Russia, beginning with the 1917 Russian Revolution, notwithstanding the conspicuous inconsistency of allowing the presence of the Russian Orthodox Church for reasons of political expediency. That revolution was one of the consequences of WWI which, "unleashed the totalitarian ideologies of Communism, Fascism, [and] Naziism, which very nearly destroyed Western civilization. Their poisonous legacy [also] lives on in radical Islamic extremism. Mixed in its toxic brew are portions of Marxism, Naziism, and Nihilism."[412] Communism not only has imposed its blasphemy on Russia, but has spread the blasphemy of atheism internationally through extensive use of state resources.

"Marxist Theology is clearly stated by Lenin, [who tells us] 'Religion is opium for the people. Religion is a sort of spiritual booze. …'

"'We Communists are atheists,' declared Chou En-lai at the Bandung, Indonesia Conference in April 1955. This Chinese communist leader captured the fundamental theological ingredient of Marxism-Leninism in one word: atheism. Today, Marxists-Leninists prefer two words: scientific atheism.

"From the university days of Karl Marx to the present, official spokesmen for Marxism have been consistent about the content of their theology – that God, whether known as a Supreme Being, Creator, or Divine Ruler, does not, cannot, and must not exist.

"God is considered an impediment, even an enemy, to a scientific, materialistic, socialistic outlook. The idea of God, insists Lenin, encourages the working class (the proletariat) to drown its terrible economic plight in the 'spiritual booze' of some mythical heaven ('pie in the sky by and by'). Even a single sip of this intoxicant decreases the revolutionary fervor necessary to exterminate the oppressing class (the bourgeois),

---

[411] A. Plummer, The Pulpit Commentary [on] Revelation, (Chicago: Wilcox & Follett Co., no date), p. 395.
[412] Steve Forbes, *Why Uncle Sam Became a Monster*, FORBES, September 2, 2013, p. 13.

Revelation Chapter 16

causing the working class to forfeit its only chance of creating a truly human heaven on earth: global communism."[413]

16:11 "their pains and their sores"

These persistent painful sores were first mentioned in 16:2. (Please see the comments there.) Wherever communism rules, as it does in the vast expanse of Russia, that society or state will painfully and persistently fall below its potential! This reality was vividly verbalized in 1932 by an Italian Senator who said: "The Russian Communists have not solved, nor will their violent and repressive methods ever enable them to solve, the fundamental problem of human society, the problem of freedom. For in freedom only can human society flourish and bear fruit. Freedom alone gives meaning to life: without it life is unbearable."[414]

Also, due to extreme centralization, "the inherent inefficiency of the communist economies prevented them from fully exploiting their vast resources and catching up to the West."[415] "Communism was a great system for making people equally poor. In fact, there was no better system in the world for that than communism. Capitalism [in contrast] made people unequally rich, and for some who were used to the plodding, limited, but secure socialist lifestyle – where a job, a house, an education, and a pension were all guaranteed even if they were meager – the fall of the Berlin Wall [which coincided with the defeat of communism in Eastern Europe] was deeply unsettling. But for many others, it was a get-out-of-jail-free card. That is why the fall of the Berlin Wall was felt in so many more places than just Berlin, and why its fall was such a world-flattening event."[416]

16:11 "they repented not of their works"

To this day, they continue their denial of God! Their anti-God propaganda continues to go forth, unabated. "The Soviet State did not in fact disappear. The U.S.S.R. shattered, rather, into a multiplicity of little successor states, most of them ruled by experienced communist autocrats whose first instinct was to reproduce and impose the systems of the authority they had hitherto wielded as Soviet managers. There was no 'transition to democracy' in most of the successor republics; that transition came – if it came at all – somewhat later. Autocratic state power, the only kind that most denizens of the domestic Soviet empire had ever known, was not so much dethroned as downsized. From the outside this was a dramatic change; but experienced from within, its implications were decidedly less radical."[417] This fits the goal allegedly sought by Gorbachev who is said to have been "letting communism fall in Eastern Europe in order to save it in Russia itself."[418]

Those who uphold the theory of atheistic communism and its implementation through Socialist political structures as something which is good, try to justify the horrors of its

---

413 http://www.allaboutworldview.org/marxist-theology.htm
414 Benedetto Croce, *Of Liberty*, FOREIGN AFFAIRS, Volume 91 No. 1, January/February 2012, p. 28.
415 Azar Gat, *The Return of Authoritarian Great Powers*, FOREIGN AFFAIRS, Volume 91 No. 1, January/February 2012, p. 47.
416 Thomas L. Friedman, The World is Flat, a Brief History of the Twenty-first Century, (New York: Farrar, Straus & Giroux, 2005), pp. 49-50.
417 Tony Judt, Postwar, A History of Europe Since 1945, (New York: Penguin Books, 2005), p. 658.
418 Tony Judt, Postwar, A History of Europe Since 1945, (New York: Penguin Books, 2005), pp. 632-633.

Revelation Verse by Verse

killings, pogroms, and gulags as "false moves along a true path."[419] The reality is, such people will not find the "true path" until they renounce atheism.

6. The bowl of God's wrath on the Euphrates 16:12-16

16:12 "And the sixth poured out his bowl upon the great river, the river Euphrates; and the water thereof was dried up, that the way might be made ready for the kings that come from the sunrising."

16:12 "the great river, the river Euphrates" (consult Map 8)

Other rivers are greater in length (for example, the Nile) and in volume of water (the Amazon, for example) but no other river can equal the Euphrates for significance. It has been a persistent fault line or boundary between empires. In the vision of the sixth-trumpet angel (9:13-14) it was the featured geographical location where the four angels had been bound. Be sure to correlate the work of the sixth wrath angel with the ministry of the four angels who were bound at the river Euphrates. (See 9:14 and comments.)

16:12 "the water thereof was dried up"

Malevolent historic forces centering on the Euphrates have been held in check by God. But now, since men continue to persist in contemptuously ignoring, defying and denying him, God sends an angel to remove those impediments which have held back incipient evil developments.

It is quite certain that the statement that "the water thereof was dried up" refers neither to the evaporation of the water nor to the diversion of the water out of the normal river channel. Though the Euphrates has been a great natural defensive barrier through the millennia of history,[420] even in ancient times it was not an insurmountable obstruction to the passage of armies. The armies of Darius, the great Persian monarch, were able to cross the Euphrates on their way west to attack Greece. Subsequently, carrying out their reprisal against the Persians, the engineers of Alexander the Great certainly coped successfully with the logistic challenge of crossing the Euphrates and other major rivers which flowed across their route of attack. Though it was the boundary between the Byzantine and the Sassanian Empires, the Euphrates certainly did not prevent their armies from crossing and attacking the neighboring empire from time-to-time. With modern military bridging techniques, the crossing of the river by the kings who shall come from the sunrising (16:12) will prove to be only a routine military undertaking.

Certainly, then, this drying up of the water of the Euphrates points to the removal of some impediment represented by the river other than a geographic one. The 120-mile-long final segment of the river is known as the Shatt al-Arab, The River of the Arabs. There, the combined waters of the Euphrates and the Tigris join together and form the political boundary between Iraq and Iran. The river has also been the east-west ethnic and linguistic boundary between Arab and Iranian Islam for many centuries. The Arabic language prevails in the Euphrates drainage basin and in North Africa all the way west to

---
419 Tony Judt, Postwar, A History of Europe Since 1945, (New York: Penguin Books, 2005), p. 563.
420 One example is found in the site on which the ancient city of Dura Europos was situated. One side of the city butted up against the right bank of the Euphrates River. The river bank there is high and perpendicular. The water literally boils past at that point. That side of the city needed no wall for safety.

Revelation Chapter 16

the shore of the Atlantic, but defiantly, the Farsi language continues to predominate on the Iranian Plateau. It is also a <u>theological boundary</u>. The Iranian Muslims on the east side of the Euphrates are Shias, while the majority of Arab Muslims on the western side of the river, except for Iraq, are Sunnis. That doctrinal-theological split has plagued Islam for many generations.

Astonishingly, throughout the entire fourteen centuries of Islamic history, linguistic, social, ethnic, and economic issues have alienated Muslims on one side of the Euphrates from those on the other side. If that long-standing division in Islam should be overcome, it might well be represented as the drying up of the Euphrates which marks multiple boundaries between Muslim people who have been enmeshed in centuries-long divisions. Achieving such an accord would make Islam a far more formidable force spiritually, politically, and militarily than it has ever been. Islam would then be in a position to exert greater influence on the kings who will come from the sunrising (16:12), especially those among them who are Muslim rulers, to participate in "the war of the great day of God, the Almighty." (16:14)

Islamic cooperation with China shows that the waters of the Euphrates barrier are drying up. Muslim countries from both sides of the Sunni-Shia divide are cooperating with China. Though Pakistan and Sudan are predominantly Sunni and Iran is overwhelmingly Shia, yet all three cooperate with Communist China. This is a clear example of the Euphrates boundary, between the main doctrinally defined factions of Islam, drying up. That development gives a clear route of ingress into the Middle East for the most significant one of the "kings" who will eventually come from the sunrising, that is, China.

Cooperation between Iran and Al Qaeda also shows that the Euphrates is drying up. The following observations seem to be valid despite the rise of ISIS and the current military offensive of Saudi Arabia in Yemen against Iran's Houthi tribal alliance. Disclosures from the 9/11 Commission have shown that the centuries-old rift between Sunni and Shia Islam may be healing in the Euphrates area, even while it continues to flare up or prevail with renewed violence in other places in the Muslim world, such as Pakistan. "Americans who go online to read the reports [of the 9/11 Commission] will actually ... discover new details about the links between al Qaeda and Iran. The conventional wisdom has been that these Sunni and Shiite cultures couldn't meet, but the report says they did so 'to cooperate against a common enemy' – the infidel U.S.

"Specifically, al Qaeda operatives trained in Iran, and al Qaeda helped Iran-backed [Shiite] Hezbollah terrorists obtain explosives. Al Qaeda was also probably involved in two attacks on U.S. troops in Saudi Arabia, including the 1996 bombing of Khobar Towers that killed 19 Americans and injured 372, both of which had previously been blamed largely on Hezbollah. This certainly sheds some useful light on State Department attempts to 'engage' Tehran's mullahs as they attempt to build a nuclear bomb."[421]

The Khomeini Revolution which overthrew the Shah of Iran in 1979 was admired throughout the Muslim world, by Sunnis as well as Shias. That admiration was so intense that some considered it an event which might herald the healing of the grievous

---
[421] *Review & Outlook, Spinning 9/11*, <u>The Wall Street Journal</u>, June 18, 2004, p. A10.

division between Sunni and Shia in the Muslim world which has plagued Islam for over thirteen centuries.

Despite the ongoing Muslim Shia-Sunni war in Iraq, in Syria, in Yemen and in Lebanon, one can gain a feel for the sense of vacillating but growing amity between those Muslim factions from an evaluation given by Bernard Lewis, a truly great scholar of Middle Eastern affairs. He wrote, "I would draw your attention to the Iranian Revolution of 1979. The word 'revolution' is much misused in the Middle East; it is used for virtually every change of government. But the Iranian Revolution was a real revolution, in the sense that the French and Russian revolutions were real revolutions. It was a massive change in the country, a massive shift of power – socially, economically, and ideologically. And like the French and Russian revolutions in their prime, it also has a tremendous impact in the world with which the Iranians shared a common universe of discourse – the world of Islam.

"I remember not long after the Iranian Revolution I was visiting Indonesia and for some mysterious reason I had been invited to lecture in religious universities. I noticed in the student dorms they had pictures of Khomeini all over the place, although Khomeini – like the Iranians in general – is a Shiite, and the Indonesians are Sunnis. Indonesians generally showed little interest in what was happening in the Middle East. But this was something important. And the Iranian Revolution has gone through various familiar phases – familiar from the French and Russian revolution – such as the conflicts between the moderates and the extremists. I would say that the Iranian Revolution is now entering the Stalinist phase, and its impact all over the Islamic world has been enormous."[422]

Though the improvement in relations across the Sunni-Shia divide in Islam is significant enough that it has the potential to fulfill the reality pointed to by the simile of the waters of the Euphrates drying up, still one should realize that the basic rift in Islam still exists. "Even though Khomeini had hoped that an Islamic revolution would spread throughout the Middle East, the Arab Sunni world was not captured by his call to arms against the region's U.S.-backed kings and dictators. Although fascinated by Khomeini's success – the Sunni Muslim Brotherhood, the mother of all Sunni fundamentalist movements, dreamed of toppling unrighteous Muslim rulers decades earlier – Sunni militants could not forgive Khomeini's allusions to the 'Hidden Imam' and the suggestion that his authority and title (Khomeini was always called the *Imam* in Iran) was somehow supernaturally charged.

"The great divide in Islamic civilization, between the Sunnis and the Shiites, who predominate only in Iran, Iraq, and Lebanon, held firm."[423] But now that Egyptian General el-Sisi has broken the power of the Muslim Brotherhood, the way for Iranian forces to project power to the west of the Euphrates River is even more open. However, though Iran's way to the Mediterranean is currently being blocked by the rise of ISIS (Islamic State of Iraq and Syria), with insight based on this prophecy, we can be sure that the impediment of ISIS ultimately will be militarily overcome. However, that will be accomplished only by great expenditure of life and fortune.

---

422 Bernard Lewis, Freedom and Justice in Islam, Imprimis, September 2006, pp. 5-6.
423 Reuel Marc Gerecht, The Islamic Paradox, Shiite Clerics, Sunni Fundamentalists, and The Coming of Arab Democracy, (Washington, D.C.: American Enterprise Institute Press, 2004), p. 32.

Revelation Chapter 16

Sunni support for Ahmadinejad, recently replaced president of Iran, in his anti-American stance demonstrated the growing cooperation among Islamic factions which is represented by the symbol of the Euphrates river drying up. "As international tension mounts over Iran's nuclear ambitions, many Mideast governments are feeling a sense of déjà vu – trapped between a belligerent leader for whom they have little sympathy and domestic populations energized by that same leader's populist anti-U.S. rhetoric. A little more than three years ago, governments in the region faced a dilemma: support the U.S. effort to topple Iraq's Saddam Hussein and incur the wrath of their populations, or snub their key economic and security patron. Many managed to muddle through. Now, as the standoff with Iran and its nuclear program gathers steam, governments in the region are facing a similar swirl of conflicting emotions and politics.

"Their conundrum is reflected in the views of people such as Magdy Farag. A 40-year-old Sunni Muslim and resident of Cairo, Mr. Farag says he has little affinity for the domestic policies of Iran's Shiite theocracy. But when it comes to Iranian President Mahmoud Ahmadinejad and his strident anti-U.S. stance, he has a different view. 'Of course I support him,' he says. 'Someone needs to stand up to America.'"[424]

America's invasion of Iraq facilitated the symbolic drying up of the Euphrates. "The Iranian highlands, as Hodgson writes, have always been extrinsically related to the politics and culture of Mesopotamia, something very much in evidence since the American invasion of Iraq in 2003, which opened the door to the re-entry of Iran into the region. Indeed, the border between Persia and Mesopotamia, which constantly shifted, was for long periods the Euphrates River itself, now in the heart of Iraq."[425] For the most likely scenario of all, see Appendix I, "Which Way Iran?"

16:12 "the kings that come from the sunrising"

It is clear that these kings are coming for war, for they are included among "the kings of the whole world" who are to be gathered "together unto the war of the great day of God, the Almighty." (16:14)

Since the reference point is "the great river, the river Euphrates," it is then obvious that the "kings which come from the sunrising" would certainly include Iran, Afghanistan, and Pakistan, all encompassed in the Iran/Persia of Ezekiel's time. (See Ezekiel 38:5.) Most probably those kings who shall come from the sunrising will include the rulers of the Far East as well. The rearmament of Japan and the great enhancement of China's military power, along with the Maoist dictum still current in Communist China, telling us that "political power comes out of the barrel of a gun," are ominous portents of this possibility. The expression "the kings of the whole world" (16:14) undoubtedly includes the U.S.A. "Kings" is probably used euphemistically for rulers.

The identity of the kings who will come from the sunrising becomes more clear if they are also ideologically defined. That definition will point predominately to the Communist and Islamic countries which lie to the east of the Euphrates. Their philosophical and religious commitments will encourage them in the attempt to eradicate America's main foothold on the eastern shore of the Mediterranean, that is, Israel.

---

[424] Karby Leggett and Yasmine El-Rashidi, *Mideast Grapples With Iran Dilemma*, The Wall Street Journal, May 11, 2006, p. A6.
[425] Robert D. Kaplan, The Revenge of Geography, (New York: Random House, 2012), p. 53.

The probability of China exerting its military power to the west of the Euphrates was graphically highlighted by the late Lee Kuan Yew, first prime minister of independent Singapore. He asked, "Why has China's peaceful rise, however, raised apprehensions [while India's rise has not]? Is it because India is a democracy in which numerous political forces are constantly at work, making for an internal system of checks and balances [while China is not such a democracy]? Most probably, yes. ...

"Suppose China were also a democracy with multiple parties and political power bases. Would a multiparty China with a yearly economic growth rate of 9% to 12% be viewed with the same equanimity as India is? Such a China would probably continue to make big strides on the economic, social and military fronts, with more sophisticated capabilities on the ground and sea and in the air and space, and would eventually become a peer competitor, if not an adversary, of the U.S. ...

"What if India were well ahead of China? Would Americans and Europeans be rooting for China? I doubt it. They still have a phobia of the 'yellow peril,' one reinforced by memories of the outrages of the Cultural Revolution and the massacres in Tiananmen Square, not to mention their strong feelings against Chinese government censorship."[426]

Among the countries which will come to participate in "the war of the great day of God the Almighty" will almost certainly be North Korea. That prediction is based on the fact that "on an island in the Suez Canal, a towering AK-47 rifle, its muzzle and bayonet pointed skyward, symbolizes one of Egypt's most enduring alliances. Decades ago, North Korea presented it to Egypt to commemorate the 1973 war against Israel, when North Korean pilots fought and died on the Egyptian side."[427]

16:13 "And I saw coming out of the mouth of the dragon, and out of the mouth of the beast, and out of the mouth of the false prophet, three unclean spirits, as it were frogs:"

16:13 "dragon ... beast ... false prophet"

In addition to the information given in Lee Kuan Yew's comments which help us understand the dragon, the beast and the false prophet, also be sure to read Appendix E, "Expanded Comments on Revelation 16:13."

"Dragon," "beast" and "false prophet" are the prophetic names of the partners in a satanic coalition, a very unholy trinity. The partners are each powerful and committed to a philosophy or doctrine which opposes Christ. There are three general characteristics applicable to each of these three wartime partners which help us identify them. **First**, each one exercises influence which is worldwide in scope, for they are able to persuade "the kings of the whole world" to participate in a colossal war. (Revelation 16:14) **Secondly**, it is important to realize that all the partners in this coalition fill their roles contemporaneously. That is, all three are on the stage of history at the same time. This is obvious since all three influence world leaders to participate in the same war. The **third** characteristic is the most frightening and ominous. Each of the three entities works by

---

426 Lee Kuan Yew, *India's Peaceful Rise*, <u>FORBES</u>, December 24, 2007, p. 33. [Note: The late Mr Yew was, at the time of writing, the Minister Mentor of Singapore.]
427 Declan Walsh, *Missiles Made in Pyongyang Sold in Cairo*, <u>The New York Times</u>, March 4, 2018, p. A1.

Revelation Chapter 16

satanic power. This reality is obvious since out of the mouth of each one of them come the spirits of demons, expressed by the repulsive simile of frogs! (Revelation 16:13-14)

16:13 "out of the mouth of the dragon"

Identification of the dragon: In the zoological hierarchy used in biblical prophetic writings to depict persons, entities and institutions[428] the serpent, or dragon, depicts the antipode of God. Thus the dragon represents the being or concept furthermost from the concept and reality of God. That is why the simile of a serpent is used to depict Satan in Revelation 12:9. Remember, in Eden it was in the form of a serpent that Satan led man away from God.

However, the entity represented by the dragon here in Revelation 16:13 is not Satan himself but, rather, it is a worldwide institution. Its being worldwide is seen in the fact that it influences "the kings of the whole world." (16:14) Because the dragon is under demonic influence (16:13), it is clear that it is energized by Satan. Therefore, this dragon is not Satan himself even though a designation is used for it which is also used for Satan. (See Revelation 12:9) Since the dragon and the other two entities are all three energized by Satan we must recognize them to be evil. However, Satan constantly tries to disguise this fact by using these entities to sponsor and subsidize various appealing aspects of the higher side of secular society such as elegant arts, architecture and grandiose music.

The satanic power which energizes the serpent is represented by the "unclean spirits" or "spirits of demons," symbolized by frogs which issue from the serpent's mouth. (Revelation 16:13-14) It also is precisely the same energizing power which animates the beast and the false prophet. Since Satan, for whom the figure of serpent is also used, is the being farthest from God, therefore, that worldwide institution which is philosophically farthest from God is represented by the dragon. Diametrically opposed to theism is atheism. Only one worldwide institution is based on atheism. <u>The dragon, therefore, seems to clearly represent communism</u>. **Thus, the dragon is corrupt government which denies God that it may itself function as God!** Because all three entities (the dragon, the beast, and the false prophet) work as satanic agents, impelled by the same influence, they are able to cooperate in instigating a global war.

"There must be no underestimate of the strength and determination of the anti-religious forces today, which are resolved to root out all religion. The communist half of the world is pledged to atheism, and regards all religion as superstition and feudalistic, 'the opiate of the masses' and the reason for their depressed state."[429] Another unmistakable evidence of the current strength of anti-Christian forces is the stunning, rapid rise of political power wielded by deviant sexually oriented groups like those designated by LGBT (Lesbian, Gay, Bisexual, Transgender - nontraditional gender identities).

Since the implementation of Perestroika (restructuring) and Glasnost (openness) in 1985 by Mr. Gorbachev, since the destruction of the Berlin Wall[430] (1990) and the Iron Curtain (1991), and since the overthrow of oppressive Communist governments in Eastern

---
428 Animals are used to depict three levels of institutions: Governmental - Dan. 7:23, Ecclesiastical - Rev. 17:13-14, and Familial - Gen. 16:12.)
429 Geoffrey Parrinder, Comparative Religion, (Westport: Greenwood Press, 1962), p. 97.
430 The fall of the Berlin Wall had a great impact. "Not only did it spark democratic transitions in Central and Eastern Europe; the end of the cold war unfroze the African landscape and encouraged democratic openings throughout the continent." - Larry Diamond, *The Next Democratic Century*, Current History, January 2014, p. 8.

Europe, many feel Communism is now a spent force. Therefore, it is no longer able, according to those who endorse such a view, to play the role that is depicted for the dragon in Revelation 16:12-16. For example, Francis Fukuyama, while he was Deputy Director of the U.S. State Department's Policy Planning Staff, optimistically wrote, "Surely the class issue has actually been successfully resolved in the West. ... The egalitarianism of modern America represents the essential achievement of the classless society envisioned by Marx. ... As a result of the receding of the class issue, the appeal of Communism in the developed Western world, it is safe to say, is lower today than at any time since the end of the First World War. ... The democratizing and decentralizing principles which he [i.e., Gorbachev] has enunciated in both the economic and political spheres are highly subversive of some of the most fundamental precepts of both Marxism and Leninism. ... If we admit for the moment that the fascist and communist challenges to liberalism are dead, are there any other ideological competitors left? ... The passing of Marxism-Leninism first from China [Fukuyama seems to refer to the relaxation which came under Deng Chou Peng. But he wrote before the Tiananmen massacre.] and then from the Soviet Union will mean its death as a living ideology of world historical significance. For while there may be some isolated true believers left in places like Managua [capital of Nicaragua], Pyongyang [capital of North Korea], or Cambridge, Massachusetts [at Harvard University], the fact [that] there is not a single large state in which it is a going concern undermines completely its pretensions to being in the vanguard of human history."[431]

Another example of this kind of exuberant optimism was expressed by the elder statesman and creator of the political concept of *containment*, George Kennan. He said, "What we are witnessing today in Russia is the breakup of much, if not all, of the system of power by which that country has been held together and governed since 1917. ... It is the end of the Russian Revolution as we have known it. ... Whatever reasons there may have once been for regarding the Soviet Union primarily as a possible, if not probable, military opponent, the time for that sort of thing has clearly passed."[432] Obviously, he wrote before Vladimir Putin's rise to power in Russia.

Christian leaders also enthusiastically and fully endorsed that optimistic view. Gene Dulin of TCM International wrote, "What a year 1989 was!!! What a way to end it!!! The revolution in Romania! It was as if God were putting a great big exclamation mark at the end of the year – a year when the Berlin Wall crumbled into souvenirs and Communism collapsed in country after country."[433] Also, Robert C. Shannon wrote in a challenging article: "Another prophecy of Jesus looms large. He assured us that the gates of hell would never prevail against the church. Now Communism has fallen, yet the church remains strong and vibrant."[434]

To assess those euphoric appraisals, we should consider the evaluation of Henry Kissinger and Andrei Sakharov. Their opinions came out in a quotation from Sakharov's book *Memoirs*. In it he tells us that, "On Feb. 5, 1987, a delegation organized by the U.S. Council on Foreign Relations came to see me. I stressed the West's vital interest in

---

431 Francis Fukuyama, "The End of History?," The National Interest, Summer 1989, pp. 9-18.
432 Evan Thomas, Newsweek, April 17, 1989, p. 34.
433 TCM International Newsletter, January 1, 1990, p. 1.
434 "Christianity in the Post-Communist World," The Christian Standard, May 6, 1990, pp. 4-5.

Revelation Chapter 16

having the U.S.S.R. become an open, democratic society. Henry Kissinger posed a blunt question: 'Is there a danger that the U.S.S.R. will first effect a democratic transformation, accelerating its scientific and technological progress and improving its economy, and then revert to expansionist policies and pose an even greater threat to peace?'

"I replied that what people should fear is not the development of an open stable society with a powerful peacetime economy in the U.S.S.R. but a disruption of the world's equilibrium and the single-minded military buildup of an internally closed and externally expansionist society."[435]

How then should we evaluate the recent retreat of Communism in Eastern Europe, in Afghanistan, and in southeast Asia? Does that retreat invalidate the analysis of Sakharov and Kissinger? Martin Sicker's recent re-evaluation of conditions immediately following the 1917 Russian Revolution may prove prophetically indicative of the outcome of recent events in the U.S.S.R. He said, "With the collapse of the tsarist regime, followed shortly by the overthrow of the provisional Kerensky government, Russia was quickly lapsing into chaos and civil war. The Bolsheviks saw an urgent need for a respite from the war in Europe [i.e., World War I] in order to be able to consolidate their control over the country. … Thus, if the Bolsheviks would have to withdraw from positions that they inherited from their tsarist predecessors in order to consolidate the revolution, these were to be seen as tactical retreats, to be reversed at a later and more suitable time."[436]

In view of these evaluations and insights, it is safe to say that Communism is not a terminally spent force but will recover the vibrancy and influence necessary to fulfill the role which is here, in Revelation 16:13, visualized under the symbol of the dragon.

The demonic power energizing the dragon, the beast, and the false prophet unmistakably implies Satan's working in human history. We Christians should not be surprised by this concept of Satan's intrusion into the historical process. After all, Scripture tells us that he is "the god of this world." (II Corinthians 4:4) Furthermore, we also know that "the whole world lieth in the evil one." (I John 5:19) In view of Satan's control, we should anticipate that Mr. Kissinger's foreboding about the future of Russia is very likely to prove accurate. Already, under the leadership of Russia's Prime Minister Putin, we see the beginning of a resurgence of communist power and influence in the world's political, economic and military affairs.

We begin to see the resurgence of Russia's political power in its influence in Italy. In a vote at the beginning of March 2018 there was a triumph for Mr. Putin and for Russia. The "Five Star Movement" is a new power in Italian politics. "They have excused Russia's incursions into Ukraine by putting the blame on the European Union and even the United Sates. They have advocated an end to the European sanctions against Russia. They have expressed skepticism about NATO, to which Russia of course does not belong.

---

435 Time, International edition, May 21, 1990, p. 49.
436 Martin Sicker, The Bear and the Lion, Soviet Imperialism and Iran, (New York: Praeger, 1988), p. 35. [Note: "Martin Sicker earned his Ph.D. in political science from the graduate faculty of the New School for Social Research in New York. He has served as a senior executive in the U.S. Government, and has taught political science at the American University and George Washington University in Washington, D.C. He has written widely in the fields of political science and international affairs and is the author of The Making of a Pariah State: The Adventurist Politics of Muammar Qaddfi, The Judaic State: A Study of Rabbinic Political Theory, and The Strategy of Soviet Imperialism: Expansion in Eurasia."]

All of that is music to Moscow's ears, as were party leaders' statements last year when they finally articulated their foreign policy. The *Time*'s Jason Horowitz wrote that they 'depicted Russia as a strategic partner that had been unfairly punished, and the United States as an abusive ally whose 70-year relationship with Italy had run its course.'"[437]

16:13 "out of the mouth of the beast"

Identification of the beast: In the Book of Revelation the beast is contrasted with the Lamb, while the harlot is contrasted with the virtuous woman, the bride of Christ. (See Revelation 5:6, 17:14, 19:6-8.) Every ideological political entity which embraces religion as part of its political system becomes bestial through its attempts to enforce its religious position. <u>This is a special beast. It is a composite entity comprised of both political and ecclesiastical elements</u>. The political elements support the ecclesiastical elements which constitute the harlot, the false church. That beast/harlot relationship mimics the union which exists between Christ, the Lamb, and the church, his bride, which he supports.

In Revelation the harlot is depicted in contrast to the pure woman, the bride of Christ. It is necessary to identify the political entity or entities upon whose power the false church, represented as a prostitute, prospers. It is that power which has thus far made it possible for the harlot to fulfill her despicable role in history. However, this composite beast does not try to deny God, as the dragon does, but tries to seize the authority established by God, for he tries to usurp the place and the role of the Lamb.

Through its folly and gullibility, the world honors the harlot, the false church, rather than the virtuous woman who is the bride of Christ, the true church. Similarly, it also honors the beast which supports the harlot (17:7). The political part of the beast hopes to be the head of the false church, represented by the corrupt woman, even as Christ, the Lamb, is head of the true church. (See Ephesians 1:22-23.) The fact that the harlot rides the beast ("the beast carries her" 17:7) shows one major cause of the frustration of the political part of the beast. It has not gotten supremacy! It is one reason why the political part of the beast, from time-to-time, tries to kill the harlot. (17:16)

Is there a worldwide religious body which through the centuries has claimed to be Christ's church which has received much of its power and influence from liaisons with political powers? Does it have a pyramidal organization culminating with supreme authority in one man? Does that individual in any way claim to act for, or in place of or as the vicar (substitute) of Jesus Christ? The beast of Revelation 16:13 is a union between political power and the harlot. It is a fundamental organic union (17:2). It should be understood then to be the hybrid political, allegedly Christian, hierarchical system represented religiously by both Roman and Eastern Catholicism in union with political power. It is a grotesque genetic monstrosity resulting from its incompatible merger. **Its rapacious nature makes the title "beast" totally appropriate.**

In a recent article Andrew Higgins has given us a clear understanding of Eastern Catholicism. He wrote, as a pillar of Putin's Russia, there is "an intimate alliance between the Orthodox Church and the Kremlin reminiscent of czarist days. Rigidly hierarchical, intolerant of dissent and wary of competition, both share a vision of Russia's future – rooted in robust nationalism and at odds with Western-style liberal democracy. ... 'The

---

437 Frank Bruni, *Italy Has Dumped America. For Russia.*, The New York Times, March 11, 2018, p. 3.

Revelation Chapter 16

state supports the church, and the church supports the state,' says Sergei Kovalyov, a Soviet-era human-rights activist. ... 'Orthodoxy has always had a special role in shaping our statehood, our culture, our morals.' Mr. Putin told bearded black-robed priests at a meeting in the Kremlin before this month's parliamentary election. ... Occasional attempts by Russian churchmen to defy state authority have been crushed."[438]

Helpfully, history also gives us clear insight into the origin of Roman (Western) Catholicism: "The Christian [read Roman Catholic] Church modeled its structure on that of the Roman Empire. The dioceses mirrored the administrative divisions of Diocletian; bishops based in the chief cities, met in synod in the provincial capitals, and those from the great Metropolitan centers were accorded special dignity."[439]

To borrow graphic language from the book of Daniel, its union of religious and political power makes this beast "diverse from all the beasts that were before it." (Daniel 7:7) If one factors out the allegedly Christian element from this hybrid, it will be "the great harlot that sitteth on many waters" (Revelation 17:1), "the woman" who is carried by the beast (Revelation 17:7), is typical of the many churches which are in a fornicatious union with civil governments, both east and west.

There is a love-hate relationship between the beast and the harlot. Normally the beast carries the harlot. (Revelation 17:7) That is the love part of the relationship. That love is an illicit, sensual, hedonistic relationship which is expressed as fornication. There is, therefore, a real union, at times, for the corrupt church is "The great harlot that sitteth upon many waters; with whom the kings of the earth committed fornication..." (Revelation 17:1-2) Therefore, the two, because of their fornication, have become, as it were, one flesh. (See I Corinthians 6:16.) Though the union is illicit because it is based on fornication, it is, nonetheless, real. Even though we can still identify the components of the resulting monstrosity, the two in their union have become one. In 17:1-2 God calls such a church/state relationship fornication, and doing so, he powerfully upholds the separation of the two institutions.

At times, however, the specifically political parts of the beast, led by its constituent "kings," (17:2) "hate the harlot, and shall make her desolate..." (17:16) The same love-hate relationship is seen in that which hinders the "man of sin" (the masculine description of the church/state union) and yet gives him his shape. (II Thessalonians 2:3-10) One may ask, why should there be a love-hate relationship? Why shouldn't they have a love relationship untarnished by any hate? It seems largely because of shattered hopes. Such a clue is given by Franklin H. Littell when he tells us, "Constantine's hope that Christianity would serve as an integrating force, of which the old gods were apparently no longer capable, was not without disappointments. The theological disputes continued to rage, and to these were added the schisms which arose on the treatment of the lapsed."[440] Thus the enamored "kings," the sovereign states and governments which fawningly give rewards to the harlot are disappointed and unfulfilled by their sinful relationship. Such adulation and deferential attention was openly given to the Roman Catholic Church in

---

438 Andrew Higgins, *Putin and Orthodox Church Cement Power in Russia*, The Wall Street Journal, December 18, 2007, pp. A1 and A18.
439 Geoffrey Baraclough, The Times Atlas of World History, (Maplewood, NJ: Hammond, Inc., 1978), p. 93.
440 Franklin H. Littell, The Macmillan Atlas History of Christianity, (New York: Macmillan Publishing Co.,Inc., 1976), p. 17.

September 2015 by President Obama's reception of the Pope at the White House, as well as the invitation given to him to address the U.S. Congress.

Eventually, occasions arise during which the political elements in this fornicatious relationship seek to break the tie by overpowering and killing the harlot. An example comes from the confiscation of the Papal States. (See comments at 14:8 and 17:8.)

At times, the emotional vacillation between love and hate in the church-state relationship has been reciprocal. For example, on the Catholic Church's side, "Many of the popes, too, disliked this accumulation of Habsburg power, even if it was often needed to combat the Turks, the Lutherans, and other foes."[441] This animosity of the Roman Catholic Church towards the political power upon which it depends is seen also in Italian history. For example, "The chronic gap between north and south, which the industrialization of the former only exacerbated, and the lack of any great contact with the world, outside the village community in so many parts of the peninsula were not helped by the hostility between the Italian government and the Catholic Church, which forbade its members to serve the state."[442]

To recapitulate, the beast <u>usurps</u> God's authority. Therefore, he is seen as "setting himself forth as God." (II Thessalonians 2:4) "And he shall speak words against the most High, and shall wear out the saints of the Most High; and he shall think to change the times and the law." (Daniel 7:25) <u>Thus, the beast does not deny God as the dragon does, rather, it tries to usurp God's role</u>. This beast is composed of a union between the corrupt church and fawning governments from which she derives much of her strength. As noted earlier, it is the rapacious persecuting nature of the corrupt church, in union with its associated political power, which makes the term "beast" appropriate.

Historically, the bestiality of the Catholic system is declared by many instances of its treatment of dissenters. For example, the Waldensians, "were persecuted by the ecclesiastical authorities and were eventually stamped out."[443] Jews were treated no better. "Some bishops were warriors. ... Although some Popes attempted to protect them, the Jews were discriminated against and confined to ghettos, and at times anti-Jewish massacres broke out. The economic factor entered, but an excuse often given was that the Jews had killed Christ. Countless individuals who dissented from the Catholic church were burned. The burning was done by the civil and not the ecclesiastical authorities, but it was in the name of Christ. A reason given was that 'heretics,' by teaching doctrines which imperilled the eternal welfare of souls, were even more dangerous than murderers who [only] took physical life. But the fact could not be gainsaid that the Christian religion was given as a reason. A faith whose primary command is love and which professes to be based upon the self-giving love of God in Christ was then, as in later centuries, in a variety of ways used to justify barbarities starkly contradicting that love."[444]

Thus, in the zoological hierarchy of the Apocalypse the beast is in opposition to the Lamb who is the Saviour and Head of the Church. Accordingly, the beast shall, "war against the

---

441 Paul Kennedy, <u>The Rise and Fall of the Great Powers</u>, (New York: Random House, 1987), p. 33.
442 Paul Kennedy, <u>The Rise and Fall of the Great Powers</u>, (New York: Random House, 1987), p. 205.
443 Kenneth Scott Latourette, <u>Christianity Through the Ages</u>, (New York: Harper & Row, Publishers, 1965), p. 116.
444 Kenneth Scott Latourette, <u>Christianity Through the Ages</u>, (New York: Harper & Row, Publishers, 1965), pp.132-133.

Revelation Chapter 16

Lamb, and the Lamb [PRAISE GOD!] shall overcome them, for He is Lord of lords, and King of kings; and they also shall overcome that are with Him, called and chosen and faithful." (Revelation 17:14)

16:13 "out of the mouth of the false prophet"

Identification of the false prophet: The false prophet promotes a corrupt theology which misrepresents God. In contrast, a true and faithful prophet is a spokesman who conveys God's message with complete integrity and fidelity. Since John received the message of the book of Revelation there have arisen myriads of false prophets. The one referred to here is a system or institution (just as the dragon and the beast stand for systems or institutions rather than one single individual) which is worldwide and is in power at the same time as the Communist and political-religious Catholic/Orthodox entities are.

This can only point to Islam which stresses prophethood more than any other worldwide religion. Islam itself is quite aware of this unique emphasis. For example, a publication from Saudi Arabia tells us, "Prophethood is not unknown to heavenly revealed religions, such as Judaism and Christianity. In Islam, however, it has a special status and significance."[445]

"The Prophet is, therefore, the archetypal paradigm, not only to be imitated in daily life, similar to the medieval *imitatione Christi* (imitation of Christ),[446] but he is also the one who, through his custom, ritual and life-praxes [customary practice or conduct], and sayings (i.e., [found in the] sunna and hadith), provides certain limitations to the interpretive possibilities of the sacred text (the Qur'an). In this, the Islamic hermeneutics is limited in a manner similar to the magisterium in the Roman Church.[447] Thus the development of the code of conduct on a personal and societal level is not so much dependent on one's own interpretation of the sacred texts but mostly on the basis of how it was interpreted and enacted by the Prophet, and how he interpreted them through his praxes and sayings."[448]

The fundamental error of Islam, out of which its other errors grow, is its Christology. Church historians often speak of Arianism finally being defeated in the ultimate triumph of Nicene Christology. However, such analysis is grossly in error. Arianism still lives. It lives aggressively and expansively under the banner of the Crescent, not under the banner of the Cross. This becomes obvious if we compare Islamic Christology with Arian Christology.

The Qur'an, which is utterly basic to any understanding of Islamic doctrine, is unmistakably clear in its presentation of Islamic Christology: "Christians say: The Messiah is the Son of Allah. That is their saying with their mouths. They imitate the

---

[445] Prophethood in Islam, (Riyadh, Saudi Arabia: World Assembly of Muslim Youth, n.d.), p. 1.
[446] See for example Thomas à Kempis, De Imitatione Christi, translated as The Imitation of Christ, by Betty I. Knott (London: Wm. Collins Sons & Co. Ltd., Fontana Books, 1963). The appearance of à Kempis' book in the early fifteenth century was no isolated occurrence, but was a manifestation of a much larger devotional movement that had already begun in the fourteenth century.
[447] Magisterium also provided the boundaries or limitations to the interpretive possibilities of the sacred text (i.e., the Bible), rather than to test a given interpretation as it is often practiced today.
[448] Charles Amjad-Ali, "Women Leadership in Islam," Al-mushir, The Theological Journal of the Christian Study Centre, Rawalpindi, Pakistan, Vol. 31, No. 4, p. 127.

sayings of those who disbelieved of old. Allah (himself) fighteth against them. How perverse are they!"[449]

One may easily see that this qur'anic quotation in essence perpetuates Arianism if he remembers that, "Arius maintained that 'the Son has a beginning but that God is without beginning' and that the Son is not a part of God."[450]

Thus the false prophet is not a **denial** of God like that of Communism; nor a **usurpation** of God's authority as in Catholicism, but a sinister and fatal **misrepresentation** of God. Islam, then, is a corrupt theology, in contrast to Communism which is a corrupt polity (i.e., government), and Catholicism which is a corrupt ecclesiology (concept of church).

While Islam's most fundamental falsity is in its Christology, the boundaries of its error extend much further. That raises the question, "how false is the False Prophet?" First, Islam is not true to its own principles. The Qur'an states explicitly, in Surah 2:256, that "There is no compulsion in religion." "Yet Mohammed used military force and strategy to defeat his polytheistic opponents, the Meccans, and his [monotheistic] Jewish rivals. Towards the end of his life, the Arab prophet was preparing a major offensive on the Christian and Byzantine provinces of Syria/Palestine, after having suffered certain setbacks during preparatory incursions. The 'holy war' [which is the pinnacle of compulsion] constituted an important factor in the prophetic life of Mohammed, therefore, and one which was often decisive for the success of his monotheistic mission."[451]

Secondly, Islam is not true to its endorsements. For example, it endorses the Bible. Surah 2:136 of the Qur'an tells us, "Say (O Muslims): We believe in Allah and that which is revealed unto us and that which was revealed unto Abraham, and Ishmael, and Isaac, and Jacob, and the tribes, and that which Moses and Jesus received, and that which the Prophets received from their Lord. We make no distinction between any of them, and unto Him we have surrendered." Though this qur'anic passage clearly endorses the Bible, Islam does not follow the Bible. If it did, it would accept the one who said "I am the way, the truth, the life."

Thirdly, it is not true to its commendations. It commends Jesus of Nazareth. Succinctly put, "it is Jesus, son of Mary, who by his person and his work transcends the other prophets. The Qur'an texts are here both explicit and astonishing. The divine mission of Jesus was sealed by manifest miracles. Alone among the prophets, Jesus is called the Messiah. Even more, he is the apostle *par excellence* of God; he is God's Word (his Logos); he is a spirit come from him (God). God makes Jesus and Mary a sign for human beings, giving them both a 'high place.' ... The entire sura (section or chapter) on Mary (XIX) magnifies the miraculous birth of her son Jesus and praises the creative and miraculous will of God for whom nothing is impossible." [452] Yet Islam does not accept what Jesus said!

---

[449] Sura 9, "Repentance," v. 30, The Meaning of the Glorious Koran, trans. Mohammed Marmaduke Pickthall, (New York: The New American Library of World Literature, Inc., 1953), p. 141.
[450] Kenneth S. Latourette, A History of Christianity, Vol. I, (New York: Harper & Row, 1975), p. 153.
[451] Joseph Hajjar, "The Bible and Christian Witness in Islamic Countries," International Review of Mission, Vol. LXX No. 279, July 1981, p. 165.
[452] Joseph Hajjar, "The Bible and Christian Witness in Islamic Countries," International Review of Mission, Vol. LXX No. 279, July 1981, p. 163.

Revelation Chapter 16

Fourthly, Islam is not true to its people. It claims that all its people are equal, but many Muslim countries are dictatorships. Also, it certainly is not true to its minorities. Verbally, Christians are, on one hand, honored but in reality are *Dhimmis* (those for whom responsibility, oversight and control is taken) who consequently have a very inferior status. "The idea that Christians should have as much right in Islamic countries to seek and make converts as Moslems have in Christian countries is routinely rejected. So are calls for the relaxation of such Islamic laws as those that prevent a Moslem woman from marrying a Christian. Discrimination against Christians living among Moslems is not confined to fundamentalist countries. Egypt's Coptic Christians complain of insidious pressure to convert to Islam." [453]

All three entities (represented by the terms Dragon, Beast, and False Prophet) have overlapping areas of common concern as well as basic elements in common. Therefore they cooperate. Yet, like strands of a rope, they certainly retain enough individuality to be distinguishable. In their areas of divergence they compete with each other, often violently. Their areas of convergence make them, as it were, a house – but it is a house divided. Thus, ultimately, their house will fall. (See Matthew 12:25-26.) Before that fall occurs, Satan finds the members of the troika (the Dragon, the Beast and the False Prophet) vehicles through which many of his goals may be achieved.

16:14 "for they are spirits of demons, working signs; which go forth unto the kings of the whole world, to gather them together unto the war of the great day of God, the Almighty."

16:14 "they are spirits of demons"

The pronoun "they" refers to "the three unclean spirits" which were introduced in 16:13. Thus, this developing and looming war ("the war of the great day of God, the Almighty") is being germinated, motivated and energized by the demonic spirit world. Revelation 16:14 emphasizes the activities of the "spirits of demons" in each of the three worldwide entities which are represented by the Dragon, the Beast and the False Prophet. (16:13) Thus, demonic activity influences the decisions of the "kings" of the whole world. Only Christian-based political analysts note and call attention to this satanic influence in the decision making processes of political leaders throughout the world. Demonic activity is also seen in the startling, rapid, worldwide growth of the occult in our time.

Precursors of the coming all-out war are seen in the sharp debates being fought in the intellectual world. These include the areas of theology, sociology, literature, philosophy, culture, and politics. This is in harmony with the warning in Colossians 2:8, which exhorts us to "See to it that no one takes you captive through hollow and deceptive philosophy, which depends on human tradition and the basic principles of this world rather than on Christ." (NIV)

16:14 "working signs"

All three entities – the Dragon, the Beast and the False Prophet – are able to deceive and beguile people at all levels of society by "working signs." However, especially in relation to the composite beast, which is composed of political power in a fornicatious relationship with the corrupt church, these signs are further identified as "the working of

---
[453] "The New Christendom," World Press Review, March 1989, p. 34.

Satan with all power and signs and lying wonders, and with all deceit of unrighteousness for them that perish; because they receive not the love of the truth, that they might be saved." (II Thessalonians 2:9-10) One category of these "signs" are the alleged miracles performed by those in Roman Catholicism enabling them to be declared to be saints.

These signs are like those of pharaoh's sorcerers and magicians who, up to a point, seemingly could duplicate the miracles which Moses performed before pharaoh. However, at the plague of lice, scripture tells us that "the magicians did so with their enchantments to bring forth lice, but they could not: and there were lice upon man and upon beast. Then the magicians said unto pharaoh, This [the miracles wrought by Moses] is the finger of God." (Exodus 8:18-19.) Ultimately, the "signs" displayed by the three demonically controlled entities will be clearly demonstrated to have been totally bogus. These signs are the very ones which Paul categorized as "lying wonders." (See II Thessalonians 2:7-10.) For a more detailed discussion of the bogus signs shown by the false prophet, see the discussion under 19:20.

Spiritual and intellectual war is one of the arenas in which we Christians are especially engaged. Two scriptures emphasize this: First, Paul wrote to the Corinthians, saying, "Though we walk in the flesh, we do not war according to the flesh (for the weapons of our warfare are not of the flesh, but mighty before God to the casting down of strongholds); casting down imaginations ["arguments" - NIV, ESV], and every high thing that is exalted against the knowledge of God, and bringing every thought into captivity to the obedience of Christ." (II Corinthians 10:3-5) Secondly, in writing to the church in Ephesus, Paul said, "Our wrestling is not against flesh and blood, but against the principalities, against the powers, against the world rulers of this darkness against the spiritual hosts of wickedness in heavenly places." (Ephesians 6:12).[454] <u>These same demonic powers will energize and guide political decisions and thus ignite the global conflict to be fought by the armed forces of the whole world. It will be a conflict impacting the life and work of every Christian, both individually and corporately</u>.

In addition to the ongoing conceptual war which is currently raging, related global temporal conflict is undoubtedly coming. This passage reminds us that it is the kings, not the Christians, of the world who are being gathered for war, though Christians will be deeply impacted by the coming conflict. In fact, the wars which currently engulf Iraq, Afghanistan, Syria and Yemen are almost certainly precursors to the world war predicted here. Many of the details of this great global struggle are given in Ezekiel, chapters 38 and 39. As yet, no war in history has fulfilled that amazing prophecy.

---

[454] For a more complete understanding of "the spiritual hosts of wickedness in heavenly places" see the comments at 11:7 under "overcome them and kill them."

Revelation Chapter 16

16:14 "the kings of the whole world to gather them together unto the war"

The book of Revelation makes it clear that a cosmic or universal conflict is already raging in which Christians are intimately involved. It is a war in which the forces of darkness "make war against the Lamb, but the Lamb will overcome them because he is Lord of lords and King of kings – <u>and with him will be his called, chosen and faithful followers</u>." (Revelation 17:14 NIV) (Compare Revelation 12:7-12.) Obviously then, this war has very serious global implications involving not only the "kings of the whole world" but also Christians, "his called, chosen and faithful followers." (17:14)

The crucial conflict predicted and described in Revelation 16:12-16 is so inclusive that we should call it the "**War of the Worlds**," not simply a world war. It is appropriate to give it that name because three worlds are clearly involved. <u>First</u>, the Heavenly or Celestial World is involved. This is obvious because it is an angel under God's command who pours out the bowl of wrath on the Euphrates River. (16:12) <u>Secondly</u>, the Terrestrial World is certainly involved, for it is "The kings of the whole world" who go to war. (16:14) <u>Thirdly</u>, the Nether World is also deeply involved, for "they are spirits of demons, working signs … which go forth unto the kings of the whole world, to gather them together unto the war of the great day of God, the Almighty…" (Revelation 16:14)

The description of the War of the Worlds, given in Revelation 16:12-16, stresses the theological and ideological motivations of the principal participants while the thirty-eighth and thirty-ninth chapters of Ezekiel emphasize the political and economic motivations of these same combatants.

16:14 "the great day of God, the Almighty"

The day when the concerted forces currently being marshaled by the Serpent, the Beast and the False Prophet to wage war and fight against God's purpose (See Romans 8:28.) are utterly defeated will be "the great day of God, the Almighty."

16:15 "(Behold, I come as a thief. Blessed is he that watcheth, and keepeth his garments, lest he walk naked, and they see his shame.)"

For the identity of the one who says "I come," please see the comments on "a great voice" at 16:1. For the vast majority of the world's inhabitants, the current development of conditions culminating in this coming global war are taking place surreptitiously without their notice, awareness or expectation. They shall be like the people in Noah's day who "knew not until the flood came and took them all away." (Matthew 24:39)

16:16 "And they gathered them together into the place which is called in Hebrew Har-Magedon."

16:16 "they gathered them together"

From verse 14 it is clear that "they" refers to "the spirits of demons," while "them" refers to "the kings of the whole world."

Revelation Verse by Verse

16:16 "the place which is called in Hebrew Har-Magedon"

Though Ezekiel does not use the place name of Har-Magedon, the war predicted in Ezekiel chapters 38 and 39 is the same war which is described in Revelation 16:12-16. Here, quite briefly, is the evidence which substantiates that conclusion.

First, the battlefield is the same. In Ezekiel, the battlefield is described as being in or on the "mountains of Israel." (Ezekiel 38:8) In Revelation, the war is centered on Armageddon. The name Armageddon comes from the Hebrew *Har-megiddo* which means the hill or mountain of Megiddo, located in the Mt. Carmel Range. (**See Map 10.**) It is then, obviously, in the mountains of Israel. The town or city of Megiddo overlooks the plain of Esdraelon, the Greek form of the Hebrew name Jezreel. The plain (NIV) of Esdraelon or Jezreel is the Valley of Megiddo. (II Chronicles 35:22) In that valley flow "the waters of Megiddo." (Judges 5:19) On the north side of the Carmel Mountain Range the Kishon River "flows through the plain of Esdraelon westward to the Mediterranean."[455]

The strategic importance of the area of Megiddo is seen from an evaluation given by Napoleon. "Even as his fleet was destroyed by Nelson in the Battle of the Nile [which took place in Aboukir Bay], [he] turned his back on that verdict and pushed on in the massive pretense that he could still conquer Syria, then Turkey, Persia, and India, and at last return to Europe with a new empire at his back to become master of the world. In February 1799 he took El Arish in the Sinai Peninsula between Egypt and Palestine, invaded Palestine a few days later, captured Jaffa on March 7, and reached the walls of Acre [slightly north of Megiddo] on March 18. 'The fate of the East is in the fort of Acre,' he said. Once Acre was in his hands he would march on to Damascus, Aleppo, and Constantinople. 'Then I will overthrow the Turkish empire and found a great new empire in the East which will preserve my place in posterity.' He never got over that vision. Twenty years later as he sat amid the rocks of St. Helena dictating his memoirs he repeated: 'Acre once taken . … I would have reached Constantinople and the Indies. I would have changed the face of the world.'"[456]

On his way to the Battle of Acre Napoleon stood at Megiddo and gazed at the great Plain of Esdraelon. There he declared, "All the armies of the world could maneuver their forces on this vast plain."[457]

Secondly, the participants in the wars predicted in the thirty-eighth and thirty-ninth chapters of Ezekiel and the sixteenth chapter of Revelation are the same.

In the **third** place, the scope of the wars described in the thirty-eighth and thirty-ninth chapters of Ezekiel is the same as that given in Revelation where we are told that the kings of the whole world will be "gathered together unto the war of the great day of God, the Almighty …" (Revelation 16:14) Similarly, the participants in the incipient war which Ezekiel foresaw will come from all over the globe.

---

455 M. C. Hazard, <u>A Complete Concordance to the American Standard Version of the Holy Bible</u>, (New York: Thomas Nelson & Sons, 1922), p. 608.

456 Barbara W. Tuchman, <u>Bible And Sword, How the British Came to Palestine</u>, (London: Macmillan, 1985), pp.165-166.

457 Http://philologos.org/bpr/files/a005.htm

Revelation Chapter 16

It is almost beyond question that the war prophesied by Ezekiel in the thirty-eighth and thirty-ninth chapters of his book and the war prophesied here in Revelation chapter 16 are the same war. At this point, one must question whether the war described to take place when the sixth trumpet angel sounds also refers to this same cataclysmic conflict. (See Revelation 9:13-21, along with the comments on that passage.) It is my conclusion that all three prophetic passages refer to the same climactic war. In the description of both conflicts predicted in chapters 9 and 16 of Revelation, the countries of the Euphrates drainage basin are specifically emphasized. The scope of the wars is the same, all three obviously being global.

There are exciting consequences growing out of the "War of the Worlds." Having concluded that the war predicted in Revelation 16:12-16 is the same war which is described in Ezekiel chapters 38 and 39, we can refer to the earlier prophecy to grasp some of the truly thrilling results which will grow out of this global conflict. (For greater detail refer to my commentary, The Definitive Battle for Palestine- from Amazon.)

Divine intervention will take place and be widely perceived as such. For example, God "will send a fire on Magog, and on them that dwell securely in the isles." (Ezekiel 39:6) Apparently, this punishment will be perceived as an obvious case of divine intervention. That will lead to the turning of those atheistic nations to God, for God says regarding this, "they shall know that I am Jehovah." (Ezekiel 39:6; compare also v. 7.)

More broadly, God says, "I will set my glory among the nations; and all the nations shall see my judgment that I have executed, and my hand that I have laid upon them." (Ezekiel 39:21) The cumulative import of these statements is summarized when God says, "I will magnify myself, and sanctify myself, and I will make myself known in the eyes of many nations; and they shall know that I am Jehovah." (Ezekiel 38:23)

The implications of this general turning to God should electrify the church! At that point in history the church will be working in a radically transformed environment. Instead of a hostile, God-denying world we shall have a universal family of nations openly acknowledging God! The evangelistic opportunity such circumstances will provide will be unprecedented. Will the church be ready?

Impact on Israel. Accompanying this international turning to God among the nations will be an equally thrilling and, eventually, even more significant event – the breaking up of the hardness of Israel. That people's consequent open acknowledgment of God will please him to the extent that he has declared, "neither will I hide my face any more from them; for I have poured out my Spirit upon the house of Israel." (Ezekiel 39:29) This inevitably implies that the Jews will turn to and accept Christ as their Messiah and Saviour, for it is in and through Christ that God's Spirit is bestowed. The message of these chapters in Ezekiel and Revelation, therefore, must be evaluated in conjunction with Romans chapter 11.

The conversion of the Jews to Jesus Christ will be one of the consequences of God's victory in this global conflict. This seems clearly implied in Ezekiel 39:22. (If anyone should think this verse implies conversion only to God but not to Christ, he should read it in the light of I John 2:23.) When the Jews come to Christ we will be on the threshold of the greatest period of Gospel victory of all time. "For if the casting away of them is the reconciling of the world, what shall the receiving of them be but life from the dead?" (Romans 11:15)

From these considerations it is obvious, contrary to popular opinion, that the Battle of Armageddon will not end the Christian era, nor human history. It will not mark the end of the career of humanity. Following that cataclysmic war, triumphant chapters of God's eternal plan will still unfold in human society.

It is probable that The Millennium (See Revelation chapter 20.) will take place between the ending of the events brought about by the pouring out of God's wrath by the sixth wrath angel and the work of the seventh and last wrath angel.

7. The bowl of God's wrath on the air 16:17-17:18

16:17 "And the seventh poured out his bowl upon the air; and there came forth a great voice out of the temple, from the throne, saying, It is done:"

16:17 "poured out his bowl upon the air"

The ensuing atmospheric disturbances will, no doubt, impact well known weather patterns. For example, the Indian monsoon might well be modified, causing either severe drought or massive flooding in Bangladesh, India and Pakistan, impoverishing millions. In the western hemisphere, such changes in the weather pattern will bring about basic changes in the occurrences of El Niño and La Niña, impacting plankton production upon which aquatic life and the fishing industry depend. Other disorders will undoubtedly ensue, like Hurricane Katrina which hit New Orleans in 2005, or the tsunami which engulfed Fukushima, Japan in 2011, or Hurricane Sandy which hit the eastern seaboard of the U.S. in October 2012, or the typhoon which inundated the Philippines in 2013. If the activity of the seventh wrath angel should take place following The Millennium, then we ought to consider the current perplexing irregularities in weather as mere warnings.

As a consequence of the seventh wrath angel's activities, "What if food were to become [radically] scarcer and more expensive, as seems now to be the trend? What if unfavorable climate change were to outrun our technical capacities [to cope with it]? Or what if melting glaciers leave societies such as China without fresh water? ... States are already taking action to minimize its consequences. ... If scientists continue to issue credible warnings about the consequences of climate change, it would be surprising if leaders did not conjure up new reasons for preemptive violent action, positioning their states for a new age of want."[458]

---

458 Timothy Snyder, *War No More, Why the World Has Become More Peaceful*, FOREIGN AFFAIRS, Vol. 91, No. 1, January/February 2012, p. 158. Whether persistent widespread climatic conditions are in the process of significant detrimental change or not, one should read Al Gore's book entitled An Inconvenient Truth (published by Melcher Media, 2006).

Revelation Chapter 16

16:17 "a great voice out of the temple, from the throne, saying, 'It is done'"

Since the great voice comes "from the throne," it is obviously the voice of Almighty God. His words, "It is done," probably refer to his final attempt to turn human society from evil by punitive measures. If that analysis is correct, as it probably is, then mankind, if these signs are ignored, will have reached a destiny determined by its own choice. There will be no further divine restraint. God will withdraw; man will be on his own, headed for eternal disaster. (See the comments at 15:1 under "seven plagues which are the last.")

16:18 "and there were lightnings, and voices, and thunders; and there was a great earthquake, such as was not since there were men upon the earth, so great an earthquake, so mighty."

16:18 "lightnings, and voices, and thunders"

It seems that this phrase points to both causes and effects. The causes are lightnings and thunders, both of which result from climatic disturbances. The voices are the effects. These are probably voices of consternation and confusion, accompanied by a sense of futility growing out of the massive disruption of normal climatic rhythms due to the work of the seventh wrath angel.

16:18 "a great earthquake"

First overhead, from the bowl poured out upon the air, and now underfoot by "a great earthquake," man's habitat will have become unstable, unpredictable and threatening. In view of the statement in the very next verse, that "the great city was divided into three parts," this "earthquake" probably implies a political/social upheaval. However, it will be an unprecedented disruption in human affairs because it will be "a great earthquake such as there had never been since man was on the earth, so great was that earthquake." (16:18 ESV)

16:19 "And the great city was divided into three parts, and the cities of the nations fell: and Babylon the great was remembered in the sight of God, to give unto her the cup of the wine of the fierceness of his wrath."

16:19 "the great city was divided into three parts"

This great city was first introduced in chapter 11. As noted in the comments on 11:8, the expression is not to be equated with the Babylon of chapter 18. Though sometimes Babylon is called "the great city" (17:18, see also 18:10, 16, 18-19, and 21), this "great city" "is called Sodom and Egypt." (See 11:8 and the comments there.) It is populated by "people, tribes, linguistic groups (tongues) and nations (ethnic groups)." (11:9) This "great city" is fallen human society while the other great city, Babylon, is the fallen church.

Human secular society is predicted to divide over how to respond to the enormous disruptive climate changes which will have grown out of the seventh wrath angel's pouring out of the contents of his bowl on the atmosphere. The seventh angel's actions will bring the culminating judgment in a series of disastrous developments which will have grown out of the activities of the previous six wrath angels.

Concerted and united human response to the series of judgmental divine interventions in the normal course of human life will become impossible because "the great city" will be divided. International forums like those which take place in the United Nations will become impossible because "the great city was divided into three parts." Where are the stress zones and the fracture lines, marking the areas where these detrimental divisions will occur? Perhaps one of the fracture lines will be the existing boundaries between the Muslim and non-Muslim worlds. Another might well be the boundaries between the Communist and Capitalist economic/political worlds.

16:19 "the cities of the nations fell"

These cities are constituent parts of "the great city." In many metropolitan centers, political harmony and economic activity will become so disordered that united administrative processes, which are essential to organized urban life, will become impossible. Thus, "the cities of the nations fell."

16:19 "Babylon the great was remembered in the sight of God to give unto her the cup of the wine of the fierceness of his wrath"

Since "Babylon the great" was instrumental in bringing about the social, the moral, the spiritual and the economic violations of divine standards, bringing boundless suffering on human society, that institution must now drink from "the cup of the wine of the fierceness ["fury" - ESV, NIV, "raging fury" - Stern] of his [God's] wrath."

There are many spiritual "Babylons." But the one in focus here is "Babylon the great." The expression points to the papal institution centered in Rome. (See the comments at 14:8, 17:1-5, and 18:2.)

16:20 "And every island fled away, and the mountains were not found."

Keep in mind that "the seventh [wrath angel] poured out his bowl upon the air." His activity brought unprecedented atmospheric upheavals. This statement that "every island fled away, and the mountains were not found" is a continuation of the description of the series of totally atypical, unprecedented, atmospheric phenomena. Here is widespread intense heavy fog, which prevents anyone from seeing the islands or the mountains. Since "every island fled away" this will be a global curse. Under those conditions air travel will be impossible. Highways will be impassible, clogged with vehicles whose drivers cannot discern the way to proceed. Harbor pilots will be unable to guide ships to their wharfs or docks. Emergency vehicles will have to travel at a crawl, if at all. Most aspects of normal human activity and economic life will be brought to a standstill

16:21 "And great hail, every stone about the weight of a talent, cometh down out of heaven upon men: and men blasphemed God because of the plague of the hail; for the plague thereof is exceeding great."

16:21 "great hail, every stone about the weight of a talent, cometh down out of heaven upon men"

The atmospheric abnormalities resulting from the seventh wrath angel pouring his bowl of wrath upon the air continues with hailstorms generating hailstones of unprecedented

Revelation Chapter 16

size and weight. If one estimates the danger from a hailstorm involving projectiles conforming to the description given in this prophecy, the results from such a storm will be utterly catastrophic. Even if one chooses the minimal weight known for the various standards for talents, the consequences would be widely destructive of structures (like houses, barns, warehouses, factories and public buildings) and certainly fatal to any living being which might be hit.

The validity of that last assertion is seen in this resume of the weight of various categories of talents: "A Greek, or Attic talent, was 26 kilograms (57 lb), a Roman talent was 32.3 kilograms (71 lb), an Egyptian talent was 27 kilograms (60 lb), and a Babylonian talent was 30.3 kilograms (67 lb). Ancient Israel, and other Levantine countries, adopted the Babylonian talent, but later revised the mass. The heavy common talent, used in New Testament times, was 58.9 kilograms (130 lb)."[459]

16:21 "men blasphemed God because of the plague of the hail; for the plague thereof is exceeding great"

Man's response to the plague of hail will be diametrically opposite to that which God desires. If we can discern a developing crescendo in the series of events which is completed by the seventh wrath angel pouring out his bowl of wrath upon the air, certainly the plague of these giant hailstones will be the ultimate disaster. We have seen social upheaval, political gridlock, collapse of cities, rank social discord, impenetrable fog and a harsh judgment of the false church. Tragically, none of those events, individually nor cumulatively, will have brought man to penitently acknowledge and serve God. Man, through utter impenitence, will set himself up for still harsher judgment. This collective human response to God's discipline proves the proverb which says, "Reprove not a scoffer, lest he hate thee: Reprove a wise man, and he will love thee." (Proverbs 9:8)

---

459 http://en.wikipedia.org/wiki/Talent_(measurement), accessed February 6, 2014.

Revelation Chapter 17

17:1 **"And there came one of the seven angels that had the seven bowls, and spake with me, saying, Come hither, I will show thee the judgment of the great harlot that sitteth upon many waters;"**

17:1 "the seven angels"

These seven angels were first introduced in 15:1; please see the notes there.

17:1 "the judgment (punishment - NIV) of the great harlot"

God views harlotry as a punishable crime. In contrast, current social legislation in many countries is trying, under the name of "sex work," to present it as a legitimate and honorable activity. "Laws regulating sex work vary widely among countries. It's illegal to buy and sell sex in the United States (with some exceptions). Germany legalized prostitution in 2002, and in December 2013 Canada's Supreme Court struck down the country's anti-prostitution measures. ... Decriminalization would allow sex workers access to government and international resources so they could better respond to threats like violence and trafficking, while also helping to ameliorate the social stigma and prejudice they so often face."[460]

17:1 "the great harlot"

The judgment or punishment which God is about to mete out is to fall on that entity which is depicted as "the great harlot." There are other ecclesiastical harlots with comparatively narrow and ordinary clienteles, as Plummer said of his own fellowship. He wrote, "Babylon [which is the harlot, 17:5] embraces much more than Rome, and illustrations of what she is lie nearer our own door."[461]

This "great harlot" is so well endowed that she doesn't need to carry on her sex-trade activities in secretive back-alley tawdry brothels. She practices her political/ecclesiastical sex trade in chancelleries, in executive mansions, in legislative assemblies, in embassies, in consulates, and in august ecclesiastical conclaves conducted in lavish and ornate settings, adorned with elegant and priceless paintings, statues and other dazzling objects of art. It is in those elegant environments that the papacy works out mutually beneficial agreements with susceptible and cooperative governments.

17:1 "that sitteth on many waters"

Those waters are clearly identified in 17:15 which tells us, "the waters which thou sawest, where the harlot sitteth, are peoples, and multitudes, and nations, and tongues." This phrase, "sitteth on many waters," expresses universality. Jeremiah used the same

---

460 Aziza Ahmad, *Think Again: Prostitution*, FOREIGN POLICY, January/February 2014, pp. 75-76.
461 A. Plummer, The Pulpit Commentary [on] Revelation, (Chicago: Wilcox & Follett Co., no date) p. 413.

description (51:13) to convey the wide extent of Babylon's influence. Here we find the reality to which the figure points in the word "Catholic" as used in the title "Catholic Church," which means the Universal Church.

The vision of the "great prostitute, who sits upon many waters" (NIV) helps us fit the visions of chapter 17 into their proper place in the succession of events in the Christian era. These visions are not limited to the Roman Empire in which the apostate church, the harlot, had its birth and early development. Rather, these visions take us on to a much later time when the apostate church has truly become international, sitting upon many waters.

17:2 "with whom the kings of the earth committed fornication, and they that dwell in the earth were made drunken with the wine of her fornication."

17:2 "the kings of the earth committed fornication"

Were the "kings" enticed by the harlot who hunts for patrons to help satiate her wantonness or did they beguile the harlot? According to 14:8 and 18:3 it is the harlot who will have taken the initiative but she finds eager and willing partners. For example, in the recent negotiations to restore full diplomatic relationships between Cuba and the U.S.A. it had been facilitated by a letter from Pope Francis to both President Obama and President Raúl Castro. "When Obama and Castro sealed the historic deal by telephone on Dec. 16, 2014, they found common ground in expressing their gratitude to the Pope. Most important, the Pope's letter offered symbolic shelter for both sides as they weighed the political costs of reconciliation. Francis' popularity as a religious figure in the U.S. gave Obama cover as he cut a deal with godless communists across the Straits of Florida, while the Pope's credibility as a Latin American shielded Castro as he got in bed with Yankee capitalists."[462]

Another example of the mutual benefit accruing both to the Roman Catholic Church and a cooperating government is given from a much earlier period during which there was a triangular relationship between the French, the Papacy and the Ottoman Empire.

The French used their close relationship with the Ottoman Porte, as the government of the Ottoman Empire was called, to vigorously promote the cause of Roman Catholic mission work in geographic Syria. One very effective incentive the French used to get Christian communities to acknowledge the authority of the Papacy was the offer of help they extended to protect those ships from piracy which were owned or operated by individuals and communities which had submitted to Rome. The Turkish pirates, for the most part, came from their base in Malta and had a tie with the Roman Catholic hierarchy. They agreed with the Papacy that they would not molest any ship whose captain had a certificate from the church authorities in Syria and Lebanon! "Inevitably the Syrian Christian whose property was exposed to the depredations of the corsairs, or who sought restitution of property already plundered by them, made his way to the French consuls. The consuls, in effect, then referred him to the [Roman Catholic] missionaries, for the tacit price of French intervention in these matters was

---

462 Elizabeth Dias, *The New Roman Empire*, TIME, September 28, 2015, p. 42.

Revelation Chapter 17

unquestionably submission to Rome."[463] Of course, the Catholic hierarchy saw to it that those who acknowledged the primacy of the Pope would also be cooperative citizens of the Porte.

For another example of kings committing fornication with the harlot, see the comments under 18:3.

17:2 "drunken with the wine of her fornication"

That wine is identified in 17:6 which tells us, "I saw the woman drunken with the blood of the saints and with the blood of the martyrs of Jesus." That "blood of the saints" is "the wine of her fornication." It is the intoxicant which inebriates those who "dwell on the earth." (17:2) In her relentless quest to bring everyone under her sway, the majority of persistent holdouts will eventually be killed. "The kings of the earth" have become drunk by imbibing that very same wine. Being drunken, they do totally irrational things. They use their persecuting expertise as an indispensable tool, not only in general statecraft but especially in opposing, controlling or destroying non-conforming Christians.

"Her fornication" consists of intimate, often clandestine, bonding with political powers in an attempt to gain influence and lavish resources to carry out grandiose schemes and to nullify any spiritual counter-movements. That bonding in some joint activities is so intimate that the distinction between church and state, at times, may be obscured.

17:3 "And he carried me away in the Spirit into a wilderness: and I saw a woman sitting upon a scarlet-colored beast, full of names of blasphemy, having seven heads and ten horns."

17:3 "a wilderness"

This is not the same wilderness as that mentioned in 12:14. This is the wilderness of spiritual depravity, though the depraved and fallen woman who inhabits it is incongruously and deceptively arrayed in costly apparel. (17:4) In contrast, the wilderness in chapter 12 is that of opposition, of isolation, of scorn, of indifference, of ridicule, and of rejection. Those conditions often lead to – and end in – persecution. Such circumstances may force the true church, at times, to seek a physical refuge in some remote area which could well and appropriately be called "a wilderness."

17:3 "I saw a woman"

This woman is in repulsive contrast to the glorious woman of chapter 12 who portrays the true church, the bride of Christ. This woman is for sale. She shamelessly sacrifices virtue for expediency. As verse 1 declares, this woman is "the great harlot," with whom "the kings of the earth committed fornication." She is the enormous fallen church which, though centered in Rome, has become universal. By this time, according to 17:1, she sits upon many waters.

---

463 Robert M. Haddad, <u>Syrian Christians in Muslim Society, An Interpretation</u>, (Westport, Connecticut: Greenwood Press Publishers, 1970), pp. 41-42.

17:3 "sitting upon a scarlet-colored beast"

This beast depicts servile governments which in reciprocity for favors rendered by the harlot are willing to support her. The support is clearly indicated by the fact that the harlot sits upon the beast. This relationship between the harlot and the beast is also emphasized in verse 7 which tells us it is "the beast that carrieth her." Such a supporting role was begun first by the Roman Empire, it was continued by its successor, the Holy Roman Empire, and now she especially gains support from the European Union, as well as from other governments as indicated by the designation "the kings of the earth." (17:2) Among those kings we must include the executive and legislative branches of the U.S.A., which sought the harlot's help in restoring diplomatic relations with Cuba. In partial reimbursement, the Pope was feted in Washington D.C., in New York and in Philadelphia. That support, both clandestine and open, constitutes that harlot's hire. (See an example under 17:2 "the kings of the earth committed fornication.") That hire is paid by secular civil governments. Collectively, they have become persecuting, vicious, and blood-stained, functioning as the secular arm of the spiritual entity. Thus, the beast is depicted as "a scarlet-colored beast."

17:3 "names of blasphemy"

These names are those of the "scarlet-colored beast," not of the harlot. Her three-fold name is given in 17:5. These names are ideological, legal, political and sociological titles and slogans. They represent legal texts and enactments made by politicians, legislators and judicial bodies. They are made by those who hold philosophies that are mysterious and abominable which are based on the assumption of total human autonomy, a stance which recognizes no higher power than that of the state itself. The category is illustrated currently in the U.S.A. by names or titles of judicial decisions, like "Roe v. Wade" which "legalizes" the killing of human fetuses and the recent U.S. Supreme Court ruling that by endorsing homosexual unions as marriage contravenes Jesus' definition of marriage which is given in Matthew 19:3-6.

17:3 "having seven heads and ten horns"

This description has been used only two times previously, in 12:3 and 13:1. However, in this third occurrence the two component parts are distinctly identified. Accordingly, we are told in 17:9 that "the seven heads are seven mountains upon which the woman sitteth." We are told in 17:10 that those mountains represent kings. Similarly, in 17:12 we are told that "the ten horns that thou sawest are ten kings who have received no kingdom as yet; but they receive authority as kings with the beast for one hour." This obviously describes a political entity which is distinct from those mentioned in 12:3 and 13:1 but which has enough similarity to them to justify the use of the same descriptive features, their heads and horns. For further details, please consult the comments made on 12:3, 13:1, 17:9 and 17:12.

17:4 "And the woman was arrayed in purple and scarlet, and decked with gold and precious stone and pearls, having in her hand a golden cup full of abominations, even the unclean things of her fornication,"

Revelation Chapter 17

17:4 **"the woman was arrayed in purple and scarlet, and decked with gold and precious stone and pearls"**

The colors "purple and scarlet, [are] the royal colors, the colors of luxury and splendor."[464] "These colors, purple and scarlet, are characteristic of the vestments of the Roman hierarchy, scarlet being particularly identified with the cardinals, who are called, 'princes of the church.'"[465] Globally using such furnishings and accouterments could only be achieved by very significant expenditures, large enough to enrich craftsmen and merchants. (See 18:3, 11, and 15.)

17:4 **"having in her hand a golden cup full of abominations, even the unclean things of her fornication"**

A "golden cup full of abominations" is a revolting and sickening incongruity. The apostle Paul has reminded us that, "in a great house there are not only vessels of gold and silver but also of wood and clay, some for honorable use, some for dishonorable." (II Timothy 2:20 ESV) It is obvious that by using a golden cup, intended for honorable use, to carry the slop generated by her repulsive abominations, the harlot, behind her facade of grandeur, in reality cares absolutely nothing about propriety or what is right. The golden cup is used to deceive observers about its contents.

What is really in the harlot's golden cup? An example comes from Pope "John XXIII, an anti-pope [who was] deposed by the Council of Constance in 1415. The most scandalous charges [against him] were suppressed: the Vicar of Christ was only accused of piracy, murder, rape, sodomy and incest."[466]

More recent confirmation of what is contained in the harlot's cup comes from the endless international arraignments and convictions of priests and bishops ultimately being fined and/or imprisoned for repeatedly committing scandalous, bestial acts of pedophilia. One of the factors causing the endless and boundless current scourge of pedophilia among priests in the Roman Catholic Church is the hierarchy's prohibition against marriage for the priesthood. This arrangement is also another key factor which helps us identify the false church. For, "the Spirit saith expressly, that in later times some shall fall away from the faith, giving heed to seductive spirits and doctrines of demons, through the hypocrisy of men who speak lies, branded in their own conscience as with a hot iron; <u>forbidding to marry</u>, and commanding to abstain from meats, which God created to be received with thanksgiving by them that believe and know the truth." (I Timothy 4:1-3)

17:5 **"and upon her forehead a name written, MYSTERY, BABYLON THE GREAT, THE MOTHER OF THE HARLOTS AND OF THE ABOMINATIONS OF THE EARTH."**

17:5 **"upon her forehead a name written"**

Several commentators say that at the time John was writing the book of Revelation, prostitutes, while on duty in the brothel, would display their trade name written on a cloth band bound around their foreheads. They undoubtedly did this to elicit business from old

---

464 William Barclay, <u>The Revelation of John</u>, Vol. II, (Philadelphia: The Westminster Press, 1976), p. 162.
465 Lee G. Tomlinson, <u>The Wonder Book of the Bible: A Commentary On the Book of Revelation</u>, (Joplin, Missouri: College Press, 1963), p. 286.
466 John Julius Norwich, <u>Absolute Monarchs, A History of the Papacy</u>, (New York: Random House, 2011), p. 453.

customers who might be seeking for them. Similarly, this theological/ecclesiastical/political prostitute, by her activities, clearly identifies herself. Yet, amazingly, Satan is able to confuse people about the identity of the false church even though her identifying features are conspicuously displayed.

Just as the beast is identified by its heads and horns (17:8), so the harlot is identified by her name which she flaunts openly. It is the name of sexual sensuality displayed universally through news reports of priests involved in pedophilia and financial scandal facilitated through the Vatican Bank to which Pope Francis called global attention, saying, shortly after beginning his pontificate, that he would have it investigated. For details on the Vatican's grievous financial improprieties, see Gerald Posner's book, <u>God's Bankers, A History of Money and Power at the Vatican</u>. Posner clearly and copiously documented the Vatican bank's violation of honesty. Still, surprisingly, most people do not recognize this institution for what it is. To make the truth even more obvious, the harlot is further identified by a three-fold name:

17:5 "mystery"

This word, "mystery," is the first segment of the harlot's name. It was identified early in the apostolic period of the Christian era. The apostle Paul alerted the Thessalonian Christians to its subtle existence when he wrote, "the mystery of lawlessness doth already work: only there is one that restraineth now, until he be taken out of the way." (II Thessalonians 2:7) Why will the leadership of churches, knowing what is right, embrace lawless policies and practices? Such behavior is mysterious. It is at least part of "the mystery of lawlessness." It is also mysterious how churches which flaunt God's will are so often able to subtly conceal that fact from the general public.

17:5 "Babylon the Great"

This second element in the harlot's name means "great confusion." The name "Babylon" is derived from the word "Babel" and it is from this association that the name means confusion. The Genesis account tells us that "the name of it [the city which was to reach to heaven] was called Babel because Jehovah did there confound the language of all the earth." (Genesis 11:9)

Accordingly, the corrupt church perpetuates a confusing mixture composed of tattered shreds and bits of biblical truth and practices with pagan ideas and rituals which have been made one of the religious anchors of their community. But because the harlot carries out her program of confusion with rituals of great solemnity, pomp and ceremony, rendered mystical by the fragrance and smoke of burning incense, by the ringing of bells, by stately processions and incantations uttered in Latin, all seems sacred. For many people, these procedures lend credence and propriety to practices and teachings which embody great error and falsehood. Multitudes think something grand, high, sacred and significant must be taking place. But, they are confused by Babylon, the epitome of confusion. When the false church reaches the pinnacle of its power, this passage predicts that it should appropriately be called "Babylon the Great."

Revelation Chapter 17

17:5 "the mother of harlots and of the abominations of the earth"

The expression "mother of harlots" constitutes the third part of her name and tells us that she has, in the course of her career, spawned equally lewd daughters. But the mother excels them all and is therefore able to call herself "great"as in "Babylon the Great." Her daughters are ethnic and national churches, which behold and covet the opulence and treasures which this mother church has amassed. They have consequently given themselves over to the same pattern of abominable theological promiscuity, leading to church-state cooperation and connivance, in hopes of achieving similar "success."

17:6 "And I saw the woman drunken with the blood of the saints, and with the blood of the martyrs of Jesus. And when I saw her, I wondered with a great wonder."

"The blood of the saints" is "the wine of her fornication" mentioned in 17:2. We know this because this verse clearly indicates that "the blood of the saints" is the intoxicating drink which has made the harlot drunk. She is "drunken with the blood of the saints." Being drunk, the harlot does not acknowledge reality nor heed exhortations which are based on facts. Thus, hopes of reformation and reclamation are only vain aspirations. Usually, we think of women as more compassionate and caring than men, but uniquely, this is an extremely vicious and murderous woman.

Foxe's <u>Book of Martyrs</u>, first published in 1563, has preserved a sweeping account of the murderous brutalities of the false church up to the middle of the sixteenth century. For evidence that this bloody persecution goes on currently, see the comments under 19:2. For a current book which catalogs the worldwide persecution of Christians, be sure to consult John L. Allen Jr.'s <u>The Global War on Christians</u>, copyrighted in 2013 and published by the Image trademark of Random House. Though Allen is the senior correspondent for the *National Catholic Reporter* as well as the senior Vatican analyst for CNN, he does not hesitate to document the bloody persecutions carried out by the Catholic Church. His discussion of Catholic persecution of Protestants in Mexico is unsparing.

17:7 "And the angel said unto me, Wherefore didst thou wonder? I will tell thee the mystery of the woman, and of the beast that carrieth her, which hath the seven heads and the ten horns."

17:7 "Wherefore didst thou wonder?"

Our wonder or "astonishment" (Stern) or "amazement" (NRSV) comes from inattention to developing trends till their reality finally bursts open before us.

17:7 "the mystery of the woman, and of the beast"

While the identity of the woman has been made clear, that of the beast may still be obscure. This is the "scarlet-colored beast, full of names of blasphemy, having seven heads and ten horns," which was mentioned in 17:3. (Please see the comments there.)

17:8 "The beast that thou sawest was, and is not; and is about to come up out of the abyss, and to go into perdition. And they that dwell on the earth shall wonder, *they* whose name hath not been written in the book of life from the foundation of the world, when they behold the beast, how that he was and is not, and shall come."

> **17:8** "The beast that thou sawest was, and is not; and is about to come up out of the abyss"

For the identity of this beast, see 16:3 under "out of the mouth of the beast." Since this beast is "to come up out of the abyss," the impetus and energizing force empowering the reappearance of this beast, at its most fundamental level, is satanic. It comes out of the abyss. (See 9:2 under "he opened the pit of the abyss.") Based on its origin, this entity will ultimately play a bestial role in European and international affairs.

This prophetic prediction seems to have had a double fulfillment. However, the very next verse (17:9) alerts us to the difficulty of identifying the beast which "was, and is not, and is about to come up out of the abyss." One of the most difficult aspects in recognizing this recurring beast is determining the proper identity of the kings mentioned in verses 9-12. The words "about to come up out of the abyss" probably had **their first fulfillment** beginning with "the coronation of Charlemagne [which took place in 800]. [It] was regarded by his contemporaries as the restoration or renewal of the Roman Empire, more than three hundred years after the deposition of Romulus Augustulus."[467] (Regarding the deposition of Romulus Augustulus, see the comments under 8:12, "third part.")

The coronation of Charlemagne marked the birth of the Holy Roman Empire. His coronation was a very dramatic moment on Christmas day in the year 800 A.D. On that august occasion "Charles Martel's grandson Charlemagne climbed the steps of St. Peter's on his knees, prostrated himself before the holy father, and was crowned Augustus, Emperor of the Romans."[468]

The emergence of the Holy Roman Empire seemed much like the resurrection of the old Roman Empire. Charlemagne, "in little more than a generation, had raised the Kingdom of the Francs from just one of the many semi-tribal European states to a single political unit of vast extent, unparalleled since the days of imperial Rome."[469]

Charlemagne was "a seven-foot, bull-necked, pot-bellied figure with the girth of a Japanese sumo wrestler, a long straight nose, thin lips, narrow black mustache, full beard. … He exudes the power of a man who has never lost a battle during sixty campaigns waged west to Spain, south to Sicily, north to the Baltic, east past Poland and Hungary, deporting ten-thousand here, massacring forty-five hundred there, baptizing whole populations into Christianity with the sword or with water – it was one or the other – governing 1,615 states all over Europe, not fearing anyone on the face of the earth. Men have never known a power like his."[470]

---

467 Hutton Webster, World History, (Boston: D.C. Heath & Co. Publishers, 1921), p 163.
468 Nigel Cliff, Holy War, (New York: Harper Collins Books, 2011), p. 22.
469 John Julius Norwich, Absolute Monarchs, A History of the Papacy, (New York: Random House, 2011), p. 55.
470 Malachi Martin, The Decline and Fall of the Roman Church, (New York: G.P. Putnam's Sons, 1981), p. 93.

Revelation Chapter 17

Long after Charlemagne, rulers of the Habsburg Empire "managed to get themselves regularly elected to the position of Holy Roman emperor – a title much diminished in real power since the high Middle Ages but still sought after by princes eager to play a larger role in German and general European affairs."[471] The actual end of the Holy Roman Empire, which had become embodied in the Habsburg Monarchy, took place on November 11, 1918 when the last occupant of the throne "'renounced' his state duties, without making a formal renunciation of the throne."[472]

After the 1918 death of the Holy Roman Empire, which was at that time embodied in the Habsburg Monarchy, **a second and more current fulfillment** of how the extinct beast will come once again into existence has taken place. In this second scenario, the words, "the beast that thou sawest was, and is not; and is about to come up out of the abyss" takes us to a point further into the twentieth and on into the twenty-first century. However, even at this more contemporary point we should be reminded that, "Charlemagne was the first ruler since the Greeks to talk of 'Europe' as a single entity. And now, many years later, the French-German alliance is the basis for the European Union, and they naturally look back to Charlemagne as a sort of patron saint. The Charlemagne Prize remains the E.U.'s highest award for people who have done most to promote the spirit of European friendship and unity."[473]

This second and far more current fulfillment of the vision of the beast which was to come up out of the abyss points to the birth of the European Union. Its birth took place because since World War II there has been and continues to be, though with notably decreasing intensity, a momentum leading to European integration. That momentum was born by the conviction of those "Europeans who passionately believed that reconstruction [from WWII] and reconciliation [after the flaming hatreds which had brought on and sustained that terrible war] had to go hand in hand with greater political unity."[474] The development of the European Union had its inception in a speech on the "United States of Europe" by Winston Churchill at the University of Zurich on September 19, 1946. The vision developed in 1951 through the European Coal and Steel Community (ECSC) to the European Economic Community in 1957 and then eventually on to the current European Union.

The European Union is "the budding European super-state of our own era, concentrated in Europe's medieval core, with Charlemagne's capital city of Aachen (Aix-la-Chapelle) still at its very center."[475] To determine whether this is the correct identity of the beast that "is about to come up out of the abyss" (17:8), we must consider the supranational, multi-state structure of the European Union. Its government is carried out by The Commission, which is, "composed of twenty-seven Commissioners, one appointed by each member country [as the number of the member countries increases or decreases, correspondingly the number of Commissioners varies].[476] The Commission supervises implementation of

---

471 Paul Kennedy, The Rise and Fall of the Great Powers, (New York: Random House, 1987), p. 32.
472 Robin Okey, The Habsburg Monarchy, (New York: St. Martin's Press, 2001), p. 395.
473 Seán Lang, European History for Dummies, 2nd Ed., (West Sussex, England: John Wiley & Sons Ltd., 2011), p. 88.
474 Matthias Matthijs, *Britain and Europe: the End of the Affair?*, CURRENT HISTORY, March 2014, p. 93.
475 Robert D. Kaplan, The Revenge of Geography, (New York: Random House, 2012), p. 139.
476 "Each member state has one commissioner. The Treaty of Nice rules, however, stipulate that after the EU has 27 members, the number of commissioners will have to be lower than the number of member states, a rotating formula which would then be decided by the European Council." - Joaquin Roy and Aimee Kanner, The A to Z of the European Union, (Toronto: The Scarecrow Press, Inc., 2009), p. xlix.

E.U. treaties, initiates and implements E.U. policy, applies E.U. law in member states, transacts negotiations with non-member states, manages E.U. funds and budgets, and acts as the international mouthpiece of the E.U., enabling the member states to speak with one voice in international forums like the W.T.O. [World Trade Organization]."[477]

In determining whether the E.U. is the revival of the old Roman Empire which is depicted by the words, "was and is not and shall come," (17:8) consider those Commissioners as the probable reality toward which those "kings" point who are mentioned in 17:9-12. If the Commissioners continue to exercise their authority according to the original concept of those who initially conceived of bringing Europe back to a status like that of the Roman Empire, Europe will be "managed by experts and officials with scant attention paid to the wishes of its beneficiaries."[478] Those Commissioners will then be functioning essentially like kings.

"The Commission is centrally involved in E.U. decision-making at all levels and on all fronts. With an array of power resources and policy instruments at its disposal, and strengthened by the frequent unwillingness or inability of other E.U. institutions to provide clear leadership, the Commission is at the very heart of the E.U. system."[479]

The revival of the Roman Empire expressed by the words "shall come" (17:8) might easily be equated with the fact that "the E.U. aims to integrate the economies, coordinate social developments and bring about political union of the member states. [Consequently], effective December 31, 1992, there was no restriction on the movement of goods, services, capital, workers, and tourists within the E.U. There are also common agricultural, fisheries, and nuclear research policies. [Failure to live up to this egalitarian standard has brought about dissatisfaction among some member states, a condition which eventually may become a fatal defection.]

"Leaders of the member nations (12 at the time) met December 9-11, 1991 in Maastricht, the Netherlands, and signed a treaty, the Maastricht Treaty, which went into effect in 1993, [which] committed the organization to launching a common currency; establishing common foreign policy; and taking a leading role in social policy among other issues. The European Central Bank was established in 1998. In 1999, 11 of the then-15 E.U. countries began using the euro. By 2002, national currencies in those 11 countries and Greece were removed from circulation and replaced with the euro as the only currency of legal tender. E.U. peacekeeping forces replaced NATO forces in Macedonia, March 31, 2003, the first such mission for the organization. A Treaty Establishing a Constitution for Europe was signed in 2004 by E.U. members but was never ratified."[480]

The political history of the beast causes wonder, because it "was, and is not; and is about to come up out of the abyss and go into perdition." (17:8) The words "is not" probably refer to the complete disintegration of the Roman Empire in the West, bringing about the fragmentation of Europe. Such dissolution of European unity occurred twice, first in 476 at the breakup of the Roman Empire and, second, in 1918 with the termination of the Holy Roman Empire. In both cases, inevitably, the Roman Catholic Church was also

---

477 John W. Wright, ed., The New York Times 2011 Almanac, (New York: Penguin Books, 2010), p. 521.
478 Tony Judt, Postwar, A History of Europe Since 1945, (New York: Penguin Books, 2005), p. 727.
479 Neill Nugent, The Government and Politics of the European Union, 6th Ed., (Durham: Duke University Press, 2006), p. 149.
480 Sarah Janssen, ed., The World Almanac, (New York City: Infobase Learning, 2013), p. 742.

Revelation Chapter 17

weakened. That reality is clear if we remember that it had been European political power, beginning with Constantine, which gave the papacy its power and strength. (See 14:8 under "Hunger for precedence.") For just one subsequent instance, remember that Pepin, son of Charles Martel and father of Charlemagne, gave the Papal States to the pope. (See also the comments under 14:8.) In return, the harlot facilitated and legitimized the efforts of her lovers' rapacious role in political power. For example, the pope put the crown on Emperor Charlemagne's head.

Just in our time it appears that the beast is again coming "out of the abyss" in the shape of the European Community, now called the European Union (E.U.), with its newly devised common economic system. How successful the E.U. may become was predicted in a confident statement by former French President Giscard d'Estaing. In 1988, he said, "Europe will be a bigger country than the U.S. Despite difficulties and setbacks, the Common Market is moving steadily, inevitably toward a unity of markets, productivity and currency. By the year 2010, the entity that is Europe will be number one in the world's economy. The U.S. will be second, China third and Japan fourth."[481]

The French president's prediction is, up to this point, obviously wrong about economic developments but has proven to be correct about the E.U. becoming "a bigger country than the U.S." By 2010 the E.U. had become "a gigantic market of nearly a half billion people."[482] In contrast, the U.S.A. in 2012 had a population of only "313,847,465."[483] We should ask if perhaps President Giscard d'Estaing's error might have been only one of timing. Will there be a greater fulfillment of his prediction at a later date, perhaps in the near future? In any case, his prescient statement of the future expansion and vigor of the new Europe did not foresee the ultimate coming breakup of the E.U., which is clearly predicted in 17:11 in the words "go into perdition." Is Brexit the beginning?

The French president's prediction of America's diminishing role, certainly in Europe if not worldwide, was confirmed in the famous statement by President Obama, during the campaign to oust Mu'ammar Qaddafi from power in Libya, that America was "leading from behind!" Later, it was again substantiated by the policy statement of the Obama administration that, to meet China's rising threat in the Pacific, America was making "a pivot to the East." Inevitably, that "pivot" implies diminished attention to the European theater of world affairs. The vigorous American foreign policy, vis a vis Europe, which was demonstrated in the term of President Reagan when Jim Baker was U.S. Secretary of State, who led America's decisive intervention in the Balkan War (which had erupted

---

481 Malcolm S. Forbes, "Fact and Comment," FORBES, (April 25, 1988), p. 31. It is important to realize that the unity of Europe will not be achieved in one unbroken crescendo of success. The Serbian-Bosnian conflict, for example, tells us in unmistakable terms that Europe is still politically weak and divided. The vulnerability of the European currency system speaks eloquently of the economic weakness still facing Europe. Millman paints this second reality in graphic colors: "When the governments of Europe decided to implement a common monetary policy, they had a long-term program in mind to overcome centuries of division by establishing a historic union. Traders didn't care about that dream. For several years during the 1980s, the European monetary system was a profitable trading opportunity. Then in 1992, European governments showed by small words and acts that they might not be quite as committed to the program of unity as they originally said they were. Traders immediately reversed course, sold off some European currencies, bought others, and in the process demolished the European monetary system. Some European officials saw in the activities of the traders evidence of a conspiracy to wreck European unity. But that view gives traders credit for being more broad minded than they are. If European unity had continued to be a profitable project, the traders would certainly have supported it." [Gregory J. Millman, The Vandals' Crown, (New York: The Free Press, 1995), p. xiii]

482 John W. Wright, ed., The New York Times 2011 Almanac, (New York: Penguin Books, 2010), p. 519.

483 Sarah Janssen, ed., The World Almanac, (New York City: Infobase Learning, 2013), p. 735.

following the breakup of Tito's Yugoslavia), will very probably not be duplicated in the very near future.[484]

As we behold the current ongoing metamorphosis of Europe we know the whole world will be highly influenced by the resultant entity which ultimately comes into being. One vital question in determining the future course and influence of the new Europe is, who will set its ideological direction and emphasis? Keep in mind that the one who rides the "beast" (See "a woman sitting upon …" - 17:3 and "the beast that carrieth her" - 17:7.) is the one who has the reigns in her hands. Consequently, in some crucial sense, the harlot will guide or direct the beast. Therefore, we should expect a dramatically increased influence of the Roman Catholic Church in her guidance of the reinvigorated Europe. It is emerging before our eyes. Right on cue, Pope Francis is beguiling political figures across a wide spectrum of countries. His ability to do this was highlighted in the December 23, 2013 issue of TIME magazine in which, in addition to putting his full-figure color photo on the cover, the editors devoted twenty-one pages to extolling the magnetism, dynamism and compassion of the new pope. They made him their "PERSON OF THE YEAR."

In the first accolade in TIME's presentation, Nancy Gibbs wrote, "Rarely has a new player on the world stage captured so much attention so quickly – young and old, faithful and cynical – as has Pope Francis. … His pulpit is visible to the ends of the earth."[485] Current adulation of Pope Francis is not limited to TIME magazine. A glossy 68-page weekly is being published in Italy under the title, "Il Mio Papa," (My Pope). It offers "a glossy medley of papal pronouncements and photographs, along with peeks into his personal life. Each weekly issue will include a pull-out centerfold of the Pope, accompanied by a quote. … The magazine also hopes to transmit the down-to-earth, no-nonsense advice that Francis offers during his weekly encounters with the faithful in St. Peter's Square and elsewhere."[486] The Vatican "looks to reassert its role as a global player after several years in which that role was reduced."[487] As pointed out before, the Vatican maintains seventy-eight papal diplomatic missions around the globe.

"Official Christianity had long overlaid and accustomed itself to ignore those strange teachings of Jesus of Nazareth from which it had arisen. The Roman church, clinging tenaciously to its possession of the title of *pontifex maximus* [the supreme pontiff],[488] had long since abandoned its appointed task of achieving the Kingdom of Heaven. It was preoccupied with the revival of Roman ascendency on earth, which it conceived of as its inheritance. <u>It had become a political body, using the faith and needs of simple men to forward its schemes.</u> (*Underlining added.*) It clung to the tradition of the Roman Empire and to the idea that it was the natural method of European unity. Europe, in a series of attempts to restore it, drifted towards a dreary imitation and revival of the misconceived failures of the past.

---

484 Students who wish to analyze the competition between nations for international leadership should read Peter Zeihan's <u>The Accidental Super Power: The Next Generation of American Preeminence and the Coming Global Disorder</u>, (New York: Twelve, Hachette Book Group, 2014).
485 Nancy Gibbs, *The Choice,* TIME, December 23, 2013, p. 44.
486 Elisabetta Povoledo, *A New Magazine for Fans of the Vatican's Biggest Star,* <u>The New York Times</u>, March 5, 2014, p. A4.
487 Herb Keinon and Eric J. Lyman, *Netanyahu in Rome: Western Sanctions Regime Against Iranians Already Unraveling,* <u>The Jerusalem Post: Christian Edition</u>, January 2014, p. 5.
488 The word pontiff comes from the Latin *pontifax* which means a bridge maker. When used in reference to the pope, it implies that he is the one who can bridge the gap between man and God.

Revelation Chapter 17

"For eleven centuries, from Charlemagne onwards, 'Emperors' and 'Caesars' of this line and that come and go in the history of Europe like fancies in a disordered mind. We shall have to tell of a great process of mental growth in Europe, of enlarged horizons and accumulating power, but it was a process that went on independently of, and in spite of, the political forms of the time, until at last it shattered those forms altogether. Europe, during those eleven centuries of the imitation Caesars which began with Charlemagne, and which closed only in the monstrous bloodshed of 1914-1918, has been like a busy factory owned by a somnambulist, who is sometimes quite unimportant and sometimes disastrously in the way. Or, rather than a somnambulist, let us say by a corpse that magically simulates a kind of life. The Roman Empire staggers, sprawls, is thrust off the stage, and reappears, and – if we may carry the image one step further – it is the church of Rome which plays the part of the magician and keeps the corpse alive."[489]

17:9 **"Here is the mind that hath wisdom. The seven heads are seven mountains, on which the woman sitteth:"**

17:9 "the mind that hath wisdom"

Please notice the following translations of 17:9: "Here is the clue for those who can interpret it" [NEB], "Here is a problem for a profound mind!" [Goodspeed], "Here is something for the intelligent to ponder" [Berkeley], "This calls for a mind that has wisdom" [NRSV]. This verse acknowledges that gaining the proper understanding and identification of the beast, the harlot, a multiple group of kings mentioned in verses 9-12, and their interactions, is difficult. At this point, each of us who seeks understanding must remember that God resists the proud but gives grace to the humble. (I Peter 5:5 and James 4:6) We also need to remember the great invitation to those who lack wisdom. We are invited to "ask of God who giveth to all liberally and upbraideth not." (James 1:5)

17:9 "seven heads"

These are the heads of the rapacious political entity known as the "scarlet-colored beast." (17:3) To gain a proper understanding of the time and reality to which this prophecy points, it is essential to realize that it does not depict the beast that "was, and is not" (17:7) but the beast which "is about to come up out of the abyss (17:8). Thus, the kings are not those of the old Roman Empire, but of the resurrected one, most probably those commissioners of the current European Union to which reference has been made already.

The structure of the European Union is extremely complicated. It often "seems incomprehensible to outsiders. Former U.S. Secretary of State, Madeleine Albright, weary of dealing with the different E.U. high-level officials responding to varied interests, once allegedly exploded in frustration: 'To understand the European Union you must be French or very intelligent ... or both.'"[490] Secretary Albright's consternation is paralleled by that of Henry Kissinger who is reported to have asked, "If I want to phone Europe – who do I call?"[491] Obviously, therefore, this is for "the mind that hath wisdom."

---

489 H. G. Wells, The Outline of History, Vol. I, (New York: Doubleday & Co., Inc, 1971), pp. 543-544.
490 Joaquin Roy and Aimee Kanner, The A to Z of the European Union, (Toronto: The Scarecrow Press, Inc., 2009), p. l.
491 Tim Marshall, Prisoners of Geography, (New York: Scribners, 2015), p. 97.

17:9 "seven mountains"

These mountains are identified in the very next verse. They are neither geological nor geographical mountains like the seven hills upon which Rome was situated, to which many commentators would point us. Rather, they are political mountains. The term points to seven prominent or outstanding "kings" or rulers.

17:9 "on which the woman sitteth"

From this description it is obvious that those political powers will give great support to the Roman Catholic Church.

17:10 "and they are seven kings; the five are fallen, the one is, the other is not yet come; and when he cometh, he must continue a little while."

17:10 "seven kings"

The reality to which the figure "seven mountains" (17:9) points is here in 17:10 explicitly identified as a group or, more probably, a succession of "seven kings." Many commentators take the position that the term "seven kings" is also figurative and should be understood as kingdoms or empires. Their position is not tenable because it is highly unlikely and biblically unprecedented that one figure of speech should only point to another figurative expression which then finally points to some objective reality.

17:10 "five are fallen, the one is, the other is not yet come"

The European Union seems to give the counterpoint which corresponds to this intricate prophetic description. The comments made here in reference to the European Union are made on the assumption that, though there are many divisions in the E.U., it is not on the brink of immediate extinction. However, on May 25, 2014 the French anti-E.U.-far-right National Front party won 25% of French votes. This catapulted Marine Le Pen, an uncompromising anti-E.U. politician, to national prominence. The night of her victory, she said, "Tonight is a massive rejection of the European Union. ... I believe this is the end of the E.U. ... I don't think the E.U. will be surviving in a few years."[492] Unknowingly, she seems to point to the reality prophesied in 17:11, which says, "the beast ... goeth into perdition."

That kind of political upset not only took place in France, but also in Britain, Austria, Sweden, Denmark and Greece, where far-right parties made strong showings. We should give full attention to the difficulties of the twenty-eight members of the E.U., as well as to this broad-based political upheaval. Still, it seems doubtful that the E.U. will prove to be ephemeral. It was "born out of the ashes of WWII in a passionate attempt to prevent the blood-drenched continent from ever going to war again."[493]

17:10 "when he cometh, he must continue a little while"

Christians must keep a vigilant eye focused on the power struggles which inevitably will continue within the hierarchy of the European Union. Undoubtedly, this "king" who though he will continue only "a little while" probably will prove to have had a notably

---

[492] Vivienne Walt, *Union Buster*, TIME, June 9, 2014, p. 31.
[493] Vivienne Walt, *Union Buster*, TIME, June 9, 2014, p. 31.

Revelation Chapter 17

longer tenure in office than those who will have preceded him. By this contrast, alert Christians will undoubtedly be able to pinpoint the office holder described here when he, in the course of events, comes to power.

17:11 "And the beast that was, and is not, is himself also an eighth, and is of the seven; and he goeth into perdition."

There will be a unique succession or perhaps concurrent cooperation of seven kings (seven cooperating E.U. Commissioners?) in the new Europe which consists of or is being formed by the European Union. During the tenure of the seventh king an eighth king will come to power with the full cooperation of the seventh. The eighth king will put policies in place which will constitute a reversion to the old classical Roman Empire, "the beast that was and is not." However, this startling resuscitation of the old Roman Empire will not endure. It will ultimately go into perdition ("destruction" - ESV, NIV, NRSV).

17:12 "And the ten horns that thou sawest are ten kings, who have received no kingdom as yet; but they receive authority as kings, with the beast, for one hour."

The reality of these kings without a kingdom, who eventually will "receive authority as kings, with the beast, for one hour," seems to be fulfilled by the European Union's system of rule, in which "The chairmanship of the Council of Ministers [is] rotated every six months, with each [participating] country getting to host a self-promoting biannual European Conference – a system already much disliked by the Union's full-time administrators. The prospect of such a circus shambling around through twenty-five different capitals, from Lisbon to Ljubljana, was plainly absurd. Moreover, a decision-taking system designed for six member-states and already cumbersome for twelve, much less fifteen, would simply grind to a halt with fifty European Commissioners (two from each country), or a European Council representing twenty-five member-states[494] – each with a power of veto."[495]

The Commissioners of the European Union seem to fulfill the description of the kings described in verses 9-12 much closer than the Emperors of the Holy Roman Empire ever did. Those Emperors served in a straight-line succession, one after the other. In contrast, the E.U. Commissioners, until their rotation puts them in power, are like the "ten kings who have received no kingdom as yet; but they receive authority as kings with the beast, for one hour." (17:12)

17:13 "These have one mind, and they give their power and authority unto the beast."

17:13 "these have one mind"

The pronoun "these" refers to the "ten kings" (17:12). Having "one mind" probably points to them being committed to one united political ideology, platform or policy, that of the European Union. Also, the words "one mind" probably point to their loyalty to European Union principles, rules and procedures.

---

494 As of February 20, 2014 there are 28 member states in the EU.
495 Tony Judt, <u>Postwar, A History of Europe Since 1945</u>, (New York: Penguin Books, 2005), p. 728.

17:13 "they give their power and authority unto the beast"

The beast is the scarlet-colored beast which we encountered at 17:3. Giving their power to the beast indicates they will not only do their utmost to promote the E.U., but will also continue the fornicatious relationship of previous European nations which supported the corrupt church.

17:14 "These shall war against the Lamb, and the Lamb shall overcome them, for he is Lord of lords, and King of kings; and they also shall overcome that are with him, called and chosen and faithful."

17:14 "These shall war against the Lamb"

Political Europe, during the time of the ten kings, will try to stifle every truly Christian movement.

17:14 "the Lamb shall overcome them ... they also shall overcome that are with him"

The words "they also shall overcome that are with him," not only tell us that some true Christians will survive in Europe, but further, with the word "overcome," this verse seems to predict a revival of true Christianity in Europe. Christ, "The Lamb," will bring about this triumph, this overcoming, through or by those who "are with him."

World War I, because of its many millions of meaningless battle-field deaths, "fundamentally undermined the faith of tens of millions of people in the liberal, moral, economic and political values that formed the foundation of the Western World."[496] Among those values which were swept away were the basic concepts of the teachings of Christ. That dismal situation was even further greatly exacerbated by the horrible trauma of World War II.

Without a peer, C. S. Lewis, stood almost alone trying to stop the avalanche of destructive skepticism in Great Britain. His powerful Christian apologetics, like those in *Mere Christianity* and in *Miracles, a Preliminary Study*, saved many from the abyss of godless unbelief. Still, empty or redeployed church buildings all over London tell us which way the tide went.

As shocking as the spiritual crisis is in Great Britain, it is much worse in mainland Europe. "It is not just religion that has disappeared from Europe – so has the memory of what a religiously ordered, or even a religiously inclined, society was like. A good definition of religion for most modern Europeans might be 'an irrational opinion, strongly held.'"[497]

Spiritually, Europe is the counterpart of galactic black holes. Victory in the face of such intense spiritual anti-gravity, as is clearly foreseen in this verse, will greatly glorify the power of Christ working in and through his people.

17:15 "And he saith unto me, The waters which thou sawest, where the harlot sitteth, are peoples, and multitudes, and nations, and tongues."

---

496 Steve Forbes, *True Catastrophes*, FORBES, August 24, 2009, p. 13.
497 Christopher Caldwell, Reflections on the Revolution in Europe: Immigration, Islam, and the West, (New York: Doubleday, 2009) p. 181.

Revelation Chapter 17

This verse explains the statement given in 17:1 about "the great harlot that sitteth upon many waters." The centuries-long life of the harlot encompasses many variations in fortune, ranging from periods of dominance to times of hobbling constriction. At the point which this verse describes, the harlot will be enjoying a period of triumph. Her influence will be worldwide, impacting peoples, multitudes, nations, and tongues ("languages" - NIV, ESV). With the enthronement of Pope Francis, a reinvigorated Roman Catholic Church seems to be entering into such a period of vigorous, worldwide impact.

17:16 "And the ten horns which thou sawest, and the beast, these shall hate the harlot, and shall make her desolate and naked, and shall eat her flesh, and shall burn her utterly with fire."

The worldwide globe-spanning success of the harlot will have been achieved through the help of the beast. (See 17:3, 17:7, and 17:17-18.) But a time in the future, like similar times in the past, will arise when the beast will hate the harlot. One example from the past of such hate was that which arose over the question of who had the right to appoint church officers. "For the church, an immediate result [of the rise of feudalism] was that each lord functioned much as had the great emperors – where possible [they indulged in] hiring and firing churchmen at will and [were] using the church as a support of personal politics. But whereas the ecclesiastical interventions of Charlemagne had integrated church and culture, the same conduct attempted by a host of minor lords seriously damaged the church and brought a series of conflicts between secular rulers and princes of the church ('investiture controversy')."[498]

"From the middle of the eleventh century until the middle of the fifteenth century these two powers, [the Holy Roman Empire and the Holy Catholic Church], that were theoretically the counterpart the one of the other, were for the most part in mortal combat. Emperors deposed popes and procured the election of others in their place. Popes excommunicated emperors and cooperated with rivals in securing changes of dynasty. Each furnished a sort of check upon the other and it is probable that this contest prevented the triumph of ecclesiastical absolutism on the one hand, and of imperial absolutism on the other."[499]

Another example from the past of the ten-horned beast hating the harlot comes from the French Revolution, the ten-year period from 1789 to 1799 when through great civil violence the government was changed from a system based on the divine right of kings to an ostensibly republican form. In 1789 the French "Assembly unilaterally abolished the annual payment of St. Peter's pence for the maintenance of the Holy See. ... On November 27, the Assembly directed that all men of the Church should swear an oath of obedience to the Constitution. ... It was the imposition of the oath that finally induced Pius to break his silence. In March 1791 and again in April he denounced the Constitution as schismatic, declared the ordinations of the new state bishops to be sacrilegious, and suspended all prelates and priests who had taken the oath. The Church in France was now split down the middle. Diplomatic relations were broken off, Avignon and the Venaissin[500] annexed yet again. Finally, on August 10, 1792, the monarchy was abolished – and the

---
498 Franklin Littell, The Macmillan Atlas History of Christianity (New York: Macmillan Publishing Co., Inc., 1976), p. 29.
499 Albert Henry Newman, A Manual of Church History, Vol. I, (Philadelphia: The Baptist Publication Society, 1939), p. 443.

bloodletting began. In Lyon a campaign of mass executions accounted for well over a hundred priests and nuns; further massacres took place in Paris, Orleans, and several other cities."[501]

17:17 "For God did put in their hearts to do his mind, and to come to one mind, and to give their kingdom unto the beast, until the words of God should be accomplished."

17:17 "God did put in their hearts to do his mind, and to come to one mind, and to give their kingdom unto the beast"

These prophetic words seem to point not just to the stunning rise but also to what has seemed like an inexorable expansion of the European Union! The "ten kings" (17:12) who "give their kingdoms unto the beast" most probably point to a group of European leaders who guide their respective countries, to seek and gain admission to the E.U. which is to be equated with "the beast." Following the admission of their countries into the E.U., those leaders may well subsequently serve as Commissioners.

17:17 "until the words of God should be accomplished"

The European political powers which constitute the E.U. will continue their illicit relationship with the corrupt church till "the judgment of the great harlot" predicted in 17:1 actually takes place. That judgment is certain to "be accomplished" because it has been announced by "the words of God."

17:18 "And the woman whom thou sawest is the great city, which reigneth over the kings of the earth."

17:18 "the woman whom thou sawest is the great city"

Here the harlot is identified as "the great city which reigneth over the kings of the earth." It is important to note that the harlot is not said to be like "the great city" but that she "is the great city." That city is Babylon, the corrupt church. Again, Satan is trying to deceive people and lead them astray by creating a counterfeit which mimics reality. The reality is "the bride, the wife of the Lamb" who is "the Holy City, Jerusalem." (Revelation 21:9-10)

17:18 "which reigneth over the kings of the earth"

The corrupt church ultimately will have gained ascendency by reigning over her supporting political powers. Her triumph will eventually generate animosity and hatred in those political entities which had previously supported her. They consequently will finally bring "the great city" down to oblivion. (17:16)

---

500 Located in southeast France. Venaissin is The Comtat Venaissin (County of Venaissin), often called the Comtat for short, the former name of the region around the city of Avignon in what is now the Provence-Alpes-Côôte d'Azur region of France. (Wikipedia)

501 John Julius Norwich, Absolute Monarchs, A History of the Papacy, (New York: Random House, 2011), pp. 376-377.

Revelation Chapter 18

VIII. *Supplementary visions*

    A.   *The origin and doom of Babylon 18:1-19:5*

18:1 "After these things I saw another angel coming down out of heaven, having great authority; and the earth was lightened with his glory."

18:1 "after these things"

An identical occurrence of this expression is found in 19:1. These words probably do not serve as a time marker. If they did, they would indicate that everything up to this point which had been prophesied to occur would have already taken place, but they have not. Rather, then, the words seem to simply mark the sequence of prophetic revelation. The words imply that after having described "these things," awesome and significant as they were, there were still more subsequent prophetic revelations of great import to be given.

18:1 "another angel coming down out of heaven, having great authority"

Being designated as "another angel" distinguishes him from the seven wrath-conveying angels about whom it was said, "one of the four living creatures gave unto the seven angels seven golden bowls full of the wrath of God, who liveth forever and ever." (15:7) This angel's "great authority" makes it possible for him to bring about, among other things, those conditions and circumstances in which the hate between the harlot and her political paramours will continue to grow. (See 17:16.)

18:1 "the earth was lightened with his glory"

This probably predicts that this magnificent angel will bring about a worldwide enlightenment, which will include a realization of the true nature of the great harlot. That realization will spark revulsion which will ultimately bring the great harlot to her destruction and ultimate extinction.

18:2 "And he cried with a mighty voice, saying, Fallen, fallen is Babylon the great, and is become a habitation of demons, and a hold of every unclean spirit, and a hold of every unclean and hateful bird."

18:2 "he cried with a mighty voice"

His voice will be powerful enough that it will be heard in spite of the deceptive propaganda of the fallen church.

18:2 "Fallen, fallen"

As previously mentioned in the comments on 9:1, the fall mentioned here in Revelation 18:2 describes the origin and character of spiritual Babylon, not its ultimate destiny and final doom which are described in later verses in this chapter. (18:9-10) The institution that is now called Babylon was once pure, noble, grand and exalted. It was once Christ's church in Rome. The reality of its original standing is not only confirmed by the apostle Paul's famous, inspired and highly regarded letter to that great church, the book of Romans, but also by two letters which Clement, a Roman church leader who flourished about 93-97 A.D., wrote to the church in Corinth. His letters were so scriptural that "the Church in Corinth long treasured [them] as scripture."[502] Also, he "contributed substantially to procedures in church government. His First Epistle [to the church in Corinth], referring to bishops and presbyters as equals, gives important evidence on the nature and function of the early ministry."[503] One instinctively wonders if Clement of Rome might have been the person to whom Paul made reference in Philippians 4:3.

But that great church fell. Once, as a church following the apostles' teaching, it was part of the new Jerusalem (See Galatians 4:26 and Hebrews 12:22.) but, abandoning that standard, it degenerated into Babylon, a center of theological, moral, spiritual and ethical confusion – confusion which is proclaimed by the meaning of its name, Babylon. (See 17:5 under "Babylon the Great.") It was a church which traded clarity of divine revelation for the confusion, ambivalence and temporizing which are born of expediency, deception and lies.

In this verse the twice emphasized fall expressed in the words "fallen, fallen is Babylon" is the same fall which Paul predicted in his second letter to the church in Thessalonica in which he wrote, "The [second] coming of our Lord Jesus Christ … will not be except the falling away come first." (II Thessalonians 2:1-3)

Surely Paul's prophecy pointed to the rise of the papacy when he said that this fall would reveal "the son of perdition, he that opposeth and exalteth himself against all that is called God or that is worshipped so that he sitteth in the temple of God setting himself forth as God." (II Thessalonians 2:3-4)

18:2   "Babylon the Great"

There are inferior, less well-known, less widespread, more nationalistic and localized Babylons, but this one is "Babylon the Great." None of the other church hierarchies which have established fornicatious relations with political powers can compare in reach and impact with this one which is centered on Rome, the Roman Catholic Church. (See comments on 18:11 under "no man buyeth their merchandise anymore.")

It is not only "Babylon the Great" which utilizes atrocious lawlessness to promote its cause, but lesser Babylons also indulge in unspeakable atrocities. A startling and repulsive example is that of "the Romanian Orthodox Church [which] proclaimed [Corneliu Zelea] Codreanu a 'national saint.'"[504] It was that Codreanu who formed the Legion of the Archangel Michael. On January 21, 1941 those Legionnaires "burnt down seven synagogues and went from house to house in the Jewish quarter, raping and torturing women to death in front of their husbands and children. … The following night, the Legionnaires rounded up an additional 200 Jews and took them to the municipal

---

502 Diarmaid MacCulloch, Christianity: The First Three Thousand Years, (New York: Viking, 2010), p. 128.
503 Franklin H. Littell, The Macmillan Atlas History of Christianity, (New York: Macmillan Co. Inc., 1976), p. 13.
504 Robert D. Kaplan, Balkan Ghosts, A Journey Through History, (New York: St. Martin's Press, 1993), p. 95.

Revelation Chapter 18

slaughterhouse, where they stripped them naked and put them through all the stages of animal slaughter on a conveyor belt."[505]

18:2 "become a habitation of demons, and a hold of every unclean spirit, and a hold of every unclean and hateful bird"

It became "a habitation of demons." Though the tragedy of its fall occurred rapidly, it did not occur instantaneously. That once great and godly church progressively became the repository of the most odious ethical and spiritual deformities, descending finally into utter apostasy. At that point, all scruples had been abandoned; deception and expediency had become its leading operating tactics. Consequently, from that juncture, the most odious methods (typified by "every unclean spirit") and repulsive means (signified by "every unclean and hateful bird") have been routinely employed. Those procedures are demonic and corrupt. Gregg quotes Hailey, who pointed out that, "Such a prison of unclean spirits stands in contrast to the holy city into which nothing unclean or abominable shall enter (21:27)."[506]

18:3 "For by the wine of the wrath of her fornication all the nations are fallen; and the kings of the earth committed fornication with her, and the merchants of the earth waxed rich by the power of her wantonness."

18:3 "by the wine of the wrath of her fornication all the nations are fallen; and the kings of the earth committed fornication with her"

For identification of the "wine of the wrath of her fornication," please see 17:2 and 17:6 with their comments. Though "all the nations are fallen," that is, fallen into the clutches of the harlot, involving them in violations of propriety and righteousness, we look at only two examples of how "the kings of the earth [have] committed fornication with her."

The first example is given to us by the history of the Spanish conquest of Central America. "In 1493, Pope Alexander VI granted the Spanish crown the exclusive right to all land in the New World beyond an arbitrary north-south line drawn 370 leagues west of the Cape Verde Islands.[507] The Spanish thus had the right to wage a 'just war' against resisting New World peoples who rejected the pope's commandment. Although he probably never believed that he could convert [the Inka/Inca emperor] Atawallpa to Christianity, Vicente de Valverde's [a Spanish friar] seemingly nonsensical pantomime [of the story of Christ] at Cajamarca served the very important purpose of giving the Pizarrists [the soldiers and other personnel of Francisco Pizarro, general of the Spanish conquering forces] a [self-assumed] legitimate right to use violence against the Inkas."[508]

That violence against the Inkas is just one example of "the wrath of her fornication." Not only had policy based on expediency come to dominate Babylon the Great, it also was adopted by the "kings of the earth," who committed fornication with her. They had concluded that if they must indulge in a fornicatious relationship with the great harlot to achieve a desired political goal, then so be it. Morality had to take second place to

---

505 Robert D. Kaplan, Balkan Ghosts, A Journey Through History, (New York: St. Martin's Press, 1993), p. 97.
506 Revelation, Four Views: A Parallel Commentary, ed. Steve Gregg , (Nashville: Thomas Nelson Publishers, 1997), p. 425.
507 The Cape Verde Islands are located in the Atlantic Ocean just west of the African country of Senegal.
508 Timothy H. Parsons, The Rule of Empires, (Oxford: Oxford University Press, 2010), p. 117.

realpolitik. Such capitulations to expediency are the same in essence as those policies of statecraft systematized and advocated by the political philosopher Niccolo Machiavelli (born 1469, died 1527). In answer to the question whether it is better for a prince to be loved or to be feared, he answered, "It is much safer to be feared than loved." He went on to state, "A prudent ruler ought not to keep faith when by so doing, it would be against his interest." He concluded by saying, a ruler "must have a mind disposed to adapt itself according to the wind, and as the variations of fortune dictate, and, as I said before, not deviate from what is good, if possible, but be able to do evil if constrained."[509]

Subordinating justice, kindness and morality to expediency was not a new phenomenon beginning with the great harlot, or with kings in a fornicatious relationship with her, or with Machiavelli. The great Indian ruler, Chandragupta Maurya, who came to power in 322 B.C., shortly after Alexander the Great's hard-won victory in northwest India, appointed Kautilya, an astute and shrewd Brahman, to be his counselor in the art of statecraft. Following that counselor's advice, "The ship of state was steered with exceptional ability … and his statecraft was not hampered by any moral scruples."[510] The moral basis of Kautilya's statecraft was "identical with that of Richelieu, who lived nearly two thousand years later: the state is a fragile organization, and the statesman does not have the moral right to risk its survival on ethical restraint."[511]

Another and much more recent example of a lewd fornicatious union, based on expediency, between the Papacy and a political leader is found in the relationship which prevailed between the Pope and Mussolini. "Pius XI and the dictator [Mussolini], who both came to power in 1922, depended on each other for support and for achieving mutual goals. They shared many political ideas; both loathed democracy and Communism. Pius gave sacred legitimacy and removed political obstacles to Mussolini's Fascist regime. Mussolini restored many ecclesiastical prerogatives that had been lost over the previous decades. Only near the end of Pius XI's pontificate, when the aging pope grew enraged with Mussolini and his friend and ally Hitler, did the unholy union begin to unravel. But the unraveling was knit up after Pacelli became Pius XII. …

"In 1924, the leader of the United Socialist Party, Giacomo Matteotti, was murdered by Fascist thugs (following a broad hint from Mussolini that they should do so), after he had criticized Fascists from the Chamber of Deputies and suggested that the recent election, marred by violence, be annulled. Mussolini's government was in trouble and the pope 'decided to do all he could to save' Mussolini and his regime. The Vatican's daily newspaper, *L'Osservatore Romano*, published an editorial reminding its Catholic readers to obey the civil authorities, as Romans 13 instructed them to do. Catholic party members were given a special warning not to help bring down the Fascist regime. The pope sent an emissary to convey his support."[512]

---

509 Niccolo Machiavelli, The Prince, (Chicago: The Great Books Foundation, 1955), pp. 55-59.
510 Vincent A. Smith, The Oxford History of India, (Oxford: Oxford University Press, 1981), pp. 94-98.
511 Henry Kissinger, World Order, (New York: Penguin Press, 2014), p. 195.
512 Kevin J. Madigan, *How the Vatican Aided Mussolini, A New Account of a Grievous Historical Record*, COMMENTARY, April 2014, pp. 33-34.

Revelation Chapter 18

18:3 "the merchants of the earth waxed rich by the power of her wantonness"

The merchants will have become rich not only by supplying the sumptuous appointments and wardrobes used by the hierarchy itself, both personally and in performing their religious rituals, but even more significantly by trade agreements negotiated by the help of the papacy. (See 18:15.) Undoubtedly, merchants would also often work as commission agents in facilitating international trade in the exquisite commodities in which the harlot constantly deals and from which she is enriched. (See 18:11ff.)

One notable example of the papacy's ability to influence the flow of trade is seen by Pope Alexander's imposition in 1494 of a Line of Demarcation defining the areas to be colonized and exploited by the Spanish and the Portugese empires.

18:4 "And I heard another voice from heaven, saying, Come forth, my people, out of her, that ye have no fellowship with her sins, and that ye receive not of her plagues:"

18:4 "I heard another voice from heaven, saying, Come forth, my people, out of her"

The voice seems to be that of Christ. He certainly has the right to make this demand of those whom he calls "my people" because he claimed ownership of the church when he said, "Upon this rock I will build **my** church." (Matthew 16:18) Christ claims ownership of the church because "he purchased [it] with his own blood." (Acts 20:28)

The identity of this "voice from heaven" as that of Christ calling to his people helps us to accurately locate and identify Babylon the Great in history. It certainly does not, as one commentator suggested, indicate that Babylon refers indefinitely to "a past, present, and future reality, and not merely as the city that shall exist in the end time."[513] On the origin and identity of Babylon the Great, please read the entire discussion which is given under 14:8.

It is amazing that Christ still had some of his people, whom he calls "my people," in Babylon, that institution which at this point had so flagrantly and egregiously departed from the divine pattern that it is now also known, in contrast to the true church, the Bride of Christ, as the false church, the Great Harlot. (17:1 and 19:2) This is a testimony to the extravagance of divine patience. Once before we have seen it similarly displayed in Christ's dealing with the church in Thyatira (2:18-28) which had been tolerating the harlot Jezebel within its fellowship. Even in that shocking circumstance, Jesus had not withdrawn that church's candlestick from its place, but exhorted those who had not condoned the teaching of Jezebel to "hold fast till I come." (Revelation 2:25)

As we have seen, the church in Rome had fallen alarmingly and tragically. Consequently, it had now become not just Babylon, confusion, but "Babylon the Great." (18:2) But, at this point it had not fallen so far that Christ did not still have some uncorrupted people in that corrupt institution. However, now it was time for those very resilient people to come out. Let it be especially noted that their coming out was not exclusively for separation but, as we shall see, it was also to undertake a great mission. (See 18:6.)

---

513 W. Hendriksen, More Than Conquerors: An Interpretation of the Book of Revelation, (Grand Rapids: Baker Book House, 1952), p. 213.

Revelation Verse by Verse

To obey Christ's command to come out of a long-standing spiritual fellowship will not be easy, even when that fellowship has become as flagrantly wicked as had the one portrayed here in Revelation as "Babylon the Great." Those adults who are ordered to "come forth" will probably have developed close ties with others in peer groups consisting of those who have also resisted the spreading, general, corporate wickedness. But if the companions are not ready to leave, then to heed Christ's call the faithful must be ready to abandon their closest associates as well as the corporate body. Undoubtedly, their children will also have developed ties with their circle of friends. Will parents be prepared to wrench them away from their closest companions?

The faith and courage with which one must be prepared to face such daunting realities, if and when he is called upon to "come forth" from a long-standing but now corrupt spiritual fellowship, are poignantly displayed in America by many congregants in the current Episcopal Church. "Since The Episcopal Church (TEC) consecrated Gene Robinson as its first openly homosexual bishop a decade ago, hundreds of [local] churches have fled the denomination. TEC is one of thirty-eight provinces in the 70-million member worldwide Anglican Communion. The departing parishes emphasize that TEC's approval of homosexuality is one outgrowth of deeper doctrinal problems: TEC leadership has questioned the authority of Scripture for decades. ... By the early 1990s, Bishop John Shelby Spong was publicly deriding the virgin birth, the resurrection of Christ, and the reliability of the Bible. Others followed, including Bishop John Chane in his 2002 Easter sermon declaring Jesus' resurrection 'at best conjectural,' Jefferts Schori has also questioned the resurrection, and adamantly denies Christ as the only way to God.

"Episcopal dioceses and TEC often have sued departing parishes for their property using the Dennis Canon – a 1979 TEC law that declared local parishes hold their property in trust for the diocese and denomination. Many parishes have argued civil trust laws don't allow an entity to declare that another group's property belongs to them. Courts in some states have agreed with that analysis, but most have ordered parishes to relinquish their property.

"The campaign has peaked under Katharine Jefferts Schori, who became in 2006 the first female presiding bishop within the Anglican Communion. Before her consecration, some departing churches offered payments to their dioceses for the properties they had built and maintained, but Jefferts Schori intervened and said TEC would not sell to congregations that intended to remain Anglican. [That refusal has come in spite of the fact that] TEC has sold buildings to Baptists, Methodists, Jews, and – in at least two cases – Muslims. ...

"TEC leadership has initiated at least 78 lawsuits against parishes and departing dioceses. (Five dioceses have left TEC.) Some lawsuits include multiple parishes. ... TEC has spent nearly $26 million on litigation: 'It's a policy of wearing people down by outspending them.' Many of the lawsuits include individual rectors and vestry members by name. Some seek punitive damages. Most suits demand church property and everything inside, as well as money in parish bank accounts.

"When members of St. James [an Episcopal church in Newport Beach, California] – founded in 1941 – considered building a new sanctuary in 1991, they worried about what

Revelation Chapter 18

would happen to their property if they withdrew from TEC. ... The congregation built a new sanctuary, but by 2004 voted to leave TEC. The diocese of Los Angeles filed suit against St. James, and named the rector and vestry members in the litigation. TEC joined the lawsuit. A California judge didn't consider the waiver letter [which the leaders of St. James had previously gotten from the attorney for the bishop of the diocese of Los Angeles] in his rulings, and awarded the multi-million dollar property to the diocese in July. In August, the court gave St. James Anglican Congregation 45 days to leave, and the church moved to a Christian school in September. The diocese is still seeking additional funds from the church. ...

"Long-time members of the church remember family weddings, baptisms, and funerals at the Newport Beach property. One church member had donated a stained glass window in memory of his son who died of Leukemia. Other members collected the ashes of family members interred on the property.

"During the Sunday morning service at St. James, rector Richard Crocker told the group: 'We are resurrection people. We are people of hope.' After the service, Marian Michaels, 82, and a member since 1965, said the loss was difficult, but 'In a way it's kind of exciting because we're waiting to see what the Lord has in store for us.'"[514]

18:4   "have no fellowship with her sins and that ye receive not of her plagues"

"In verse 4, two reasons are given for separation from Babylon: (1) to avoid ... becoming a participant in **her sins**; (2) to avoid receiving a portion in **her plagues**."[515] Their association in a corrupt fellowship had reached the limit. To extend it any further would jeopardize their own standing with God.

18:5   "for her sins have reached even unto heaven, and God hath remembered her iniquities."

Her sins have reached a flagrant and notorious level where they cannot be ignored, denied or covered up. The knowledge of the scandalous condition of that church will have become known at every level of society, even the highest, "unto heaven."

18:6   "Render unto her even as she rendered, and double unto her the double according to her works: in the cup which she mingled, mingle unto her double."

18:6   "Render unto her even as she rendered"

To whom is this command given? If one simply follows the sequence found in verses 4-6, he finds that this command is clearly addressed to those whom Christ calls, "my people." (18:4) Christ has a special role for them to fill. Thus, not only must those who are faithful to Christ leave the corrupt corporate body called Babylon, they must now openly oppose the evil of that body of which they were once a part.

Barclay disagrees with this conclusion. He wrote, "The instructions to take vengeance on Rome is not an instruction to human beings; it is an instruction to the angel, the divine instrument of justice. Vengeance belongs to God, and to God alone."[516] However, Barclay

---
514 Jamie Dean, WORLD, December 28, 2013, pp. 34-40.
515 Revelation, Four Views: A Parallel Commentary, ed. Steve Gregg , (Nashville: Thomas Nelson Publishers, 1997), p. 429.
516 William Barclay, The Revelation of John, Vol. II, (Philadelphia: The Westminster Press, 1976), p. 173.

overrides the clear grammar of this passage in which the subject of the verb, "render," is that group whom Jesus calls "my people," the ones who are to "render even as she rendered." He takes this position by assuming that the activities detailed in verses 6 and 7 constitute vengeance, which is prohibited for Christians to render. (See Romans 12:19 and Hebrews 10:30.) However, we should consider that they will be rendering clarity and justice, not vengeance. That clarity will be in response to the deceit and hypocrisy of the harlot and the justice will be in distinction to the robbery and thuggery of the harlot.

Barnes takes the position that the activities which are to be carried out against the harlot are to be enacted by the nations in which Christ's persecuted people live. He says, "It would seem to be a call on the nations that had been so long under her sway, and among whom, from time to time, so much blood had been shed by her, to arise now in their might, and to inflict deserved vengeance."[517] The position suggested by Barnes is negated by verse 9 which tells us that the kings, rulers of the nations, will weep and wail over the fall of Babylon the Great. Obviously, then, they will not have intentionally brought about that fall.

18:6 "double unto her the double according to her works: in the cup which she mingled, mingle unto her double"

The presentation of the truth will have clarity which will be the double of the deceit and hypocrisy with which the harlot will have mislead multitudes through the centuries.

The cup referred to is that which was first mentioned in 17:4. It is a golden cup depicting sincerity, honesty and probity. While the use of the cup by the harlot was feigned, it will be appropriately used by the Bride of Christ.

18:7 "How much soever she glorified herself, and waxed wanton, so much give her of torment and mourning: for she saith in her heart, I sit a queen, and am no widow, and shall in no wise see mourning."

Initially, the torment will be that of shame, repudiation, rejection and humiliation when her satanic lifestyle becomes openly, graphically and irrefutably exposed through the decisive and insightful revelations made by those who will have come out of her, as well as by other Christian observers. Recollection of her arrogant boast, recorded in this verse, that I "shall in no wise see mourning" will only intensify her torment. Ultimately, she will be consigned to that place from which the smoke goes up forever. (See Revelation 19:2-3.)

18:8 "Therefore in one day shall her plagues come, death, and mourning, and famine; and she shall be utterly burned with fire; for strong is the Lord God who judged her."

18:8 "in one day shall her plagues come, death, and mourning, and famine"

Plummer, quoting Alford, tries to coordinate these judgments with the crimes or conditions for which they will be imposed. He wrote, "*Death*, for her scorn of the prospect of widowhood; *mourning*, for her inordinate reveling; *famine*, for her

---

[517] Albert Barnes, Notes, Explanatory and Practical on the Book of Revelation, (New York: Harper & Brothers Publishers, 1852), p. 437.

Revelation Chapter 18

abundance."[518] In any case, her judgment will come very suddenly, "in one day." (See the comments on 18:21.)

18:8   "she shall be utterly burned with fire"

This is not a call to those whom Christ designates as "my people" (18:4) to become arsonists or incendiaries burning down the buildings and worldwide infrastructure of the false church. Gregg quotes Henry Morris, who said, "The scriptures do not describe the source of such a devastating fire, but it surely can be no ordinary fire."[519]

However, we have previously encountered this extraordinary category of fire in 11:5. There, we found that the fire is the word of God, for fire is one of the graphic similes portraying God's word. As noted in that earlier passage, here are three examples:

(1) "Is not my word like fire? saith Jehovah; and like a hammer that breaketh the rock in pieces?" (Jeremiah 23:29) (2) "Wherefore thus saith Jehovah, the God of hosts, Because ye speak this word, behold, I will make my words in thy mouth fire, and this people wood, and it shall devour them." (Jeremiah 5:14) (3) "Behold, the name of Jehovah cometh from far, burning with his anger, and in thick rising smoke: his lips are full of indignation, and his tongue is as a devouring fire." (Isaiah 30:27)

18:9   "And the kings of the earth, who committed fornication and lived wantonly with her, shall weep and wail over her, when they look upon the smoke of her burning,"

18:9   "the kings of the earth"

Though "kings" are specifically stated, all governments which have indulged in a fornicatious relationship with the harlot are, no doubt, intended.

18:9   "weep and howl"

Such lamentations undoubtedly will be stimulated by the major loss of lavish private income and adequate state revenue since one of the greatest sources of cash flow underpinning state budgets will have been disrupted. Along with the great economic decline will come the loss of the costly perquisites enjoyed by holders of high office. Now, rulers will also be faced with the painful problem of promptly developing alternative income streams with which to meet their state expenditures. Failure to quickly find replacements will probably spark protests and civil disobedience, perhaps even rebellion.

18:9   "the smoke of her burning" (See also 18:18 where this phrase occurs again.)

The Great Harlot has performed her nefarious work behind a smokescreen of subterfuge and deception. Consequently, few people will have understood the reality of what had been going on. As the fire of divinely revealed truth exposes the reality and the extent of that subterfuge, behind which the illicit union of church and state will have been carried out, then that subterfuge itself will become visible, as "the smoke of her burning." To express it another way, the burning will reveal her smokescreen, "the smoke of her burning." At this point, "her burning" is not burning in hell but that produced by the

---
518 A. Plummer, The Pulpit Commentary [on] Revelation, (Chicago: Wilcox & Follett Co., no date), p. 432.
519 Revelation, Four Views: A Parallel Commentary, ed. Steve Gregg , (Nashville: Thomas Nelson Publishers, 1997), p. 431.

purging fire and burning which will have come from the fire of God's word. (Jeremiah 5:14)

18:10 "standing afar off for the fear of her torment, saying, Woe, woe, the great city, Babylon, the strong city! for in one hour is thy judgment come."

18:10 "the fear of her torment"

The uncovering of the crimes of the corrupt church will have been brought about by those whom Christ calls "my people." (18:4) They will now have rendered unto her even as she rendered. (18:6) Next, political leaders will fear a similar disastrous exposé of their own scandalous and illicit activities.

18:10 "the great city, Babylon, the strong city! for in one hour is thy judgment come"

The destruction of this spiritual Babylon will come with breathtaking suddenness like that which befell the ancient city of Babylon in 538 B.C. The last king of that Babylon was Nabonidus. He "was a highly educated monarch, who brought far too much intelligence and imagination and not enough of the short-range wisdom of this world to affairs of state. ... No doubt he realized the weakness and disunion of his empire ... and had some conception of unification in his mind. Events were marching too rapidly for any such development. His innovation had manifestly raised the suspicion and hostility of the priesthood of Bel. They sided with the Persians. 'The soldiers of Cyrus entered Babylon without fighting.' Nabonidus was taken prisoner, and Persian sentinels were set at the gates of the temple of Bel."[520]

18:11 "And the merchants of the earth weep and mourn over her, for no man buyeth their merchandise any more;"

18:11 "the merchants of the earth weep and mourn over her"

Behind the scenes, the corrupt false church had become a dominating player in the world's commodity markets and in worldwide commerce. In some cases, it would play this role as an end user, but more significantly, as a facilitator and financier in the broader scope of world trade. Once the harlot can no longer function in that facilitating role, trade and traders, "the merchants" of this verse, will be disastrously impacted. Their utter ruin would lie just ahead. With interconnected bishoprics (located in many major cities throughout the world) having highly organized administrative staffs, Babylon the Great will have been in an ideal position to spot advantageous trading opportunities and play the lucrative role of middle-man and financier.

18:11 "no man buyeth their merchandise any more"

A coming crisis leading to a breakdown in world trade is clearly implied. Up to this juncture, the impact of the economic activity of the false church will have been far greater than most of us have ever imagined. "Roman Catholicism is totally intertwined with the heartbeat of Europe's economic system. It is estimated by some scholars that the

---

520 H. G. Wells, The Outline of History, Vol. I, (New York: Doubleday & Co., Inc., 1971), p. 186.

Revelation Chapter 18

Vatican owns one-third of Europe's real estate."[521] Further specificity is gained by the research of an Italian scholar who tells us, "Another aspect of the Vatican's real estate patrimony are the 'colonies,' prudent real estate investments abroad into marquee buildings in various parts of Europe – downtown Paris, London townhouses on the Thames, dreamy apartments in Lausanne and other parts of Switzerland. The market value of these properties amounts to approximately 591 million [billion?] euros."[522]

But because "The Catholic Church is one of the oldest, largest and richest institutions on earth, with a following 1.2 billion strong,"[523] that corrupt church is capable of facilitating very significant trade in valuable merchandise. For an example from history, the city of Florence was a center "where merchants achieved [not only] access to the sea through Pisa, … [but also] great expansion and banking through connection with the papacy."[524]

The Roman Catholic Church can assist merchants and traders by easing negotiations, facilitating trade arrangements and devising exchange deals through "the Vatican Bank, an institution [which] even U.S. Treasury officials privately say is corrupted. Soon after he was elected he [Pope Francis] named a special commission to investigate the bank, which in turn handed the matter off to an independent firm for an audit. Francis also issued initiatives to counter money laundering [which, therefore, had obviously been going on] and increase the monitoring of the Vatican's finances. In October, the bank disclosed an annual report for the first time in its 125-year history."[525] The sheer size and scope of the Roman Catholic Church makes it possible for its elite hierarchy to negotiate advantageous deals worldwide.

"If [Pope] Francis' spiritual empire were a country, it would be the third largest in population after China and India."[526] One scholar has called it "the [world's] largest global Christian community." To give a specific example, she went on to say that "Brazil has the world's largest Catholic population, with over 160 million adherents."[527]

Specific categories of merchandise, in the trade of which the Roman Catholic Church takes a significant, advantageous and valuable, behind-the-scenes part, are listed in the next two verses. However, among those trade items are several which may need clarification. The demand for the commodities which make up the list will vary depending upon conditions which will change during the long cavalcade of years.

18:12 "merchandise of gold, and silver, and precious stone, and pearls, and fine linen, and purple, and silk, and scarlet; and all thyine wood, and every vessel of ivory, and every vessel made of most precious wood, and of brass, and iron, and marble;"

In economics, all the items of merchandise listed in verses 12 and 13 except, perhaps, "slaves and souls of men," come under the category of commodities. Most often, however, even slaves, of both the varieties mentioned here, were heartlessly and brutally

---

521 Revelation, Four Views: A Parallel Commentary, ed. Steve Gregg , Quoting Robert Caringola, (Nashville: Thomas Nelson Publishers, 1997), p. 432.
522 Gianluigi Nuzzi, Merchants in the Temple, (New York: Henry Holt & Co., 2015), p. 122.
523 Nancy Gibbs, *The Choice*, TIME, December 23, 2013, p. 44.
524 Franklin H. Littell, The Macmillan Atlas History of Christianity, (New York: Macmillan Co. Inc., 1976), p. 60.
525 Howard Chua-Eoan and Elizabeth Dias, *The People's Pope*, TIME, December 23, 2013, p. 54.
526 Taken from multiple sources, TIME, December 23, 2013, p. 58.
527 Sherron George, *Report on Pope Francis and the 2013 World Youth Day*, International Bulletin of Missionary Research, Vol. 38, No. 2, p. 74.

shipped and traded as commodities. Commodity prices are volatile and often fluctuate wildly, being impacted by the uncertainties and instabilities of transport, supply and demand. From this list of twenty-eight commodities in verses 12 and 13, most of which are luxury items, comment is given only on those for which there is either need for clarification or historic information of great interest.

18:12 "purple ... scarlet"

"The purple color – *porphura* – was obtained from a species of shellfish found on the coasts of the Mediterranean, which yielded a reddish-purple dye, much prized by the ancients. Robes dyed in that color were commonly worn by persons of rank and wealth, Mark 15:17, Mark 15:20; Luke 16:19. The purple color contains more blue than the crimson, though the limits are not very accurately defined, and the words are sometimes interchanged. Thus the mock robe put on the Saviour is called in Mark 15:17, Mark 15:20, *porphuran* – 'purple,' and in Matthew 27:28, *kokkine* – 'crimson.'"[528]

18:12 "silk"

Among fabrics, silk probably is the most extravagant. Its price often fluctuated because of conditions prevailing in various historic periods. For example, at one point, the stimulus for the silk trade came from the wealth and opulence of Rome, where ostentation and extravagance increased with prosperity. Pliny, in his *Natural History*, describes the vast amount of labor involved in acquiring silk fabrics and then says, "So has toil to be multiplied; so have the ends of the earth to be traversed: and all that a Roman dame may exhibit her charms in transparent gauze."[529] (Doesn't that help us understand the relevance of I Peter 3:1-6?) Silk was "sold for $800,000 a pound in the Sybaritic markets of Rome."[530] (No, I didn't inadvertently hit an extra cipher or two when I entered that figure. The author wrote, "eight-hundred-thousand dollars per pound"!)

The Alexandrian Greek monk, Cosmas, writing between 535 and 550 A.D., explained that the land route from China was a great shortcut for shipment of silk compared to the sea route. Thus it was preferred. He says, "loads of silk passing through the hands of different nations in succession by land reach Persia in a comparatively short time, whilst the distance from Persia by sea is vastly greater."[531]

18:12 "all thyine wood "("scented wood - ESV," "citron wood - NIV")

This wood is "mentioned only in Rev. 18:12 among the articles which would cease to be purchased when Babylon fell. It was called citrus, citron wood, by the Romans. It was the Callitris quadrivalvis of botanists, of the cone-bearing order of trees, and of the cypress tribe of this order. The name of this wood is derived from the Greek word *thuein*, 'to sacrifice,' and it was so called because it was burnt in sacrifices, on account of its fragrance. The wood of this tree was reckoned very valuable, and was used for making articles of furniture by the Greeks and Romans. Like the cedars of Lebanon, it is disappearing from the forests of Palestine."[532]

---

528 Barne's Notes on the Bible, http://biblehub.com/commentaries/revelation/17-4.htm, accessed 4/3/14.
529 Owen and Eleanor Lattimore, Silks, Spices, and Empire (New York: Dell Publishing Co., Inc., 1968), p.25.
530 Nancy Hatch Dupree, An Historical Guide to Afghanistan, (Kabul: Afghan Tourist Organization 1971) p. 26.
531 Owen and Eleanor Lattimore, Silks, Spices, and Empire (New York: Dell Publishing Co., Inc., 1968), p. 18.
532 Easton's 1897 Bible Dictionary, http://www.biblestudytools.com/dictionary/thyine-wood, accessed 4/1/14.

Revelation Chapter 18

"Thyine wood is a 15th-century English name for a wood from the tree known botanically as Tetraclinis articulata (syn. Callitris quadrivalvis, Thuja articulata). The name is derived from the Greek word *thuon*, 'fragrant wood,' or possibly *thuein*, 'to sacrifice,' ... Craftsmen who worked in citrus wood and ivory had their own guild (collegium).

"The New International Version translates the passage 'citron wood'; the Amplified Bible translates it as 'scented wood.'"[533]

"Thyine: An African tree; akin to Greek thyon; a tree the wood of which was burned as perfume, of or pertaining to the sandarac tree, or its fragrant wood. Thyine wood: the fragrant and beautiful wood of the sandarac tree of Morocco. ... The possession of thyine wood was supposed to bring good luck and its sacredness arose from the fact that from it was produced the incense used by the priests."[534]

18:13 "and cinnamon, and spice, and incense, and ointment, and frankincense, and wine, and oil, and fine flour, and wheat, and cattle, and sheep; and merchandise of horses and chariots and slaves; and souls of men."

18:13 "cinnamon, and spice"

How the spice trade stimulated the economy may be understood if we realize that, "Before the first Europeans dropped anchor in Asia, they could obtain spices only at exorbitant prices and from Arabs who brought them overland. Pepper was worth its weight in gold. In England during the Middle Ages cloves served as currency. In Germany, a pound of nutmeg could buy seven oxen. The spice trade supplied much of the wealth that helped bring about the Italian Renaissance. For centuries spices were a significant force in the global economy."[535]

18:13 "frankincense"

Just prior to the beginning of Muhammad's electrifying and epochal prophetic career, yet another event conspired to bring poverty to many thousands of Arabians. It was a dramatic decline in the market for frankincense, the unique high-value export from Oman. In part, the cause of this economic collapse is thought to have been "the spread of Christianity. The new religion, it seems, had less need than pagan faiths for incense as a means of reaching heaven."[536] The failure of the frankincense trade not only decimated the economy in the growing areas in Oman but also in all the transhipment points throughout Arabia.

18:13 "slaves and souls of men" (See addendum on page 304.)

Translators and commentators have had difficulty clearly identifying the unique difference which distinguishes these two categories of slavery. The first category, "slaves," comes from the Greek word *somaton*, which relates to peoples' physiques or bodies. This points to the slavery of hard, unremitting physical labor, such as excavating

---

[533] http://en.wikipedia.org/wiki/Thyine_wood, accessed 4/2/14.
[534] Webster's New International Dictionary of the English Language, 2nd ed. Unabridged, (Springfield, MA: G&C Merriam Co., 1943).
[535] Clayton Jones, World Monitor, July 1990, p. 59.
[536] Dana Adams Schmidt, Yemen, The Unknown War, (New York: Holt, Rinehart and Winston, 1968), p.101.

in a mine, growing and picking cotton, planting and cutting sugar cane or – under a lash – manning an oar in the hold of a slave ship.

The second category of slavery, that is "souls of men," is translated from the Greek word *psukas*, meaning souls or spirits. Therefore, this second form of slavery touches the human spirit much more deeply than the first category of slavery does. It probably points to the many forms of sexual slavery, such as enticing and trapping young girls into brothels as prostitutes and children into becoming victims of pedophilia. The act of sexual union touches the human spirit far more deeply than does unremitting, hard physical labor. As scripture reminds us, "he who is joined to a prostitute becomes one body with her, for, as it is written, the two will become one flesh." (I Corinthians 6:16 ESV)

These two forms of slavery, both of which are physical, spiritual, ethical and moral monstrosities, from time-to-time have been promoted by the harlot for greatly enhanced profit, along with trafficking in a wide spectrum of more ordinary commodities. (See addendum on page 304.) "Not only Constantinople but papal Rome had a thriving slave market, and Spain was a major supplier as well as Rus."[537] Papal involvement in slavery was in harmony with the general moral and spiritual degradation of the fallen church. For example, in the era of The Crusades "it became a leading aim with the popes to enrich their relations, [members of their family], especially their illegitimate children. Hence, *nepotism* [favoring one's relatives for appointment to church office] was practiced in such a way as to scandalize Christendom. It came to be said, even by faithful Catholics, that in the Roman Curia everything could be had for money. The enforcement of celibacy on the clergy and the vast increase of the number and the membership of monastic orders, in the absence of any proper ethical principles, led to an appalling increase in immorality. The most horrible licentiousness became widely prevalent and the moral influence of clergy and monks was highly corrupting."[538]

That "horrible licentiousness" which was accompanied by "an appalling increase in immorality" is still typical of the harlot. For example, "Pope Francis said on Friday [April 11, 2014] that he took personal responsibility for the harm done by priests who sexually abused children, and he pledged that the Roman Catholic Church would confront the issue unflinchingly and impose sanctions when necessary. 'The Church is aware of this damage,' he said. 'It is personal moral damage, carried out by men of the church.'"[539]

18:14 "And the fruits which thy soul lusted after are gone from thee, and all things that were dainty and sumptuous are perished from thee, and men shall find them no more at all."

The pronoun "thy" refers back to the "merchants" mentioned in 18:11. Habitually, they were overpowered by greed in their impatient efforts to generate enough money to support their very luxuriant, sumptuous and decadent lifestyles. Negotiating deals to that end had become the dominating motivation in their innermost beings. Thus, their souls "lusted" after "the fruits," that is, the extortionate profits, and the "dainty and sumptuous"

---

537 Philip Longworth, Russia, the Once and Future Empire From Pre-History to Putin, (New York: Saint Martin's Press, 2005), p. 30.
538 Albert Henry Newman, A Manual of Church History, Vol. I, (Philadelphia: The Baptist Publication Society, 1939), p. 520.
539 Elisabetta Povoledo, *Pope Takes Responsibility in Priests' Abuse Scandal, Francis Goes Further than Predecessors*, The New York Times, April 12, 2014, p. A7.

Revelation Chapter 18

consumer items one may buy with extreme profits. God will not allow trade which ignores ethics and morality to flourish forever.

18:15 "The merchants of these things, who were made rich by her, shall stand afar off for the fear of her torment, weeping and mourning;"

Merchants' and traders' economic activities will have been called to a much higher standard, one which the majority of merchants will find daunting, considering their background of rapacious economic activity in harmony and cooperation with the Great Harlot. Regrettably, their fear will not lead to "Godly sorrow [which] worketh repentance." On the contrary, their fear will lead to "the sorrow of the world [which] worketh death." (II Corinthians 7:10)

18:16 "saying, Woe, woe, the great city, she that was arrayed in fine linen and purple and scarlet, and decked with gold and precious stone and pearl!"

The words "Woe, woe" are the expression of repeated lamentations by the merchants. Though it will have become unmistakably clear that God will not accept expediency as a basis for economic activity, these merchants still long and pine for the fruits generated by their former rapacious unrestrained forms of entrepreneurial activity.

18:17 "for in an hour so great riches is made desolate. And every shipmaster, and every one that saileth any wither [to whatever place]**, and mariners, and as many as gain their living by sea, stood afar off,"**

18:17 "in an hour so great riches is made desolate"

The decisive and critical hour is that of the sudden, abrupt and dramatic destruction of the harlot. When the prophecy tells us that in one hour great riches are to be made desolate, it seems to portray a financial collapse, perhaps of the Vatican Bank which, because of the highly centralized system in the Catholic Church, would impact dioceses worldwide. Like the great financial collapses of 1929 and 2008, fortunes will have vanished overnight.

18:17 "every shipmaster, and every one that saileth any wither, and mariners, and as many as gain their living by sea, stood afar off"

The universal impact of the destruction of Babylon, also known as the harlot, will be understandable if we remember that the institution is universal, as expressed in Revelation 17:1 and 17:15, she is the harlot who sits on many waters. That description indicates that the false church has had a global presence with offices staffed by personnel in many major cities throughout the world dedicated to, among other things, facilitating deals for merchants and maritime freight companies. Of course, the harlot gets a handsome fee for her work. Consequently, her destruction will impact every aspect of global trade.

18:18 "and cried out as they looked upon the smoke of her burning, saying, What city is like the great city?"

18:18 "the smoke of her burning"

Please see the comments on this same terminology at 18:9. This smoke is to be clearly distinguished from that mentioned in 19:3.

18:18 "the great city"

That city is Babylon the Great, the false church, which is also known as the harlot. (Revelation 17:18) Also be sure to read the comments under "Babylon the Great" at 18:2.

18:19 "And they cast dust on their heads, and cried, weeping and mourning, saying, Woe, woe, the great city, wherein all that had their ships in the sea were made rich by reason of her costliness! for in one hour is she made desolate."

18:19 "were made rich by reason of her costliness"

Her costliness not only reflects the money spent on consumer items for personal wants and pleasures, but that which is allocated to maintaining a worldwide administrative structure through which, in addition to her spiritual activities, global trade was expedited.

18:19 "for in one hour is she made desolate"

These words speak of the suddenness and abruptness with which destruction will fall upon the false church. One wonders if indicative developments leading up to that calamity will give forewarning before the fateful hour arrives.

18:20 "Rejoice over her, thou heaven, and ye saints, and ye apostles, and ye prophets; for God hath judged your judgment on her."

18:20 "Rejoice over her, thou heaven, and ye saints, and ye apostles, and ye prophets"

This exultant rejoicing is in triumphant contrast to the lamentations highlighted in 18:16-19.

18:20 "God hath judged your judgment on her"

At last! God has responded to the prolonged and sustained pleas from not only the saints at large but from the apostles and prophets for judgment, justice and relief.

18:21 "And a strong angel took up a stone as it were a great millstone and cast it into the sea, saying, Thus with a mighty fall shall Babylon, the great city, be cast down, and shall be found no more at all."

Can such a pulsating, successful and influential, global institution collapse and become inoperable almost instantaneously? The suddenness of its fall is expressed by "one day"(18:8) and by "one hour" (18:10, 18:17 and 18:19). We have examples of such dramatic collapses in the sudden fall and dissolution of the Soviet Union (December 26, 1991) and the great banking house of Lehman Brothers which collapsed shortly after the worldwide economic crisis which erupted in 2008.

Revelation Chapter 18

18:22 "And the voice of harpers and minstrels and flute-players and trumpeters shall be heard no more at all in thee; and no craftsman, of whatsoever craft, shall be found any more at all in thee; and the voice of a mill shall be heard no more at all in thee;"

18:22 "And the voice of harpers and minstrels and flute-players and trumpeters shall be heard no more at all in thee"

The long era during which the false church was the patron of great classical musical extravaganzas and operas will have abruptly and decidedly ended. They will no longer be able to utilize the magnificent, creative work of men like George Frideric Handel to mask the repulsive wickedness of the Great Harlot. In 1706 Handel traveled to Italy where he composed sacred music for the Roman clergy.

The decree against harpists, minstrels, flutists and trumpeters certainly does not indicate that God is in opposition to fine music but that he is against using music as part of a smokescreen which hides hideous immorality, duplicity and rapacious greed.

18:22 "no craftsman, of whatsoever craft, shall be found any more at all in thee"

There will be no architects, sculptors, embroiderers, carvers, or engravers like those who through the centuries were hired to magnificently adorn the buildings of the Vatican. Further, there will be no more subsidizing great masters, like Rubens to paint graphic and stunning altar pieces or like Michelangelo to create artistic masterpieces like his renowned ceiling in the Sistine Chapel. The magnificent work of these and many other highly gifted artists, beyond providing great esoteric beauty, served as a smokescreen or a subterfuge, hiding the reality of Babylon the Great.

18:23 "and the light of a lamp shall shine no more at all in thee; and the voice of the bridegroom and of the bride shall be heard no more at all in thee: for thy merchants were the princes of the earth; for with thy sorcery were all the nations deceived."

18:23 "the light of a lamp shall shine no more at all in thee; and the voice of the bridegroom and of the bride shall be heard no more at all in thee"

The destruction of the harlot will be so totally all-encompassing that even "pastoral" activities on the local level (like marriage ceremonies) will cease. Whether the lamp which is mentioned here represents those that would normally be lit for marriage ceremonies, or whether it means the papacy will not be able to illuminate their buildings, is not clear.

18:23 "thy merchants were the princes of the earth"

Usually, only people of wealth, such as these "merchants," would have the means by which they could attain a position from which political power could be gained and exercised. As Proverbs tells us, "The rich ruleth over the poor." (Proverbs 22:7) In confirmation of that proverb, Isaiah stated that in the maritime empire of Tyre, her merchants were princes and her traffickers were the honorable of the earth. (See Isaiah 23:8.)

18:23 "with thy sorcery were all the nations deceived"

The pronoun "thy" refers to "Babylon, the great city,"(18:21) which is to be equated with the Mother of Harlots. (See 17:5.) The word "sorcery" is a translation of the Greek word *pharmakeia*, from which our English word "pharmacy" is derived. As used here in 18:23, it points to a drug, potion or narcotic which overpowers someone's sense of right and propriety, a strong type of a Mickey Finn. Translators have struggled to convey the meaning concisely. While most translations express the idea with the word "sorcery," the NIV and the Stern translations give it as "magic spell." The Phillips New Testament rendered it as "witchery." The Message expressed it as "black magic arts." The Amplified translation chose "magic spells and poisonous charm" to express the idea.

Gregg quotes Barnes as saying, "It is a common representation of Papal Rome that she has *deceived* or *deluded* the nations of the earth ... and no representation ever made accords more with the facts as they have occurred. The word *sorceries* here refers to the various arts, the tricks, imposters, and false pretenses by which this has been done."[540]

At the diplomatic level, the papacy, through the centuries, has presented political offers and guidance which have entranced or bewitched her political paramours. The extensive wide-ranging diplomatic corps maintained by the papacy, coupled with her clerical staff stationed in major cities throughout the world, makes it possible for an alert papacy to globally monitor conditions and the political pulse. On the basis of that advanced knowledge, often outstripping the efforts of secular diplomatic outposts, her suggestions – though sometimes devious – have been luring. This has most recently been demonstrated in the papacy's role in July 2015 of restoring diplomatic relations between Cuba and the U.S.A. Pope Francis "acted as the chief advocate for renewing diplomatic ties between Washington and Havana, officials said."[541]

18:24 "And in her was found the blood of prophets and of saints, and of all that have been slain upon the earth."

When the smokescreen finally blows away, one will be able to see the gruesome reality which will have become visible.

The fall of Babylon the Great, the Mother of Harlots, will have come about through the preaching of Christ's Gospel by the church whose ranks will have been enlarged by those who will have come out of Babylon, the harlot. (See 18:4 and comments.) That will also be one of the many great factors in bringing about The Millennium which is highlighted in chapter 20.

Addendum to Revelation 18:13 on Slavery and the Roman Catholic Church

The reality of the endorsement and practice of slavery by the Roman Catholic Church is a historical fact that is largely suppressed by that church. "The thought of the sixteenth century Jesuit social theorist, Robert Bellarmine, who mixed a clear sense of Catholic distinction from Protestantism with a philosophy synthesizing Augustine and Thomas Aquinas, [was] that slavery

---

540 Revelation, Four Views: A Parallel Commentary, ed. Steve Gregg, (Nashville: Thomas Nelson Publishers, 1997), p. 436.
541 www.cnn.com/2014/12/17/politics/pope-cuba/index.html, accessed 8/21/15.

Revelation Chapter 18

was a natural part of the created order. ... Protestants regarded the Reformation as a new birth of freedom, while Jesuits led Catholics in abominating it as an upwelling of heresy. Amid this context, Jesuits of the [Maryland] colony honored Ignatius [Loyola, founder of the Jesuits] as a mainstay of the Catholic counterattack on the Protestant reformers of the sixteenth century. They believed that he had checked a Protestant wave from rolling across all Europe and had founded the Society of Jesus for the specific purpose of insuring that the Roman Catholic Church would always have the warriors it needed for the ongoing struggle against Protestant perfidy. This interpretation of their heritage was so strong among the Jesuits of Maryland that they responded to the argument of abolitionism by looking not at the merits of the case but at its source. Jesuits ultimately regarded abolitionism as if it were just another Protestant error in three centuries of sectarian rivalry. ... The legacy of this perspective on Ignatius and his heritage was a severe resistance to abolitionism by nineteenth century Jesuits. They saw it as a movement which, having originated among Protestants, was automatically heretical."[542]

"This theological perspective quite comfortably accommodated a division of American society into rulers and ruled, masters and slaves. It encouraged the Jesuits to think that Africans could not function as moral agents without the guidance of white Catholic slave owners." [543]

"The Jesuits defended the Catholic proposition that while the Word of God was indeed contained *in* scripture, it was not contained *by* scripture. Decisive to them were the interpretations of scripture handed down by popes, ecumenical councils, and the totality of eighteen and more centuries of Church tradition. Thus arose the Jesuit conviction that such 'individualistic' readings of scripture as abolitionism were simply misinterpretations by people who could not have the Spirit because they did not embrace the true Church's whole tradition."[544]

"A scrutiny of the twenty-one general councils of the Roman Catholic Church reveals that at least four of them produced canons which sanctioned slavery."[545]

"In their own battles against the consequences of the human fall, Jesuits often displayed a tendency to mistrust their own sense impressions, manipulating their observations to make them deductively subservient to the theories postulated by reason and 'the higher faculties' of the mind. What they observed was placed at the service of what they already believed. In this way, their belief in the doctrine of concupiscence prompted them to see black people as born to be slaves rather than born to be fully human."[546]

"The Jesuits, Dominicans, and others nonetheless supported and participated in the horrors of the Atlantic slave trade. The slave traders and missionaries in Angola worked closely together with little difficulty. The holiest of Catholic institutions in Luanda – the Holy House of Mercy – took its share from the slave trade. The bishop, like the colonial governor, the civil and ecclesiastical officials, the army, and the municipal council, received his income from precisely this source."[547]

---

542 Thomas Murphy, S.J., Jesuit Slave Holding in Maryland, 1717-1838, (Rutledge, New York: 2001), pp. 131, 136.
543 Thomas Murphy, S.J., Jesuit Slave Holding in Maryland, 1717-1838, (Rutledge, New York: 2001), p. 142.
544 Thomas Murphy, S.J., Jesuit Slave Holding in Maryland, 1717-1838, (Rutledge, New York: 2001), p. 144.
545 Thomas Murphy, S.J., Jesuit Slave Holding in Maryland, 1717-1838, (Rutledge, New York: 2001), p. 146.
546 Thomas Murphy, S.J., Jesuit Slave Holding in Maryland, 1717-1838, (Rutledge, New York: 2001), p. 153.
547 Eugene D. Genovese, Roll, Jordan, Roll, (New York: Pantheon Books, 1974), p. 176.

Revelation Chapter 19

Introduction: The climax of chapter 19 (19:15-21) is a complement or an addendum to chapter 16:12-16, especially to 16:14 which tells of "the war of the great day of God, the Almighty." This chapter portrays the victorious two-level (See 19:11 and 19:15.) participation of Christ, the King of Kings (19:16) in this great coming war. The dawning of The Millennium will be one of the very significant developments growing out of this incipient global conflict.

19:1 "After these things I heard as it were a great voice of a great multitude in heaven, saying, Hallelujah; Salvation, and glory, and power, belong to our God:"

19:1 "After these things"

The same expression opens the eighteenth chapter. Please see the comments there.

19:1 "a great voice of a great multitude"

Though the voice was that of a great multitude, the participants composing that multitude obviously spoke in harmony, with clarity and unanimity, thus making it possible for John to understand the message. The "great voice" was not a babble.

19:1 "a great multitude in heaven"

This multitude probably includes the spirits of Christians who will have died "normal" deaths, as well as the spirits of those who have been martyred for Christ, along with the spirits of the faithful Old Testament saints.

After his crucifixion, when Jesus "ascended on high, he led captivity captive and gave gifts unto men." (Ephesians 4:8) Before Jesus took captivity captive, the spirits of the faithful who had previously died were held captive in the place known as "Abraham's bosom." (Luke 16:22-23) Those Old Testament saints could not be allowed into heaven before the completion of "the redemption that is in Christ Jesus: whom God set forth to be a propitiation through faith in his blood to show his righteousness because of the passing over of the sins done aforetime in the forbearance of God." (Romans 3:24-25) The faithful who had previously died before that redemption was completed, constituted the members in that temporary captivity in "Abraham's bosom" whom Jesus liberated by triumphantly taking them as his captives to reside in heaven. Subsequently, because Jesus made that intermediate condition unnecessary, when Christians die our spirits go directly into the presence of Christ (II Corinthians 5:8, Philippians 1:23). Be sure to read the additional comments at 1:18 under "I have the keys of death and Hades."

19:1 "saying, Hallelujah"

The word "Hallelujah" is a Hebrew word which means "Praise ye Jehovah." The four occurrences of the word "Hallelujah" in verses 1, 3, 4, and 6 in Revelation chapter 19 "are the only times that the word appears in the New Testament."[548]

19:2 "for true and righteous are his judgments; for he hath judged the great harlot, her that corrupted ["who corrupted" – ESV, NIV] the earth with her fornication, and he hath avenged the blood of his servants at her hand."

19:2 "true and righteous are his judgments"

The pronoun "his" refers back to the noun "God" in 19:1. The righteousness of "his judgments" is based on the principle enunciated by Paul in his second letter to the church in Thessalonica in which he said, "It is a righteous thing with God to recompense affliction to them that afflict you." (II Thessalonians 2:6)

19:2 "he hath judged the great harlot"

These words of doom are in splendid contrast with the triumphant announcement in 19:7 that "the marriage of the Lamb is come." The severity of the harlot's judgment is made clear in the very next verse.

19:2 "that corrupted the earth with her fornication"

Beyond those corporate borders directly controlled by the harlot, worldwide she will have also become a highly-esteemed social and religious establishment. Therefore, her heavily compromised morals and ethics will have very adversely influenced moral and ethical standards throughout global society, indicated by the words "the earth."

19:2 "he hath avenged the blood of his servants at her hand"

To this day, the system called "the harlot" continues to be shamelessly vicious. To confirm this, one only has to monitor what has been happening in Mexico and Poland in recent times, both areas where Roman Catholicism dominates.

For example, "Hostilities between Mexico's Catholics and Protestants reached a new high last month [February 1990] when an inter-denominational prayer meeting attended by some 160 evangelicals in the Mexico City area was violently broken up by a mob of several thousand Catholics armed with stones, machetes, and sticks. Virtually all those attending the meeting were injured. 'It was a miracle no one was killed,' said Roxanne Menezes, a young Christian worker who described the scene as 'nightmarish.' … Catholic officials in the neighboring suburbs of Xicalco and Magdalena, where most of the mob originated, have made it clear that evangelicals are not welcome. They refused to comment on the Ajusco incident, but a local priest referred reporters to local government official Guillermo Gutierrez. A report in the influential daily newspaper Uno mas Uno quoted Gutierrez as affirming the expulsion: 'We are all Catholic … In the case someone who lives [in this community] might decide to change religion, the person could be expelled and would have to sell his possessions.' … In 1989 alone, attacks against evangelicals took the lives of at least five believers, injured dozens more, caused

---

548 Revelation, Four Views: A Parallel Commentary, ed. Steve Gregg, (Nashville: Thomas Nelson Publishers, 1997), p. 441.

Revelation Chapter 19

hundreds to flee homelands, and destroyed or closed countless churches. Pentecostal leader and CONEMEX [Mexico's Fellowship of Evangelicals] vice president Aroldo Espinoza, who represents more than 300 churches in central Mexico, reported that in his denomination alone more than 30 churches in the state of Hidalgo are closed and unable to function due to threats of violence against those congregations."[549]

A European example comes from Poland. There, "Social discontent may erupt one of these days – a dreadful specter for a government that traces its lineage to a mass trade union. Maciej Giertych, one of Roman Catholic Primate Jozef Glemp's closest advisers, recently made his attitude toward minorities clear: 'If any Polish citizen does not consider himself a Pole [which is to say, a Polish Catholic] let him leave the country or let him be loyal to the hosts whose guest he happens to be.' In the meantime, various right-wing groups have mushroomed, most of them preaching the authoritarian, jingoistic and anti-Semitic doctrines of the prewar National Democrats."[550]

Utterly no cry from the papacy has been heard repudiating events like those just cited which have taken place in Mexico, Poland, and other countries. Why no repudiation? Because those events are a true reflection of the rapacity of the bestial system.[551]

19:3 **"And a second time they say, Hallelujah. And her smoke goeth up for ever and ever."**

"Her smoke" refers to that which rises from her judgment. (19:2) This smoke is to be distinguished from "the smoke of her burning" mentioned in 18:9 and 18:18. (Please see the comments there.) That smoke seems to point to the smokescreen behind which the Great Harlot will have done her work. This smoke, in contrast, rises from the punishment of those who motivated, inspired, participated in and guided the abominable, great, church-centered distortion, aberration and corruption, known as The Harlot. It is smoke which rises from "the eternal fire which is prepared for the devil and his angels." (Matthew 25:41, See also Revelation 20:14 and 21:8.) This is the second occurrence in the book of Revelation of "smoke" being used to refer to the punishment of flagrant unrepentant sinners. It was first used in 14:11; please see the comments there under "the smoke of their torment goeth up for ever and ever."

19:4 **"And the four and twenty elders and the four living creatures fell down and worshipped God that sitteth on the throne, saying, Amen; Hallelujah."**

19:4 "the four and twenty elders"

They seem to be a select group of glorified Christians who have been chosen for duty at the throne of God. (Please see the earlier discussion about them at 4:4.)

19:4 "the four living creatures"

The redemption of the animal kingdom is shown by the presence of the four living creatures in this panorama of heaven. (Please see the discussions of this phenomenon at 4:6, 6:1-2 and 15:7.)

---

549 Christianity Today, March 19, 1990, p.44
550 U.S. News & World Report, March 26, 1990, p. 41.
551 For further substantiation of the nature of the system read David A. Yallop, In God's Name (New York: Bantam Books, 1984).

19:5 "And a voice came forth from the throne, saying, Give praise to our God, all ye his servants, ye that fear him, the small and the great."

19:5 "a voice came forth from the throne"

Though it came from the throne, this was not the voice of God for it speaks of God with the third person pronouns "his" and "him." It was probably the voice of one of the twenty-four elders mentioned in verse 4 who are gathered around the throne.

19:5 "give praise to our God"

The words "give praise to our God," like the exhortation to "Praise ye Jehovah" found in Psalms 135:1, are simply the translation of the Hebrew word "Hallelujah." (See the comments at 19:1 under "saying, Hallelujah.")

B.   The marriage of the Lamb 19:6-10

19:6 "And I heard as it were the voice of a great multitude, and as the voice of many waters, and as the voice of mighty thunders, saying, Hallelujah: for the Lord our God, the Almighty, reigneth."

This triumphant affirmation that "the Lord our God, the Almighty, reigneth" raises the question: "How can we keep the conviction that 'the Almighty reigneth' when there is so much wrong in our world?" The assurance that God is reigning comes from the fact that pivotal developments in his declared plan and under his oversight are observably taking place despite ongoing wrong. This is in addition to the amazing fact that the immeasurably vast physical universe continues to exist and function in a precise and predictable manner. (See "upholding all things by the word of his power," Hebrews 1:3.)

The development which is highlighted in verse 7 is the announcement of the marriage of the Lamb (See 12:7.) which implies the ongoing existence of the church, whose role is to participate as the bride in that marriage. In spite of all that is wrong in society and in history, one of the anchor points which has stood fast is the ongoing existence of the true church, Christ's bride. Notwithstanding all her enemies (sometimes necessitating flight into a wilderness - see 12:6), her weaknesses, her flaws and her shortcomings, she still exists. Because of that fact, the announcement will be made that "the marriage of the Lamb is come" which reminds us that "our God, the Almighty reigneth." Just as Jesus said about his church, "the gates of Hades shall not prevail against it." (Matthew 16:18)

19:7 "Let us rejoice and be exceeding glad, and let us give the glory unto him: for the marriage of the Lamb is come, and his wife hath made herself ready."

19:7 "the marriage of the Lamb is come"

The Stern Translation, which is corroborated by the Good News Translation, renders this phrase as "the time has come for the wedding of the Lamb." Those translations make an important distinction. It is not the marriage itself which has come, but the time for the marriage which has come. As we shall see in the discussion under 19:9, the actual marriage event comes later and is described in Revelation 21:2. Therefore, consider the

Revelation Chapter 19

declaration in 19:7 as a wedding announcement for a glorious event scheduled to take place sometime in the near future.

The church will constitute the bride of Christ (II Corinthians 11:2 and Ephesians 5:29-32), along with the Old Testament saints. (See the comments on 19:9 about others who will also be part of the bride.) When that marriage is consummated, all who compose the bride of Christ will have an infinitely closer union with him. It is thrilling to even imagine the enhanced understanding, insight and power implied by that union.

19:7 "his wife hath made herself ready"

The Greek word *gunay*, may be translated as either wife or bride. The context should determine the choice. Since the marriage between Christ and his bride is imminent but has not been consummated at this point, the use of the word "wife" is inappropriate. The RSV, the NIV and the ESV all have, therefore, correctly translated the word as "bride."

Christ's bride will not have become entirely ready till the completion of the war which is clearly predicted in this chapter. Only after the conclusion of that conflict will the evangelism be able to take place, the fruit of which will make it possible for the bride to become fully ready.

19:8 "And it was given unto her that she should array ["clothe" - ESV] herself in fine linen, bright and pure: for the fine linen is the righteous acts of the saints."

While the true church, the bride of Christ, will have been tempted to turn from the way, like the harlot has, the bride's "righteous acts" testify to her steadfastness and purity. (See the specifics in Matthew 25:34-40.) This is in glaring contrast with the abominable acts of the harlot, only a few of which have been cataloged in 19:2.

19:9 "And he saith unto me, Write, Blessed are they that are bidden to the marriage supper of the Lamb. And he saith unto me, These are true words of God."

19:9 "he saith unto me"

The speaker seems to be the one whose "voice came forth from the throne." (19:5) The one speaking to John identifies himself in verse 10 as one of John's fellow-servants.

19:9 "Blessed are they that are bidden ["invited" - ESV, NIV] to the marriage supper of the Lamb"

Invitations will have been sent, but the feast, "the marriage supper of the lamb," will come later, highlighted in the account given in chapter 21. Who will constitute the group to be invited or "bidden to the marriage supper of the Lamb?" Those recipients of invitations "to the marriage supper of the Lamb" cannot be Christians or Old Testament saints like Noah, Abraham and Moses, along with myriads of other faithful servants of God who lived in the pre-Christian eras, for they, collectively along with the church, will constitute the bride. Certainly, the bride will not receive an invitation like those which will be sent to the guests.

The issue of the inclusion of Old Testament saints, along with Christians, being those who together will constitute Christ's bride, is highly relevant. The Old Testament saints are to be included because they, like New Testament Christians, will also have been saved through the blood of Christ. The power of his blood to forgive sins was applied retroactively for their benefit. That truth comes from the fact that Christ's death also took "place for the redemption of the transgressions that were under the first covenant, [so] they that have been called may receive the promise of the eternal inheritance." (Hebrews 3:15) As we have previously seen in the comments on "a great multitude in heaven" at 19:1, this truth is also emphasized by Paul in Romans 3:24-25. When that redemption of the Old Testament saints was completed, they became "just men made perfect." (Hebrews 12:23) Their inclusion along with New Testament Christians is also made clear from Jesus' statement "that many shall come from the east and the west, and shall sit down with Abraham, and Isaac, and Jacob, in the kingdom of heaven." (Matthew 8:11)

But, what about those guests, "they that are bidden"? Who will they be? We are indebted to Peter through whom we learn that "angels desire to look into" the things which "have been announced" unto us. (I Peter 1:12) One of the greatest announcements of all time will be, "the marriage of the Lamb has come, and his Bride has made herself ready." (Revelation 19:7 ESV) Probably, God will honor the angels' long-standing desire by inviting them to be guests at the marriage supper of the Lamb. It will be a gala celebration without precedent and beyond description!

19:10 "And I fell down before his feet to worship him. And he saith unto me, See thou do it not: I am a fellow-servant with thee and with thy brethren that hold the testimony of Jesus: worship God; for the testimony of Jesus is the spirit of prophecy."

19:10 "I fell down before his feet to worship him"

Be sure to read the comments on 22:8 which record a second occurrence of John's misplaced worship. Here, the person before whom John prostrated himself apparently was the messenger who is identified in 19:5 and 19:9.

John's inclination toward paying homage to him probably arose because he was overwhelmed by the awareness of some of the enhanced potential which would grow out of the closer, more intimate union with Christ which this marriage implies. He knew this could only be brought about through divine wisdom and power, attributes which John mistakenly thought were possessed by the visiting messenger.

19:10 "he saith unto me, See thou do it not: I am a fellow-servant with thee"

As previously mentioned, the one who spoke to John seems to have been the one mentioned in 19:5 whose "voice came forth from the throne." Even though that person had been exalted to a position very near the throne of God, he still humbly acknowledged his utter inferiority to God, claiming to be only John's "fellow servant."

19:10 "thy brethren that hold the testimony of Jesus"

The brethren who hold the testimony of Jesus cannot be those who are half-convinced followers of Jesus. They must "hold the testimony of Jesus" in the face of increasing numbers of more astute and subtle philosophical arguments against the validity of the propositions which underlie the Gospel of Christ. Additionally, there are also waves of assaults motivated by raw and very explicit sensuality. Since all these attacks deny even

Revelation Chapter 19

the most basic truths which we Christians acknowledge, we can only "hold the testimony of Jesus" if we do so with resolution, courage and keen insight. Only then can we uphold and effectively make known "the testimony of Jesus." This tenacious and courageous stand must be maintained in the face of ongoing and increasing attacks such as those which were previously noted at 11:7 under "overcome them and kill them." The death of Christians may well take gruesome forms, for in 20:4 we are told of those who will have been "beheaded for the testimony of Jesus." Let all of us resolve to be faithful unto death, no matter what form that death may take. Those who are faithful to Christ will have to "hold the testimony of Jesus" in the face of at least four categories of attacks:

First, there are attacks coming from the sensualists who are marshaling more and more political and social pressure to silence Christians. (See 13:18 under "the number of the beast; for it is the number of a man.") The followers of Christ must uphold biblically-based spiritual and ethical standards in the face of propositions which promote transgender bathrooms, same-sex marriage, sex outside of marriage and the perversions involved in all the transgender sexual activities.[552] As we face the future, we will repeatedly encounter the acronym "LGBT," which stands for lesbian, gay, bisexual and transgender. The issue of sexual morality even reaches into high school biology text books which teach unmarried female students which drugs are effective in inducing an abortion should they become pregnant.[553] At the same time, the U.S. government has allotted huge sums to fight sexually transmitted diseases without any moral campaign to prevent such infections. San Francisco is considered to be ground zero for HIV in the United States. It is seeking, at great public expense, to become the first city in the world with no infections, **no stigma** and no deaths, though with shortened lives.[554] "There is no cure, so patients must swallow pills for the rest of their lives. Antiviral medications are also expensive – [up to $60,000 a year] – and come with unpleasant side effects."[555]

Second, Christians must face the blatant, aggressive denials of Christian doctrine endlessly advocated and enforced through lethal and brutal procedures by Islam. For the most fundamental doctrinal attacks by Islam on the identity of Jesus, see Appendix F, "The Christology of Islam."

Third, we must face the renewed atheistic attacks of communism. (Please see the comments at 16:13 under "out of the mouth of the dragon.")

Fourth, we must face attacks based on several categories of devious and quasi-scientific research which pose a danger to understanding the truth of the basic concepts upon which the Gospel is based. This form of attack is integrated into Neo-Darwinian evolution. For a discussion of this widespread powerful attack on the basics of the Christian faith, see Appendix G, "Darwin at the University."

---

552 Kasim Reed, mayor of Atlanta, Georgia, "announced Tuesday [1/6/15] that he had fired the chief of the city's Fire Rescue Department, Kelvin Cochran, after Mr. Cochran gave workers a religious book he wrote containing passages that condemn homosexuality. ... That move sparked a debate about religious liberty and freedom of expression: Last month, the 1.4-million-member Georgia Baptist Convention began an online petition that called for Mr. Cochran's reinstatement and suggested that his First Amendment rights had been violated. ... At a news conference Mr. Reed said that ... Atlanta's non-discrimination policy is 'non-negotiable.'" - Richard Fausset, *Atlanta Ousts Fire Chief Who Has Antigay Views*, The New York Times, January 7, 2015, p. A13.

553 For example, Campbell Biology: Concepts and Connections used by the Gilbert, Arizona School District. See Rick Rojas, *In Arizona, a Textbook Fuels a Broader Dispute Over Sex Education*, The New York Times, November 28, 2014, pp. 18 and 20.

554 Adapted from Alice Park, *The End of AIDS*, TIME, December 1-8, 2014, p. 45.

555 Sophia Lee, *Recycling a Tragedy*, WORLD, October 3, 2015, p. 48.

19:10 "the testimony of Jesus is the spirit of prophecy"

To explain his urgently uttered prohibition against John's attempted worship, the messenger pointed out that the focus of the centuries of biblical prophecy was not on him but on Jesus since "Jesus is the spirit of prophecy." Therefore, he is the one before whom everyone should fall prostrate. Not only is Jesus the focal point to which the entire prophetic message points, but as was emphasized in the comments on 1:1, Christ is also the central figure in delivering the divine revelation.

C. Christ defeats the Beast and the False Prophet 19:11-21

19:11 "And I saw the heaven opened; and behold, a white horse, and he that sat thereon called Faithful and True; and in righteousness he doth judge and make war."

19:11 "I saw the heaven opened"

At crucial times in the progress of human affairs, to understand events, to see connections between seemingly isolated and unrelated developments, to see comprehensive, significant, meaningful patterns, we must be able to evaluate everything from a heavenly perspective. At this point, John was honored by being allowed to behold significant events which were taking place in heaven, events which would impact developments on earth. Thankfully, he was not ordered, as he was once before (10:4), to conceal the vision from us.

19:11 "a white horse, and he that sat thereon"

The mention of the white horse takes us back to 6:1-2 where it was previously featured. As Barnes pointed out, white horses were ridden by conquerors on the day of their triumph. "The preference of white to denote triumph or victory was early referred to among the Hebrews. Thus, Judges in verse 10 of the Song of Deborah says, 'Speak, ye that ride on white asses, ye that sit in judgment, and walk by the way.' [Judges 5:10 KJV] The expression, then, in the passage before us, would properly refer to some kind of *triumph*, whether of the gospel or of victory in war."[556] This victory probably refers to that which will be gained by a war fought on two levels. One war will be fought by proclamation of the Gospel and the other by divine participation in temporal warfare.

Attempting to identify the one "that sat thereon" brings us to a pleasant point of agreement. As endlessly divergent as interpretations of Revelation often are, on this matter there is great unanimity and agreement among commentators. This is so, whether they belong to the Historicist, Preterist, Futurist, Spiritual or some other school of interpretation. They all seem to agree that the rider on the white horse is Christ. As Gregg has noted, "Few persons appearing in Revelation are more universally identified by expositors than the rider upon this white horse."[557] Doubtless this concord has grown out of the fact that in verses 11-16 many attributes of the rider are given which can hardly point to anyone other than Jesus Christ.

---

[556] Albert Barnes, Notes, Explanatory and Practical on the Book of Revelation, (New York: Harper & Brothers Publishers, 1852), p. 166.
[557] Revelation, Four Views: A Parallel Commentary, ed. Steve Gregg, (Nashville: Thomas Nelson Publishers, 1997), p. 449.

Revelation Chapter 19

19:11 "he that sat thereon [is] called Faithful and True"

In his letter to the church at Laodicea, Jesus claimed these attributes for himself. He said, "These things sayeth the amen, the faithful and true witness, the beginning of the creation of God." (Revelation 3:14) These attributes are said, in numerous other passages, to belong to Christ. Note, for example, John 14:6, I Thessalonians 5:24, II Thessalonians 3:3, II Timothy 2:13, Hebrews 2:17 and 3:2.

19:11 "he doth judge and make war"

This judgment must be clearly differentiated from the judgment of the "great white throne" which is highlighted in 20:11-12. This judgment seems to point to a sifting to find those who would be willing to capitulate to Christ as he and his army confront people with the truth of the Gospel, that confrontation being part of a two-level war. (See 19:15.) The other aspect of this war is a gigantic clash of arms in which angelic armies will take part. (See 19:14.)

19:12 "And his eyes are a flame of fire, and upon his head are many diadems; and he hath a name written which no one knoweth but he himself."

19:12 "his eyes are a flame of fire"

This description has occurred twice previously in 1:14-15 and in 2:18. Please see the comments in those places.

19:12 "upon his head are many diadems" ["crowns" - KJV, NIV]

As Barclay has pointed out, the Greek word for the crown on his head "is *diadema* which is the royal crown."[558] As the book of Hebrews makes clear, though it does not utilize the word *diadema*, the one wearing these crowns or diadems is Jesus Christ, the very one who has been "crowned with glory [Gr. *doksa*] and honor [Gr. *timay*]." (Hebrews 2:9)

There are two facts which tell us unmistakably that he is presently reigning or ruling as king over his kingdom. First, Christ is riding the royal steed (verse 11) and, secondly, he is wearing the royal crown. There isn't the slightest indication that the rule of Christ from the time of his initial coronation (his being exalted, Acts 2:33) has at any time been interrupted. No lacuna or gap in his dominion is known to have taken place. On Christ's coronation and reign, please see the exposition at 20:3 under the discussion of I Corinthians 15:25-26. When Jesus returns the second time in total triumph, he will "come in his glory." (Matthew 25:31)

19:12 "he hath a name written which no one knoweth but he himself"

This secret name was probably engraved or embossed on his dazzling crown. Since it was written, presumably it could be read, but its meaning was unknown up to the time John was given this vision of Christ in glory. It is part of the "mystery of Christ" (Ephesians 3:4) and of "the mystery of God." (See Colossians 2:2.) It may be like a word from a foreign language, written in a familiar script. Though such a word may be sounded out, its meaning would still be illusive. Ultimately, it is probable that the mystery of Christ's

---

558 William Barclay, The Revelation of John, Vol. II, (Philadelphia: The Westminster Press, 1976), p. 4.

unknown name will be revealed on the pattern of previous mysteries. (See I Corinthians 2:9-10.)

19:13 "And he is arrayed in a garment sprinkled with blood: and his name is called The Word of God."

19:13 "he is arrayed in a garment sprinkled with blood"

Instead of "sprinkled with blood," the KJV, the ESV, the NRSV and the NIV all render it "dipped in blood." Plummer helpfully says, "Probably the similarity of this passage [that is, Revelation 19:13 with Isaiah 63:3] has caused the reading 'sprinkled with blood,' which is found in a few manuscripts. In the original passage in Isaiah, the *blood* is doubtless the *blood* of his enemies; but it is possible that there is here a reference to the blood of Christ himself, which he shed in his warfare with Satan."[559]

19:13 "his name is called The Word of God."

This chapter highlights three names of the rider on the white horse: **First**, in verse 12, a name is given which is known only to the rider himself. **Secondly**, here in verse 13, the name by which he is called is "The Word of God." **Finally**, in verse 16, his name, expressing triumph, is "King of Kings and Lord of Lords."

From the fact that one of his names is "The Word of God," we see that the famous designation for Christ, which is uniquely used in the first chapter of John's Gospel, is a name. As noted in the discussion of the authorship of Revelation, Plummer has pointed out that "Only in St. John's writing does this title appear – a strong argument in favor of his authorship of the Apocalypse (cf. John 1:1; I John 1:1)."[560]

19:14 "And the armies which are in heaven followed him upon white horses, clothed in fine linen, white and pure."

These armies, rather than being as Barnes thought, the "hosts of the redeemed,"[561] are doubtless to be identified with the legions mentioned by Jesus when he pointedly asked Peter, "Do you think I cannot call on my Father, and he will at once put at my disposal more than twelve legions of angels?" (Matthew 26:53 NIV) This identification becomes utter certainty according to what Jesus revealed when he previously said "the Son of man shall come in the glory of his Father with his angels; and then shall he render unto every man according to his deeds." (Matthew 16:27)

From II Kings 6:8 and 6:15-17 we read of a historical event during which, through angels, God took a direct hand in the flow of history rather than his usually more remote role. The mention here of "the armies which are in heaven" which are to follow Christ seem to point to a similar coming intervention in human affairs by explicit divine power, projected through angels. (See II Thessalonians 1:7.)

It is highly probable that it will be by means of these heavenly armies of angels that the overt divine intervention predicted by Ezekiel in his prophecy of this incipient war will

---

[559] A. Plummer, The Pulpit Commentary [on] Revelation, (Chicago: Wilcox & Follett Co., no date), p. 449.
[560] A. Plummer, The Pulpit Commentary [on] Revelation, (Chicago: Wilcox & Follett Co., no date), p. 449.
[561] Revelation, Four Views: A Parallel Commentary, ed. Steve Gregg, (Nashville: Thomas Nelson Publishers, 1997), p. 450.

Revelation Chapter 19

take place. For examples: In Ezekiel 38:16, Ezekiel quotes God as saying "I will bring thee [Gog] against my land." In Ezekiel 38:22, God is quoted as saying, "with blood will I enter into judgment with him." According to Ezekiel 39:3, God tells Gog, "I will smite thy bow out of thy left hand." Further, God is quoted in Ezekiel 39:6 as saying, "I will send a fire on Magog."

19:15 "And out of his mouth proceedeth a sharp sword, that with it he should smite the nations: and he shall rule them with a rod of iron: and he treadeth the winepress of the fierceness of the wrath of God, the Almighty."

19:15 "out of his mouth proceedeth a sharp sword, that with it he should smite the nations"

Christ will lead in fighting a two-level war. The first level is fought by the "sharp sword" of his mouth, in conjunction with which he will rule with "a rod of iron." The second level of this war is that in which Christ will tread "the winepress of the fierceness of the wrath of God."

A sharp sword is a well-known simile used to depict the word of God. (See Hebrews 4:12 and Ephesians 6:17.) Here, it probably is used to depict a prophetic passage in God's word like that in Ezekiel chapter 39. Smiting with it probably means to bring it to pass, to bring the nations to the fulfillment of their prophesied destiny. This function of God's word was foreseen long ago by Isaiah, who wrote, "with righteousness he shall judge the poor, and decide with equity for the meek of the earth; and he shall strike the earth with the rod of his mouth, and with the breath of his lips he shall kill the wicked." (Isaiah 11:4 ESV) (See also the comments on 19:21.)

19:15 "and he shall rule them with a rod of iron"

If one should think that the description in this section of Revelation implies the second, final return of Christ to the earth, Jay Adams, as quoted by Gregg, gave clear guidance when he noted, "That this does not describe a physical coming such as the second advent is apparent. ... Christ is nowhere else said to return upon a *horse* [as he is in 19:11 depicted as doing]. He did not ascend this way, and he is to return *as he ascended*. [See Acts 1:11.]"[562]

The "rod of iron" is most probably to be equated with the measuring rod which was highlighted in 11:1. (Please see the comments there.) It is another simile for the word of God which has been called a sword, but is here also called a "rod of iron." It refers to scripture by which we may determine whether concepts, conditions or practices in our lives, the church or society are legitimate and appropriate or not. This function of scripture is clearly set forth in the following passages: Isaiah 8:20, I Corinthians 4:6, II Timothy 3:16-17 and Hebrews 8:5. It is probably called the "rod of iron" because its truth is inflexible. Spiritual reality revealed by God's word is just as rigid and unforgiving (See Galatians 1:8.) as "natural laws" like that of gravity. When the nations submit to King Jesus' rule of the "rod of iron," we will be in The Millennium!

---

562 Revelation, Four Views: A Parallel Commentary, ed. Steve Gregg , (Nashville: Thomas Nelson Publishers, 1997), p. 450.

19:15 "he treadeth the winepress of the fierceness of the wrath of God, the Almighty"

As emphasized before, this passage portrays a war fought at two levels. As depicted here by the "winepress of the fierceness of the wrath of God," there will be a widespread, global, physical war. Simultaneously, it will be accompanied by an all-out war for men's hearts, indicated by the "sharp sword" which comes out of Christ's mouth. Any subterfuge, hypocrisy, mental dishonesty or other effort to disregard the truth will be met by a fierce response from God and his army. For the identification and the character of this winepress, see the comments at 14:18-19.

19:16 "And he hath on his garment and on his thigh a name written, KING OF KINGS, AND LORD OF LORDS."

19:16 "he hath on his garment and on his thigh a name written"

As the practice still is today, battle uniforms have identifying name tags. This rider has his name written in two places: "on his garment and on his thigh." When mounted, as he is here depicted to be, the name displayed on his thigh would be more visible.

19:16 "KING OF KINGS, AND LORD OF LORDS"

Probably this is the name which is written both "on his garment and on his thigh." The identity of this king was previously and unmistakably given in 17:14, which says, "the Lamb shall overcome them, for he is Lord of lords and King of kings." Triumphantly and encouragingly, that verse goes on to say, "they also shall overcome that are with him, called and chosen and faithful." (Revelation 17:14)

19:17 "And I saw an angel standing in the sun; and he cried with a loud voice, saying to all the birds that fly in mid heaven, Come and be gathered together unto the great supper of God;"

19:17 "I saw an angel standing in the sun"

Plummer, probably correctly, concluded that "standing in the sun" is equivalent to the expression "in mid heaven (as in ch. viii. [verse] 13, etc.)"[563] On the meaning of "in mid heaven" please see the comments on 14:6 under "in mid heaven."

19:17 "he cried with a loud voice, saying to all the birds that fly in mid heaven, Come and be gathered together unto the great supper of God"

This "great supper of God" stands in unique distinction by its stark contrast to "the marriage supper of the Lamb," which was highlighted in 19:9. By Ezekiel, centuries earlier, this "great supper of God" was prophesied to eventually take place. Ezekiel recorded, "And thou, son of man, thus saith the Lord Jehovah: Speak unto the birds of every sort, and to every beast of the field, Assemble yourselves, and come; gather yourselves on every side to my sacrifice that I do sacrifice for you, even a great sacrifice upon the mountains of Israel, that ye may eat flesh and drink blood. Ye shall eat the flesh of the mighty, and drink the blood of the princes of the earth, of rams, of lambs, and of

---

563 A. Plummer, The Pulpit Commentary [on] Revelation, (Chicago: Wilcox & Follett Co., no date), p. 450.

Revelation Chapter 19

goats, of bullocks, all of them fatlings of Bashan. And ye shall eat fat till ye be full, and drink blood till ye be drunken, of my sacrifice which I have sacrificed for you. And ye shall be filled at my table with horses and chariots, with mighty men, and with all men of war, saith the Lord Jehovah." (Ezekiel 39:17-20)

19:18 "that ye may eat the flesh of kings, and the flesh of captains, and the flesh of mighty men, and the flesh of horses and of them that sit thereon, and the flesh of all men, both free and bond, and small and great."

This verse gives added specificity to the gruesome defeat which Ezekiel's prophecy predicts for those godless hordes who ultimately will invade the land of Israel with the intent to destroy Israel. The essence of Ezekiel's account of the defeat of the invading armies is captured in the following verses from his prophecy: "And thou, son of man, prophesy against Gog [See comments on Revelation 20:8.], and say, Thus saith the Lord Jehovah: Behold, I am against thee, O Gog, prince of Rosh, Meshech, and Tubal: and I will turn thee about, and will lead thee on, and will cause thee to come up from the uttermost parts of the north; and I will bring thee upon the mountains of Israel; and I will smite thy bow out of thy left hand, and will cause thine arrows to fall out of thy right hand. Thou shalt fall upon the mountains of Israel, thou, and all thy hordes, and the peoples that are with thee: I will give thee unto the ravenous birds of every sort, and to the beasts of the field to be devoured. Thou shalt fall upon the open field; for I have spoken it, saith the Lord Jehovah." (Ezekiel 39:1-5)

"And it shall come to pass in that day, that I will give unto Gog a place for burial in Israel, the valley of them that pass through on the east of the sea; and it shall stop them that pass through: and there shall they bury Gog and all his multitude; and they shall call it the valley of Hamon-gog. And seven months shall the house of Israel be burying them, that they may cleanse the land. Yea, all the people of the land shall bury them; and it shall be to them a renown in the day that I shall be glorified, saith the Lord Jehovah. And they shall set apart men of continual employment, that shall pass through the land, and, with them that pass through, those that bury them that remain upon the face of the land, to cleanse it: after the end of seven months shall they search. And they that pass through the land shall pass through; and when any seeth a man's bone, then shall he set up a sign by it, till the buriers have buried it in the valley of Hamon-gog." (Ezekiel 39:11-15)

19:19 "And I saw the beast, and the kings of the earth, and their armies, gathered together to make war against him that sat upon the horse, and against his army."

19:19 "I saw the beast"

Undoubtedly, this beast is to be identified with the one which is a partner in the unholy trinity mentioned in 16:13. Here, in 19:19-20 we are told of the ultimate destiny of two of the members of that trinity, the beast and the false prophet. The destruction of the third entity, the dragon, is described in 19:21 as "the rest were killed," and in 20:7-9 under "the names of Gog and Magog."

19:19 "the kings of the earth, and their armies"

Centuries earlier, an inclusive roster of these kings was given by Ezekiel: "Thus saith the Lord Jehovah: Behold, I am against thee, O Gog, prince of Rosh, Meshech, and Tubal: and I will turn thee about, and put hooks into thy jaws, and I will bring thee forth, and all thine army, horses and horsemen, all of them clothed in full armor, a great company with buckler and shield, all of them handling swords; Persia, Cush, and Put with them, all of them with shield and helmet; Gomer, and all his hordes; the house of Togarmah in the uttermost parts of the north, and all his hordes; even many peoples with thee." (Ezekiel 38:3-6)

In addition to that roster of world rulers, Ezekiel added "I will send a fire on Magog, and on them that dwell securely in the isles." The isles probably, among others, refer to Borneo, Islamic Indonesia and the southern island of Mindanao in the Philippines where the majority of the people also give their allegiance to the false prophet.

19:19 "to make war against him that sat upon the horse, and against his army"

For the identity of the one mounted on "the horse," see the comments on 19:11. "His army" is composed of the angelic host mentioned in 19:14 who complement the church which, under the leadership of Christ, is fighting evil. (Compare II Thessalonians 1:7.)

Christians are armed for their part in this war. (See Ephesians 6:11-18 and II Corinthians 10:3-5.)

19:20 "And the beast was taken, and with him the false prophet that wrought the signs in his sight, wherewith he deceived them that had received the mark of the beast and them that worshipped his image: they two were cast alive into the lake of fire that burneth with brimstone:"

19:20 "the beast was taken"

This beast is a composite one, formed through a love-hate relationship between the political beast and the ecclesiastical harlot. Normally the political part of the beast carries the harlot. (Revelation 17:7) That is the love part of the relationship. That love is an illicit sensual hedonistic relationship which is expressed as fornication. There is, therefore, a real union, at times, for the corrupt church is "the great harlot that sitteth upon many waters; with whom the kings of the earth committed fornication ..." (Revelation 17:1-2) Therefore, the two, because of their fornication, have become, as it were, one flesh. (See I Corinthians 6:16.) Though the union is illicit because it is based on fornication, it is, nonetheless, real. Even though we can still identify the components of the resulting monstrosity, the two in their union have become one, and thus united they form "the beast." Since God calls such a church/state relationship fornication, a prohibited union, he powerfully upholds the separation of the two institutions.[564]

---

[564] For details on the fornicatious relationship between the Roman Catholic Church and various political powers, see the very detailed and inclusive account given by Gerald Posner in God's Bankers, A History of Money and Power at the Vatican, (New York: Simon & Schuster, 2015).

Revelation Chapter 19

19:20 "and with him the false prophet that wrought the signs in his sight"

The false prophet points to the founder of Islam. The fact that he "wrought the signs ["miracles" - KJV, "miraculous signs" - NIV] in his [that is, the beast's] sight" is in harmony with the statement in 16:14 that he along with his evil companions went about their worldwide mission by "working signs." These phenomena are similar to some of the "signs and lying wonders" about which Paul warned the Thessalonian Christians. (II Thessalonians 2:9) However, these signs, miracles, or miraculous signs do not point to paranormal miracles, that is, to miracles which result in healings, resurrections or events like walking on water, which even currently are not scientifically explainable. Rather, the signs to which reference is made seem to point to the astonishing miraculous success of establishing the Islamic movement despite its open, blatant and total inconsistency, deceit and dishonesty. Keep in mind that Muhammad, who is here designated "the false prophet" and who initiated the Islamic movement, appeared several centuries after the distortion of Christianity did, the outcome of which is here compositely designated as "the beast." So, historically, the bogus miracles involved in the rise of Islam took place in "his [that is, in the beast's] sight."

To further understand this phenomenon, please review the facts which were given previously in the discussion of 16:13.

19:20 "wherewith he deceived"

It is astonishing to the point of being miraculous that in the face of such obvious inconsistencies and falsehoods the Arab prophet could be persuasive enough to gain worldwide credence. The use of force, along with the threat of death against anyone who tried to prevent Muhammad from realizing his dream of global dominion, often not only deterred them from speaking out but most often brought them to their knees in obedience.

19:20 "he deceived them that had received the mark of the beast and them that worshipped his image"

The deceptive power of the false prophet not only brought the vast swath of nations from the Indus River in the east to the Atlantic Ocean at Morocco under the sway of Islam, but this description also points us to Russia being deceived by the false prophet (See the comments on Revelation 13:16 under "a mark on their right hand or upon their forehead.") and, therefore, it clarifies the basis for the mysterious affinity between Russia and Islam. To identify "them that worshipped his image," see the comments on 13:14.

19:20 "they two ["these both" - KJV, "the two of them" - NIV] were cast alive into the lake of fire that burneth with brimstone"

The statements "they two,"or "these both," or "the two of them" refer to "the beast [which] was taken, and [along] with him the false prophet." It is these two who were cast into the "lake of fire." That statement probably refers to their ultimate rather than their immediate destiny.

19:21 "and the rest were killed with the sword of him that sat upon the horse, even the sword which came forth out of his mouth: and all the birds were filled with their flesh."

Revelation Verse by Verse

19:21 "the rest were killed"

The destruction of the third entity, the dragon, is described here, in 19:21, as "the rest were killed," and in 20:7-9 they, that is, "the rest," are specified under the names of "Gog and Magog." The two entities comprising "the rest" are specified in 19:19 as "the kings of the earth and their armies," the principal ones among them being Gog and Magog. (See the exposition at 20:8.)

19:21 "the sword which came forth out of his mouth"

Mention of "the sword" points us to the word of God. (Hebrews 4:12 and Ephesians 6:17) It is by his word that God directs "the armies which are in heaven [which] followed him." (19:14) It is by this directed army that "the rest were killed." This points to direct divine intervention in the affairs of men. This is one specific fulfillment of the declaration in Daniel 4:25, "that the Most High ruleth in the kingdom of men." (See the comments on 19:15.)

19:21 "and all the birds were filled with their flesh"

This is pointing to the fulfillment of the prophecy in Ezekiel 39:1-5.

Revelation Chapter 20

D. The binding and loosing of Satan 20:1-10

20:1 "And I saw an angel coming down out of heaven, having the key of the abyss and a great chain in his hand."

20:1 "an angel coming down out of heaven"

As previously pointed out, according to Hebrews 1:14, angels are "ministering spirits, sent forth to do service for the sake of them that shall inherit salvation." The first two verses of this chapter indicate that the mission upon which this angel was being sent, when completed, would render one of the greatest services to the heirs of salvation for all time.

Referring to "an angel coming down out of heaven," one commentator wrote, "The messenger [the word angel means messenger] from heaven ["having the key of the abyss"] is Jesus. It is he who has the key of death and Hades (Revelation 1:18; 3:7)."[565] He came to that conclusion by assuming that death and Hades together constitute the abyss. However, please see the definition of "the abyss" at 20:3, under the words "cast him into the abyss," which makes it clear that death and Hades should be differentiated from the abyss. That being the case, the "angel coming down out of heaven having the key of the abyss" is not Christ.

20:1 "having the key of the abyss"

The first mention of this key was made in 9:1-11. On that occasion the key was used to open the abyss, giving Satan the opportunity to unleash the Islamic movement on human society. From this, the twentieth chapter of the book of Revelation, it becomes clear that not only the calamity growing out of Islam was unleashed by the opening of the pit, but also many additional social and spiritual plagues emerged which owe either their origin or their enhanced power to the opening of the abyss. At this point, according to 20:3, the key is going to be used to lock or seal the abyss.

20:1 "a great chain in his hand"

According to 20:2, this chain will be used to bind Satan for a thousand years. A chain of iron or steel links would be of no use in binding Satan since he is a spirit-being. Therefore, this prophesy probably points to a chain of circumstances, of facts, of disclosures, of evidences and of logical arguments – all either described in, based on or deduced from the Bible – which will totally immobilize and neutralize Satan's deceptions, arguments and allurements.

---

565 Fred P. Miller, <u>Revelation: A Panorama of the Gospel Age</u>, (Claremont, Florida, Moellerhaus Publisher, 1991), p. 206.

This chain will be comparable to – only greater than – that which is implied, though not specifically mentioned, in 11:11. There it was noted that the two witnesses, that is the Gentile and Jewish churches, would gain the ability to successfully counteract, thus binding, the anti-God concepts which had seemingly negated the power of the Gospel message. That spiritual victory would clearly be the result of a divine initiative, for the passage says, "the breath [or "Spirit" - KJV] of life from God entered into them."

Here, it is thrilling to anticipate a chain of doctrinal biblical truth of such clarity, veracity, relevance and power that it will bind Satan for a thousand years! We should remember that angels are "ministering spirits sent forth to do service for the sake of them that shall inherit salvation." (Hebrews 1:14) Certainly, as noted above, the angel who comes with "a great chain in his hand" to bind Satan fits that category!

20:2 **"And he laid hold on the dragon, the old serpent, which is the Devil and Satan, and bound him for a thousand years,"**

20:2 "laid hold on the dragon, the old serpent, which is the Devil and Satan"

The idea of the angel laying hold on the dragon is that of apprehending him, of stopping him in his tracks, of thwarting his planning and preventing him from implementing further activities. The work which this angel will perform will be an extension of the work of Christ about which John previously told us when he wrote, "To this end was the Son of God manifested, that he might destroy the works of the devil." (I John 3:8)

20:2 "bound him for a thousand years"

Theologians and biblical commentators usually refer to this "thousand years" as The Millennium. The word millennium comes from two Latin words: "mille" which means one thousand and "annus," meaning a year, from which we get our word annual. So, the word "millennium" means one thousand years. When we talk about The Millennium we mean this special period of one thousand years, or at least a very long time, spanning a period of approximately ten centuries. This coming historic period is given great emphasis in verses 2-7 in which it is emphasized six times.

This passage predicts that at some point during the Christian period of world history, a unique and singular era lasting one thousand years, will eventually dawn, during which Satan, being bound, will be immobilized. Being bound implies that during that entire period, for a thousand years, he will be unable to mislead people or nations, will be unable to influence legislative bodies or those making judicial decisions, and will be unable to dominate the media or popularize evil. Further, it means he will no longer be able to obscure the distinction between right and wrong or truth and error, and, thus, The Millennium will be a period during which sin, in all of its various and deceiving manifestations, will be clearly recognized as evil. Even the current avalanche of gay, homosexual, lesbian and transgender acceptance and endorsement will be completely nullified and repudiated.

Today, the distinction between right and wrong has become so entangled in specious arguments that the truth is obscured. To many, evil often appears righteous while, vice versa, righteousness often appears evil. For example, such confusion has become rampant

Revelation Chapter 20

because of the determined, aggressive governmental campaigns to legalize and regularize abortion and same-sex marriage. Because these deviations from righteousness (See Romans 1:26-27.) have technically become legal, many people have been deceived into thinking that they must also be righteous. These days, because of Satan's hyperactivity, it often becomes very difficult for the average person to know where to take his moral and ethical stance. (Please see Hebrews 5:14 and Philippians 1:9-10.) However, all moral and ethical confusion and obscurity will be removed when Satan is bound during The Millennium.

When the moral and spiritual atmosphere becomes clear because of the binding of Satan, inevitably the message of Christ's Gospel will be understood and felt with much greater ease, clarity and power. Then, undoubtedly, vast multitudes of people living under those greatly improved conditions will yield their hearts to Christ. Thus, we should expect that the true church will thrive and flourish during The Millennium.

20:3 **"and cast him into the abyss, and shut it, and sealed it over him, that he should deceive the nations no more, until the thousand years should be finished: after this he must be loosed for a little time."**

20:3 "cast him into the abyss, and shut it, and sealed it over him"

As noted before, (See 9:11 under "the angel of the abyss.") originally Satan seems to have been an angel who at some point rebelled against God. Thus he entered that category of angels which Jude identified as "Angels that kept not their own principality, but left their proper habitation, he hath kept in everlasting bonds under darkness unto the judgment of the great day." (Jude 1:6) The words "everlasting bonds under darkness" give the definition of "the abyss," which is also to be equated with the "pits of darkness" about which Peter tells us in II Peter 2:4. The abyss is the place where Satan is to be bound during The Millennium. It is also called "his [Satan's] prison." (Revelation 20:7)

20:3 "that he should deceive the nations no more"

The word "nations" is translated from the Greek word, *ethne*, which denotes ethnic groups or people groups, rather than political entities. It is frightening to realize that Satan frequently deceives entire ethnic groups. A prime example was Satan's success in turning the extensive and varied Turkish ethnic group into avid adherents to Islam beginning with Islam's victory over China at the Battle of Talas in 751. The Turks, like the Kurds, inhabit areas which spread across several different political boundaries. Whenever a whole people group becomes mesmerized by Satan, evil will have gained tremendous power and momentum.

20:3 "until the thousand years should be finished"

During The Millennium, "the thousand years," we can expect a very long period during which Satan can no longer deceive the nations as he has repeatedly done in the past. What a felicitous world it will be when there will be no deception. Rather, social and economic justice will prevail.

Also, because Satan will be in the abyss, we can expect a long period of peace. Notice that at the end of this period there will be war again. As Revelation 20:7-8 says, "when the thousand years are finished, Satan will be loosed out of his prison and they shall come forth to deceive the nations that are in the four corners of the earth, Gog and Magog to gather them together to the war." This implies that during The Millennium there will be no war. Think what an impact that will have on the average person's standard of living! Further, it will present an unparalleled congenial environment for the spread of the Gospel.

If the great military budgets of the whole world were channeled into civilian use, we could nearly have our streets paved with sterling silver. To cite just one example, that of America, "The cost of air and naval platforms is becoming prohibitive. The price of a new *Gerald R. Ford*-class aircraft carrier is $12 billion with no aircraft or other equipment on its deck. The price tag according to the latest design of a *Zumwalt*-class destroyer is close to $4 billion. The F-22 Raptor costs $200 million a plane and the F-35 Joint Strike Fighter $135 million. In addition to the cost of projecting air and naval power around the world – and particularly in East Asia – there is a very real imperial fatigue felt by the American public, and by some influential sections of the defense and foreign policy elite in Washington, following the ruinous cost in lives, diplomatic prestige, and monetary expense of the wars in Afghanistan and Iraq."[566]

The results of a millennium without war, which is implied in 20:7-8, would be truly splendid. Presently, war budgets drain astronomical sums from other programs, sums which if wisely, properly and honestly utilized, could greatly enhance living conditions for everyone. If those resources were channeled into raising the living standard for all people, it could usher in a real utopia. Millions of residents in horrible slum areas in major cities around the world could be given such basic benefits as weather-proof fundamental housing, clean drinking water and proper sanitation facilities. If there were no war, undoubtedly governments throughout the world would greatly reduce taxes and Christians would therefore, at that point, have much greater resources to devote to spreading Christ's Gospel and to showing "forth the excellencies of him who called [them] out of darkness into his marvelous light." (I Peter 2:9) However, as genuinely victorious as The Millennium will be, it will not be the ultimate, eternally abiding victory promised to Christians, for during The Millennium the curse of death will not yet have been nullified; neither will sin have yet been totally and eternally eliminated.

Understandably, Christians who have meditated deeply on this exciting biblical passage long for the arrival of the period which is prophesied here to one day dawn upon the world. (See Appendix H for additional scriptures which point forward to The Millennium.)

Traditionally, there are three views of The Millennium. First, there is The Pre-millennial View. The full statement of that position is that Jesus Christ will return before (pre) The Millennium. According to this view, The Millennium is predicted to result from Christ's return to begin his reign on the earth.

The second position is called The Post-millennial View. It affirms that Christ's uninterrupted reign began at his resurrection. It will be from his divine rule which was

---

[566] Robert D. Kaplan, Asia's Cauldron, the South China Sea and End of a Stable Pacific, (New York: Random House, 2014), p. 23.

Revelation Chapter 20

announced on Pentecost (Acts 2:36) that The Millennium will ultimately develop. The second and final return of Jesus will occur following (post) The Millennium.

Finally, there is a third view known as <u>The A-millennial View</u>. The a-millennial position, as the name implies, is that there will be no special period known as The Millennium. Those who embrace this view believe that the whole Christian age is The Millennium. They often base that assumption on Jesus' question found in Matthew 12:29 in which he asked, "How can one enter into the house of the strong man, and spoil his goods, except he first bind the strong man? And then he will spoil his house." With his question about the binding of the strong man, Jesus explained how he had performed the miracle of healing the demoniac who previously could neither see nor speak. (He had been "blind and dumb"- Matthew 12:23.) First of all, he said in essence, "I have bound the strong man." Who was that strong man? He was the devil who had put his poor victim in grievous trouble, making that demon-possessed man one of his slaves. Jesus went into that house, bound Satan, the strong man, the tyrant, and gave freedom to the one whom Satan had bound. The a-millennialists, on the basis of that one dramatic incident, conclude that the binding of Satan described in Revelation 20:2 is already underway, having begun during the ministry of Jesus, and will continue on during the whole Christian period.

However, the historic truth about Satan's being bound does not support the a-millennial view. Undoubtedly, during his ministry, Jesus bound Satan on many occasions. For Scripture tells us in Acts 10:37-38 that Jesus "went about doing good, and healing all who were oppressed of the Devil."

Was that binding of Satan, which obviously Jesus did, the same binding which is implied in Revelation 20, where for a thousand years Satan is going to be immobilized? Obviously not. Even in the closing days of Jesus' ministry Satan became hyperactive. For example, Luke 22:3 tells us, "Satan entered into Judas who was called Iscariot, being of the number of the twelve…" How ironic! Satan entered into one of the closest associates of Jesus, the only one who could bind him. Consequently Judas was willing to sell his Master for thirty paltry pieces of silver!

Also, Satan was hyperactive in the apostolic age. That was made clear when Peter asked, "Ananias, why hath Satan filled thy heart to lie to the Holy Spirit and to keep back part of the price of the land?" (Acts 5:3) Satan certainly was working then, at one of the greatest moments of triumph in the early church, when liberality and generosity had triumphed over greed and selfishness. Even then, Satan got in. Later, Peter exhorted Christians to "be sober, be watchful: your adversary the devil, as a roaring lion, walketh about, seeking whom he may devour." (I Peter 5:8) Furthermore, even later on during the apostolic age, the whole world came into Satan's grasp. I John 5:19 makes that point clear by telling us, "the whole world lieth in the evil one."

The binding of Satan which Jesus did during his ministry was magnificent, but it was localized and temporary. Jesus carried out those occasions of binding Satan not only to relieve many cases of acute human suffering but also, especially, to certify his own identity. (John 20:30-31) The binding which Jesus did during his ministry was not the binding which is predicted in Revelation 20 during which, for an entire millennium, the devil is going to be immobilized.

Ponder again the statement in Revelation 20:2-3: "He laid hold on the dragon, the old serpent, which is the Devil and Satan and bound him for a thousand years, and <u>cast him into the abyss, and shut it, and sealed it over him, that he should deceive the nations no more</u>."

During the intervening centuries, since Jesus went back to God, have the nations been deceived or not? A person doesn't have to be an academic historian or political scientist to affirm that the nations have been terribly deceived and continue being deceived to the present time. We Americans should not imagine that our own nation has been spared from Satan's attacks. We need to pray for our statesmen and our leaders that they may avoid the subtle influences of the deceiver who is currently loose in our world and to whom they also may fall prey. (See I Timothy 2:1-2.) Our prayers are necessary because Satan, the devil, the old dragon, has ways of deceiving politicians as well as us ordinary mortals. Even though politicians may act with full sincerity and with great erudition, they may still be in complete error.

Obviously, the binding which Jesus did on many notable occasions was not the prolonged binding of Satan which is implied in this intriguing twentieth chapter of Revelation. We still look forward to the fulfillment of this marvelous vision.

Finally, we should understand that the events predicted in this passage are to occur during the Christian dispensation, not in some fanciful hypothetical post-church era. It will be an era which dawns largely because of the triumph of the church in promoting the Gospel of Christ.

20:3 "after this he must be loosed for a little time"

Immediately upon the completion of the unique one-thousand-year period known as The Millennium, Satan "must be loosed." After triumph there must be testing. That testing will be severe to prove whether the gains made by the church will have been properly and solidly achieved. Will the advances prove to have been genuine, or will they have been superficial fruits of opportunism? (See the comments on 20:7.) At the end of The Millennium Satan will instigate another war, the final paroxysm of satanic destruction. It will prove to be a time of severe testing for God's people.

20:4 "And I saw thrones, and they sat upon them, and judgment was given unto them: and I saw the souls of them that had been beheaded for the testimony of Jesus, and for the word of God, and such as worshipped not the beast, neither his image, and received not the mark upon their forehead and upon their hand; and they lived, and reigned with Christ a thousand years."

20:4 "I saw thrones, and they sat upon them, and judgment was given unto them"

The grammar of the ASV is clumsy. The English Standard Version clarifies the grammar by saying, "I saw thrones, and seated on them were those to whom the authority to judge was committed."

Revelation Chapter 20

The word "thrones" indicates that Christ is sharing his sovereignty. This reality is also stressed later in this verse where we are told, "<u>they</u> ... reigned with Christ." When the time comes during which Satan can "deceive the nations no more," governing decisions will be under Christ's oversight, who will share those responsibilities with those who have stood most steadfastly and resolutely with him.

Especially notice that verse 4 says, "Judgment was given unto them." The pronoun "them" refers to those who had been willing to lay down their lives for Jesus Christ in opposition to evil. The identity of those who will participate in making governing decisions was clarified by Paul when he told us that "the saints shall judge the world." (I Corinthians 6:2) It is obvious that The Millennium will be one period during which a unique category of saints will function in that role.

20:4 "I saw the souls of them that had been beheaded for the testimony of Jesus and for the word of God"

Jesus taught that there will be a general, bodily, physical resurrection which will be totally inclusive, including believers as well as unbelievers. (See John 5:28-29.) Jesus will continue reigning until that climactic event takes place. In contrast, the resurrection described here in Revelation 20:4 with the words "they lived" is called "the first resurrection." (20:5) The first resurrection is not a physical resurrection. It is important to note that John says, "I saw the souls of them that had been beheaded for the testimony of Jesus, and for the word of God." <u>He didn't see their bodies, but their souls</u>.

This great passage gives immeasurable comfort to Christians when they suffer for their faith. The words "they lived" tell us that though the persecutors had intended to deliver Christians to death and extinction, in fact, they will have delivered them to a more meaningful life than they had experienced before they were martyred. This new life is distinctly different from that of the physical resurrection, the ultimate renewal of life in the body. That event will take place for both the just and the unjust. (Acts 24:15) Not only did Jesus predict it (John 5:28-29) but it is also certified to ultimately take place by the fifteenth chapter of I Corinthians and by this very vivid account in Revelation 20:12-13. Prior to that ultimate climactic event, this blessing, which is called "the first resurrection" (Revelation 20:5), will have been bestowed on those who had been martyred in the service of Jesus Christ. It will be a highly spectacular event which will take place before the general resurrection and the final judgment which are described in 20:11-15.

20:4 "such as worshipped not the beast, neither his image, and received not the mark upon their forehead and upon their hand"

This description identifies that elite group of Christians who will have sustained their faith through the most severe testing. For clarification of the "mark upon their forehead and upon their hand," see the commentary on 13:16.

20:4 "they lived, and reigned with Christ a thousand years"

When we are told that "they lived and reigned," the pronoun "they" points to the martyrs, as well as those who resisted the terrible pressure to worship the beast or his image or to receive the mark upon their forehead or upon their hand. They will be given a category of activity which will make them partners with Christ as he governs the universe and continues to lead the church during The Millennium.

These events are to take place while Christ is reigning, for these victors are to reign with Christ. According to Acts 2:30-33, Christ began his reign by being exalted to the throne of God. Since his exaltation, Christ has continued to reign from the throne of David (as has been discussed in more detail under 20:3). His exaltation was confirmed by having been seated upon the throne of David from which he is presently ruling. It was through his resurrection that he was exalted to a reigning position at the right hand of God. (Please see Colossians 3:1, Hebrews 10:12, and I Peter 3:21-22.) His reign will continue on through The Millennium and beyond, "for he must reign, till he hath put all his enemies under his feet. The last enemy that shall be abolished is death." (I Corinthians 15:25-26) Though today we often see the church in a condition of weakness and frustration, we should look forward to a time when it will be magnificently triumphant.

20:5 "The rest of the dead lived not until the thousand years should be finished. This is the first resurrection."

20:5 "The rest of the dead lived not until the thousand years should be finished"

This statement applies to both the non-Christian and the Christian dead. Though the Christian dead will not experience the bodily resurrection till some time after the completion of The Millennium, in the interim their state is one of bliss, expressed by the words "the joy of thy Lord." (See Matthew 25:20-23.)

20:5 "this is the first resurrection"

This "first resurrection" (See the comments on the phrase, "they lived" at 20:4.) certainly cannot, as some commentators suggest, refer to the resurrection which comes by being raised with Christ through baptism "so we also might walk in newness of life." (Romans 6:4) Every Christian has experienced that resurrection, while only an elect group, "the souls of them that had been beheaded for the testimony of Jesus, and for the word of God," (20:4) will experience "the first resurrection." Thus, in clear contrast to the resurrection to be experienced by all Christians, this "first resurrection" will only have been experienced by those who have been martyred and those who have successfully resisted and withstood the great temptation to receive the mark on their foreheads or on their hands. (See Revelation 20:4.) Furthermore, quite obviously, "the first resurrection" is not, as some have suggested, to be equated with Christ being "the first born from the dead." (Colossians 1:18)

20:6 "Blessed and holy is he that hath part in the first resurrection: over these the second death hath no power; but they shall be priests of God and of Christ, and shall reign with him a thousand years."

20:6 "the second death"

The existence of the "second death" is mentioned four times in Revelation: in 2:11, here at 20:6, then in 20:14, and finally, in 21:8, where its definition is very tersely given.

Revelation Chapter 20

20:6 "they shall be priests of God and of Christ"

While all obedient believers in Christ are priests (See I Peter 2:5 and 2:9.), the priesthood of this elect group of victors will be unique and special. In some way, their ministry in this special priesthood will most probably help facilitate the halcyon days which will characterize The Millennium.

20:6 "shall reign with him a thousand years."

One wonders what these hero priests will be assigned to do following the period of their one-thousand-year-long co-regency with Christ. One cannot imagine that they would be either sidelined or demoted. Probably, therefore, they will be promoted to even more glorious service. (See Daniel 7:27.)

20:7 "And when the thousand years are finished, Satan shall be loosed out of his prison,"

Please see the comment on 20:3 where we are assured that Satan will be loosed only "for a little time," but it will be a time of widespread vicious attacks on the church. (See 20:9 and comments.)

20:8 "and shall come forth to deceive the nations which are in the four corners of the earth, Gog and Magog, to gather them together to the war: the number of whom is as the sand of the sea."

20:8 "shall come forth to deceive the nations"

It is through these nations, after they have been deceived, that Satan will make his final attack, not on Israel as depicted in Ezekiel chapters 38 and 39, but on the church. (See Revelation 20:9.) Even though the roster of attacking nations is nearly identical, both here and in Ezekiel, this culminating satanic attack will usher in the final judgment.

20:8 "the nations which are in the four corners of the earth, Gog and Magog"

Are these terms, "the nations which are in the four corners of the earth" and "Gog and Magog," to be understood as equivalents or as two distinct groups of participants comprising the army which will, according to the next verse, hurl itself against the Christians? Probably the undesignated "nations which are in the four corners of the earth" are distinct from and in addition to "Gog and Magog." On the expression "the four corners of the earth," see the discussion under Revelation 7:1. Here the discussion of Gog and Magog is given in inverse order:

MAGOG. Magog appears in the table of nations in Genesis 10:2. Since he was one of the sons of Japheth, we know the name here represents an ethnic people group, a nation in the ethnic sense. In addition to the mention of Magog here in Revelation 20:8, the name is only found in Genesis 10:2 and in Ezekiel 38:2 and 39:6.

According to Ezekiel chapters 38 and 39, the original place of residence for Magog was in the "uttermost parts of the north." That location is determined by using the mountains of Israel as the reference point. However, it seems by the time the events prophesied through Ezekiel occur, Magog will have been displaced. In his former location will be "Gog of the land of Magog." (Ezekiel 38:2)

333

Revelation Verse by Verse

Note how the phrase "Gog of the land of Magog" is rendered by several other translators who seem to have understood the same import: In *The Bible in Living English*, translated by Steven T. Byington, "Gog in the country of Magog." *Today's English Version* reads: "Gog ... in the land of Magog." *The Holy Bible in the Language of Today*, translated by William F. Beck, renders it, "Gog in the land of Magog" and James Moffatt translated it, "Gog [in the land of Magog]."

However, some translations render the passage in such a way that one wonders if Magog has been displaced. First, notice *The Septuagint Version of the Old Testament*, translated by Bremton, which says, "Gog and the land of Magog." *The Septuagint Bible* translated by Thomson renders it, "against Gog and the land of Magog." *The Jerusalem Bible* expresses it this way, "Gog and the country of Magog."

This disparity of views notwithstanding, the issue may be resolved with assurance. It is very instructive to notice in the account in Ezekiel chapters 38 and 39 that while Magog is very closely linked with Gog, it is not said that Magog will come from the uttermost parts of the north as Gog will, though he will be involved in the invasion of Israel. This seems to imply that Magog has forfeited his former place of residence to Gog. Therefore, not only from textual evidence but also from contextual implications, it seems better to conclude that "Gog of the land of Magog" is the correct rendering of the passage.

Though Magog seems no longer to live in his ancestral area, still he (i.e., the people descended from him) will actively involve himself in the war described in Ezekiel chapters 38 and 39, eventually bringing upon himself divine judgment, for God says, "I will send a fire on Magog ." (Ezekiel 39:6)

The most probable candidate for the identity of Magog is the Mongol people even though only two consonants of the name Magog (that is, M and G) coincide with the consonants of the name Mongol. However, the geographical evidence for the Mongols being identified as Magog is quite strong. The Mongols are a group of distinct people united by a common language and nomadic traditions more than by physical characteristics. "All Mongols recognize their kinship to each other in varying degrees through legend, written history, and especially language. Dialects vary from east to west more than from north to south, but very few are unintelligible to other Mongols."[567] Geographically, the Mongols certainly fit the biblical description, "Gog of the land of Magog." At one time, the Mongols controlled practically all the area which ultimately came under the sovereignty of the former Soviet Union. Slavic Russia now controls the area and is now the leader of or is the "prince of Rosh, Meshech, and Tubal." (Ezekiel 38:2)

"The Mongol forces crossed the Volga in the autumn of 1237 and attacked the principalities of central Russia, capturing town after town, including Moscow, which was then comparatively unimportant. ... In the summer of 1240 the Mongols resumed their attack, and in December they captured and destroyed Kiev, the ancient capital of Russia. The way [at that point] lay open into central Europe."[568] Apparently only the death of Ugedei, the chief of the Mongols, and the ensuing struggle for power kept the Mongols from subduing Europe. "The Mongol military machine, after all, was capable of

---

567 Owen Lattimore, "Mongols," The New Encyclopaedia Britannica, 15th ed. (1979), Macropaedia Vol. 12, p. 370.
568 John Andrew Boyle, "Mongols," Collier's Encyclopaedia Vol. 16, (1969), p. 455D.

Revelation Chapter 20

conquering China, Turkestan, and Persia, all areas with immense populations and gargantuan walled cities. (The Mongols subdued China in sixty years, Russia in three.)"[569]

If Magog points us to the Mongols, which seems to be the case, then the prophecy in Ezekiel chapters 38 and 39 points to a major group of far eastern participants in the great coalition which will invade Israel. That possibility, of course, is buttressed by Revelation 16:12-16 which emphasizes the participation of "the kings that come from the sunrising." From close examination it seems highly likely that the war prophesied in Ezekiel 38 and 39 is distinct from this one predicted in Revelation chapter 20 (See the comments under 20:9.), though the main participants are the same. The war described by Ezekiel should be paralleled with that prophesied in Revelation 16:12-16 and in Revelation chapter 19.

In summary, it seems the Mongols should be considered the people with whom to identify Magog. First, because of the etymological evidence for the association of the names. Secondly, the parallel passage in Revelation 16:12-16 points us to major participation in the war predicted in Ezekiel 38 and 39, as well as in this war, by forces from the Far East. They will be "the kings that come from the sunrising." Thirdly, the geographic and cultural impact of the Mongol occupation of Russia was extensive and prolonged. So profound was that impact that a famous proverb came into being in France, and later in other western countries, which says, "Scratch a Russian and find a Tatar."[570]

"Far to the west, [i.e., west of the then Mongol capital of Peking] the Khan of the Golden Horde in South Russia and the Il-Khan in Persia were autonomous territorial rulers, but they were subject to the supreme authority of the Great Khan, the head of their family and overlord of their Empire. In time, the Khanates of the West became independent and Islamic – but by that time the oriental civilization of **the united Mongol Empire had profoundly affected them**. [emphasis added]"[571] The pronoun "them" refers to the people of Iran and Russia.

As a logical deduction from this conclusion, Christian analysts should give the closest attention to developments in inner Asia, China, and other countries among the Pacific Rim nations.[572]

GOG. (This name occurs only in Ezekiel 38:2, 38:3, 38:14, 38:16, 38:18, 39:1, 39:11 and Revelation 20:8.) Thus, if the translation "Gog of the land of Magog" is correct, as it seems to be, then the land once occupied by Magog was subsequently occupied by the expansion of the Russian Empire. Since Gog is the leader of Tubal, Meshech, Togarmah and the other members of the coalition which will invade Israel, the name Gog would seem to point to the Slavs who rule Russia. That the name Gog does refer to a nation is confirmed here in Revelation 20:7-8 which says, "The nations which are in the four corners of the earth, Gog and Magog." Gog and Magog clearly seem to be etymologically related. Probably Gog is a derivative from Magog. Though Gog is apparently the

---

569 Charles J. Halperin, Russia and the Golden Horde, (Bloomington: Indiana University Press, 1985), p. 48.
570 Charles J. Halperin, Russia and the Golden Horde, (Bloomington: Indiana University Press, 1985), p. viii.
571 Bernard Lewis, Islam in History Ideas, People, and Events in the Middle East, (Chicago: Open Court Publishing Company, 1993), p. 202.
572 Whether China, through the influence of free-market capitalism which it has embraced, will become a democratic open country friendly with western democratic countries and, therefore, no threat through military confrontation in the Middle East or in the South China Sea is a most serious issue. To judge the likely resolution of this deeply significant matter every serious student should read Lawrence F. Kaplan, Trade Barrier, Why Trade Won't Bring Democracy to China, The New Republic: July 9 & 16, 2001, p. 23.

derivative, the people to whom it applies have come to dominate not only the homeland of Magog, but the peoples of the great coalition which eventually will invade Israel. **Gog, therefore, most probably refers to Slavic Russia.** In many ways Slavic Russians are a Mongol derivative. It should be noted that their forms of society and government have been largely derived from the Mongols just as the name Gog seems to have been derived from Magog. "The invading hordes under the leadership of the famous Ghenghis Khan brought to the Russian people those institutions which they had delivered to other conquered races: a system of taxation (yasak), a political discipline which established absolute obedience to the authority of the Khan."[573]

Theological Clues. In addition to geographical and ethnic clues, there are also theological clues which point to the Russian Federation, which recently replaced the former Soviet Union, as the leading participant from the north who will participate in this coming war against Israel. Ezekiel 38:3 says, "Thus saith the Lord Jehovah: Behold, **I am against thee, O Gog**, [emphasis added] prince of Rosh, Meshech, and Tubal:" God's opposition to these people is not without cause, since they have been against him since 1917. From that time aggressive anti-God regimes have governed the vast Russian Eurasian land mass, first the Soviets and now the Russian Federation.

Atheism is the central concept of communism. In the communistic telling of things, religion is the opiate of the people, the ultimate foolishness, the ultimate lie. They are against the very concept of God. The Russian Orthodox Church is only tolerated as an adjunct to the atheistic state. The domination of the Communist party ended, at least temporarily, with the collapse of the Soviet Union. However, communist philosophy, aggressively promoted, has denied millions of people access to the knowledge of God and the freedom to serve him. It is not surprising, then, that Ezekiel portrayed God as against Gog and his associates. It is very questionable whether the religious relaxation which has taken place in Russia following the collapse of the Soviet Union will continue. As that relaxation ends, we probably will see a revival of an aggressive campaign against any pro-God activity in Russia, except in the subservient state-recognized Russian Orthodox church.

Military Disaster. In the war as depicted in Ezekiel, Gog and his forces will be destroyed by an overwhelming military calamity. In contrast, here they will be confronted by and destroyed by divine judgment. In Ezekiel, the extent of the coalition's military disaster is seen in the fact that it shall require seven months to bury the corpses of their soldiers! (cf. Ezekiel 39:11-20) Though civilian areas will inevitably share the pain and destruction of the war, those resident populations will not be completely annihilated. We are also told that God "will send a fire on Magog, and on them that dwell securely in the isles." (Ezekiel 39:6) But, apparently, this punishment will be perceived as an obvious case of divine intervention and will lead to the turning of those nations to God. This conclusion is logical because God is recorded as saying regarding that development, "they shall know that I am Jehovah." (Ezekiel 39:6, compare also v. 7.) Further, God declares, "I will set my glory among the nations; and all the nations shall see my judgment that I have executed, and my hand that I have laid upon them." (Ezekiel 39:21) It is difficult to miss the cumulative import of these statements. It is summarized when God says, "I will

---

573 Anatole G. Mazour, <u>Russia Past And Present</u>, (New York: D. Van Nostrand Company, Inc., 1951), p. 75.

Revelation Chapter 20

magnify myself, and sanctify myself, and I will make myself known in the eyes of many nations; and they shall know that I am Jehovah." (Ezekiel 38:23)

20:9 "And they went up over the breadth of the earth, and compassed the camp of the saints about, and the beloved city: and fire came down out of heaven, and devoured them."

20:9 "they went up over the breadth of the earth"

This statement seems not only to describe the broad, extensive areas from which the forces composing this mighty army will come, but also where they will have an impact.

20:9 "compassed the camp of the saints about, and the beloved city:"

How the fortunes of the church will have changed! Christians will go from the triumph of The Millennium to becoming defendants in a beleaguered camp and in a besieged city. The same constellation of nations which banded together, according to Ezekiel's account, come malevolently together once again according to this account in Revelation.

However, please note that <u>at this point the Revelation account clearly diverges from that in Ezekiel 38 and 39</u>. In Ezekiel's prophecy, the war ends with great evangelistic victories, both among the Jews and the Gentiles. Here, the church is encircled and in dire danger of extinction, at which point God brings the Christian age to a close with fire from heaven and eternal judgment. Though God used fire in the account in Ezekiel (38:22, 39:6), its purpose was to swing the battle decisively against the invading coalition, bringing about a new day for the Gospel. <u>It is important to note that in Ezekiel's account, fire did not introduce final eternal judgment as it does here</u>.

Though at this juncture the church is beleaguered, consisting only of the surrounded "camp of the saints," it still is, as God sees it, "the beloved city" which is the new Jerusalem. (Revelation 3:12)

20:9 "fire came down out of heaven, and devoured them."

This is not a fire which might be used to divert a civilization from annihilation, but one to engulf it and utterly destroy it. This is the fire Jesus mentioned which would be used when "the tares are gathered up and burned." (Matthew 13:40) This is the fire which will rage "at the revelation of the Lord Jesus from heaven with the angels of his power in flaming fire." (II Thessalonians 1:7) This is the "fierceness of fire which shall devour the adversaries." (Hebrews 10:27) This is the fire which is "reserved against the day of judgment and destruction of ungodly men." (II Peter 3:7) This is the fire by which the heavens "shall be dissolved, and the elements shall melt with fervent heat." (II Peter 3:12) This is like the fire which consumed the residents of Sodom and Gomorrah who "are set forth as an example, suffering the punishment of eternal fire." (Jude verse 7) This is the fire to be experienced by those who "shall be tormented with fire and brimstone in the presence of the holy angels and in the presence of the Lamb." (Revelation 14:10) This is the fire in which the fearful, the unbelieving, the abominable, the murderers, the fornicators, the sorcerers, the idolaters and all liars shall have part, "the lake that burneth with fire and brimstone." (Revelation 21:8)

20:10 "And the devil that deceived them was cast into the lake of fire and brimstone, where are also the beast and the false prophet; and they shall be tormented day and night for ever and ever."

Here again is that unholy trinity of the devil, the beast and the false prophet which we encountered in chapter 16. However, here, instead of the "dragon" who mimicked Satan, we find Satan, "the devil," himself.

Somewhere between the events described in 20:10 and in 20:11, we will have reached the point at which time merges back into eternity. It is the point at which the culmination of the Christian period of history, known as "the last days," will have been completed. (On the use of the phrase "the last days" to indicate the entire Christian period of history, often called the Christian dispensation, please see the discussion at 4:1 under "the things which must come to pass hereafter.") It will simultaneously mark the beginning of the period described by inspiration through Paul as "the ages to come." Please read the discussion of this exhilarating transition in the exposition of 4:1.

E. The judgment of the Great White Throne 20:11-15

20:11 "And I saw a great white throne, and him that sat upon it, from whose face the earth and the heaven fled away; and there was found no place for them."

20:11 "a great white throne, and him that sat upon it"

The "great white throne" is the throne from which final judgment will be rendered. From Jesus' own statement we know he is the one who will sit on that throne. He said, "The Son of man shall come in the glory of his Father with his angels; and then shall he render unto every man according to his deeds." (Matthew 16:27) This identification of the one who is to sit on the "great white throne" is in harmony with further statements made by Jesus that "neither doth the Father judge any man, but he hath given all judgment unto the Son," (John 5:22) and that "he [the Father] gave him authority to execute judgment because he is a son of man." (John 5:27) The "great white throne" will be "the throne of his glory." (See Matthew 25:31-34.)

20:11 "from whose face the earth and the heaven fled away; and there was found no place for them"

Undoubtedly, this is the cataclysmic finale to which Peter pointed when he said, "The day of the Lord will come as a thief; in the which the heavens shall pass away with a great noise, and the elements shall be dissolved with fervent heat, and the earth and the works that are therein shall be burned up. Seeing that these things are thus all to be dissolved, what manner of persons ought ye to be in all holy living and godliness, looking for and earnestly desiring the coming of the day of God, by reason of which the heavens being on fire shall be dissolved, and the elements shall melt with fervent heat?" (II Peter 3:10-12)

Though all the familiar planetary and terrestrial phenomena will have been changed (See 21:1.), at the resurrection every human who has been redeemed through Christ will have survived to inhabit a new and incorruptible body. (I Corinthians 15:52) The resurrection body will "be conformed to the body of his glory." (Philippians 3:21) Those reincarnated

Revelation Chapter 20

human beings, those who will have been redeemed by Christ, will inhabit the "new heavens and the new earth wherein dwelleth righteousness." (II Peter 3:13)

20:12 "And I saw the dead, the great and the small, standing before the throne; and books were opened: and another book was opened, which is the book of life: and the dead were judged out of the things which were written in the books, according to their works."

20:12 "I saw the dead, the great and the small, standing before the throne"

Obviously, at this point, the general physical resurrection will have taken place. The resurrection, as Jesus said, will include "all that are in the tombs." (John 5:28) It will be totally inclusive. No category shall be exempt. It will include "the great and the small." Accompanying that momentous event, a preliminary evaluation will have simultaneously occurred. It will have been, as it were, a separation of the sheep from the goats. (See Matthew 25:32.)

Every human who has ever lived will have been bodily called forth. This will also include all those whose bodies will have disintegrated into their separate atomic components. (See "the sea gave up the dead that were in it"- 20:13.) "They that have done good [shall come forth] unto the resurrection of life; and they that have done evil, unto the resurrection of judgment." (John 5:29) Since God keeps track at the atomic level of the material which makes up our physical bodies (See Psalm 139:15-16.), he is able to call our bodies back into being from any atomic-level dispersion they may have undergone during or following the death process.

The picture of those standing before the great white throne is that of those whose condemnation will have been announced because they rejected God's provision for the forgiveness of sin and salvation. For those who have rejected Christ, there is no doubt about their destiny, for each one of them has "been judged already, because he hath not believed on the name of the only begotten Son of God." (John 3:18) Then the question naturally arises, if the doom of the lost is already determined and sealed, why have them stand in judgment?

First of all, each person in this category will stand before the white-throne bar of judgment so the reason for his consignment to eternal doom might be universally declared. This declaration is necessary so that God's righteousness in judgment (See Acts 7:31.) might be unmistakably shown or made clear. (See Romans 3:26.)

Secondly, this judgment of the doomed will assign the severity of each one's punishment. While their doom is eternal, their punishment will differ. The coming of the Lord for those who are unfaithful will take place in a day when that person "expecteth not, and in an hour when he knoweth not, and [the Lord] shall cut him asunder, and appoint his portion with the unfaithful. And that servant, who knew his Lord's will and made not ready, nor did according to his will, shall be beaten with many stripes; but he that knew not, and did things worthy of stripes shall be beaten with few stripes." (Luke 12:46-48)

There will also be **a distinctly separate and unique judgment** of those who have accepted Christ. This will occur despite the fact that Jesus said, "He that heareth my word, and believeth on him that sent me, hath eternal life, and cometh not into judgment, but hath passed out of death into life." (John 5:24) The judgment out of which the believer has passed or from which he is exempt is the white-throne judgment. But among the believers there will still be a judgment or evaluation, not to decide upon their destiny, but to determine their status. Paul reminded the church in Rome of this awesome fact when he wrote that "each one of us shall give account of himself to God." (Romans 4:12) This judgment was clearly implied by the apostle James when he wrote, "Be not many of you teachers, my brethren, knowing that we shall receive heavier judgment." (James 3:1) The apostle Paul reminded the church in Corinth that "We must all be made manifest before the judgment seat of Christ; that each one may receive the things done in the body, according to what he hath done, whether it be good or bad." (II Corinthians 5:10) Knowing that we are to face such an evaluation of our Christian lives, it behooves us to follow John's exhortation in which he wrote, "Watch out that you do not lose what you have worked for, but that you may be rewarded fully." (II John 8 NIV; See also I Corinthians 3:12-15.)

20:12 "books were opened: and another book was opened, which is the book of life"

This opening of the books seems to mirror a judgment scene recorded in Daniel 7:10 in which it was said, "the judgment was set, and the books were opened." Most probably the books which were opened were identified by Jeremiah when he said, "The sin of Judah is written with a pen of iron, and with the point of a diamond: it is graven upon the tablet of their heart." (Jeremiah 17:1) The apostle Paul refers to this category of books when he wrote, "they show the work of the law written in their hearts." (Romans 2:15) When the books will be opened, the memory of every repressed and covered up sin and crime which has been recorded in smothered consciences will be brought back into vivid view, except for those who in their obedience to the Gospel of Christ were baptized, "not [for] putting away of the filth of the flesh, but the interrogation of a good conscience ["an appeal to God for a good conscience" - ESV] toward God through the resurrection of Jesus Christ." (I Peter 3:21)

On "the book of life," please see the comment at 20:15.

20:12 "the dead were judged out of the things which were written in the books, according to their works"

"The books" are the consciences of individual human beings. The conscience is the tender spiritual adjudicator whose judgment no man can avoid. The permanency of the record in the human conscience is seen in the fact that "men that speak lies [are] branded in their own conscience as with a hot iron." (I Timothy 4:2) It is the facility of the conscience which makes it possible for "our heart [to] condemn us." (I John 3:20)

We can repress and forget what has been "written in the books." But we cannot delete or erase what has been written there. Only God can do that. On judgment day, those faint, repressed and forgotten memories of unforgiven sins will be recalled, revived and made brilliantly visible before each person. When that occurs, it will be "the day when God shall judge the secrets of men." (Romans 2:16) "If our heart condemn us, God is greater than our heart and knoweth all things. Beloved, if our heart condemn us not we have boldness toward God." (I John 3:20-21)

Revelation Chapter 20

20:13 "And the sea gave up the dead that were in it; and death and Hades gave up the dead that were in them: and they were judged every man according to their works."

This verse portrays the totally inclusive scope of the resurrection of the dead. Physical death is here summarized under two categories: (1) maritime related deaths, and (2) deaths by all other causes. Those two categories of death describe only the physical aspect of the general physical resurrection which Jesus described by saying, "The hour cometh, in which all that are in the tombs shall hear his voice, and shall come forth; they that have done good, unto the resurrection of life; and they that have done evil, unto the resurrection of judgment." (John 5:28-29)

Just as the earth and sea will give up the countless human bodies which are buried in them, so there will also be a spiritual factor accompanying this physical resurrection. That aspect is here portrayed when we are told that "Hades gave up the dead that were in them." Hades is the place or condition in which the conscious spirits of unsaved humanity are detained till they are reunited with their resurrection bodies to stand for judgment before the great white throne. Please see the discussions of Hades under Revelation 1:18 and under 19:1 following the phrase "a great multitude in heaven."

20:14 "And death and Hades were cast into the lake of fire. This is the second death, even the lake of fire."

This implies that not only will the persons who are detained in either one of these realms be cast into the lake of fire, but the entities themselves, which are known as "death and Hades," will also be cast into that fiery lake, no longer to be a threat to mankind.

20:15 "And if any was not found written in the book of life, he was cast into the lake of fire."

The book of life was mentioned first by Moses when making intercession for his people. He told God that should he be unwilling to forgive Israel's sin, "Blot me, I pray thee, out of thy book which thou hast written." (Exodus 32:32) David prophetically pled with God on Christ's behalf concerning those who would crucify the Messiah. He said, "Let them be blotted out of the book of life, and not be written with the righteous." (Psalm 69:28) This seems to be the same book to which Daniel referred when he prophesied, "At that time thy people shall be delivered, everyone that shall be found written in the book." (Daniel 12:1) It is almost certain that Malachi referred to this book when he wrote, "They that feared Jehovah spake one with another; and Jehovah harkened, and heard, and a book of remembrance was written before him, for them that feared Jehovah, and that thought upon his name." (Malachi 3:16) Jesus referred to the book of life when he said, "Rejoice not, that the spirits are subject unto you; but rejoice that your names are written in heaven." (Luke 10:20) The apostle Paul indicated that faithful Christians' names would be there, like those of his "fellow-workers, whose names are in the book of life." (Philippians 4:3) This elite record is mentioned in Revelation, not only here in 20:15, but also in 3:5, 13:8, 17:8, 20:12 and 21:27.

Revelation Verse by Verse

In Mary A. Kidder's great hymn, which she wrote in 1876, she expresses both the prayer, which should be on each of our hearts, and its answer. She wrote:

"Lord, I care not for riches, neither silver nor gold;
I would make sure of Heaven, I would enter the fold.
In the book of Thy kingdom, with its pages so fair,
Tell me, Jesus, my Saviour, is my name written there?

Oh! that beautiful city, with its mansions of light,
With its glorified beings, in pure garments of white;
Where no evil thing cometh to despoil what is fair;
Where the angels are watching, yes, my name's written there."

Revelation Chapter 21

F.   The New Heaven and New Earth 21:1-8

21:1 "And I saw a new heaven and a new earth: for the first heaven and the first earth are passed away; and the sea is no more."

21:1   "I saw a new heaven and a new earth"

The old heaven and earth will have become too blood-stained, ravaged, polluted and haunted with memories of despicable centuries of war and plunder to simply be remodeled into a congenial habitation for the eternally redeemed of mankind. Should God preserve the old geographic, oceanic and atmospheric arrangement, memories of the past would dull the ecstasy of heaven. Only "a new heaven and a new earth" will suffice.

The transformation from the old to "a new heaven and a new earth" will be the momentous occasion during which "creation itself will be liberated from its bondage to decay and brought into the glorious freedom of the children of God. We know that the whole creation has been groaning as in the pains of childbirth right up to the present time." (Romans 8:21-22 NIV)

21:1   "the first heaven and the first earth are passed away; and the sea is no more"

The words "first heaven" undoubtedly refer to the current astronomical heaven, the fifth meaning of the word "heaven" listed in the summary given in the introduction to chapter 15. Lest anyone should suppose that the word "earth" may point only to the concept of terra firma, meaning solid ground or dry land, here it is made clear that the meaning of the word is more inclusive, encompassing the entire globe. To make that point unmistakable, the vision also says, "the sea is no more." The sea, which is to be no more, is the global sea of the present world. This declaration is certainly not telling us that there will be neither sea nor ocean in the new creation. This description is that of the old earth and sea, not of the new ones. Thus, the description tells us that the old earth, including the sea, the ones currently present, will pass away, not that the new order will have no sea. When they shall pass away no one will be able to say as William Faulkner did in a famous statement about World War I, "The past isn't dead. It isn't even past."[574]

When the present global arrangement is replaced, an entirely new astronomy, oceanography and geography will have to be developed. This understanding is assured by God's statement recorded in 21:5 that "I make all things new." All the current familiar navigational reference points like the Cape of Good Hope, the Strait of Gibraltar, the Strait of Malacca and countless others, will no longer be there.

Additionally, the "new earth" not only will introduce redeemed humans to a new era of exploration but to an entirely new horticulture. The colors of flowers will be more

---
574 Richard Rubin, *100 Years of Gratitude*, The New York Times, Travel, August 24, 2014, p. 7.

dazzling and their fragrances more enchanting. The new vegetables and fruits will be more appealing, appetizing and nutritious. The redeemed animal kingdom will not only have rapport but close fellowship with humans. (See the discussion at 4:6 under "four living creatures" and especially 6:1-2 under "one of the four living creatures.")

The phrase "passed away" is the second declaration in Revelation that the present physical order will be eliminated, destroyed and abandoned. This statement was anticipated in 20:11, which says, "The earth and the heaven fled away; and there was found no place for them." As noted before in comments on 20:11, God gave the apostle Peter the prophetic ability to describe the violent end of the present terrestrial and galactic universe. He has told us, "The heavens that now are, and the earth, by the same word have been stored up for fire, being reserved against the day of judgment and destruction of ungodly men." (II Peter 3:7) Giving further detail, Peter goes on to tell us that "The heavens shall pass away with a great noise and the elements shall be dissolved with fervent heat, and the earth and the works that are therein shall be burned up." (II Peter 3:10)

It is amazing that David Jeremiah, widely regarded preacher though he is, would so erroneously write, "Peter is not talking about destroying the earth, he is telling us that, at the end of the Millennium, as God is preparing for the eternal state, He is going to do a refreshing of the earth."[575]

21:2 "And I saw the holy city, new Jerusalem, coming down out of heaven from God, made ready as a bride adorned for her husband."

21:2 "the holy city, new Jerusalem, coming down out of heaven from God"

Its identity. The holy city, new Jerusalem, is the city which Abraham had longed for centuries earlier. (Hebrews 11:10) It was also anticipated very early in the visions of Revelation, at 3:12, where it is identified as "the city of my God." This "new Jerusalem" is called "the Jerusalem that is above" in Paul's epistle to the Galatians (See Galatians 4:26.), while in the epistle to the Hebrews it is called "the heavenly Jerusalem." (Hebrews 12:22-23)

Its character. "Holy." The exclusion of wickedness is especially emphasized three times: 21:8, 21:27 and 22:15. No human being in and by himself is holy enough to gain entrance. Only those who through the "sanctification of the Spirit unto obedience and sprinkling of the blood of Jesus Christ" (I Peter 1:2) having been made holy, will be allowed to enter. Graciously, that cleansing is offered to everyone. (Please see Revelation 22:17.)

Its occupants. The citizens of the "new Jerusalem," "the Jerusalem that is above," the "heavenly Jerusalem," through the centuries, will have been garnered in **two locations**. First, its citizens are those truly redeemed people in the widely scattered congregations of Christ's church throughout the globe. Secondly, as those saints die, their spirits go to be with Christ at God's right hand. (Be sure to see the discussion under "a great multitude in heaven" at 19:1.) Eventually, all the citizens of the "new Jerusalem" will have been assembled in that heavenly locale. That congregation, eventually and triumphantly,

---
[575] David Jeremiah, Answers to Questions About Heaven, (San Diego, Calif.: Turning Points for God, 2013), p. 141.

Revelation Chapter 21

according to this vision, being the composite "new Jerusalem," will come down out of heaven "as a bride adorned for her husband." She will inhabit the new earth which will have been freshly created and gloriously decorated to become the venue for the marriage of the Lamb.

21:2 "made ready"

This is accomplished by the work of preaching and teaching (Titus 3:1-7), but above all by the work of renewal through the Holy Spirit (Titus 3:5).

21:2 "a bride adorned for her husband"

The blessings which are enumerated in Revelation 21:3-7 are only part the fruit which will be produced by this holy matrimonial union, the ultimate fellowship between God and man. The announcement of this wedding was given in 19:7 but it is here, both chronologically and spatially (in the new heaven and the new earth), that the actual marriage takes place. The adornment will probably consist, in part at least, of those rewards mentioned in II John verse 8 and in I Corinthians 3:14.

21:3 "And I heard a great voice out of the throne saying, Behold, the tabernacle of God is with men, and he shall dwell with them, and they shall be his peoples, and God himself shall be with them, and be their God:"

21:3 "a great voice out of the throne"

This voice seems to be the voice of Christ. (See the comments on 20:11.)

21:3 "the tabernacle of God is with men"

"The [Greek] word used for *dwelling place* is *skene,* literally a *tent* [tabernacle]; but in religious use it had long since lost any idea of an impermanent residence."[576]

The intimacy between God and men, which was the norm in Eden, will not only be restored but greatly enhanced. This marvelous development will bring to an end the seemingly interminable period during which "no man hath beheld God at any time." (I John 4:12) In the new world, the redeemed "shall see God's face." (Revelation 22:4) That is the time when we "shall see him even as he is." (I John 3:2)

21:3 "he shall dwell with them, and they shall be his peoples, and God himself shall be with them, and be their God"

Complete intimacy between God and man will dominate this coming endless period. Such fellowship will fulfill the highest aspiration of the great African American Methodist preacher, Charles A. Tindley (1851-1933) and countless others like him. Tindley expressed his yearning when he composed the sublime hymn entitled "Nothing Between." The chorus, like a fervent imploring prayer says, "Nothing between my soul and the Saviour, so that his blessed face may be seen; nothing preventing the least of his favor, keep the way clear! Let nothing between."

When God himself shall dwell with redeemed man, it will constitute the ultimate, intimate fellowship between man and his creator. We should try to visualize man's

---

576 William Barclay, The Revelation of John, Vol. II, (Philadelphia: The Westminster Press, 1976), p. 228.

expanded and enhanced potential which will be attained because of that fellowship with God. It will be the fulfillment of David's exuberant and exultant cry that "in thy presence is fulness of joy: in thy right hand there are pleasures for evermore." (Psalm 16:11)

21:4 "and he shall wipe away every tear from their eyes; and death shall be no more; neither shall there be mourning, nor crying, nor pain, any more: the first things are passed away."

The changes in the new heaven and the new earth are not to be limited to astronomy, geography, entomology and botany, but will reach the level of the most important and intimate human experiences. Every negative, discouraging, disappointing and painful experience, up to and including death, all of those experiences which will have caused sorrow and tears will be eliminated. Since "every tear" shall be wiped away, it is implied that sorrows, growing out of past tragedies, will be completely assuaged. However, all of this healing and consolation will not happen instantaneously, since at least one aspect of victory over man's painful past will be gained incrementally. (See 22:2 under "the leaves of the tree were for the healing of the nations.")

21:5 "And he that sitteth on the throne said, Behold, I make all things new. And he saith, Write: for these words are faithful and true."

21:5 "he that sitteth on the throne"

The one on the throne is Christ. (See the comments on 20:11.)

21:5 "I make all things new"

Christ's declaration that "I make all things new" enhances the statement in verse 1 that "the first heaven and the first earth are passed away." His making all things new, in addition to the rebirth of those categories of existence already mentioned, will, for example, also bring a total revolution in entomology. Pesticides will no longer be necessary to suppress insects which ravage trees, vegetables and flowers because such insects will no longer exist! As a consequence, the distinction between organic and non-organic farming will simply disappear.

21:5 "write: for these words are faithful and true"

John had already received not only a mandate, but an order, to transcribe the visions which he was privileged to behold. That mandate was given at the outset of the special revelations which are the basis for the book of Revelation. At that point God said to him, "Write therefore the things which thou sawest, and the things which are, and the things which shall come to pass hereafter." (Revelation 1:19) However, this vision is of such great significance and importance that Christ repeats his previous order. It has the connotation of saying, "John, be sure you do not miss the description of this vision in your written account." We may, for example, think that the blessings here enumerated are impossible of being attained. However, they may truly be anticipated knowing the one who sits on the throne. It is a vision of hope, anticipation and clarity which would especially strengthen anyone who may be enduring persecution. (On the statement that "these words are faithful and true," please see the comments on the same assertion at Revelation 22:6.)

Revelation Chapter 21

21:6 **"And he said unto me, They are come to pass. I am the Alpha and the Omega, the beginning and the end. I will give unto him that is athirst of the fountain of the water of life freely."**

21:6 "They are come to pass"

Several translations have rendered the phrase "they are come to pass" as "it is done." The pronoun "it" refers to a group of developments, while "they" refers to those developments individually. In either case, the group of developments referred to has not yet taken place historically. The words "come to pass" or "it is done" refer to Christ's fiat or command which decrees six things that are to take place:

1. The creation of the new heaven and the new earth will occur. (21:1)

2. The Holy City will come down out of heaven. (21:2)

3. The tabernacle of God is with men. (21:3)

4. Every tear is wiped away. (21:4)

5. Death is abolished. (21:4)

6. All things are made new. (21:5)

21:6 "I am the Alpha and the Omega"

See the comments at 1:8, and especially at 22:13. Here, the self-identification seems clearly to refer to Christ.

21:6 "I will give unto him that is athirst of the fountain ["spring" - ESV, NIV] of the water of life freely"

This will be the glorious fulfillment of Jesus' statement that "I came that they may have life, and have it abundantly." (John 10:10) In the Garden of Eden God made ongoing life, not its initial endowment, possible through "the tree of life." (Genesis 2:9) In heaven, access to "the tree of life" will not only be restored, (See comments at 2:7, 22:2 and 22:14.) it will be augmented by "the fountain [or spring] of the water of life." This heavenly artesian fountain or spring eventually flows so copiously that it becomes "a river of water of life." (22:1)

Glorious as that first garden was, this second Eden will be a great enhancement, more marvelous than the first. Though the first Eden had four rivers (Genesis 2:10-14), none of them flowed with "the water of life." This fountain will be the ultimate fulfillment of the promise Jesus made to the Samaritan woman when he said, "Whosoever drinketh of the water that I shall give him shall never thirst; but the water that I shall give him shall become in him a well of water springing up unto eternal life." (John 4:14)

21:7 "He that overcometh shall inherit these things; and I will be his God, and he shall be my son."

21:7 "He that overcometh shall inherit these things"

There are two prerequisites for overcoming, both of which have been stressed previously. Those who up to this point had triumphed, had not only overcome "because of the blood of the Lamb … [but also] **(1)** because of the word of their testimony; and [because] **(2)** they loved not their life even unto death." (Revelation 12:11)

The things which the victors shall inherit have been highlighted in the first five verses of this chapter. In verse 1 it is the new heaven and the new earth; in verse 2 it is citizenship in the new Jerusalem; in verse 3, it is the ecstasy of God's personal presence with the redeemed; in verse 4, it is the assurance that sorrow, mourning, crying and pain will be eternally eliminated; and in verse 5, it is the prospect of luxuriating in a completely new creation.

21:7 "I will be his God, and he shall be my son"

This statement seems to imply that from this point, redeemed man, as sons of God, will share in deity. Therefore, from this juncture, in a very profound way "as we have borne the image of the earthy ["earthly man" - NIV], we shall also bear the image of the heavenly." (I Corinthians 15:49)

21:8 "But for the fearful, and unbelieving, and abominable, and murderers, and fornicators, and sorcerers, and idolaters, and all liars, their part shall be in the lake that burneth with fire and brimstone; which is the second death."

21:8 "for the fearful, and unbelieving, and abominable, and murderers, and fornicators, and sorcerers, and idolaters, and all liars"

This list of eight repugnant deviations from God's purpose for man and from the level of behavior the people of Christ must embody, are examples of temptations and practices which every victorious Christian will have overcome. (See "he that overcometh" at 21:7.) **(1)** Victors must overcome fear, or as Stern, NRSV, ESV, and NIV express it, we must overcome cowardice. Sometimes acting upon the will of God is hazardous, dangerous and risky. We may advance with trembling but we must not turn our backs on activity which God puts before us. **(2)** If we yield to the temptation to doubt, which is expressed by the sin of being "unbelieving" or "faithless" (ESV), we cannot and will not carry out God's express purpose. Looking at God's past fidelity should encourage us to undertake even those responsibilities which may be very daunting. **(3)** Whatever thought or activity which comes under the definition of being "abominable," "vile" (Stern), "polluted" (NRSV), or "detestable" (ESV) must be renounced by every Christian who seeks victory. **(4)** Murder is a sin which unequivocally debars one from eternal life. For as John has told us, "Whosoever hateth his brother is a murderer: and ye know that no murderer hath eternal life abiding in him." (I John 3:15) (See also the discussion at 22:15.) **(5)** Not only must we be victors over anger which leads to murder, but over lust which leads to fornication or being "sexually immoral" as Stern, ESV and NIV express it. The King James expresses it as being "whoremongers." **(6)** Victors must turn their backs on

Revelation Chapter 21

sorcerers, that is on "those involved in the occult and with drugs"(Stern) or "who practice magic arts." (NIV) (See especially 22:15.) **(7)** All forms of idolatry must be consistently avoided, even "covetousness, which is idolatry." (Colossians 3:5) (See also 22:15.) **(8)** No matter what pressure we may be under or what enticements may be before us, those who seek victory must not compromise, disguise or change the truth because lying is forbidden. (See also 21:27 and 22:15.)

21:8 "their part shall be in the lake that burneth with fire and brimstone; which is the second death"

The pronoun "their" refers to anyone, even professed followers of Christ, whose lifestyle incorporates any of the above-named eight practices which God vehemently denounces. For such a person, instead of being one "that overcometh," (21:7) he is one who has capitulated to sin and compromised God's standard of holiness. He will, consequently, be faced with the ultimate expression of the wrath of God, which is the second death. As Johnson pointed out, one of the most fearful aspects of the second death is that it "has no resurrection."[577]

G.　The wife of the Lamb and New Jerusalem 21:9-27

21:9 "And there came one of the seven angels who had the seven bowls, who were laden with the seven last plagues; and he spake with me, saying, Come hither, I will show thee the bride, the wife of the Lamb."

21:9 "one of the seven angels who had the seven bowls, who were laden with the seven last plagues"

For identification of "the seven angels who had the seven bowls," see 15:1.

21:9 "Come hither, I will show thee the bride, the wife of the Lamb"

Though it came through the help of an angel, this vision of the bride was God-sent. But with John, as is the case with everyone, God demands that the recipient take a step ("come hither") in the direction of greater truth and understanding before he will bless anyone with additional comprehension.

21:10 "And he carried me away in the Spirit to a mountain great and high, and showed me the holy city Jerusalem, coming down out of heaven from God,"

21:10 "he carried me away in the Spirit to a mountain great and high"

This is reminiscent of the deeper insight John gained about Jesus when he was taken to that high mountain where, right in front of him, Jesus was transfigured. (Matthew 17:1-8) The "bride, the wife of the Lamb" (21:9) is here in verse 10 depicted as a city, "the holy city Jerusalem." It is visible from "a mountain great and high." Christians should already know that, because as citizens of that city we have been made "to sit with him [Christ] in the heavenly places, in Christ Jesus." (Ephesians 2:6)

If one really wants to see or comprehend Christ's bride, "the holy city Jerusalem," one needs an elevated observation point. To get a proper undistorted view like John, one has

---
[577] B. W. Johnson, A Vision of the Ages, (Hollywood: California, Old Paths Book Club, n.d.), p. 195.

to climb that "mountain great and high." One's observation point, that is, his ability to perceive and understand, will have to be higher than the average person's conceptual stance. The bride of Christ is glorious, "having the glory of God." (21:11) To really see her, to comprehend her true reality, one must gain an elevated conceptual vantage point, a point of true perspective, here represented as "a mountain great and high." If we are not willing to climb that mountain, as John did, we will never gain the true understanding, or the true view, of the church. For most of us, climbing that mountain will very probably be arduous, involving long hours of study and prayer. One of our prayers should be "Open thou mine eyes that I may behold wondrous things out of thy law." (Psalm 119:18)

21:10 "showed me the holy city Jerusalem, coming down out of heaven from God"

These visions of "the holy city Jerusalem" depict the church. (See Galatians 4:26 and Hebrews 12:22-23.) Though by these visions we behold the church triumphant, the descriptions emphasize those virtues, qualities and characteristics of the church which will have led it to that position of victory. (See the discussion of "two locations" at 21:2.)

21:11 "having the glory of God: her light was like unto a stone most precious, as it were a jasper stone, clear as crystal:"

21:11 "having the glory of God: her light was like unto a stone most precious"

The church, the new Jerusalem, in all phases of its existence, should be luminous (Matthew 5:14-16 and Philippians 2:15), but not with a self-generated light. The light must emanate from "the glory of God." "The Shekinah that once rested on the temple in earthly Jerusalem has departed from that institution and come to alight upon the church, the new temple of the Holy Spirit and the new city of God."[578]

Because the church is to enlighten the society in which it lives, each of the seven churches featured in the book of Revelation is represented as a candlestick or a lamp stand. (See 1:20.) Like precious stones which focus sunlight in dazzling and alluring ways, so the church is to "show forth the excellencies of him who called [it] out of darkness into his marvelous light." (I Peter 2:9)

21:11 "a jasper stone, clear as crystal"

Please see the comments at 4:3 concerning the jasper stone.

21:12 "having a wall great and high; having twelve gates, and at the gates twelve angels; and names written thereon, which are the names of the twelve tribes of the children of Israel:"

21:12 "having a wall great and high"

The concepts and values which separate the church from the world are represented here by "a wall great and high." Those concepts and values are neither trivial nor incidental. They are both "great," that is, significant, and "high," dealing with the most important and consequential issues.

---

[578] <u>Revelation, Four Views: A Parallel Commentary</u>, ed. Steve Gregg, (Nashville: Thomas Nelson Publishers, 1997), p. 493.

Revelation Chapter 21

21:12 "having twelve gates"

See the comments on 21:21.

21:12 "at the gates twelve angels"

These angels are from that group which rejoices when sinners repent and gain entrance through those gates into the city. As Jesus said, "There is joy in the presence of the angels of God over one sinner that repenteth." (Luke 15:10)

21:12 "names written thereon, which are the names of the twelve tribes of the children of Israel"

Those names seem to commemorate the very first ones to have passed through those gates. This is in harmony with the fact that the Gospel went "to the Jew first, and also to the Greek." (Romans 1:16) Also, we should never forget "that through Israel God made a way for the world to enter the city of God, for 'salvation is of the Jews' (John 4:22)."[579] For the identification of which Jewish tribal names will be written thereon, see Revelation 7:4 and the comment at "every tribe of the children of Israel."

21:13 "on the east were three gates; and on the north three gates; and on the south three gates; and on the west three gates."

Entrance is open to people regardless of the direction from which they may come. The directions – east, north, south and west – show that access is open to people to enter this heavenly city, not only from any geographic quadrant of the globe, but also from every religious, racial, and philosophical background, many of which are often divergent from and frequently contradictory to the truth of the Gospel of Christ. The position from which people come is irrelevant. It doesn't matter in which geographical or conceptual place they may have been, there is a corresponding gate through which they may enter this glorious city. As Jesus said, "They shall come from the east and west, and from the north and south, and shall sit down in the kingdom of God." (Luke 13:29) However, admission is granted at all the gates on the same terms. At none of the gates are discounted terms of entry offered. The fundamental condition for entrance is given in 22:14 which tells us, "Blessed are they that wash their robes, that they may have the right *to come* to the tree of life, and may enter in by the gates into the city." This shows that Jesus is the door. (See John 10:7.)

21:14 "And the wall of the city had twelve foundations, and on them twelve names of the twelve apostles of the Lamb."

This description is in complete harmony with Paul's statement that the household of God is "built upon the foundation of the apostles and prophets, Christ Jesus himself being the chief cornerstone." (Ephesians 2:20) The apostles and prophets are foundational in the sense that through them God initially defined the doctrinal and conceptual truths upon which the church is built. It was through their work that "the house of God, which is the church of the living God, [became] the pillar and ground ["buttress" - ESV, "foundation" - NIV] of the truth." (I Timothy 3:15) Further, they also gave the initial inspirational and

---

[579] Revelation, Four Views: A Parallel Commentary, ed. Steve Gregg , (Nashville: Thomas Nelson Publishers, 1997), p. 494.

guiding examples. We see this function in the life of Paul, who said, "The things which ye both learned and received and heard and saw in me, these things do: and the God of peace shall be with you." (Philippians 4:9)

21:15 "And he that spake with me had for a measure a golden reed to measure the city, and the gates thereof, and the wall thereof."

We encountered this measuring reed much earlier in the Revelation account. (Please see Revelation 11:1-2 with the accompanying comments.) Here, the measuring reed is called "golden" because the standards with which it measures, evaluates and corroborates are invaluable. Therefore, we should say to God, "I have rejoiced in the way of thy testimonies, as much as in all riches." (Psalm 119:14) In Revelation 19:15 (See the comments there.) it is called "a rod of iron" because truth is inflexible, truth not being relative but objective and certain. From 21:17, we learn that John's angel guide, who was showing him the bride (21:9), was using the same measuring device which John was to use, showing the universality of truth.

21:16 "And the city lieth foursquare, and the length thereof is as great as the breadth: and he measured the city with the reed, twelve thousand furlongs: the length and the breadth and the height thereof are equal."

21:16 "the city lieth foursquare, ... he measured the city with the reed, twelve thousand furlongs"

The physical dimensions given here are based on the ancient Greek unit of measurement called the *stadia*, from which we get the word "stadium." As previously noted at 14:20, a *stadia* was "about 606 English feet; it was the length of the race-course at Olympia, and the eighth part of the Roman mile."[580] Older translations have given this unit of measure as a "furlong," which is 660 feet. The ESV and NIV have simply carried the Greek word *stadia* over without translating it.

To have a basis for comparison, note the statistics given by Josephus: "Alexandria was 30 stadia by 10; Jerusalem was, in circuit, 33 stadia; Thebes, 43; Nineveh, 400; Babylon, 480; the holy city, 48,000!"[581] Twelve thousand stadia is 1,377 miles, while twelve thousand furlongs is 1,500 miles. As one commentator graphically noted, such "a city with that area would stretch nearly from London to New York. Surely we are meant to see that in the holy city *there is room for everyone*."[582]

21:16 "the length and the breadth and the height thereof are equal"

The church possesses a reassuring uniformity because truth is the same in every place and in every direction. While there is infinite variety in details, the essentials are the same everywhere. Thus, no matter which philosophical, conceptual or theological direction one comes from to enter "the holy city Jerusalem," he will find a consistent, unifying basic norm. The standards are the same, "the length and the breadth and the height thereof are equal." Not only are the divinely given doctrinal concepts definite and certain, they are

---

580 A. Plummer, The Pulpit Commentary [on] Revelation, (Chicago: Wilcox & Follett Co., no date), p. 351.
581 C. Clemance, The Pulpit Commentary [on] Revelation, (Chicago: Wilcox & Follett Co., no date), p. 515.
582 William Barclay, The Revelation of John, Vol. II, (Philadelphia: The Westminster Press, 1976), p. 238.

Revelation Chapter 21

also reasonable and factual, rather than capricious, whimsical or arbitrary. It measures the same on all sides, it is foursquare. God does not show favoritism to anyone. Entrance is gained only by embracing the truth and requirements of the Gospel. Accordingly, Jesus said, "Enter ye in by the narrow gate: for wide is the gate and broad is the way that leadeth to destruction, and many are they that enter in thereby. For narrow is the gate, and straightened the way, that leadeth unto life, and few are they that find it." (Matthew 7:13- 4)

21:17 "And he measured the wall thereof, a hundred and forty and four cubits, according to the measure of a man, that is, of an angel."

21:17 "he measured the wall thereof, a hundred and forty and four cubits"

Because some popular preachers present the measurements given in chapter 21 as the dimensions of heaven, it is vitally important to remember that these statistics are not those of heaven, but of "the holy city Jerusalem, coming down out of heaven." (21:10)

The measurement given for the wall is for its height. In older translations the word "cubit" has been given for the translation of the Greek word *paichon*. The English word "cubit" is a derivative from the Latin *cubitus*, meaning the elbow. A cubit was the length from the elbow to the tip of the middle finger, on average 1.5 feet. The computation based on that standard comes to 216 feet. Comparatively, the wall is not high. It is for definition, not defense. The height of the city wall is utterly minuscule compared to the height of the city itself, which measured 12,000 stadia, that is, 1,377 miles. (See 21:16.)

Though comparatively low, it represents the very definite separation wall between the church and the world. (See II Corinthians 6:14-18, James 1:27, I John 2:15-17, and I John 4:5-6.) Those distinct values lead to unique lifestyles for those who embrace them. However, the dividing wall is not so high that the church cannot be seen. Thus we understand that the church is neither monastic nor cloistered. The reality, the purpose, the direction, the truth, the purity, the hope, and the eternal values of the church tower far above the separation wall which stands between it and the world. Citizens of the world, struggling in a ridiculous, meaningless, directionless and sensual environment resulting from imbibing atheistic philosophies, can look across that dividing wall and see the church towering appealingly above the drab, monotonous, parched and fruitless desert-like condition in which they live.

21:17 "according to the measure of a man, that is, of an angel"

The translators of the KJV and ASV, all of whom are represented by the quote given here, have put us on a dead-end street by saying "the measure of a man, that is, of an angel." It isn't clear whether the angel refers to a man or to the measure. Later translations help us out of this corner. The ESV renders it, "by human measurement, which is also an angel's measurement." The NIV and the NRSV render it, "by man's measurement, which the angel was using." Stern translated it, "by human standards of measurement, which the angel was using."

21:18 "And the building of the wall thereof was jasper: and the city was pure gold, like unto pure glass."

Revelation Verse by Verse

Even the first encounter with the church, at the wall of the new Jerusalem, is tantalizing, like jasper. But the city is much higher than the wall and is visible to everyone on the outside. Therefore, the closer one comes, awe and inspiration increase exponentially. It becomes like the attraction of "pure gold, like unto pure glass."

21:19 "The foundations of the wall of the city were adorned with all manner of precious stones. The first foundation was jasper; the second, sapphire; the third, chalcedony; the fourth, emerald;"

> **21:19 "The foundations of the wall of the city were adorned with all manner of precious stones."**

The foundations are the apostles. (See 21:14.) For the astonishing and invaluable work which they have done, they are going to be adorned ("decorated" - NIV) with precious stones. Those stones will probably be fashioned into medallions or pendants.

> **21:19 "The first foundation was jasper; the second, sapphire; the third, chalcedony; the fourth, emerald."**

The correlation between the twelve apostles and the twelve precious stones is not given. Translators have spent countless hours and devoted tremendous expertise to translate the names of these precious stones in terms which correspond to the ones currently familiar. Following is a tabulation which using the ASV as a base, draws from nine other translations and gives all the variations. The nine additional translations and their abbreviations are these: the King James Version (KJV), the English Standard Version (ESV), the New International Version (NIV), the New Revised Standard Version (NRSV), the Moffatt translation (Moff), Beck's American Translation (Beck), Complete Jewish Bible translated by David H. Stern (Stern), The Berkeley Version of the New Testament (Berk), and the New Testament by Edgar J. Goodspeed (Good).

21:20 "the fifth, sardonyx; the sixth, sardius; the seventh, chrysolite; the eighth, beryl; the ninth, topaz; the tenth, chrysoprase; the eleventh, jacinth; the twelfth, amethyst."

Table Comparing Precious Stones in Several Versions/Translations

	Revelation 21:19-20											
ASV	Jasper	Sapphire	Chalcedony	Emerald	Sardonyx	Sardius	Chrysolite	Beryl	Topaz	Chrysoprase	Jacinth	Amethyst
KJV	"	"	"	"	"	"	"	"	"	"	"	"
ESV	"	"	agate	"	onyx	carnelian	"	"	"	"	"	"
NIV	"	"	"	"	"	carnelian	"	"	"	"	"	"
NRSV	"	"	agate	"	onyx	carnelian	"	"	"	"	"	"
Moff	"	"	agate	"	onyx	"	"	"	"	"	"	"
Beck	"	"	agate	"	"	carnelian	"	"	"	"	"	"
Stern	diamond	"	"	"	"	carnelian	"	"	"	"	turquoise	"
Berk	"	"	white agate	"	"	"	"	"	"	"	"	"
Good	"	"	"	"	"	"	"	"	"	"	"	"

Revelation Chapter 21

21:21 "And the twelve gates were twelve pearls; each one of the several gates was of one pearl: and the street of the city was pure gold, as it were transparent glass."

21:21 "the twelve gates were twelve pearls; each one of the several gates was of one pearl"

Every person who enters these gates, regardless of the place or direction from which he began his journey, will have found the pearl of great price. This is the pearl about which Jesus spoke when he said, "The kingdom of heaven is like unto a man that is a merchant seeking goodly pearls and having found one pearl of great price, he went and sold all that he had and bought it." (Matthew 13:45-46)

21:21 "the street of the city was pure gold, as it were transparent glass"

The "street of the city" is not only paved with gold, but with "pure gold." That means gold which has been refined until it has become transparent! This stupendous golden street is only reached by the "narrow road that leads to life." (Matthew 7:14 NIV) The transparency of the gold may also point to greatly enhanced eyesight which will be granted to us in our resurrection body. Remember that "it is written, things which eye saw not, and ear heard not, and which enter not into the heart of man, whatsoever things God prepared for them that love Him." (I Corinthians 2:9)

21:22 "And I saw no temple therein: for the Lord God the Almighty, and the Lamb, are the temple thereof."

21:22 "I saw no temple therein"

The concept of a temple is that of a place where God's presence may be encountered. The Jewish temple was a sacred place where God was not only entreated to be present, but actually was present from time-to-time.

21:22 "the Lord God the Almighty, and the Lamb, are the temple thereof"

The church has no need for a temple because God's continual presence has made such a devoted area redundant. God and the Lamb are both present, fulfilling constantly the central purpose of the temple, thus no other temple is needed. The continual and perpetual presence of Christ with the church, is assured only so long as it yields to his will. Then, as he said, "I am with you always." (Matthew 28:20)

21:23 "And the city hath no need of the sun, neither of the moon, to shine upon it: for the glory of God did lighten it, and the lamp thereof is the Lamb."

21:23 "the city hath no need of the sun, neither of the moon, to shine upon it: for the glory of God did lighten it"

This should be the level of enlightenment in the church. It is a fulfillment of Isaiah's prophecy which says, "The sun shall be no more thy light by day; neither for brightness shall the moon give light unto thee: but Jehovah will be unto thee an everlasting light, and thy God thy glory." (Isaiah 60:19) The city "is illuminated by the one who declared himself to be the 'light of the world.' (John 8:12)"[583] Any congregation of the Lord's

---

583 <u>Revelation, Four Views: A Parallel Commentary</u>, ed. Steve Gregg, (Nashville: Thomas Nelson Publishers, 1997), p. 497.

church which does not have the presence of both God and the Lamb should be named "Ichabod," which means there is no glory. (See I Samuel 4:21.)

It is this same glory of God which permeates the scripture so that ecstatically we say to God, "the opening of thy words giveth light; it giveth understanding unto the simple." (Psalm 119:130)

21:23 "the lamp thereof is the Lamb"

It is through Jesus, the Lamb, that we experience "the glory of God" by which the church is enlightened.

21:24 "And the nations shall walk amidst the light thereof: and the kings of the earth bring their glory into it."

21:24 "the nations shall walk amidst the light thereof"

The word "nations" is the translation of the Greek word *ethne*, which means an ethnic or people group, not a political entity. These are individuals from the nations who will have responded to the message of those who went to them in obedience to Christ, who said, "Go ye therefore and make disciples of all the nations [*ethne*], baptizing them into the name of the Father and of the Son and of the Holy Spirit: teaching them to observe all things whatsoever I commanded you: and lo, I am with you always, even unto the end of the world." (Matthew 28:19-20) The assurance that "the nations shall walk amidst the light thereof" predicts the success of the church's evangelistic efforts.

21:24 "the kings of the earth bring their glory into it"

People or citizens constitute the glory of kings and other categories of world rulers. As we are told in Proverbs 14:28, "In the multitude of people is the king's glory." The policies and principles embraced by a political entity as its fundamental operating basis will encourage men and women of principle, either by revulsion or attraction, to seek entry into the new Jerusalem. Revulsion will come should the king or leader commit the government to wickedness. As Proverbs tells us, "It is an abomination to kings to commit wickedness; for the throne is established by righteousness." (Proverbs 16:12)

There are historic examples of tyrants who by force have tried to Christianize their citizens and in that way bring the glory of their domain into the holy city, the church. All of their efforts have led to grievous distortions of the concept of Christ's church because they violated the eternal principle announced to Zerubbabel which tells us, "Not by might nor by power, but by my Spirit, saith Jehovah of Hosts." (Zechariah 4:6) The New Testament examples of conversion to Christ emphasize persuasion in conspicuous contrast to coercion. The following passages highlight that emphasis: Acts 2:40, Acts 9:8, Acts 17:4, Acts 18:4, Acts 28:23, and II Corinthians 5:11.

Though he was not the first tyrant to have done so, Charlemagne, who was crowned by the pope in 800 A.D., is noted for "baptizing whole populations into Christianity with the sword or with water – it was one or the other – governing 1,615 states all over Europe, not fearing anyone on the face of the earth. Men have never known a power like his."[584]

---

584 Malachi Martin, The Decline and Fall of the Roman Church, (New York: G.P. Putnam's Sons, 1981), p. 93.

Revelation Chapter 21

His efforts led to the strengthening and expansion of the horrible ecclesiastical distortion embodied in the church known as the Roman Catholic Church.

Another example of a king who tried to force his people to become Christians is that of Prince Vladimir of Kiev who in 988 A.D. ordered the mass baptism of his subjects in the Dnieper River. That was the decisive turning point of the southern Slavic people, incorporating them into a distorted form of the church, the Russian Orthodox Church. That doctrinal commitment has remained largely intact right into the twenty-first century despite the current threatening encroachments by Islam into Russia.

In inspiring contrast to the two examples just cited, as a consequence of a legitimate action by their king, the Armenians were probably the first people as a nation to have accepted Jesus Christ. There are differing accounts of how the Gospel first reached Armenia. One venerable and very widely accepted account tells us that Abgar, the Armenian king, was afflicted with leprosy. Having heard of Jesus, he sent a messenger with an appeal for him to come and exercise his power to heal. According to the account, Jesus sent a return message in which he said, "When I have been taken up, I will send to you one my disciples to heal your suffering, and give life to you and those with you." Accordingly, "After the Lord's Passion and Ascension, His promise was fulfilled by the Apostles, who sent Addai, one of the seventy-two elect, on a missionary assignment to Edessa [Abgar's capital]."[585] The conversion of the Armenian people was mostly from Zoroastrianism.

21:25 "And the gates thereof shall in no wise be shut by day (for there shall be no night there):"

21:25 "the gates thereof shall in no wise be shut by day"

Hopeful and eager entrants are welcomed as long as the period lasts which is defined by the word "day." This "day" is not the 24-hour day, the day defined by the rotation of the earth. This "day" is the sunlight period of history. (See 12:1 under "the woman's glorious wardrobe.") This is the same period which is called "today" in Hebrews 3:13. During this whole extensive era, the Christian dispensation, the gates to "the holy city, new Jerusalem," that is, the church, will remain open.

It is appropriate at this point to reiterate the comment which was made at 21:10 that these visions of "the holy city Jerusalem" are depicting the church. Though through these visions we behold the church triumphant, the descriptions emphasize those virtues, qualities and characteristics of the church which will have led it to victory in all historic periods.

21:25 "there shall be no night there"

This absence of night should not be confused with a verbally similar statement in 22:5. This statement, and a very similar one in 21:23, refers to the absence of night or darkness in new Jerusalem, which is the church, while 22:5 refers to eternal light in heaven. That such a sustained and enlightened condition in the church should be normal is emphasized by several scriptural statements. First, Paul said to the Ephesian church, "Ye were once

---
585 Aziz S. Atiya, A History of Eastern Christianity, (Millwood, N.Y.: Kraus Reprint, 1980), pp. 244-245.

darkness, but are now light in the Lord: walk as children of light." (Ephesians 5:8) To the church in Colossae Paul wrote, "He has rescued us from the dominion of darkness and brought us into the kingdom of the Son he loves." (Colossians 1:13 NIV) To the church in Thessalonica Paul wrote, "You are not in darkness, brothers, for that day to surprise you like a thief. For you are all children of light, children of the day. We are not of the night or of the darkness." (I Thessalonians 5:4-5 ESV)

21:26 "and they shall bring the glory and the honor of the nations into it:"

"When people enter the Church, they must bring their gifts with them; writers bring their power in words, artists their power in colour, sculptors their knowledge of line and form and mass, musicians their music. There is no gift which Christ cannot use."[586] (See also the comments on 21:24.)

21:27 "and there shall in no wise enter into it anything unclean, or he that maketh an abomination and a lie: but only they that are written in the Lamb's book of life."

21:27 "there shall in no wise enter into it anything unclean, or he that maketh an abomination and a lie"

This statement of exclusion basically reiterates that which was emphasized in 21:8. (See especially the comments on 22:14.) The following two translations should help us feel the impact even more forcefully. The ESV renders it, "nothing unclean will ever enter it, nor anyone who does what is detestable or false, but only those who are written in the Lamb's book of life." The NIV tells us, "nothing impure will ever enter it, nor will anyone who does what is shameful or deceitful, but only those whose names are written in the Lamb's book of life." On the issue of lying, see also 22:15.

21:27 "only they that are written in the Lamb's book of life"

On the "book of life," see the discussion under 20:15.

---

586 William Barclay, The Revelation of John, Vol. II, (Philadelphia: The Westminster Press, 1976), p. 247.

Revelation Chapter 22

H. The River of Life and the Tree of Life 22:1-5

22:1 "And he showed me a river of water of life, bright as crystal, proceeding out of the throne of God and of the Lamb,"

22:1 "he showed me a river of water of life"

Beginning as an artesian "spring" (NIV) or "fountain" (ASV) (21:6) and then becoming "a river of water of life," this life-giving stream flows "out of the throne of God and of the Lamb." Its flow seems to have increased from that of a spring to that of a river as the need required. The need would have increased because increasing numbers of people responded to the invitation which is verbalized in 22:17.

This vision incorporates a powerful reminder that the source and origin of life is "the throne of God and of the Lamb." All of man's research, experimentation, and resources have not been able to develop an alternative. The river's life-giving water will sustain all living beings in the new creation. This is the fulfillment of Psalm 46:4 which says, "There is a river, the streams whereof make glad the city of God, the holy place of the tabernacles of the Most High." The water is infused with life by the Holy Spirit. (See John 6:63 and 7:38-39.)

22:1 "bright as crystal, proceeding out of the throne of God and of the Lamb"

The water of life is "bright as crystal." It sparkles with unexpected, unimaginable, surprising and endless potential. As radical Islam continues to sway more and more of the Muslim world, the average Muslim will lose all sense of enchantment with the meaning, expectancy and possibility of life. This became clear when, "After the Madrid bombings, a spokesman for al-Qaeda left a message: 'You love life, and we love death.' The horror is that greatness is tied to death rather than to achievement in life."[587] Such Muslims constitute a huge ghoulish death cult whose ghastly and gruesome murders are blood sacrifices to a fiendish, Frankensteinish, deified enormity. We must never forget the source of life. It is neither self-generated nor does it spontaneously burst into existence as the followers of Darwin would have us to believe. Exclusively, it proceeds "out of the throne of God and of the Lamb."

22:2 "in the midst of the street thereof. And on this side of the river and on that was the tree of life, bearing twelve manner of fruits, yielding its fruit every month: and the leaves of the tree were for the healing of the nations."

---

587 Shelby Steele, *Life and Death*, The Wall Street Journal, August 22, 2006, p. A12.

Revelation Verse by Verse

22:2 "[a river is] in the midst of the street thereof. And on this side of the river and on that was the tree of life"

Sinful man was expelled from the first garden but here, redeemed man is given access to a garden far more stunning and grand than the first.

The street probably portrays only the main avenue promenade, esplanade, or boulevard of heaven. It will be the ultimate fulfillment of Isaiah's vision in which he said, "A highway shall be there, and a way, and it shall be called The way of holiness; the unclean shall not pass over it; but it shall be for *the redeemed*: the wayfaring men, yea fools, shall not err *therein*." (Isaiah 35:8)

If "the tree of life" should prove to be one single tree, it would be enormous, with huge branches reaching completely across the river and shading the street even on the other side of the life-giving river. More probably, the words depict the "tree of life" as a genus or species with individual plantings along both sides of the river.

By eating its "fruit" one will be imbued with life. This is the ultimate tree of life. It corresponds to its predecessor in the original Garden of Eden which would have bestowed eternal life on anyone who might have eaten its fruit. (See Genesis 3:22.) If one will have drunk "the water of life" from the river, will that life be further enhanced by eating fruit from the "tree of life"? Perhaps "the water of life" will endow or sustain physical life, while "the tree of life" will grant the life of social and ethnic concord, since it is "for the healing of the nations."

The portrayal of heaven as a beautiful garden is so captivating that it deeply influenced city planners in New Julfa, the Christian section of the beguiling Iranian city of Isfahan. Between 1604 and 1614 the dictatorial Safavid Iranian monarch, Shah Abbas, ordered the deportation of between 60,000 and 70,000 families of Armenian and Georgian Christians from the far north of his empire to populate and develop sparse areas on the southern litoral of the Caspian Sea and in the desert oasis of Isfahan. Those Christians (who had been forced to become residents in Isfahan, the new capital of Shah Abbas), enchanted by this account in the book of Revelation, left memorials to their faith in the nomenclature of the street grid of their area in Isfahan.

A look at some of those names makes it quite sure that those town planners were reading the Book of Revelation when they laid out portions of the city. The river (which, of course, the planners did not lay out) is called The River of Life! While that name reflects the far greater concept of the River of the Water of Life (Revelation 22:1), it also reflects the very obvious ecological fact that all agriculture in Isfahan has, through the centuries, been dependent on the river. Thus in a very real sense, the river gave life to the city. Just how dependent life is on the river was sadly illustrated in the years 1868-1870 when the rains failed. During the ensuing famine 12,000 perished in Isfahan.[588] It was this keen awareness of the role of the river which gave birth to "… the custom of the Armenians at Epiphanytide[589] to conduct a very solemn and gorgeous ceremony of Blessing the Waters of the Zayandehrud [the river which gives life] in Isfahan."[590]

---
588 Robin E. Waterfield, Christians in Persia (London: George Allen & Unwin Ltd., 1973), p. 115.
589 "A feast on January 6 in commemoration of the coming of the Magi as the first manifestation of Christ to the Gentiles." Webster's New International Dictionary of the English Language, 2nd ed. Unabridged, (Springfield, MA: G&C Merriam Co., 1943).
590 Robin E. Waterfield, Christians in Persia (London: George Allen & Unwin Ltd., 1973), p. 67.

Revelation Chapter 22

In addition to the name of the river, on the south bank of the Zayandehrud (The River of Life) is the street Khyaban-e-Dalan-e-Behisht, which means The Avenue Which Leads to the Threshold of Heaven or Threshold of Heaven Avenue! On the other side of the River of Life is Kyaban-e-Bagh-e-Jannat, i.e., The Avenue Which Leads to The Garden of Heaven! In the south part of Julfa is a street called Kyaban-e-Hoseynabad, i.e., The Avenue Which Leads to The Abode of Beauty! Another street is Kyaban-e-Shahzadeh Ebrahim, i.e., The Avenue of The Royal Heirs of Abraham! (Certainly they are the only ones who can set foot on the threshold of heaven's door! cf. Rom. 4:1-12.) But to reach the ultimate, but by no means exhausting the examples, there are two parallel streets with extremely notable names. The first is Behisht Aieen Avenue which means The Avenue Which is The Mirror of Heaven. Appropriately enough, just two streets away is Hasht Behisht Boulevard, The Boulevard of the Eight Heavens! As I did, you may find it surprisingly harmonious with such striking nomenclature that the four royal gardens established by order of King Shah Abbas were made accessible by a street still called The Avenue of the Four Gardens and that "the water channels which ran the whole length of the avenue down to the river were faced with onyx."[591]

22:2 "the tree of life, bearing twelve manner of fruits, yielding its fruit every month: and the leaves of the tree were for the healing of the nations"

One wonders if this tree of life will simultaneously bear "twelve manner of fruits" each month or whether it will sequentially produce the same fruit but perhaps of a different flavor or variety in each of the twelve months.

Time will have left its mark on eternity. Ethnicity will continue into eternity despite the fact that innumerable clashes and wars will have taken place during historic time because of ethnic strife. But in heaven there will be no danger of ethnic strife erupting again because the marvelous tree of life has leaves "for the healing of the nations (*ethnon*)." One wonders why God will not have healed the persistent ethnic rifts all at once, rather than on a monthly basis. Conceivably, God wants us to remember our miserable condition before he saved us.

When we are told that "the leaves of the tree were for the healing of the nations," it probably does not indicate that those leaves were to be eaten. Rather, circumstances will be such that the redeemed from all ethnic backgrounds will gather in the shade cast by the leaves of the tree of life. As people from various and diverse ethnicities associate there with each other, the old concepts of fear, repugnance and revulsion, born out of centuries of ethnic competition, rivalry, strife and war, will heal. Their association in the shade of that marvelous tree will be therapeutic.[592] It will result in "the healing of the nations." Those leaves will have far greater healing power than the balm of Gilead (Jeremiah 8:22 and 46:11) or that of the balm which Joseph's brothers carried to Egypt as a gift for Pharaoh. (See Genesis 43:11.)

Each ethnic group will learn that the new birth (John 3:5) had transformed everyone present, even those who had previously been among their mortal ethnic enemies. They will have found that people from their rival ethnic enemies had been completely

---

591 Roger Stevens, <u>The Land of the Great Sophy</u>, (London: Methuen & Co. Ltd., 1962), p. 385.
592 The leaves of this marvelous tree are "for the healing of the nations." The word "healing" is the translation of the Greek word *therapeian*, from which our words "therapy" and "therapeutic" are derived.

transformed by "the washing of regeneration and renewing of the Holy Spirit." (Titus 3:5) Redeemed men and women will be present there from groups which had waged the most vicious forms of ethnic war. Here in their radically new persons, they will be discovered to have become loving, winsome, generous, welcoming, gracious and noble. Those old fears, hatreds, suspicions and divisions will heal by intimate association and fellowship with former enemies in the shade of the leaves of the tree of life. Probably God chose this repetitive process so redeemed mankind would never forget who it was that had saved them from the horribly destructive morass of ethnic strife.

From the words "yielding its fruit every month" it is obvious that in heaven the continuation of our gloriously enhanced human existence will still be demarcated by periods called "months." Exhilaratingly different than human experience on this side of heaven, the heavenly cavalcade of event-filled "months" will not end or terminate in death, for as we have been assured, "death shall be no more." (21:4) Also, that series of periods which are to be known as "months" will not be finite but infinite, recurring eternally. How that eternal parade of "months," rolling on perpetually, is to be differentiated from the succession of months with which we are currently familiar, is not entirely clear. On the whole issue of time versus eternity, please see the discussion at 6:10 under "how long?"

Some commentators think that "bearing twelve manner of fruits yielding its fruit every month" implies twelve varieties of trees. However, there is no textual support for that idea. It appears that a single species of tree will bear twelve varieties of fruit during a twelve-month cycle. In any case, it seems that "the primary thought is that the tree is ever fruitful."[593]

22:3 **"And there shall be no curse any more: and the throne of God and of the Lamb shall be therein: and his servants shall serve him;"**

22:3 "there shall be no curse any more"

The future is secure! There will never be a rebellion by a heavenly being such as that which occurred when Satan made a lunge for dominance. (Please see the comments at 9:11 and 20:3.) That rebellion brought a prolonged curse causing incalculable suffering during the entire human experience.

22:3 "the throne of God and of the Lamb shall be therein"

The location of "the throne of God and of the Lamb" is defined only by the adverb "therein." Most probably we are to understand the reality to which it points is "the holy city Jerusalem" in its triumphant state. More specifically, the throne of God and of the Lamb will be located where the tree of life and the river of life will be.

22:3 "his servants shall serve him;"

In what capacity will we serve him? (Please see the comments at 22:5 under "they shall reign forever and forever.")

22:4 **"and they shall see his face; and his name shall be on their foreheads."**

---
[593] Lee G. Tomlinson, The Wonder Book of the Bible: A Commentary On the Book of Revelation, (Joplin, Missouri: College Press, 1963), p. 364.

Revelation Chapter 22

22:4   "they shall see his face"

This promise is a great enhancement to the blessing granted to Moses. To him God, using many anthropomorphisms, said "Thou canst not see my face; for man shall not see me and live. And Jehovah said, Behold, there is a place by me, and thou shalt stand upon the rock: and it shall come to pass, while my glory passeth by, that I will put thee in a cleft of the rock, and will cover thee with my hand until I have passed by: and I will take away my hand, and thou shalt see my back; but my face shall not be seen." (Exodus 33:20-23)

As Christians, we exult in the hope that when "he shall be manifested we shall be like him; for we shall see him even as he is." (I John 3:2) In this ringing declaration, John simply calls attention to Jesus' promise that "the pure in heart" are blessed, "for they shall see God." (Matthew 5:8)

22:4   "his name shall be on their foreheads"

(Please see the discussion at 3:12 under "I will write upon him the name of my God.")

22:5   And there shall be night no more; and they need no light of lamp, neither light of sun; for the Lord God shall give them light: and they shall reign for ever and ever."

22:5   "there shall be night no more; and they need no light of lamp, neither light of sun; for the Lord God shall give them light"

Compare this verse with the comments on 21:23 and 21:25. From this verse it seems something much more stunning will replace the captivating beauty of our present sunrises and sunsets. Undoubtedly, the new beauty will be so splendid that we will experience no nostalgia for the present arrangement. The new light will emanate from "the Lord God [who] shall give them light."

22:5   "they shall reign for ever and ever"

Our lives in eternity will not be given to idleness. Under the oversight of Christ we "shall reign for ever and ever" in "the world to come." (Hebrews 2:5) That world is also described as "the ages to come." (Ephesians 2:7) Sometimes those ages are referred to in the singular, as "the age to come." (Hebrews 6:5) Reigning does not describe a state of inactivity but of deep involvement in authoritative oversight. The redeemed shall even reign over angels according to I Corinthians 6:3, which tells us that "we shall judge angels." This judgment will obviously not be exercised in adjudicating criminal cases, since sin will not be there. (See 21:27.) Therefore, it will probably consist of judging the comparative levels of the angels' diligence, efficiency and performance.

I.   Corroboration and exhortation 22:6-20

22:6   "And he said unto me, These words are faithful and true: and the Lord, the God of the spirits of the prophets, sent his angels to show unto his servants the things which must shortly come to pass."

22:6   "These words are faithful and true"

This assurance was given previously at 21:5. Certainly we who live in the twenty-first century should be able to testify that the "words" in the predictions given in the book of

Revelation "are faithful and true." The words of Revelation convey facts, not fables; realities not myths. This assertion is substantiated historically because many realities and developments which were predicted have come to pass during the many centuries subsequent to John's transcription of these prophecies. Here are a few examples:

(1) The prophecies foresaw the great barbarian invasions which befell the Roman Empire. (For example, see 8:9-10 and the comments.)

(2) Subsequent to the barbarian invasions the fall of the great Roman Empire was clearly predicted. (See 8:12 and comments.)

(3) John transcribed the visions of the rise of the Byzantine Empire and its fall. (See 13:1 and following.)

(4) The visions predicted the rise of Byzantium's successor, the Russian Empire. (See 13:11 and 16:2 and following.)

(5) The rise and career of Islam were clearly predicted. (See 9:1-2 and following.)

(6) The emergence and career of a flagrantly corrupt form of Christianity, growing out of the true church was vividly predicted. (See the comments on 18:2 and following.)[594]

22:6 "the Lord, the God of the spirits of the prophets"

The "spirits of the prophets" seems to refer to "that spiritual part of the nature of the prophets by which they are made to discern and to communicate God's will."[595] Though Plummer's comment is certainly helpful, it should be enhanced by insight from Acts 2:4 which tells us that the apostles "were all filled with the Holy Spirit, and began to speak with other tongues, as the Spirit gave them utterance." Also, Peter has told us that no prophecy of scripture "had its origin in the will of man, but men spoke from God as they were carried along by the Holy Spirit." (II Peter 1:21 NIV)

22:6 "sent his angels to show unto his servants the things which must shortly come to pass"

The role of angels in the divine revelatory process is stressed several times in the Revelation account. (See the comments at 22:16.) Though the revelations were initially given to John, they were (through him) to be given to "his servants." The pronoun "his" points to "the Lord God" of verse 5.

22:7 "And behold, I come quickly. Blessed is he that keepeth the words of the prophecy of this book."

22:7 "I come quickly"

This proclamation is made from the divine perspective which is given to us by Peter who has informed us "that one day is with the Lord as a thousand years, and a thousand years as one day." (II Peter 3:8) We must ask God to help us view history and our lives from his perspective. (See also 22:12.)

---

594 The demonstrable truth of Christ's message exposes the lie of Hitler when he called the Christian message "proven untruth." - David Motadel, Islam and Nazi Germany's War, (Cambridge: The Belknap Press of Harvard University, 2014), p. 64.
595 A. Plummer, The Pulpit Commentary [on] Revelation, (Chicago: Wilcox & Follett Co., no date), p. 546.

Revelation Chapter 22

Jesus will not come as quickly as many presume. For example, many people reading or hearing about the destructive chaos caused by the civil war in Syria, the merciless aggression of ISIS in northern Iraq and eastern Syria, the murderous exploits of Boko Haram in Nigeria and northwestern Africa, or the rising crime and lawlessness in Western societies, often exclaim in utter despair, "these are the last days!" Their emotional and fearful utterances distort the meaning of Jesus' statement that "I come quickly." They use a biblical expression, "the last days," which means the final period of human history, to express their foreboding that we are right on the very threshold of eternal doom.

From "the words of the prophecy of this book" one will learn that there are many eras of human history yet to emerge before time ends. One of the most notable of those eras will be The Millennium. (See 20:1-7.) Many people, without understanding the meaning of the biblical expression "the last days," which was first spoken at the beginning of the Christian era (See Acts 2:17.), often utter that phrase to express hopeless frustration and despair. At the same time they frequently seem to wash their hands of any personal responsibility to improve conditions as though time were so short that it would be ridiculous to make any attempt. (On the use of the phrase "the last days" to indicate the entire Christian period of history, often called the Christian dispensation, please see the discussion at 4:1 under "the things which must come to pass hereafter.")

22:7 "Blessed is he that keepeth the words of the prophecy of this book"

Stern has rendered the phrase "he that keepeth the words" as "he who obeys the words of the prophecy written in this book." The phrase "he that keepeth the words" or "he who obeys the words" probably means that the one viewing and evaluating history and the coming scenarios of human experience by "the words of the prophecy of this book" will then order his life by the insights given in the prophecies of Revelation. Such a person, then being confident and certain of where he is in the flow of human events, will know how to order his life to achieve his maximum potential. A great blessing indeed!

22:8 "And I John am he that heard and saw these things. And when I heard and saw, I fell down to worship before the feet of the angel that showed me these things."

22:8 "I John am he that heard and saw these things"

John had not described apparitions, imaginations or phantom ideas, but genuine scenes from coming reality. By means of divinely given visions, he actually "heard and saw these things." The messages of Revelation are not composed of illusions. To give more certainty to the message, he wrote "I John." It was his way of signing the document. Thus, he dropped his previous reticence, which is very conspicuous in his Gospel, to give full self-disclosure. (See John 21:7 and 21:20.) Here, he openly tries to convince the reader of the truth, validity and reality of the vision which he has transcribed. (See also 22:6.)

22:8 "I fell down to worship before the feet of the angel that showed me these things"

"It is remarkable that, in verses 8 and 9, John made precisely the same mistake (seeking to worship the angel) for which he had been sternly rebuked earlier (cf. 19:10), and now receives the same rebuke again. This may give us some notion of the extent to which the magnificence of the visions distracted him [by being captivated and enthralled] and interfered with his normal rational activity."[596]

22:9 "And he saith unto me, See thou do it not: I am a fellow-servant with thee and with thy brethren the prophets, and with them that keep the words of this book: worship God."

This helps us conceive of angels in proper perspective. Though angels have been agents in the process of divine revelation (See 22:6 under "sent his angels to show …"), they are not divine and, therefore, should not be worshipped.

22:10 "And he saith unto me, Seal not up the words of the prophecy of this book; for the time is at hand."

22:10 "Seal not up the words of the prophecy of this book"

Christians are not members of a mystery cult where the deepest and most profound knowledge is only to be divulged to a secretly initiated, elite hierarchy. We are not members of an occult group or of a Masonic lodge. On the contrary, these deep revelations of God's truth and man's future, "the words of the prophecy of this book," are to be made widely available, even to the most humble Christian. This is to be done despite the fact that the message of this book may well spark opposition and persecution.

22:10 "the time is at hand"

The time which is "at hand" is the current period of history during which these visions are applicable, useful and profitable. The time which is "at hand" is the Christian era. Whether it is a time when the church is under attack or at peace, John is commanded not to seal the words of the prophecy of this book. All Christians desperately need to understand where we are and what we are to expect in our segment of the flow of history.

22:11 "He that is unrighteous, let him do unrighteousness still: and he that is filthy, let him be made filthy still: and he that is righteous, let him do righteousness still: and he that is holy, let him be made holy still."

22:11 "He that is unrighteous, let him do unrighteousness still: and he that is filthy, let him be made filthy still"

A point is coming when the opportunity for a new birth, for regeneration and for repentance, will have passed. Those who have made an implacable commitment to evil will finally be given unimpeded freedom to pursue their head-long rush to eternal disaster. It will be a finality even more definitive, fearful and consequential than God's closing of the door on Noah's ark. (Genesis 7:16)

22:11 "he that is righteous, let him do righteousness still: and he that is holy, let him be made holy still"

In dramatic contrast to those who vote for unrighteousness, everyone who will have made his life-choice on the side of righteousness and holiness is encouraged to continue in

---

[596] <u>Revelation, Four Views: A Parallel Commentary</u>, ed. Steve Gregg, (Nashville: Thomas Nelson Publishers, 1997), p. 501.

Revelation Chapter 22

pursuit of the fulfillment of his marvelous decision. The triumph of righteousness and holiness will be eternal.

22:12 "Behold, I come quickly; and my reward is with me, to render to each man according as his work is."

22:12 "I come quickly"

His coming will happen quickly. Several translations render it "soon." The word "quickly" conveys the idea of "suddenly." (Please see the comments at 22:7.) Sadly, many will be caught unprepared, like those in Noah's time who "knew not until the flood came and took them all away." (Matthew 24:39)

22:12 "my reward is with me, to render to each man according as his work is"

(See 20:12 under "a distinctly separate and unique judgment.")

22:13 "I am the Alpha and the Omega, the first and the last, the beginning and the end."

Understanding the meaning of the declarations in this verse will take us to the limits of our cognitive powers and probably beyond. They bring us to the point where time tries to comprehend eternity, where the finite tries to understand the infinite, where the limited attempts to grasp the meaning and scope of the unlimited, where man tries to comprehend God.

22:13 "I am the Alpha and the Omega"

If we try to verbally express the meaning of infinity, eternity and true deity, the alphabet is too limited. We are helpless -- both before alpha and following omega! It is vain to try to express meaning which exceeds the full scope of the alphabet, which usually limits the scope of mental comprehension and verbal expression. God is both the beginning (the alpha) and the consummation (the omega) of meaning. (See also the comments at 1:8.)

22:13 "the first and the last"

If we are searching for the ultimate origin, the true beginning, "the first" of all existence and meaning as well as the climactic consummation of all being and existence, "the last" of everything, we can find them only in God! (See 1:17.)

22:13 "the beginning and the end"

Is the Eternal One finite? Can he be defined, confined or restricted by a "beginning" or an "end"? Obviously not! God's statement that he is "the beginning and the end" simply tells us that there is nothing and no one which or who is anterior to or subsequent to God! We need not look in any direction for meaning and reality beyond God.

22:14 "Blessed are they that wash their robes, that they may have the right to come to the tree of life, and may enter in by the gates into the city."

22:14 "Blessed are they that wash their robes"

Those who wash their robes are privileged to enjoy the fulfillment of David's cry to God, "Purify me with hyssop, and I shall be clean: wash me, and I shall be whiter than snow."

(Psalm 51:7) It is because of having gone through that purification process that God can say, "Though your sins be as scarlet, they shall be as white as snow: though they be red like crimson, they shall be as wool." (Isaiah 1:18) It can only be achieved by divine power and grace, for God tells us that, "Though thou wash thee with lye, and take thee much soap, yet thine iniquity is marked before me." (Jeremiah 2:22)

"To wash your robe means to have recourse to the cleansing fountain of the blood of Jesus Christ. That blood not only removes all guilt, but also has merited for us the purifying and sanctifying Spirit. Hence, we must have recourse to it *constantly*."[597]

The phrase, "they that wash their robes" "shows the human part in salvation ... we have to take that sacrifice to ourselves."[598] (See also the comments on 7:14.)

22:14 "that they may have the right to come to the tree of life"

The tree of life does not cleanse one of his sin. It grants and perpetuates life. One must have been cleansed, must have washed his robes, in order to gain access to the priceless tree of life.

22:14 "may enter in by the gates into the city"

Those who will be allowed to enter will be granted the rights of citizenship. They may then enjoy all the privileges, benefits and perquisites of heaven's full-time permanent occupants. (See the discussion of the gates at 21:12-13 and 21:25-27.)

22:15 "Without are the dogs, and the sorcerers, and the fornicators, and the murderers, and the idolaters, and every one that loveth and maketh a lie."

22:15 "Without are the dogs"

Dogs have one especially repulsive habit which undoubtedly has consigned them to being mentioned as a type of those who will be excluded from heaven. That may well be why they are cited here as an example of those who will be "without." Both Proverbs 26:11 and II Peter 2:2 tell us, as repulsive as it is, that dogs return to their vomit! Similarly, one who has come to believe that Jesus is the Christ, has repented of his sinful life style and has been baptized into Christ and then goes back to his old life style, is returning to his vomit. Such a one is going to be banned from heaven. He is going to be "without." This fearful exclusion is also emphasized in 21:8 and 21:27.

Some of the commendable traits of dogs are also acknowledged in scripture. Their value as herd dogs or shepherd dogs is noted in Job 30:1 as "the dogs that guard my sheep." Their compassion is also noted (See Luke 16:21.) as well as their humility. (See Mark 7:28.)

22:15 "the sorcerers"

The apostle Paul highlighted the advantageous and the exclusive position which had been given to the Jews through verbal revelation when he said, "they have been entrusted with the very words of God."[599] Israel's possession of revealed scripture was utterly unique!

---

597 W. Hendriksen, More Than Conquerors: An Interpretation of the Book of Revelation, (Grand Rapids: Baker Book House, 1952), p. 253.
598 William Barclay, The Revelation of John, Vol. II, (Philadelphia: The Westminster Press, 1976), p. 255.
599 Romans 3:2 NIV

Revelation Chapter 22

Other people have sorcery in many forms: seances, divinations, mediums, necromancy, witchcraft, auguries, conjurations, soothsaying, fortune telling, astrology, horoscopes, magic, incantations, spells, clairvoyance, psychic phenomena, crystal gazing, telepathy, wizardry, voodoo, shamanism, demonology, black art, occultism, omens, trances, hypnosis, chants, jinxes, hexes, palm reading, Tarot Card reading and Ouija boards.

Some relevant passages on the occult are: Leviticus 19:26-28, Deuteronomy 18:10-13, I Samuel 15:23, Micah 5:12, Malachi 3:5, Galatians 5:20, Revelation 18:23 and 21:8.

22:15 "the fornicators"

The word "fornicators" identifies those who indulge in the satisfaction of sexual desire between males and females, uninhibited by divine principles. Only within those guidelines is such indulgence legitimate. (See Hebrews 13:4.) In God's sight it is only within the divinely established parameters of marriage, between one man and one woman, that the union of male and female may legitimately and rapturously be finalized. (See Matthew 19:4-5.)

The spectrum of violations of divinely given marriage concepts is very broad, ranging from Bacchanalian types of orgies (Numbers 25:1-9) to private, lustful vision. About that level of fornication, Jesus said that, "Everyone who looketh on a woman to lust after her hath committed adultery with her already in his heart." (Matthew 5:28)

Expanding on Jesus' teaching, the apostle Paul has told us, "This is the will of God, *even* your sanctification, that ye abstain from fornication; that each one of you know how to possess himself of his own vessel in sanctification and honor, not in the passion of lust, even as the Gentiles who know not God." (I Thessalonians 4:3-5) The NIV renders the passage this way: "It is God's will that you should be sanctified: that you should avoid sexual immorality; that each of you should learn to control his own body in a way that is holy and honorable, not in passionate lust like the heathen, who do not know God."

22:15 "the murderers"

Murder is not simply to be equated with killing. Under strict judicial processes the Mosaic Law legitimized executions. For example, Deuteronomy 17:6 tells us that "at the mouth of two witnesses, or three witnesses, shall he that is to die be put to death; at the mouth of one witness he shall not be put to death." Death, by legal execution, is clearly upheld in Romans 13:4 which tells us that a ruler does not bear "the sword in vain: for he is a minister of God, an avenger for wrath to him that doeth evil."

While the parameters are not so carefully and explicitly drawn, it is clear that killing in war was allowed when it was waged under the sections of Mosaic Law which governed that type of conflict. That there were rules of war is made clear in I Kings 2:5 which tells of Abner who "shed the blood of war in peace" and was executed for that transgression.

Murder is killing motivated by repulsive and impulsive urges such as sexual lust, greed, envy, anger, jealousy, embarrassment or revenge. It is killing which is carried out by an individual or individuals with no judicial scrutiny or permission by any state authority. It is killing which takes place without due process of law.

22:15 "the idolaters"

In addition to the practice of open idolatry such as one may observe in a Hindu temple, totally innocuous items are often made into idols. Accordingly, the veneration of "the idols of gold, and of silver, and of brass, and of stone, and of wood; which can neither see, nor hear, nor walk" (9:20) is also condemned.

22:15 "everyone that loveth and maketh a lie"

Probity, veracity, reliability and honesty must not be compromised. (See 21:8 and 21:27.)

22:16 "I Jesus have sent mine angel to testify unto you these things for the churches. I am the root and the offspring of David, the bright, the morning star."

22:16 "I Jesus have sent mine angel to testify unto you these things for the churches."

In the book of Revelation, the role of angels in the revelatory process, that is, bringing the divine message to man, has been repeatedly emphasized. (For examples, see 17:7, 18:1, 18:21, 21:9 and 22:6 along with their comments.)

22:16 "I am the root and the offspring of David, the bright, the morning star."

The self identification which Jesus gives at this point is an enhancement of his earlier disclosure recorded at 2:28 in which he said to those in Thyatira who had (1) held fast, (2) had overcome and (3) had kept his works unto the end, that he would give them authority over the nations and also endow them with "the morning star." Here, Christ gives an even greater disclosure of himself showing that "the morning star" arises out of "the root and offspring of David." This enriches our understanding of one of the great endowments we now enjoy, "which is Christ in you, the hope of glory." (Colossians 1:27) Peter points out that to be endowed with "the morning star," which he calls the "day-star," gives illuminating guidance, enhancing our understanding of the message of the prophets. He wrote, "We have the word of prophecy made more sure; whereunto ye do well that ye take heed, as unto a lamp shining in a dark place, until the day dawn, and the day-star arise in your hearts." (II Peter 1:19)

22:17 "And the Spirit and the bride say, Come. And he that heareth, let him say, Come. And he that is athirst, let him come: he that will, let him take the water of life freely."

22:17 "Spirit ... bride ... he that heareth"

There are three partners who invite outsiders to enter into the heavenly city. Of these three, "the Spirit" is divine. He delivers his invitation to the human heart. Repeatedly and universally, he "will convict the world in respect of sin, and of righteousness, and of judgment." (John 16:8) At those moments "our heart [will] condemn us." And knowing that "God is greater than our heart and knoweth all things" (I John 3:20), we are impelled to seek forgiveness. The voice of the Spirit is like that still small voice which Elijah heard. (I Kings 19:12) One of the most dangerous things anyone can do is "resist the Holy Spirit" (Acts 7:51) or to harden his heart when he hears the Spirit's voice. (Hebrews 4:7)

Revelation Chapter 22

The second one to whom God has given the privilege of inviting others to "take the water of life freely" is the bride. She is the church in its corporate sense. There are vast areas so distant and widespread into which the invitation to "Come" is to be given that only the corporate effort of congregations, whether singly or in cooperation with fellow congregations, can effectively project the Lord's invitation. Historically, the bride, which is the church, has functioned exemplarily in this role. (See Acts 13:1-3.)

Finally, individual evangelism is both mandated and motivated because it is Jesus who tells us, "He that heareth, let him say, Come." Christians give the most powerful invitations when they give it by "the word of their testimony." (12:11) These individual invitations take place in many venues. The first is within the home. As Moses commanded Godly Jewish parents to make divine truth known to their children (Deuteronomy 4:9), so Christian fathers are instructed to nurture their children "in the chastening and admonition of the Lord." (Ephesians 6:4) It is at their parents' knees that children should first hear of God's gracious invitation to "Come."

Also, individual Christians should invite their neighbors to "Come." In this we should follow the example of the Samaritan woman who said to her neighbors, "Come, see a man, who told me all things that ever I did: can this be the Christ?" (John 4:29) Also, we individual Christians must not forget to invite our friends. When we do, we follow the example of Phillip who found "Nathaniel and sayeth unto him, 'We have found him of whom Moses and the law and the prophets wrote, Jesus of Nazareth.'" (John 4:45)

22:17 "he that is athirst, let him come"

Long ago, the prophet Jeremiah said, "Ye shall seek me, and find me, when ye shall search for me with all your heart." (Jeremiah 29:13) In harmony with Jeremiah's defining statement, Jesus said, "Blessed are they that hunger and thirst after righteousness, for they shall be filled." (Matthew 5:6) Thus, even without an explicit invitation, some sinners are "invited" by the impulsion of an inner thirst to come to Christ for cleansing, meaning, significance and assurance.

22:17 "he that will, let him take the water of life freely."

We must do everything in our power to assist those who are confronted by opposition or impediments in their desire to yield their lives to Christ so they may drink of the water of life.

22:18 "I testify unto every man that heareth the words of the prophecy of this book, if any man shall add unto them, God shall add unto him the plagues which are written in this book:"

22:18 "I testify unto every man that heareth the words of the prophecy of this book, if any man shall add unto them"

Since "the words of the prophecy of this book" answer our deepest and most profound questions, and since they help us "assign meaning and order to absurd chaos,"[600] this book of Revelation was obviously destined to have a global circulation and impact. Therefore, someone moved by opportunism may wish to attach or add some personal

---
600 Theo Pauline Nestor, *With Enough Ink*, LIV FUN, Autumn 2014, p. 31.

concept to its text which he wants to propagate. Others may wish to make additions which would warp or nullify some of the teachings of this book which they may have found disturbing or unpalatable.

22:18 "God shall add unto him the plagues which are written in this book:"

While there are many other plagues mentioned in Revelation, certainly the three mentioned in Revelation 18:8 are basic. They are: "death, and mourning, and famine."

22:19 "and if any man shall take away from the words of the book of this prophecy, God shall take away his part from the tree of life, and out of the holy city, which are written in this book."

22:19 "if any man shall take away from the words of the book of this prophecy"

We cannot pick and choose. Some may want to blunt sections of "the words of the book of this prophecy" because the complete message may well cause opposition which will have painful social, professional and economic consequences. If we frankly and honestly, though winsomely, expound and teach the message of Revelation, even then, in many circumstances we probably will bring upon ourselves vicious opposition. Jesus helped us understand the working principle from which that opposition will arise when, speaking of the world, he said, "me it hateth, because I testify of it, that its works are evil." (John 7:7)

Areas from which opposition will undoubtedly arise will be those where the dominant ideology is defined by Islam, by Roman Catholicism, by Russian Orthodoxism or a host of smaller churches which are also in fornicatious relationships with political powers. Teaching the ultimacy of deity, which dominates the entire book but is given special focus in 22:13, will bring the scorn and hatred of all the proponents of those philosophies and political and social ideologies, whatever their garb, which are based on atheism. Atheists find their nihilism attractive because it gives them unrestrained liberty for sensualism.

Another area from which strident opposition has arisen against those who refuse to "take away from the words of the book of this prophecy" is the voice of those insisting that deviant sex is moral and proper. "Holding the line isn't as easy as it used to be. A rash of high profile lawsuits across the country against cake bakers, florists, and photographers declining to serve gay weddings have underscored some of the challenges for Christians and others navigating a swiftly changing social tide. ... Any company or organization with religious objections to promoting or endorsing homosexuality could face similar dilemmas as legal demands for affirming homosexuality grow."[601]

22:19 "God shall take away his part from the tree of life, and out of the holy city, which are written in this book."

"Here we are told specifically that it is possible for some to have their part in the Book of Life taken away."[602] This truth indicts those who affirm "once saved, always saved" as false witnesses.

---

601 Jamie Dean, *Losing Their Shirts: Christian Small-Business Owners Across the Country are Under Threat as Gay Activists Try to Force Them to Affirm Homosexuality*, WORLD, May 2, 2015, p. 40.
602 Revelation, Four Views: A Parallel Commentary, ed. Steve Gregg, (Nashville: Thomas Nelson Publishers, 1997), p. 504.

Revelation Chapter 22

22:20 **"He who testifieth these things saith, Yea: I come quickly. Amen: come, Lord Jesus."**

Jesus' declaration that "I come quickly" is the fulfillment of John's entreaty, "Come, Lord Jesus." Compare John's prayer with Paul's plea when he said "maranatha" as recorded in I Corinthians 16:22. The word "maranatha" is Aramaic but is written in Greek which means, "come quickly Lord."

22:21 **"The grace of the Lord Jesus be with the saints. Amen."**

"Bearing in mind that the theme of the book is the conflict between good and evil, we may well conclude our study of it by joining in the prayer of John, that the help of the Lord Jesus may be on the side of his saints to enable them to overcome and then receive their reward."[603]

---

603 A. Plummer, The Pulpit Commentary [on] Revelation, (Chicago: Wilcox & Follett Co., no date), p. 548.

Appendix A

Correlating Seventeen Eschatological Passages in the New Testament With the Account Given in Revelation

I.   Matthew 16:27: "For the Son of man shall come in the glory of his Father with his angels; and then shall he render unto every man according to his deeds."

On the fulfillment of this prophecy and its correlation with the Revelation account, see the commentary on Revelation 19:11-16.

16:27 "the Son of man shall come in the glory of his Father"

"The glory of his Father" corresponds to the statement in Revelation 19:12 that "upon his head are many diadems."

16:27 "with his angels"

See especially "the armies which are in heaven followed him" in the commentary on Revelation 19:14.

16:27 "then shall he render unto every man according to his deeds"

Please see the comments on Revelation 19:11 and 19:15 under "he doth judge and make war."

II.   Matthew 24:1-51 (See the parallel passages in Mark 13:1-37 and Luke 21:5-36.)

24:1 "And Jesus went out from the temple, and was going on his way; and his disciples came to him to show him the buildings of the temple."

24:2 "But he answered and said unto them, See ye not all these things? verily I say unto you, There shall not be left here one stone upon another, that shall not be thrown down."

24:2 "See ye not all these things?"

The "things" which were under consideration were "the buildings of the temple." (24:1) This identification is also made unmistakably clear by both Mark's and Luke's accounts. Mark wrote, "Jesus said unto him [that is to one of his disciples], Seest thou these great buildings? There shall not be left here one stone upon another, which shall not be thrown down." (Mark 13:2) Luke wrote, "And as some spake of the temple, how it was adorned with goodly stones and offerings, he said, As for these things which ye behold the days will come, in which there shall not be left here one stone upon another, that shall not be thrown down." (Luke 21:5-6)

24:2 "I say unto you, There shall not be left here one stone upon another, that shall not be thrown down"

Jesus correctly predicted the total destruction of the Jewish temple. This prophecy does not point to an eschatological event but to the Roman suppression of the Jews which involved the destruction of their temple. Repeatedly in the commentary, it has been pointed out that the destruction of the temple took place <u>before</u> the book of Revelation was written.

24:3 "And as he sat on the mount of Olives, the disciples came unto him privately, saying, Tell us, when shall these things be? and what *shall be* the sign of thy coming, and of the end of the world?"

24:3 "Tell us, when shall these things be?"

This is the first part of the disciples' triple question. The "things" about which they asked refer to Jesus' statement in verse 2 that "there shall not be left here one stone upon another, that shall not be thrown down." Those words point to the complete destruction of the Herodian Jewish temple in Jerusalem. Jesus' answer in verses 15-22 elaborates on the temple's destruction along with some of its related consequences.

24:3 "the sign of thy coming"

Second, the disciples asked, "What shall be the sign of thy coming?" Jesus answered that question in segments found in verses 4-5, verse 11, verses 23-27, and finally, in verse 32.

24:3 "the end of the world"

Third and last of all, the disciples asked concerning "the end of the world." Jesus' answer is given in segments found in verses 6-14. Jesus' second coming and the end of the world will both be eschatological events as has been noted in the commentary.

24:4 "And Jesus answered and said unto them, Take heed that no man lead you astray."

This is not advice causing one to become cynical but to be wary, cautious and discerning. Should some imposter persuade people that he himself is the Christ, as one who has appeared either the first or the second time, he could then enlist people in the most grotesque and unrighteous plots and schemes.

24:5 "For many shall come in my name, saying, I am the Christ; and shall lead many astray.

The most notorious imposter who appeared in apostolic times as a false Christ was Simon bar Kokhba. "Reputedly of Davidic descent, he was hailed as the Messiah by the greatest rabbi of the time, Akiva ben Yosef, who also gave him the title Bar Kokhba ('Son of the Star'), a messianic allusion. Bar Kokhba took the title nasi ('prince') and struck his own coins, with the legend 'Year 1 of the Liberty of Jerusalem.'"[604] (See also the comments at 24:24.)

---

[604] "Bar Kokhba," *Encyclopedia Brittanica* Online, http://www.britannica.com/EBchecked/topic/52477/Bar-Kokhba, Accessed June 10, 2015.

Appendix A

24:6 "And ye shall hear of wars and rumors of wars; see that ye be not troubled: for *these things* must needs come to pass; but the end is not yet."

24:6 "ye shall hear of wars and rumors of wars"

Actual war and threatening or incipient war, with the exception of the period of The Millennium (See the commentary on 20:1-7.), will characterize human society till Jesus' final return.

24:6 "*these things* must needs come to pass"

These words indicate that there is an inevitability about the outbreak of war. Some of the causes for war are well known. For example, competition for control of trade routes, for possession of natural resources and control of choke points in the world's transport system – such as the current contest between the U.S.A. and China over free access to travel and shipping in the South China Sea – constantly bring contention and war. Also, clashing, competitive ideological systems, such as Catholic vs. Protestant and Communism vs. a free market society, may lead to war. In times of natural disasters such as famines (24:7), danger of war is greatly exacerbated. Famine may be both the cause and the result of war.

24:6 "the end is not yet"

The "end" is the one about which the disciples asked, "the end of the world." (24:3)

24:7 "For nation shall rise against nation, and kingdom against kingdom; and there shall be famines and earthquakes in divers places."

The discreet conditions which are itemized in verses 7-12 will be those which the followers of Christ will have to face from time-to-time and from place-to-place as history marches to its ultimate climax.

24:7 "nation shall rise against nation, and kingdom against kingdom"

Jesus foresaw that war, except for the period known as The Millennium (See the commentary on 20:1-7.), would plague human society throughout its entire existence. (Please see the comments at Revelation 14:20 under "the bridle's of the horses.")

24:7 "there shall be famines and earthquakes in divers places"

The famines which Jesus predicted, except for occasional failures in the weather cycle, would usually develop as one of the tragic consequences of war during which agriculture and transportation would be disastrously disrupted. Whether the "earthquakes in divers places" point to political upheavals or to tectonic upheavals – or both – is not clear, though almost without exception, war causes political earthquakes.

24:8 "But all these things are the beginning of travail."

As disastrous as wars and famines accompanied by earthquakes are, worse is yet to come. These phenomena are only "the beginning" of an extended period of human history marked by turmoil which Jesus calls "travail." The Greek word *odinon*, which is translated "travail" in the ASV is rendered "sorrows" in the KJV, and "birth pains" in the NIV and ESV, and "sufferings" in the RSV.

24:9 "Then shall they deliver you up unto tribulation, and shall kill you: and ye shall be hated of all the nations for my name's sake."

24:9 "Then shall they deliver you up unto tribulation, and shall kill you"

Repeatedly, the "travail" (24:8), through the centuries, would reach a murderous apex. According to verse 10, among the perpetrators of the murder of those who follow Christ will be some who will have defected from the church.

24:9 "hated of all the nations"

Any exception to this universal hate-motivated opposition will only be temporary. Among other causes, the hatred grows from ethical stances taken by Christians. As Jesus said, the world "hateth me because I testify of it that its works are evil." (John 7:7) For example, as we Christians take our stance against the current tidal wave of grossly deviant and aggressive sexual practices categorized by the letters LGBT[605], and where "60% [of the citizens] support same-sex marriage,"[606] we must face expressions of intense hatred. For further information on the rising vicious opposition to Christian ethics see J. Paul Nyquist's <u>Prepare: Living Your Faith in an Increasingly Hostile Culture</u>. "He points out that the nation's culture war is over, Christians have lost, and persecution is on its way."[607]

24:10 "And then shall many stumble, and shall deliver up one another, and shall hate one another."

24:10 "then shall many stumble"

We must pray for our own steadfastness because as the heat and pressure of persecution rises, many followers of Christ will find conditions intolerable and unbearable. (See Matthew 6:13 and 26:41.)

24:10 "shall deliver up one another, and shall hate one another"

After capitulating, some defecting Christians will be enlisted as informers who will point marauding enemies to Christ's intrepid followers.

24:11 "And many false prophets shall arise, and shall lead many astray."

Every Christian must identify basic doctrinal anchor points which will stabilize him/her in times of extreme doctrinal turbulence. (See 24:5 and 24:24.)

---

605 Lesbian, Gay, Bisexual, Transgender.
606 Paul Krugman, *Democrats Being Democrats*, <u>The New York Times Op-Ed</u>, June 15, 2015, p. A19.
607 <u>WORLD</u>, June 27, 2015, p. 45.

Appendix A

24:12 "And because iniquity shall be multiplied, the love of the many shall wax cold."

24:12 "iniquity shall be multiplied"

Some of the iniquities which "shall be multiplied" have already been specified as the appearance of imposters (v. 5), war (v. 6-7), famines (v. 7), tribulation (v. 9), and martyrdom (v. 9).

24:12 "the love of many shall wax cold"

This will be one of the results of a deteriorating moral and spiritual environment. As David asked by inspiration, "When the foundations are being destroyed, what can the righteous do?" (Psalm 11:3 NIV)

24:13 "But he that endureth to the end, the same shall be saved."

The faithful follower of Christ cannot compromise the essentials of his faith, no matter how grievous his conditions may become. Jesus here reiterates the teaching which he had given earlier when he told the disciples, "Ye shall be hated of all men for my name sake: but he that endureth to the end, the same shall be saved." (Matthew 10:22)

24:14 "And this gospel of the kingdom shall be preached in the whole world for a testimony unto all the nations; and then shall the end come."

24:14 "this gospel of the kingdom shall be preached in the whole world for a testimony unto all the nations"

The global preaching of the "gospel of the kingdom" will take place in defiance of grievous and daunting conditions which have been enumerated in verses 5-13. That achievement will be a testimony to the unquenchable faithfulness of many of Jesus' disciples.

24:14 "then shall the end come"

In this verse Jesus answers his disciples' third question which was, "What shall be the sign of thy coming and of the end of the world?" (24:3) How close is the end? The calculation must be based on the fact that it cannot take place till "the Gospel of the kingdom shall be preached in the whole world." One method by which we may estimate the progress of worldwide Gospel preaching is by Bible translation. As of June 2015, statistics given by the American Bible Society indicate that there are still 1,859 languages for which no translation has yet been begun, that is, 37% of the 6,901 world languages.[608]

24:15 "When therefore ye see the abomination of desolation, which was spoken of through Daniel the prophet, standing in the holy place (let him that readeth understand),"

24:15 "When therefore ye see"

Here, Jesus turns his teaching from the remote, "the end of the world," (24:3) to the immediate, that which they would "see." The fact that the disciples with whom Jesus was discussing these momentous issues would "see" one of the most dramatic and

---

[608] These statistics have been taken from <u>Christianity Today</u>, June 2015, p. 18.

consequential near-term developments take place made it clear that a critical part of Daniel's prophecy would be fulfilled during their lifetime. They would "see" it come to pass.

24:15 "the abomination of desolation, which was spoken of through Daniel the prophet"

That "spoken of through Daniel the prophet" to which Jesus referred is found in Daniel 9:24-27.[609] Jesus quotes the expression "the abomination of desolation" from Daniel 9:27, which says "upon the wing of abomination shall come one that maketh desolate; and even unto the full end, and that determined, shall wrath be poured out upon the desolate."

The "one that maketh desolate," about whom Daniel prophesied, points to Titus, the Roman general who led the attack on and destruction of Jerusalem in 70 A.D. The mention in Daniel 9:27 of "the one that maketh desolate" describes "the prince that shall come [and] shall destroy the city and the sanctuary." (Daniel 9:26)

In an earlier prophecy, Daniel, under the symbol of the fourth kingdom, forewarned his countrymen of the rise of Rome and its unmitigated power. Israel's high priests, following the resurrection of Jesus, either forgot or did not understand or did not believe Daniel's prophecy about the Roman Empire. It says, "The fourth kingdom shall be strong as iron, forasmuch as iron breaketh in pieces and subdueth all things; and as iron that crusheth all these, shall it break in pieces and crush." (Daniel 2:40) Consequently, politically, socially and economically, Israel was completely crushed and subdued in both 70 and 135 A.D. because it defied Rome.

Jewish leaders not only ignored Daniel's prophecies, they also ignored the example of Rome's military power and brutality which it demonstrated in its suppression of Carthage. That famous city had become "the greatest maritime power the world had hitherto seen. She claimed the Western Mediterranean as her own, and seized every ship she could catch west of Sardinia." Even so, Carthage could not resist Roman power. In the third and final Punic War(149-146 B.C.), "the Carthaginians suffered horribly from famine; but they held out until the town was stormed. The street fighting lasted for six days, and when at last the citadel capitulated, there were fifty thousand Carthaginians left

---

609 While there is no necessity to discuss the 70 weeks of Daniel for this exposition, still, in brief, I give the fine and very clear exposition of Jim Knutson, long-time preacher in the Church of Christ in Siletz, Oregon. Jim makes it clear that he is indebted to David Vaughn Elliott for some of this exposition. In Daniel 9:25 the angel is quoted as saying " Know therefore and discern, that from the going forth of the commandment to restore and build Jerusalem unto the anointed one, the prince, shall be seven weeks, and three-score and two weeks." Jim has pointed out that there were four decrees or commandments from which the count could be made. First, was Cyrus' decree (Ezra 1:1-4), second was Darius' decree (Ezra 6:1-12), third was Artaxerxes' decree (Ezra 7:11-26 and Ezra 9:9), and fourth, a second decree by Artaxerxes (Nehemiah 2:1-10). Jim points out that "They [the Jews of Jesus' time] had four different dates to count from, which gave them a range of time in which [they should have] expected the Messiah. After centuries of expectation they [should have] had some idea of when to be looking for His appearance. About the first decree, Jim commented "Cyrus' command concerned the temple, which was the most important part of Jerusalem." About the second decree, Jim's comment is "As with the first, this second decree dealt with the temple. The decree was issued to stop the opposing forces ('It will be built again ... in times of distress' Daniel 9:25), this time they completed and dedicated the temple, aided by the prophesying of Haggai and Zechariah." Concerning the third decree, Ezra was to "appoint magistrates and judges" (Ezra 9:25) and "repair the ruins" (Ezra 9:9). The fourth decree refers to the "final act of a Persian monarch [which] dealt with the building of Jerusalem's walls. Nearly 100 years had followed the first decree, and the walls were still in ruins. Now, finally, Nehemiah moved the people to rebuild the walls." "Which of these four decrees' to restore and rebuild Jerusalem is the one referred to in Daniel's prophecy (9:25)? ... The first two are much too early, the fourth is several years too late. Nobody suggests [the advent of] any Messiah for those three dates, thus the only one of the four dates to examine is the third one. ... Most scholars place Jesus' baptism in 26 A.D. That is precisely the year we arrive at when adding 483 years to Artaxerxes' decree of 457 B.C. (Ezra 7:11-26); and Jesus proceeded to accomplish what Gabriel said would be accomplished during the 490 years; namely: 'To finish the transgression, to make an end of sins, to make reconciliation for iniquity, to bring in everlasting righteousness, to seal up vision and prophecy, and to anoint the most Holy.' (Daniel 9:24)"

Appendix A

alive out of an estimated population of half a million. These survivors went into slavery, the whole city was burnt, the ruins were plowed to express final destruction, and a curse was invoked with great solemnities upon anyone who might attempt to rebuild it."[610]

By pointing his disciples to Daniel's prophecy, Jesus gave them a clear time-marker. The destruction of Jerusalem would follow the crucifixion by which "the anointed one [Jesus himself, see Acts 10:38] [would] be cut off and shall have nothing." (Daniel 9:26) Quite literally, he had nothing. Even his clothes were taken by the soldiers who crucified him. (See John 19:23-25.)

24:15 "standing in the holy place"

This refers to the city of Jerusalem, the Holy City. (See Nehemiah 11:1 and Isaiah 52:1.) This does not refer to the Holy place in the temple. Had Jesus' disciples waited until Roman soldiers had advanced into the Holy place in the temple, it would have been far too late to have fled.

24:16 "then let them that are in Judaea flee unto the mountains:"

"In 66 CE a Jewish revolt broke out in Palestine which drew its inspiration from the traditions of Jewish self-assertion and rage against outside interference which looked back to the heroic era of Judas Maccabeus. The comforts provided by Roman rule were not enough to persuade everyone in the Jewish community that they should outweigh the constant reminder from the Roman authorities that Jews were not masters of their own destinies. The rebels eventually took control in Jerusalem and massacred the Sadducee elite, whom they regarded as collaborators with the Romans. The Jewish Christian Church, interestingly, fled from the city; it was distant enough [doctrinally and emotionally] from the world of Jewish nationalism to wish to keep out of this struggle. The result of the revolt was in the long term probably inevitable: the Romans could not afford to lose their grip on this corner of the Mediterranean and they put a huge effort into crushing the rebels. In the course of the capture of Jerusalem, whether by accident or by design, the great Temple complex went up in flames, never to be restored; its site lay as a wasteland for centuries. Jewish fury accumulated at this highly unusual destruction of one of the Mediterranean world's most renowned shrines and in 132–5 they rose again in revolt. Now the Romans erased the name of Jerusalem from the map and created a city, Aelia [tribe, people] Capitolina. It took its name with deliberate offensiveness from a new temple of Jupiter, the chief god of the Roman pantheon as worshipped on the Capitoline Hill in Rome itself (the temple was built apparently on a site which encompassed the place of Jesus' crucifixion and burial, although this was probably coincidental). So, Aelia Capitolina was not even intended to be a Greek city; it was a Roman colony."[611]

24:16 "let them that are in Judea flee"

Not only were the Christians living in and close to Jerusalem to flee, but Jesus' command applied to <u>all</u> Christians in the entire province of Judea. Jesus' command is in vivid contrast to his previously repeated order to his followers to stay in Jerusalem. (Luke 24:49, Acts 1:4) That previous order kept Jesus' followers in Jerusalem for the feast of

---
610 H. G. Wells, <u>The Outline of History</u>, Vol. I, (New York: Doubleday & Co., Inc, 1971), pp. 162, 376.
611 Diarmaid MacCulloch, <u>Christianity: The First Three Thousand Years</u>, (New York: Viking, 2010), pp. 106-107.

Pentecost which occurred fifty days after his death. It was essential that the church start at that place and at that time to give it an international impact from its very inception. It would have that impact because of the influence of those Jews from sixteen nations (Acts 2:9-11) who would obey the Gospel on that day and then return home to share the Gospel message. But here the church was ordered, when the signs were right, to flee from the city and province of its birth. The purpose for fleeing was to prevent the church – while still in its infancy – from suffering a major crippling blow by being caught among those whom Rome would destroy.

24:17 "let him that is on the housetop not go down to take out things that are in his house:"

Following ancient construction methods, houses in Jerusalem usually had flat roofs with a balustrade around the perimeter. (See Deuteronomy 22:8.) Thus, the enclosed space "on the housetop" provided a private area like a courtyard for family use. Jesus' counsel to "not go down to take out things that are in his house" probably led to the Christian Jews in Jerusalem keeping on hand at all times a small bag or backpack of the most basic essentials needed for emergency evacuation.

24:18 "and let him that is in the field not return back to take his cloak."

This instruction seems to imply that the Christians would take their emergency packs with them even when they went out to do field work.

24:19 "But woe unto them that are with child and to them that give suck in those days!"

Pregnant women and nursing mothers would require special assistance to keep up with their fleeing families and friends. Because of the urgency, their flight would be much more arduous than that of the pregnant virgin Mary during her trip from Nazareth to Bethlehem.

24:20 "And pray ye that your flight be not in the winter, neither on a sabbath:"

Jesus clearly implies that the prayers of his followers could impact the timing of a major international event so it would occur neither in winter nor on a sabbath. Therefore, by prayer we, too, may often have some control over our future circumstances.

Flight in winter would be much more rigorous than it would be in other seasons of the year. Flight on a sabbath day would expose the Christian Jews to their non-Christian Jewish compatriots who would be keeping the Sabbath. Fleeing on that day would make them conspicuous. Then, it would not be a secret flight. They would be exposed and considered traitors to the Jewish cause.

24:21 "for then shall be great tribulation, such as hath not been from the beginning of the world until now, no, nor ever shall be."

This tribulation refers to the terrible fate which befell those unfortunate Jews who were trapped in Jerusalem because they did not believe in Christ and consequently did not follow his instruction to flee when the armies of Titus gathered in 70 A.D. to besiege Jerusalem. About that siege, Jesus prophesied that no fully comparable suffering had ever

Appendix A

occurred in the past nor would ever occur in the future. That means, for example, that the horrible sufferings, unspeakable as they were, of the people of Carthage (See comments on 24:15), and of thousands of Russians trapped in Stalingrad when the Germans besieged that city during World War II, did not equal the suffering which the citizens of Jerusalem endured under the Roman siege.

It should clearly be noted that those who suffered in the agony of the Roman siege of Jerusalem were not Christians, but unbelieving Jews. Jesus had instructed his disciples to flee from Jerusalem when they saw the Roman troops massing outside the city walls. (Matthew 24:15-16) The majority of Christians, followers of Jesus, did flee from the besieged city. It should also be noted that this tribulation has no connection to any period of tribulation just prior to Jesus' return. This tribulation occurred in 70 A.D. and therefore cannot be considered an eschatological event.

At the time of Jesus' triumphal entry into Jerusalem, he clearly foresaw that city's gruesome, imminent suffering. The account says, "when he drew nigh he saw the city and wept over it, saying, 'If you, even you, had only known on this day what would bring you peace—but now it is hidden from your eyes. The days will come upon you when your enemies will build an embankment against you and encircle you and hem you in on every side. They will dash you to the ground, you and the children within your walls. They will not leave one stone on another, because you did not recognize the time of God's coming to you.'" (Luke 19:41-44 NIV) This warning of the coming catastrophe was not given privately to his disciples but openly and publicly in the hearing of some of the leaders, the Pharisees (Luke 19:39), in an attempt to turn them from their madness.

While Jesus was openly and clearly trying to save the Jewish people from the destruction of their corporate existence, the Jewish leaders totally misread his efforts. The apostle John recorded their misbegotten and misdirected thinking: "Then the chief priests and the Pharisees called a meeting of the Sanhedrin. 'What are we accomplishing?' they asked. 'Here is this man performing many miraculous signs. If we let him go on like this, everyone will believe in him, and then the Romans will come and take away both our place and our nation.' Then one of them, named Caiaphas, who was high priest that year, spoke up, 'You know nothing at all! You do not realize that it is better for you that one man die for the people than that the whole nation perish.' He did not say this on his own, but as high priest that year he prophesied that Jesus would die for the Jewish nation, and not only for that nation but also for the scattered children of God, to bring them together and make them one. So from that day on they plotted to take his life." (John 11:47-53 NIV)

Previously, with the same great emotional intensity which later brought Jesus to tears, he had tried to avert the terrible disaster which was about to befall Jerusalem. He said "O Jerusalem, Jerusalem, that killeth the prophets, and stoneth them that are sent unto her! How often would I have gathered thy children together, even as a hen gathereth her own brood under wings, and ye would not!" (Luke 13:34)

24:22 "And except those days had been shortened, no flesh would have been saved: but for the elect's sake those days shall be shortened."

24:22 "except those days had been shortened, no flesh would have been saved"

"With [the Roman Emperor] Vespasian it was a matter of honor to complete the subjugation of the Jews. His son Titus, with an army of eighty thousand, besieged Jerusalem in A.D. 70. Josephus, the historian, took sides with the Romans against his own people and cooperated with Titus. His writings constitute the only detailed account we possess of this terrible struggle.

"Besides the ordinary population of Jerusalem, hundreds of thousands of Jews had flocked to the city from Judea, Syria, and even Mesopotamia. The besieged held out with fanatical obstinacy. The horrors of famine, pestilence, and cannibalism were added to the destructive fury of the Roman Army. As one part of the city after another fell into the hands of the Romans, the inhabitants were remorselessly executed. Over a million are said to have been slaughtered and over a hundred thousand to have been taken captive. Multitudes were sent into the most degrading slavery. Thousands of the choicest young men were selected for gladiatorial exhibitions. The temple was destroyed, although Titus is said to have wished to preserve it."[612]

24:22 "for the elect's sake those days shall be shortened"

Here is a clear example of divine intervention in human history. Had a total annihilation of the Jews of Jerusalem and Judah been allowed, it would have had an adverse impact on the Christian Jews, "the elect," who had fled from the epicenter of the battle. Had the battle gone on till every Jew in Jerusalem had been killed, it probably would have led to an empire-wide suppression and execution of Jews, Christian as well as non-Christian.

24:23 "Then if any man shall say unto you, Lo, here is the Christ, or, Here; believe *it* not."

This warning was given because of the extreme rigors which would arise from the coming Roman military offensive. People would be tempted to grasp at fantasies and false hopes held forth by charlatans and opportunists. (Compare v. 26.)

24:24 "For there shall arise false Christs, and false prophets, and shall show great signs and wonders; so as to lead astray, if possible, even the elect."

Please compare 24:4-5 and 24:11.

24:24 "there shall arise false Christs, and false prophets"

Jesus did not specify the time-span during which these imposters would arise. Presumably, it would be during the whole Christian period of history. Therefore, in addition to the comments at 24:5 regarding Simon bar Kokhba, think also of the centuries-long succession of popes, claiming to be Christ's vicar, that is, his substitute!

24:24 "shall show great signs and wonders"

Those signs and wonders, shown by the vicars of Christ, involved ostentatious wealth, mysterious pomp and ceremony, carried out with clouds of incense smoke and chants.

---

[612] Albert Henry Newman, A Manual of Church History, Vol. I, (Philadelphia: The Baptist Publication Society, 1939), p. 117.

Appendix A

24:24 "to lead astray, if possible, even the elect"

The papal deception has been immeasurably successful. It has unquestionably produced the largest church in Christendom. It has attained that status by leading multitudes astray.

24:25 "Behold, I have told you beforehand."

Jesus' predictions were not a guesstimate, but a declaration of future certainty.

24:26 "If therefore they shall say unto you, Behold, he is in the wilderness; go not forth: Behold, he is in the inner chambers; believe *it* not."

The Messiah's triumphant final coming will neither be remote, "in the wilderness," nor secretive, "in the inner chambers." Therefore, there will be no need to seek him either in hidden or remote places. (Compare v. 23.)

24:27 "For as the lightning cometh forth from the east, and is seen even unto the west; so shall be the coming of the Son of man."

With these words Jesus gives his ultimate answer to his disciples' question, "What shall be the sign of thy coming?" (24:3) Anyone who should claim to be the returning Messiah but does not come in this globally spectacular manner would be a fraud and an imposter. Jesus' second coming will not be concealed or secret but will be like the lightning flashing from one horizon to the other. The lightning and accompanying thunder will make the "coming of the Son of man" visually and audibly unmistakable.

24:28 "Wheresoever the carcase is, there will the eagles be gathered together."

24:28 "the carcase" ("the corpse" - ESV)

The carcase, or carcass (NIV), or corpse refers to the Jewish nation. Because Jews by and large had rejected the Messiah, the Anointed One of Daniel 9:24-27, the Jewish body politic no longer surged with divinely endowed vitality. Spiritually, the Jewish body politic was comatose. It had become a carcass, a corpse.

24:28 "there will the eagles be gathered together"

Most probably "the eagles" refer to the ornamental crests depicting eagles which were fixed on the top of the Roman army's regimental flag poles. Another possibility is that it refers to the carrion birds which flocked or gathered together to gorge on the flesh of hundreds of thousands of corpses which the Roman army piled at the base of Jerusalem's walls. The second idea should be rejected because had the Christians waited to flee till the rotting corpses were piling up, it would have been too late to escape.

24:29 "But immediately after the tribulation of those days the sun shall be darkened, and the moon shall not give her light, and the stars shall fall from heaven, and the powers of the heavens shall be shaken:"

24:29 "immediately after the tribulation of those days"

The days referred to are those of the tribulation associated with the destruction of Jerusalem. Therefore, this verse does not describe eschatological events at the end of the Christian age as does Matthew 24:14, which says, "This gospel of the kingdom shall be preached in the whole world for a testimony unto all the nations; and then shall the end come."

24:29 "the sun shall be darkened, and the moon shall not give her light, and the stars shall fall from heaven, and the powers of the heavens shall be shaken:"

The terms "sun," "moon," "stars" and "powers of the heavens" refer to positions of Jewish leadership in political, religious, social and economic arenas. They were ultimately paralyzed and completely incapacitated, that is "darkened," following the Roman occupation of Palestine beginning in 63 B.C., which ultimately culminated in the destruction of Jerusalem and the Jewish temple in 70 A.D. Roman control became even more severe and limiting following the suppression imposed after the second Jewish rebellion under the leadership of bar Kokhba which lasted from 132 to 135 A.D. Following that second Jewish revolt, Jews were even prohibited from entering Jerusalem. The only national Jewish religious activity in Palestine was that which was only tenuously allowed to be exercised in a very limited way at the village of Jamnia. Only then did the Jewish "sun," "moon," "stars" and "powers of the heavens" begin once more to shine, that is to function, but only very feebly.

24:30 "and then shall appear the sign of the Son of man in heaven: and then shall all the tribes of the earth mourn, and they shall see the Son of man coming on the clouds of heaven with power and great glory."

24:30 "the sign of the Son of man in heaven"

Though one might think this sign is the same phenomenon which is described in verse 27, more probably it points to another reality. Jesus had prophesied that the temple would be destroyed. He indicated the severity of that destruction when he said that not one stone would be left on top of another. (Matthew 24:1-2) When his prophecy was fulfilled, his reputation was so greatly enhanced that it became "the sign of the Son of man [who was then] in heaven." The "sign" was that the Son of man, who would then be in heaven, had been totally correct in his predictions about Jerusalem.

24:30 "all the tribes of the earth mourn"

These are the Jewish tribes of the Dispersion. (See John 7:35, James 1:1 and I Peter 1:1.) They had previously been scattered widely over the earth by the Assyrian and Babylonian invasions of Israel and Judah. Now, by the Roman conquest and destruction of Jerusalem, many additional thousands of Jews were flung into exile and dispersed broadly among many nations. Luke reported Jesus as saying "They shall be led captive into all the nations." (Luke 21:24) They, that is, Jews from "all the tribes," would mourn over the

Appendix A

great tragedy that had befallen Jerusalem and the Jewish nation, a tragedy in which they found themselves deeply and irremediably entangled.

Their situation would become a stark fulfillment of Deuteronomy 28:64-67: "Then the LORD will scatter you among all nations, from one end of the earth to the other. There you will worship other gods – gods of wood and stone, which neither you nor your fathers have known. Among those nations you will find no repose, no resting place for the sole of your foot. There the LORD will give you an anxious mind, eyes weary with longing, and a despairing heart. You will live in constant suspense, filled with dread both night and day, never sure of your life. In the morning you will say, 'If only it were evening!' and in the evening, 'If only it were morning!'– because of the terror that will fill your hearts and the sights that your eyes will see."

24:30 "they shall see the Son of man coming on the clouds of heaven with power and great glory"

The Jewish people would come to "see," that is to understand, that what had happened had been the work of Christ. In an exalted super-human way, "on the clouds of heaven," his word would have been fulfilled which redounded to his "great glory." But even so, they would not humble themselves and accept the Messiah.

24:31 "and he shall send forth his angels with a great sound of a trumpet, and they shall gather together his elect from the four winds, from one end of heaven to the other."

24:31 "he shall send forth his angels with a great sound of a trumpet"

These "angels" should be understood in the most basic sense of the Greek word, *anggelon*, as messengers; that is, as Christians declaring the Gospel of Christ. (See the discussion of the seven angels of the churches in the province of Asia at 1:4 in the commentary.) Not only were the surviving unbelieving non-Christian Jewish people scattered as a result of the destruction of Jerusalem, but so were the Christians. In that manner they were sent forth, being dispersed widely. Jesus had instructed his followers to flee when they saw the Roman army massing for its attack on the city. (Matthew 24:15-22) Subsequently, Jerusalem was no longer a Christian center as it had previously been. (See Acts 15:2-4.) Following Rome's attack on Jerusalem, the destruction was so great that some said there was no evidence that the place had been inhabited. However, the Roman emperor Hadrian vowed to rebuild it as a center for the Roman army, named for the god Jupiter. Consequently, the apostles no longer lived there but worked in far-flung places, as John in Ephesus, as Peter and Paul in Rome, and as Thomas in Khorasan (in far eastern Iran, at Taxila, in present-day Pakistan). From Taxila Thomas took the Gospel all the way to South India to Madras/Chennai, where he was martyred.

Thus, it was by the destruction of Jerusalem that Jesus was to "send forth his angels." His angels were the Christians, messengers who declared the Gospel. In a much greater way, the destruction of Jerusalem dispersed the Christians than had the martyrdom of Stephen. About that earlier occasion, the record tells us "they therefore that were scattered abroad went about preaching the word." (Acts 8:4) Their dispersion served as a prototype of the scattering of the Christians which resulted from the destruction of Jerusalem.

The "great sound of a trumpet" almost certainly refers to the sound of the Roman army's trumpets which guided and directed the troops during the battle for Jerusalem. Prior to its destruction, Jerusalem had been the premier Christian center. It was the site upon which the church had its birth and the center to which appeals were made in settling Christian doctrinal disputes. (See Acts 15.) Following its destruction in 70 A.D., Jerusalem was no longer the premier center of Christian activity. Rather, we see Christian centers like Alexandria and Antioch having much greater preeminence.

24:31 "they shall gather together his elect"

The dispersion of the Christians initiated a great evangelistic movement resulting in an unprecedented in-gathering of new converts to Christ, "his elect," into the church.

24:31 "from the four winds, from one end of heaven to the other"

These are global geographical terms which depict how widespread the evangelistic consequences of the dispersion of the Christians from Jerusalem would be.

24:32 "Now from the fig tree learn her parable: when her branch is now become tender, and putteth forth its leaves, ye know that the summer is nigh;"

This expression is a simile for the coming of the Roman army. Botanically, the approach of summer is easily detected by the appearance of tender new branches and new leaves on a fig tree; similarly, there were signs of the coming violent attack on Jerusalem which would be focused on the temple. Of special note among those signs were the rejection of the Anointed One (See comment on Daniel 9:26 at Matthew 24:15.) and the abomination of desolation standing in the holy place, that is, the Roman army being present in the Holy City.

24:33 "even so ye also, when ye see all these things, know ye that he is nigh, *even* at the doors."

24:33 "he is nigh, *even* at the doors"

Both the King James Version and the New International Version translate the phrase "he is nigh" as "it is near." Similarly, the Stern Translation[613] renders "he is nigh, even at the doors" as "the time is near, right at the door." In this place, though the translators of the NRSV put "he is near, at the very gates" in the text, they point out that it may be rendered as "it is near, at the very gates." The R.S.V. Interlinear Greek-English New Testament[614] renders the passage, "it is on (at) [the] doors."

Though a large number of translations use the words "he is nigh," still, that rendering is certainly wrong. The very next verse makes "he is nigh" an impossibility, for such a rendering would have Jesus' final triumphant return taking place during the apostolic generation! If we understand Jesus to have said "the time is near" or "it is near" – both expressions referring to the destruction of Jerusalem, the imminence of which was expressed in verse 32 as "the summer is nigh" – then the potential time clash is resolved. The narrative doesn't shift to Jesus' second coming till verse 36.

---

613 David H. Stern, <u>Complete Jewish Bible</u>, (Jerusalem, Israel: Jewish New Testament Publications, Inc., 1998).
614 Alfred Marshall, <u>The R.S.V. Interlinear Greek-English New Testament</u>, (Grand Rapids, MI: Zondervan Publishing House, 1958), p. 109.

Appendix A

In understanding this, we must also consider Luke's account in which he recorded Jesus as saying, "When ye see these things coming to pass, know ye that the kingdom of God is nigh." (Luke 21:31) Behind the Roman inclusion of the Jewish homeland in 63 B.C. into the expanding Roman Empire and Rome's subsequent imposition of strict, direct control over Jewish citizenry, was divine oversight. That divine impetus is indicated by the statement that "the kingdom of God is nigh." This expression refers to this one specific moment of God's rule in human affairs. It was an event in human history that should help everyone know "that the most high ruleth in the kingdom of men." (Daniel 4:17, 4:25)

Therefore, the statement that "the kingdom of God is nigh" does not point to the establishment of the church, "the kingdom of heaven." That had taken place in 33 A.D., thirty-seven years before the destruction of Jerusalem. Neither does it point to an end-time event as Nolland indicated when he said, "Luke thinks here of the eschatological consummation of the kingdom of God."[615]

24:34 "Verily I say unto you, This generation shall not pass away, till all these things be accomplished."

The Roman attack on and the destruction of Jerusalem would take place while the generation to whom Jesus was speaking was still alive. That generation would not yet have passed away.

24:35 Heaven and earth shall pass away, but my words shall not pass away."

By this statement, Jesus is assuring his disciples that they could totally rely on what he was telling them. Though encompassing all he had said and taught, his assurance was especially applicable to his prediction about Jerusalem. His prediction was more fixed and unmovable than the astronomical "heaven and earth" which would eventually pass away. (See Revelation 21:1-5.) Much sooner, as he had just predicted, the constellations of Jewish powers, "heaven and earth" (See 24:29.), would pass away.

24:36 "But of that day and hour knoweth no one, not even the angels of heaven, neither the Son, but the Father only."

"That day" denotes a remote time. It is to be contrasted with "the time is near" (v. 32). From the next verse it is clear that "that day" points to "the coming of the Son of man."

24:37 "And as *were* the days of Noah, so shall be the coming of the Son of man."

24:38 "For as in those days which were before the flood they were eating and drinking, marrying and giving in marriage, until the day that Noah entered into the ark,"

We must not allow routine activities in the normal course of life to engulf, consume or distract us so we become oblivious to impending significant global events. Jesus rebuked many for such misplaced emphasis. He said, "Hypocrites! You know how to interpret the appearance of the earth and the sky. How is it that you don't know how to interpret this present time?" (Luke 12:56 NIV)

---

615 John Nolland, Word Biblical Commentary, Vol. 35C (Dallas, TX: Word Books Publisher, 1993), p. 1009.

24:39 "and they knew not until the flood came, and took them all away; so shall be the coming of the Son of man."

Noah's flood occurred at a time of negligence, induced by indifference and ignorance, "they knew not." The flood was globally inclusive, it "took them all away." Similarly, all of mankind shall be impacted by "the coming of the Son of man."

24:40 "Then shall two men be in the field; one is taken, and one is left:"

The expressions "one is taken" and "one is left" refer to a believer and an unbeliever. They do not imply that those serving Christ will make up fifty percent of the population at the time of "the coming of the Son of man." (24:39) Jesus implied that the numerical balance between his followers and those who had rejected him would be, startlingly, the inverse of any fifty/fifty assumption. He made that clear at the time when he asked, "When the Son of man cometh, shall he find faith on the earth?" (Luke 18:8) Jesus' pessimistic question is fully justified by the prediction in 24:37 which says, "as were the days of Noah, so shall be the coming of the Son of man." On that occasion only eight people were saved.

The expression "one is taken," is found in both verses 40 and 41. That event will occur at "the coming of the Son of man." (24:39) Therefore, it should be equated with I Thessalonians 4:17, which says, "we that are alive, that are left, shall together with them be caught up in the clouds, to meet the Lord in the air: and so shall we ever be with the Lord." Theologians call that future event "The Rapture." This being "taken," this being "caught up in the clouds to meet the Lord," is also described as "our gathering together unto him." (II Thessalonians 2:1)

This "Rapture," this being "taken," will not occur to rescue believers from intense worldwide persecution just prior to The Millennium as many pre-millennial expositors affirm. This being "taken" is a terminal event to be compared with the time when "Jehovah said unto Noah, Come thou and all thy house into the ark." (Genesis 7:1) (See the discussion of the Rapture in the commentary at 7:14-17 and 11:12.)

24:41 "two women *shall be* grinding at the mill; one is taken, and one is left."

24:42 "Watch therefore: for ye know not on what day your Lord cometh."

His coming will occur when daily activities will be proceeding as usual. For example, normal field work will be going on, as indicated by the words "then shall two men be in the field" (v. 40), which suggests plowing, sowing and harvesting. Ongoing domestic work, such as "grinding" grain to make flour as indicated by v. 41, will also be carried out as usual. We must "watch," that is, stay alert and not allow our senses to be dulled by the routine of daily life and work.

24:43 "But know this, that if the master of the house had known in what watch the thief was coming, he would have watched, and would not have suffered his house to be broken through."

Appendix A

Obviously, just as there are clues about an impending robbery, such as dogs barking, unusual sounds or drafts caused by someone opening a door or window, so Jesus gives us clues of the imminence of his coming about which we should remain alert.

24:44 "Therefore be ye also ready; for in an hour that ye think not the Son of man cometh."

Through prophecy there were clear signs of the Son of man's coming at Bethlehem. And, derived from Jesus' instruction to his disciples, there also would be obvious indications of the coming destruction of Jerusalem. His final coming, though it will be surprising, like the coming of a thief, and occurring "in an hour that ye think not," may still be anticipated by those who expect his return. If this were not so, he would not exhort us to be ready. Paul, expounding on Jesus' instruction, tells us, "you know very well that the day of the Lord will come like a thief in the night." (I Thessalonians 5:2 NIV) For those who do not anticipate Jesus' return, it will be a frightening event. In panic they will appeal to the mountains to fall on them. (See Revelation 6:16ff.)

24:45 "Who then is the faithful and wise servant, whom his lord hath set over his household, to give them their food in due season?"

This expression, "the faithful and wise servant," probably points to every parent, every teacher and every preacher "whom his lord hath set over his household." The household is "the house of God, which is the church of the living God, the pillar and ground of the truth." (I Timothy 3:15) Their duty is "to give them their food in due season." Giving them their food means to teach and preach the message of Christ faithfully to build up and strengthen the brethren.

We must not let fascination and anticipation with the Lord's future return captivate us to the point that we become negligent in our present responsibilities.

24:46 "Blessed is that servant, whom his lord when he cometh shall find so doing."

The blessing is described in the very next verse.

24:47 "Verily I say unto you, that he will set him over all that he hath."

This promise is fully confirmed in Revelation 22:3-5.

24:48 "But if that evil servant shall say in his heart, My lord tarrieth;"

The "evil servant" is relying on one-dimensional thinking. He only sees the time factor. He concludes that since in all this long time such an event has not happened, God must have changed plans, and therefore concludes that it will never happen! The "evil" or "wicked" servant's conclusion that Christ is delaying his return, saying "My lord tarrieth," is based on the same specious thinking which Peter exposed. Such unbelievers ask, "Where is the promise of his coming? For, from the day that the fathers fell asleep, all things continue as they were from the beginning of the creation." (II Peter 3:4) Peter goes on to remind everyone that previous judgments came after mercifully long delays. Delays are not granted to induce indifference, negligence or profligacy but to give all of us time to correct our thinking and our behavior. Such delays are tokens of God's goodness which is intended to lead us to repentance. (See Romans 2:4.)

24:49 "and shall begin to beat his fellow-servants, and shall eat and drink with the drunken;"

Anyone who holds the Lord in disdain will not hold himself back from flagrant depravity and the imposition of cruelty on his fellow servants.

24:50 "the lord of that servant shall come in a day when he expecteth not, and in an hour when he knoweth not,"

The "evil servant" (v. 48) has cut himself off from anticipation and expectancy ("he expecteth not") and knowledge ("he knoweth not"). Such a person has made himself extremely vulnerable.

24:51 "and shall cut him asunder, [cut him in pieces - ESV] and appoint his portion with the hypocrites: there shall be the weeping and the gnashing of teeth."

See Revelation 20:10, 21:8 and 22:15.

III.   Matthew 25:31-34

25:31 "But when the Son of man shall come in his glory, and all the angels with him, then shall he sit upon the throne of his glory:"

25:31 "the Son of man shall come in his glory"

See the comments on Revelation 1:7 and 19:12. His glory is expressed in Revelation 19:12 by telling us "upon his head are many diadems."

25:31 "all the angels with him"

See the comments on Revelation 19:14.

25:31 "then shall he sit upon the throne of his glory"

Please see the comments on Revelation 20:11.

25:32 "and before him shall be gathered all the nations: and he shall separate them one from another, as the shepherd separateth the sheep from the goats."

25:32 "before him shall be gathered all the nations"

This statement is in full harmony with the picture given in Revelation 20:11-12.

25:32 "he shall separate them one from another, as the shepherd separateth the sheep from the goats"

The picturesque scene of universal judgment under the figure of a shepherd dividing the sheep from the goats is fully substantiated under the more prosaic description in Revelation 20:13, which anticipates the time when the sea will have given up the dead which were in it; and when death and Hades will have given up the dead which were in

Appendix A

them "and they were judged every man according to their works." The words "every man" takes in both sheep and goats. On the distinction of the judgment which will be meted out to both categories, see the comments on Revelation 20:12 under "I saw the dead, the great and the small, standing before the throne."

25:33 "And he shall set the sheep on his right hand, but the goats on the left."

Jesus clearly identified his sheep. He said, "My sheep hear my voice, and I know them, and they follow me: and I give unto them eternal life; and they shall never perish, and no one shall snatch them out of my hand." John 10:27-28

25:34 "Then shall the king say unto them on his right hand, Come, ye blessed of my Father, inherit the kingdom prepared for you from the foundation of the world:"

The invitation to those who are designated as the "blessed of my Father" will mark the greatest triumph of all time and eternity. It is a triumph which totally thwarts Satan's attempts to destroy mankind, the pinnacle of God's creation. The victors will be invited to inherit that kingdom which has been "prepared for you from the foundation of the world." This kingdom seems to be something distinct from the church, which is also called "the kingdom of heaven." In reading Christ's letters to the seven churches, it is obvious that encroachments of sin had not yet been overcome. But in this kingdom, there will be no sin to mar the perpetual fellowship with Christ and God!

IV. John 14:2-3

14:2 "In my father's house are many mansions; if it were not so, I would have told you; for I go to prepare a place for you."

14:2 "In my father's house are many mansions"

In the book of Revelation we get glimpses into only a few of those mansions. One which is emphasized again and again is the throne room. See, for example, Revelation 3:21, chapters 4 and 5, 6:16-17 and 7:15-17. We also learn of "the temple of my God" in 3:12. Another glimpse of one of the mansions is God's tabernacle, mentioned in Revelation 21:3. In addition to these glimpses, in Revelation 21:16 we are given a description of the city which "lies foursquare" and whose dimensions are enormous and which will accommodate "many mansions."

14:2 "I go to prepare a place for you"

The place is the new heaven and the new earth. See Revelation 21:1.

14:3 "And if I go and prepare a place for you, I come again, and will receive you unto myself; that where I am, there ye may be also."

One may understandably ask, "What has Jesus been doing since he ascended?" (John 20:17, Acts 1:10-11) John gives us Jesus' answer to that question here at 14:3. He is preparing a stupendously glorious place for his loyal followers in which everything will be new. (Revelation 21:5)

Revelation Verse by Verse

V.   **John 21:22**

21:22 "Jesus sayeth unto him, If I will that he tarry till I come, what is that to thee? Follow thou me."

This is just one of the many occasions at which Jesus assures us he will come again. (See Matthew 16:27-28, 23:39, 25:1-13, 25:19, 25:31-46, 26:64, Mark 8:28, 13:1-37, Luke 9:26, 12:37, 17:22-37, 18:8, 19:11-13, 19:15, 21:5-36, John 14:3, 14:18, 14:28-29, Acts 1:11, Philippians 3:20, II Peter 3:10, I John 3:2, Revelation 1:4, 2:25, 3:3, 22:7, 22:12, 22:20.) In addition to these references, there are many assurances of Jesus' second coming which are not listed here.

VI.   **Acts 1:9-11**

1:9 "And when he had said these things, as they were looking, he was taken up; and a cloud received him out of their sight."

Probably his being "taken up" portrays the manner in which Christ's faithful followers will be taken up at his final triumphant coming. We are told that "we that are alive, that are left, shall together with them be caught up in the clouds, to meet the Lord in the air: and so shall we ever be with the Lord." (I Thessalonians 4:17) This event corresponds to "one is taken." (Matthew 24:40) This is the biblical Rapture. (See the commentary on 7:14-17 and 11:12.)

1:10 "And while they were looking stedfastly into heaven as he went, behold, two men stood by them in white apparel;"

As noted in the commentary on 1:14-15, the whiteness which John saw is also a symbol, used by Isaiah, of sinlessness. Isaiah said, "Though your sins be as scarlet, they shall be as white as snow; though they be red like crimson, they shall be as wool." (Isaiah 1:18)

1:11 "who also said, Ye men of Galilee, why stand ye looking into heaven? this Jesus, who was received up from you into heaven shall so come in like manner as ye beheld him going into heaven."

"In like manner" may not imply there will be similarity in every detail. The main point is that he will return by coming through the air. That is, "he shall descend from heaven." (I Thessalonians 4:16)

VII.   **Acts 3:19-21**

3:19 "Repent ye therefore, and turn again, that your sins may be blotted out, that so there may come seasons of refreshing from the presence of the Lord;"

Repentance is necessary for salvation, to have one's sins "blotted out." Also, widespread repentance will transform society, eliminate criminal activity, increase prosperity and reduce taxes. Such conditions will be notable features of the "seasons of refreshing."

3:20 "and that he may send the Christ who hath been appointed for you, *even* Jesus:"

Appendix A

God mercifully delays the second coming to give man time to respond to his gracious offer of salvation.

3:21 "whom the heaven must receive until the times of restoration of all things, whereof God spake by the mouth of His holy prophets that have been from of old."

3:21 "whom the heaven must receive"

(See Philippians 3:20 and Colossians 3:4.) "Here St. Peter corrects the popular view that the Messiah should remain on earth, John xii.34."[616]

3:21 "until the times of restoration of all things"

"The word restoration in this place ... is limited by the expression 'all things whereof God spake by the Holy prophets,' and consequently it consists in the fulfillment of the Old Testament predictions; and the remark gives assurance that Jesus will not return again till all these predictions have been fulfilled."[617]

"Peter seems to be saying, 'Jesus will remain in heaven until all the things the prophets predicted are fulfilled.'"[618]

The NIV helps us understand the phrase the "restoration of all things." It says, "He must remain in heaven until the time comes for God to restore everything, as he promised long ago through his holy prophets." Stern, in the *Complete Jewish Bible*, renders it "He has to remain in heaven until the time comes for restoring everything." This passage should be aligned with Revelation 21:1, "a new heaven and a new earth," and 21:5, "I make all things new."

VIII. I Corinthians 15:51-53

15:51 "Behold, I tell you a mystery: We all shall not sleep, but we shall all be changed,"

Here, death is referred to as sleep because it will be followed by the resurrection, a great awakening. The Christian who experiences the resurrection will undergo a fundamental change. That change will be two-fold, the description of which is given in verses 53-54.

15:52 "in a moment, in the twinkling of an eye, at the last trump: for the trumpet shall sound, and the dead shall be raised incorruptible, and we shall be changed."

15:52 "in a moment, in the twinkling of an eye, at the last trump"

The transformation which is in this verse referred to as a "change" will not be incremental or evolutionary but will occur in the tiniest segment of time, "in the twinkling of an eye." It will be a culminating event which will instantaneously take place at "the last trump." There will be a terminating event in human history which will take place as if God marked off the epochal periods of history by trumpet signals. One such period is described in Revelation 8:2-14:20. But history is finite. It will come to a conclusion which will be highlighted by God's final trumpet blast, "the last trump."

---

616 R. J. Knowling, The Acts of the Apostles, Vol. II, (London: Hodder & Stoughton, 1900), p. 115.
617 J. W. McGarvey, New Commentary on Acts of Apostles, Vol. I, (Cincinnati: The Standard Publishing Co., 1892), p. 63.
618 Gareth L. Reese, A Critical and Exegetical Commentary on the Book of Acts, (Joplin, MO: College Press, 1976), p. 166.

15:52 "the dead shall be raised incorruptible"

This raising of the dead to incorruptibility refers to the resurrection of the Christian dead. Their resurrection is part of the total global resurrection about which Jesus spoke when he said, "The hour cometh, in which all that are in the tombs shall hear his voice, and shall come forth; they that have done good, unto the resurrection of life; and they that have done evil unto the resurrection of judgment." (John 5:27-29) The theme of the general resurrection comes forth clearly and dramatically in the Revelation account. It tells us that "the sea gave up the dead that were in it; and death and Hades gave up the dead that were in them: and they were judged every man according to their works." (Revelation 20:13)

For the Christian dead, the resurrection will change their status to one of incorruptibility. This fundamental change from the corruption of sin and death is a development called "the fashioning anew of the body of our humiliation." (Philippians 3:21) It will free us from all contamination and decay, a phenomenon which is described as "being conformed to the body of his glory." (Philippians 3:21)

15:53 "For this corruptible must put on incorruption, and this mortal must put on immortality."

When this takes place, the recipients of incorruption and immortality will take on the image of God according to the original intent, as expressed in Genesis 1:27. Then "we shall be like him." (I John 3:2)

IX.   Philippians 3:20-21

3:20 "For our citizenship is in heaven; whence also we wait for a Saviour, the Lord Jesus Christ:"

We Christians have dual citizenship. Obviously, we are citizens of the countries in which we reside. However, temporal governments often fall below the standard to which God holds them. According to that standard, civil government is to take "vengeance on evil-doers" and to give "praise to them that do well." (I Peter 2:14) When that standard is ignored or breached, Christians often suffer. In such grievous circumstances we can patiently endure injustice knowing that the day will come when we will become residents in the realm to which our second citizenship entitles us.

3:21 "who shall fashion anew the body of our humiliation, *that it may be* conformed to the body of his glory, according to the working whereby he is able even to subject all things unto himself."

3:21 "who shall fashion anew"

This fashioning anew is equivalent to being "raised incorruptible." (I Corinthians 15:52) This fashioning anew is included in the sweeping assertion that "he maketh all things new." (Revelation 21:5)

Appendix A

3:21 "the body of our humiliation"

We are often humiliated, not only by the limitations genetically imposed on imagination and creativity, but even more acutely we are humiliated when our present bodies, due to sickness, injury or old age, no longer allow us to function as we formerly did.

X.   I Thessalonians 4:13-17

4:13 "But we would not have you ignorant, brethren, concerning them that fall asleep; that ye sorrow not, even as the rest, who have no hope.

> Death can only be referred to as sleep when it is visualized with a resurrection in view. Among the faithful Jews, the hope of a personal resurrection is found as far back as Daniel, who by revelation wrote that "many of them that sleep in the dust of the earth shall awake, some to everlasting life, and some to shame and everlasting contempt." (Daniel 12:2) Daniel was assured that he would personally experience the resurrection. He was told "Go thou thy way until the end be; for thou shalt rest, and shalt stand in thy lot, at the end of the days." (Daniel 12:13)
>
> Devastating pagan nihilism made a deep impact upon many Jews who collectively found philosophical support in that error by associating together in the sect of the Sadducees. Luke, the author of the book of Acts, reports that "the Sadducees say that there is no resurrection, neither angel, nor spirit; but the Pharisees confess both." (Acts 23:8) If one reads the inscriptions on the tombstones of believing Jews, he will find a sharp "contrast between the simple faith and earnest hope which they express, and the grim proclamation of utter disbelief in any future to the soul, not unmixed with language of coarsest materialism, on the graves of so many of the polished Romans! ... That civilization was doomed which could inscribe over its dead such words as: 'To eternal sleep;' 'To perpetual rest;' or more coarsely express it thus, 'I was not, and I became; I was, and am no more. Thus much is true; who says other, lies; for I shall not be,' adding, as it were by way of moral, 'And thou who livest, drink, play, come.' ... We can understand how a religion which proclaimed a hope so different, must have spoken to the hearts of many even at Rome, and much more, how that blessed assurance of life and immortality which Christianity afterwards brought, could win its thousands, though it were at the cost of poverty, shame, torture, and the arena."[619]

4:14 For if we believe that Jesus died and rose again, even so them also that are fallen asleep in Jesus will God bring with him.

4:14 "we believe that Jesus died and rose again"

> These two assertions are absolutely central and fundamental to a Christian's belief. We know and believe that Jesus actually died. The cumulative evidence from the Gospel accounts is massively overwhelming. He was not simply grievously wounded and subsequently revived in the coolness of the sepulchre. He actually died and his lifeless body was placed in the sepulchre. Consequently, his post-crucifixion appearances can only be explained as a true resurrection, not a resuscitation.

---

[619] Alfred Edersheim, The Life and Times of Jesus the Messiah, Vol. I, (Grand Rapids, MI: Wm. B. Eerdmans Publishing Co., 1943), p. 69.

It is amazing that the virus of unbelief, revealed by denying the resurrection, had infected some of the Christians who made up the church in Corinth. To those congregants Paul asked, "How say some among you that there is no resurrection of the dead?" (I Corinthians 15:12) Paul made it clear that such denial repudiated not only unassailable eyewitness testimony of the resurrection of Jesus (I Corinthians 15:4-8), but the testimony of botany as well. He rebuked those unbelievers in the church at Corinth reminding them that the seed "which thou thyself sowest is not quickened except it die: and that which thou sowest, thou sowest not the body that shall be, but a bare grain, it may chance of wheat, or of some other kind; but God giveth it a body even as it pleased him, and to each seed a body of its own." (I Corinthians 15:36-38)

4:14   "them also that are fallen asleep in Jesus will God bring with him"

The death of a Christian does not lead to extinction of his being; rather, the spirit of the Christian at death goes to be with Christ. (See Philippians 1:23.) When Jesus makes his final triumphant return (See Acts 1:11.) he will bring with him the spirits of his followers who have been faithful unto death. God, bringing with Christ the Christians who have fallen asleep, is intimated in Revelation 21:10 by "the holy city Jerusalem, coming down out of heaven from God."

4:15   For this we say unto you by the word of the Lord, that we that are alive, that are left unto the coming of the Lord, shall in no wise precede them that are fallen asleep.

4:15   "we that are alive, that are left unto the coming of the Lord"

The words "we that are alive" refer to those Christians who will be alive when Jesus returns.

4:15   "shall in no wise precede them that are fallen asleep"

Those Christians who are living when Christ returns will not be given precedence ("shall in no wise precede") over those faithful ones who will have died prior to Jesus' second coming. It seems that the spirits of Christians whom Jesus will bring with him at the time of his victorious return will experience the triumph during which "death is swallowed up in victory"(I Corinthians 15:54) before those will who are still alive at Jesus' return.

4:16   For the Lord himself shall descend from heaven, with a shout, with the voice of the archangel, and with the trump of God: and the dead in Christ shall rise first;

4:16   "the Lord himself shall descend from heaven"

The Lord to whom reference is made is the Lord Jesus Christ. On the occasion of the second coming, he will not make his appearance by utilizing a representative but will come personally. It will be "the Lord himself."

4:16   "with a shout"

The "shout" is rendered in the ESV as "a cry of command" and in the NIV as "a loud command." Probably it will be the same "shout" or "command" that Jesus gave at the tomb of Lazarus when "he cried with a loud voice, Lazarus, come forth!" (John 11:43) However, the command will be to all mankind, not only to Lazarus.

Appendix A

4:16 "with the voice of the archangel"

The title "archangel" means "ruling angel." Obviously therefore, there is a hierarchy among the angels. Near the top is Gabriel, who declared his position of authority when he told Zacharias, "I am Gabriel. I stand in the presence of God." (Luke 1:19 NIV) Outranking him is the angel who is in charge of the entire angelic host. Though the archangel's name occurs in the ninth verse of the book of Jude as "Michael," here his name is not given, we are simply told that he is "the archangel." At the return of Jesus the archangel will, by his "voice," make it clear to everyone who the divine personage is who has arrived from on high.

4:16 "and with the trump of God"

This trumpet signal fully conforms to Paul's exposition of eschatological events which he gave to the church in Corinth in which he said, "Behold, I tell you a mystery: We all shall not sleep, but we shall all be changed, in a moment, in the twinkling of an eye, at the last trump: for the trumpet shall sound, and the dead shall be raised incorruptible, and we shall be changed. For this corruptible must put on incorruption, and this mortal must put on immortality." (I Corinthians 15:51-53) Will the appearance of Jesus and the voice of the archangel, along with the attention-demanding signal from God's trumpet, occur simultaneously around the entire globe or will those events occur serially as each segment of the earth's surface is lightened by the sun?

4:16 "the dead in Christ shall rise first"

This statement emphasizes the affirmation in verse 15 that "we that are alive … shall in no wise precede them that are fallen asleep." Those Christians who are alive when Jesus returns will not receive immortality before those do who have died in Christ and whose spirits Jesus will bring with him at his second coming.

4:17 then we that are alive, that are left, shall together with them be caught up in the clouds, to meet the Lord in the air: and so shall we ever be with the Lord."

As I have noted in the commentary on Matthew 24:40, theologians call this future event "The Rapture." This being "taken," this being "caught up in the clouds to meet the Lord," is also described as "our gathering together unto him." (II Thessalonians 2:1) The ecstasy of this rapture was captured in poetry and song by H. L. Turner in the great hymn "Christ Returneth," in which he wrote "Oh, joy!, oh, delight! should we go without dying. No sickness, no sadness, no dread and no crying, Caught up thru' the clouds with our Lord into glory, When Jesus receives 'His own.'"

This "Rapture," this being "taken," will not occur to rescue believers from intense worldwide persecution just prior to The Millennium as many pre-millennial expositors affirm. This being "taken" will be a terminal event to be compared with the time when "Jehovah said unto Noah, Come thou and all thy house into the ark." (Genesis 7:1) (See also the discussion of the Rapture in the commentary at 7:14-17 and 11:12.)

Revelation Verse by Verse

XI. II Thessalonians 1:7-10

1:7 **"And to you that are afflicted rest with us, at the revelation of the Lord Jesus from heaven with the angels of his power in flaming fire,"**

1:7 " to you that are afflicted rest with us"

The rest or relief does not imply the immediate cessation of persecution but the mental calm which comes from the assurance that justice will ultimately be rendered. When one suffers unjustly, the temptation is to conclude there is no divine oversight or governance of the universe. While injustice may prevail during our lifetime, here we are assured that, ultimately, justice will be meted out. This prophecy takes us to the judgment before the great white throne, described in Revelation 20:11-15.

1:7 "at the revelation of the Lord Jesus from heaven"

The NIV makes it clear that restitution for injustice will often not occur during our lifetime but will take place at Jesus' second coming. Then, he will "give relief to you who are troubled, and to us as well. This will happen when the Lord Jesus is revealed from heaven in blazing fire with his powerful angels." (II Thessalonians 1:7 NIV)

1:7 "with the angels of his power in flaming fire"

These angels will come as agents of justice under the oversight of the archangel who is mentioned in I Thessalonians 4:16. These angels are to be equated with "the armies which are in heaven" at Revelation 19:14 and with "his army" at Revelation 19:19.

1:8 **"rendering vengeance to them that know not God, and to them that obey not the gospel of our Lord Jesus:"**

1:8 "rendering vengeance to them that know not God"

The ignorance of those who "know not God" is deliberate. Those who flaunt such flagrant denial will suffer "vengeance." On the other hand, God clearly is gracious to those who truly have had no opportunity to know him: "If you say, 'But we knew nothing about this,' does not he who weighs the heart perceive it? Does not he who guards your life know it? Will he not repay each person according to what he has done?" (Proverbs 24:12 NIV) Paul clearly indicates in Romans 2:7 that the principle stated in Proverbs 24:12 continues to be applicable during the Gospel age.

1:9 **"who shall suffer punishment, *even* eternal destruction from the face of the Lord and from the glory of his might,"**

While the suffering and injustice endured by persecuted Christians will ultimately cease, the punishment of those who have inflicted injustice and torture on the followers of Christ will be eternal. (See the comment on Revelation 19:3.)

1:10 **"when he shall come to be glorified in his saints, and to be marvelled at in all them that believed (because our testimony unto you was believed) in that day."**

Appendix A

1:10 "he shall come to be glorified in his saints"

Simply the presence alone of those people who are known as "his saints" will glorify Christ. It will demonstrate that Christ has thwarted Satan's most powerful efforts at total destruction and catastrophe. There will be myriads of people, "his saints," who will have escaped Satan's destructive embrace because of the salvation which Christ has brought. In addition, those saints will give ecstatic and rapturous expressions as the heirs of salvation which will glorify Christ. They will say "Hallelujah; salvation, and glory, and power, belong to our God …" (Revelation 19:1-5)

1:10 "to be marvelled at in all them that believed"

We marvel even now because of the astonishingly specific predictions about what will take place when Jesus comes. Those coming events have been described repeatedly by revelation through scripture. Still, beholding the realities will cause us to marvel much more. As Paul said, "Things which eye saw not, and ear heard not, and which entered not into the heart of man, whatsoever things God prepared for them that love him." (I Corinthians 2:9)

XII. II Thessalonians 2:8

2:8 "And then shall be revealed the lawless one, whom the Lord Jesus shall slay with the breath of his mouth, and bring to nought by the manifestation of his coming;"

This passage should be equated with Revelation 19:11-16. Note especially that while here it is "the breath of his mouth" by which Jesus will slay the lawless one, in Revelation 19:15 we are told that "out of his mouth proceedeth a sharp sword, that with it he should smite the nations."

XIII. I Timothy 6:14

6:14 "That thou keep the commandment, without spot, without reproach, until the appearing of our Lord Jesus Christ:"

The standard for obedience to Christ, not only for Timothy but for every Christian, is to be spotless and above reproach. This standard will not only prevail till "the appearing of our Lord Jesus Christ" but eternally. (See Revelation 21:27.)

XIV. II Timothy 4:1:

4:1 "I charge *thee* in the sight of God, and of Christ Jesus, who shall judge the living and the dead, and by his appearing and his kingdom:"

4:1 "I charge *thee* in the sight of God, and of Christ Jesus"

Timothy is to take an oath of utter, total and complete fidelity in the execution of his ministry, not only in relation to the highest present reality, that is, God and Christ Jesus, but also in relation to the eschatological work of Christ when he will "judge the living and the dead" which will occur at "his appearing" and that of "his kingdom." (See Revelation 20:11-15.)

4:1 "who shall judge the living and the dead"

A writer of history often delivers judgments on the actions and intentions of those involved in bringing about historic events. Usually such judgments do not distress those participants because they will not be called to give account. In dramatic contrast, this judgment will call the participants back to stand trial.

4:1 "by his appearing and his kingdom"

His appearing refers to his second coming which was announced at the time of his ascension. On that occasion two angels told the apostles that "this Jesus, who was received up from you into heaven, shall so come in like manner as ye beheld him going into heaven." (Acts 1:11) Every writer of the books making up the New Testament concurs in the reality of this future climactic event. While the following list is not inclusive, it substantiates the statement about every writer calling attention to this coming dramatic development: Matthew 25:1-13, 25:19, Mark 8:38, Luke 9:26, John 14:28-29. Paul writes of the second coming in I Corinthians 1:7-8, 4:5, 11:26 and 15:23, Philippians 3:20-21, Colossians 3:4, I Thessalonians 1:10, 2:19, 3:13, 4:15-17, 5:2-3, 5:23, II Thessalonians 1:7-10, 2:1-3, 2:8, I Timothy 6:14-15, II Timothy 4:1, 4:8, Titus 2:13 and Hebrews 9:28. James highlights the event in James 5:7-9. Peter showcases it in I Peter 1:7, 1:13, 4:13 and 5:4; II Pet 3:3-4, 3:10-14. John takes up the theme again in I John 3:2 and Jude stresses it obliquely in Jude 6 when he mentions "the judgment of the great day" and in verse 24 in which he calls attention to the one "that is able to guard you from stumbling, and to set you before the presence of his glory without blemish in exceeding joy." It is referred to repeatedly in the book of Revelation, for example, 1:7, 3:11, 16:15, 22:12 and 22:20.

XV. Titus 2:13

2:13 "Looking for the blessed hope and appearing of the glory of the great God and our Saviour Jesus Christ;"

The ASV's choice of the word "looking" doesn't convey the intense anticipation that Stern gives in his *Complete Jewish Bible* in which he translated the idea as "continuing to expect the blessed fulfillment…" Stern's translation is upheld by the Literal English Translation which accompanies the Nestle Greek Text in which the Greek word *prosdechomenoi* is translated as "expecting." We are to ardently look for or expect the fulfillment of two great sustaining realities of Christian life. The first one is the blessed and sustaining hope which has been engendered in our hearts and minds by Christ's message. That hope is the anticipation that "this corruptible shall have put on incorruption and this mortal shall have put on immortality." (I Corinthians 15:53-54) The second reality, the coming of which we avidly await, though currently invisible, will dramatically be fulfilled by the "appearing of the glory of the great God and our Saviour Jesus Christ." That will be the moment when "we shall be like him for we shall see him even as he is." (I John 3:2) Titus 2:13 is one of the many references that declare the deity of Christ. See the scripture list at Revelation 15:3 under "great and marvelous are thy works, O Lord God."

Appendix A

XVI. Hebrews 9:28

9:28 "So Christ also, having been once offered to bear the sins of many, shall appear a second time, apart from sin, to them that wait for him, unto salvation."

While the first coming of Jesus took place to deal with the universal calamitous problem of sin, his next and final coming will be to fulfill the great anticipation of those who "wait for him, unto salvation." Salvation, in the sense of being forgiven and of being reconciled to God, is the invaluable present possession of everyone who has accepted and obeyed the message of Jesus. Even though we are saved, we still "wait for him, unto salvation." This salvation is the consummation of all the promises to individual Christians relating to God's plan for redeemed man. This coming blissful status will include immortality and deity. The participation in deity is clearly affirmed when John says "we shall be like him, for we shall see him even as he is." (I John 3:2) The potential of this coming ecstasy for the heirs of salvation exceeds the capacity of our enlightened understanding to grasp. Our future status will be so stunning that, at the present, there is no adequate simile.

XVII. II Peter 3:3-11

3:3 "knowing this first, that in the last days mockers shall come with mockery, walking after their own lusts,"

3:3 "in the last days mockers shall come with mockery"

Mockers who ridicule Christianity are nothing new. Celsus, an anti-Christian philosopher writing about 180 A.D. alleged that Jesus was the bastard son of Mary by a Roman soldier named Panthera. We know of the calumny of Celsus through the refutation written by Origen (c. 185 - c. 254), a great Alexandrian Christian scholar.

Tragically, Jews incorporated Celsus' lie under the title "Toledot Yeshu" into the Talmud. By this means it was widely circulated in Europe and the Middle East during the medieval period, turning thousands of Jewish people away from Jesus because of this grotesque and utterly false libel.

From Peter's prophecy it seems that at some period just prior to Jesus' return, lampooning mockery against Christ and his message will become even more subtle and destructive. The verse-by-verse commentary calls attention to this present-day phenomenon with extensive references at Revelation 11:7 under the title "overcome them and kill them."

3:3 "walking after their own lusts"

An example of one who made lust the fundamental consideration of ethical behavior is given by the philosopher Bertrand Russell, who in one of his more restrained expositions said: "Economic causes compel men, as a rule, to postpone marriage, and it is neither likely that they will remain chaste in the years from 20 to 30 nor desirable psychologically that they should do so; but it is much better that, if they have temporary relations, that they should not be with professionals but with girls of their own class, whose motive is affection rather than money. For both these reasons, young unmarried people should have considerable freedom as long as children are avoided."[620]

3:4 "and saying, Where is the promise of his coming? for, from the day that the fathers fell asleep, all things continue as they were from the beginning of the creation."

3:4 "Where is the promise of his coming?"

The rendering of the NIV brings the meaning of the verse into clearer focus. It says, "They will say, 'Where is this coming he promised?'" The error of their calculations is to evaluate the promise in the context of an attenuated time scale. They have selected a period of history during which they know that no divine appearance occurred. On the basis of that phony analysis, they predict that a divine visitation will never occur.

3:4 "from the day that the fathers fell asleep"

The skeptics' analysis of history is skewed by analyzing an arbitrary and limited period. The arbitrary period of history which they have selected only goes back to some known point in their patriarchal genealogy, to the point at which "the fathers fell asleep." It does not encompass the scope of the entire human experience.

3:4 "all things continue as they were from the beginning of the creation"

The skeptics have analyzed the period beginning at some point at which "the fathers fell asleep." Then they subtly ask us to accept their rank assumption that the conditions which prevailed in that brief period of analysis are applicable all the way from "the beginning of the creation." This is deceptive slight of hand because it supposedly evaluates the historical record from its very inception.

3:5 "For this they willfully forget, that there were heavens from of old, and an earth compacted out of water and amidst water, by the word of God;"

3:5 "they willfully forget"

Peter gives us an exposé as well as an indictment with this brief accusation. A modern example of skeptics who "willfully forget" is found in those who assert that "natural selection," should such a highly questionable phenomenon exist, accounts for the existence of all life and matter. However, they "willfully forget" that "natural selection" could not function unless there were something previously existing from which to make a selection. Therefore, it is obvious that, "natural selection explains 'only the survival of the fittest, not the arrival of the fittest.'"[621] Thus, even conceptually, the evolutionary theory of the origin of the universe does not address the question of the ultimate origin of all existing matter and life.

3:5 "there were heavens from of old, and an earth"

Evidence for previous orders of terrestrial and sidereal existence and their destruction are found in the fossils on earth and in the burnt out stars in the planetary system.

---

620 Bertrand Russell, Why I Am Not a Christian, (New York: Simon & Schuster Inc., 1957), p. 171.
621 Stephen C. Meyer, Darwin's Doubt, the Explosive Origin of Animal Life and the Case for Intelligent Design, (NY: Harper Collins, 2013), p. x.

Appendix A

3:5 "compacted out of water and amidst water"

Though Peter does not give us a scriptural reference substantiating this statement, it is fully corroborated by Genesis 1:1-2.

3:5 "by the word of God"

Every attempt to explain, by non-theological means, why there is something rather than nothing has proven to be ludicrously inadequate. Matter and life are not self-generated. Their existence requires the initiative of an outside power, that is, a creator. The origin of matter cannot be explained without going beyond the boundaries of matter. Only a divine fiat, "the word of God," can explain the existence of matter and life.

3:6 "by which means the world that then was, being overflowed with water, perished"

3:6 "by which means"

This adverbial clause points us back to "the word of God."

3:6 "the world that then was, being overflowed with water, perished"

The fossil record gives adequate evidence that a previous order of existence was destroyed by water. Ancient petrified life forms are encased in water-carried sediment. This universal archeological record substantiates the scriptural record of the universal flood.

3:7 "but the heavens that now are, and the earth, by the same word have been stored up for fire, being reserved against the day of judgment and destruction of ungodly men."

3:7 "the heavens that now are, and the earth"

As noted before, by reference to fossils and burnt out stars, both of these realities which "now are" show the marks of having been brought into their current status from a previous order of existence.

3:7 "stored up for fire"

The second global and galactic destruction will be far more definitive than the previous one. It will be so inclusive that God will look upon his new handiwork and say "I make all things new." (Revelation 21:5)

3:7 "day of judgment and destruction of ungodly men"

The focal point and purpose of the coming global and violent astronomical dissolution is to render "judgment" and consequent "destruction of ungodly men."

3:8 "But forget not this one thing, beloved, that one day is with the Lord as a thousand years, and a thousand years as one day."

The "one thing" is illustrated by two realities, both of which indicate that time is relative. The limitations of time as experienced by humans, whether a trivial period of "one day" or whether an extensive period of "a thousand years," impose no limitations to the Eternal One. See the discussion in the commentary at Revelation 6:10 under "how long?"

3:9 "The Lord is not slack concerning his promise, as some count slackness; but is longsuffering to you-ward, not wishing that any should perish, but that all should come to repentance."

3:9 "The Lord is not slack concerning his promise"

"His promise" is the one mentioned in verse 4, "the promise of his coming." The idea of "his coming" is a declaration that God personally will intervene in human society to stop its continued course of increasing flagrant wickedness. Since no divine intervention has occurred in some arbitrarily defined period of history, it is assumed none will occur in the foreseeable and conceivable future.

3:9 "is longsuffering to you-ward"

Divine patience, here called "longsuffering," is dangerously misinterpreted as divine carelessness or indifference. In reality, God is delaying judgment with the hope that man – seeing the futility, the brutality and destructiveness of his unrestrained capitulation to the basest sensual desires – will end his rebellion because it leads to personal and societal grief, vacuity and ruin. But the hope for self-generated moral recovery is a vain hope, especially when divine patience is interpreted as indifference.

3:9 "not wishing that any should perish, but that all should come to repentance"

God says, "I take no pleasure in the death of the wicked." (Ezekiel 33:11) This means God is not vindictive or sadistic. God wants man to be eternally triumphant. God, with even the faint hope that man may be self-correcting, both personally and societally through repentance, has delayed judgment as long as possible.

3:10 "But the day of the Lord will come as a thief; in the which the heavens shall pass away with a great noise, and the elements shall be dissolved with fervent heat, and the earth and the works that are therein shall be burned up."

3:10 "the day of the Lord will come as a thief"

The choice of "a thief" as the simile for the occurrence of ultimate divine judgment is astonishing. There are many aspects of the coming of a thief which cannot be transferred to illustrate or describe the final coming of divine presence into the human experience. A thief's exploits are totally selfish and malevolent. The coming of a thief has no positive or redemptive intent or purpose. The work of thieves is totally negative and destructive. Though this final and definitive divine coming of God into human history will be destructive, it is a destruction to stop evil, not to perpetuate it or profit from it. Thus, though God's climactic intrusion into human affairs and the human environment will be both instantaneous and destructive, it will be benevolent in the sense that it sets an uncompromising termination point for evil. Only the unpredictability and the suddenness with which thieves carry out their projects are transferable to describe the ultimate coming of divine judgment upon human society.

3:10 "the heavens … the elements … and the earth"

Sometimes the word "heaven" is used in reference to places of high political status, as pointed out in the commentary on Revelation 6:14, in which it is said, "the heaven was

Appendix A

removed as a scroll when it is rolled up ..." About that statement the comment was made that, "This certainly does not point to an atmospheric or astronomical collapse, but indicates that the whole political structure, in this verse represented by 'every mountain and island,' will be discredited, repudiated and overthrown."

In Peter's use of "the heavens," since it is associated with "the elements" and "the earth," the word points us to the astronomical sense of the word heaven, meaning the planets and their associated sidereal bodies. The concept that the entire astronomical complex will be destroyed is in harmony with Revelation 21:5 in which God is quoted as saying, "I make all things new."

"The elements" are thought by some commentators to refer here to the stars or heavenly bodies but that is not credible because it would just repeat the meaning which is conveyed by "the heavens." "The elements" refer to the basic materials which make up the universe. Though the systematization and classification of fundamental elements, which is displayed in the periodic table, did not exist at the time Peter penned this prophecy, the Greek word *stoicheia,* translated here as "elements," is undoubtedly used to express the most fundamental components of material existence.

"The earth" refers to the only humanly inhabitable astronomical body. The only astronomical body on which conditions exist making human life and activity possible, is our familiar globe, our earth, which rotates on its axis every twenty-four hours and circumnavigates the sun once every year.

3:11 "Seeing that these things are thus all to be dissolved, what manner of persons ought ye to be in *all* holy living and godliness,"

3:11 "these things are thus all to be dissolved"

"Things" is the inclusive word referring to "the heavens … the elements... and the earth." The most stable reference points to which humans may point are defined by and consist of these three realities. Here, we are informed that the stability which we associate with these three centers of existence is itself a fleeting concept. If we are searching for ultimate, eternal, inviolable, consistent and unmovable reality, we must look beyond "these things" to God because all "these things" will "be dissolved."

3:11 "what manner of persons ought ye to be in *all* holy living and godliness"

The knowledge of the temporal nature of all material existence should guide our search for permanence. That search can only lead us to God.

Appendix B

Anchor Points in the Book of Revelation's Panorama of History

There are three seven-fold predictive visions in Revelation: the seven seals (6:1-8:2), the seven trumpets (8:2-14:20) and the seven bowls [or vials] (15:1-17:18). These should not be understood to predict three uninterrupted, non-overlapping, end-to-end series of sequential events. The trumpet series of visions does not take up the time-line at the point to which history was carried in the vision of the seven seals. Similarly, the seven-bowls vision does not pick up the time line at the point to which it was carried in the seven-trumpet vision. Rather, there is significant time line overlap in the three series of visions. When the time line of a later vision overlaps the time line of a previous one, it does not repetitiously highlight previously expounded developments or events but delineates other and distinct phenomena in that period which were not described by the earlier vision.

The seven-seals' vision (Revelation 6:1-8:2) takes us to a point in time somewhere beyond the epochal development of the conversion of the Jews to Christ (Revelation 7:2-8) and the subsequent and consequent global Gospel triumph among the Gentiles (Revelation 7:9-17). Those two epochal events are still (from the time of this writing) to occur in the future, however, probably in the near future. Therefore, there is a great time line overlap between the two epochal seal-related events described in 7:2-17 and the event announced when the fifth trumpet is sounded (Revelation 9:1-11). In the later vision, we are taken back to the sixth century A.D., to the birth of Muhammad, his career and the early history of Islam. This obviously overlaps the scope of the time line depicted by the seven seals. In the seven-bowl series of prophetic visions, the sixth vision (Revelation 16:12) takes us to the current triumph of Shi'ism in Iraq. That event has opened the way for the kings from the east, that is, "from the sunrising," Iran being the first among them, to make their way to the Battle of Armageddon (Revelation 16:16). While there is time line progress depicted in each of the three series of seven visions, there is also time line overlap between them.

We who are living in the first quarter of the twenty-first century should be able to see, from the insights available to us from Romans chapter 11, that the conversion of the Jews to Christ, depicted in Revelation 7:2-8, is imminent. (See the book God's Game Plan by B.L. Turner.) If one evaluates that approaching event from a more inclusive biblical perspective, he will see that such a development is also significantly and uniquely epochal. First of all, that fact becomes clear by noting the great emphasis given to it by the Jewish prophets who predicted it in an impressive series of prophecies. The following partial selection shows the importance which the prophets gave to the Jews' tragically long-delayed but ultimate acknowledgment of the Messiah.

Revelation Verse by Verse

The Conversion of Israel to Jesus Christ was Foreseen by the Major Prophets

Isaiah, for example, repeatedly alerts his readers' attention to the coming epochal conversion of the Jews to the Messiah, though it would occur many centuries beyond the period of his ministry, since he prophesied from 740-681 B.C. Note his following prophecies:

"With joy shall ye [the dispersed of Judah and Ephraim] draw water out of the wells of salvation." (Isaiah 12:3)

"For Jehovah will have compassion on Jacob, and will yet choose Israel, and set them in their own land: (See Isaiah 11:11-12.) and the sojourner shall join himself with them, and they shall flee to the house of Jacob." (Isaiah 14:1)

"In that day shall Israel be the third with Egypt and with Assyria, a blessing in the midst of the earth; for that Jehovah of hosts hath blessed them, saying, 'Blessed be Egypt my people, and Assyria [essentially modern Iraq] the work of my hands, and Israel mine inheritance.'" (Isaiah 19:24-25)

"In days to come shall Jacob take root; Israel shall blossom and bud; and they shall fill the face of the world with fruit." (Isaiah 27:6)

"And the remnant that is escaped of the house of Judah shall again take root downward, and bear fruit upward. For out of Jerusalem shall go forth a remnant, and out of Mt. Zion they shall escape: the zeal of Jehovah of hosts will perform this." (Isaiah 37:31-32)

"Fear not; for I am with thee [that is, with Israel]: I will bring thy seed from the east, and gather thee from the west; I will say to the north, Give up; and to the south, Keep not back; bring my sons from far, and my daughters from the end of the earth; every one that is called by my name, and whom I have created for my glory, whom I have formed, yea, whom I have made." (Isaiah 43:5-7)

"Yet now hear, O Jacob my servant, and Israel, whom I have chosen: Thus saith Jehovah that made thee, and formed thee from the womb, who will help thee: Fear not, O Jacob my servant; and thou, Jeshurun [the upright one], whom I have chosen. For I will pour water upon him that is thirsty, and streams upon the dry ground; I will pour my Spirit upon thy seed, and my blessing upon thine offspring: and they shall spring up among the grass, as willows by the watercourses. One shall say, I am Jehovah's; and another shall call himself by the name of Jacob; and another shall subscribe with his hand unto Jehovah, and surname himself by the name of Israel." (Isaiah 44:1-5)

"Verily thou art a God that hidest thyself, O God of Israel, the Saviour. ... Israel shall be saved by Jehovah with an everlasting salvation: ye shall not be put to shame nor confounded world without end." (Isaiah 45:15-17)

"In Jehovah shall all the seed of Israel be justified, and shall glory." (Isaiah 45:25)

Jeremiah, whose ministry covered the period from 626 to 585 B.C., also prophesied of the same epochal event: He tells us, "Thus saith Jehovah the God of Israel: like these good figs, so will I

Appendix B

regard the captives of Judah, whom I have sent out of this place into the land of the Chaldeans, for [their] good. For I will set mine eyes upon them for good, and I will bring them again to this land: and I will build them, and not pull them down; and I will plant them, and not pluck them up. And <u>I will give them a heart to know me, that I am Jehovah: and they shall be my people, and I will be their God; for they shall return unto me with their whole heart</u>." (Jeremiah 24:5-7)

"In those days and in that time, saith Jehovah, the children of Israel shall come, they and the children of Judah; they shall go on their way weeping, and <u>shall seek Jehovah their God</u>." (Jeremiah 50:4)

Ezekiel, who prophesied from 593-571 B.C., also in several passages predicts the same epochal developments about which Isaiah and Jeremiah prophesied: "Therefore say, Thus saith the Lord Jehovah: I will gather you from the peoples, and assemble you out of the countries where ye have been scattered, and <u>I will give you the land of Israel</u>. And they shall come thither, and they shall take away all the detestable things thereof and all the abominations thereof from thence. And I will give them one heart, and <u>I will put a new spirit within you; and I will take the stony heart out of their flesh, and will give them a heart of flesh; that they may walk in my statutes, and keep mine ordinances, and do them: and they shall be my people, and I will be their God</u>. But as for them whose heart walketh after the heart of their detestable things and their abominations, I will bring their way upon their own heads, saith the Lord Jehovah." (Ezekiel 11:17-21)

"Therefore say unto the house of Israel, Thus saith the Lord Jehovah: I do not this for your sake, O house of Israel, but for my holy name, which ye have profaned among the nations, whither ye went. And I will sanctify my great name, which hath been profaned among the nations, which ye have profaned in the midst of them; and <u>the nations shall know that I am Jehovah, saith the Lord Jehovah, when I shall be sanctified in you before their eyes</u>. For I will take you from among the nations, and gather you out of all the countries, and <u>will bring you into your own land</u>. And I will sprinkle clean water upon you, and <u>ye shall be clean: from all your filthiness, and from all your idols, will I cleanse you. A new heart also will I give you, and a new spirit will I put within you</u>; and I will take away the stony heart out of your flesh, and I will give you a heart of flesh. And <u>I will put my Spirit within you</u>, and cause you to walk in my statutes, and ye shall keep mine ordinances, and do them. And ye shall dwell in the land that I gave to your fathers; and <u>ye shall be my people, and I will be your God</u>." (Ezekiel 36:22-28)

"And I will set my glory among the nations; and all the nations shall see my judgment that I have executed, and my hand that I have laid upon them. So the house of Israel shall know that I am Jehovah their God, from that day and forward. And the nations shall know that the house of Israel went into captivity for their iniquity; because they trespassed against me, and I hid my face from them: so I gave them into the hand of their adversaries, and they fell all of them by the sword. According to their uncleanness and according to their transgressions did I unto them; and I hid my face from them. Therefore thus saith the Lord Jehovah: <u>Now will I bring back the captivity of Jacob, and have mercy upon the whole house of Israel</u>; and I will be jealous for my holy name. And they shall bear their shame, and all their trespasses whereby they have trespassed against me, when they shall dwell securely in their land, and none shall make them afraid; when I have brought them back from the peoples, and gathered them out of their enemies' lands, and am sanctified in them in the sight of many nations. And they shall know that I am Jehovah their God, in that I caused them to go into captivity among the nations, and have gathered them unto their own land; and I will leave none of them any more there; neither will I hide my face any more from them; for I have poured out my Spirit upon the house of Israel, saith the Lord Jehovah." (Ezekiel 39:21-29)

The Conversion of the Jews to Christ Was Foreseen Also By the Minor Prophets

Both Micah and Zechariah as well as Hosea prophesied in harmony with the remarkable series of statements from the major prophets, which have just been quoted. Accordingly, **Hosea**, who prophesied from 750-715 B.C., said, "For the children of Israel shall abide many days without king, and without prince, and without sacrifice, and without pillar, and without ephod or teraphim: afterward shall the children of Israel return, and seek Jehovah their God, and David their king, and shall come with fear unto Jehovah and to his goodness in the latter days." (Hosea 3:4-5)

Micah, who prophesied from 735-700 B.C., said, "The remnant of Jacob shall be in the midst of many peoples as dew from Jehovah, as showers upon the grass." (Micah 5:7) Micah also pointed ahead to the conversion of Israel when he wrote, "He will again have compassion upon us; he will tread our iniquities under foot; and thou wilt cast all their sins into the depths of the sea. Thou wilt perform the truth to Jacob, and the lovingkindness to Abraham, which thou hast sworn unto our fathers from the days of old." (Micah 7:19-20)

Zechariah, who prophesied from 520-480 B.C., also foresaw Israel's future in complete concurrence with the vision of the other major and minor prophets. He said, "Sing and rejoice, O daughter of Zion; for, lo, I come, and I will dwell in the midst of thee, saith Jehovah. And many nations shall join themselves to Jehovah in that day, and shall be my people; and I will dwell in the midst of thee, and thou shalt know that Jehovah of hosts has sent me unto thee." (Zechariah 2:10-11)

He went on to say, "It shall come to pass that, as ye were a curse among the nations, O house of Judah and house of Israel, so will I save you and you shall be a blessing: fear not but let your hands be strong." (Zechariah 8:13)

Zechariah further prophesied giving us God's promise about the redemption of the Jewish people. He said that, "I will pour upon the house of David, and upon the inhabitants of Jerusalem, the spirit of grace and supplication; and they shall look unto me whom they have pierced; and they shall mourn for him, as one mourneth for his only son, and shall be in bitterness for him, as one that is in bitterness for his first-born." (Zechariah 12:10)

The Conversion of the Jews to Christ and Its Impact Was Foreseen By John

In full accord with God's prediction given to us by five Jewish prophets and the apostle Paul, an across-the-board turning of the Jews to Jesus is clearly predicted in Revelation 7:2-8 as a major climactic event. Those Jews are said to have been sealed on their foreheads. That undoubtedly refers to being sealed by the Holy Spirit, a phenomenon which is mentioned in II Corinthians 1:22 and in Ephesians 1:13 and 4:30, a clear indication that they would have become Christians.

Appendix B

What will be the impact of this future widespread turning of the Jews to Christ? The answer is given in the victorious vision in the immediately following verses of the seventh chapter of Revelation. In that passage, we are told that there will be, "A great multitude which no man could number, out of every nation and of all tribes and peoples and tongues, standing before the throne and before the lamb, arrayed in white robes, and palms in their hands; and they cry with a great voice, saying, Salvation unto our God who sitteth on the throne and unto the lamb." (Revelation 7:9-10)

The Conversion of the Jews to Christ Was Prophesied Also By the Apostle Paul

In harmony with all those prophetic statements just cited from the Major and Minor prophets, the apostle Paul wrote that, "a hardening in part hath befallen Israel, until the fullness of the Gentiles has come in, and so all Israel shall be saved: even as it is written, there shall come out of Zion the Deliverer; He shall turn away ungodliness from Jacob: and this is my covenant unto them, when I shall take away their sins." (Romans 11:25-27)

Further Insight From Paul About the Jewish Conversion to Christ

Anticipating and substantiating the climactic vision given to John, Paul also foresaw the impact which the turning of the Jews to Christ would have on the Gentiles. He prophesied it would be like life from the dead for the Gentile population of the world. That is the import of Romans 11:15 which says, "For if the casting away of them [that is, the Jews] is the reconciling of the world, what shall the receiving of them be, but life from the dead?"

His inspired prediction is in complete harmony with the vision in Revelation which describes the collective body of Gentile converts to Christ as "a great multitude which no man could number, out of every nation and of all tribes and peoples and tongues, standing before the throne and before the Lamb, arrayed in white robes, and palms in their hands; and they cry with a great voice, saying, salvation unto our God who sitteth on the throne and unto the Lamb." (Revelation 7:9-10) Thus, the time horizon of the seven seals' series of visions is very extensive, stretching at least two-thousand years, from the apostolic age to the opening years of the twenty-first century, and, probably, beyond.

Statements in the epistle to the Romans make it clear that two pinnacle events of the seven-seals-series-of-visions, that is, first, the conversion of the Jews to Christ and second, the consequent global conversion of Gentiles to Christ, are closely related. As noted before, Paul's statement as recorded in Romans 11:15 says, "For if the casting away of them is the reconciling of the world, what shall the receiving ["acceptance" - NIV] of them be, but life from the dead?" (ASV)

The first pinnacle event is the receiving or acceptance of Jesus the Messiah by the Jews and the second pinnacle event is the emergence of the Gentiles, as it were, "from the dead." Paul obviously was looking forward to a time when physical Israel was going to be received or accepted. As God, for a time, because of their unbelief, rejected or cast them out of the central part or role in carrying out his eternal purpose, so one day he will receive or accept them into that noble role! This means they are going to accept Christ, which constitutes the only basis for their being received.

Instead of the word "receiving," which is used in the ASV version of Romans 11:15, other translations use synonyms which emphasize this obvious meaning. Moffatt's translation says, "For if their exclusion means that the world is reconciled to God, what will their **admission** mean? Why, it will be life from the dead!" Williams' translation also makes this point clear by saying, "For if the rejection of them has resulted in the reconciling of the world, what will the result be of the final **reception** of them but life from the dead?"

Thus we can confidently look forward to a time, before Christ's final triumphant return, when ethnic Jews will submit to Christ in large numbers. That, in turn, will result in greater numbers of Gentiles coming to Christ, a greater response than at any time in previous history! Please do not miss the fact that the words "life from the dead" refer to the blessing which will come to the Gentiles through the turning of Israel to Christ.

It is surprising that Barnes, whose commentary was first published in 1864, failed to see the cause-and-effect relationship between the turning of the Jews to Christ and the resulting innumerable host of Gentiles who, consequently, would yield themselves to Christ. Barnes, unfortunately, was completely wrong when he wrote, "This must be regarded, I think, as an episode, having no *immediate* connection with what precedes or what follows. It seems to be thrown in here — while the impending judgments of the sixth seal are suspended, and before the seventh is opened — to furnish a *relief* in the contemplation of so many scenes of woe, and to cheer the soul with inspiring hopes from the view of the great number that would ultimately be saved."[622]

Romans 11:15 gives additional emphasis to the truth which was highlighted just three verses earlier, in Romans 11:12. Kenneth Taylor expresses the idea forcefully in his paraphrase. He rendered it, "Now if the whole world became rich as a result of God's offer of salvation, when the Jews stumbled over it and turned it down, think how much greater a blessing the world will share in later on when the Jews, too, come to Christ."

In sharp contrast to Barnes' incomprehension about this epochal development, in 1875 Moses E. Lard very perceptively highlighted this imminent upcoming development when he commented on Romans 11:15. He wrote, "But when the Jews are received back into the divine favor, what event will then occur among the Gentiles that can, with propriety, be characterized as life for the dead? I answer, their general conversion. The Gentiles are now in countless numbers dead in sin, dead to righteousness, dead to Christ. Their more general regeneration will certainly be life from the dead."[623]

The impact of the general Jewish conversion to Christ on the Gentile population of the world, so powerfully called to our attention by Mr. Lard is also emphasized by other commentators. For instance, Thomas wrote, "If, then, the sin of Israel led to the salvation of the Gentiles, much more will their restoration be the means of blessing to the entire world. Their reception back again is to be of infinitely greater value to the world than their fall."[624]

---

622 Albert Barnes, Notes, Explanatory and Practical on the Book of Revelation, (New York: Harper & Brothers Publishers, 1864), p. 198.
623 Moses E. Lard, Commentary On Paul's Letter to the Romans, (Des Moines, Eugene S. Smith, no date), p. 359.
624 W. H. Griffith Thomas, Romans, A Devotional Commentary, Vol. II, (London, The Religious Tract Society, no date), p. 198.

Appendix B

Barclay also clearly saw the extensive impact which the conversion of the Jews to Christ would have on the Gentiles when he wrote, "If the rejection of the Jews had done so much, if, through it the Gentile world has been reconciled to God, what superlative glory must come when the Jews come in. If the tragedy of rejection has had results so wonderful, what would the happy ending be like, when the tragedy of rejection had changed to the glory of reception? Paul can only say that it would be like life from the dead."[625]

This future epochal evangelistic triumph, which will grow out of the turning of the Jews to Christ, will be a fulfillment of Zechariah's startling prophecy in which he said, "Thus saith Jehovah of hosts: In those days it shall come to pass, that ten men shall take hold, out of all the languages of the nations, they shall take hold of the skirt of him that is a Jew, saying, We will go with you, for we have heard that God is with you." (Zechariah 8:23)

Anticipating Jewish Acceptance of Jesus Christ

When may we anticipate the realization of the Jewish acceptance of Jesus of Nazareth as their Messiah, as predicted in the remarkable chain of prophetic utterances, itemized just above, and which is climactically highlighted in Revelation 7:2-8? This inquiry is no idle guessing game. On the contrary, God wants Gentile Christians to anticipate this epochal shift in order to take a central role in bringing about this historically transformative development. Paul made this clear when he wrote, "By the grace shown to you [Gentile Christians] they [the Jewish people] may now obtain mercy." (Romans 11:31)

From statements made both by Jesus and by Paul, it becomes clear that we Christians living in the first quarter of the twenty-first century are standing on the threshold of that dramatic event which will prove to have been one of the most momentous developments in all history.

That exuberant assurance is given because it appears that the hardening which has kept the major part of genetic Israel from acknowledging Jesus of Nazareth as their Messiah is in the process of breaking up. We gain this understanding from Paul's inspired prognosis of Jewish history which is given in the eleventh chapter of Romans. In Romans 11:25, the word "fullness" in the expression, "the fullness of the Gentiles be come in," comes from the Greek noun *playroma* (πληρωμα). Jesus used a very closely related word, recorded in Luke 21:24, when he said, "Jerusalem shall be trodden down of the Gentiles until the times of the Gentiles be fulfilled." The words "be fulfilled" are from the Greek verb *playrothosi* (πληρωθωςι). Both Greek words, *playroma* and *playrothosi*, are built on the Greek verb *playroo* (πληροω) and have the same meaning. On the basis of this identity, it seems highly probable that Paul, by inspiration, was commenting on Jesus' prophecy and has, therefore, given us a time-marker for the occurrence of the breaking up of the hardness of Israel. Thus, when Jerusalem, after centuries of being under Gentile rule and domination, came under exclusive Jewish control as a consequence of the 1967 Arab/Israeli war, it was a signal that the hardness of Israel against Christ would begin to dissipate.

In Romans 11:25, the expression "the fulness of the Gentiles be come in" does not point to "the general conversion of the world to Christ, as many take it; for this would seem to contradict the latter part of this chapter, and throw the national recovery of Israel too far into the future:

---
625 William Barclay, <u>The Letter To The Romans</u>, (Philadelphia, The Westminster Press, 1957), p. 159.

besides, in Romans 11:15, the apostle seems to speak of the receiving of Israel, not as following, but as contributing largely to bring about the general conversion of the world — but 'until the Gentiles have had their *full* time of the visible Church all to themselves while the Jews are out, which the Jews had till the Gentiles were brought in.'"[626]

The NIV rendered the second half of Romans 11:25 rather carelessly. It says, "Israel has experienced a hardening in part until the full number of the Gentiles has come in." Those translators took the liberty to translate the Greek noun *playroma*, which means fullness, as "full number."

The American Standard Version, the Douay-Rheims Bible, the English Standard Version, the King James Version, the Literal Version of the Bible, the Modern King James Version and the New King James Version have all translated Romans 11:25 correctly. All the other translations with which I am acquainted, have inserted their interpretation rather than giving us a faithful, accurate translation.

Jesus said, that Jerusalem would be under Gentile domination "until the times of the Gentiles be fulfilled." (Luke 21:24) The apostle Paul shows that simultaneously with the end of Gentile sovereignty over Jerusalem the hardness in the hearts of Jews would begin to end.

Gentile sovereignty over Jerusalem ended with the six-day war in 1967. That was some 49 years ago. Even though some have denied that Jerusalem came totally under Jewish control in 1967, the evidence in support of that affirmation is incontrovertible. Almost half a century has elapsed since Jewish sovereignty over Jerusalem was established, and indeed, evidence that the hardness in Jewish hearts against the Gospel of Christ is beginning to wane is becoming more and more evident.

In both the Eastern and Western hemispheres, as the church marches toward these epochal triumphs, it at times will encounter opposition so fierce that it often will have to maintain a very low profile or even go into hiding. Such an unhappy reality is graphically depicted in the twelfth chapter of Revelation. In addition to external opposition, the fulfillment of the purpose of the church will also have been impeded by great internal controversies, like those fought out over the issues involved in the development of the institutions of monarchical and metropolitan bishops, a strife out of which the Papacy developed. In such times, it seemed the true church was nowhere to be found. But, according to the twelfth chapter of Revelation, the church was in a wilderness, seeking shelter from scorn, contempt and satanic attack. It was marginalized, ignored and hardly known, yet all the while pregnant with the formation of new converts, all the while simultaneously confronted by mortal danger.

A Special Note on History

We Christians need to realize that a proper, accurate and thorough understanding of history may, at some points, be extremely difficult to acquire. One of the ways God distinguishes himself from mankind is by claiming, "I am God, and there is none like me; declaring the end from the beginning." (Isaiah 46:9-10) While God is able to predict the end from the beginning, we mortals very frequently cannot declare the beginning even from the end. For example, it is very difficult

---

626 From JFB Commentary (e-Sword).

Appendix B

to precisely pinpoint the event with which either World War I or World War II started. In such a challenging environment we should especially appreciate the book of Revelation because it highlights the critical and important developments in history to which we should pay special attention.

One example of the difficulty of clearly understanding history comes from a scholar who devoted many years and awesome qualifications to narrating the history of The Thirty Years' War. He wrote, "The course of European diplomacy in the 1620s (and to a lesser extent in the 1630s) is littered with repudiated negotiations and unratified treaties. That is also why the history of the first decade of The Thirty Years' War ... is so impossibly complicated."[627]

Those complications were augmented by the scope and duration of that war. "Religious antagonism and political friction together produced The Thirty Years' War. It was not so much a single conflict in Germany as a series of conflicts, which ultimately involved nearly all Western Europe. At one time Sweden took a prominent part in the struggle under her heroic king, Gustavus Adolphus, who came to the aid of the Protestant princes against the Holy Roman Emperor."[628]

Another testimony to the difficulties one may encounter in getting a clear understanding of history is given by the great scholar Bernard Lewis who wrote, "There are many uncertainties in historical research and often a major achievement of research may be to raise doubt where there was certainty before. Uncertainty may be beneficial in that it invites further research and further thought. But uncertainty disguised as certainty is dangerous."[629]

The book of Revelation itself in 17:9 warns us that some historical developments are hard to understand. (See the comments on 17:9 under 5:4.) This reality is underscored by the relevant observation that, "historians can make their own contribution by reminding their readers of the complexity of all historical developments, and by pointing to the paths not taken, or forgotten."[630]

In spite of those difficulties, Christians have an advantage because of scriptural prophetic historical anchor points to which we can relate and by which we can, therefore, evaluate historical events and developments. Accordingly, we are kept from endorsing the erroneous view of those theologians, historians, philosophers and analysts who proclaim that we live in the post Christian era. Neither should we endorse the equally erroneous position of those who assert that the most significant event in history has already occurred, identified by one historian as the fall of the Soviet Union, and, who therefore, have concluded that we are at the end of history. In contrast, to cite one example, Christians are confident that we will have a very significant part in bringing the future victory to pass which is described in Revelation 7:9-10, which says, "After this I looked and there before me was a great multitude that no one could count, from every nation, tribe, people and language, standing before the throne and in front of the Lamb. They were wearing white robes and were holding palm branches in their hands. And they cried out in a loud voice: 'Salvation belongs to our God, who sits on the throne, and to the Lamb.'" (NIV) The role we twenty first-century Christians may play in bringing that great victory to pass will

---

627 Geoffrey Parker, The Thirty Years' War (New York: Military Heritage Press, 1987), p. 48.
628 Hutton Webster, World History, (Boston, D.C. Heath & Co. Publishers, 1921), p. 276.
629 Bernard Lewis, Notes On A Century: Reflections of a Middle East Historian, (New York: Viking, 2012), p. 143.
630 J. H. Elliott, History In the Making, (New Haven, Yale University Press, 2012), p. 79.

depend upon our grasping the scope of that task and our realistic commitment to achieving that triumph.

———

Appendix C

The Birth of the Muslim Empire

(See Map 7)

The Jewish scholar, S. D. Goitein, analyzing the rise of Islam, said "The hundred years' war of Muhammadan conquests were [years of] a great catastrophe for the countries affected. Millions of people were reduced to slavery and dragged from one part of the world to another. However, this great mixing of classes and races had also the beneficial effect that fresh minds were prepared for the new Arabic-speaking civilization of the Middle East."[631]

Goitein's "hundred years' war" gives only a view of Islam's opening years of devastating conquest. After Muhammad's death in 632 A.D., the first priority was achieving doctrinal, political and military unity in the Arabian Peninsula. During his ten-year rule in Medina, Muhammad had for the first time in recorded history unified Arabia. However, upon his death that unity evaporated into renewed tribalism and widespread return to other local loyalties. That defection from Islam was considered apostasy, and as such, was intolerable. From June 632 to July or August 633 A.D., war to suppress apostasy was waged with great brutality and ferocity under orders of the first Caliph, Abu Bakr. The Caliph gave command of the Muslim army to Khalid ibn al Waleed who proved to be one of Islam's greatest military leaders during the opening decades of the Muslim era. The War of Apostasy, the *Ridda* War, lasted about fourteen months. The no-holds-barred ferocity of that war comes clearly before us in the record of the vicious battle of Yemama. It was a battle against Musailama who was one of those deemed by Muhammad and his followers to be false prophets, working in opposition to and in defiance of Islam. The victor in the 14-month-long vicious war was clearly Abu Bakr and his army. Just as the victory was decisive, so were the consequences. "When the rebels were defeated by Khalid with great slaughter, the authority of Medina was much more firmly established than it ever had been in the days of Muhammad himself."[632]

Let us calculate the beginning of Islam's multi-continental conquest with the second battle of the Yarmuk[633] in 636 A.D. It was that battle which brought the whole eastern seaboard of the Mediterranean under Muslim control. If we limit the Muslim conquest to one hundred years from that date (636) it would exclude two highly consequential conflicts. First, in 750 A.D., the Battle of the Zab River, a tributary flowing from the northeast to the Tigris River, brought the Umayyad Caliphate to a violent and abrupt end and gave birth to the Abbasid Caliphate. One year later, in 751 A.D., the Battle of Talas gave dominance of all Central Asia to the Muslims.

---

[631] S.D. Goitein, Jews and Arabs, Their Contacts Through the Ages, (New York: Schocken Books, 1967), p. 151.
[632] John Bagot Glubb, The Great Arab Conquests, (London: Quartet Books, 1980), p. 124.

[633] The Yarmuk River is the major eastern tributary to the Jordan River. It flows through a very steep and precipitous gorge from the highlands of the Anti-Lebanon Mountains, now in western Jordan.

Revelation Verse by Verse

The first Woe (Revelation 9:1-11) embraces the birth and the first 150 years of the career and history of Islam. Many may wonder why that relatively brief period of 150 years is called a period of Woe. First of all, it deserves that title because it was a period of vast military conquest and occupation engulfing an enormous area. Consequently, myriads of people were killed and many others either had to capitulate by becoming Muslims or be plunged into acute and ongoing poverty, degradation and suffering.

By 712 A.D. Islam's thrust to the east, under the generalship of Muhammad bin Qasim, had triumphed all the way to the Indus River valley. That left all of Baluchistan, Sindh and the southern part of the Punjab, basically the southern half of what is today Pakistan, occupied by Islam's victorious Arab Army. That was a great blow to the Buddhist culture previously dominant in the Indus drainage basin all the way from the Himalayas to the Indian Ocean.

Prior to that eastern conquest, all of Sassanian Iran, including the area now called Afghanistan, and all of the Iranian plateau, up to the Zagros Mountains, its western border, fell to Islam as a consequence of the Battle of Nehawand in 642 A.D. The Tigris-Euphrates watershed had previously been conquered.

The Muslim victory at the Second Battle of the Yarmuk (636 A.D.) forced the Byzantines to pull their forces all the way north to the formidable barrier of the Taurus mountain range. Subsequently, that mountain range served as the boundary between Islamdom and Byzantium till the Muslim Turkish Army decimated the Byzantine Army at the Battle of Manzikart in 1071 A.D. As a result of that pivotal battle, all of Asia Minor, shortly thereafter, fell into the hands of Islamic Seljuk and Ottoman Turks who had previously begun to enthusiastically embrace Islam after the Battle of Talas in 751 A.D.

From Asia Minor the Ottoman Turks crossed the Dardanelles into the Greek Peninsula, often referred to as the Balkan Peninsula. Ironically, their crossing took place by the invitation of Byzantium! The Byzantines hoped the Turks would help them repel an invasion by the Avars and then return to Asia Minor, which they never did.

In 1389 the Serbs were subjected to Islamic hegemony as a consequence of the Battle of Kosovo, which took place on a battlefield which became known as The Field of Blackbirds because of the countless carrion birds which congregated there to strip the bones of the fallen Serbian soldiers. Next, the Hungarians, though they fought courageously at the Battle of Mohacs in 1526, were defeated and subjected to Muslim rule.

Only three years later, in 1529, the Muslim Ottomans were at the walls of Vienna. Their attack failed because the Saffavid Persians attacked the eastern border of the Ottoman Empire, requiring the Turkish troops at Vienna to rush in defense of their eastern border. However, in 1683, the Ottomans were again besieging Vienna in another unsuccessful attempt to break through Europe's last line of defense. That proved to be the highwater mark of Ottoman-Turkish-Muslim power in the west.

That Second Battle of the Yarmuk (636 A.D.), to which reference has already been made, not only gave all the eastern seaboard of the Mediterranean to the Muslims, but gained for them the entire area from the Taurus mountains in the north to the border of Egypt in the south.

Appendix C

Subsequently, Egypt was viciously and audaciously snatched from the Byzantine Empire by the Arab general Amr ibn al-Aasi in 658 A.D.

After the fall of Egypt, Muslim armies swept west through Berber North Africa, reaching the Atlantic in 681 A.D. Under the leadership of General Tariq in 712 A.D., all of Spain except a tiny mountainous enclave in the far northwest, basically the current Basque homeland, had been conquered. The famous mountain of Gibraltar is named after General Tariq. In Arabic it is called Jebel Tariq, meaning the mountain of Tariq. The English rendition reduced the Arabic to our familiar "Gibraltar."

By 732 A.D. the Muslim army based in Spain had rampaged across the Pyrenees Mountains to Tours, halfway through France. However, near Tours they were defeated by the army of Charles Martel and forced to pull back to the south side of the Pyrenees Mountain barrier.

In summary, by 712 A.D., like a monstrous leviathan, Islam held in its grasp the very extensive territory, stretching more than 5,000 miles, all the way from the Indus River in the east to the Spanish-Moroccan Atlantic seaboard in the west. Buddhism in what is now Pakistan and Afghanistan, Zoroastrianism in what is now Iran, and Christianity which had a major presence all the way from Afghanistan to and through North Africa to the Atlantic Ocean, lay in the grip of Islam. Both Buddhism and Zoroastrianism shortly vanished from those areas which fell under the governance of Islam. In contrast, the presence of Christianity continued on into the twenty-first century but has now been brought to the threshold of extinction by radical Islam in the Muslim Middle East.

By the time at which Islam reached the Atlantic, it not only had its own vibrant, very widespread economic community, but its own language and its own religion. Since the Germanic tribes, which earlier had infiltrated into Europe were quasi-Christian, they, their plundering of Rome notwithstanding, often sought to integrate with European culture. In stark contrast, the Muslims, with few exceptions, held the West, its culture, its language and its religion in utter contempt. Thus the "great Arab conquests were not only battle victories but also revolutionary repudiations of the Roman and Persian world orders."[634]

During the first century and a half of its history, Islam's dynamism enabled it to achieve world conquest far exceeding that of the Persians under Cyrus and Darius or that of the Greeks under Alexander the Great. That dynamism did not die with the overthrow of Islam's Umayyad caliphate in 750 A.D. Its doctrinally inspired, dominating missionary spirit continued to be very vibrant. That missionary impetus, combined with military power on the borders and with governmental power within the areas which had been conquered, imparted great resilience and kinetic energy to the Islamic movement.

Ongoing military expansion was both preceded and followed up by intense Muslim missionary activity. The Chinese Tang Dynasty's military expansion to the west had been decisively stopped and thrown back by the Muslim victory at a great battle on the Talas River in Kyrgyzstan in 751 A.D. The Chinese withdrew all the way back to the eastern slopes of the Pamir mountain range. What is today China's Xinjiang Province, subsequent to the Battle of Talas, was known for many years as Chinese Turkestan, reflecting the predominant ethnic makeup of the area. The pivotal

---
634 Charles Hill, *Trial of a Thousand Years*, Hoover Digest, 2011, No. 3, p. 51.

Battle of Talas exposed the previously Christianized Turks to the full force of both ideological and military Islam. The military ardor of Islam was magnetically attractive to the Turks whose martial exploits preceded the rise of Islam by centuries. The Christian Turks began to lose the power to expand evangelistically and soon lost all presence in the rising sea of Muslim Turks.

Islam's eventual defeat of and occupation of the Jewish Khazar kingdom exposed south-central Russia, the Caucasus region, to Muslim infiltration and expansion. Similarly, the defeat of the Nubians in battles to the south of the great rapids on the Nile River opened north-east Africa to Muslim domination. Islam continues to prevail in Sudan and all the way east to and including the Horn of Africa.

Islam also expanded into south-east Asia into the very extensive areas which, till the end of WWII, were known as the Indies (related to India). Those areas became known as the Indies because they had previously been dominated by Hinduism and Indian culture. "When Marco Polo was in Sumatra in 1293, he observed that the inhabitants were 'all savage idolaters, a very cruel and very evil people,' but he also saw a new development at Parlak in the north-east corner of the island where 'all the people used to worship idols, but by reason of the many Saracen[635] merchants who frequent there with their ships, they have converted them all to the abominable law of Muhammad.'"[636]

A movement with such a vast area under its control, and working under the guidance of the angel of the abyss, has generated such momentum that its impact will be felt for centuries. Doubtless, it will be one of the major contributors to the rise of the Woe which erupts during the oversight of the sixth trumpet angel.

---

[635] Tom Holland, drawing his information from the work of D. F. Graf and M. O'Conner, entitled, *The Origin of the Term Saracen and the Rawwafa Inscriptions*, informs us that, "It is telling that Roman authors, from the fourth century onwards, begin to use a new word to designate the Arabs, one that seems ultimately to have derived from *Shirkat*: 'Saracens.' Although the Romans themselves appear to have been wholly ignorant of the original meaning, and although the stereotype they had of the 'Saracens' remained the reassuringly traditional one, of nomads, bandits and savages, the use they made of the new name did nevertheless hint at a new and emerging order." Tom Holland, In the Shadow of the Sword: The Battle for Global Empire and the End of the Ancient World, (London: Little, Brown, 2012), p. 236.

[636] David Bentley-Taylor, The Weathercock's Reward, Christian Progress in Muslim Java, (London: Overseas Missionary Fellowship, 1967) p. 9.

Appendix D

The Fall or Collapse of Babylon

When it was discovered that a group of documents known as the Isidorian Decretals were forgeries, it was a great blow to the counterfeit church. "About the middle of the ninth century there arose, from the region around Rheims, the *Decretals of Isidore,* professing to have been compiled by one Isidore Mercator and to be a collection of decisions of councils and Popes from Clement of Rome late in the first or early in the second century to the eighth century. They included The Donation of Constantine. Some of the material was genuine, but much was spurious. The *Decretals* depicted the Popes as claiming supreme authority from the beginning, permitted all bishops to appeal directly to the Pope, thus limiting the authority of archbishops, and regarded bishops and Popes as free from secular control. In an uncritical age it [the group of documents known as the *Decretals*] was accepted as genuine and, although not the work of the Popes, was used to reinforce their claims."[637]

An especially dramatic step in the fall of the false church (mentioned earlier in the discussion under Revelation 12:15) came with the discovery that the document known as The Donation of Constantine was a forgery. "Probably written about the middle of the eighth century, it purported to be from early in the fourth century and [to have been written] by the Emperor Constantine. It described the latter's conversion, baptism, and miraculous healing from leprosy through Pope Sylvester I, and said that out of gratitude he was making over to the Pope and his successors his palace in Rome and 'the city of Rome and all the provinces, districts, and cities of Italy or of the Western regions.'"[638]

"The forged Donation much fired the imagination of later popes and clerical supporters of their power, who saw it as a manifesto for a world in which Christ's church would be able to rule all society."[639]

Another milestone in the fall of both the false church in the West and in the East took place as a result of the dramatic end of relationships between the church centered on Rome and that centered on Constantinople. "While both claimed to be heirs of the Roman Empire, the Holy Roman Empire and the Byzantine Empire had become clearly separate and the fiction that they were the Western and Eastern wings of the same realm was progressively more difficult to maintain. ... [Their separation became unmistakable and irreversible when] on July 16, 1054, the Papal legates dramatically laid on the altar of St. Sophia, as it stood ready for the Eucharist, a sentence of excommunication of the Patriarch and his supporters and left the cathedral, shaking the dust off their feet."[640] That rupture between the false churches of both East and West has

---

[637] Kenneth Scott Latourette, A History of Christianity, Vol. I, (New York: Harper & Row, Publishers, 1975), p. 342.
[638] Kenneth Scott Latourette, A History of Christianity, Vol. I, (New York: Harper & Row, Publishers, 1975), p. 341.
[639] Diarmaid MacCulloch, Christianity: The First Three Thousand Years, (New York: Viking, 2010), p. 351.
[640] Kenneth Scott Latourette, A History of Christianity, Vol. I, (New York: Harper & Row, Publishers, 1975), pp. 571-573.

come to be known by church historians as The Great Schism. The "Pope and [the] Oecumenical Patriarch did not declare the excommunication revoked for another nine hundred years after the events of 1054, and even now in many areas the reconciliation between Orthodoxy and Western Catholicism is distinctly shaky."[641]

Another epochal development in the fall of Babylon was marked by the work of Martin Luther. Luther's work was preceded by the landmark preparatory labors of Wyclif and Hus, to whom mention has been made in the discussion of "the wine of her fornication." (Revelation 14:8) "It was on October 31, 1517 … that Martin Luther nailed his notice to the church door at Whittenburg, announcing that he was prepared to defend, in open debate, ninety-five theses which claimed to establish the invalidity and illegality of indulgences. It would not have been a difficult task. The idea that a spiritual grace could be sold commercially for hard cash was obviously nonsense, and in recent times [that is, just before Luther nailed his theses on the church door] new and improved indulgences had come onto the market. It was now possible, for example, to acquire them in respect of sins not yet committed – to lay up, as it were, a credit balance of advance absolution; alternatively, indulgences could be bought on behalf of deceased relatives: the more money paid, the shorter their time in purgatory.

"By now the Church was teetering on the edge of an abyss, yet still [Pope] Leo failed to see that Luther's crusade was more than a 'monkish squabble.' The man was clearly an irritant; but Savonarola had been a good deal worse and was now almost forgotten. This tiresome German would doubtless go the same way. Meanwhile, in November 1518, the Pope published a bull: all who denied his right to grant and issue indulgences would be excommunicated. But no one in Germany took any notice. Reverence for the papacy, as Guicciardini lamented, 'had been utterly lost in the hearts of men.' Half-heartedly, Leo tried to enlist the help first of the General of the Augustinian Order and then of Luther's protector, the Elector Frederick III of Saxony, to bring the monk to order; but neither attempt was successful. Then in 1520 he published another bull, *Exsurge Domine*, condemning Luther on forty-one separate counts. This, Luther publicly burned – and was consequently excommunicated. On October 11, 1521, the pope bestowed the title Fidei Defensor – Defender of the Faith – on King Henry VIII of England, in recognition of his book *The Defense of the Seven Sacraments Against Martin Luther*."[642]

That the fall of Babylon is even yet not total, but is ongoing, becomes clear if we understand the nature, the origin and the power behind the perpetuation of that institution. As political Rome declined, it became unable to render many governmental functions. That opened an opportunity for the church, based on the city of Rome, to begin functioning in those vacated segments of civil life which had previously been cared for by the Roman civil government. The Roman church could easily step into that expanded role because by that time, "The Christian Church [had] modeled its structure on that of the Roman Empire. The dioceses mirrored the administrative divisions of [Emperor] Diocletian; bishops based in the chief cities, met in synod in the provincial capitals, and those from the great Metropolitan centers were accorded special dignity."[643]

---

641 Diarmaid MacCulloch, Christianity: The First Three Thousand Years, (New York, Viking, 2010), p. 374.
642 John Julius Norwich, Absolute Monarchs, A History of the Papacy, (New York: Random House, 2011), pp. 292-293.
643 Geoffrey Baraclough, The Times Atlas of World History, (Maplewood, NJ: Hammond, Inc., 1978), p. 93.

Appendix D

The mimicking of the Roman Empire by the Roman Catholic Church went much further. "Within three centuries, the Roman Church had transformed the administrative organization of the Roman Empire into an ecclesiastical system of bishoprics, dioceses, monasteries, colonies, garrisons, schools, libraries, administrative centers, envoys, representatives, courts of justice, and a criminal system of intricate laws all under the direct control of the pope. His Roman palace, the Lateran, became the new Senate. The new senators were the cardinals. The bishops who lived in Rome and the priests and deacons helped the pope administer this new *imperium*. This bureaucracy elected the head of the *imperium*, and they carried on the tradition from pope to pope."[644]

Thus, greatly modified Christianity "stepped onto the empty throne of the Roman Empire."[645] In doing so, it gained power, pomp and grandeur which it subsequently never wanted to forfeit. This is just one of the reasons the Roman Catholic Church even yet maintains "seventy-eight papal diplomatic missions around the globe."[646]

The move of the church based in Rome into its new function as a secular governing institution was a development based largely on the theology of Augustine, Bishop of Hippo. Augustine, by his persuasive theological dissertation, *The City of God*, laid the foundation for theological Babylon, the misbegotten concept in which the church wields secular power to coerce people into submission to its dictates. That Augustine fell into this grievous error, is also confirmed by his role in the Donatist controversy of justifying brutality in his effort to stamp out the very vigorous Donatist Movement.[647]

This glaring breach of the boundary which Jesus clearly demarcated between the church and civil government when he said "Render unto Caesar the things that are Caesar's and unto God the things that are God's," (Mark 12:17) was based on despicable motives and impulses. Those who dared to lead the church into violation of Jesus' teaching, were "petty men, motivated by greed for money and power."[648] They were filled with arrogance, jealousy, greed and worldly ambition.

A few decades after the founding of the church, a clear distinction began to be drawn between elders and bishops, even though at the church's beginning those two titles were both used for the occupants of the same office. (See Acts 20:17 and v. 28.) Subsequently, those who exclusively called themselves bishops to the exclusion of the lower category of church office holders, then known only as elders, sought for even higher distinction. That distinction came with the term Metropolitan Bishop, referring to bishops whose offices of authority were situated in the most important cities, the metropolises (the mother cities), such as Alexandria, Antioch, Caesarea, Constantinople and Rome. The Metropolitan Bishops saw themselves as archbishops, that is ruling bishops, superior even to other bishops serving in towns and cities of less economic, cultural or political significance.

---

644 Malachi Martin, The Decline and Fall of the Roman Church, (New York: G.P. Putnam's Sons, 1981), p. 105.
645 Malachi Martin, The Decline and Fall of the Roman Church, (New York: G.P. Putnam's Sons, 1981), p. 71.
646 Malachi Martin, The Decline and Fall of the Roman Church, (New York: G.P. Putnam's Sons, 1981), p. 292.
647 "By 412 Augustine had lost patience and he backed harsh new government measures against the Donatists. He even provided theological reasons for the repression: he pointed out to one of his Donatist friends that Jesus had told a parable in which a host had filled up places at his banquet with an order, 'compel them to come in.' That meant that a Christian government had the duty to support the Church by punishing heresy and schism, and the unwilling adherents which this produced might be the start of a living faith. This was a side of Augustine's teaching which had much appeal to Christian regimes for centuries to come." Diarmaid MacCulloch, Christianity: The First Three Thousand Years, (New York: Viking, 2010), p. 304.
648 Malachi Martin, The Decline and Fall of the Roman Church, (New York: G.P. Putnam's Sons, 1981), p. 56.

Their hunger for precedence stemmed from the most ignoble motives. Among them was the desire for adulation coming from common Christians who, from time to time, were obliged to appeal to the bishop for his intervention in some stressful and complicated issue. As the church moved from a congregational to a hierarchical organizational pattern, the governing political authorities saw that beguiling a Metropolitan Bishop by flattery or financial advantage was an effective method of eliciting the cooperation of the broad body of Christians to their political purposes. For example, among the benefits Constantine bestowed on the clergy was the use of "all the imperial facilities: roads, stations, convoys, guards, garrisons, lawyers, judges, courts, forts, public buildings [and] treasuries."[649] In the vacuum created by the decisive fall of Roman political power in 476, it was a small step for the Bishop of Rome, now sometimes called a pope, to step into the void and begin the exercise of outright political power.

---

[649] Malachi Martin, The Decline and Fall of the Roman Church, (New York: G.P. Putnam's Sons, 1981), p. 50.

Appendix E

Expanded Comments on Revelation 16:13
The Dragon, the Beast and the False Prophet Form a Coalition of Evil

I.   The evil forces represented by the dragon, the beast and the false prophet multiply their power through a subtle coalition.

    A.   The basis of their coalition:

First, there is a recognizable basis for the participation of Communism and Catholicism in the coalition, despite their seeming incompatibility. Their emerging coalition is seen, for example, in developments in Central and South America. In those countries, "...aligning many Latin American Catholic clergy on the side of the poor is a class battle against rich governments. Many clergy believe that revolution is the only option open to the Roman Catholic Church if it really wants to help the poor. It is clear that the 'Pope' wants the Third conference in Puebla to put a halt to the leftist-Marxist trend in the clergy."[650]

Currently there are 500 million Roman Catholics in Latin America. Even in 1979 when the number of Roman Catholics was only 300 million, there were some 150,000 <u>comunidades de base</u> (basic communities). A look at that phenomenon will give us insight into the emerging coalition between Catholicism and Communism in Latin America. For example, "...many supporters of the comunidades have enthusiastically adopted the language and goals of the 'theology of liberation', a peculiar blend of Marxian economic analysis and Gospel imperatives, best articulated by Peruvian Priest Gustavo Gutierrez in the early 1970s. Observes Volta Redonda Bishop Waldyr Calheiros de Novais: 'The comunidades are the theology of liberation put into practice.' ...Ultimately, the future of the comunidades could well depend less on their theology than on whether they can avoid the appearance of being merely adjuncts of Marxist revolution in the hemisphere."[651]

It has become clear that Pope Francis embraces the economic concepts enshrined in comunidades de base (basic communities). "During the 1970s, Francis, instead ['of ideologies which hide and defame reality'] embraced an Argentine derivation of liberation theology, which was known as the theology of the people. ... [He became] increasingly outspoken against politicians whom he thought did too little for the poor. ... Francis is not condemning capitalism in total, but he is criticizing the indifference it fosters toward the poor. ... Ken Hackett, the United States ambassador to the Holy See, argues that Francis' economic views have been wrongly simplified and scoffs at the suggestion that the pope is a socialist as a 'naive characterization.' ... [However,] inside the grandiose marble nave of St. Peter's Basilica ... the ritual, grandeur and continuity of the service – and the sheer weight of gold leaf and marble in

---

650 David Vaughn Elliott, <u>The Central American Call</u>, February 1979.
651 <u>Time</u>, May 7, 1979, p. 88.

the basilica – seemed to make a mockery of Francis' goal to create 'a poor church of the poor.'"[652]

Marxists see very clearly what the implications of liberation theology are. For example, the official Communist party of Zimbabwe, the Zimbabwe African National Union-Patriotic Front (ZANU) some time ago published a party document entitled "Society and the Church." In this document "ZANU admonishes the churches to follow the liberation theology model of Latin America and to turn to 'Marxism for a discovery of their true vision and true vocation.'

"Some observers wonder if ZANU, now that Zimbabwe is a one-party state, will extend the same control over the churches that it now exerts over the media and labor unions. The party has also set up youth brigades and people's militias."[653]

The coalition between Communism and Catholicism is also seen in church-state relationships in Russia. The Russian Orthodox Metropolitan Filaret of Kiev "… declares that the Soviet State is not an atheistic state. It consists of believers and non-believers." For example, Father Vladimir Shtepa of the Orthodox Church in the city of Oster (in the Ukraine) says, "The main principle of Christianity and Marxism is the same. Believers try to enter the kingdom of God, and Marxists strive for true Communism. The bright future for man and the kingdom of God – aren't they the same?"[654]

The emergence of the coalition between Catholicism and Communism took a major leap forward at the unprecedented summit meeting between Mr. Gorbachev and Pope John Paul II in the Vatican on December 1, 1989. It resulted in the Pope agreeing to "do his part to restrain the Uniates [i.e., the Ukrainian Uniate Catholic Church. The word Uniate implies a church which has united with the Vatican without accepting the Latin liturgy.] from pushing for a separate Ukrainian state …"[655] In reciprocity the Kremlin has given official recognition of the Roman Catholic Church in the U.S.S.R. and freedom for the church to function in that Communist state.

The development of the coalition is buttressed by philosophical accommodations. David Lyon, referring to the book by Peter Hebblethwaite, *The Christian - Marxist Dialogue and Beyond*, says the author "… notes the tendencies for 'Christians' to become more and more Marxist (especially in the liberation theologies and Christians for Socialism). 'Read the Gospels from a class point of view', say some. Hebblethwaite replies: 'Look at the world through these spectacles and it will soon begin to take on a Marxist shape.' Hebblethwaite concludes by noting Teilhard de Chardin's hope for a 'synthesis between a transformed Marxism and a renewed Christianity.'"[656] Though only a dozen people attended his funeral, Pierre Teilhard de Chardin (1881 - 1955) was a "… great Jesuit paleontologist whose works received widespread attention after his death."[657]

These empirical references to the coalition between Communism and Catholicism are in harmony with biblical statements. For example, in Revelation 16:13-14 the three entities are not

---

652 Jim Yardley, *A Humble Pope, Challenging the World*, The New York Times, September 19, 2015, p. A7.
653 World Pulse, April 29, 1988, p. 5.
654 Time, Dec. 3, 1979, p. 103.
655 Newsweek December 4, 1989, pp. 88-89.
656 The Evangelical Times, Surrey, England (April 1979).
657 Sydney E. Ahlstrom, A Religious History of the American People (New Haven: Yale University Press, 1974) p. 1014.

Appendix E

only on the stage of history simultaneously, motivated by the same demonic power, but are also engaged cooperatively in the same destructive activity, "to gather them (i.e., "the kings of the whole world") together unto the war of the great day of God."

In Ezekiel 38:13, the "young lions of Tarshish" seem to be allied with the Communist powers: Gog, Magog, Meshech, and Tubal. Though it is disputed, the best identity for Tarshish is Spain. To be more specific, the name should probably be identified with the ancient city of Tartessus which was located in what is now Spain, on the southwest coast, between Huelva and the Strait of Gibraltar. Tartessus was one of the most renowned mining and metal refining centers of the ancient world. If we connect that with the fact that the word Tarshish comes from a Phoenician word, "for 'mine' 'smeltery'; from the Babylonian word for 'smelting plant'; or 'refinery,'"[658] the identification, though not entirely certain, is very strong. If this conclusion is correct, then a notoriously Catholic country will ally itself with the Communist bloc in this predicted war.

There is also a developing coalition between Communism and Islam. We are all witnesses to the rapidly growing roster of Islamic countries cooperating with Russian Communism. This became particularly obvious during the Soviet invasion of Afghanistan. "At the end of 1979, the Soviet Union, which had already by a series of sponsored subversions obtained a dominant position in Afghanistan, decided that armed force was necessary to maintain it. The Soviet army and air force, therefore, embarked on a full-scale invasion of the country, in the course of which they violated an international boundary, arrested and executed the government of the country – which incidentally they themselves had no small share in installing – and resorted, in order to maintain themselves, to the most brutal repression of the Afghan civil population.

"One would have thought that this was a clear-enough case of aggression. The aggression was certainly clear, but the menace was clearer and the response accordingly subdued. At the United Nations General Assembly, at gatherings of Third World or non-aligned states, even at Islamic summit conferences, it proved impossible to muster general support for an explicit condemnation of Soviet aggression and occupation. Instead, the most that could be accomplished was mildly worded reproaches, avoiding such offensive terms as 'aggression' and 'occupation' and for the most part even avoiding the mention of the Soviet Union by name, but merely 'requesting' or 'urging' the removal of 'foreign troops' from Afghanistan. **Notable in the discussions leading to these resolutions was the active lobbying of Syria, South Yemen, the PLO, and sometimes also Algeria and Libya on behalf of the Soviet Union.**"[659] (Emphasis added.)

Superficially, nothing would seem to be more incompatible than the affinity, which has become obvious, between Islam and Communism. If one compares only the confession of faith which Muslims recite daily, "There is no God but God and Mohammed is his prophet," with the communist dictum that "Religion is the opiate of the people," it would seem that no coalition could be possible.

However, the growing list of Muslim nations cooperating with Communism belies the conclusion one is tempted to make from such a superficial analysis. Consider what has happened to the ideological alignment of Libya, the Yemen Republic, Syria, and Iraq. Also, keep in mind the growing list of Islamic countries which embrace some form of Islamic Socialism. That

---

[658] Madeleine S. Miller and J. Lane Miller, Harper's Bible Dictionary (New York: Harper & Brother, Publishers, 1961, p. 727.
[659] Bernard Lewis, Islam And The West, (New York: Oxford University Press, 1993), p. 149.

socialism may well be the forerunner of some variety of full-blown communism. Also, events in Iran which were engineered by the Muslim religious leaders have brought the Communist Tudeh political party much closer to the threshold of dominant power in the country.

The ideological affinity of Islamic Libya with communism became more clear as time passed. This was seen particularly in the late Mu'ammar al-Qaddafi's sense of affinity for Communist China. Some call this a Confucian-Islamist alliance. The most passionate call for such cooperation came from Mu'ammar al-"Qaddafi, who in March 1994 declared: 'The new world order means that Jews and Christians control Muslims and if they can, they will after that dominate Confucianism and other religions in India, China, and Japan. ... What the Christians and Jews are now saying: We were determined to crush Communism and the West must now crush Islam and Confucianism. Now we hope to see a confrontation between China that heads the Confucianist camp and America that heads the Christian crusader camp. We have no justifications but to be biased against the crusaders. We are standing with Confucianism, and by allying ourselves with it and fighting alongside it in one international front, we will eliminate our mutual opponent. We, we as Muslims, will support China in its struggle against our mutual enemy. ... We wish China victory.'"[660]

In a statement which is a bit more oblique than that of Mr. Qaddafi, yet just as significant and just as indicative of the developing coalition between Islam and Communism, "President Mohammad Khatami [president of Iran from 1997 - 2005], on the second day of a five-day visit to China, called for an 'Asian convergence' aimed at standing up to Western dominance and globalization. Mr. Khatami called China and Iran two of the world's greatest civilizations, saying they needed to work together to forge the world of tomorrow, 'hampering the domination of the world's unipolar system.'"[661]

The relationship of Pakistan and China also shows the proclivity of Muslim countries for close relationships with the leading communist country. In a discussion of Pakistan's experimental nuclear blasts in the Baluchistan desert on May 28, 1998, Michael Hirsh, Economics Correspondent for *Newsweek*, wrote: "Pakistani Prime Minister Nawaz Sharif, after all, made a point of thanking the Chinese for their technical help on the bomb."[662]

Hirsh's observation of the relationship of China and Pakistan in developing Pakistan's nuclear capability is fully confirmed by Jaswant Singh who at the time was Senior Advisor on Defense and Foreign Affairs to Indian Prime Minister Atal Bihari Vajpayee and was also a Member of Parliament for the Bharatiya Janata Party. He wrote: "India's May 1998 tests violated no international treaty obligations. ... Moreover, the forcing of an unconditional and indefinite extension of the NPT [Non Proliferation Treaty] on the international community made 1995 a watershed in the evolution of the South Asian situation. India was left with no option but to go in for overt nuclear weaponization. The Sino-Pakistani nuclear weapons collaboration – a flagrant violation of the NPT – made it obvious that the NPT regime had collapsed in India's neighborhood.."

---

660 Samuel P. Huntington, The Clash of Civilizations and the Remaking of World Order, (New York: Simon & Schuster, 1996), pp. 239-240.
661 *World Briefing*, The New York Times, June 24, 2000, p. A5.
662 Michael Hirsh, "The Great Technology Giveaway?," Foreign Affairs, September/October 1998, p. 2.

Appendix E

Singh went on to give more details on the China-Pakistan relationship. He wrote, "In 1997 more evidence surfaced on the proliferation [of cooperation] between China and Pakistan and about U.S. permissiveness on this issue. During Chinese President Jiang Zemin's recent visit to Washington, the United States insisted on a separate agreement with China on Chinese proliferation [of assistance] to Iran and Pakistan, which the Chinese signed instead of professing their innocence. Both the U.S. unease and the Chinese signature attest to Chinese proliferation as a threat to India's security. After all these assurances, China continued to pass missile technology and components to Pakistan. Despite this, the Clinton administration was still willing to certify that China was not proliferating or – even worse for India – that the United States was either unable or unwilling to restrain China. As the range of options for India narrowed, so, too, did the difficulties of taking corrective action."[663] In short, China supports Pakistan's military strength as a counterbalance to India's growing military strength.

If more corroboration is needed, Nancy Bernkopf Tucker, professor of history at Georgetown University and the Georgetown School of Foreign Service gives it. She wrote, "American intelligence sources contend that China sold missile, nuclear, and chemical technology to Pakistan and Iran before and after its 1992 pledges to adhere, informally, to the international Missile Technology Control Regime (MTCR) and officially, to the nuclear Non-Proliferation Treaty. Its assistance to Pakistan has been egregious and may well have been a prime factor in India's decision to carry out nuclear weapons tests in May, as well as in Pakistan's ability to respond in kind immediately."[664]

There are three specific areas of underlying compatibility that makes this proliferating phenomenon possible. These specific points of convergence, before I enumerate them, should be seen in a broad context in which many non-white peoples, Muslim and non-Muslim, cooperate with Communist Russia. Keep in mind that following World War II, and largely because of that war, scores of peoples who had lived under Western colonial domination became politically free. Thus, "since all these nations were breaking away from Western countries, ... their ally was [by that very fact] the Soviet Union. This most stagnant and static of societies, by almost any standard the least revolutionary of the major powers, was perceived, however inaccurately, as a broker of and sympathizer to revolution. Thus the successes of indigenous people were seen in the minds of Western policy makers as part of a giant game plan designed in Moscow."[665]

First is the concept of the classless society. "Muslims share the communist concept of a classless society. In pilgrimages to Mecca, for instance, every Muslim worshiper dresses identically. The richest oil baron wears the same simple white robe as an insignificant, poverty-stricken pilgrim. And as with the Communists, being classless for Muslims is largely a matter of appearance. Muslim princes and Soviet tyrants live more royally than the poor, who simply remain poor."[666]

Second is the ideal of the just society. "Muhammad envisioned an economic system tied to the laws of Islam, which he believed would create the just society. But since Islamic law is meant to

---

663 Jaswant Singh, "Against Nuclear Apartheid," Foreign Affairs, September/October 1998, pp. 44, 46.
664 Nancy Bernkopf Tucker, "A Precarious Balance: Clinton and China," Current History, September 1998, p. 247.
665 David Halberstan, The Next Century, (New York: William Morrow and Company, Inc., 1991), p. 56.
666 Ishak Ibraham, Black Gold and Holy War, (Nashville: Thomas Nelson publishers, 1983), p. 113.

be the law of the state, that leads to a level of political control matched only in Marxist societies and other dictatorships."[667]

Third and finally, there is the idea of the totally possessive society. "Islam is not just a religion, it is a whole way of life. It is often a tight institution involving social, legal and political loyalties. Even though the law of apostasy with disinheritance and death is not always carried out, nevertheless persecution can take many other forms."[668]

To summarize some of the pertinent unique societal features under Islam which give it compatibility with communism, I quote from an Afghan historian who succinctly states the case: "Though the Arabs failed in their attempts to conquer the whole of Afghanistan by force of arms, yet their missionary activities had better chance in this country. In the medley of religions, cults, beliefs and superstitions that existed in Afghanistan at this time, Islam infused a new life and worked a mighty change both in the social and cultural life of the people. The Islamic conception of one Supreme God, equality and brotherhood of man completely revolutionized the outlook of the Afghans. The new democratic faith, setting little value on birth, broke down all social barriers, and came as liberator of the depressed classes, who had been living under tyrannies of social and political inequities for centuries." [Underlining added.][669] It is, thus, the goal of Islam to address the solution of social inequities on a class basis which, among other factors, allies it with the professed goals of Communism.

Principles of feudalism seem to form one of the more fundamental bases of this remarkable cooperation. This becomes clear if we remember that feudalism is based on force as are Communism, Catholicism, and Islam. *Time* magazine well expressed this reality for Communism: "The glue of Soviet hegemony is force and intimidation, not shared purpose."[670]

Force as an operating principle in Islam grows out of its concept of the relationship between religion and politics. "To apply the notion of the division between church and state to Islam would run counter to the whole Islamic concept of religion and way of life; and, as we know, this has caused great difficulty in our time in Islamic countries that have tried to adopt Western, and therefore, at bottom, Western Christian, constitutions and social systems."[671] Historically, whenever and wherever religion and state form a single entity, orthodoxy (whatever from time-to-time that may be defined to be) has always been imposed by force.

The stance of New Testament Christianity is starkly different from the Islamic concept. "Unlike Islam and Judaism, Christianity started on its career in this world in conditions in which the members, and even the leaders, of the early Christian Church found themselves remote from politics. ... And the people among whom it originally spread were in walks of life in which they had little political power and no hand at all in military affairs."[672]

---

667 Ishak Ibrahim, Black Gold and Holy War, (Nashville: Thomas Nelson publishers, 1983), p. 113.
668 Christian Goforth, "The Entree of Media Through Stress Factors in Muslim Culture," Conference on Media in Islamic Culture Report, (Marseilles: International Christian Broadcasters and Evangelical Literature Overseas, 1974), p. 110.
669 Mohammed Ali, A Short History of Afghanistan (Kabul: by the author, 1970 Printed in Pakistan by the Punjab Educational Press, Lahore), p. 6.
670 Time, December 29, 1980.
671 Arnold Toynbee, Christianity Among the Religions of the World (New York: Charles Scribner's Sons, 1957), p. 12.
672 Arnold Toynbee, Christianity Among the Religions of the World (New York: Charles Scribner's Sons, 1957), p. 67.

Appendix E

The use of force by current ideologically based political systems to ensure conformity is a revival of an old concept in new and often more dangerous trappings. "In the twentieth century, fanaticism has come back into our life, animating, this time, not our ancestral Western Christianity but our twentieth-century [and on into the twenty-first century] Western ideologies, Nationalism and Communism. The ideologies claim that, whereas Christianity is old and outworn, they are new and have a mission to fulfill in our time. In truth, however, the ideologies are merely new variations on a very old religion, the religion of manworship, the worship of collective human power, which is an older religion than Christianity and was, in fact, in the Roman Empire, Christianity's earliest adversary. Communism is a worship of collective human power on a worldwide scale, and in this respect it is a modern counterpart of the worship of the goddess Rome and the god Caesar."[673]

The compulsive, oppressive and suppressive nature of feudalism as it operated in Catholic polity is stressed by Marion Gibbs. He says: "Over against the divided peasantry and the townsmen with their petty local interest and outlook, stood the greater landlords, the barons, prelates and the king. They were an organized political group, conscious of the community of their class interests.

"Idealizing and sanctioning the relationships of this divided society, more closely integrating it to the other feudal kingdoms of Christendom, was the power of organized religion — the Catholicism of the Roman Church. Its mystifying conception of justice cloaked all social contradictions and gave colour to all social activities. The Church itself as a landholding institution was an inseparable part of the economic, social, and political structure of feudal society.

"On the contrary, the significant development of the twelfth century was the depression of large numbers of peasants to serfdom or villeinage, and the emergence of a legal theory of their unfree status.

"Events in the thirteenth century, however, tell us that whether a villein did his labour services or paid cash for them, was a matter for his lord to decide. He was still a villein."[674]

Bolstering the role of Catholicism in the feudal organization of society was the power inherent in ownership of land. "Otto's successors, notably Henry II (Emp.: 1002-1024), Henry III (Emp.: 1035-1056) and Henry IV (Emp.: 1065-1106) carried on the tradition of meddling in church disputes and wasting strength in trans-alpine military interventions. The critical issue was control of the major episcopal and arch-episcopal posts, since the church was the wealthiest landowner."[675]

A coalescence similar to those developing between Catholicism and Communism and between Islam and Communism is also evident between Catholicism and Islam. Arne Rudvin, Bishop of the Church of Pakistan, has carefully documented this trend. He says, "The Second Vatican Council made much use of the concept of LOGOS SPERMATIKOS [The Scattered Word or the Sowing Word], and on this basis took up a definitely positive attitude

---

673 Arnold Toynbee, Christianity Among the Religions of the World (New York: Charles Scribner's Sons, 1957), p. 79.
674 Marion Gibbs, Feudal Order (New York: Henry Schuman 1953), pp. 8, 9, 90 - 91.
675 Franklin H. Littell, The Macmillan Atlas History of Christianity, (New York: Macmillan Co. Inc., 1976)., p. 31.

towards Islam. In the document on the missionary work of the Church we read: 'But whatever truth and grace are to be found among the nations, as a sort of secret presence of God, this activity frees from all taint of evil and restores to Christ its maker, who overthrows the devil's domain and wards off the manifold malice of vice. And so, whatever good is found to be sown in the hearts and minds of men, or in the rites and cultures peculiar to various peoples, is not lost. More than that it is healed, ennobled and perfected for the glory of God, the shame of the demon, and the bliss of men.'

"The document on the Church, de ecclesia, develops this line of thinking yet further and includes non-Christian religions within the history of salvation. We read: 'But the plan of salvation also includes those who acknowledge the Creator. In the first place among these are the Muslims who, professing to hold the faith of Abraham, along with us adore the one and merciful God, who on the Last Day will judge mankind. Nor is God Himself far distant from those who in shadows and images seek the unknown God, for it is he who gives to all men life and breath and every other gift (cf. Acts 17:25-28) and who as Saviour wills that all men be saved (cf. I Tim. 2:4). Those also can attain everlasting salvation who, through no fault of their own, do not know the Gospel of Christ or His Church, yet sincerely seek God, and moved by grace, strive by their deeds to do His will as it is known to them through the dictates of conscience.'"[676]

The cooperation between Catholicism and Islam which is developing rapidly in our time will be understandable if we keep the fundamental character of those two world religions clearly before us. That character is revealed by a glimpse of both systems in an earlier period. "At the beginning of the eighth century the world was polarized between the two super-powers representing Christianity and Islam. Their ideological doctrines were welded to power-politics pursued by the classical methods of propaganda, subversion and military conquest."[677]

We see the cooperation between Catholicism and Islam translated into political policy. For example, "Seeking to secure the rights of the Roman Catholic Church in a future Palestinian state, the Vatican signed an agreement today (February 15, 2000) with the Palestine Liberation Organization that would protect freedom of religion and the legal status of Christian churches. ... It was Mr. Arafat's ninth visit with the pope, who has never concealed his sympathy for the Palestinian cause. 'John Paul II once again expressed the solidarity of the Holy See for the Palestinian people, who are still waiting to see their legitimate aspirations realized,' the Vatican spokesman, Joaquin Navarro-Valls, said after the meeting. ... The wording in today's document on that issue reads like a reproach to Israel and a reaffirmation of the Vatican's support for a Palestinian state. It also seeks to bind Palestinian leaders to recognize the rights and privileges of the church."[678]

II. The Hyperactivity of Evil is frightening.

A. Iran is Now Trying to Heal Islam's Historic Rift.

The critical dates in the development of the Sunni/Shia rift in Islam:

---

[676] Arne Rudvin, "The Gospel and Islam: What Sort of Dialogue is Possible?," Al-Mushir, volume XXI, (Autumn 1979, No. 3 & 4), p. 110.
[677] Arthur Koestler, The Thirteenth Tribe (New York: Random House, 1976), p. 58.
[678] Alessandra Stanley, Vatican and P.L.O. Sign Pact Guaranteeing Church's Rights, The New York Times, February 16, 2000, p. A12.

Appendix E

656 **Caliph Uthman [Othman], Islam's third Caliph, was murdered by Arab troops.** This led to a power struggle in Islam.

656 **Ali ibn Talib becomes Islam's fourth Caliph.** "Ali [was] one of the most respected of all Muslims. He was the son of Muhammad's uncle, Abu Talib, who had raised the Prophet, and the husband of Muhammad's daughter Fatima, who bore him two sons."[679]

Contention over Ali's appointment as fourth caliph led to the Battle of Siffeen, the first civil war in Islam. "One of the chief complaints against [his immediate predecessor] Othman [Uthman] had been to the effect that all the provincial governors chosen by him had been his near relatives from [the] Beni Umaiya [tribe]. But Ali was from Beni Hashim. He could not have been accused of nepotism if he had left Othman's governors in office, at least for a time. Instead of doing so, however, he immediately dismissed them all. Muawiya [governor of Damascus], however, refused to resign his post."[680]

657 "Ali entered Kufa [in Iraq] in January 657, seven months after the murder of Othman, and thereafter made the city his capital."[681]

657 **The Battle of Siffeen** (July) was the first civil war in Islam. It was fought between the forces of Caliph Ali and those of Muawiya, governor of Damascus. (Siffeen was located a little north of Ragga [Raggah/Rakka] which is on the west bank of the Euphrates near the confluence of the Balikh River.) On his accession to the caliphate, Ali ordered all regional governors to submit their resignations. "The governor of Syria, however, replied that he would tender his allegiance to Ali as soon as the murderers of Othman had been punished. Seeing that further negotiation was useless, Ali left Kufa [his capital] at the head of 50,000 men. He moved up the Tigris from Medain to Mosul and then, turning west by Sinjar, arrived at Raqqa on the Euphrates. Crossing the river, he moved up on the west bank. A little way above Raqqa, he met the Syrian army led by Muawiya at Siffeen."[682]

Muawiya had objected to Ali holding the office of caliph because he had refused to seek and prosecute the murderers of Caliph Othman, Islam's third caliph and Ali's immediate predecessor. Othman had appointed Muawiya, his relative, to be governor of Damascus.

Both sides concluded that the only way to resolve the stalemate and determine who would become the next reigning caliph was to resort to war. During the ensuing battle, the Battle of Siffeen, the forces of Ali were clearly winning which led Muawiya to call for a decision by arbitration based on the Koran.[683] Ali accepted the proposal and by doing so forever lost the momentum of battle and the opportunity for a decisive military decision in his favor. That Ali accepted Muawiya's ruse so dismayed some 12,000 of his troops that they defected from Ali's army, becoming the nucleus of the Kharijite [Seceder] Movement. They "formed an independent

---

679 Desmond Stewart, Early Islam, (New York: Time Incorporated, 1967), p.59.
680 John Bagot Glubb, The Empire of the Arabs, (London: Hodder & Stoughton, 1963), p. 34.
681 John Bagot Glubb, The Great Arab Conquests, (Englewood Cliffs, NJ: Prentice-Hall Inc., 1963), p. 323.
682 John Bagot Glubb, The Great Arab Conquests, (Englewood Cliffs, NJ: Prentice-Hall Inc., 1963), p. 324.
683 Most probably, the Koran in its final rendition, did not exist at this early date. However, "that does not mean, of course, that a proto-Qur'an did not exist in some form or another, prior to that point." Andrew Rippin, Forward, In John Wansbrough Quranic Studies, (Amhurst, New York: Promethius Books, 2004) p. xvii.

community in northern Arabia. In 658 A.D. most of them were killed and the remnants dispersed."[684]

658   **Founding of Umayyad Caliphate.** Following the Battle of Siffeen, Muawiya annexed Egypt and declared himself Caliph. He ruled Syria, Palestine and Egypt from Damascus. Till his murder, Ali ruled Iraq and Persia from Kufa. Thus, Islam was divided, having two opposing caliphs.

661   **Ali was murdered** by Abdul Rahman ibn Muljam, a Kharijite. This left Muawiya to be the sole Caliph.

680   **Upon the death of Muawiya** (April), **Yazid,** Muawiya's unworthy son, became Caliph in Damascus.

680   **Hussain** (Ali's son), after his father was murdered, became rival caliph by invitation of the people of Iraq. He made the 800 mile trip from Mecca to Kufa in August or September.

680   **Hussain and his family were surrounded by cavalry near Karbala.** (Oct. 2, first day of the Arabic month of Muharram) They were forbidden and prevented from getting water from the nearby Euphrates River.

680   **Hussain proposed three life-saving alternatives to Ubaidullah:** (Oct. 4) (1) Return to Medina, (2) Go to Damascus to be judged by Yazid, or (3) Fight infidels on some distant border. All these alternative suggestions were flatly refused.

680   **Hussain and his companions were decapitated and their bodies mutilated.** (Oct. 10) Their heads were sent to Yazid in Damascus. Yazid touched the mouth of Hussain with his staff. "An old man at the court cried out, 'Blasphemy! I have seen the Prophet kiss those very lips.' It was a tragic day for Islam. The believers were irrevocably split, creating a schism that has continued to haunt the Moslem world through the centuries."[685] That was the beginning of the Shia movement, the Shi-at Ali, meaning the partisans of Ali.

Every year the Shiites have "a period [in the month of Muharram] of public mourning that commemorates the killing of Imam Hussain, the Prophet Muhammad's grandson, during a battle 1,300 years ago in Karbala, Iraq. That military defeat solidified a split between what became the two main branches of Islam, the Shiite and the Sunni.

"Now Iran, the world's only Shiite Islamic government, is reaching across the divide, hoping to unite Arab Muslims, the vast majority of whom are Sunni, and draw them beneath an overarching banner of Islam to fight common enemies in Israel and the West. …

"As Iran's leadership pursues an aggressive, confrontational foreign policy, it is effectively trying to become a regional superpower seeking to fill the void left by the collapse of Arab nationalism and by the absence of any one dominant nation. While the United States and Europe hope that

---

684 Carlton S. Coon, Caravan: The Story of The Middle East, (New York: Henry Holt and Company, 1956), p. 120.
685 Thomas J. Abercrombie, "Early split still divides Moslem world," Seattle Times, Sunday, May 27, 1979, p. H10.

Appendix E

the United Nations Security Council will help tame Iran, officials here [in Tehran, Iran] see such outside pressure as adding to their bona fides among Arab Muslims."[686]

The persistent centuries-old Sunni-Shia factional divide may be temporarily pushed aside to achieve a goal common to both factions. "On the subject of the need to overthrow the existing world order, Islamists on both sides – Sunni and Shia – have been in general agreement. However intense the Sunni-Shia doctrinal divide erupting across the Middle East in the early twenty-first century, Sayyid Qutb's views were essentially identical to those put forward by Iran's political ayatollahs. Qutb's premise that Islam would reorder and eventually dominate the world struck a chord with the men who recast Iran into the front of religious revolution. Qutb's works circulate widely in Iran, some personally translated by Ayatollah Ali Khamenei."[687]

A new power alignment, one clearly predicted to arise by the great Jewish prophet Ezekiel (See chapters 38 and 39.), is clearly developing, a development to which America's leaders seem unaware or indifferent. The Tehran-Moscow-Beijing triumvirate is aligning itself to dominate the world militarily, economically, philosophically and politically. By destroying Sunni Islamic military/political power in Iraq (by the Bush administration's war against Saddam Hussein's Iraq), followed by the decision of the Obama administration to pull American forces totally out of Iraq, America has opened the way for Iranian-Shia power, with Moscow's blatant assistance, to expand all the way to the Mediterranean.[688] U.S. negotiators are now offering Iran military assistance to defeat ISIS, providing Iran will not continue its head-long development of atomic weapons. The defeat of ISIS will put Iranian forces, along with their allies, in position to attempt the destruction of Israel. It is just such a war which Ezekiel clearly prophesied would occur.

While America's leadership has been slow or remiss in seeing the trend of developments involving the Muslim world, Iran's supreme leader, Ayatollah Ali Khamenei, has manifested deep understanding of current events. He said, "Today what lies in front of our eyes and cannot be denied by any informed and intelligent individual is that the world of Islam has now emerged out of the sidelines of social and political equations of the world, that it has found a prominent and outstanding position at the center of decisive global events, and that it offers a fresh outlook on life, politics, government and social developments."[689]

B.   Evil works in cycles. This is indicated by the words "bound" and "loosed" in Revelation 20:1-3. In current history we are presently beholding the hyperactivity of three of Satan's agencies. Additionally, general wickedness (for example, that seen in the revolution in sexual norms), not necessarily or directly connected with either Communism, Catholicism or Islam, is also obviously hyperactive. Our Scripture pictures the three anti-Christian entities at a period of expansion and aggressive activity. This means that Communism, Catholicism and Islam are in a period of hyperactivity.

However, in recent times Communism has suffered a number of serious setbacks: The Sino-Soviet rift of 1963, the emergence of the autonomy of Euro-Communism, the Vietnam-Cambodia War, the China-Vietnam War. Expressed in another way, it has been pointed out that,

---
686 Michael Slackman, *Iran the Great Unifier? The Arab World is Wary*, The New York Times Week in Review, February 5, 2006, p. 3.
687 Henry Kissinger, World Order, (New York: Penguin Press, 2014), p. 155.
688 Russia has openly and continuously supported the Bashar al-Assad regime with military supplies delivered through the Syrian Mediterranean port of Tartus.
689 Henry Kissinger, World Order, (New York: Penguin Press, 2014), p. 146.

"Indeed, states on the fringe of the Soviet orbit have already slipped away. Albania, Yugoslavia, and more significantly, China, were all once part of the Soviet system and are now distinctly separate."[690]

The most serious setback of all was the dissolution of the Soviet Union itself. "The last great world empire broke up in 1991. On December 25 President Mikhail Gorbachev, having become a leader without a country, announced his immediate resignation. A few minutes later the Soviet hammer and sickle flying over the Kremlin was lowered and replaced by the flag of Russia."[691]

These events have served to make the West less cautious, to cause it to lower its guard. The dramatic resurgence of unified Communism, when it occurs, as it most probably will, shall, then, only be more threatening. We may be witnessing the beginning of Russian Communist resurgence with the beginning of the Putin presidency.

One can comprehend the power of a newly unified communist block, encompassing essentially the territory of the former Soviet Union, if he reviews their achievements before the breakup of the Soviet Union. Let us, then, briefly review their significant gains, especially strategic vis-a-vis philosophical gains. Since Communism is committed to the use of force, it is such gains which really count.

Former President Richard Nixon gave valuable insight and perspective. He said, "The Third World War began before the Second World War ended. While the United States demobilized its armies and the other major allies began to rebuild their countries, the Soviet Union embarked on a drive for brazen imperial conquest. In less than five years, Moscow annexed Latvia, Lithuania, Estonia, and parts of Finland and Japan, imposed communist puppet governments on the peoples of Poland, Czechoslovakia, Hungary, Romania, Bulgaria, and Northern Korea, and made unsuccessful attempts to grab Greece, Turkey, and parts of Iran. Over the next thirty years, the Kremlin created satellite states in East Germany, Cuba, Vietnam, Cambodia, Laos, Angola, Mozambique, Ethiopia, Yemen, Afghanistan, and Nicaragua. Without ever issuing a formal declaration, the Kremlin has been at war against the free world for over forty years."[692] While many of these gains have been partially or completely forfeited due to the collapse of the Soviet Union, they show what such a united force may do in the future.

Catholicism is prospering. Notwithstanding the financial troubles of the Vatican, the hierarchy recently has been able to show its power by reaffirming and reimposing the practice of celibacy on the clergy. This should inform us afresh about who is animating the Roman Catholic system. Please see I Timothy 4:1-3 and Hebrews 13:4.

Pope John Paul negotiated a tremendous victory in his meeting with Mr. Gorbachev on December 1, 1989. Out of that meeting the Kremlin gave official recognition of the Roman Catholic Church in the U.S.S.R. and freedom for the church to function in that communist state. In addition we have seen the power of the Catholic system in Mexico and in Poland. These are indicative of widespread gains made under the charismatic leadership of Pope John Paul and now by every move under the dynamic inspiration of Pope Francis.

---

690 James Dale Davidson and Sir William Rees-Mogg, Blood in the Streets, (New York: Summit Books, 1987), p. 144.
691 1992 Britannica Book of the Year, Daphne Daume, ed., (Chicago: Encyclopaedia Britannica, Inc., 1992), p. 443.
692 Richard Nixon, 1999 Victory Without War, (New York: Simon and Schuster, 1988), p. 26.

Appendix E

Islam also is in a period of revival. From Mindanao to Morocco Islam is reasserting itself.

It is reasserting itself economically through the use of oil money. Though the Asian economic depression has exacerbated an oil glut driving prices down, this is almost certainly a temporary phenomenon.

It is reasserting itself politically through nationalism and Islamic socialism.

It is reasserting itself religiously through reimposing Nizam-e-Mustafa, that is, the polity of Mohammed. This is to be achieved through the imposition of Shari'a, the repressive medieval Muslim law code. Afghanistan gives us an example of what this can mean if we look at the country since the Taliban have come to power.

Islam is reasserting itself evangelistically by reaching into new areas. In North America there is not only an Islamic center in Washington D.C., but also one in Eugene and another in Corvallis, Oregon and others in many cities and towns in between. There are now more Muslims in America than Methodists. Islam is also violently encroaching into the northern areas of Christian Africa. This is seen especially in northern Nigeria where Christian institutions are under attack by Boko Haram. Islam is also beginning to use the mass media extensively as well as sending greater numbers of missionaries to reach out with its message.

Appendix F

The Christology of Islam

Note: Unless otherwise indicated, all quotations from the Koran are from <u>The Glorious Koran, An Explanatory Translation</u> by Marmaduke Pickthall.

The Christology of the Koran may be summarized by fifteen Koranic statements about Jesus, eleven of which are in harmony with the biblical account, while four are not. The source of the harmonious statements may well have been God directing Muhammad's utterances as he did Balaam's when he "put a word in Balaam's mouth." (Numbers 23:5)

Though the Koran affirms eleven crucial positive truths about Jesus, unfortunately the broad body of Muslims, the *umma*, lives in total ignorance of the fundamental import of these remarkable, biblically-true statements. When Muslims truly understand the meaning of these statements, doubtless many will submit their lives to Christ! However, any Muslim who comes to a proper and true understanding of these statements about Jesus will have to do so in the face of resolute, devious and subtle efforts by Islamic propagandists to distort the facts.

Miracle Worker

<u>The first Koranic statement</u> about Jesus which conforms to the biblical account asserts that he performed miracles.[693] Miracles constitute one way in which God lets us know that a given development is a divine initiative or a message has divine approval. Surah 2:87 tells us, "We gave Jesus the son of Mary Clear (Signs) and strengthened him with the Holy Spirit. ..." (Yusuf Ali Trans.)

This affirmation that Jesus performed miracles (signs), is corroborated in Surah 2:253 which tells us, "Those apostles we endowed with gifts, some above others: To one of them Allah spoke; others he raised to degrees (of honor); To Israel Jesus the son of Mary We gave Clear (Signs), and strengthened him with the Holy Spirit. ..." (Yusuf Ali, Trans.)

The Koran's account focuses on three of the most significant signs or miracles Jesus performed. It says, "by My permission [1] thou didst heal him who was born blind [2] and the leper by My permission; [3] and how thou didst raise the dead, by My permission." (Surah 5:110)

The Koranic emphasis that Jesus worked miracles is in harmony with the Gospel statement in John 20:30-31. There, John recorded that "Many other signs therefore did Jesus in the presence of the disciples, which are not written in this book: but these are written, that ye may believe that Jesus is the Christ, the Son of God; and that believing ye may have life in his name."[694]

---

[693] Miracles are also called signs, wonders and powers. All of these designations point to the same phenomenon. See Hebrews 2:3-4.
[694] See also Hebrews 2:3-4.

Some of Muhammad's contemporaries cast doubt on the validity of his message because he performed no miracles. In Surah 13:7 the Koran has preserved both those skeptics' arguments and Muhammad's rebuttal. It tells us, "Those who disbelieve say: If only some portent were sent down upon him from his Lord!" The first answer to this objection was given in a revelation regarding Muhammad. It said, "Thou art a warner only, and for every folk a guide." In a second rebuttal, Muhammad asserted that "this Qur'an is not such as ever could be invented in despite of Allah; but it is a confirmation of that which was before and an exposition of that which is decreed for mankind – Therein is no doubt – from the Lord of the worlds. Or say they: He hath invented it? Say: Then bring a Surah like unto it, and call (for help) on all ye can besides Allah, if ye are truthful." (Surah 10:38-39) (See also Surah 81:19-21)

Strengthened by God's Spirit

The second Koranic statement about Jesus which is in harmony with the biblical account is that God strengthened him by the Holy Spirit. This comes from the two Koranic references cited previously, that is, 2:87 and 2:253, both of which assert that God "strengthened him with the Holy Spirit." In these two references from the Koran, please note the implicit Trinitarian connotation, showing God, Christ and the Holy Spirit working together.

These Koranic affirmations are in harmony with the Gospel record given by Luke which tells us, "When the devil had completed every temptation, he departed from him for a season. And Jesus returned **in the power of the Spirit** into Galilee." (Luke 4:13-14) The biblical account also tells us that "God anointed him with the Holy Spirit and with power." Consequently, he "went about doing good and healing all that were oppressed of the devil; for God was with him." (Acts 10:38)

"God anointed him [Jesus] with the Holy Spirit and with power" at his baptism. On that occasion, when he came up "out of the water, he saw the heavens rent asunder, and the Spirit as a dove descending upon him: and a voice came out of the heavens, Thou art my beloved Son, in thee I am well pleased." (Mark 1:10-11)

Union With God's Spirit

The third Koranic assertion about Jesus which is compatible with the New Testament account is that he is a spirit from God. Surah 4:171 tells us, "The Messiah, Jesus son of Mary, was only a messenger of Allah, and His word which He conveyed unto Mary, and **a Spirit from Him.**"

The Koranic statement that Jesus is "a Spirit from Him" is in harmony with a New Testament affirmation about Jesus to which Christians have given scant attention. Through inspiration, the apostle Paul said, "Now **the Lord is the Spirit**, and where the Spirit of the Lord is, there is freedom." (II Corinthians 3:17 NIV) The expression "the Lord is the Spirit" conveys the same truth expressed in the phrase "the Spirit of life in Christ Jesus." (Romans 8:2)

Though not recognized by Muslims, this Koranic passage clearly expresses the Trinitarian idea of the unity of God. Here, God ("Allah"), Christ ("Jesus son of Mary") and the Holy Spirit ("a Spirit from Him") work together as one deity. This plurality in unity in Koranic theology is also clearly seen in the use of the plural pronouns "we" and "us" in reference to God. For example, in reference to Jesus, the Koran quotes God as saying, "We may make of him a revelation for

Appendix F

mankind and a mercy from Us." (Surah 19:21) It reminds us of the affirmation of the Trinity in Isaiah 48:16.

The Messiah

<u>In the fourth place</u>, in harmony with the biblical account, the Koran repeatedly calls Jesus the Messiah! For instance, in Surah 3:45 we read, "O Mary! Lo! Allah giveth thee glad tidings of a word from **Him, whose name is the Messiah, Jesus, son of Mary,** illustrious in the world and the Hereafter, and one of those brought near (unto Allah)." The other references in the Koran to Jesus as the Messiah are: Surah 4:157, 4:171-172, 5:19, 5:72, 5:75 and 9:30-31.

Whether Muhammad had any true understanding of what the title "Messiah" means or not, it is completely certain that almost no present-day Muslim understands the significance of this term. However, Christians should certainly know that the title "Messiah" means The Anointed One. The Old Testament term in Hebrew is "Messiah," (see Daniel 9:24-25), while the New Testament translation is rendered by the Greek word, "Christ." As Israel's prophets, priests and kings were anointed with special oil to set them apart for the work of their respective offices,[695] accordingly, Acts 10:38 records that "God anointed him [i.e., Jesus] with the Holy Spirit and with power: who went about doing good, and healing all that were oppressed of the devil; for God was with him." By anointing Jesus, God honored him by making him the occupant of the three offices of Prophet, Priest and King. (See also Hebrews 1:9.)

The New Testament account of Jesus being anointed by God is a fulfillment of a prophecy by Isaiah who ministered from 740 to 681 B.C. Looking forward to the work of Christ, he said, "The Spirit of the Sovereign LORD is on me, because the LORD has anointed me to preach good news to the poor. He has sent me to bind up the brokenhearted, to proclaim freedom for the captives and release from darkness for the prisoners, to proclaim the year of the LORD's favor and the day of vengeance of our God, to comfort all who mourn, and provide for those who grieve in Zion – to bestow on them a crown of beauty instead of ashes, the oil of gladness instead of mourning, and a garment of praise instead of a spirit of despair. They will be called oaks of righteousness, a planting of the LORD for the display of his splendor." (Isaiah 61:1-3 NIV) This is the very scripture which Jesus used when he preached at Nazareth. On that occasion he clearly identified himself as the one to whom the prophecy pointed. (See Luke 4:16ff.)

The Righteous One

<u>The fifth Koranic affirmation</u> about Jesus, which is in conformity with the biblical account, is that he was righteous. This assertion is made in two Surahs. First, Surah 3:46 says, "He will speak unto mankind in his cradle and in his manhood, and **he is of the righteous**." This Koranic declaration of Jesus' righteousness is again emphasized when, according to the Koran, the angel said to Mary, "I am only a messenger of the Lord, that I may bestow on thee a **faultless son**." (Surah 19:19)

In Christian theology, it is clear that Christ's sinlessness was utterly essential to his being man's Saviour. These Koranic statements of the righteousness and faultlessness of Jesus are in harmony with repeated affirmations in the New Testament about Jesus' righteousness. There he is called,

---
[695] For priests, see Exodus 40:13; for kings and prophets, see I Kings 19:15-16.

Revelation Verse by Verse

"Him who knew no sin." (II Corinthians 5:21) It is affirmed that in all points, he was "tempted like as we are, yet without sin." (Hebrews 4:15) Further it is stated that he was "holy, guileless [without deceit], undefiled, separated from sinners." (Hebrews 7:26) He "did not sin, neither was guile found in his mouth." (I Peter 2:22) He was "manifested to take away sins; and in him is no sin." (I John 3:5) His sinlessness made it possible for him to become "sin on our behalf; that we might become the righteousness of God in him." (II Corinthians 5:21)

In stark contrast to the sinlessness of Jesus, the Koran emphasizes the sin of Muhammad two times. First, he is ordered to pray for the forgiveness of his sin. Thus Surah 47:19 says, "So know (O Mohammad) that there is no god save Allah, and ask forgiveness for thy sin and for believing men and for believing women." Secondly, the sinfulness of Muhammad is also confirmed in Surah 48:1-2 in which Muhammad is told, "Lo! We have given thee (O Mohammad) a signal victory, that Allah may forgive thee of thy sin that which is past and that which is to come, and may perfect His favour unto thee, and may guide thee on a right path."

The Word of God

Sixth in the remarkable series of Koranic statements which point to the utterly unique role of Jesus is one which tells us that Jesus is the Word of God. The Koran says that Jesus is, "a messenger of Allah, and **His word** which He conveyed unto Mary." (Surah 4:171) Also, the Koran calls Christ, "a word from him." (Surah 3:45)

Everyone with biblical literacy surely can relate this statement to the well-known passages about Jesus in John 1:1 and 1:14. In those verses the inseparably intimate relationship of Christ and God is revealed by Christ being called the Word of God. Their inseparable and unitary relationship is seen in the fact that we cannot impugn the word of an individual without impugning the individual himself, so one cannot diminish the stature of Christ, the Word of God, without diminishing the person of God.

The Second Adam

The seventh Koranic assertion about Jesus which is in harmony with the biblical account is, Jesus is like Adam! The Koran says, "Lo! The likeness of Jesus with Allah is as the likeness of Adam." (Surah 3:59) This duplicates the biblical testimony that, "The first man Adam became a living soul. The last Adam became a life-giving spirit." (I Corinthians 15:45) The biblical account also affirms that, "death reigned from Adam until Moses, even over them that had not sinned after the likeness of Adam's transgression, who is a figure of him who was to come." (Romans 5:14)

Muhammad's acknowledgment that Jesus is as Adam came from an intense dialogue between him and a delegation of Christians from Najran. About eight years after Muhammad's *Hijra*, also spelled *Hegira*, (the Arabic term for Muhammad's flight from Mecca to Medina in 622 A.D., the event which marks the beginning of the Muslim Era) the church at Najran sent a delegation of leading Christians to Medina to meet Muhammad. The members of that delegation seemed to have had two objectives. First, they hoped to win Muhammad for Christ. But, should their attempt fail, they wanted to negotiate a treaty, pact or covenant with Muhammad which would

Appendix F

guarantee freedom for the church, at least for the church at Najran in the southwest corner of the Arabian Peninsula, to continue its existence.

Some sixty members of the huge church in Najran[696] formed the delegation which made the arduous journey from Najran to Medina to make their appeal to Muhammad. Two leaders from that delegation were allowed to personally meet Muhammad to present their case before him.

"When the two divines spoke to him [Muhammad] the apostle said to them, 'Submit yourselves.' [The word 'Islam' means submission, thus Muhammad was ordering them to become Muslims.] They said, 'We have submitted.' He said: 'You have not submitted, so submit.' They said, 'Nay, but we submitted before you.' [They meant we have submitted to God.] He said, 'You lie. Your assertion that God has a son, your worship of the cross, and your eating pork hold you back from submission.' They said, 'But who is his father, Muhammad?' The apostle was silent and did not answer them. So God sent down concerning their words and their incoherence the beginning of the sura of the Family of Imran ..."[697]

When the two delegates said to Muhammad, "Nay, but we submitted before you." it was because the word Muslim, meaning "one who has submitted." It was a name which the Christians in Najran had used to define themselves long before their meeting with Muhammad. By using that name they meant to affirm that they had submitted to God through Christ. Muhammad had plagiarized the name for his budding movement and by the time the men from Najran were visiting Muhammad the name had been infused with the meaning of submitting to Muhammad and his doctrine. Of course, the delegates from Najran had not and would not submit in that sense.[698]

When the Christians asked, "But who is his father, Muhammad?," they confronted Muhammad with the central truth of the gospel, the identity of Christ, the true Christology! Muhammad could not answer their inquiry. But that night he had a vision which is recorded in the 59th verse of the third Surah of the Koran. It says, "Lo! the likeness of Jesus with Allah is as the likeness of Adam. He created him of dust, then He said unto him: Be! and he is."[699] Though this statement in no way subverts the affirmation that Jesus is the Son of God, still, because of it, Muhammad felt exonerated in his refusal to submit to Christ.

Though Muhammad had little or no formal education, he was a highly intelligent man. He must have realized at least some of the implications of the parallel which he had drawn between Adam and Christ. **First**, just as Adam was the source of life for the whole human race, so Christ in an even more significant sense must also be the source for universal life. **Second**, he must have realized that as Adam is related to all men, so Christ is the only truly universal messenger from God. Since Muhammad could claim neither of those distinctions for himself, he must have realized

---

696 The stunning number of members was 40,000. That census come from two sources: (1) "The reduction of the number of Christians of Najran from 40,000 to 4,000 in the space of about eighty years is one of the few definite details we have of the diminution of Christians under Islam." [Laurence E. Browne, The Eclipse of Christianity in Asia From the time of Muhammad till the Fourteenth Century, (Cambridge: The University Press, 1933), p. 36.] (2) "The people of Najran having increased in number to 40,000..." [The Origins of the Islamic State, Being a Translation From the Arabic of Kitab Futuh Al–Buldan of al-Imam abu-l 'Abbas Ahmad ibn-Jabir al-Baladhuri, trans. Philip Khuri Hitti (Beirut: Khayats, 1966), p. 103.]

697 Ibn Ishaq, The Life of Muhammad, Trans A. Guillaume, (Karachi: Oxford University Press, 1967), pp. 271-272.

698 The shift in the use of the word Muslim has been noted by others: "In the Qur'an *muslim* basically means 'monotheist" and it could therefore be applied to Christians, Jews and other monotheists but, ... gradually, the Qur'anic term *muslim* underwent a kind of shrinkage, so it applied now only to those monotheists who followed Qur'anic law and no longer applied to Jews and Christians. ..." Fred M. Donner, Muhammad and the Believers, (Cambridge: Harvard University Press, 2010), p. 204.

699 Quoted from the translation by Marmaduke Pickthall.

that Christ was far greater than he was. He should, therefore, have openly and contritely acknowledged the supremacy of Christ. Not to have submitted to Christ, knowing only these two obvious facts, was an enormous inconsistency.

Christ's similarity to Adam is obvious from three observations: (1) neither of them had a human father, (2) both are related to the whole human race and (3) both, in distinct ways, are fountains of life for every human being. Adam is the fountain through which everyone's physical life has flowed, while Jesus is the fountain from which man's spiritual and eternal life flows. Though Muhammad may not have had a way to know, Christians know that Jesus is "the true light, even the light which lighteth every man, coming into the world." (John 1:9)

Added Insight

A further enhancement of the understanding of the relation between Christ and Adam comes from an interesting account in the Koran about the origin of Satan. Surah 17:61 says, "And when We said unto the angels: Fall down prostrate before Adam and they fell prostrate all save Iblis [the Koranic title for Satan], he said: Shall I fall prostrate before that which Thou has created of clay?"

This concept of the Adam-Christ relationship is so important that it is expounded in more detail in Surah 38:72-79 which says, "When thy Lord said unto the angels: lo! I am about to create a mortal out of mire, and when I have fashioned him and breathed into him of My spirit, then fall down before him prostrate. The Angels fell down prostrate, every one, saving Iblis; he was scornful and became one of the disbelievers. He said: O Iblis! What hindereth thee from falling prostrate before that which I have created with both My hands? Art thou too proud or art thou of the high exalted? He said: I am better than him. Thou createdst me of fire, whilst him Thou didst create of clay. He said: Go forth from hence, for lo! thou art outcast, and lo! My curse is on thee till the Day of Judgment."

Since Muhammad proclaimed Jesus is as Adam, then shouldn't Jesus, the greater Adam, be worshiped as the first Adam was? And should not Muhammad himself, knowing this, have prostrated himself before Jesus?

Virgin Born

In the eighth place, the Koran explicitly upholds the virgin birth of Jesus. This is powerfully portrayed through Mary's perplexity when she asks the heavenly messenger, "How can I have a son when no mortal hath touched me, neither have I been unchaste? He said: So (it will be). Thy Lord saith: It is easy for Me. And (it will be) that We may make of him a revelation for mankind and a mercy from Us, and it is a thing ordained." (Surah 19:20-21)

We should thank God that Muhammad did not buy into the polemic attack made against Jesus by Celsus, an anti-Christian philosopher, who writing about 180 A.D. alleged that Jesus was the bastard son of Mary by a Roman soldier named Panthera. We know of the calumny of Celsus through the refutation written by Origen, (c.185 - c. 254) a great Alexandrian Christian scholar.

Appendix F

Tragically, Jews incorporated Celsus' lie into the Talmud under the title *Toledot Yeshu*, turning thousands of Jewish people away from Jesus because of this grotesque and utterly false libel.

Revelation

The ninth concurrence between the Koranic depiction of Jesus and that of the Gospels is that Jesus is a revelation. The Koran quotes God as saying of Jesus, "We may make of him a revelation for mankind." (Surah 19:21) This is in harmony with the Koranic statement that Jesus is "Allah's messenger." (Surah 4:157) This is stressed also in Surah 4:171 in which Jesus is again called "a messenger of Allah."

The Gospels make it clear that Jesus is the revelation of God and of the will and purpose of God at the most profound level. The Gospels quote Jesus as saying, "He that hath seen me hath seen the Father;… the words that I say unto you I speak not from myself: but the Father abiding in me doeth his works. Believe me that I am in the Father, and the Father in me: or else believe me for the very works' sake." (John 14:9-11)

Mercy

The tenth compatibility between the Koranic presentation of Jesus and the Gospel record is that Jesus is a mercy. In addition to being "a revelation for mankind," he is also destined to be "a mercy" from God. (Surah 19:21) The Gospel account certifies that Jesus is the epitome of mercy, as well as the promoter of mercy. For example, Jesus taught, "Blessed are the merciful: for they shall obtain mercy." (Matthew 5:7) When criticized for dining with tax collectors and sinful people, Jesus retorted, "They that are whole have no need of a physician, but they that are sick. But go ye and learn what this meaneth, I desire mercy and not sacrifice: for I came not to call the righteous, but sinners." (Matthew 9:12-13) He also taught that mercy should generate further mercy. In a parable, in reference to one whose indebtedness had been forgiven, Jesus said, "Thou wicked servant, I forgave thee all that debt, because thou besoughtest me: shouldest not thou also have mercy on thy fellow servant, even as I had mercy on thee?" (Matthew 18:33) Jesus was consistently angry at those who refused to temper justice with mercy. He said, "Woe unto you, scribes and pharisees, hypocrites! For you tithe mint and anise and cummin, and have left undone the weightier matters of the law, justice, and mercy and faith: but these ye ought to have done, and not to have left the other undone." (Matthew 23:23)

God's Viceroy

Finally, in the eleventh place, as the greater Adam, the Koran in Surah 2:30 surprisingly calls Jesus God's Viceroy on earth! The Arabic word in the Koran which has been translated Viceroy is *khalifa* (usually rendered as "caliph" in English). Normally, *khalifa* is translated as successor but obviously the word cannot carry that significance here because God has not forfeited his sovereignty nor appointed a successor. God is still fully sovereign though he has appointed a Viceroy, one who shares his divine royalty.

A startling Koranic passage about Jesus says, "When thy Lord said unto the angels: Lo! I am about to place a viceroy [*khalifa*] in the earth, they said: Wilt Thou place therein one who will do harm therein and will shed blood, while we, we hymn Thy praise and sanctify Thee? He said:

Revelation Verse by Verse

Surely I know that which ye know not and He taught Adam all the names, then showed them to the angels, saying: Inform me of the names of these, if ye are truthful. They said: Be glorified! We have no knowledge saving that which Thou has taught us. Lo! Thou, only Thou, art the Knower, the Wise. He said: O Adam! Inform them of their names, and when he had informed them of their names, He said: Did I not tell you that I know the secret of the heavens and the earth? And I know that which ye disclose and which ye hide and when We said unto the angels: Prostrate yourselves before Adam, they fell prostrate, all save Iblis. He demurred through pride, and so became a disbeliever. And We said: O Adam! Dwell thou and thy wife in the Garden, and eat ye freely (of the fruits) thereof where ye will; but come not nigh this tree lest ye become wrongdoers." (Surah 2:30-35)

Since the angels were to prostrate themselves before the lesser Adam, should the command not apply also to the greater Adam, that is to Jesus Christ, the prophet who, as God's Viceroy, shares God's royalty? Jesus, being God's Viceroy, is clearly substantiated in Christian theology by the throne statements about him in the New Testament. They imply his divine sovereignty. The book of Hebrews tells us, "But of the Son he saith, Thy throne O God, is forever and ever; ..." (Hebrews 1:8) The writer of Revelation says, "And he showed me a river of life, bright as crystal, proceeding out of the throne of God and the Lamb." (Revelation 22:1)

Four Negative Statements About Christ.

In stark contrast to the eleven biblically-true Koranic affirmations about Jesus, amazingly, there are four Christological Koranic denials regarding him. These denials form the doctrinal stance concerning Jesus which Muslim clerics ordinarily emphasize. The intensity of their emphasis leads the average Muslim to think these denials frame the whole truth about Jesus! The four Koranic denials of the Gospel testimony about Jesus may reflect the influence of Waraqa bin Nawfal, the Ebionite preacher in Mecca. He was also cousin to Khadija, Muhammad's highly respected first wife.

I. The Koran Denies the Death of Jesus

Even though the Koran asserts that Jesus did not die, in glaring contrast, Christians affirm the reality of his death every week through observance of the Lord's Supper. The crucial Koranic statement is, "Their saying [is]: We slew the Messiah, Jesus son of Mary, Allah's messenger – They slew him not nor crucified, but it appeared so unto them; and lo! Those who disagree concerning it are in doubt thereof; they have no knowledge thereof save pursuit of a conjecture; they slew him not for certain." (Surah 4:157)

This verse flagrantly and contemptuously challenges the historical testimony upholding the record of the death, burial and resurrection of Christ. Among many other accounts in the New Testament, a powerful and graphic summary is given in I Corinthians 15:3-8. By daringly alleging that Christians who affirm the reality of the crucifixion "have no knowledge thereof save the pursuit of a conjecture," the Koranic message not only undermines one of the essential affirmations of the Gospel of Christ, but also repudiates the bases of both the evidentiary process of Western legal systems as well as the process by which sound history may be established, that is, determining historical truth by the testimony of eyewitnesses.

Appendix F

When the Koran speaks about "those who disagree concerning it," it must be clearly emphasized that there was no disagreement between Jews, Jewish leaders, Roman officials and the followers of Christ about the reality of the death of Jesus. Disagreement was only over whether he had arisen from the dead. The testimony of eyewitnesses (Roman soldiers - John 19:31-37, Jews, officials as well as commoners - Matthew 27:62-66, along with Christians - John 20:24-29) has always been united, testifying that Jesus really died by crucifixion. It requires great temerity and audacity for one living six centuries after the event to deny the united harmonious testimony of both the friends and enemies of Jesus who were present when he died.

Not only does the Koranic denial of the death of Jesus fly in the face of the united contemporary testimony, but it falsifies Jesus' own statements. Here are a few excerpts from what Jesus said about his own death: "From that time began Jesus to show unto his disciples, that he must go unto Jerusalem, and suffer many things of the elders and chief priests and scribes, and be killed, and the third day be raised up." (Matthew 16:21) "I am the good shepherd; and I know mine own, and mine own know me, even as the Father knoweth me, and I know the Father; and I lay down my life for the sheep. ....Therefore doth the Father love me, because I lay down my life, that I may take it again. No one taketh it away from me, but I lay it down of myself. I have power to lay it down, and I have power to take it again. This commandment received I from my Father." (John 10:14-18) "And I, if I be lifted up from the earth, will draw all men unto myself. But this he said, signifying by what manner of death he should die." (John 12:32-33) "Then saith Jesus unto them, All ye shall be offended in me this night: for it is written, I will smite the shepherd, and the sheep of the flock shall be scattered abroad. But after I am raised up, I will go before you into Galilee." (Matthew 26:31-32)

"And Jesus saith unto them, All ye shall be offended: for it is written, I will smite the shepherd, and the sheep shall be scattered abroad. Howbeit, after I am raised up, I will go before you into Galilee." (Mark 14:27-28)

II. The Koran Denies that Jesus is God

The Koran insists that Jesus is not God! It states that, "They surely disbelieve who say: Lo! Allah is the Messiah, son of Mary. The Messiah (himself) said: O Children of Israel, worship Allah, my Lord and your Lord. Lo! Whoso ascribeth partners unto Allah, for him Allah hath forbidden paradise. His abode is the Fire. For evil-doers there will be no helpers. They surely disbelieve who say: Lo! Allah is the third of three; when there is no God save the One God. If they desist not from so saying a painful doom will fall on those of them who disbelieve." (Surah 5:72-73) (See also Surah 9:31.)

As we have seen, the denial that Jesus is divine flies in the face of clear Koranic indications of Christ's deity. The biblical record made Christ's deity clear. It affirms that God not only sent down, he came down! That is the clear import of Matthew 1:23 which says, "And they shall call his name Immanuel; which is, being interpreted, God with us." The deity of Jesus is confirmed by John's gospel in its message of "the Word." We learn that "the Word" was God (John 1:1), then through the birth of Jesus, the Word "became flesh." (John 1:14) This divine visit to mankind is called the incarnation in Christian theology. (See also Titus 2:13, Hebrews 1:8, I John 5:20 and Revelation 22:1.)

Revelation Verse by Verse

Plurality in Unity

By denying the deity of Jesus, Islam not only repudiates the clear Koranic indications of plurality in the unity of God, which were carefully noted previously, but it insists on a monotheism so strict, so unitary and so monolithic that one cannot explore the fullness of God. It is a monotheism even more unitary than the mathematical number 1, the values of which are factored out all the time by fractions such as 1/2 and 1/3. These fractions do not deny or compromise the unity of the numeral 1 which is written above the line. They simply affirm that within the unity of the numeral 1 are inherent values and factors which may be considered independently. To express this concept theologically, is to say that there is a fullness in the One who is God, for "in him dwelleth all the fullness of the Godhead bodily." (Colossians 2:9)

Three Tests

In denying that Jesus is God, Islam repudiates its own criteria for recognizing deity. According to the Koran there are three proofs of deity. The **first** proof is the power to create and the **second** is the power to reproduce creation. These criteria are found in Surah 10:35 which tells us, "Say: Is there of your partners (whom ye ascribe unto Allah) one that produceth Creation and then reproduceth it? Say: Allah produceth Creation, then reproduceth it. How then, are ye misled!" The **third** proof of deity is whether the entity under consideration is able to and actually does answer prayer. That criterion is given in Surah 7 which will be considered later.

To understand Surah 10:35 even more clearly, which was quoted from Marmaduke Pickthall's *The Meaning of the Glorious Koran*, consider it from the following translations: A.J. Arberry rendered it, "Say: 'is there any of your associates who originates creation, then brings it back again?' Say: 'God - He originates creation, then brings it back again; …" Sher Ali translated it, "Say, 'Is there any of your associate gods who originates creation and then reproduces it?' Say, 'It is Allah *alone* Who originates creation and then reproduces it. …" Yusuf Ali gives this rendering, "Say: 'Of your partners, Can any originate creation and repeat it?' Say: 'It is God who originates Creation and repeats it: …" N.J. Dawood's translation says, "Say: 'Can any of your idols conceive Creation, then renew it? Allah conceives Creation, then renews it. …"

Jesus Created

The Koran itself testifies that Jesus created. Therefore, Jesus meets the first Koranic criterion for being acknowledged as Deity. The Koran makes it very clear that Jesus created living organisms, not just lifeless matter. Surah 5:110 gives this description, "When Allah saith: O Jesus, son of Mary! Remember My favour unto thee and unto thy mother; how I strengthened thee with the holy Spirit, so that thou spakest unto mankind in the cradle as in maturity; and how I taught thee the Scripture and Wisdom and the Torah and the Gospel and how thou did shape of clay as it were the likeness of a bird by My permission, and didst blow upon it and it was a bird by My permission, and thou didst heal him who was born blind and the leper by My permission; and how thou didst raise the dead, by My permission; and how I restrained the Children of Israel from (harming) thee when thou camest unto them with clear proofs, and those of them who disbelieved exclaimed: This is naught else than mere magic."

Appendix F

This concept is so basic and fundamental that we should see how other translators have rendered it. N.J. Dawood translated the key assertion this way, "… by My leave you fashioned from clay the likeness of a bird and breathed into it so that, by My leave, it became a living bird. …" Yusuf Ali has given it to us with equal clarity. His translation says, And behold! thou makest Out of clay, as it were, The figure of a bird, By My leave, And thou breathest into it, And it becometh a bird …" A.J. Arberry concurs with the other translators. His rendering is, "…and when thou createst out of clay, by My leave, as the likeness of a bird, and thou breathest into it, and it is a bird, by My leave …"

The following three Koranic passages also stipulate that the power to create is one of the criteria by which we recognize and identify Deity. Surah 7:191-192: "Attribute they as partners to Allah those who created naught, but are themselves created, And cannot give them help, nor can they help themselves?" Surah 16:17: "Is He then Who createth as him who createth not? Will ye not then remember?" Surah 22:73: "O Mankind! A similitude is coined, so pay ye heed to it: Lo! those on whom ye call beside Allah will never create a fly though they combine together for the purpose. And if the fly took something from them, they could not rescue it from him. So weak are (both) the seeker and the sought!"

Biblical Testimony

Long before the Koran was ever known, the Bible made it clear that Jesus created. This is seen in the miracle of the feeding of the 5,000 which is recorded in Matthew 14:13-21. The Koran may refer to this miracle in Surah 5:112-115. The essential part of Matthew's account says "he [Jesus] directed the people to sit down on the grass. Taking the five loaves and the two fish and looking up to heaven, he gave thanks and broke the loaves. Then he gave them to the disciples, and the disciples gave them to the people. They all ate and were satisfied, and the disciples picked up twelve basketfuls of broken pieces that were left over. The number of those who ate was about five thousand men, besides women and children." (Matthew 14:19-21 NIV) It is obvious that without a miracle of creation, "the five loaves and the two fish" were utterly inadequate to have satisfied the hunger of that throng of people consisting of 5,000 men, along with many women and children.

Jesus Restored Creation

The second Koranic criterion by which Muslims should recognize Deity is whether a being is able to restore creation. We find this criterion in Surah 10:35 which puts the issue succinctly. It asks, "Is there of your partners (whom ye ascribe unto Allah) one that produceth Creation and then reproduceth it? Say: Allah produceth Creation, then **reproduceth** it. How then, are ye misled!"

To understand this passage even more clearly, consider the following translations: A.J. Arberry rendered it, "Say: 'is there any of your associates who originates creation, then **brings it back again**?' Say: 'God - He originates creation, then brings it back again; …" Sher Ali translated it, "Say, 'Is there any of your associate gods who originates creation and then **reproduces it**?' Say, 'It is Allah *alone* Who originates creation and then reproduces it. …" Yusuf Ali gives this rendering, "Say: 'Of your partners, Can any originate creation and **repeat it**?' Say: 'It is God who originates Creation and repeats it: …" N.J. Dawood's translation says, "Say: 'Can any of your idols conceive Creation, then **renew it**?' Allah conceives Creation, then renews it.…"

The Koran is very explicit that Jesus indeed did reproduce, repeat, bring back again, and renew creation! In Surah 5:110 it is recorded that Allah said to Jesus, "thou didst raise the dead, by My permission." The biblical record tells us that Jesus raised Jairus' daughter (Mark 5:22-43), the widow's son (Luke 7:11-17) and Lazarus (John 11:1-53).

Jesus Answered Prayer

The **third** Koranic standard by which we may recognize Deity is whether that being is able and willing to help when we pray to him. This is clearly stated in Surah 7:191-194 which says, "Attribute they as partners to Allah those who created naught, but are themselves created, and cannot give them help, nor can they help themselves? And if ye call them to the Guidance, they follow you not. Whether ye call them or are silent is all one to them. Lo! those on whom ye call beside Allah are slaves like unto you. Call on them now, and let them answer you, if ye are truthful."

Jesus meets this stipulation. We may call on him and he has the power and the love to answer and to help. The Koran itself makes that clear. From Surah 5:112-115 which we have already seen in another connection, the Koran asserts that Jesus answered the prayers of his disciples. When Jesus' disciples called on him, saying, "We wish to eat thereof," he answered them! The Koranic passage says, "When the disciples said: O Jesus, son of Mary! Is thy Lord able to send down for us a table spread with food from heaven? He said: observe your duty to Allah, if ye are true believers. (They said:) We wish to eat thereof, that we may satisfy our hearts and know that thou hast spoken truth to us, and that thereof we may be witnesses. Jesus, son of Mary, said: O Allah, Lord of us! Send down for us a table spread with food from heaven, that it may be a feast for us, for the first of us and for the last of us, and a sign from Thee. Give us sustenance, for Thou art the Best of Sustainers. Allah said: Lo! I send it down for you. And whoso disbelieveth of you afterward, him surely will I punish with a punishment wherewith I have not punished any of (My) creatures."

Of the many examples that Jesus answers prayer which are found in Christian Scripture, I cite only Mark 4:35-41: "That day when evening came, he said to his disciples, 'Let us go over to the other side.' Leaving the crowd behind, they took him along, just as he was, in the boat. There were also other boats with him. A furious squall came up, and the waves broke over the boat, so that it was nearly swamped. Jesus was in the stern, sleeping on a cushion. The disciples woke him and said to him, 'Teacher, don't you care if we drown?' He got up, rebuked the wind and said to the waves, 'Quiet! Be still!' Then the wind died down and it was completely calm. He said to his disciples, 'Why are you so afraid? Do you still have no faith?' They were terrified and asked each other, 'Who is this? Even the wind and the waves obey him!'" (NIV)

In view of these facts, (1) Jesus creates, (2) Jesus recreates and (3) Jesus answers prayer, what should Muslims think of Jesus? He has met all the criteria set by the Koran to recognize deity, so every follower of the Koran should believe that Jesus is not only human but divine as well!

Appendix F

III. The Koran Denies the Trinity

The Koran puts the denial of the Trinity this way: "Disbelievers are they surely who say: 'God is the third of the trinity;' but there is no god other than God the one. And if they do not desist from saying what they say, then indeed those among them who persist in disbelief will suffer painful punishment." (Surah 5:73 Ahmed Ali Translation)

As pointed out above in the paragraphs titled "Union With God's Spirit" and "Plurality in Unity," the Koran itself has statements which imply the Trinitarian concept of God. Biblical Trinitarian statements depict not the association of three Gods but the profundity and fulness of the One God. The biblical concept of the Trinity, among many other references, is found powerfully presented in the following two passages: "Come ye near unto me, hear ye this; from the beginning **I** have not spoken in secret; from the time that it was, **there am I**; and now **the Lord Jehovah** hath sent **me** and **his Spirit**." (Isaiah 48:16) "And **I** will pray **the Father**, and he shall give you another Comforter, that he may be with you for ever, even **the Spirit of truth**: whom the world cannot receive; for it beholdeth him not, neither knoweth him: ye know him; for he abideth with you, and shall be in you." (John 14:16-17)

IV. The Koran Denies that Jesus is the Son of God

In the Koran Jesus is repeatedly called "the son of Mary," never "the Son of God." "And the Jews say: Ezra is the son of Allah, and the Christians say: The Messiah is the son [ibn] of Allah. That is their saying with their mouths. They imitate the saying of those who disbelieved of old. Allah (Himself) fighteth against them. How perverse are they! (Surah 9:30) See also Surah 19:35 and Surah 23:91. The Biblical declaration that Jesus is the Son of God is summarized in Romans 1:1-4 and Hebrews 1:1-5.

For the Christian view on the question of Jesus being the son of God, please read the section entitled "The Second Adam."

Holding a true Christology, that is, the correct understanding of Jesus or the true narrative about Jesus, is of prime importance for at least three reasons:

First, it is of prime importance because it is the basis for salvation. Jesus said, "Except ye believe that I am *he*, ye shall die in your sins." (John 8:24b ASV).

John tells us, "Many other signs therefore did Jesus in the presence of the disciples, which are not written in this book: but these are written, that ye may believe that Jesus is the Christ, the Son of God; and that believing ye may have life in his name." (John 20:30-31 ASV)

Second, it is of prime importance because it is the focal point of biblical prophecy. The apostle John emphasizes that "the testimony of Jesus is the spirit of prophecy." (Revelation 19:10 NIV)[700]

---

700 See also Acts 3:24.

Third, it is of prime importance because it is a benchmark by which to make correct spiritual evaluations. "Who is the liar but he that denieth that Jesus is the Christ? This is the antichrist, *even* he that denieth the Father and the Son." (I John 2:22 ASV, See also I John 4:3.)

In view of the significance of a proper Christology, we can never agree with the Roman emperor Constantine's sentiment about Jesus. He made his view clear during the Arian controversy, just before the Council of Nicea in 325. He expressed it in a letter "to Arius and Alexander of Alexandria, urging them to give up the 'trifling matter' of their quarrel concerning the divinity of the Son."[701]

Conclusion

With the eleven positive biblically-true affirmations in Koranic Christology, perhaps one day those positive statements about Jesus will overpower the false statements about him found in the Koran. When that day arrives, it is nearly certain that there will be a massive turning of Muslims in obedience to the Gospel of Christ.

Paul urged the Christians in the church at Colossae to pray that a door might be opened for the Word. He said, "pray for us, too, that God may open a door for our message, so that we may proclaim the mystery of Christ, for which I am in chains. " (Colossians 4:3 NIV) So we need to pray earnestly and continually that a door may be opened in the Muslim world for the Word. Certainly, the eleven biblically-true statements about Jesus, which are found in the Koran, will be one of the means by which a great door for the Gospel may be pushed wide open for Muslims. All of us need to pray regularly and fervently to that end.

---

[701] Peter J. Leithart, Defending Constantine, (Downery Grove, IL: University Press, 2010), p. 80.

Appendix G

Darwin at the University

Christians must face philosophical attacks based on several categories of quasi-scientific research which challenge the truth of the most basic concepts upon which Christ's Gospel is based. Those neo-Darwinian[702] forms of attack are especially dangerous because as materialistic speculative philosophies they often masquerade as empirical science. This danger comes in various guises presumably based on: ethnology, paleology, genetics, anatomy, embryology, geology, anthropology, astronomy, biology and other sciences, all presented in a neo-Darwinian evolutionary framework. But, is the conclusion which they present "really science – or is it actually a kind of mythology?"[703]

The apostle John expressed the Christian doctrinal stance as those who "hold the testimony of Jesus." (Revelation 19:10) That testimony must be held in the face of assertions like those found in the following series of polemical attacks from an evolutionary biologist on the faculty of the University of Washington. His assertions constitute an aggressive vendetta presented in an annual lecture which he calls, "The Speech." Though it consists of eight allegations presented to vulnerable incoming freshman students, it challenges all of us:

1. To begin, he alleges that "no biologist, and no biology course, can help being 'evolutionary.'"

2. Further, in discussing religion and evolution, he asserts that "the former [is] concerned with values, the latter with facts."

3. However, for those of us who hold steadfastly to the concept and reality of God, the evolutionary professor offers us a fallacious palliative which says, "God might well have used evolution by natural selection to produce his creation."

4. Next, the materialistic professor also alleges that "as evolutionary science has progressed, the available space for religious faith has narrowed."

5. He then audaciously and blatantly contends that "an entirely natural and undirected process, namely random variation plus natural selection, contains all that is needed to generate extraordinary levels of non-randomness."

---

[702] "The overall synthesis of Mendelian [Gregor Mendel, 1822-1884, Austrian botanist] genetics with Darwinian theory came to be called 'neo-Darwinism.'" - Stephen C. Meyer, <u>Darwin's Doubt, the Explosive Origin of Animal Life and the Case for Intelligent Design</u>, (NY: Harper Collins, 2013), p. 158. "Neo-Darwinism is the basis of modern evolutionary thought." - Michael J. Behe, <u>Darwin's Black Box</u>, (NY: Touchstone, 1996), p. 24.

[703] Lee Strobel quoting Jonathan Wells [holds Ph.D. in molecular and cell biology, is a post-doctoral research biologist], <u>The Case for a Creator</u>, (Grand Rapids, MI: Zondervan, 2004), p. 36.

6. Hard on the heels of those daring positions, he claims that, "Living things are indeed wonderfully complex, but [are] altogether within the range of a statistically powerful, entirely mechanical phenomenon."

7. His aggressive philosophical attack goes on to say that "no literally supernatural trait has ever been found in Homo sapiens; we are perfectly good animals, natural as can be and indistinguishable from the rest of the living world at the level of structure as well as physiological mechanism."

8. Finally, he capped off his attack by the challenge that "the more we know of evolution, the more unavoidable is the conclusion that living things, including human beings, are produced by a natural, totally amoral process, with no indication of a benevolent controlling creator."[704]

Before responding individually and consecutively to the calumnies in Professor Barash's "Darwin-only science curriculum,"[705] it should be pointed out that the average Christian, evaluating the environment in which he lives, thoughtfully asks: 1) Could there be an intricate harmonious design, such as the one we witness daily in man's habitat, without a **designer**?[706] 2) Could there be such obvious meticulous coordination as any layman may observe in our universe without a **coordinator**?[707] 3) Could the harmony between human needs and the response offered by our benign global environment be achieved with no **conductor**?[708] 4) Could life suddenly spring into existence out of inanimate substances[709] with no **initiator**?[710] 5) Could the complicated, intricate, reciprocal interchange that the average person sees at many levels of the environment in which we live exist and continue with no **facilitator**?[711] 6) Could the human

---

704 This series of statements has been excerpted from David P. Barash, *God, Darwin and My College Biology Class*, The New York Times, Sunday Review, September 28, 2014, p. 5.

705 The wording is taken from Stephen C. Meyer, Darwin's Doubt, the Explosive Origin of Animal Life and the Case for Intelligent Design, (NY: Harper Collins, 2013), p. xii.

706 Darwin, in his *On the Origin of Species*, claimed that evolution had "refuted the scientific argument for design. He did this by explaining away any presumed vestiges of an actual designing intelligence, showing instead that these 'appearances of design' had been produced by a purely undirected process – indeed, one that could mimic the powers of a designing mind." - Stephen C. Meyer, Signature in the Cell, (New York: Harper Collins, 2009), p. 9. Lee Strobel, quoting Alister McGrath [studied molecular biodynamics at Oxford and is the author of the three-volume A Scientific Theology], asks "Is it a pure coincidence that the laws of nature are such that life is possible? Might this not be an important clue to the nature and destiny of humanity?" - Lee Strobel, The Case for a Creator, (Grand Rapids, MI: Zondervan, 2004), p. 127. "Richard Dawkins has noted, for example, that the digital information in DNA bears an uncanny resemblance to computer software or machine code. He explains that many aspects of living systems 'give the appearance of having been designed for a purpose' nevertheless, neo-Darwinists regard that appearance of design as entirely illusory, as did Darwin himself, because they think that purely mindless, materialistic processes such as natural selection and random mutations can produce the intricate designed-like structures in living organisms. In this view, natural selection and random mutation mimic the powers of a designing intelligence without themselves being intelligently directed or guided." - Stephen C. Meyer, Darwin's Doubt, the Explosive Origin of Animal Life and the Case for Intelligent Design, (NY: Harper Collins, 2013), p. 339.

707 Strobel, quoting Patrick Glynn [a Harvard Ph.D. and recovered atheist], says "All the seemingly arbitrary and unrelated constants in physics have one strange thing in common – these are precisely the values you need if you want to have a universe capable of producing life." - Lee Strobel, The Case for a Creator, (Grand Rapids, MI: Zondervan, 2004), p. 126. "The very success of science in showing us how deeply ordered the natural world is provides strong grounds for believing that there is an even deeper cause for that order." - Richard Swinburne quoted by John C. Lennox, God's Undertaker, Has Science Buried God?, (Oxford, England: Lion Hudson pl, 2007), p. 47.

708 Strobel comments, "The 'coincidences' that allow the fundamental properties of matter to yield a habitable environment are so improbable, so far-fetched, so elegantly orchestrated, that they require a divine explanation." - Lee Strobel, The Case for a Creator, (Grand Rapids, MI: Zondervan, 2004), p. 151.

709 "The term 'molecular evolution' is now commonly used to describe the emergence of the living cell from non-living materials." John C. Lennox, God's Undertaker, Has Science Buried God?, (Oxford, England: Lion Hudson PLC, 2007), p. 100.

710 "Astronomy leads us to a unique event, a universe which was created out of nothing, one with the very delicate balance needed to provide exactly the right conditions required to permit life, and one which has an underlying (one might say 'supernatural') plan." - Arno Penzias, Physics Noble Prize-Winner, quoted by John C. Lennox, God's Undertaker, Has Science Buried God?, (Oxford, England: Lion Hudson PLC, 2007), p. 57.

711 "The extraordinary fine-tuning of the laws and constants of nature, their beauty, their discoverability, their intelligibility – all this combines to make the God hypothesis the most reasonable choice we have. All other theories fall short." - Lee Strobel, Quoting Robin Collins, The

Appendix G

eye's many fully integrated and interdependent features have gradually come into being and be maintained without an **integrator**? That question is entirely appropriate because, "the hurdles for gradualism become higher and higher as the structures are more complex, more interdependent."[712]

Richard Dawkins,[713] on page 6 of his well-known book, The Blind Watchmaker, wrote, "Darwin made it possible to be an intellectually fulfilled atheist."[714] One wonders at what level of intellect one is working if he can be fulfilled with conclusions based on assumptions which prove to be obviously specious.

In harmony with that series of six penetrating questions, uniquely qualified non-Christian analysts and thinkers also recognize the fact "that certain things are so remarkable that they have to be explained as non-accidental."[715] That resounding assertion is also made independently by highly qualified Christian analysts, one of whom has written, "There are telltale features of living systems and the universe that are best explained by an intelligent cause – that is, by the conscious choice of a rational agent – rather than by an undirected process."[716]

Nevertheless, scientists are willing to spend huge sums of public money seeking for a purely mechanical explanation for the dawn of life on earth. One reminder of that fact comes from a statement by the European Space Agency explaining their attempt to land a robotic probe on the small comet known as 67P/Churyumov-Gerasimenko. The effort is known as the Rosetta mission. The Rosetta scientists hold the possibility that their effort may "provide information about whether comets could have brought life's basic building blocks to earth, such as amino acids, which make proteins. 'The possibility is that comets brought not just water, but – trapped in the water – organic components that are the missing link for explaining the emergence of life on earth,' said Jean-Pierre Bibring, lead lander scientist."[717] It must seem "to them, life is like a soup mix: just add water!"[718]

One by one let us consider Professor Barash's points:

1. Why, as Professor Barash claims, is the evolutionary concept so pervasive that embracing it becomes so inevitable that no biology course can help being "evolutionary?" One overriding reason is that "almost everyone in our secular cultures has been brow beaten into regarding the reductive research program as sacrosanct, on the ground that anything else would not be science."[719]

Case for a Creator, (Grand Rapids, MI: Zondervan, 2004), p. 149.
712 Michael J. Behe, Darwin's Black Box, (NY: Touchstone, 1996), p. 203.
713 "The evolutionary biologist Richard Dawkins, a prominent atheist, is a member of the British Humanist Association, the country's [Great Britain's] pre-eminent non-religious organization, with a membership of over 12,000 which sponsors a good deal of anti-religious political activity." - T. M. Luhrmann, *Religion Without God*, The New York Times, December 25, 2014, p. A21.
714 Stephen C. Meyer, Darwin's Doubt, the Explosive Origin of Animal Life and the Case for Intelligent Design, (NY: Harper Collins, 2013), p. 409.
715 Thomas Nagel, Mind and Cosmos, (New York: Oxford University Press, 2012), p. 7. Nagel is University Professor in the Department of Philosophy and the School of Law at New York University. He says of himself, "My speculations about an alternative to physics as a theory of everything do not invoke a transcendent being." (p. 12)
716 Stephen C. Meyer, Signature in the Cell, (New York: Harper Collins, 2009), p. 4.
717 Gautam Naik, Rendezvous *With a Comet*, The Wall Street Journal, November 13, 2014, p. A9.
718 Lee Strobel, The Case for a Creator, (Grand Rapids, MI: Zondervan, 2004), p. 154.
719 Thomas Nagel, Mind and Cosmos, (New York: Oxford University Press, 2012), p. 7. Nagel explains his expression "reductive research program" as "a reduction of biology to chemistry and physics." (p. 44)

Revelation Verse by Verse

Three examples will help us understand what Nagel meant by his phrase, "brow beaten." First, "In August 2004, a technical journal ... called the *Proceedings of the Biological Society of Washington* published the first peer-reviewed article, explicitly advancing the theory of intelligent design in a mainstream scientific periodical. After the publication of the article, the Smithsonian's Museum of Natural History erupted in internal controversy, as scientists angry with the editor – an evolutionary biologist with two earned Ph.D.'s – questioned his editorial judgment and demanded his censure."

Another example is found "In 2005, [when] a federal judge would rule that public-school science students in Dover, Pennsylvania, could not learn about the idea that life pointed to an intelligent cause, because the idea was neither scientific nor testable."

As a final example, "In 1981, in *Mclean v. Arkansas Board of Education*, opponents of creationism, represented by attorneys working for the American Civil Liberties Union (ACLU), sued the state of Arkansas, arguing that a law that required teachers to teach creationism alongside Darwinian evolution in public-school science classrooms was unconstitutional."[720]

In the face of the kind of pressure seen in the three examples just given, Professor Barash may be right to allege that "no biologist, and no biology course, can help being 'evolutionary.'" "What is clear, in Galileo's time and ours, is that criticism of a reigning scientific paradigm is fraught with risk, no matter who is engaged in it."[721]

"It can be highly dangerous to think outside the evolutionary box. For, to question evolution is, in the eyes of many, to question what is, to them, sheer fact by virtue of philosophical necessity; and thus the questioner runs the risk of being classified – if not certified – as a member of the lunatic fringe."[722]

An astonishing aspect of scientific community life helps explain the inability of many members to accept truth. This was pointed out by Barry Commoner, Senior Scientist and Director of the Critical Genetics Project at the Center for Biology of Natural Systems at Queens College, City University of New York. He said, "To some degree the theory [of neo-Darwinism] has been protected from criticism by a device more common to religion than science: dissent, or merely the discovery of a discordant fact, is a punishable offense, a heresy that might easily lead to professional ostracism. Much of this bias can be attributed to institutional inertia, a failure of rigour, but there are other, more insidious, reasons why molecular geneticists might be satisfied with the status quo; the central dogma has given them such a satisfying, seductively simplistic explanation of heredity that it seemed sacrilegious to entertain doubts. The central dogma was simply too good not to be true."[723]

2. Next, Professor Barash insidiously claims that the basic contrast between religion and evolution is that "the former [is] concerned with values, the latter with facts." In his jauntily audacious assertion, we should not miss the point that, by his dichotomy, he puts evolution and its concepts outside of the scope of values. Thus with his indiscriminate broom, Professor Barash

---

720 All three examples are taken from Stephen C. Meyer, Signature in the Cell, (New York: Harper Collins, 2009), pp. 1, 31 and 416.
721 John C. Lennox, God's Undertaker, Has Science Buried God?, (Oxford, England: Lion Hudson PLC, 2007), p. 25.
722 John C. Lennox, God's Undertaker, Has Science Buried God?, (Oxford, England: Lion Hudson PLC, 2007), p. 97.
723 John C. Lennox, God's Undertaker, Has Science Buried God?, (Oxford, England: Lion Hudson PLC, 2007), p. 135.

Appendix G

has swept both religion and evolution into a garbage heap of total insignificance, religion without facts and evolution without value!

Christians are not willing to acknowledge the validity of the theory of evolution even in the restricted realm given to it in this argument to which Professor Barash has, perhaps inadvertently, consigned it. But we do rejoice that he sees that religion and values are inseparable. Also, in the dichotomy which Professor Barash has drawn, certainly anyone may see the "conflict between two metaphysical interpretations of the nature of reality and the significance of human life."[724]

One also wonders if the evolutionary process is considered to be goal-directed. If so, by whom or by what it is directed? On the other hand, if it is not goal-directed, then why did the process continue till it reached the human level?

3. When Professor Barash tells Christians that "God might well have used evolution by natural selection to produce his creation," we wonder if he had ever thought that God probably used a process which is infinitely more efficient and less time consuming than "evolution by natural selection." Darwinism claims that natural selection "has a building effect so powerful that it can begin with a bacterial cell and gradually craft its descendants over billions of years to produce such wonders as trees, flowers, ants, birds, and humans."[725]

Certainly, a more efficient method than that proposed by evolution would be necessary to guarantee the coordination needed to sustain human life. Should man have appeared, but not simultaneously the cornucopia of fauna and flora required to sustain human life, all would have been in vain. The hit-and-miss system envisioned by evolution, even were it true, could not have brought about the coordinated, life sustaining support system, based on animal and vegetable resources, upon which man's survival depends. Another aspect of the coordination needed to sustain human life when it first appeared is the absolute necessity that both male and female should appear at the same time and in the same place.

4. What Professor Barash labels "evolutionary science" is deceptively mislabeled. The quality of pronouncements by evolutionists which are labeled as "science" was highlighted by evolutionary biochemist George Wald who in 1954 argued that "Time is in fact the hero of the plot. ... Given so much time, the impossible becomes possible, the possible probable, and the probable virtually certain."[726]

For believers in neo-Darwinism, time has become their great evolutionary wizard. A contemporary evolutionary medical doctor helps us understand the central role their wizard plays in bringing about the marvels of the human body. He tells us, "The origins of our inner ear lie hundreds of millions of years back in evolution, when primitive fish began to develop hollows in the skin that were sensitive to waves of pressure from water around them, as well as to water's movement as they pitched and rolled. With time the nerves became more refined, the hollows became tubes of sea water, and those tubes eventually closed off and buried themselves in the head. Further on in evolution, bones that were originally related to the jaw migrated and

---

[724] Ian G. Barbour, Science Ponders Religion, (New York: Appleton-Century-Crofts, 1960), p. 200., as quoted by Charles B. Thaxton, Walter L. Bradley and Roger L. Olsen in The Mystery of Life's Origin: Reassessing Current Theories, (Dallas, TX: Lewis & Stanley, 1992), p. 208.
[725] Phillip E. Johnson, Darwin on Trial, (Downers Grove, IL: Inter Varsity Press, 1991), p. 16.
[726] Stephen C. Meyer, Signature in the Cell, (New York: Harper Collins, 2009), p. 195.

miniaturized, becoming the amplifying bones of the ear. The tubes dedicated to sensing rotational movement became our semi-circular canals (balance), and it's theorized that parts involved in sensing the pressure waves became our cochleas (hearing)." What is the proof given by our evolutionary doctor that all of these miraculous transformations actually occurred? He tells us, "In the composition of their salts, the fluids of our inner ear still carry the memory of that primordial ocean."[727] That description reveals the quality of much evolutionary research. The fluid of the inner ear is saline; therefore, it must have come from the primeval ocean. That conclusion exceeds even the bounds of gullibility.

The "available space for religious faith," contrary to Professor Barash's claim, has not narrowed. Rather, the exclusion of God, which is inherent in neo-Darwinism, has created a barren desert of materialism where religion is needed more than ever. Thus, religion has progressively become more important. It is clear that man cannot prosper in a totally materialistic environment. Just as Jesus said, "Man shall not live by bread alone." (Matthew 4:4)

5. Professor Barash's statement that "random variation" is able "to generate extraordinary levels of non-randomness," asks us to believe an assertion even more preposterous than the proposition that water flows uphill! Of course he sees the reconciliation of this absurdity by stating that it is brought about by "natural selection."[728] He asks us to believe that preposterous assertion while he completely ignores the countervailing truth, which has been pointed out by many analysts, that "natural selection," should such a highly questionable phenomenon exist, could not function unless there were something previously existing from which to make a selection. Therefore, it is obvious that, "natural selection explains 'only the survival of the fittest, not the arrival of the fittest.'"[729] Thus, even conceptually, the evolutionary theory of the origin of the universe does not address the question of the ultimate origin of all existing matter and life.

The evolutionary concepts of "random variation" and "natural selection" have simply been deified by "endowing matter and energy with creative powers that they cannot be convincingly shown to possess."[730] The powerlessness of "natural selection" is not surprising when we realize its attributes as expounded by Richard Dawkins, one of its greatest advocates. He wrote, "Natural selection, the blind, unconscious, automatic process which Darwin discovered and which we now know is the explanation for the existence and apparently purposeful form of all life, has no purpose in mind. It has no mind and no mind's eye, it does not plan for the future. It has no vision, no foresight, no sight at all."[731]

---

[727] Gavin Francis, The Mysterious World of the Deaf, The New York Review of Books, November 20, 2014, p. 45. It seems that Dr. Francis' exposition of the evolutionary process would qualify for the term "truthiness" coined in 2005 by the comedic pundit Stephen Colbert in 2010. The term was entered in the New Oxford American Dictionary in which they gave the meaning, "The quality of seeming or being felt to be true, even if not necessarily true." - Dave Itzkoff, Of Truthiness and Pesky Consequences, The New York Times, December 18, 2014, p. C1.

[728] Pierre Grasse of the Sorbonne in Paris has "...observed that fruit flies remain fruit flies in spite of the thousands of generations that have been bred and all the mutations that have been induced in them. In fact, the capacity for variation in the gene pool seems to run out quite early on in the process, a phenomenon called genetic homeostasis. There appears to be a barrier beyond which selective breeding will not pass because of the onset of sterility or exhaustion of genetic variability. If there are limits even to the amount of variation the most skilled breeders can achieve, the clear implication is that *natural* selection is likely to achieve very much less. It is not surprising that he argued that microevolution could not bear the weight that is often put upon it." - John C. Lennox, God's Undertaker, Has Science Buried God?, (Oxford, England: Lion Hudson PLC, 2007), p. 108.

[729] Stephen C. Meyer, Darwin's Doubt, the Explosive Origin of Animal Life and the Case for Intelligent Design, (NY: Harper Collins, 2013), p. x.

[730] John C. Lennox, God's Undertaker, Has Science Buried God?, (Oxford, England: Lion Hudson PLC, 2007), p. 50.

[731] John C. Lennox, God's Undertaker, Has Science Buried God?, (Oxford, England: Lion Hudson PLC, 2007), p. 78.

Appendix G

The "random variation" and the extremely long periods of time needed for that variation to bring about evolution's desired "selection" indeed requires unimaginably long ages, reaching into billions of years. However, judging from the thousands of fossil remnants preserved in the Cambrian geological level of stone formations, life appears to have occurred "far too suddenly to be readily explained by the gradual activity of natural selection and random variations."[732]

If rigorous adherence to the boundaries of neo-Darwinism precludes the conclusion they want, those committed to neo-Darwinism seem free to fudge as Richard Dawkins has been noted to do. For example, "Whether in the analogies he drew to animal breeding or the computer simulations he used to demonstrate the supposed ability of mutation and selection to generate new genetic information, Dawkins repeatedly smuggled in the very thing he insisted the concept of natural selection expressly precluded: the guiding hand of an intelligent agent."[733]

6. When Professor Barash tells us, that, "Living things are indeed wonderfully complex, but [are] altogether within the range of a statistically powerful, entirely mechanical phenomenon," he is offering us a copious serving of "word salad"[734] which he has tossed together by using a mixture of "jargon laced descriptions of unobserved past events."[735] That jargon is composed of words from "fact-free science."[736] To this he adds a generous measure "of the fuzzy word-pictures typical of evolutionary biology."[737] Obviously, then, his salad, as someone has said, "blurs the distinction between theory and evidence." He is willing to make "judgments that exceed the bounds of the data."[738] There are absolutely no statistics which give us the "statistically powerful, entirely mechanical" phenomenon he talks about.

He concludes by telling us, "living things [are an] entirely mechanical phenomenon." He ignores the fact that "the gap between non-living chemicals and even the most primitive living organism is absolutely tremendous."[739] Are humans and animals only machines, being an "entirely mechanical phenomenon?" Do not animals, as well as humans, respond to fear and love? Does not this indisputable fact place men and animals in quite a different category than that used to classify automobiles, refrigerators and lawnmowers? Try patting your automobile on its hood and see if it responds as your dog does when you pat him on his head. When you put gasoline in your car's tank, does your car express appreciation as your dog does when you put food in his dish?

The teaching that man is an "entirely mechanical phenomenon" is the concept which led China under Mao to treat her citizens as "rustless screws in the revolutionary machine."[740] That Chinese

---

732 Stephen C. Meyer, Darwin's Doubt, the Explosive Origin of Animal Life and the Case for Intelligent Design, (NY: Harper Collins, 2013), p. 36.

733 Stephen C. Meyer, Darwin's Doubt, the Explosive Origin of Animal Life and the Case for Intelligent Design, (NY: Harper Collins, 2013), p. 185.

734 For the statements about "word salad," see Stephen C. Meyer, Darwin's Doubt, the Explosive Origin of Animal Life and the Case for Intelligent Design, (NY: Harper Collins, 2013), p. 227.

735 Stephen C. Meyer, Darwin's Doubt, the Explosive Origin of Animal Life and the Case for Intelligent Design, (NY: Harper Collins, 2013), p. 227.

736 An insightful expression coined by Maynard Smith. See Michael J. Behe, Darwin's Black Box, (NY: Touchstone, 1996), p. 156.

737 Michael J. Behe, Darwin's Black Box, (NY: Touchstone, 1996), p. 68.

738 Lee Strobel, The Case for a Creator, (Grand Rapids, MI: Zondervan, 2004), p. 128. An example of judgments that exceed the bounds of the data is found when one realizes that "the statements of Dawkins, Coyne, and many others about all the evidence (molecular and anatomical) supporting a single, unambiguous animal tree are manifestly false." - Stephen C. Meyer, Darwin's Doubt, the Explosive Origin of Animal Life and the Case for Intelligent Design, (NY: Harper Collins, 2013), p. 124.

739 Lee Strobel, The Case for a Creator, (Grand Rapids, MI: Zondervan, 2004), p. 39.

740 Evan Osnos in his Age of Ambition as quoted by David Brooks, *The Ambition Explosion*, The New York Times, November 28, 2014, p. A29.

phenomenon could prove to be a prelude to the destiny of the whole human enterprise should neo-Darwinism triumph globally.

7. Professor Barash did not define what he meant by the term "supernatural traits" in Homo sapiens. Does man's ability to triumph in the face of fear and selfishness rise high enough to meet his concept?

Does man have no "traits" which excel those of animals? This question in no way minimizes animal traits which are astounding, such as beavers' ability to construct dams, spiders' ability to spin webs, vast clouds of starlings' ability to swoop and soar in perfect unison, wings beating only an inch or two from their fellow birds' wings yet without any accident, and weaver birds' ability to weave beautifully plaited nests which hang from limbs which reach out over water? But do not man's abilities to observe, to analyze, to create, and to imitate far excel the marvelous works of those creatures? Do not those unique abilities set mankind apart?

Even Richard Dawkins, who "is the best modern popularizer of Darwinism around," and who "writes with passion because he believes Darwinism is true and also believes that atheism is a logical deduction from Darwinism,"[741] believes there is a clear distinction between man and animals. Surprisingly, he wrote, "What makes us *humane*? What are the qualities that we admire and aspire to: qualities that make us human, as opposed to brutish?

"We have big brains. Other species are marked out by other qualities. Swifts and albatrosses are spectacularly good at flying, dogs and rhinoceroses at smelling, bats at hearing, moles, and aardvarks and wombats at digging. Human beings are not good at any of those things. But we do have big brains; we are good at thinking, remembering, calculating, imagining, speaking. Other species can communicate, but no other species has true language with open-ended grammar. No other species has literature, music, art, mathematics or science. No other species makes books or complicated machines such as cars, computers and combine harvesters. No other species devotes substantial lengths of time to pursuits that don't contribute directly to survival or reproduction."[742]

8. Finally, Professor Barash asserts "that living things, including human beings, are produced by a natural, totally amoral process, with no indication of a benevolent controlling creator." That assertion totally skirts the challenge made by Paul Wesson in 1996 who called everyone's attention to the fact that regarding "large evolutionary innovations … none has ever been observed and we have no idea whether any may be in progress." Looking to the far past, he noted, "there is no good fossil record of any."[743]

In the final analysis, men may ignore or deny the evidence, no matter how clear it is. As Paul said of atheists in his day, "They refused to have God in their knowledge." (Romans 1:28) That persistent refusal has continued till the present time, though disguised under a cloud of current

---

741 Michael J. Behe, Darwin's Black Box, (NY: Touchstone, 1996), p. 33.
742 Richard Dawkins, *This Organ Separates Humans from Animals*, New Republic, January 20, 2014, p. 1. An especially informative and helpful exposition of the distinction between humans and animals is given at www.middletownbiblechurch.org, entitled "Similarities & Differences Between Men and Animals (Ch. 8)" from "Science, the Scriptures and the Saviour" document by George Zeller.
743 John C. Lennox, God's Undertaker, Has Science Buried God?, (Oxford, England: Lion Hudson PLC, 2007), p. 106. As one very astute analyst commented, "Evolutionary projection has no direct evidence, is highly speculative and is sometimes barely distinguishable from science fiction." - Carl F. H. Henry, God, Revelation and Authority, Vol. 6, Part 2, (Waco, Texas: Word Books, Publisher, 1983), p. 173.

Appendix G

nomenclature. Once that line of denying the existence of God is crossed, the only possible stance left is a purely "materialistic hypothesis that all we have is matter/energy and the forces of physics, [and] then there is only one option – matter/energy together with the forces of nature over time have produced life, that is, evolution of some sort."[744] "As science advanced in the late nineteenth century, it increasingly excluded appeals to divine action or divine ideas as a way of explaining phenomena in the natural world. This practice came to be codified in a principle known as methodological naturalism. According to this principle, scientists should accept as a working assumption that all features of the natural world can be explained by material causes without recourse to purposive intelligence, mind, or conscious agency."[745] In stark contrast, "Christians have always believed that God testifies to his existence through the book of nature and the book of Scripture."[746]

Christian witness to the truth should be convincing enough to make it impossible for people, like those in the former Soviet Union, to live in "different realities," being defined by "multiple truths." We must make reality so clear that no one will be able to say "that there is no such thing as objective truth." We must very clearly make it impossible for neo-Darwinism to "replace facts with disinformation." We must make the truth so clear that no one will "simply give up on the search for truth." Therefore, the Christian presentation must take the persuasive form of "reality-based discourse."[747]

---

744 John C. Lennox, God's Undertaker, Has Science Buried God?, (Oxford, England: Lion Hudson PLC, 2007), p. 96.

745 Stephen C. Meyer, Darwin's Doubt, the Explosive Origin of Animal Life and the Case for Intelligent Design, (NY: Harper Collins, 2013), p. 19. Professor Thomas Nagel explains this philosophical prejudice against God by telling us that, "The priority given to evolutionary naturalism in the face of its implausible conclusions about other subjects is due, I think, to the secular consensus that this is the only form of external understanding of ourselves that provides an alternative to theism — which is to be rejected as a mere projection of our internal self conception on to the universe without evidence." - Thomas Nagel, Mind & Cosmos, (New York: Oxford University Press, 2012), p. 29.

746 Jay Wesley Richards [holds three advanced degrees in philosophy and theology, including a Ph.D. from Princeton] quoted by Lee Strobel, The Case for a Creator, (Grand Rapids, MI: Zondervan, 2004), p. 189. In modern times few have read "the book of nature" as perceptively as did William Paley. He shared his understanding in his classical book, Natural Theology. Though Richard Dawkins, Oxford scientist and dedicated evolutionist, tried to discredit Paley, Behe reminds us that "The main argument of the discredited Paley has actually never been refuted. Neither Darwin nor Dawkins, neither science nor philosophy has explained how an irreducibly complex system such as a watch might be produced without a designer. Instead, Paley's argument has been sidetracked by attacks on its injudicious examples and off-the-point theological discussions. Paley, of course, is to blame for not framing his argument more tightly. But many of Paley's detractors are also to blame for refusing to engage his main point, playing dumb in order to reach a more palatable conclusion." Michael J. Behe, Darwin's Black Box, (NY: Touchstone, 1996), p. 213.

747 The statements in quotation marks in this paragraph have been taken from Peter Pomerantsev, *Russia's Ideology: There Is No Truth*, The New York Times, December 12, 2014, p. A29.

Appendix H

Scriptures Which Point to The Millennium

The following six passages should encourage us to anticipate the remarkably extended period during which Christ's ongoing rule, with the exception of the elimination of death, will have become totally triumphant.

First, we are told in I Corinthians 15:25-26 that "He must reign, till He hath put all his enemies under his feet. The last enemy that shall be abolished is death." Jesus Christ is reigning now. His reign will neither have been interrupted, postponed, diverted nor delayed before The Millennium begins. We know Christ is reigning, not only from this passage in I Corinthians, but also from the proclamation which Peter made on the day of Pentecost, in which he said, "God had sworn with an oath to him [the patriarch David] that of the fruit of his loins he would set one upon his throne; he foreseeing this spake of the resurrection of Christ." (Acts 2:30-31) As surely as Christ is on that throne, he is reigning. Peter's declaration of Christ's glorification is also substantiated by Luke 24:26, which asks, "Did not the Christ have to suffer these things and then enter his glory?" (NIV) Christ's exaltation to occupy David's throne is the glorious position from which he currently exercises real power and authority over human affairs. Especially, his reign includes being "head over all things to the church." (Ephesians 1:22)

When Paul wrote to the Christians in the church at Colossæ, he reminded them that Jesus has "delivered us [Christians] out of the power of darkness, and translated us into the kingdom of the Son of his love." (Colossians 1:13) The Christian's citizenship in that kingdom has neither been cancelled, revoked nor rescinded. This means that the church of Christ and the kingdom of Christ presently have the same boundaries. That truth was not only given through the apostle Paul but through John as well. Writing to "the seven churches" which were in the Roman province of Asia, he said, Jesus "made us to be a kingdom." (Revelation 1:6) He went on to identify himself by saying "I, John, your brother and partaker with you in the tribulation and kingdom." (Revelation 1:9) John also tells us that those whom Christ had purchased unto God with his blood, consisting of "men of every tribe, and tongue, and people, and nation" (Revelation 5:9), he had "made to be a kingdom." (Revelation 5:10 NIV) Thus, we Christians should be grateful for having received "a kingdom that cannot be shaken." (Hebrews 12:28 ESV) With an uninterrupted reign, Christ continues to rule over that kingdom. Thus, that kingdom is the one "which shall never be destroyed nor shall the sovereignty thereof be left to another people." (Daniel 2:44)

The concept of Christ's kingdom cited in the paragraph above, drawn exclusively from scripture, gives a radically different picture than the one drawn by Hal Lindsey when he wrote, "This restoration [of the nation of Israel, flourishing in prosperity] would take place after a worldwide dispersion and long-term desolation of the land of Israel. However, it would occur shortly before the events which will culminate with the personal, visible return of the Messiah, Jesus Christ, to set up an everlasting Kingdom and bring about the spiritual conversion of Israel."[748] On the contrary, that everlasting kingdom was established at the very beginning of the Christian era. Thus, it is not to be established at a supposed, but totally erroneous, return of Christ immediately following the founding of the state of Israel.

The Gospel of Christ will ultimately see a day of global victory, notwithstanding the persistent worldwide Islamic aggressive resistance to and denials of the Gospel. It is just such a victory, which is to result from the testimony of Christ's two witnesses (See 11:5-12 and comments.), which will also culminate in the dawning of The Millennium. This reality was also foreseen by Daniel. He not only portrayed the kingdom of God as a stone quarried or cut out without hands, obviously describing a divine initiative, but saw the destiny of that stone. He saw it as though it had already become "a great mountain, and [had] filled the whole earth." (See Daniel 2:34-44.) Apparently, it is that global victory which ushers in The Millennium. Christ will continue his rule through The Millennium and beyond till "He hath put all his enemies under his feet." (I Corinthians 15:25)

Currently Christ is putting his enemies, who are also the enemies of mankind, under his feet. Scripture says the ultimate victory will be his triumph over death. Thus, as felicitous as The Millennium will be, it is clear that the crowning victory will be achieved following The Millennium. It will be in the new heaven and the new earth that death will finally have been abolished. (See Revelation 21:1-4.) When that ultimate triumph takes place, Jesus will then relinquish his reign, giving all authority back to the Father that He may be all in all. (See I Corinthians 15:25-28.) So, according to I Corinthians 15, we should anticipate a time, known as The Millennium, during which the enemies of both God and man are put under the feet of Christ. What a triumphantly marvelous time that will be! Social and economic justice will prevail, in short, all injustice will have been overcome and wars will have ceased.

Secondly, it is also clear from Matthew 6:10 that there will dawn a period of victory for the kingdom of Christ on earth. It will be known as The Millennium. Though this passage in Matthew is very familiar, we may not have thought seriously about its implications regarding The Millennium. So consider deeply what Jesus taught us to pray when we implore God, saying, "Thy kingdom come. Thy will be done, as in heaven, so on earth." Surely Jesus has not taught us to pray for an impossibility. What would it mean if the will of God were carried out on earth as it is in heaven? Obviously, it would be just such a golden age as that which is clearly implied in Revelation chapter 20. We need, therefore, to pray for the triumph of Jesus and his Gospel during our part in the human drama. It is challenging, surprising and humbling to realize the transforming role our prayers are intended to have!

In the third place, consider the implications of I Corinthians 6:2, which asks us, "know ye not that the saints shall judge the world?" According to this passage, a time is coming when Christianity is going to prevail to the extent that Christians will be the ones sitting in the seats of judgment and in the legislative councils, making governing decisions throughout the whole world. This implies a global victory for the Gospel, a superlative global triumph for Jesus Christ in the affairs of mankind. Such a condition is precisely that which will prevail during The Millennium.

---

[748] Hal Lindsey, The Late Great Planet Earth, (Grand Rapids, Michigan: Zondervan Publishing House, 1976), p. 41.

Appendix H

Fourthly, please consider Isaiah 11:9 where we read, "They shall not hurt nor destroy in all my holy mountain; for the earth shall be full of the knowledge of Jehovah, as the waters cover the sea." If one reads the whole passage given in Isaiah 11:1-9 it becomes clear that it is anticipating the Christian period of human history, that is, the Christian age or dispensation. Verse 9 highlights the apex or the consummation of the Christian age when it tells us, "The earth shall be full of the knowledge of Jehovah as the waters cover the sea." Obviously, that triumphant moment has not yet arrived. For example, it is no longer legal to present the biblical creation account of the origin of the universe in many, if not most, American public schools. Consequently, children don't even know that God Almighty created the world, let alone what God desires of them. But this passage predicts a time in the future when the knowledge of Jehovah shall cover the earth as the waters cover the sea. Though that era is still in the future, we should eagerly anticipate its coming in the period called The Millennium.

In the fifth place, in Romans 11:11-15, we also find the prophecy of a coming golden age, like that predicted in Revelation 20:1-6. Paul begins by asking, "Did they [the Jewish people] stumble that they might fall?" Then he answers, "God forbid: but by their fall salvation is come to the Gentiles [See Acts 13:46], to provoke them [the Jewish people] to jealousy. Now if their fall is the riches of the world, and their loss the riches of the Gentiles; how much more their fullness?" When he asks, "How much more?" he means how much more riches and how much more gain will accrue to the world when the Jewish people eventually turn to Christ.

In verse 13 Paul goes on to say, "But I speak to you that are Gentiles. Inasmuch then as I am an apostle of Gentiles, I glorify my ministry; if by any means I may provoke to jealousy them that are my flesh and may save some of them [referring to genetic Jews]. For if the casting away of them is the reconciling of the world, what shall the receiving of them be, but life from the dead?" This anticipated "life from the dead" doesn't point to new life for the Jewish people but rather predicts the great blessing of a golden age which will come to the whole world as a result of the Jewish people being brought to Jesus Christ. So, we have the same implication in Romans 11 which we have encountered in Matthew 6:10, I Corinthians 6:2, I Corinthians 15:25 and Isaiah 11:9, which is emphasized in more detail in Revelation 20:1-6.

Finally, in the sixth instance, please consider Isaiah 2:1-4. Though this passage has been quoted widely in preaching for many decades, there has been little emphasis upon its millennial implications. The first verse says, "The word that Isaiah the son of Amoz saw concerning Judah and Jerusalem. And it shall come to pass in the latter days, [that is, in the latter days of Judah and Jerusalem] that the mountain of Jehovah's house shall be established on the top of the mountains, and shall be exalted above the hills." This passage is not talking about a tectonic mountain-building process, an earthquake, or volcanic activity, but something much more significant.

"The mountain of Jehovah's house," his house, at that time being the Jewish temple, was Mt. Moriah, the location where Abraham centuries earlier had prepared to sacrifice Isaac. Prophetically, it was known as Mt. Zion. Isaiah implied that something of such supreme importance would take place at that location, inconspicuous mountain though it was, which would propel it to a status greater than that possessed by any other mountain in the world. Dwarfing earlier important events which had taken place there, or on other mountains, Mt. Moriah would be "established on the top of the mountains" and "be exalted above the hills."

Furthermore, verse 2 goes on to tell us that, "all nations shall flow unto it and many peoples shall go and say, Come ye, and let us go up to the mountain of Jehovah, to the house of the God of Jacob." That is the prophetic description of a great evangelistic movement, the one which actually began on the day of Pentecost as chronicled in the second chapter of the book of Acts.

Isaiah's famous passage also says that those people would go up to Mt. Zion (Mt. Moriah) in anticipation that God "will teach us of his ways, and we will walk in his paths: for out of Zion shall go forth the law." That law was not the law of Moses which was declared from Mt. Sinai, a completely different mountain.

The ultimate triumphant pinnacle in Isaiah's prophecy appears in verse 3 which predicts that, "he will judge between the nations, and will decide concerning many peoples; and they shall beat their swords into plowshares and their spears into pruning hooks; nation shall not lift up sword against nation, neither shall they learn war any more."

In meditating on the twentieth chapter of Revelation, especially verses 7 and 8, we should again contemplate some of the implications of a war-free world, implications which were also foreseen much earlier by Isaiah. War is to be abolished during the whole ten-centuries-long period of time called The Millennium. It is only subsequent to The Millennium that Satan gets his foothold again, enabling him to usher in one final destructive war-filled era. But for a coming long period of time, for a thousand years, there will be no war. What is predicted so clearly in Revelation was prophesied centuries earlier by Isaiah as well. Thus, on the basis of many scriptures, culminating in this famous passage in Revelation, we can anticipate a long period during which the cause of Christ will flourish and prevail!

Appendix I

Which Way Iran?

Iran has continuously been in the international spotlight, especially since the Khomeini Revolution of 1979. During that upheaval, on November 4, 1979, the entire diplomatic staff of the American Embassy was arrested and held hostage till the inauguration of President Ronald Reagan in 1981. Their imprisonment marked the turbulent transition from a long, cordial relationship between America and Iran during the reign of Shah Reza Pahlavi to the despotic rule of Mullah Khomeini, whose hatred for America is epitomized in his characterization of the United States as "The Great Satan." Since then, hostility has continuously characterized the relationship between Iran and America. Through harsh embargoes, America finally forced Iran to the negotiating table to get them either to abandon or substantially delay the development of nuclear weapons. A resulting agreement went into effect on January 17, 2016.

As far back as the magnificent Achaemenid Empire founded by Emperor Cyrus (reigned 559-530 B.C., II Chronicles 36:22 et al.), the people and governments controlling the Iranian Plateau have shown themselves to be exceptionally resilient and dynamic. However, when Emperor Darius (Ezra 4:5 et al.) pushed Iranian western conquest all the way to Greece, he triggered a terrible retribution, carried out by the military genius Alexander the Great (the notable "horn" of Daniel 8:5), bringing all of Iran under Greek control. Iranian vibrancy again asserted itself by the expulsion of the Greeks and the founding of the Iranian-Persian-Parthian Empire in 247 B.C. (See Acts 2:9.) Eventually, another branch of the Iranian people replaced the Parthians by establishing the Sassanian Empire in 226 A.D. Both the Parthians and the Sassanians were robust enough to repeatedly contest the eastern border of the Roman Empire. The Gospel of Christ made very significant inroads among the Iranian people despite the dominant Zoroastrian religion which was continuously endorsed by Iranian governments from the time of Cyrus till the rise of Islam. The Magi, who brought gifts to Christ in his infancy, were Zoroastrian priests.

In 642 A.D., a Muslim-Arab army, fighting with the fanatical zeal of Muhammad's vision of world conquest, defeated the Iranian-Persian-Sassanian army in the Battle of Nehawand, bringing all Iran under Muslim control. Even at that low point, Iranian resiliency was clearly seen in their refusal (in contrast to Syria, Egypt and all of northern Africa) to adopt Arabic as the Iranian national language, keeping their native Farsi in that critical role. Also, to spite their Arab conquerors, they embraced the Shia branch of Islam, hated by the Arabs. Next, Iran flexed its muscles dramatically in decisively defeating the Arabs at the Battle of the Zab River in 750 A.D., bringing the Arab Umayyad Caliphate (governed from Damascus) to a decisive and disastrous end. The center of Islamic power then shifted to the new Iranian-dominated Abbasid Caliphate, governing from the resplendent city of Baghdad which they built on the Tigris River. However, subsequently the Abbasid Caliphate slowly declined till in 1258 A.D. the Mongol-Turks destroyed Baghdad and wrested power from the waning Abbasids.

Revelation Verse by Verse

In spite of such dramatic setbacks, Iranian dynamism was not effaced. A new inland capital was founded at Isfahan. There, the great Iranian emperor, Shah Abbas, enhanced the magnificence of his capital city, Isfahan, to such a level that the idiom "Isfahan nisf Jahan" became colloquial. It means "Isfahan is half the world!" Iranian military power directed from Isfahan was able to force the army of the Ottoman Empire to abandon its first siege of Vienna in 1529 by attacking Ottoman Turkey on its eastern border. Subsequently, a breakdown of indigenous Iranian political power created a vacuum which ultimately divided Iran, giving Russia dominance in the north and Britain control in the south. But again, Iranian resilience emerged under the leadership of Reza Khan, a military officer who became prime minister in 1923 and was declared Shah in 1925. During World War II, Reza Khan was forced into exile by Britain and America due to his pro-Axis leanings and his son, Mohammed Reza Pahlavi, came to the throne. His rule was openly and whole-heartedly pro-Western. The Khomeini Revolution of 1979 brought the Shah's reign to a tragic end, forcing him into a short period of desperate exile, during which he died of cancer while vainly seeking permission to enter the United States for treatment.

Surprisingly, the Khomeini Revolution has been able to harness the remarkably persistent and dynamic Iranian centuries-long resilience to promote its own goals. Its immediate aim is to become the unquestioned dominating imperial power in the Middle East. For several decades, the competition between Saudi Arabia and Iran for Middle Eastern dominance has been growing. The balance now clearly favors Iran. In Iran's labor force, the engineering, scientific, technical and mechanical sectors are capably filled by home-grown talent, while in sharp contrast, Saudi Arabia is largely dependent upon third-country nationals. Iran has successfully weathered a long, bleak period of greatly reduced earnings from oil exports due to the sanctions imposed by the West. On the other hand, Saudi Arabia is just beginning to feel sharp constrictions due to the recent dramatic collapse of world oil prices. To cope, the Saudi Regime has reduced the lavish subsidies it pays to its own citizenry out of oil revenues, sparking internal unrest and criticism. Somehow, Iran has risen above "the oil curse," while Arabia has not. "Nations rich in natural resources, especially oil, tend to stagnate culturally and intellectually."[749]

For several months, on its southern border, Saudi Arabia has been bombing Yemen in an unsuccessful attempt to break the power of the Shia Houthi ruling coalition. The Houthis favor Iran from whom they receive major financial and military support. To Saudi Arabia's north is Iraq, a Shiite-controlled ally of Iran. To Saudi Arabia's northwest is Syria, whose brutal ruler is also a very close ally of Iran. In short, Arabia is nearly surrounded by pro-Iranian powers.

Further, Arabia has no naval presence in the Persian Gulf comparable to Iran's. They seem to be relying on protection from America's 5th fleet, which is based in Bahrain. By recently executing the leading Shia cleric of Arabia's important Shia community, Arabia's leaders infuriated Iran, resulting in the burning of the Arabian Embassy in Tehran. The burning of the embassy was not the result of a popular uprising. It was conceived and carried out by the Revolutionary Guard and their close subsidiary, the Basij, the most radical elements of Iran's fractious system of government. In a very hasty response, Arabia broke all diplomatic relations with Iran just at the time they should have been making every diplomatic effort to avoid open conflict.

---

749 Eric Weiner, The Geography of Genius, (New York: Simon Schuster, 2016), p. 90.

Appendix I

Everything points to an imminent, major, dramatic realignment in the Middle East. Iran has her Shiite proxies well-established in key locations throughout the region: Hezbollah in Lebanon, Hassan al Asad in Syria, the ruling Shiite government of Iraq in Baghdad, the Houthis in Yemen and the important Shia minority on Arabia's strategic east coast. Arabia has been frantically trying to get Sunni Muslim powers to pledge allegiance to the Arabian cause at this extremely tense moment. So far, the only significant commitment has been made by Sudan. While Pakistan professes loyalty to Saudi Arabia, she has counseled Arabia to negotiate with Iran and has made no commitment of troops to Arabia should war erupt. Perhaps a critical upheaval may come from the great existing tension within the royal house of Saudi Arabia. Should the present power structure in Arabia be brought down from within, it would invite attacks on Arabia's borders from the great Shiite coalition.

Should the Saudi Arabian regime collapse like a house of cards, or should open warfare erupt between Iran and Saudi Arabia, it is almost certain that the Shiite cause would prevail. Such a development would open the way for Iranian ground forces to directly confront Israel, whom the mullahs epitomize as "The Little Satan," in contrast to America, "The Great Satan." We may not have to wait for Iran to out-live the restrictions imposed by the recent Nuclear Arms Agreement so they may develop nuclear weapons with which to obliterate Israel. They may well attempt such an apocalyptic attack by conventional forces. Thus, along with Russia, which is already gathering awesome forces on Israel's border, Iran may consummate the role depicted for it in the 38th and 39th chapters of Ezekiel by non-nuclear war. The ultimate upshot of that coming war will be the dawn of an unparalleled opportunity for Gospel triumph! Let us pray that we may make the necessary preparations to be used significantly by God at that epochal turning point in history!

Map 1

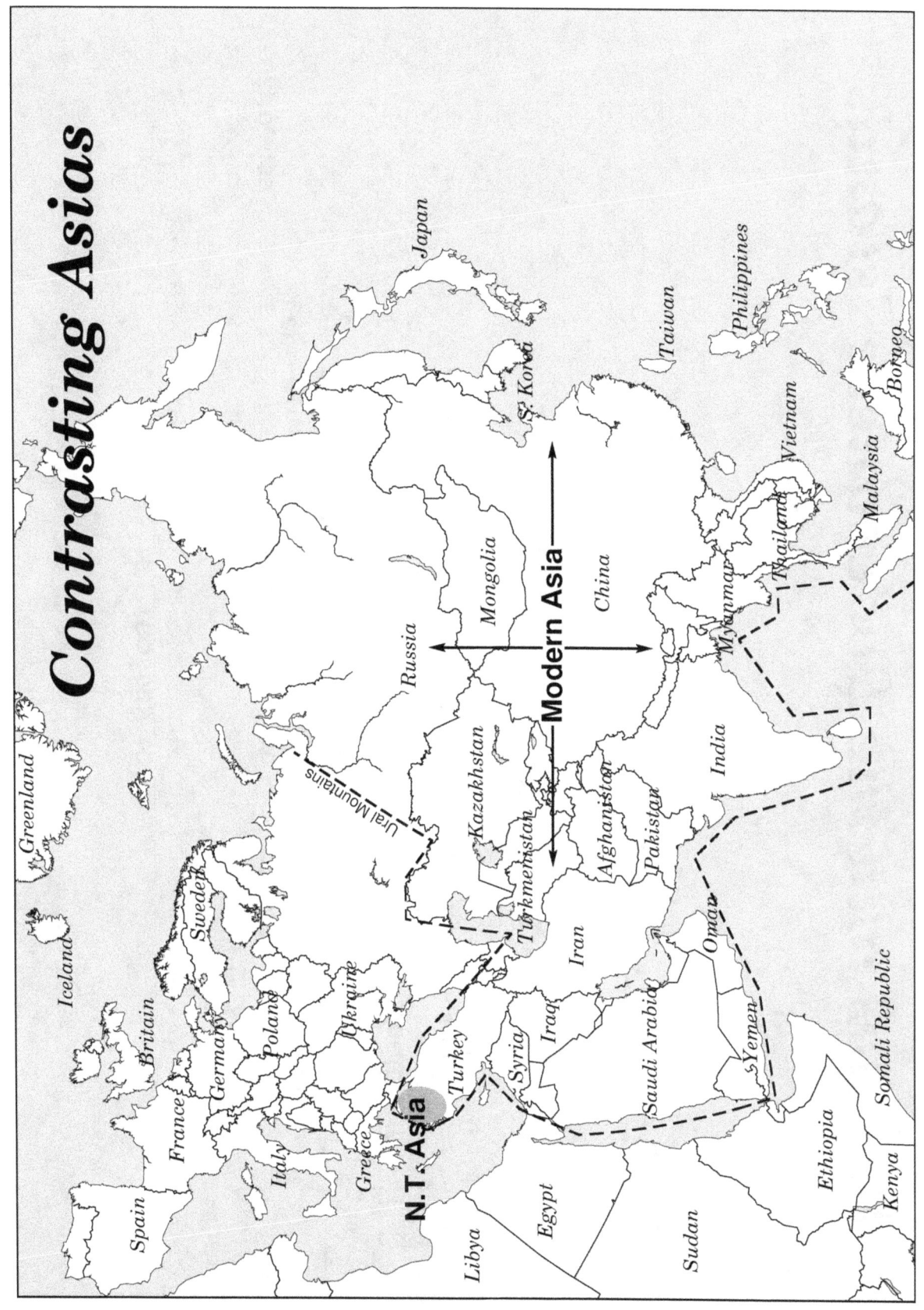

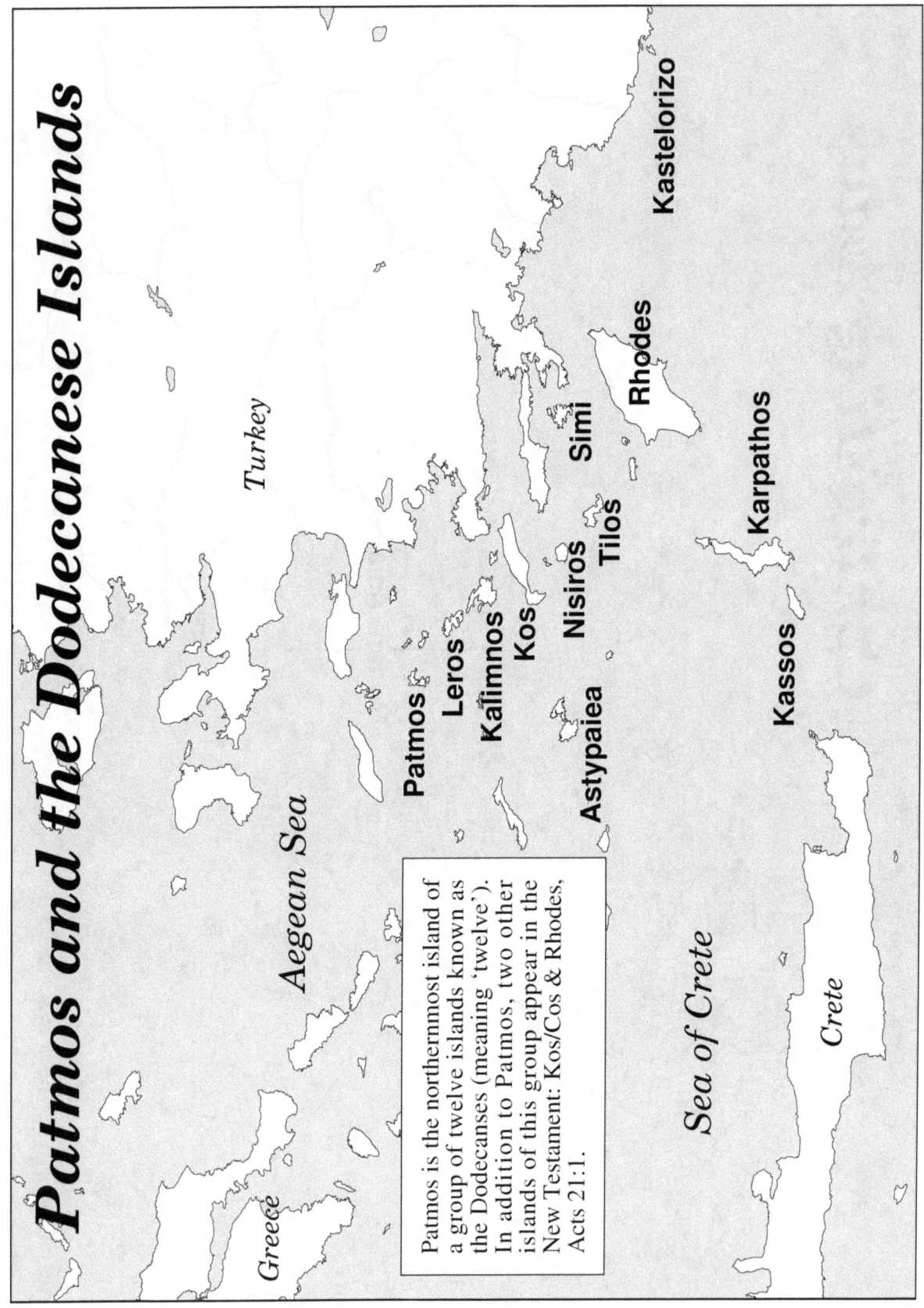

Map 3

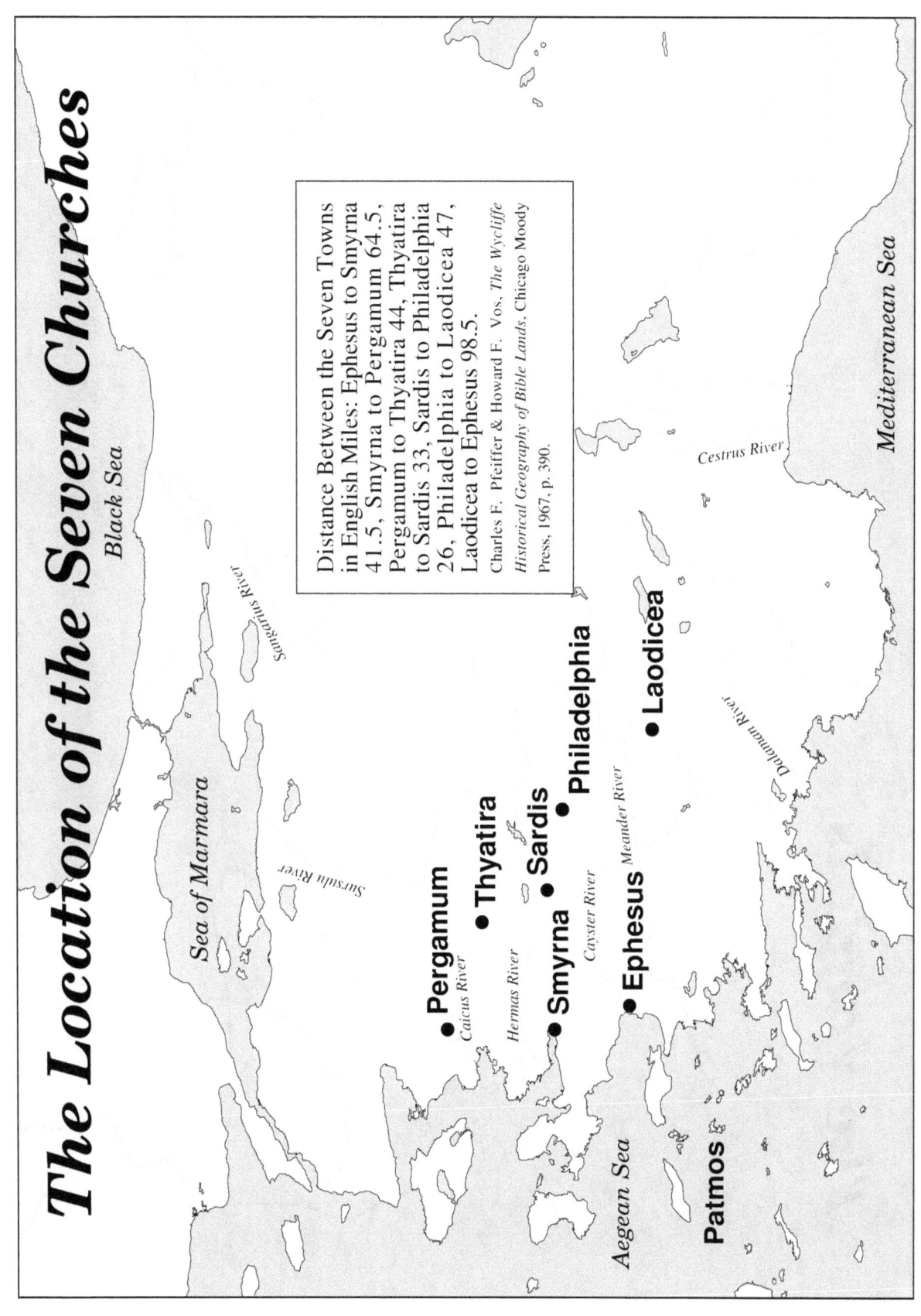

Map 4a

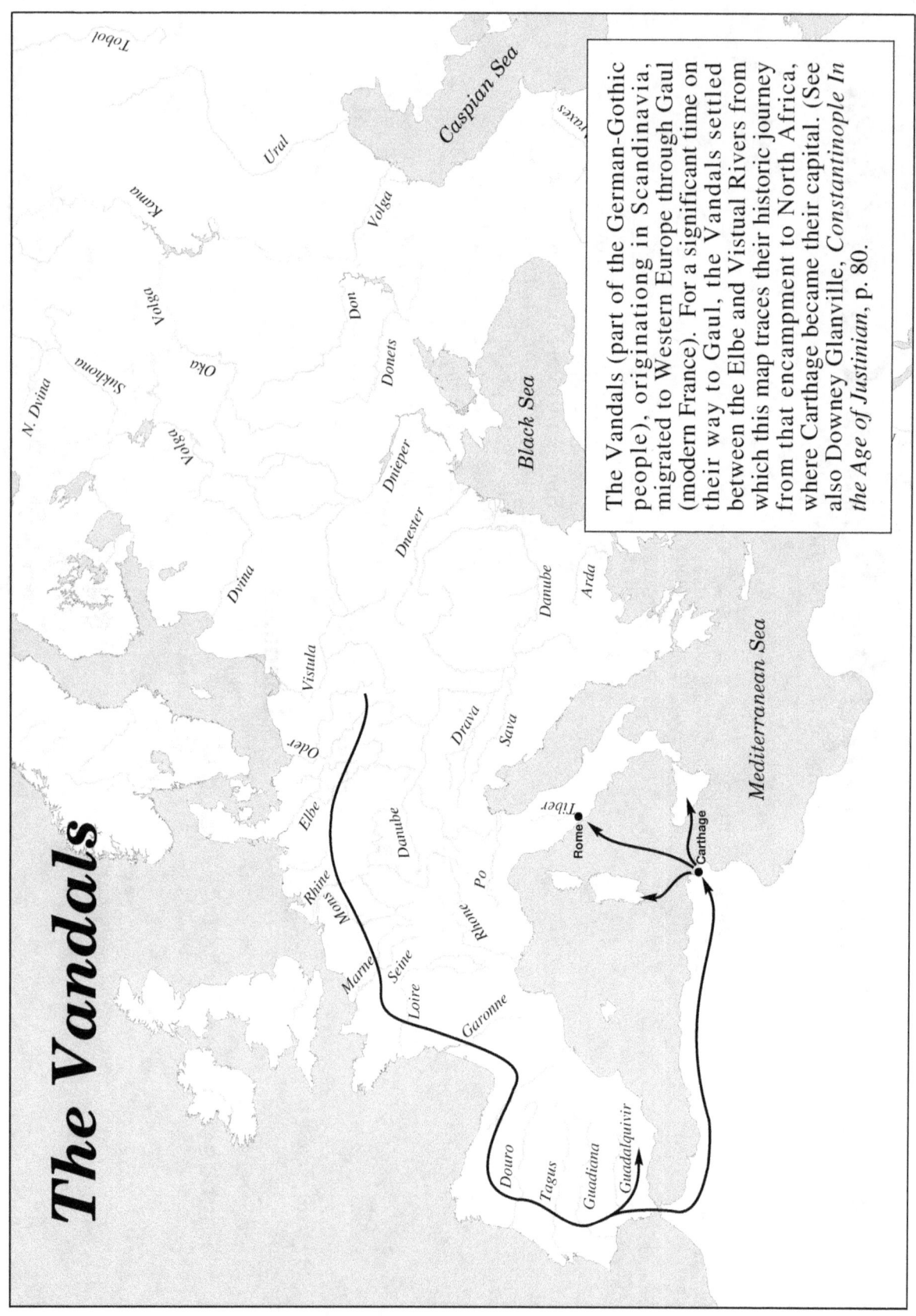

Map 4b

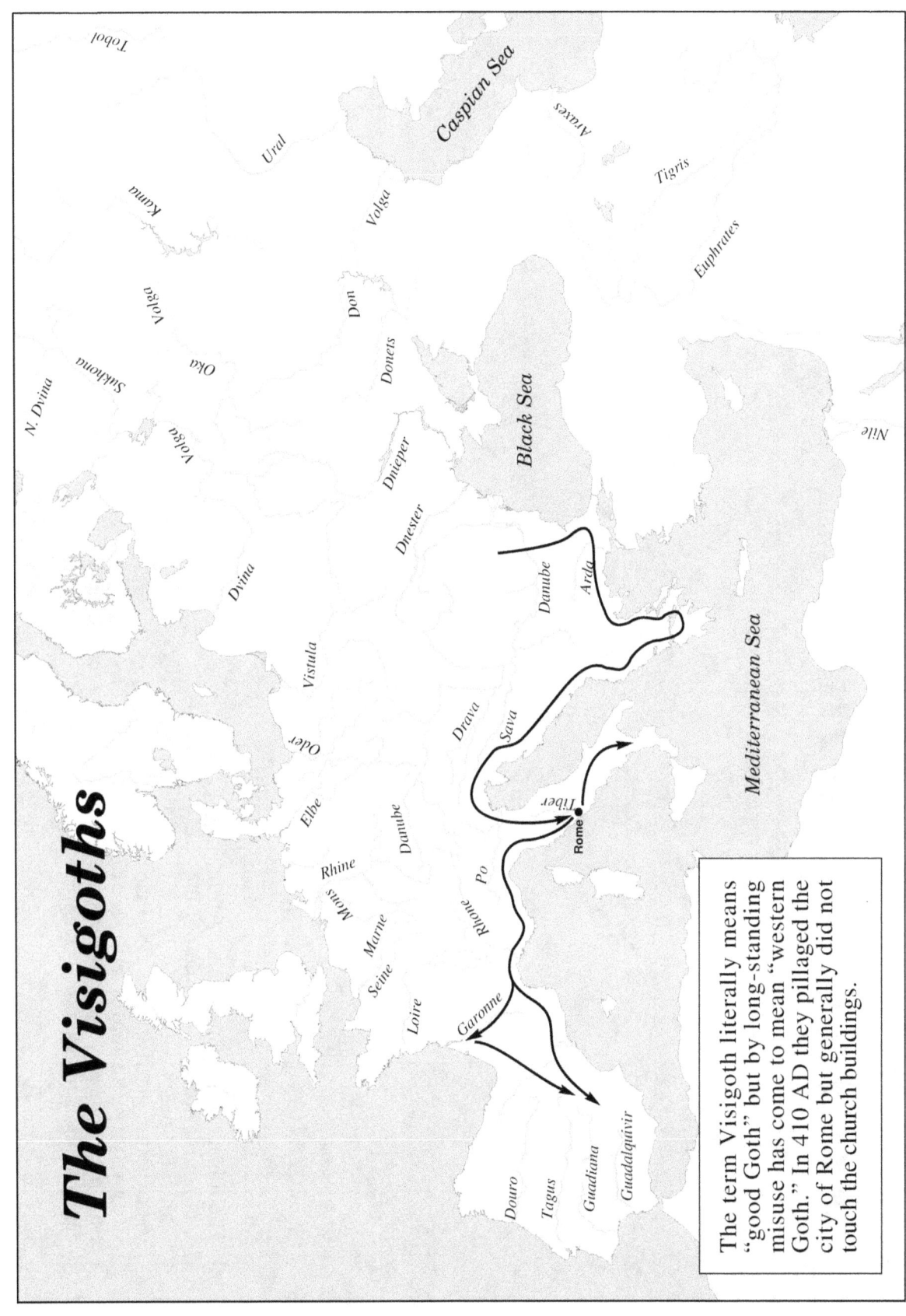

Map 4c

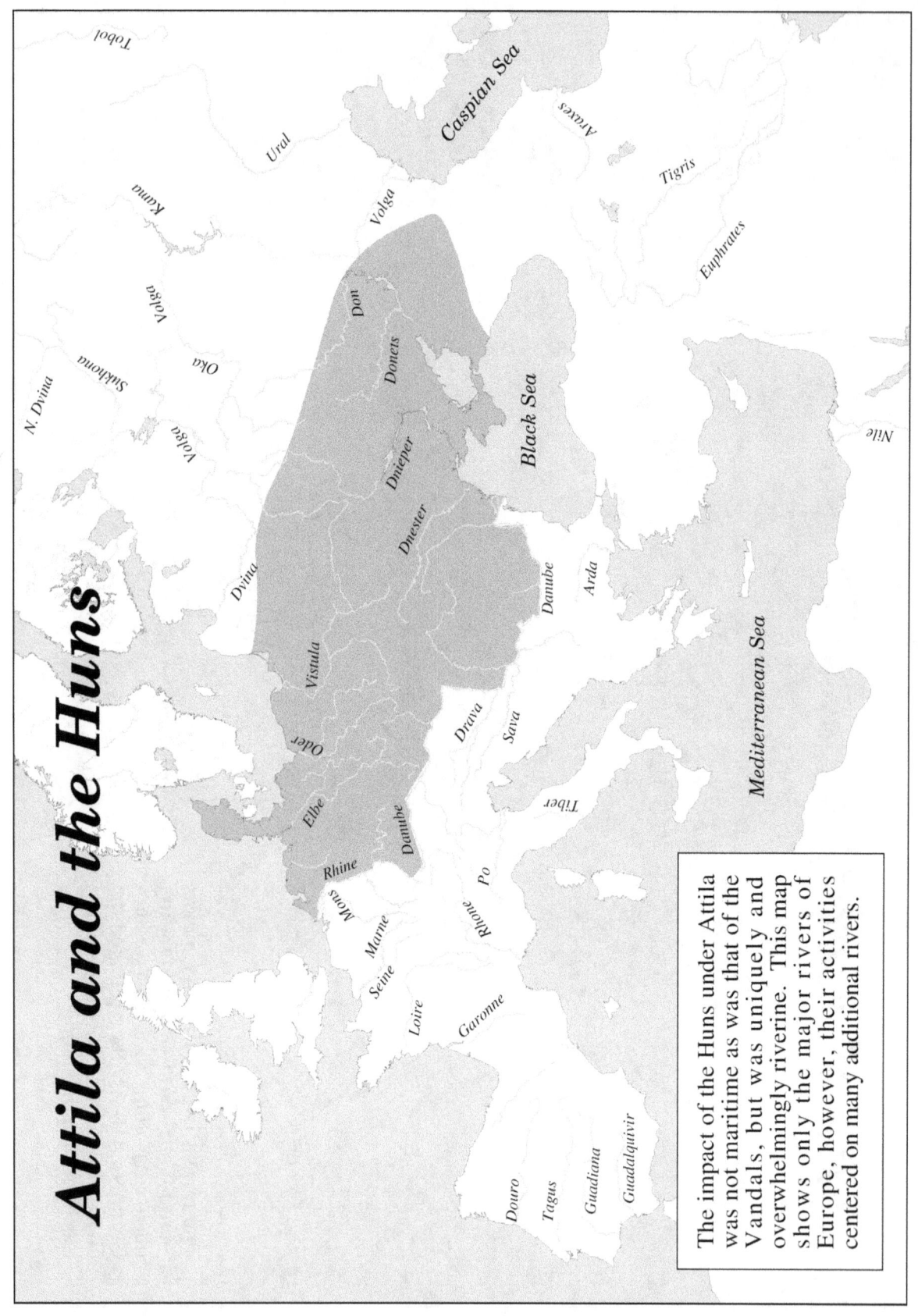

Map 5

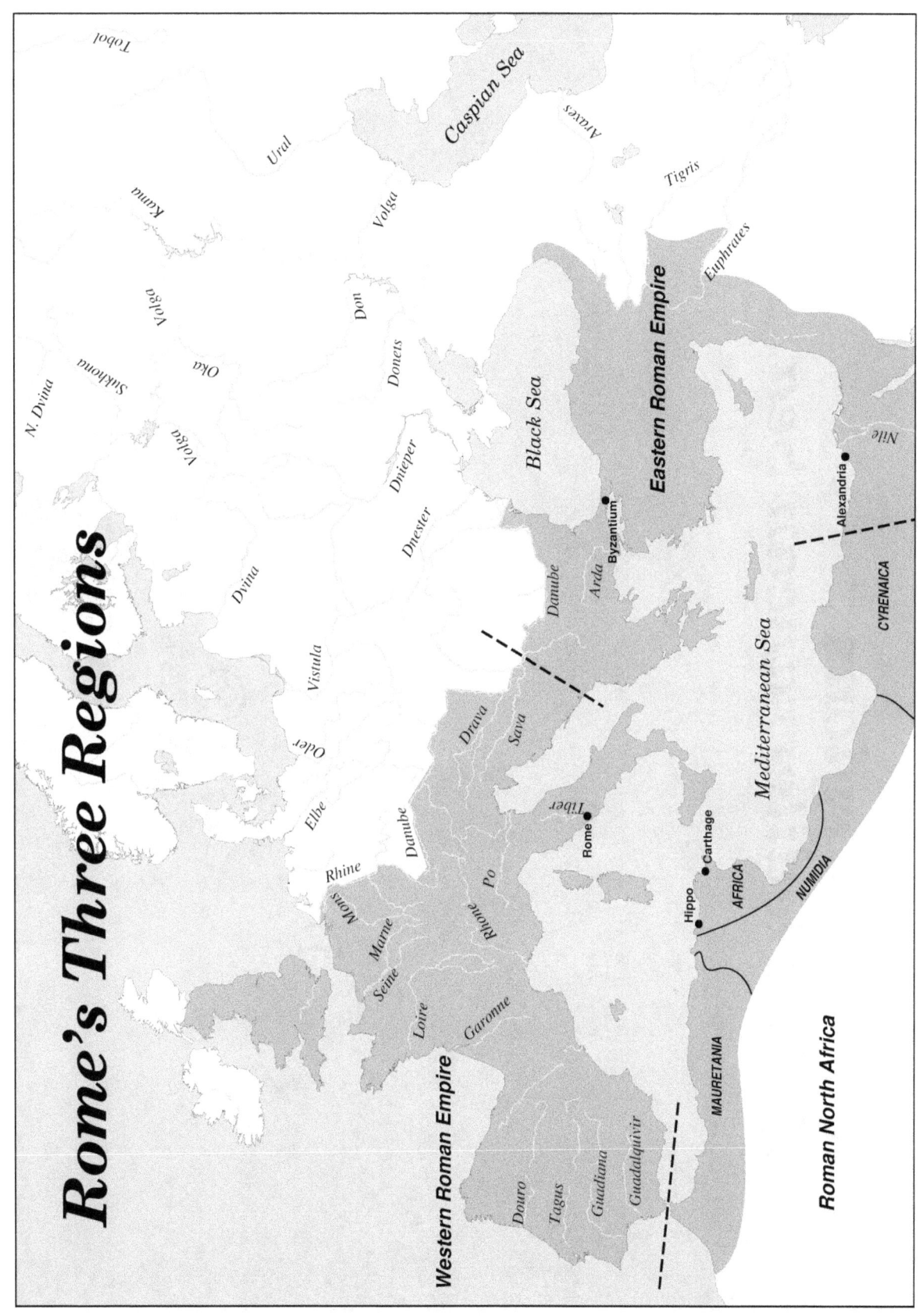

Map 6

Map 7

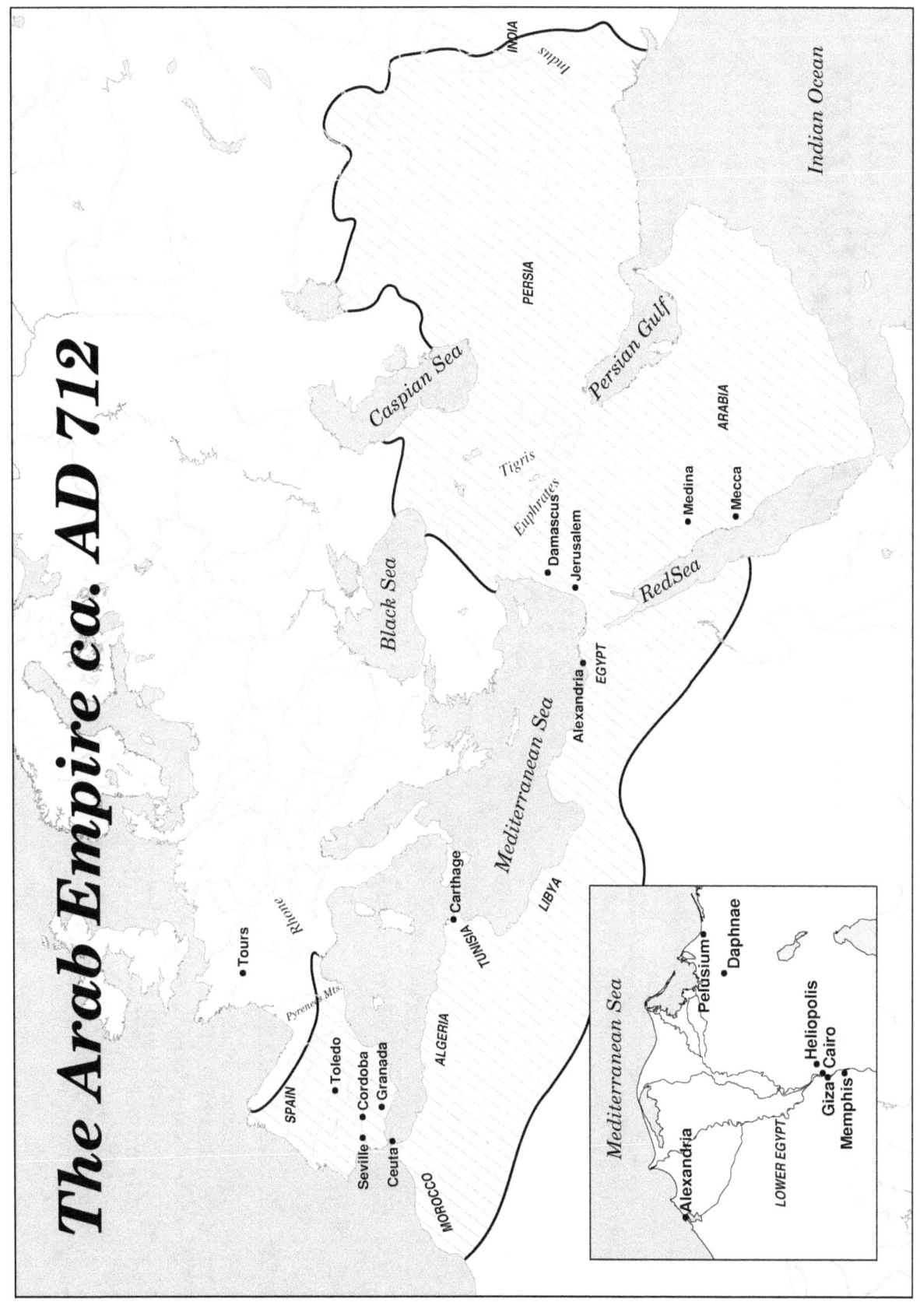

Map 8

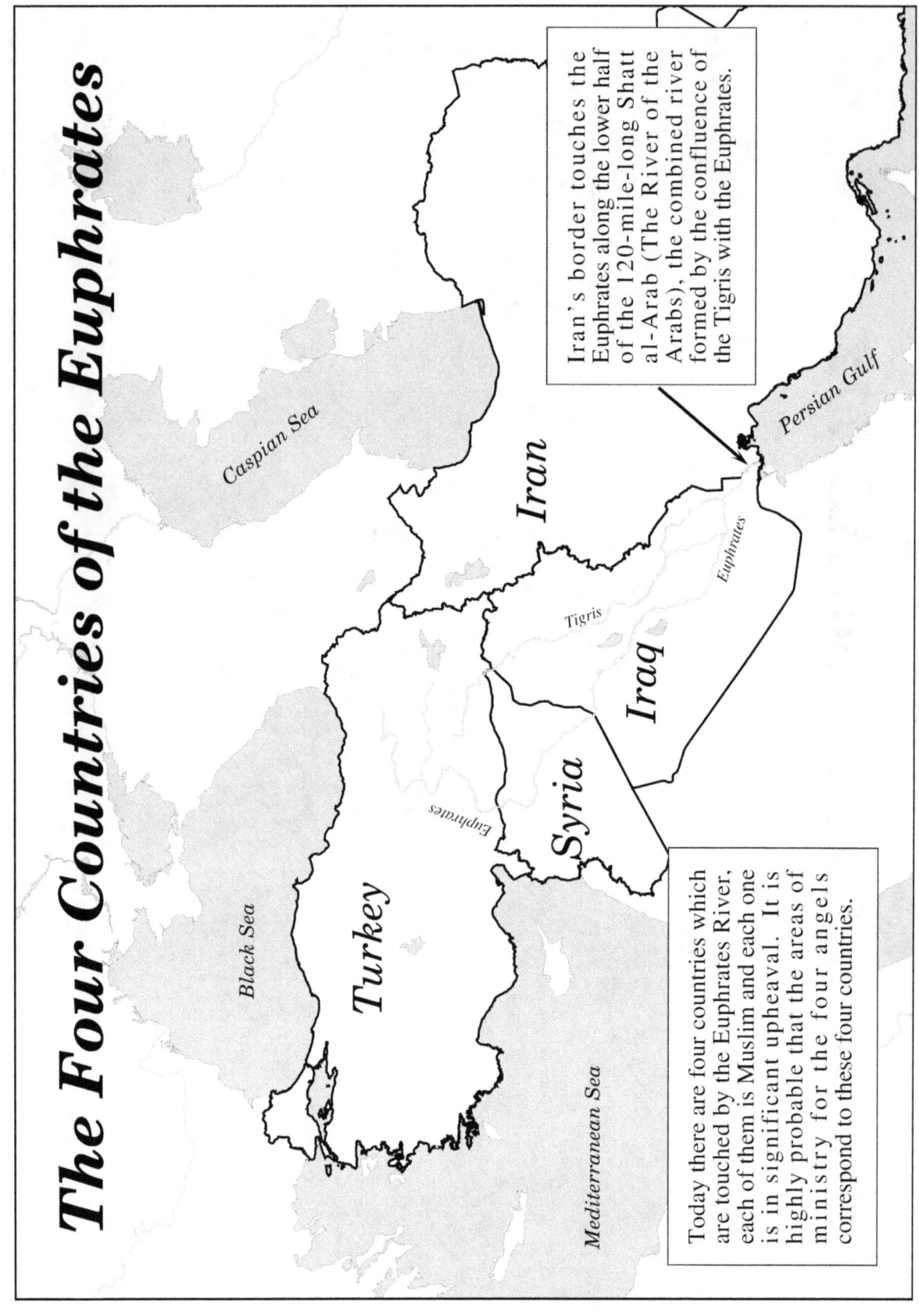

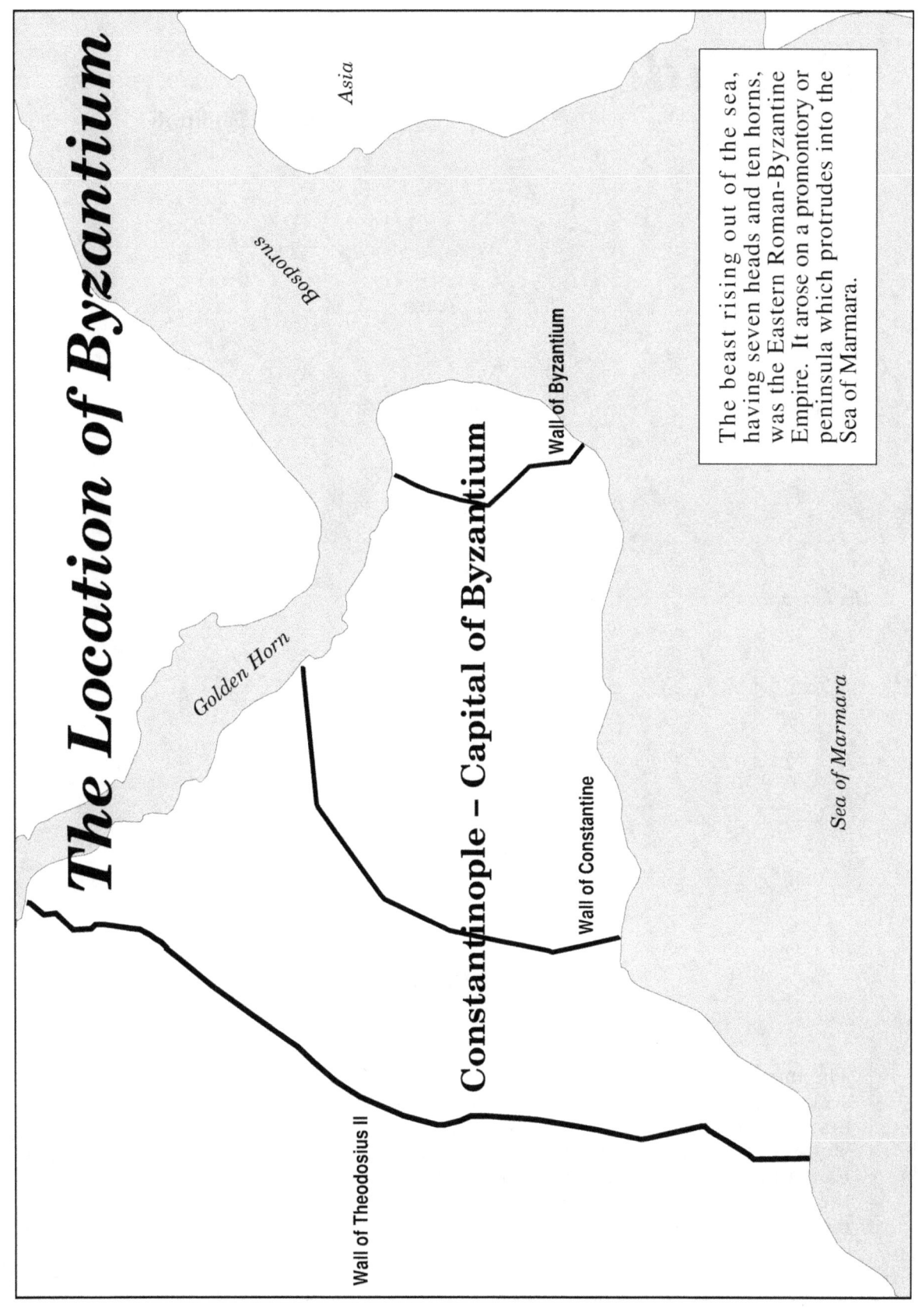

Map 10

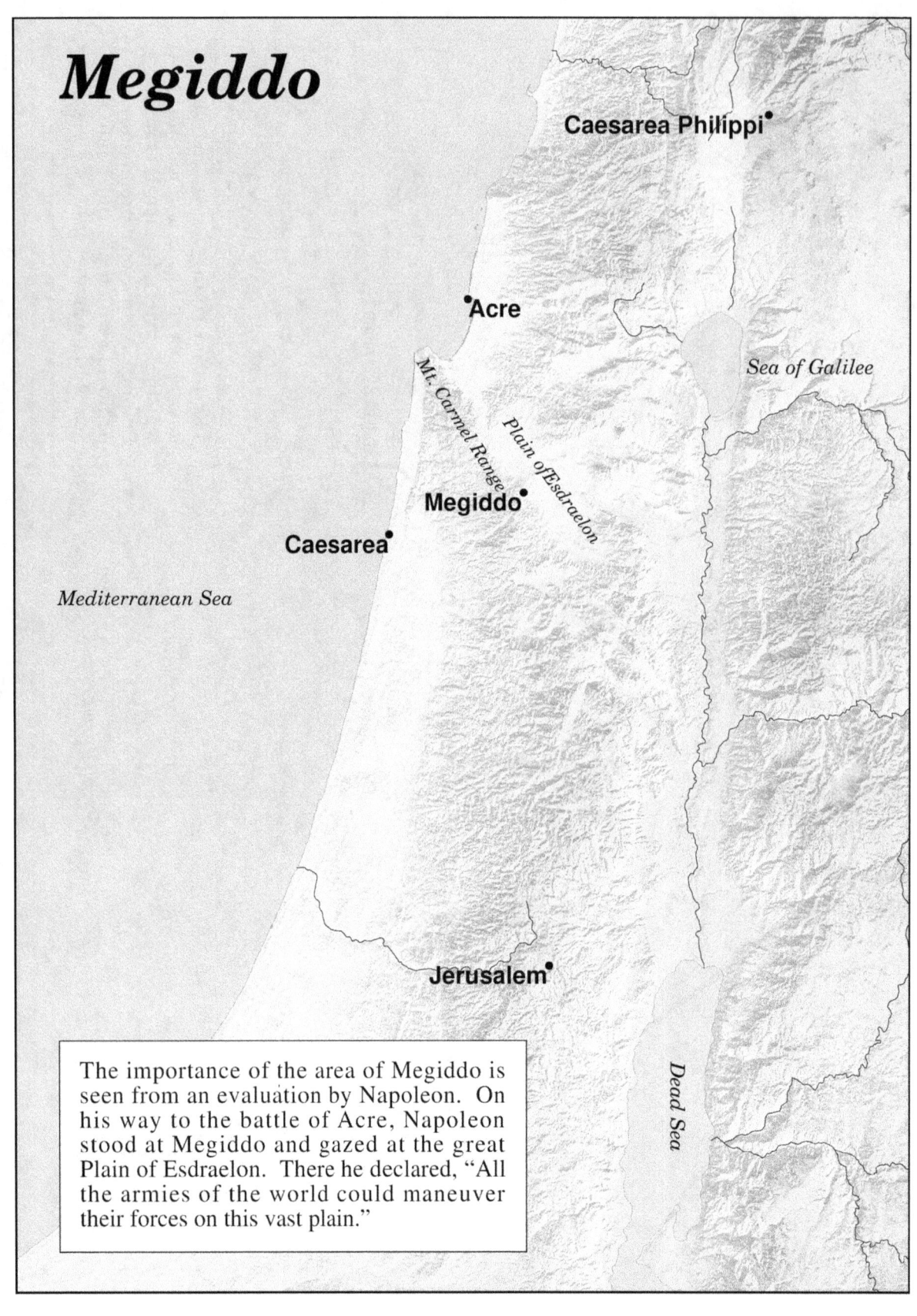

Alphabetical Index

a-millennial	329
Aachen (Aix-la-Chapelle)	127, 279
Abaddon	130, 142
Abbasid Caliphate	36, 137, 143, 419, 469
Abdul Rahman	436
Abdul-Muttalib	131
Abdullah	131
abominable	151, 274, 277, 291, 311, 313, 337, 348, 422
abomination	220, 275, 356, 358, 380, 388, 411
abortifacients	93, 211
abortion	211, 315, 327
Aboukir Bay	264
Abraham	22, 23, 106, 141, 155, 174, 204, 244, 260, 309, 313, 314, 344, 361, 412, 434, 467
Abraham Lincoln	204
Abraham's bosom	22, 23, 309
absolutism	287
Abu Talib	131, 133, 435
abyss	129, 130, 133, 135, 142, 164, 167, 230, 278-281, 283, 286, 325, 327, 330, 422, 424
acceptance of Christ	105
accuser	41, 184
Achaemenid Empire	469
Adam	31, 129, 174, 181, 445-448
Adam, first	181, 444
Adam, second	181, 444
Adolphus, Gustavus	417
Adriatic	121, 178
Aegean Sea	9, 14, 29, 32, 120, 194, 195, 202
Aelia Capitolina	381
afflicted	13, 400
Afghanistan	214, 251, 255, 262, 328, 420, 421, 429, 432, 438, 439
Africa	11, 117-121, 126, 159, 178, 214, 215, 301, 365, 421, 422, 428, 439, 469

agents of judgment..144
agents of justice...400
ages to come..41, 72, 73, 338, 363
agriculture..135, 147, 206, 210, 243, 360, 377
Ahmadinejad...251
Al Qaeda...113, 249
al-Qaddafi, Muammar...281, 430
Alaric..120, 121
Albania..438
Alcuin...127
alethinos..56, 63
Alexander the coppersmith..27-29
Alexander the Great...248, 292, 421
Alexander, Pope..222, 291, 293
Alexandria..36, 91, 120, 195, 198, 352, 388, 425
Alexandrinus manuscript..236
Algeria..178, 429
Ali ibn Talib..435
alive........................13, 22, 26, 33, 38, 49, 227, 242, 283, 322, 323, 381, 389, 394, 398, 399
all things new..343, 346, 396, 405, 407
Allah...139, 259, 260, 442-445, 447-453
Allahu akbar..132
alpha...14, 347, 367
Alpha and the Omega...14, 347, 367
Alps..124, 164
altar..37, 96, 115, 116, 143, 157, 158, 226, 244, 305, 423
Amazon River..163, 248
Amen...13, 62-64, 86, 110, 311, 317, 373
American Civil Liberties Union (ACLU)...458
Amina...131
Anagastes..123
Anatolia..198
angel......6, 7, 9, 10, 20, 23, 25, 32, 35, 40, 42, 43, 49, 51, 54, 55, 62, 75, 76, 79, 83-85, 103-105, 109, 110, 115, 116, 119, 122, 125, 127, 129, 130, 133, 142-144, 151, 152, 154-156, 159, 169,

Alphabetical Index

170, 183, 184, 218, 219, 223, 224, 226, 227, 229, 231, 232, 235-238, 241-246, 248, 263, 265-269, 271, 277, 289, 290, 295, 304, 305, 311, 314, 317, 318, 320, 322, 325-327, 337, 338, 349-353, 363-366, 370, 375, 387, 389, 392, 397-400, 402, 422, 443, 446, 447

angel of the abyss..130, 142, 327, 422
angel of wrath..237, 242, 244
Angola...307, 438
animal kingdom..76, 77, 87, 236, 311, 344
animal sacrifice..83
Anointed One..141, 380, 381, 385, 388, 443
anti-Christ..72
anti-God concepts..89, 167, 326
anti-Semitism..134, 204
Antioch..32, 57, 179, 195, 198, 231, 388, 425
Antipas..37, 38, 47, 60, 189
Apollos..40
Apollyon..130, 142
apostate church..272
apostle John..5, 7, 14, 25, 26, 32-34, 54, 56, 60, 103, 191, 229, 383
apostles. 8, 22, 25-28, 70, 72, 83, 89, 106, 130, 154, 157, 174, 175, 190, 290, 304, 351, 354, 357, 364, 387, 402
apostolic.............1, 8, 11, 30, 33, 36, 46, 53, 62, 117, 174, 175, 213, 215, 276, 329, 376, 388, 413
apostolic era..36, 174
Apostolic Fathers..8, 53
aqueducts..119, 125
Arab prophet..260, 323
Arabia..132, 135, 139, 249, 259, 301, 419
Arabian Peninsula..419, 445
Arabic..36, 132, 135-137, 213, 248, 421, 444, 447, 469
Arabic-speaking civilization..419
Arabs..123, 131, 134, 140, 141, 144, 203, 234, 248, 301, 422
arbitrary period of history..404
archangel..115, 143, 290, 398-400
Archippus..62
Arianism..259, 260
Aristotle..126

Revelation Verse by Verse

Arius	191, 260
Armageddon	148, 242, 264, 266, 409
Armenians	92, 357, 360
armies which are in heaven	318, 324, 375, 400
Asher	107
Asia	1, 6, 9-11, 14, 15, 17, 18, 25-30, 32, 33, 35, 36, 39, 42, 49, 53-55, 63, 119, 121, 143, 158, 204, 255, 301, 328, 335, 387, 419, 420, 422
Asia Minor	14, 32, 36, 420
Asia, Central	9, 204
Assyria	386, 410
astronomers	101, 245
astronomical	99, 169, 230, 328, 343, 389, 405, 407
Atawallpa	291
atheism	165, 246, 248, 253, 336, 372, 462
Atlantic	91, 117, 179, 241, 249, 291, 307, 323, 421
atmospheric	99, 173, 230, 231, 237, 266, 268, 343, 407
atmospheric heaven	173, 231
Attalus	10, 35, 36, 49, 56
Attila	121-124, 230
Augusta	118
Augustine	118-120, 126, 127, 159, 163, 425
Augustus	178, 278
Austria-Hungary	214
author	7, 8, 41, 56, 139, 165, 196, 227, 300, 397
Avars	203, 420
avenge	82, 97
Babel	276
Babylon	104, 105, 130, 142, 159, 166, 183, 193, 203, 219, 220, 222, 267, 268, 271, 272, 276, 277, 288-291, 293-296, 298, 300, 303-306, 352, 386, 423-425
Babylon the Great	130, 203, 219, 267, 268, 275-277, 289-291, 293, 294, 296, 298, 304-306
Baghdad	127, 137, 469, 471
Bahrain	470
Baker, Jim	281
Bakr, Abu	419

Alphabetical Index

Balaam 31, 38, 39, 49, 87
balance 94
Balearic Isles 120
Balikh River 435
Balkan Peninsula 117, 420
Balkan War 281
Baltic 124, 204, 278
Baluchistan 420, 430
Bangladesh 266
Baptists 294
barley 93, 94, 113
Basil 208
Basque 421
Battle of Acre 264
Battle of Armageddon 148, 266, 409
Battle of Kosovo 420
Battle of Manzikart 420
Battle of Nehawand 221, 420
Battle of Nehwand 469
Battle of Siffeen 435, 436
Battle of Talas 327, 419-422
Battle of the Nile 264
Battle of Yarmuk 419, 420
Battle of Yemama 419
Batu 206
bear 89, 197
beast ..28, 36, 39, 74, 77, 95, 133, 135, 164, 167, 194-200, 202-210, 223, 224, 232-234, 239-241, 245, 246, 252, 253, 255-259, 261-263, 273, 274, 276-288, 315, 316, 320-323, 330, 331, 338
beast coming up out of the sea 194, 197, 198, 200
beast that carrieth her 274, 277, 282
beast, first 202, 206-208, 240
Bede 126
beginning and the end 22, 347, 367
beginning of the creation of God 62, 64, 317

beheaded	91, 92, 210, 315, 330-332
Bel	298
beloved city	337
Beni Umaiya	131, 435
Berber	138, 203, 421
Bering Sea	204
Berlin	35, 37, 247
Berlin Wall	247, 253, 254
Bernard Lewis	138, 250, 417
Bethlehem	181, 190, 222, 382, 391
Bharatiya Janata Party	430
Big Bang	97
binding of Satan	327, 329, 330
biodiversity	163
birth control	93
bisexual	253, 315
Bishop of Rome	200, 426
Bishop Simon	221
bishops	10, 46, 89, 90, 92, 180, 221, 257, 258, 275, 287, 290, 416, 423-425
Bittugur	123
black horse	93, 94
Black Sea	194, 195, 202
Blasphemy	32, 58, 194, 197, 245, 246, 268, 269, 273, 274, 277, 436
Bleda	123, 124
blessed are the dead	98, 225
blissful status	403
Blue Nile	243
Boethius	126
Bohemians	90
Boko Haram	365, 439
Boniface	118-120
Book of Life	54, 55, 203, 278, 339-341, 358, 373
book of the future	79, 80, 83, 152
books	7, 80, 127, 136, 139, 165, 167, 222, 315, 339, 340, 402

Alphabetical Index

books were opened..339, 340
booze...246
Bosporus...194, 195, 197, 198
bowls..82, 231, 236, 238, 271, 289, 349, 409
Brahman..292
brass...20, 42, 148, 169, 299, 370
Brazil...163, 299
breastplates...140, 147, 235
breath of his mouth...401
breath of life...167, 168
bride adorned..176, 215, 344, 345
bride of Christ...176, 192, 215, 256, 273, 293, 296, 313, 350
bride, the wife of the Lamb...176, 181, 288, 349
bridles..213, 228
brimstone...133, 147, 223-225, 322, 323, 337, 338, 348, 349
Britain...215, 284, 286
Brown, Dan..165
Buddhism...193, 421
Buddhist culture..420
budgets...280, 297, 328
Bulgaria...123, 438
Bulgars..203, 234
burned with fire...296, 297
burnt out stars...404, 405
Bush, President George...437
buy or to sell...210
Byzantine 49, 63, 117, 133, 138, 144, 145, 151, 194-203, 206, 207, 209, 232, 233, 240, 248, 260, 364, 420, 421, 423
Byzantine Empire 117, 141, 144, 145, 151, 194, 195, 197-201, 203, 205-207, 209, 232, 233, 240, 364, 421, 423
Byzantine government..197
Byzantium.......................................36, 132, 145, 194, 197, 207, 209, 221, 233, 364, 420
C. S. Lewis..286
Caesar..15, 37, 38, 196, 200, 209, 220, 221, 425

Caesarea 425
Caesarea of Cappadocia (Kayseri) 198
Caesaropapism 200, 201
Caiaphas 12, 13, 19, 383
Cairo 251
Cajamarca 291
Caligula 15
Caliph Uthman 435
Cambodia 243, 437, 438
Cambridge 254
camels 50, 51, 134
camp of the saints 337
Canada's Supreme Court 271
candelabra 18
candlesticks 18, 19, 23, 25, 30, 76, 160, 161
cannibalism 384
Cape Bon 119
Cape Verde Islands 291
capital punishment 44, 97
capitalism 247, 335, 427
Capitalist 268, 272
captains 99, 100, 321
captives 112, 309
captives of Judah 411
captivity 22, 23, 105, 204, 262, 309, 411
Cardinal Gasparri 220
cardinals 275, 425
Carolingian Renaissance 127
Carrington Event 245
carrion birds 100, 385, 420
Carthage 117, 118, 120, 122, 141, 178, 380, 383
Casaroli 205
Caspian 124, 205, 360
Cassiodorus 126

Alphabetical Index

Castro, Raul...272
cataclysmic conflict..145, 213, 265, 266
Catherine the Great...204
Catholic. 90, 113, 119, 187, 189-191, 258, 259, 272, 277, 292, 299, 306, 307, 310, 377, 427, 429, 433, 438
Catholic Church. 200, 205, 217, 219, 220, 257, 258, 272, 275, 277, 280, 282, 284, 287, 290, 299, 302, 303, 357, 425
Catholic hierarchy..272, 273
Catholicism...................220, 256, 257, 260, 262, 298, 310, 372, 424, 427, 428, 432-434, 437, 438
Catholics...90, 180, 190, 302, 310
cattle..77, 301
Caucasus...124, 204, 207, 240, 422
cavalry...50, 51, 140
celibacy..217, 302
Celsus..165, 403, 446, 447
Celts..234
Cephas..25
certificate...37, 272
chain..325, 326
Chaldeans...411
Chane, Bishop John...294
Changan..193
chariots...140, 141, 145, 301, 321
charlatans...384
Charlemagne...126, 127, 164, 278, 279, 281, 283, 287, 356
Charlemagne Prize...279
Charles the Bald..127
chaste...403
chasten...62, 68
Chechen war..240
Chechnya...204, 207
cherubim...31, 71
Chiang Kai-shek..215
China..161, 182, 187, 193, 194, 215, 241, 243, 249, 251, 252, 254, 266, 281, 299, 300, 327, 335, 377, 421, 430, 431, 437, 438, 461

Revelation Verse by Verse

China-Pakistan relationship	431
Chinese	193, 215, 234, 246, 252, 421, 430, 431, 461
Chinese Nationalists	215
choke points	241, 377
Chou En-lai	246
Christendom	113, 190, 302, 433
Christian - Marxist dialogue	428
Christian age	1, 72, 73, 90, 213, 329, 337, 386
Christian center	387, 388
Christian dispensation	79, 170, 182, 330, 338, 357, 365
Christian era	72, 73, 87, 109-111, 174, 193, 213, 227, 228, 272, 276, 313, 365, 366, 417
Christian evangelism	90, 92, 193
Christian period of history	213, 338, 365, 384
Christian Turks	422
Christian world	193, 194, 227

Christians. 1, 13-16, 23, 32-35, 38, 44, 46, 47, 53-55, 57-61, 63, 67, 73, 75, 76, 82, 89-92, 95-97, 105, 110-113, 116, 133, 136, 138, 139, 145, 158-161, 171, 173, 177, 179, 182-189, 191-193, 196-200, 202, 203, 209, 216, 220, 221, 224-226, 233, 234, 242, 255, 259, 261-263, 273, 276, 277, 284-286, 296, 309, 311, 313-315, 322, 323, 328, 329, 331-333, 337, 341, 349, 357, 360, 363, 366, 371, 372, 378, 381-383, 385, 387, 388, 396, 398-400, 403, 412, 415-417, 426, 428, 430, 442-446, 448, 449, 453, 455, 459, 463, 465, 466

Christology	259, 260, 315, 441, 445, 454
Christopher Hitchens	165
Christotokos	191
church and state	220, 221, 223, 273, 297, 432
Church Fathers	53
church in Corinth	28, 73, 173, 176, 202, 290, 340, 398, 399
church in France	287
church in Persia	221
church in Rome	130, 162, 175, 180, 219, 290, 293, 340
churches of Asia	6, 10, 26, 32, 49, 55
Churchill, Winston	279
Chuzas	189
cinnamon	301
circumcision	25

Alphabetical Index

citizenship...54, 61, 169, 178, 348, 368, 396, 465
City of God..61, 120, 126, 159, 193, 350, 351, 359, 425
city of my God...60, 61, 229, 344
civil government..195, 196, 222, 274, 396, 424, 425
civilizational crisis..228
Clemens...15
Clement of Alexandria..8, 91
Clement of Rome...290, 423
climate...163, 266, 267
climatological phenomena...117
clouds...12, 13, 19, 148, 163, 230, 384, 387, 390, 394, 399
coats of mail...140
Codreanu...290
collectivization..210
colonialism...214
Colossae...17, 57, 62, 67, 358
commerce..195, 202, 298
Commission...243, 249, 279, 280
Commissioners..279, 280, 285, 288
commodities..165, 293, 299, 300, 302
Common Market...281
Communism..........187, 246, 247, 253-255, 260, 292, 315, 336, 377, 427-430, 432, 433, 437, 438
Communist.......................182, 240, 246, 247, 251, 253-255, 259, 268, 272, 336, 428-431, 438
Communist China..187, 215, 249, 251, 430
compendium...156
compromise..16, 35, 38, 157, 310, 349, 370, 379
comunidades de base...427
concordat...220
CONEMEX..311
conflict, temporal..262
conflict, universal..263
conformed to the Gospel...193
Confucianism..430
conquer..52, 87, 88, 90, 113, 264

conquering 30, 87-90, 135, 180, 198, 291, 335
consequences of sin 83
Constantine 92, 119, 189, 194-197, 200, 221, 222, 257, 281, 423, 426
Constantinople 122, 123, 133, 144, 145, 191, 194-199, 201, 205-207, 209, 245, 264, 302, 423, 425
Constitution for Europe 280
consumer items 303, 304
contraceptives 186, 211
conversion 58, 88, 104, 106, 108, 136, 139, 179, 181, 193, 213, 215, 222, 265, 356, 357, 412-416, 423
conversion of the Jews 88, 104, 265, 409, 410, 412, 413, 415
Coptic Christians 261
Copts 198
Corinth 28, 73, 173, 175, 176, 192, 202, 262, 290, 340, 398, 399
Cornelius 116
Cornelius Gallus 138
corrupt church 166, 217, 225, 257, 258, 261, 276, 286, 288, 298, 299, 322
corsairs 272
Corsica 120
Cosmos 59, 101, 457, 463
Council of Constance 223, 275
Council of Ministers 285
Council of Nicea 53, 190, 191
counterfeit 98, 180, 182, 219, 288, 423
craftsman 305
creationism 458
creatures 76, 77, 81, 82, 85-87, 94, 109, 121, 216, 236, 289, 311, 344
Crete 119
crimson 20, 98, 300, 368, 394
criticism 89, 202
Croesus 49-51
crown 34, 60, 74, 75, 77, 87, 88, 90, 139, 140, 173-175, 225, 317
crown of life 34, 54, 60
crucifixion 12, 26, 166, 309, 381, 397

Alphabetical Index

crusade..92, 222, 424
Crusaders...213, 430
Crusades..1, 180, 213, 214, 302
crying..177, 226, 346, 348, 399
Ctesiphon..199, 221
Cuba..272, 274, 306, 438
culminating event...395
cultural relativism..227
Cultural Revolution..187, 252
cultural vitality...228
culture..7, 89, 124, 134, 193, 227, 251, 257, 261, 287, 378, 420-422
cumulative evidence...397
curse...31, 33, 38, 148, 268, 328, 362, 381, 412, 446, 470
Cush..100, 322
Cyprus..119
Cyrenaica...178
Cyril..191, 207, 208
Cyrillic..207, 208
Cyrillic Bible...208
Cyrus...49-51, 298, 380, 421, 469
Czar...205, 209, 210, 240, 246, 256
Czech Republic..208, 222
Czechoslovakia..438
Czechs..207, 222, 223
Dacian king..178
Dagestan..204
Damascus...19, 21, 54, 131, 137, 198, 231, 264, 435, 436, 469
Dan (tribe of)..106, 107
Dan Brown...165
Daniel..12, 19-21, 45, 341, 379-381, 397
Danube...117, 122, 123, 207
Dar al-Islam...139
Dardanelles..195, 420
Darius..248, 380, 421, 469

Revelation Verse by Verse

Dark Ages 113, 125
Darwin 456, 457, 460
DaVinci Code 165
Dawkins, Richard 165, 457, 460-462
day and night 77, 111, 112, 184, 224, 338
day of judgment 337, 344, 405, 446
death 3, 12, 13, 15, 22, 23, 27, 32, 34, 35, 38, 44, 46, 47, 49, 54, 70, 75, 79, 81, 83, 84, 89, 90, 92, 93, 95, 98, 99, 107, 118, 121, 123, 125, 126, 131, 136-139, 144, 146, 147, 162, 166, 170, 174, 181, 185, 190, 196-199, 203, 204, 206, 208-210, 213, 218, 219, 221, 225, 231, 232, 235, 242, 254, 279, 290, 296, 303, 309, 314, 315, 323, 325, 328, 331, 332, 334, 339-341, 346-349, 359, 362, 369, 372, 382, 392, 395-398, 406, 419, 428, 432, 436, 444, 448, 449, 465, 466
death shall be no more 346, 362
deceive the nations 72, 327, 328, 330, 331, 333
decriminalization 271
Dedan 100
deity 46, 61, 82, 190, 226, 348, 367, 372, 402
delays 391, 392, 395
Delphi 50
democracy 240, 247, 252, 256, 292
denarius 94
Denmark 90, 124, 284
Dennett, Daniel 165
deposed 117, 125, 275, 287
desolate 189, 257, 287, 303, 304, 380
despot 97
destiny 34, 36, 71, 143, 219, 267, 289, 319, 321, 323, 339, 340
devil 6, 34, 52, 177, 181, 184-186, 188, 189, 224, 311, 326, 329, 330, 338
devilish 37, 184
Dhimmi 138, 139, 261
diadems 177, 178, 194, 197, 317, 375, 392
Dinzic 123
dioceses 257, 294, 303, 424, 425
Diocletian 47, 92, 96, 201, 257, 424
discrimination 211, 261, 315
disease 44, 151, 239

Alphabetical Index

dispersion	9, 25, 39, 339, 386-388
Disraeli, Benjamin	190
dissenters	163, 198, 209, 258
dissolved	337, 338, 344, 406, 407
divine intervention	144, 231, 265, 268, 318, 324, 336, 384, 406
divine patience	155, 244, 293, 406
division in Islam	249, 250
Dnieper River	205, 207, 357
Doctrina Jacobi	141
doctrinal anchor points	378
doctrines of demons	275
dogs	87, 368, 391, 462
dolphins	245
Domitian	8, 14-16, 91, 178
Donation of Constantine	189, 423
Donatist controversy	119, 159, 425
Donatist Movement	159, 425
door	57, 59, 68, 69, 71, 76, 251, 271, 351, 361, 367, 388, 424
Doxology	77
dragon	176-179, 182-186, 188, 189, 194, 196-199, 204, 206, 213, 252-256, 258, 259, 261, 315, 321, 324, 326, 330, 338
drug addiction	149
drug culture	227
Dulin, Gene	254
E.U.	214, 279-281, 283-286, 288
eagles	187, 385
earth	12-14, 19, 21, 25, 59, 70-72, 74, 80-82, 84-86, 88-91, 95, 97-100, 103, 104, 116-118, 127, 129, 134, 135, 146, 152-155, 160-164, 166, 167, 171, 172, 178, 179, 184-186, 188, 189, 195, 198-200, 202-210, 216, 218-220, 223, 224, 226, 227, 229, 230, 233, 238-240, 244, 245, 247, 257, 267, 272-278, 282, 288, 289, 291, 293, 297-300, 305, 306, 310, 316, 319-322, 324, 328, 333, 335, 337-339, 341, 343-348, 356, 357, 386, 387, 389, 390, 393, 395, 397, 399, 404-407, 410, 447-449, 457, 466, 467
earthquake	60, 98-100, 116, 168-170, 172, 235, 267, 377, 467
East China Sea	241
East Germany	438

Eastern Catholicism...256
Eastern Europe..247, 253, 255
Eastern Roman Empire...194, 197
Eastern Roman-Byzantine Empire...194
Eastern Rome...117
ecclesia...434
ecclesiastical perversion..220
economic...18, 29, 32, 33, 42, 93-95, 104, 116, 127, 130, 132, 147, 163, 169, 180, 202, 238, 241, 245, 246, 249, 251, 252, 254, 255, 258, 263, 268, 279, 281, 286, 297, 298, 301, 303, 304, 327, 372, 386, 403, 421, 425, 427, 431, 433, 439, 466
economy...32, 42, 93, 95, 148, 203, 210, 255, 281, 301
ecstasy...43, 343, 348, 399, 403
ecumenical council...200
Eden...31, 87, 177, 253, 345, 347, 360
Edessa..198, 357
Egypt....36, 117, 135, 144, 165, 166, 178, 187, 190, 195, 198, 203, 214, 232, 234, 235, 243, 250, 261, 264, 267, 269, 362, 410, 420, 421, 436, 469
Egyptians...144, 203, 235
Einstein...101
El Arish...264
El Niño...266
elders...10, 31, 74-77, 80-82, 85, 86, 109, 110, 170, 171, 216, 311, 312, 425
Elias..208
Elijah..54, 162, 371
embankment...383
end of the ages..72, 73
end of times...72
England...117, 126, 301, 424
English Channel...117
entrepreneurial activity..303
Epaphras..62
Ephesus...10, 14, 16, 17, 25-31, 52, 57, 63, 65, 85, 136, 173, 191, 195, 262, 387
Ephraemi manuscript..236
epidemic..94, 239
Episcopal church..294

Alphabetical Index

eschatological event	376, 383, 386, 399
Esdraelon	264
Esther	30
Estonia	204, 438
eternal good tidings	218, 219
eternally triumphant	406
eternity	1, 11, 72, 79, 97, 338, 361-363, 367
ethics	110, 130, 186, 193, 222, 244, 290-292, 302, 303, 310, 315, 327, 378, 403
Ethiopia	100, 132, 145, 243, 438
ethnic strife	361, 362
Euphrates	91, 92, 117, 143, 144, 169, 179, 193, 237, 248-252, 263, 265, 420, 435, 436
Europe	11, 92, 103, 118, 119, 122, 123, 125-127, 143, 201, 214, 227, 228, 239, 247, 254, 255, 264, 278-283, 285, 286, 298, 299, 334, 356, 417, 420, 421
Europe, new	281, 282, 285
European	117, 122, 124, 141, 175, 214, 252, 278-282, 285, 286, 288, 301, 311, 417, 421
European Central Bank	280
European Coal and Steel Community (ECSC)	279
European Economic Community	279
European Russia	206
European super-state	279
European Union	175, 214, 241, 274, 279, 281, 283-285, 288
Eusebius	26
evangelicals	310, 311
evangelistic triumph	415
Eve	87, 181
evolution	196, 456, 458, 459, 461, 463
evolution, Neo-Darwinian	315, 455
evolutionary biology	461
evolutionary theory	404, 460
exaltation	16, 73, 85, 168, 230, 332
excommunicated	287, 424
expediency	134, 246, 273, 290-292, 303
extinction	30, 121, 220, 284, 289, 331, 337, 398, 421
eyesalve	66, 67

Revelation Verse by Verse

eyewitness..398, 448, 449
Ezekiel..20, 61, 71, 84, 100, 137, 142, 155, 182, 183, 251, 264, 265, 318-322, 333, 335-337, 411, 437
fallen church...203, 267, 273, 289, 302
fallen is Babylon...130, 203, 219, 289, 290
false prophet............38, 132, 133, 141, 210, 230, 252, 253, 255, 259-263, 316, 321-323, 338, 427
famine...94, 95, 123, 146, 296, 360, 372, 377, 379, 380, 384
fantasies..384
Farag..251
Fascist...254, 292
Fatima..435
fear not..6, 21, 22, 34, 412
fearful...94, 116, 337, 348, 349, 365, 367, 368
feast of Pentecost..381
fellow-servant..314, 366
feudalism..287, 432, 433
financial scandal..276
Finland..204, 438
fire..20, 33, 41, 42, 55, 66, 75, 76, 92, 113, 116, 117, 119, 133, 147, 151, 152, 161-164, 208, 223-226, 232, 242, 245, 265, 287, 296-298, 311, 317, 319, 322, 323, 334, 336-338, 341, 344, 348, 349, 400
fire came down...337
first and the last..21, 22, 32, 367
first born of the dead..12, 13
first commandment..55
first earth..343, 346
first fruits unto God and unto the Lamb..106, 213, 216
first heaven...343, 346
first resurrection..331, 332
flat earth..103
flight..33, 138, 196, 203, 312, 382, 444
flood...83, 263, 367, 389, 390, 405
Florence..299
flour...301, 390
forehead...104, 210, 223, 240, 275, 323, 330, 331

Alphabetical Index

foreheads..................104-106, 135, 136, 211, 215, 216, 275, 332, 363, 412

fornication.38, 42, 43, 148, 149, 180, 217, 219, 220, 222, 223, 257, 272-275, 277, 291, 297, 310, 322, 348, 369, 424

fornicators..................166, 337, 348, 368, 369

Fort Sumter..................214

fortunes..................303, 337

fossil record..................405, 462

fountains..................113, 122, 168, 219, 230, 243

four and twenty elders..................74, 77, 82, 170, 171, 311

four corners of the earth..................103, 328, 333, 335

four living creatures..................76, 77, 81, 82, 86, 87, 94, 109, 216, 236, 289, 311, 344

foursquare..................352, 353, 393

fourth kingdom..................380

France..................32, 35, 92, 100, 124, 215, 284, 288, 335, 421

Francis, Pope..................180, 220, 272, 276, 282, 287, 299, 302, 306, 427, 428, 438

Francisco Pizarro..................291

Francs..................278

frankincense..................301

French..................214, 215, 227, 272, 279, 281, 283, 284, 287

French consuls..................272

French Revolution..................250, 287

freshwater..................237, 243

frogs..................252, 253

Fukushima..................266

Fukuyama..................254

function of scripture..................157, 319

furlong..................228, 352

future.....5, 6, 30, 34, 46, 72, 73, 78-81, 83, 88, 107, 111, 130, 134, 152, 155, 169, 210, 211, 213, 215, 233, 240, 241, 255, 256, 281, 282, 287, 293, 313, 315, 362, 366, 382, 383, 385, 397, 399, 402, 412, 413, 415, 417

Gabriel..................115, 380, 399

Gad..................107

Gaiseric..................119, 120, 122

Galatia..................29

Galatians..................35, 344

Galen 36
Gamaliel 58
Gaul 8, 32, 118, 121, 123
Gauls 35, 234
gay couples 93, 211
gemstones 74
General el-Sisi 250
General Tariq 421
Genseric 118-120
Gentile 105, 106, 108, 158-162, 166, 167, 415, 416
Gentile sovereignty 416
Gentiles 25, 57, 59, 73, 88, 91, 103, 106, 108, 110, 337, 369, 413-416, 467
geographic 6, 11, 18, 42, 142, 159, 204, 227, 248, 272, 335, 343, 351
geography 6, 42, 119, 158, 343, 346
geomagnetic storm 245
German 90, 94, 95, 100, 111, 119, 120, 122-125, 180, 207, 214, 215, 271, 279, 301, 383, 417, 421, 424
Germanic people 122
Germany 90, 94, 95, 100, 122, 215, 271, 301, 417, 424
Ghenghis Khan 336
ghettos 258
Giacomo Matteotti 292
Gibbs, Marion 433
Gibraltar 421, 429
Giscard d'Estaing 281
Glasnost 253
glass 76, 232, 234, 295, 353-355
global 19, 25, 103, 104, 147, 153, 158, 163, 164, 186, 187, 203, 207, 214, 226, 238, 239, 241, 245, 247, 253, 262, 263, 265, 268, 276, 277, 282, 299, 301, 303, 304, 309, 310, 320, 323, 343, 372, 388, 389, 396, 413
global church 158
global conflict 147, 214, 262, 265, 309
global earth 103, 239
global society 186, 310
global trade 303, 304

Alphabetical Index

Global War..103, 187, 253, 263, 277
glory of God...64, 86, 176, 236, 350, 355, 356, 434
goats...321, 339, 392, 393
God hypothesis...165
God of Israel...20, 410
Gog..100, 319, 321, 322, 324, 328, 333-336, 429
Goitein, S. D..419
gold.......50, 66, 74, 76, 139, 140, 148, 169, 180, 235, 242, 274, 275, 299, 301, 303, 353-355, 370
Golden Horde..206, 335
Golden Horn..194
golden reed..352
Gomer..100, 322
Gonderic...118
Gondophares, King...193
Gorbachev, Mikhail...240, 241, 247, 253, 254, 428, 438
Gospel concept..193
Gospel triumph...72, 88, 95, 106, 108, 109, 164, 170, 409, 471
Gospel victory...103, 106, 108, 265
Goths...118, 119, 122
government.....89, 91, 117, 138, 179, 183, 186, 195-197, 211, 220, 221, 250, 253, 257, 258, 260, 271, 272, 274, 279, 287, 290, 297, 328, 336, 356, 396, 437
grapes...226, 227
grapes of wrath...227
great city...159, 165, 166, 168, 267, 268, 288, 298, 303, 304, 306
great harlot......................................257, 271, 273, 287-289, 291-293, 297, 303, 305, 310, 311, 322
Great Schism...424
great supper of God..320
great tribulation...43, 44, 110-113, 116, 382
great white throne..317, 338, 339, 341, 400
Greece...35, 120, 147, 242, 248, 280, 284, 438, 469
Greek.5, 7, 10, 14, 35, 36, 38, 43, 44, 51, 56, 59, 63-65, 68, 69, 74, 88, 94, 96, 97, 112, 119, 121, 126, 130, 138, 141, 142, 149, 151, 160, 178, 190, 197, 205, 207, 214, 217, 228, 229, 234-236, 240, 242, 264, 269, 300-302, 306, 313, 317, 327, 345, 351-353, 356, 373, 377, 381, 387, 388, 402, 415, 416, 420
Greek Orthodox church..205, 217, 240

Revelation Verse by Verse

Gregory	126
Grunbaum	97
Guillaume	130, 132
Hades	22, 23, 95, 167, 309, 312, 325, 341, 396
Hadrian	91, 117, 387
hail	116, 117, 172, 232, 235, 268, 269
Hail Mary	190
Hallelujah	82, 309-312, 401
Hamon-gog	321
Hanbali school	139
Handel, George Frideric	82, 305
Hannibal	121
Hapsburg Empire	164, 214, 258, 279
Har-Magedon	263, 264
harlot	180-182, 220, 256-258, 271-277, 281-283, 286-289, 291-293, 296-298, 302-306, 310, 311, 313, 322
harlotry	222, 271
Harpagos	50
harps	74, 82, 83, 216, 232, 233
Harris, Sam	165
Harun al-Rashid	127
Hashim, Beni	131, 132, 435
Hassan al Asad	471
Havana	306
he that heard and saw	365
he that is holy	55, 56, 366, 367
heads and horns	177, 196, 197, 274, 276
healing of the nations	346, 359-361
heaven	12, 13, 19, 21, 30, 41, 45, 53-55, 57, 60, 61, 71, 73, 76, 79, 80, 82, 83, 85, 86, 99, 110, 112, 115, 122, 127, 129, 130, 132, 133, 151, 153-155, 157, 162, 163, 167-170, 172, 173, 176-179, 183, 184, 186, 195, 202, 203, 208, 215, 216, 218, 219, 225, 226, 229-231, 233, 235, 238, 246, 247, 268, 276, 282, 289, 293, 295, 301, 304, 309, 311, 314, 316, 318, 320, 324, 325, 337, 338, 341, 343-350, 353, 355, 357, 360-362, 368, 386-389, 393-396, 398, 400, 402
heavenly Jerusalem	159, 181, 215, 344
Hebblethwaite, Peter	428

Alphabetical Index

Hellenism	177
Henry II	433
Henry III	433
Henry IV	433
Heraclius	141, 197, 199
Herakleios	197, 199
hermeneutics	259
Herod Antipas	189
Herodian Jewish temple	376
Herodotus	49, 51
Hezbollah	249, 471
Hidden Jews	161
Hierapolis	17, 62
hierarchy among the angels	115, 399
Higgins, Andrew	256
Hijaz	132
Hijrah	132
Hinduism	193, 194, 422
hippie movement	227
Hippo	118, 120, 425
historical process	255
history of Islam	409, 420
Hitchens, Christopher	165
Hitler	1, 180, 204, 292

holy city...8, 17, 158, 159, 166, 176, 215, 228, 288, 291, 344, 347, 349, 350, 352, 353, 356, 357, 362, 372, 373, 381, 388, 398

holy place	18, 96, 181, 359, 381, 388
Holy Roman Emperor	279, 417
Holy Roman Empire	164, 274, 278-280, 285, 287, 423
Holy See	180, 220, 287, 427

holy Spirit.11, 29, 33, 34, 73, 81, 85, 105, 136, 157, 181, 183, 202, 216, 226, 329, 345, 350, 356, 359, 362, 364, 371, 412, 441-443, 450

Homo sapiens	456, 462
homosexual union	274

homosexuals............44, 182, 274, 294, 315, 326, 373
honor of the nations............358
Horn of Africa............422
horses............51, 87, 95, 134, 135, 139-141, 147, 148, 228, 301, 316, 318, 321, 322, 377
Hosea............107, 412
hour of trial............59, 60
house of Israel............85, 107, 265, 321, 411, 412
house of Judah............57, 182, 410, 412
housetop............382
Houthi............249, 470, 471
how long............72, 82, 97, 98, 104, 156, 208, 244, 362
Huelva............429
humiliation............112, 139, 296, 396, 397
Hun............120, 122-124, 126, 203, 230
Hunayn Ibn Ishaq............36, 127, 130, 131
hundred and forty and four thousand............106, 215, 216
Hungarians............207, 420
Hungary............122, 214, 215, 278, 438
Hurricane Katrina............266
Hus, Jan............222, 223, 424
Hussain............436
hydroelectric............243
I come quickly............60, 365, 367, 373
ideological............194, 250, 251, 254, 256, 263, 274, 282, 377, 422, 429, 430, 433, 434
idolaters............166, 337, 348, 368, 370, 422
idols............38, 42, 43, 134, 148, 169, 370, 422
Ignatius............32, 179, 231
Il-Khan............335
image..19, 37, 56, 64, 65, 83, 97, 174, 195, 208-210, 223, 224, 232-234, 239-241, 246, 283, 322, 323, 330, 331, 348
image of the beast............209
immediate............379, 400, 414
immortality............396, 397, 399, 402, 403
impenitence............148, 269

Alphabetical Index

Imperialism	134, 255
in the Spirit	16, 73, 105, 174, 202, 231, 273, 349
incense	37, 75, 82, 96, 115, 116, 276, 301, 384
incorruptible	338, 395, 396, 399
incorruption	396, 399, 402
India	135, 137, 161, 193, 194, 214, 252, 264, 266, 292, 299, 387, 422
Indian Ocean	420
Indies	264, 422
Indus River	323, 420, 421
industry	195, 215, 266
infrastructure	125, 151, 169, 297
inheritance	23, 26, 282, 314, 410, 432
iniquities	295, 379, 412
injustice	180, 396, 400, 466
Inka/Inca	291
investiture controversy	287
Iran	99, 100, 137, 144, 182, 193, 198, 209, 214, 221, 248-251, 335, 387, 420, 421, 470, 471
Iranian Revolution	250
Iraq	139, 144, 214, 248-251, 262, 328, 365, 409, 410, 429, 435-437, 470, 471
Irenaeus	8, 15, 32
iron	113, 140, 147, 275, 299, 325, 340, 380
Isaiah	20, 34, 67, 72, 87, 89, 98, 142, 183, 305, 319, 355, 360, 394, 410, 411, 443, 467, 468
Isfahan	360, 470
Ishaq, Hunayn ibn	36, 127, 130, 131
Isidore Mercator	423
Isidorian Decretals	423
ISIS	193, 249, 250, 365, 437
Islam	30, 98, 100, 105, 127, 131-139, 142, 143, 145, 182, 187, 193, 194, 198, 207, 213, 221, 227, 240, 246, 248-251, 259-261, 315, 322, 323, 325, 327, 335, 357, 359, 364, 372, 419-422
Islamic civilization	250
Islamic history	137, 143, 249
Islamic movement	323, 325, 421
Islamic socialism	429, 439

Revelation Verse by Verse

Israel...20, 38, 39, 54, 61, 70, 85, 99, 100, 103, 106, 107, 134, 154, 161, 187, 191, 192, 216, 234, 251, 264, 265, 269, 320, 321, 333-336, 341, 350, 351, 369, 380, 386, 410-416, 434, 436, 437, 443, 449, 450, 465, 466, 471

Israel shall blossom...410

Issachar..108

Italy...120, 121, 123, 125, 126, 220, 282, 305, 423

Jacob...81, 105-108, 174, 260, 314, 410-413, 468

James...21, 25, 33, 66, 70, 166, 340

Jamnia..33, 386

Jan Hus..222, 223, 424

Japan..215, 251, 266, 278, 281, 430, 438

Japanese-Russian War..215

Jehovah. 11, 12, 31, 34, 39, 61, 71, 77, 89, 145, 161, 164, 171, 174, 265, 276, 297, 310, 312, 320-322, 336, 337, 341, 355, 356, 363, 399, 412, 415

Jehovah of hosts...356, 410, 412, 415

Jeremiah...134, 138, 271, 340, 371, 410, 411

Jerome...32, 126, 140

Jerusalem 8, 9, 21, 25, 27, 28, 30, 33, 34, 57, 60, 61, 104, 105, 107, 111, 130, 158, 159, 166, 176, 180, 181, 192, 198, 213, 215, 218, 229, 288, 290, 334, 337, 344, 345, 348-350, 352-354, 356, 357, 362, 380-389, 398, 412, 415, 416

Jerusalem that is above..176, 180, 181, 192, 344

Jesus is divine..234

Jewish converts..104, 105, 215-217

Jewish leadership...386

Jewish lexicographer..217, 218

Jewish nationalism...381

Jewish rebellion...33, 386

Jewish revolt...381, 386

Jewish sovereignty...416

Jewish synagogues..90

Jewish temple...28, 33, 158, 355, 386

Jewish thought..217

Jewish/Gentile church..167-169, 182, 202

Jews. 15, 25, 26, 29, 32, 33, 58, 59, 88, 92, 103-106, 108, 111, 136, 139, 141, 144, 154, 161, 180, 203, 213, 214, 218, 258, 265, 290, 294, 337, 351, 369, 381-386, 397, 412-416

Alphabetical Index

Jezebel	10, 42-44, 46, 49, 293
Jezreel	264
Jihad	187, 213
jizya	136, 138, 139
Joannitius	127
John Chrysostom	122
John the Baptist	215
Joseph	107, 108, 190, 196, 362
Josephus	352, 384
Judah	57, 80, 81, 107, 182, 340, 384, 386, 412
Judaism	46, 89, 215, 218, 259
Judas Maccabeus	381
judgment	7, 14, 28, 39, 40, 43, 54, 113, 117, 142, 144, 155, 171, 195, 210, 213, 219, 223, 231, 232, 234, 235, 237, 243, 244, 265, 267, 269, 271, 288, 296-298, 304, 310, 311, 316, 317, 319, 327, 330, 331, 333, 334, 336-341, 344, 363, 367, 371, 391-393, 396, 400, 402, 405, 406, 411, 414, 458, 466
judgment day	145, 238, 340
judgment seat	340
Jupiter	381, 387
just	85, 109, 118, 224, 244, 291, 314, 331
justice	43, 55, 74, 97, 98, 113, 124, 171, 232, 234, 244, 292, 296, 304, 327, 400, 433, 466
justifier	85, 109
Justin Martyr	8
Justinian	195, 200
Ka'ba	131
Karbala	436
Kautilya	292
Kawadh-Siroy	199
Kazakhstan	240
Kennan, George	254
key of David	55, 57
key of Hades	22
key of the abyss	130, 133, 230, 325
keys of death	22, 23, 309
Khadija	137

Khamenei, Ayatollah..437
Khan..470
Khan of the Golden Horde...335
Kharijite..436
Kharijite [Seceder] Movement...435
Khazar kingdom...422
Khomeini Revolution...249, 469, 470
Khorasan..387
Khusrau..198, 199
Kiev...194, 204-209, 240, 246, 334, 357, 428
Kievan Rus...204, 205, 209, 240
King Henry VIII...424
King of kings...259, 263, 286, 309, 318, 320
kings...12, 13, 45, 73, 74, 91, 99, 100, 156, 171, 194, 248, 249, 251-253, 257, 259, 261-264, 272-274, 278, 280, 283-288, 291, 292, 296, 297, 321, 322, 324, 335, 356, 409, 429
kings of the earth.....................12, 13, 100, 171, 257, 272-274, 288, 291, 297, 321, 322, 324, 356
Kipchak...206
Kirkuk...92
Kissinger, Henry..254, 255, 283
knock..68-70
knowledge of God..262, 336
Kokhba, Simon bar..376, 384, 386
Koran...130, 139, 140, 435
Korean War...214, 215
Koreish...131
kosmos..59
Kremlin..256, 257, 428, 438
Kufa..435, 436
Kurds...234, 327
Kyrgyzstan..240, 421
L'Osservatore Romano..292
La Niña..266
lake of fire...55, 164, 322, 323, 338, 341

Alphabetical Index

Lamb....41, 55, 74, 75, 81-83, 85, 87, 100, 101, 106, 108-110, 113, 168, 175, 181, 185, 203, 213, 215, 216, 218, 223, 224, 233, 256, 258, 259, 263, 286, 288, 310, 312-314, 320, 337, 345, 348, 349, 351, 355, 356, 358, 359, 362, 413, 417

Lamb's book of life	55, 358
lamentations	297, 303, 304
lamp stands	18, 30, 76
land of Israel	103, 321, 411, 465
Laodicea	16, 17, 62-68, 317
Laos	243, 438
last days	72, 338, 365
last trump	395, 399
Latin	113, 117, 126, 127, 130, 138, 205, 207, 222, 276, 282, 326, 353
Latin America	272, 427, 428
Latin American Catholic clergy	427
Latin liturgy	428
Latvia	204, 438
Law of the Sea	241
lawless one	401
Lebanon	250, 272, 300, 471
Lee Kuan Yew	252
Legion of the Archangel Michael	290
Lehman Brothers	304
Leibniz	97
Lenin	1, 206, 210, 246, 254
leopard	89, 197
Lepanto	242
Levi	107, 108
Lewis, Bernard	138, 250, 417
Lewis, C. S.	286
LGBT	253, 315, 378
liars	337, 348
liberation theology	427, 428
Libya	100, 138, 178, 281, 429, 430
licentiousness	302

Licinius ... 92
light 21, 30, 53, 54, 74, 76, 111, 161, 174, 176, 227, 229-231, 305, 328, 350, 355-358, 363, 386
lightning ... 21, 75, 116, 117, 130, 172, 208, 230, 235, 267, 385
lights in the world ... 30, 76
Lindsey, Hal ... 465
lion ... 52, 77, 80, 81, 89, 107, 153, 197, 208, 224, 329
Lion that is of the tribe of Judah ... 80, 81, 107
Lisbon ... 285
literature ... 7, 44, 95, 193, 261, 462
Lithuania ... 204, 438
little book ... 151-153, 155, 156
Little Sisters of the Poor ... 201
living creatures ... 76, 77, 81, 82, 85-87, 94, 109, 216, 236, 289, 311, 344
Ljubljana ... 285
locusts ... 134-139, 141
Logos Spermatikos ... 433
London ... 146, 286, 299, 352
Lord God the Almighty ... 355
Lord of lords ... 259, 263, 286, 318, 320
Lord's day ... 16
Louata ... 138
Lucy ... 189
lukewarm ... 65
Lutheran Reformation ... 90
Lutheranism ... 90
Lutherans ... 258
Lydia ... 10, 49, 56, 63
Lydia, the lady ... 42
Lydian ... 49-51
Lyon ... 8, 32, 288
Maastricht Treaty ... 280
Macedonia ... 25, 29, 32, 65, 280
Machiavelli ... 292
Madras/Chennai ... 193, 387

Alphabetical Index

Magdalena..310
Magi..361, 469
magic...149, 306, 349, 369, 450
magicians...262, 283
magisterium..259
Magnesia...36, 117
Magog..265, 319, 321, 322, 324, 328, 333-336, 429
Magyars..207
Mahan..121
Malthus, Thomas...146
man of sin..40
Managua...254
Manasseh..107, 108
mandate...19, 93, 104, 170, 195, 196, 201, 213, 346
manna...40, 41
mansions...271, 342, 393
manuscripts..7, 74, 126, 236, 318
many waters..20, 216, 257, 271-273, 287, 303, 312, 322
Mao Tse-tung...1, 215, 251, 461
Maoist dictum...251
Marcellinus Comes..123
mariners..303
maritime trade..241, 303, 305
mark of the beast..210, 239-241, 322, 323
mark upon their forehead...210, 330, 331
Marmara, Sea of..194, 195, 201, 202
marriage 93, 137, 173, 175, 180, 186, 217, 274, 275, 305, 310, 312-315, 320, 327, 345, 369, 378, 389, 403
marriage of the Lamb..175, 310, 312, 314, 345
marriage supper..313, 314, 320
Martel, Charles...164, 278, 421
Martin Luther..90, 153, 223, 424
martus..38
Marx, Karl..1, 246, 254

Marxism..246, 254, 428
Marxism-Leninism...246, 254
Marxist...239, 246, 427, 428, 432
Mary..26, 181, 189-192, 196, 260, 382
Mary, sister of Martha..59
materialism...148, 149, 237, 397
Mauretania...118, 178
Maurya, Chandragupta...292
Meander Valley...63
measure...9, 81, 82, 94, 144, 152, 157, 158, 180, 214, 352, 353
measured the city...352
measured the wall..353
measuring rod...157, 319
Mecca..131, 132, 137, 260, 431, 436, 444, 448
Medina...130, 132, 135, 137, 419, 436, 444, 445
Mediterranean..........35, 63, 117, 119-122, 194, 195, 202, 250, 251, 264, 300, 380, 381, 419, 420
Megiddo..237, 264
Mekong River..243
menorah..18
merchants..180, 195, 275, 291, 293, 298, 299, 302, 303, 305, 422
mercy...43, 55, 74, 115, 151, 171, 242, 415
Meshech..100, 321, 322, 334-336, 429
Mesopotamia...138, 198, 251, 384
Messiah. .87, 89, 160, 176, 191, 217, 218, 259, 260, 265, 341, 376, 385, 387, 395, 409, 410, 413, 415, 442, 443, 448, 449, 453, 465
Messianic Jew..218
Methodists...294, 439
Methodius..207, 208
Metropolitan Bishop..159, 416, 425, 426
Mexico..211, 277, 310, 311, 438
Mexico City...310
Micah...412
Michael...183, 290, 399
Michelangelo..305

Alphabetical Index

Mickey Finn..306
Middle East.........................9, 11, 134, 187, 215, 249, 250, 335, 403, 419, 421, 437, 470, 471
Midianite..38, 134
mighty men...99, 321
Milan..92
Miletus..14, 17
Millennium. 1, 13, 72, 104, 109, 126, 145, 266, 306, 309, 319, 326-333, 337, 344, 365, 377, 390, 399, 465-468
mind........................11, 45, 52, 55, 71, 80, 105, 148, 162, 179, 184, 283, 285, 288, 292, 387, 402
Mindanao..322, 439
miracles, see signs...260, 262, 323, 441, 442
Moab, Moabite..38
mockery..166, 403
Mohammad Khatami...430
Mohammed...260, 429, 439
Mohammed Reza Pahlavi..470
monarchianism..46, 89
monarchical bishops..10, 416
Mongol Tatars...205
Mongol-Turks..469
Mongolia...204, 215
Mongols..234, 239, 334-336
monophosites..198
moon..98, 99, 125, 127, 129, 173-175, 355, 386
moral and ethical standards..186, 310
morality..291, 292, 303, 315
Mordecai..30
Morocco..138, 178, 301, 323, 439
Mosaic Law...55, 369, 370
Mosaic tabernacle...116
Moscow...100, 194, 204-206, 241, 246, 334, 431, 437, 438
Mosul..435
mother of harlots...277, 306
mount Zion..107, 159, 171, 215, 216

mountain great and high..349, 350
mourning...296, 303, 304, 346, 348, 372, 443
mouth 20, 21, 39, 40, 54, 56, 65, 148, 155, 156, 161-163, 185, 188, 197, 200, 202, 217, 218, 252, 253, 256, 259, 278, 297, 315, 319, 320, 323, 324, 369, 395, 401
Mozambique..438
Mt. Carmel..264
Mt. Moriah..467, 468
Mt. Zion...410, 467, 468
MTCR (Missile Technology Control Regime)..431
Muawiya..435, 436
Muhammad. 130-133, 136, 137, 140, 142, 148, 230, 301, 323, 409, 419, 420, 422, 431, 435, 436, 441-446, 448, 469
Muhammad bin Qasim..420
Muhammad, biography of 130, 132
Muharram...436
multitude 20, 106, 108-110, 134, 145, 161, 169, 271, 276, 286, 287, 296, 309, 312, 314, 321, 327, 341, 344, 356, 384, 385, 413, 417
murder..83, 97, 123, 149, 275, 348, 369, 370, 378
murderers..258, 337, 348, 368, 369, 435
Musailama..419
Muscovy...205
Muslim wars of conquest...213
Muslim world..127, 134, 143, 187, 227, 238, 249, 250, 268, 359
Muslims.......132, 134, 135, 138, 139, 142, 145, 198, 213, 249, 260, 294, 359, 419-421, 429-431, 434-437, 439, 441, 442, 445, 451, 452, 454
Mussolini..220, 292
Mutawa...187
my people...293, 295-298, 410-412
Mylapore..193
mysterious...250, 274, 276, 323, 384
mystery.....................................23, 57, 67, 81, 153, 155, 173-175, 222, 275-277, 317, 366, 395, 399
mystery of Christ..57, 174, 317
mystery of God...67, 155, 317
mystery of lawlessness..222, 276
mystical..276

Alphabetical Index

Nabonidus, King	298
Nadao	123
Najran	444, 445
names of blasphemy	194, 197, 273, 274, 277
Naphtali	107
Naples	222
Napoleon	214, 264
narrative	27, 156, 177, 193, 194, 388
Nationalism	196, 256, 433, 436, 439

nations 156, 158, 166, 169, 171, 172, 175, 181, 217, 219, 226, 234, 241, 243, 244, 265, 267, 268, 271, 286, 287, 291, 296, 300, 305, 306, 319, 323, 326-328, 330, 331, 333, 335-337, 346, 356, 358-361, 370, 378, 379, 382, 386, 387, 401, 412, 415

natural selection	404, 455, 459-461
naval war	164
naval warfare	121, 237, 242
Nazarenes	221
Nazareth	38, 165, 190, 215, 217, 260, 282, 371, 382, 415
Naziism	246
Neanderthal Man	189
Nebraska Man	189
Neo-Darwinian evolution	315, 455
nepotism	302, 435
Nestorian	36, 193, 198
Nestorius	191
new heaven and a new earth	339, 343, 345-348, 393, 466
new Jerusalem	60, 61, 130, 176, 215, 229, 290, 337, 344, 345, 348, 350, 354, 356, 357
new song	74, 82, 216

New Testament...8, 15, 29, 35, 53, 56, 90, 100, 153, 157, 162, 236, 269, 310, 314, 356, 402, 432, 442, 443, 448

New Testament Christians	314
new world	71, 291, 345, 430
Newton	97, 101
Nicaragua	254, 438
Nicene Christology	259
Nickolaus	30, 31

Revelation Verse by Verse

Nicolaitans..30, 31, 39, 49
Nicomedia..201
Nigeria...365, 439
night..............19, 26, 51, 77, 111-113, 125, 184, 224, 229, 284, 290, 338, 357, 358, 363, 387, 391
Nihilism..72, 246, 372, 397
Nile..117, 138, 243, 248, 264, 422
ninety-five theses..424
Nineveh...197, 352
Nixon, Richard...438
Nizam-e-Mustafa..439
no wind..103
Noah...83, 151, 263, 313, 367, 389, 390, 399
North Africa..11, 117-120, 126, 159, 178, 248, 421
North Korea...254
Northern Korea..438
Norway..90
NPT (Non Proliferation Treaty)..430
Nubians..422
number of his name..210, 232-234
number of the beast...210, 315
number seven..18, 82
Numidia...118
oath...113, 154, 287, 401
Obama Care...201
Obama, President..258, 272, 281, 437
Odoacer...164
Odovacar..125, 126
oikoumene...59
oil..94, 124, 301
ointment...301
Old Glagolitic...207
Old Testament saints..309, 313, 314
Omar..138
omega..14, 347, 367

Alphabetical Index

Onesiphorus..25
opium...246
Oracles..49, 50
ordinances...411
Origen..26, 403, 446
Orleans...266, 288
Orthodox Church...................................195, 205, 217, 240, 246, 256, 290, 336, 357, 428
Oster..428
Ostrogoths..123, 126
Othman (Uthman), Caliph..435
Ottoman Empire..144, 272, 420, 470
Ottoman Porte..272
Ottoman Turkey..470
Ottoman Turks..145, 201, 420
Ottomans...242, 420
overcometh..31, 34, 35, 40, 45, 54, 60, 70, 348, 349
Pacelli..292
Pacific..9, 194, 241, 281, 335
Pacific Rim..335
pain..................................91, 109, 110, 112, 141, 176, 180, 245-247, 336, 343, 346, 348, 378
Pakistan...193, 249, 251, 266, 387, 420, 421, 430, 431, 433, 471
pale horse...93, 95
Palestine..26, 33, 141, 214, 260, 264, 265, 300, 381, 386, 434, 436
palms...108, 109, 135, 413
Panthera..403, 446
papacy.................92, 189, 214, 220, 271, 272, 281, 290, 292, 293, 299, 305, 306, 311, 416, 424
papal deception..385
Papal States..180, 220, 258, 281
papyrus..36
parchment..36
Paris..288, 299
Parthia..26
Parthian...91, 92, 179, 193, 198, 221, 469
Parthian Empire..91, 92

Revelation Verse by Verse

Parthian Iran	193
patience of the saints	224
Patmos	7, 13-15, 32, 60, 79, 84, 91, 178
Patriarch of Constantinople	122, 205
pattern	75, 96, 116, 176, 193, 209, 220, 224, 266, 277, 293, 318, 426

Paul....1, 7, 10, 11, 21, 22, 25-29, 31, 40-45, 52, 54, 55, 57, 62, 64, 65, 67, 69, 72, 73, 75, 81, 83-85, 91, 96, 108, 118, 119, 148, 154, 157, 159, 160, 162, 165, 166, 173-176, 180, 181, 183, 185, 191, 192, 195, 202, 216, 222, 231, 232, 238, 262, 275, 276, 290, 310, 314, 323, 331, 338, 340, 341, 344, 351, 352, 357, 358, 369, 373, 378, 387, 398-402, 412, 413, 415, 416

Peace of Westphalia	214
pedophilia	275, 276, 302
Pentecost	16, 28, 79, 81, 85, 108, 213, 219, 329, 382
Pentecostal	311
peoples	12, 19, 41, 71, 72, 89, 108, 156, 166, 171, 271, 286, 287, 321, 322, 336, 345, 412, 413
Peor	39
Perestroika	253
Pergamum	10, 16, 17, 29, 31, 35-40, 42, 47, 49, 60, 63
periodic table	407
permanence	407
persecuting power	93, 222
persecution	13, 14, 32, 33, 46, 60, 89-96, 110-113, 116, 117, 141, 151, 163, 170, 176, 177, 179, 182, 183, 186, 187, 189, 198, 203, 213, 221, 230, 273, 277, 346, 366, 378, 399, 400
persecution of the church	96, 151, 170, 182, 221
Persia	46, 49, 89, 92, 100, 132, 179, 195, 197, 221, 251, 264, 300, 322, 335
Persian	51, 52, 91, 92, 137, 179, 213, 221, 248, 298, 380, 421, 469
Persian Gulf	178, 470
Persians	49, 50, 123, 136, 248, 298, 420, 421
Person of the Year	282
Perun	208

Peter. 1, 7, 21, 22, 25, 28, 38, 39, 67, 72, 81, 83, 85, 106, 153, 157, 183, 222, 226, 231, 314, 318, 327, 329, 338, 344, 364, 365, 370, 387, 395, 402

Peter the Great	206
Peter Waldo	90
Petrograd	206
Pharisees	55, 244, 383, 397

Alphabetical Index

Philadelphia	16, 17, 26, 33, 45, 55-61, 63, 65, 274
Philippi	32, 42, 81
Philippians	65
Philippines	266, 322
philosophical arguments	169, 314
philosophy	169, 237, 252, 261, 336, 463
Phrygia	29, 63
Picts	117
pigeons	245
pillar	60, 167, 188, 256, 351, 412
pillars	25, 60, 151, 152
Piltdown-Man	189
piracy	121, 241, 272, 275
Pisan Pope	222
plagues	111, 145, 147, 148, 169, 231, 232, 234-236, 245, 267, 293, 295, 296, 325, 349, 372
Pliny	63, 91, 140, 202, 300
PLO (Palestine Liberation Organization)	429, 434
Poland	161, 278, 310, 311, 438
Poles	207
political	29, 46, 49, 98-100, 103, 104, 116, 125, 132, 134, 163-165, 173, 177, 180, 182, 183, 189, 195, 196, 198, 205, 209, 217, 219, 220, 223, 230, 233, 234, 237, 240-242, 246-248, 252, 254-259, 261-263, 267-269, 271, 272, 274, 276, 278-280, 282-286, 288, 289, 291, 292, 298, 306, 315, 322, 327, 330, 336, 356, 372, 377, 386, 406, 407, 417, 419, 424-426, 430, 432-434, 437
political nationalism	196
political power	120, 163, 179, 194-196, 200, 204, 205, 217, 219, 220, 225, 251-253, 256-258, 261, 273, 281, 284, 288, 290, 305, 372, 426, 432, 437, 470
politics	196, 201, 221, 251, 261, 287, 432, 434, 437
Polo, Marco	422
Polycarp	32-34, 38, 179, 231
pope	92, 180, 200, 220, 222, 258, 272-276, 281, 282, 287, 291-293, 299, 302, 306, 356, 384, 423-426
Pope Alexander	291, 293
Pope Francis	180, 220, 272, 276, 282, 287, 299, 302, 306, 427, 428, 438
Pope John Paul II	428, 438
Pope Pius V	180

Pope Pius VI ... 287
Pope Pius XI ... 180, 292
Pope Pius XII ... 292
Pope Sylvester I ... 423
population figures ... 106
post-millennial ... 13, 328
pour my Spirit ... 410
poverty ... 32, 34, 65, 67, 203, 301, 397, 420
power centers ... 193, 198
Prague ... 222, 223
prayers of all the saints ... 115
pre-millennial ... 13, 328, 399
pre-millennialism ... 13
preacher ... 10, 40, 62, 222, 344, 345
preaching ... 10, 15, 27, 29, 32, 43, 90, 108, 162, 163, 193, 218, 219, 226, 306, 311, 345, 379, 387
Precious Stones ... 74, 180, 350, 354
presbyters ... 290
present time ... 330, 343, 389, 462
prevail ... 18, 22, 23, 58, 66, 116, 145, 167, 246, 254, 312, 327
principalities ... 53, 183, 195, 262, 334
prison ... 6, 22, 23, 34, 35, 84, 113, 126, 196, 291, 327, 328, 333
Proconsular Africa ... 118
profits ... 132, 302, 303
progressive revelation ... 174
promise of his coming ... 391, 404, 406
prostitute ... 43, 256, 272, 275, 276, 302
Protestant ... 90, 146, 187, 306, 307, 377, 417
Protestant Bible commentators ... 152
Protestant Reformation ... 152, 222
Protestants ... 310
Protestants in Mexico ... 277
province of Asia ... 1, 6, 9, 10, 14, 17, 18, 25, 27-30, 33, 35, 36, 42, 49, 53, 158, 387
Punic ... 116
Punic War, Second ... 121, 122

Alphabetical Index

Punic War, Third	117, 380
punishment	44, 98, 133, 134, 155, 217, 224, 244, 265, 271, 311, 336, 337, 339, 400, 452, 453
Punjab	420
purchase unto God	82, 83
purple	42, 180, 274, 275, 299, 300, 303
purple and scarlet	180, 274, 275, 303
Put	100, 322
Putin	211, 240, 241, 246, 254-257
Pyongyang	254
Pyrenees Mountains	421
Pytho	50
Qaddafi, Muammar	281, 430
Qur'an	139, 259, 260
Quraish	131, 132
rain	162, 163, 224, 230, 267
rain forests	163
Ramsay	63
random variation	455, 460, 461
Rapture	1, 110-113, 167, 390, 394, 399
Raqqa	435
Reagan	281, 469
realpolitik	292
red dragon	177, 197, 213
red horse	88-90
redeemed man	84, 345, 348, 360
redemption	23, 41, 75-77, 84, 87, 108, 152, 309, 311, 314, 412
reference point	251, 333, 343, 407
refined	20, 66, 207, 355
Reformation	11, 90, 151-153, 222
reign for ever and ever	170, 363
reigned with Christ	210, 330, 331
remnant	52, 191, 193, 410, 412, 436, 461
remote	6, 169, 379, 385, 389
render	295, 296, 298, 306, 312, 318

renewing 105, 362

Reprove 62, 68, 269

rest 11, 76, 77, 89, 96, 98, 224, 225, 387, 397, 400

restitution 272, 400

restoration 68, 87, 395, 414, 465

resurrection .. 12, 22, 79, 81, 213, 219, 278, 294, 295, 328, 331, 332, 338-341, 349, 355, 380, 395-398

resurrection of judgment 339, 341, 396

resurrection of life 339, 341, 396

resurrection, general 331, 339, 341, 396

Reuben 107

revelation 231, 289, 290, 316, 337, 364, 366, 369, 397, 400, 401, 442, 446, 447

rewards 61, 85, 178, 180, 257, 345

Reza Aslan 165

Reza Khan 470

Rheims 423

Rhine 117, 124

Rhodes 14, 15, 35

Riazan 239

rich 22, 32, 38, 41, 43, 65-67, 85, 100, 105, 131, 175, 198, 209, 218, 242, 247, 291, 293, 299, 303-305, 352, 414

Richard Dawkins 165, 456, 457, 463

Richelieu 292

rituals 83, 197, 208, 276, 293

river of water of life 347, 359

rivers 117, 122, 124, 206, 230, 243, 248, 347

rod of iron 45, 157, 181, 189, 319, 352

Roe v. Wade 274

Roman 117

Roman army 384, 385, 387, 388

Roman Catholic Church 205, 217, 220, 257, 258, 272, 275, 280, 282, 284, 287, 290, 299, 302, 322, 357, 425, 427, 428, 434, 438

Roman Catholic Primate 311

Roman Church 91, 195, 259, 282, 290, 424, 425, 433

Roman citizenship 47, 178

Alphabetical Index

Roman Curia 189, 302

Roman emperors 91, 125

Roman Empire 49, 59, 60, 91, 92, 96, 117, 119, 122, 123, 125, 126, 144, 145, 147, 164, 177, 179, 182, 183, 189, 194, 195, 197, 205, 217, 257, 272, 274, 278-280, 282, 283, 285, 287, 364, 380, 389, 423-425

Roman government 14, 32, 42, 46, 91

Roman hierarchy 275

Roman mile 228, 352

Roman persecution 32, 91, 92, 116, 117, 164, 177, 213

Roman Republic 35, 36

Romania 254, 438

Romanian Orthodox Church 290

Romanov, Michael 205

Rome 27, 32, 36, 37, 39, 46, 49, 60, 63, 91, 117, 119-122, 130, 146, 162, 164, 175, 177, 178, 180, 194, 197, 198, 200-203, 205, 210, 213, 217, 219, 220, 222, 268, 271-273, 278, 283, 284, 290, 293, 295, 300, 302, 306, 340, 380-382, 387, 389, 397, 421, 423-426

Romulus Augustulus 117, 125, 278

Root of David 80, 81, 107

rose again 397

Rosetta mission 457

Rosh 100, 321, 322, 334, 336

routine 389, 390

Royal Road 92

Rudvin 433

Russell, Bertrand 403

Russia 99, 100, 119, 204-208, 210, 211, 214, 215, 233, 237, 239-241, 246, 247, 254-256, 323, 334-336, 357, 422, 428, 431, 438, 470, 471

Russian Empire 204, 205, 208-210, 335, 364

Russian Federation 241, 336

Russian Orthodox Church 240, 246, 336, 357

Russian Orthodox Metropolitan 205, 428

Russian state 206, 209, 239

sackcloth 98, 99, 159-161

sacrifice 83

Saddam Hussein 251

Revelation Verse by Verse

Sadducee...381, 397

sadistic..95, 406

Saffavid Persians...420

Saint Sophia..195, 423

saints 67, 70, 74, 75, 82, 96, 115, 116, 157, 159, 171, 175, 176, 202-204, 224, 225, 232, 244, 258, 262, 273, 277, 304, 306, 309, 313, 314, 331, 337, 344, 373, 400, 401

saints shall judge the world..75, 159, 331

Sakharov, Andrei..254, 255

Salvation 69, 109, 110, 153, 183-185, 218, 219, 309, 325, 326, 339, 351, 368, 395, 401, 403, 413, 414, 417

Sam Harris...165

same-sex marriage...93, 186, 217, 315, 327, 378

San Francisco..315

sanctuary...380

Sanhedrin..383

Saracen..141, 422

Sarai..205

Sarajevo..214

Sardian..51

Sardinia..120, 380

Sardis..16, 17, 42, 49-54, 60, 197

Sassanian..92, 179, 198, 209, 221, 248, 420, 469

Sassanian Empire..92, 469

Sassanian Iran..198, 209, 420

Satan...26, 32, 33, 37, 38, 41, 45, 58, 59, 69, 72, 87, 105, 129, 130, 133, 142, 164, 167, 171, 177, 179-184, 186, 188-190, 194, 198, 199, 202, 224, 230, 231, 253, 255, 261, 262, 276, 288, 318, 325-331, 333, 338, 362, 393, 401, 437, 468, 469, 471

Satan, Great..469, 471

Satan, Little...471

Satan's rebellion..142

satanic..35, 37, 58, 59, 133, 143, 164, 168-170, 172, 177, 182, 186-188, 200, 206, 252, 253, 261, 278, 296, 330, 333, 416

satanic coalition..252

Saudi Arabia..187, 249, 259, 470, 471

Savonarola..424

Alphabetical Index

Sayyid Qutb	437
Scandinavia	90, 119
scarlet	20, 98, 180, 273-275, 277, 283, 286, 299, 300, 303, 368, 394
scarlet-colored beast	273, 274, 277, 283, 286
scattered	26, 344, 383, 386, 387, 411, 433, 449
Schori, Katharine Jefferts	294
science	22, 455-459, 461-463
scientific	36, 246, 255, 315, 323, 455, 456, 458, 470
scientific community	458
scorpion	134, 136, 137, 141
Scribes	55, 244
Scythia	26
Scyths	122
sea gave up the dead	339, 341, 396
sea is no more	343
sea of glass	76, 232, 234
seal	6, 74, 79-83, 103-108, 135, 136, 153, 154, 216, 238, 244, 325, 327, 330, 339, 366, 380, 412-414
Seal not up the words	6, 366
seal of God	105, 135, 136
second coming	13, 40, 145, 376, 385, 388, 394, 395, 398-400, 402
second death	34, 35, 332, 341, 348, 349
secular society	166, 186, 203, 253, 267
seed of Israel	410
seek understanding	80
Seleucia-Ctesiphon	221
Seleucid	36
self-generated	350, 359, 405, 406
Seljuk	420
sensualism	31, 43, 46, 149, 166, 372
sensuality	43, 276, 314
separation	56, 219, 241, 257, 293, 295, 322, 339, 353, 423
Septuagint	10, 63, 334
Serbia	214, 215, 233, 281, 420

Revelation Verse by Verse

Serbs..233, 420
serfdom...433
seven bowls...409
seven churches. 5, 6, 9-12, 14, 16-20, 23, 25, 32-34, 40, 47, 49, 51, 55, 70, 76, 82, 129, 158, 350, 393, 465
seven diadems..177, 178, 197
seven heads...177, 194, 196-198, 273, 274, 277, 283
seven lamps of fire...76
seven last plagues..231, 349
seven mountains...274, 283, 284
seven plagues...231, 232, 235, 236, 267
seven seals..73, 79-81, 87, 107, 238, 409, 413
Seven Spirits..9, 11, 12, 49, 51, 75, 76, 81, 82
seven stars..20, 23, 25, 49, 51, 129
seven trumpets...115, 116, 238, 409
seventh seal...115
sex work..271
sexual slavery..302
sexual union...217, 302
sexually transmitted diseases..315
Shah Abbas...360, 361, 470
Shah of Iran...249, 469, 470
Shannon, Robert C..254
Shapur II, Emperor..221
Shari'a...138, 439
Sharif, Nawaz, P.M. of Pakistan..430
sharp sword..319, 320, 401
Shatt al-Arab..144, 248
Sheba..51, 100
sheep...301, 339, 368, 392, 393
shepherd..69, 113, 168, 221, 368
Shi-at Ali..436
Shi'ism...409
Shia..249, 250, 436, 437, 469-471

Alphabetical Index

Shiites	250, 436
shipping	32, 195, 241, 242, 377
shipping lanes	241, 242
shut by day	357
Sicilians	122
Sicily	119-122, 278
sickle	213, 225-227
sign in heaven	177, 229, 231
signs	5, 208, 210, 232, 261-263, 267, 322, 323, 382, 383
silence	115, 229
silk	161, 202, 203, 299, 300
Silk Road/Route	161, 202
silver	148, 169, 198, 242, 275, 299, 328, 329, 370
Simeon	107, 108
Simon, Bishop	221
Sinai	75, 191, 236
Sinai Peninsula	264
Sinaitic manuscript	236
Sindh	420
Singapore	196, 252
Singh, Jaswant	430, 431
sinlessness	20, 56, 234, 394
Sino-Soviet rift	437
Sistine Chapel	305
slavery	204, 301, 302, 306, 307, 381, 384, 419
slaves	97, 113, 187, 204, 242, 299, 301, 329
Slavic	207, 208, 233, 334, 336, 357
Slavic language	207
Slavic Russia	334, 336
Slavs	203, 207, 208, 335
sleep	21, 395, 397, 399
Slovaks	207
small and great	321
smoke of her burning	297, 303, 304, 311

smoke of their torment ... 224, 311
smokescreen ... 133, 134, 297, 305, 306, 311
Smyrna ... 6, 16, 17, 25, 26, 32-34, 38, 54, 56, 58, 63, 65
social ... 7, 46, 58, 94, 99, 104, 109, 116, 130, 132, 139, 163, 182, 193, 196, 205, 227, 238, 249, 250, 252, 267-269, 271, 280, 310, 311, 315, 325, 327, 360, 372, 373
societal behavior ... 151
societal commitment ... 151
society ... 12, 46, 89, 92, 95, 100, 123, 126, 127, 143, 144, 148, 149, 151, 155, 156, 162, 166, 186, 188, 193, 200, 203, 228, 231, 232, 244, 247, 253-255, 261, 266-268, 286, 295, 310, 312, 319, 325, 336, 350, 377, 379, 394, 423
sociology ... 261
Sodom ... 155, 165, 166, 244, 267, 337
solace ... 113
solar ... 237, 245
solar flare ... 245
Solomon's temple ... 51, 60, 213
Solzhenitsyn ... 228
Somalia ... 241
Son of God ... 42, 166, 183, 185, 191, 226, 326, 339
son of man ... 12, 13, 19, 225, 226, 234, 318, 320, 321, 338, 375, 385-387, 389-392
son of perdition ... 72, 222, 290
song of Moses ... 216, 233, 234
Song of the Lamb ... 216, 233
sorcerers ... 262, 337, 348, 349, 368, 369
sorceries ... 148, 149, 169, 306
sorcery ... 305, 306, 369
souls ... 77, 96, 138, 210, 258, 299, 301, 302, 330-332
South America ... 194, 220, 427
South China Sea ... 241, 377
Soviet empire ... 247
Soviet State ... 247, 428
Soviet Union ... 204, 240, 241, 254, 304, 334, 336, 417, 429
Spain ... 100, 118, 120, 121, 147, 214, 278, 302, 421, 429
Spaniards ... 214, 234
Spanish conquest ... 291

Alphabetical Index

Spanish Peninsula	117
spew	65, 148
spherical world	103
spice	301
spirit of prophecy	6, 314, 316
spirits of demons	253, 261, 263
spirits of the prophets	364
Spong, Bishop John Shelby	294
St. Catherine's Convent	236
St. Helena	264
St. Peter's Basilica	220, 427
St. Peter's pence	287
St. Peter's Square	282
St. Petersburg	204, 206
stadia	228, 352, 353
Stalin	1, 111, 210, 250, 383
Stalingrad	111, 383
standard for obedience	401
stars	20, 23, 25, 49, 51, 98, 99, 125, 129, 131, 173-175, 178, 179, 230, 386
starvation	151
state control	210
state-sponsored persecution	117
statutes	411
Stenger, Victor J.	165
sterilization	93, 180
stony heart	411
Strait of Gibraltar	118, 119, 121, 343
Strait of Malacca	241, 343
Strait of Sicily	119, 121
subjugated	145
Sudan	100, 187, 249, 422, 471
Sultan Mehmed the Conqueror	207
Sumatra	422

sun. 20, 21, 72, 98, 99, 112, 119, 125, 129, 133, 151, 152, 173-175, 180, 189, 218, 224, 245, 320, 355, 363, 386, 399

Sunni 131, 249-251, 434, 436, 437, 471

Sunni-Shia 131, 249, 250, 434, 437

Sunspot 245

sup 68, 69

supernatural 238

Sura 134, 260

Surah 130-132, 137, 139, 140, 260, 441

Sweden 90, 284, 417

Switzerland 196, 299

swoon 32

sword of my mouth 39, 40

synagogue of Satan 26, 32, 33, 58, 59

synagogues 21, 33, 73, 90, 214, 290

Syria 29, 32, 54, 62, 63, 99, 119, 132, 135, 138, 144, 195, 198, 214, 250, 260, 262, 264, 272, 365, 384, 429, 435, 436, 469-471

tabernacle 18, 96, 111, 112, 116, 174, 202, 231, 235, 345, 347, 359, 393

Tajikistan 240

taken up 357, 394

Talas River 421

talent 30, 268, 269

talent, Babylonian 269

talent, Egyptian 269

talent, Greek or Attic 269

talent, Roman 269

Taliban 113, 439

Talmud 403, 447

Tang Dynasty 193, 421

Tarshish 100, 429

Tartessus 429

Tatar 204-206, 335

Tatarstan 204

Taurus mountain 36, 420

Alphabetical Index

Taxila..193, 387

TCM International..254

Teilhard de Chardin...428

temple...9, 18, 28, 33, 37, 43, 60, 96, 111, 157, 158, 172, 180, 181, 183, 184, 202, 214, 222, 226, 235, 236, 238, 266, 267, 290, 298, 350, 355, 370, 375, 376, 381, 384, 386, 388, 393, 467

Temple complex...381

temple of God...9, 157, 158, 172, 183, 184, 202, 222, 235, 290

ten diadems...194, 197

ten horns...177, 194, 196-198, 273, 274, 277, 285, 287

terminating event...395

termination point for evil..406

Tertullian..8, 32

testimony......5-8, 14, 15, 28, 73, 74, 91, 96, 98, 122, 140, 160-162, 164, 165, 170, 176, 181, 182, 185, 189, 191, 192, 201, 210, 215, 235, 293, 314-316, 330-332, 348, 371, 379, 386, 398, 400, 417

Thailand...243

theism...253, 463

Theodoric...126

Theodosius...122

theological..159, 191, 193, 198, 201, 217, 222, 223, 246, 249, 257, 263, 276, 277, 290, 336, 352, 425

theology...56, 90, 158, 169, 246, 259-261, 425, 427, 428, 443, 448, 449

Theophanes..199

theotokos..190, 191

third part of men..144, 145, 147

third Rome...205, 210

Third World...429

Thirty Years' War..94, 95, 214, 417

Thomas, apostle...26, 81, 193, 387

thought processes...105

thousand years...210, 325-333, 365

three gates..351

throne....9, 11, 12, 37, 41, 49, 69-71, 73-77, 79, 81, 82, 85, 96, 100, 101, 108-113, 115, 116, 143, 168, 170, 181, 183, 197, 198, 200, 208, 216, 227, 229, 232, 236, 245, 246, 266, 267, 279, 311-314, 317, 332, 338-341, 345, 346, 356, 359, 362, 392, 393, 400, 413, 417, 425, 448, 465

Revelation Verse by Verse

throne of God 76, 111, 143, 181, 232, 311, 314, 332, 359, 362

throne of grace 115, 116

throne of the beast 245

thrones 20, 70, 74, 75, 170, 195, 210, 330, 331

thunder 75, 87, 116, 153, 154, 156, 172, 208, 216, 235, 267, 312, 385

Thyatira 10, 16, 17, 42-46, 52, 70, 293, 370

thyine wood 299-301

Tiananmen Square 252, 254

Tigris 137, 144, 248, 419, 420, 435, 469

time…1, 5, 6, 9, 11, 17, 27-30, 33, 34, 41, 43, 46, 49, 54, 72, 79, 97, 98, 101, 103, 143, 144, 154, 155, 158-160, 163, 168, 171, 172, 174, 177, 182, 187-189, 201, 237, 238, 244, 258, 265, 275, 283, 287, 293, 312, 314, 326, 327, 330-332, 338, 345, 361, 362, 365-367, 383, 388-391, 393, 395, 399, 402, 405, 409, 411, 413-416, 449, 453, 459, 466-468

time line 409

time scale 404

time zones 204

Timothy 10, 25-28, 401

Tischendorf 74, 236

Titus, General 28, 111, 158, 380, 382, 384

Togarmah 100, 322, 335

Toledot Yeshu 403, 447

tongues 12, 41, 108, 109, 156, 166, 245, 267, 271, 286, 287, 364, 413

torture 35, 60, 112, 113, 196, 397, 400

totalitarian government 202

trade routes 377

transformed 105, 225, 236, 265, 362

transgender 253, 315, 326

transgressions 314, 411

travail 176, 377, 378

tree of life 31, 159, 347, 351, 359-362, 368, 372, 373

tribes 13, 14, 41, 70, 106-108, 123, 132, 156, 166, 234, 260, 267, 350, 351, 386, 413, 421

tribulation 6, 14-16, 32, 34, 35, 43, 44, 65, 110-113, 116, 378, 379, 382, 383, 386, 465

triumph 18, 29-31, 41, 54, 55, 59, 72, 73, 79, 85, 88, 109, 110, 121, 161, 163, 164, 170, 177, 182, 186, 234, 259, 286-288, 316-318, 329, 330, 337, 367, 393, 398, 409, 415, 418, 462, 466, 471

triumphal entry 383

Alphabetical Index

true..8, 55, 56, 58, 61-64, 67, 82, 97, 105, 133, 149, 159, 166, 182, 185, 193, 203, 209, 228, 233, 244, 256, 259, 273, 286, 293, 310, 312, 313, 316, 317, 327, 346, 350, 364, 367, 397, 416

true church..................182, 193, 203, 228, 256, 273, 293, 312, 313, 327, 364, 416

trumpet 16, 20, 71, 75, 115, 116, 119, 120, 122, 125, 127, 129, 143, 151, 155, 169, 170, 231, 238, 248, 265, 305, 387, 388, 395, 399, 409, 422

truth....15, 26, 40, 55, 56, 71, 83, 90, 157, 167, 176, 185, 188, 189, 202, 219, 229, 260, 262, 275, 276, 296, 297, 314, 315, 317, 319, 320, 326, 329, 349, 351-353, 366, 371, 373, 391, 414, 442, 445, 448, 453, 455, 458, 460, 463, 465

tsarist regime...255
Tubal...100, 321, 322, 334-336, 429
turbans...140, 242
Turfan...193
Turkestan...335, 421
Turkey...8, 9, 144, 215, 264, 438, 470
Turkish...................35, 100, 143, 145, 146, 207, 213, 242, 264, 272, 327, 420
Turkish pirates...272
Turkmenistan..240
Turks.......................................30, 135, 143-145, 201, 234, 258, 327, 420, 422
twelve angels...350, 351
twelve foundations..351
twelve gates..350, 351, 355
twelve manner of fruits...359, 361, 362
twelve pearls...355
twenty-four elders..74-77, 312
twinkling of an eye...395, 399
two candlesticks..160, 161
two olive trees...160
two prophets..166, 167
two witnesses.................................159-165, 167-169, 182, 201, 326, 369
two-edged sword...20, 21, 35, 36, 40
Tyre..142, 183, 305
U.S...93, 251, 272, 274, 281, 306, 377
U.S. Congress...258
U.S. government...93, 187, 211, 315
U.S.S.R...241, 247, 255, 428, 438

Ubaidullah 436
Ukraine 204, 205, 241, 428
Umayyad Caliphate 137, 419, 421, 436, 469
unbelieving 111, 159, 171, 337, 348, 383, 387
underground church 182
Uniates 428
union of ecclesiastical and political power 219
United Nations 268, 429, 437
United Nations Security Council 437
Universal Church 70, 272
universe 59, 71, 72, 79, 85, 101, 112, 171, 250, 312, 332, 344, 400
University of Washington 455
Urals 206, 207
Uzbekistan 240
Vajpayee, Atal Bihari, P.M. of India 430
Valerian 46, 89, 91
Valla, Lorenzo 189
Vandal invasion 118, 119
vandalism 120
Vasco da Gama 127, 214
Vatican 180, 205, 220, 276, 277, 282, 292, 299, 305, 428, 433, 434, 438
Vatican Bank 180, 276, 299, 303
Vatican City 220
Vatican Palace 220
Vaticanus manuscript 236
vellum 36
vengeance 118, 149, 196, 295, 296, 396, 400, 443
Venice 119
verbal unity 162
Vespasian 384
vicar 256, 275, 384
Vicente de Valverde 291
Victor J. Stenger 165
Victorinus 15

Alphabetical Index

victors	232, 233, 242, 332, 333, 348, 393
Vienna	420, 470
Vietnam	214, 215, 243, 437, 438
villeinage	433
vindictive	406
virginity	217
Visigoths	120, 121
Vladimir	207, 208, 240, 357
Vladimir, Grand Principality of	206
Vladivostok	204
Volga River	205, 334
Wahabi	213
Waldensens	92
Waldensians	258
Waleed, Khalid ibn al	419
wall great and high	350
war	1, 39, 40, 72, 82, 90, 92, 94, 95, 99, 100, 103, 104, 111, 117, 119, 121, 122, 135, 139, 140, 144, 146-148, 151, 162, 164, 169, 183-185, 187, 189, 194, 198, 199, 202, 203, 206, 213-215, 221, 226-228, 231, 233, 237, 240-244, 249-253, 255, 258, 260-266, 277, 279, 281, 284, 286, 291, 309, 313, 316-322, 327, 328, 330, 333-337, 343, 361, 362, 365, 370, 377-380, 383, 415-417, 419
War of Apostasy, Ridda War	419
War of the Worlds	263, 265
war, conceptual	262
warfare	147, 239, 262, 316, 318
wash their robes	31, 159, 351, 368
Washington	274, 306, 328, 431, 439
wealth	51, 65-67, 85, 202, 300, 301, 305, 384
weather cycle	377
weather patterns	162, 163, 243, 266
wells of salvation	410
Western Catholic Church	219
Western Europe	11, 92, 118, 126, 201, 228, 239, 417
Western Rome	117
Western world	254, 286

whales	245
wheat	93, 94, 301, 398
white garments	54, 66, 67, 74
white horse	87-90, 316, 318
white robes	41, 75, 108-110, 413, 417
white stone	40, 41
Wilberforce, William	204
wild beasts	28, 95
wilderness	54, 151, 180-182, 187-190, 273, 312, 385, 416
wine	50, 67, 69, 94, 219, 223, 267, 268, 272, 273, 277, 291, 301, 424
wine of her fornication	272, 273, 277, 424
wine of the wrath of God	223
wine of the wrath of her fornication	219, 291
winepress	214, 227, 228, 319, 320
witness	5-8, 12, 13, 37, 38, 47, 62, 64, 110, 160, 161, 185, 193, 238, 317, 369
Woe	127, 129, 133, 142, 144, 148, 151, 155, 169, 170, 186, 298, 303, 304, 420, 422
woman, drunken	273, 277
Word of God	5-7, 14, 15, 21, 27, 40, 66, 96, 153, 161, 162, 210, 297, 318, 319, 324, 330-332, 404, 405, 444
world population	108, 143, 145-147, 151, 162, 243
world rulers	183, 195, 262, 322, 356
world trade	298
World Trade Organization (W.T.O.)	280
world war	104, 169, 214, 262, 263
World War I	103, 206, 214, 215, 227, 228, 233, 242, 246, 254, 255, 286, 343, 417
World War II	111, 146, 147, 214, 279, 284, 286, 383, 417, 422, 431, 470
wormwood	124
worship	8, 15, 33, 37, 38, 58, 59, 75, 77, 78, 82, 83, 85, 86, 109, 110, 130, 132, 148, 149, 153, 157, 169, 170, 190, 199, 203, 206-210, 219, 222-224, 234, 239, 240, 290, 311, 314, 316, 322, 323, 330, 331, 365, 366, 381, 387, 422
worshiped	86, 109, 110, 170, 210
worshipful adoration	75, 85
wrath angel	144, 237, 241-243, 245, 248, 266-269
wrath of God	74, 88, 98, 224, 226, 227, 231, 236, 238, 289, 319, 320, 349
writer	6-8, 138, 146, 165, 180, 186, 187, 402

Alphabetical Index

writer of Revelation	7, 8
Wyclif	222, 223, 424
Xicalco	310
Xinjiang	193, 421
Yarmuk, Second Battle of	419, 420
Yazdgerd II	92
Yazid	436
Yeltsin, Boris	239-241
Yemen	100, 131, 249, 250, 262, 429, 438, 470, 471
Yosef, Akiva ben	376
Yugoslavia	233, 282, 438
Zab River	137, 419, 469
Zacharias	115, 399
Zagros Mountains	420
ZANU (Zimbabwe African National Union)	428
zealous	33, 62, 68
Zechariah	107, 412, 415
Zemin, Jiang, President of China	431
Zimbabwe	428
Zion	107, 159, 171, 215, 216
Zionism	134
Zoroastrian	136, 137, 141, 193, 221, 357, 421, 469

About the Author

Following the typical American primary and secondary education, the writer graduated from San Jose Bible College with a Bachelor of Theology Degree in 1947. In 1956, after having served nine-and-one-half years in evangelistic Christian ministry at Vancouver, Washington, and having taught four years in a Portland, Oregon-based Bible college, he entered the graduate school of the University of Pennsylvania, where in 1959 he completed his M.A. Degree in South Asia Regional Studies. His thesis was *A Contribution to the English Historical Cartography of Iran in the Early Islamic Period.*

Following the completion of his studies at the University of Pennsylvania, he and his family sailed to Pakistan in August 1960 where they spent the next fifteen years in Christian evangelism, both urban and rural. During the early part of his stay in Pakistan, he also studied history and political science at the University of the Punjab in Lahore, Pakistan.

While living in Pakistan, Turner made several study and preaching trips to various sites throughout much of India. Also, due to a war between India and Pakistan in 1971, he and his family spent six months in Afghanistan during which he became acquainted with further aspects of that country's history and geography.

Toward the end of 1975, the Turners were no longer allowed to renew their visas and consequently had to terminate their residential mission work in Pakistan. On their way back to America, Lee and his youngest son Jonathan, traveling by Jeep, pursued a six-month study-tour of the Middle East which included Afghanistan, Iran, Turkey, Jordan and Syria. During that tour Lee sent a series of letters home entitled *Travel Letters From The Center Arena of History.* Since 1975, Lee has made 22 trips back to Pakistan and several additional trips to India. As a board member of IDES, a U.S. Christian relief organization, he visited Sudan and Egypt several times, and in India he traveled to war-torn Imphal in the remote, far northeastern corner of that great country, to help implement relief projects.

The ministry continues to the present day in the form of radio and internet broadcasting of the Gospel, along with visits to Pakistan. While still in Pakistan in 1971, the Turners began a shortwave radio outreach in the Urdu language in order to reach more people for Christ. Those broadcasts have continued uninterruptedly and go out under the name of Awaz-e-Haq (The Voice of Truth). The work has expanded so that the programs can be heard on internet radio (available 24/7 all over the world!) and is carried on by a small group of dedicated and skilled brethren under the name of Key Communications, directed by Jonathan Turner. Urdu Christian literature and Bibles are also made available to listeners through local Christians in Pakistan.

For additional information, see www.keycom.org.

www.ingramcontent.com/pod-product-compliance
Lightning Source LLC
Chambersburg PA
CBHW080751300426
44114CB00020B/2698